Border of Hope, Fence of Despair

For Maxine

An Autobiography

Thank you!

Laszlo S. Lichter

Laszlo S. Lichter

Border of Hope, Fence of Despair
Copyright © 2020 Laszlo S. Lichter
Written by Laszlo S. Lichter

All rights reserved. No part of this book may be used or reproduced by any means, graphic, electronic, or mechanical, including taping, photocopying, or by information storage retrieval system without the written permission of the author(s) except in the case of brief quotations embodied in critical articles and reviews.

ISBN: 9798695834390

"*Border of Hope, Fence of Despair* is a must-read for anyone living in a country like Canada, where we take freedom for granted. We were toddlers at the time Laszlo's story ends in the book. During the next 40 years we lived in Hungary we learned very little about the events leading to 1956. People were afraid of talking about the Hungarian Revolution. We heard talk every year after October 23 that some people got into trouble because they tried to remember that great event, not just behind closed doors. It was a great coincidence that as new Canadians, we found not only wonderful friends but also a missing piece of history when we met Rozsa and Laszlo."

-Laszlo Podor

"I finished reading *Border of Hope, Fence of Despair* a few weeks ago. What an amazing memoir! The author was my High School Principal and although I knew he and his family escaped from Hungary, I had no idea what they endured to get to Canada. The struggle and determination of Laszlo and his family is described in detail in the book. The impossibility of a decent life under the Communist Government in Hungary became more and more evident. I was on the edge of my seat as I read this riveting account of their lives and escape. It is also a wonderful love story of his courtship and marriage to Rozsa. Laszlo did not hold back. It is an emotional and gripping book."

- Lisa Annand

"I am not a history buff, but as soon as I got my hands on this book I just couldn't put it down. I was hooked; every chapter was like watching a movie in my mind. If it ever gets to the big screen I'll be there in the front row."

-Vicki Burns

"This book is a great love story. It shows the power of the human spirit to overcome extreme odds and obstacles to follow one's heart and principles. It would make a good movie."

-Margaret McCain

"It was refreshing to read your honest account of your time under Communist occupation of your home land. A book like this would be ideal to be taught in schools so all of us could understand how blessed we are in the Country we live in."

-B.A. McLellan

"I could not stop reading this book. Oh, those terrifying times and yet the horrors continue as you failed your escape attempt and get arrested. Compared to all the trials you write about, our problems seem so trivial. You two were very brave then and now too to relive those times by writing this book. Thank you for sharing those experiences."

-Janet Killawee

"A fantastic read. Based on a true story. This book has shown me the meaning of true love, loyalty and bravery. Recommended for reading."

-Mavis Fahey-Hawkins

"It is a remarkable accomplishment."
-George Norrie

I just finished reading *Border of Hope, Fence of Despair* and I loved it! WOW! Your story telling is amazing. I laughed at the funny little things like the ingenious way you got the lunch tickets. I cried at the tender moments when Rozsa went to the hospital to have Ildi and you got there. Your journey was a true love story but also very poignant and insightful. Your writing style is engaging and your voice was vivid. You instilled in your reader the weight of important, danger and drama of Europe at that time in history. The harrowing escape to Austria gave the reader your depth of resolve and a sense of how dangerous that time had been. Your epilogue was so emotional and thank you for letting the reader know what happened to the people in your story. Please don't stop writing!!! You have a gift that should be shared in my opinion. Thank you again for sharing your story with me. I have so enjoyed your book."
-Yvonne Lantz

"This is a riveting story of determination, anguish and love. From the early pages of the book, you can feel the fiery spirit of Laszlo and his deep affection for Rozsa. The descriptions of the surroundings and the aura of the village being taken over by Communist rule make you feel you are there. You can clearly imagine the plight of this young man and his determination to make a better life for his family. It is a beautifully written testament to this period of history. It is also a moving story of love. To decide to escape from your country and leave your relatives behind takes courage and careful planning but to do this with a young woman and your infant child marks the plight facing them. The book gives more than a moment of pause to those of us who have always experienced freedom."
-Kathy Gayle Didkowsky

"As I am reading your book the *Border of Hope, Fence of Despair* I am shocked by the cruelty and brutality. It was way beyond my wildest imagination. I have read those pages again since I could hardly believe my eyes. Your book is a serious page turner especially for those who do not appreciate their freedom. Your book should be mandatory reading for those sitting in the malls waiting for their luck to change. I cherish every page you wrote."
-Betty Knodell

"A deeply personal story from a man who recounts his boyhood life from love to marriage and eventual nail-biting escape from Communist Hungary. A story that places a very personal perspective of what life was behind the iron curtain. Mr. Lichter offers a history that evokes a sense that one has just read someone's personal diary. A wonderful read."
-William Reive

"Oh my dear! I can't imagine living through some of the atrocities described in those chapters. You Hungarians are a strong breed of humans! I am so happy you and your family made it all the way to Canada. I am so happy that I had the privilege of hearing a portion of it firsthand so many years ago and now to be able to read the details through the pages of your book. Incredible indeed! I do hope you will have a book signing when it becomes available. I for one will be there."
-Hazelle Pettipa

"I found this book amazing. It is such an excellent read. Your recollections of the past are so clear that I can see your deeds, feel your pain, and understand your motivation to manipulate. Your determination to create a good life for your family in Canada is admirable. Thank you for sharing your memories with me."

-Roseanna Isenor

"This is a book that makes you count your blessings."

-Betti McLellan MacLean

"Your writing has brought many emotions to the surface, the forefront being compassion and understanding. The writer has enabled me to see a firsthand glimpse into a world I could only imagine, and now I have a much clearer understanding. The strength of your convictions for a better life and protecting your loved ones, show clearly in your writing. I feel your book will help people to be more appreciative of their own freedom that, so often, are taken for granted. Hats off to you for your successes. I smiled at the floundering of a young man in love. I cried for the injustices your loved ones suffered. I laughed at the bountiful harvest above your bed. I was in awe of the ingenious way you handled your oppressors. And I cheered when you crossed the border."

-Susie Rose Smith

"The writing is excellent! So much so, that I get clear images of what the author is describing. I wanted to take my time and give it the attention it so well deserves. You obviously took such care in writing it, and it is evident in each word you carefully chose. I couldn't put the book down, and even dreamt about it last night. My heart broke when I was reading about life in Communist Hungary and the many millions whose fate was unlike ours. I had a hard time understanding how inhumanly your family and many others were treated. I had not heard about what was happening in Hungary until I was much older and my parents spoke of all the suffering. Thanks to this book I have an even closer understanding from reading *Border of Hope, Fence of Despair* our dear neighbours."

-Allison DesJardins

"Thank you for sharing your life and your remarkable journey to freedom. It will leave a lasting impression on me and I'm sure I will always remember it. It is so hard to fathom, being a born Canadian, the hardships so many had to endure. We all need to remember not to take freedom for granted."

-Krista Faulkner

"This book made me smile and cry and my heart raced too. It really shows Canadians how privileged we are. I am looking forward to going to your first reading."

-Lori Smith

"I have finished reading your book and I struggle to express my admiration of you and your family for the way you endured that tyranny. Through your words I feel like I know you and your family. I felt all the emotions, pain, sorrow, happiness, anguish and hope. I realize that your faith in God carried you through all your trials and tribulations. I can only try to imagine the exhilaration you and your wife felt upon crossing the line to freedom. I would be remiss if I didn't acknowledge the fortitude, love and dedication of your wife. Without her, I don't think your journey to freedom would have been successful. This was an incredible story. Thank you for giving us a true understanding what real hardship and injustices you and your countrymen had to experience."

-Mary Young Wilfred Clooney

"I found your book wonderful. Knowing you made it so much more interesting. It should be made public, maybe in podcast."

-Gloria McCluskey

"I finished reading this book and found it very interesting. Before reading it I never really understood or appreciated the challenges that you, my dear Father and others faced back then. Growing up in Canada, with everything we take for granted does not let one really comprehend the hardships that others experience elsewhere. Nor does it allow a person to really understand what it would have been like for you and others to grow up in a Communist occupied country, where the State trusts no one, and does everything possible to turn neighbour against neighbour. I compliment you on your writing. Congratulations and thank you for sharing your recollections."

-Guy Lichter

"This book is a page turner start to finish. Laszlo has a knack for telling a story and holding the reader's attention. You can't but read this book about his family's escape from Communism, without comparing it to events in today's unsettled political climate. We truly can learn from history if we choose."

-Debbie Mountenay

"I truly enjoyed this book, it was one of those books that you couldn't wait to see what happens next. It is a testimony of true love, persistence and a desire for a better life. It saddened me to read about the pain and suffering your family and friends endured. I highly recommend this book."

-Pam Starrat

Prologue

My fifty-fourth birthday came, just a few months before I was to retire from my chosen profession, teaching. As my family celebrated the non-event, my mind searched desperately for a solution.

"I may have many years to go before the Merciful Lord ends my life. What am I to do between now and then?" I asked myself. Although I have been involved in Municipal politics, as a councillor, at that time, I did not see that as something worth doing for the rest of my life. It was then that I have decided to turn my energies to writing, so I allowed my gray matter to play back images of my life's episodes that were recorded only in my mind. An insignificant, yet exciting life that truly began in 1948.

That was the year when I met my wife to be; when my Sun began to shine; when my short life's hopes surged; and I have begun to experience happiness. Not even the tragedies, that were yet to come, were ever able to cast a permanent shadow on the happiness that filled me; a happiness that never left me.

That birthday is now ten years behind me; politics of any type is only a distant memory, as are the two books that I wrote since then. *Dreams and Broken Promises* and *When The Dreams Vanish,* both considered "novelograpics" (a strange hybrid of novel and biography). My two books remain unpublished, maybe due to my lack of effort to find a willing publisher. A few copies, I have printed for relatives, gather dust on some bookshelves, waiting for a time when their owners will feel the urge to read them again.

My thousands of hours of work were appreciated by some, including my wife, Rozsa, who always stood beside me, encouraged me to keep on writing, if for no other reason than to get me to the point of writing this biography.

So I am ready to begin...

Dedication

To my two companions who crossed the border with me, back in '56.

Rozsa, who remained by my side, before and ever since. Who listened to my reading of each chapter and then took the trouble to read them again. She offered many changes and never failed to correct my mistakes, but without ever offending.

And to Ildiko, who as a child, heard parts of our story, but never fully understood why I acted as I did. Maybe now that the whole story is told, as accurately as memory permitted, she will be able to grant her forgiveness.

Laszlo S. Lichter
January 26, 1998

Chapter 1

The scorching August Sun baked our un-paved street for three solid weeks. The temperature reached forty degrees Centigrade, but neither that, nor the almost unbearable dust could dampen my friends' enthusiasm from playing soccer. So they ran; kicked at the home-made soccer ball; screamed at each other when their team was doing poorly; shouted in jubilation when they finally scored a goal and looked for a substitute when one or another team member could no longer perform in the summer heat.

"Do you want to play Laszlo?" shouted my street's team captain.

I just stood there, as I stood by our gate for the last hour, hoping against hope that I will be allowed to play. It was not the first time in the last eleven years that I had waited for those words, but the invitation came rarely. I was too short, too skinny, too slow and the boys, who lived on Sip Street had no desire to be saddled with a player whose coordination left a lot to be desired. Neither did they desire to be beaten by the team of Sohaz street, but now they were one player short and I have waited too long to turn down the invitation.

So I accepted the team captain's summons; stood between the two rocks that marked our team's goal posts and my heart beat with fear each time the enemy approached. I tried, I truly tried to out-guess the opponents, but my efforts failed, time and time again. Since I took up my post, one player or another kicked the inflated pig bladder past me.

My team captain urged me: "Keep your eye on the ball. Don't let them score again!" A chorus of voices joined him: "Don't be so clumsy!" shouted the disappointed members of my team. "Atta boy! Keep it up," shouted members of the opposition.

I stood between my rocks, sweat poured off my whole body, dust mingled with my body fluids forming mud that caked my skin. My eyes tried to watch the ball, but they were drawn away by the sight of the approaching girls.

There were two of them. I judged them to be around thirteen years old. They carried a large wicker basket. Their arms strained with the effort of carrying the contents that hid under the blanket. There were two of them as I said, but for me there was only one. Some magic trick made the other girl disappear, while the one, whose sight my eyes held like vice-grips, appeared to be much closer then she really was.

I no longer remembered to watch the ball; I no longer heard the boys' shouting. I wiped the sweat from my face with dirty hands to better see.

Her blond hair was braided in two pony tails; her sweet face contained a trace of a smile and a frown. Her blouse, which was decorated with sun-flowers, stuck to her young body; her skirt flung this way and that with each step she took. Her skin was like milk; her ears tiny petals; her cherry lips parted slightly as she sucked in the hot air; her blue eyes sparkled like precious stones.

She approached the gate, just ten feet from where I stood, and as the gate swung open, as she stepped inside, as she disappeared, I heard my captain speak.

"What in hell is wrong with you? Are you sick Laszlo? Did you get a sun-stroke?" Then I felt his hand on my shoulder and he whispered in my ear: "I will never ask you to play again. You are too sickly."

Those words would have devastated me at any other time, but this time they carried no meaning. My reply, if that is what it was, came in a whisper: "I saw her! I really did Lajcsi."

"Who did you see?" asked my bewildered leader.

"The girl I love...My wife to be...The future Mother of my children." My stammered declarations must have convinced him that I suffered a sun-stroke, so he led me to the gate of our house; with his hands he urged me gently to enter my home and to leave the game of soccer to those who do not get so easily afflicted by the least physical exertion. I obeyed him, thus ending my short soccer career and my life truly began.

***

During the next six weeks my life centered around my studies at the Gymnasium of Economics, where I was in my third year of study, hoping to graduate in 1950. My determination to excel was greater than ever: I wanted to impress the girl I loved; the young lass who was no longer a stranger.

Shortly after the last organized soccer game I have ever played, I set about finding out who that sweet creature was. Fate smiled upon me. The daughter of our River Captain and her family moved into the house, across the street, I found out from my parents and from that moment on I was determined to make her acquaintance. It was a lot easier than I ever expected.

Her brother, Joe, was about my age; a student, one grade below mine, in the same school I attended. Thus we became friends and I became his helper. I carried water for the Buja family from the well; I chopped wood when that became necessary; I helped in any way I could. My help Joe accepted willingly and since I promised myself to stick to the truth as much as my memory permits, I am not reluctant to admit that it was not at all difficult to exploit his laziness, thus making myself indispensable, at least to Joe.

"Will you bring a bucket of water from the artesian well? Or will you cut some wood for the stove? Or will you give me a hand with my homework?" came his requests quite often and I was overjoyed to oblige.

Each time I entered the Buja home my heart began to beat faster. I hoped to get introduced to Rozsa, whose name I learned from Joe, but for days I saw her only from a distance. Each time I set eyes upon her, my determination to make her love me became even stronger.

Then my first opportunity arrived and I extended my shaking hand to hold hers, just for a moment, and with quivering voice I stammered out my name:

"My name is Laszlo...Laszlo Lichter," I told her and forgot to let go of her tiny, warm, well shaped hand.

"Mine is Rozsa Buja. I heard a lot about you from my brother. Joe says you are quite a worker..." her voice trailed off and to my greatest disappointment she withdrew her hand, turned around and walked away.

"Did I make a good impression?" I wondered and my skeptical mind turned against me. "How could you? You are rather short and skinny. Not really much to look at. She must have giggled hearing your shaking voice. Next time you must compose yourself. You must portray a better image," that was one part of my mind speaking, but another part argued with the latter. "You did quite well...She said you were quite a worker. That ought to count for something. Next time you will screw up your courage and maybe invite her to see a movie." While the argument continued between the skeptical and the hopeful regions of my mind, I set about to complete the task that Joe and I began. When the last piece of wood got split, I said good-by to Joe and expressed my hope that I will be able to help him again.

His words of parting and the laughter that followed them bothered me not in the least: "You can be certain of that!"

***

During the first three months I saw her almost daily; spoke to her briefly when she appeared at the scene of the never ending tasks that Joe found for me to do. She was always pleasant, but never lingered long enough for me to marshal my courage to ask her to a movie.

Then a day came when Joe got bored supervising my clumsy attempts at cutting logs and left me to do the work alone.

"I guess you can manage this small task, you really do not need me," Joe announced and when I nodded my head in agreement, he added sheepishly: "I have so many other things to do...Maybe I should attend to some other task." His words barely finished, he scooted away.

I did not mind working alone, although the logs were quite heavy and the cross-saw cut better by one person on each end, but one of its handles wasn't touched by anyone or days, so it really made little difference that Joe disappeared. At least that is what I thought for the next thirty minutes, then my hope began to soar and I blessed Joe for his absence.

I saw Rozsa enter the fenced back-yard, where I worked. With each step that brought her closer my heart-beat thundered and I feared that she might become frightened.

"I thought Joe and you worked together?" Rozsa's sweet voice sang out the innocent question.

"We do..." I assured her, "...but Joe had some other chore to do. So I am cutting these logs alone."

"Do you mind if I hold on to the other end of the saw? It might make it easier for you Laszlo," her words were music to my ears.

"I would love you to do that..." I stated without thinking and just the use of the word 'love' made me blush, I am sure.

She held on to the wooden handle of the saw with both hands and her bare arms sticking out of her silk blouse began to pull the saw, while I pushed my end. Then we reversed the process and it was my turn to pull the saw. Her whole body moved closer, yet not closer at all, for I had to take a step back to my greatest regret.

After twenty minutes or so of cutting with the saw, Rozsa and I finished the last log. We wiped perspiration from our foreheads, and with a sigh Rozsa sat down on the pile of wood.

"This is harder work than I thought. I am not surprised at Joe's reluctance to do as told by father. Why do you help him Laszlo?" she asked and turned her face toward me, expecting an honest answer.

"I like to help Joe..," I began, but her smile that betrayed a good dose of skepticism stopped the flow of my words.

"Do you really?" she asked and smiled again.

"Well I don't mind to help him and to tell the truth I like to be here, at your house."

"Well you are welcome, any time Laszlo," she replied and my heart's joyous beat quickened greatly. I opened my mouth to invite her to a movie, but our ears heard no sounds; my fear of her rejection kept me silent.

"Were you going to say something Laszlo?" she asked innocently and I, the love struck boy, decided to change the subject.

"I was just going to ask you about your school." I chose the safest topic I could.

"Well there is not that much to tell..," she began, "I am in grade seven at the Roman Catholic Nun's school for girls. Each and every morning we attend Mass together and we are made to stand beside the empty pews." I listened to her words, fascinated by her charming voice and did not interrupt her.

During this first sharing I have learned that many times during the morning Mass, Rozsa had fainted. She explained, without appearing to complain that the nuns showed no mercy to any of the students. She revealed, but without bragging, that she studied diligently, took her studies very seriously. She spoke matter of factly about school discipline the nuns held paramount; about the praise they heaped incessantly on anyone showing real scholarship. Told me how they frowned upon laziness; tolerated no failure; how even the smallest pleasures of life had to be approved by her home-room teacher, without whose signature even a parental, written permission, wasn't sufficient to allow a student to attend a movie in either of the two cinemas of Baja. In both cinemas one could expect the lights to come on, a few minutes after the beginning of the show, and a teacher, with the assistance of a policeman would look for those written permits.

"God have mercy on any student who is found in the cinema without that precious document, bearing the signatures of parent and home-room teacher." Rozsa stopped, perhaps having realized that her long, straight-forward telling about her life created an aura of intimacy never ever granted to me before; or perhaps her lips became dry from the telling. The latter must have been the real reason for her stopping and I saw her delicately wet her lips with her pink tongue and I was overwhelmed by the desire to take her into my arms; to tell her how much I love her; to tell her about my plan of making her fall in love with me; of wanting her become my wife, the Mother of my children.

She may have sensed the coming of my bold move, shifted slightly her position and began to speak:

"The last time I was given permission by my home-room teacher to see a movie was on June 6. Although I had written permission from my Mom, three times before, during the last school year, Sister Anne just looked at the piece of paper each time and gave it back with a comment: 'Maybe when you really earn it. Your grades are good, but some of the other girls do even better.' Then early in June I gave her one more slip of paper that bore the signature of my Mother. It was a permission slip to allow me to see the movie, The Hunchback of Notre-Dame. This time Sister Anne signed my cherished piece of paper and as she handed it to me she spoke: 'Congratulations. This time you deserve my approval, and besides this is your twelfth birthday. Isn't it?'"

"Did Rozsa try to tell me something?" I wondered and to my greatest surprise my words rolled off my tongue without effort.

"I know June 6 was some time ago, but I didn't know you then. I wish you a belated Happy Birthday Rozsa. And now that I know, I would like to give you a gift. Do you think you could accept my invitation to a movie? That is if your parents approve and the same goes for your home-room teacher." I held my breath awaiting her answer and congratulated myself, not only on finding my courage, but also on my invitation's timing.

"I would really like that, I really do," came her reply and her words made me overjoyed.

"Do you think your parents will approve?"

"I am sure they will," Rozsa assured me.

"But they hardly know me. It is true that Joe introduced us; that my parents and yours are friends, but I hardly had the chance to speak to them."

"Deeds speak louder than words Laszlo. They may not know from Joe all you did to help out, but they sure know that from me."

"From you, Rozsa?" I was really astonished and deliriously happy.

"Yes, from me. Whenever I came back and saw you doing Joe's jobs I felt obligated to let them know who did the lion's share," she stated and I couldn't miss the radiance of her face, the kindness of her words, the maturity of her thinking, all of which made me feel joy, experience elation, yet I felt totally confused. To cover my feelings and confusion I have decided to change the subject.

"June 6 was your twelfth birthday? Did you say that? I was sure you were somewhat older."

"Well, in that you are wrong Laszlo. What made you think I am older?" her question surprised me. I did not know what answer to give.

"Tell me Laszlo..," she teased me and I searched for words that would not betray my thoughts.

"You seem so mature."

"Mature in what way?" she continued her teasing.

"The way you think. How seriously you take your studies and the way you look." I dared not tell her more, but she wasn't going to allow me to stop, so I continued.

"Your blond hair in its two braids do not look childish; your blue eyes shine with intelligence; your beautiful face is radiant with understanding; your lovely ears hear all that is spoken and your brain's and heart's perception is not that of a twelve year old."

"Aren't you a flatterer Laszlo?"

"I spoke only the truth."

We parted shortly after and two weeks later Rozsa made her announcement: "I have two signatures on my permission slip, if you still want to take me to a movie."

"Indeed I do," I stated gladly, one step closer to my dream and we have made our plan.

***

Rozsa's parents' house faced ours, as I mentioned before. Faced it in a way. Our houses were built from bricks, covered with clay and white-washed with lime. Each house was built in the form of a rectangle; one long side faced an adjacent property and had no windows at all. The other long side faced a fenced yard with its doors and few windows. One short side faced the street and had two windows or more, while the back end faced another house providing them with privacy by having only one small opening from the huge attic that was accessible only by a ladder.

Our few windows allowed no glimpse at Rozsa house, which was across the street from our high, solid brick fence with one small gate in it. Many a nights I left my room that I shared with my brother, George, crossed the large yard to reach the small gate which I opened slightly to be able to see the two windows across the street. Behind those two windows slept Maria and Jozsef Buja, Rozsa's parents and beyond their room Rozsa and Joe rested in the room they shared. So I stood by our gate and through the small opening I created, I watched the house. I imagined one of its occupants doing her home-work. In my mind I could see her eyes scanning the pages of her book; her slender fingers holding a pencil or a pen, writing in her note-book; I could imagine her finishing her work, satisfied that all her home assignments were completed well; I could picture her talking to her brother; having a late night snack; changing into her night-gown with practiced modesty, while her brother she made to turn away. I imagined her kneeling beside her bed to say her evening prayer, just before slipping under her down-filled bedding. I strained my ears to hear her prayer, but not even my imagination made it possible for me to know if her supplication to the Almighty included my name or not. When I sensed that my beloved fell asleep I returned to my room, slipped into my bed and began my own prayer: "Dear Lord I have so much to thank You for and so much to ask of You. Please allow Rozsa to fall in love with me..," I always began and when I finished my nightly prayer I usually fell into a blissful sleep and dreamt about the only girl I could ever love.

Laszlo S. Lichter

***

    I put on a suit, the only suit I had and walked across the street to greet Rozsa's parents and to thank them for their permission to take their only daughter to a movie. We began our walk, side by side, hands swinging, but not touching. My steps had a special spring to them like never before; I ascribed this change to the presence of Rozsa, who walked beside me telling me about her day at school.

    We walked the short length of Sip Street rather slowly. I wanted the time to never end. My eyes saw things so differently. The dilapidated brick fences of various homes seemed to take on a charm I have never noticed before; the communal well, with its worn handle, made shiny by the hundreds of hands that pumped it daily grew in importance; the swirling dust of the street, whipped up by the wind, no longer bothered me as it did before. We turned the corner and entered another short street that bore the name of Klapka Gyorgy and we talked about our families.

    There were no side-walks on either streets, just plain looking, sometimes poorly kept homes with their glass windows soaking up Rozsa's image. When we entered Honved Street our feet carried us over the uneven, broken stones of the side-walk and then Rozsa stumbled. I grabbed her arm to steady her lithe body and even after she regained her balance I was loath to let her arm go, but she was too young to walk with anyone arm in arm, so I reluctantly gave in, let her arm go and blessed those who were too lazy to fix the potholes.

    She stumbled a couple more times before we traversed the long street of Hajnald and each time I gave her the assistance she needed and myself the most exquisite happiness I have ever experienced in my sixteen years of life.

    We walked by the beautiful Church of Priests; crossed the small park with its large statue, surrounded by wooden benches; stared into poorly decorated store windows before we reached Urania, the larger of two cinemas in our city.

    The movie lasted for two hours. This time neither teacher nor policemen checked for permission slips that we both obtained and carefully placed in easily accessible pockets. I no longer remember the title of the movie, nor the story line, possibly due to the fact that while Rozsa watched intently the screen I watched nothing but her beautiful face and felt nothing other than her nearness. I didn't want the movie to end; I didn't want to give her back to her parents. I cherished each moment I spent with her and wished with all my heart for twice as many pot-holes on our walk back to her home.

    On the way home she never stumbled. She kept her eyes on each spot where she placed her magnificent feet and for a while we walked in silence.

    "Did you enjoy the movie Laszlo?" she finally broke the spell and I don't know why I whispered.

"It was the most beautiful movie I ever saw."

I saw her allow herself a knowing smile and her eyes twinkled with mischief when she replied.

"You probably never saw a movie before."

"Yes I did. I saw many of them."

"And this one was the best you ever saw?"

"It is true Rozsa," I replied and pronounced her name with reverence.

"Well maybe we were not together," she replied more seriously and I fell into the unintended trap.

"We were together and I loved every minute of it."

"I am glad to hear that..," Rozsa's voice trailed off noting the seriousness of my declaration.

Before I said good-night to her, front of their gate, she looked deeply into my eyes and in her sweet voice she thanked me.

I waited until she entered her house feeling devastated about our parting, but then my spirits rose.

"She came to a movie with me. She allowed me to touch her arm, not once, but three times on the way to the movie. Maybe she will accept another invitation," I consoled myself and flew across the street, skipped across the yard, danced into my bedroom and sang out my prayer of thanks to the Almighty.

***

The memory of that precious evening sustained me for many weeks. My mind kept going back to the joyous moments of holding Rozsa's arm; watching her face in the light of the cinema's projector's beam that illuminated her beautiful features. I had to command myself to do my own chores and that of Joe; to pay attention to my studies; and I took great delight in every opportunity I had to talk with Rozsa and with her parents.

Rozsa's Mother had two sisters, Margit and Eta. All three of them lived in Baja when Rozsa's Mother met her husband to be. They fell in love and waited impatiently for

Mr. Buja to finish his studies at the Military academy. At an early age his father passed away, his Mother raised him alone. She had a few suitors, amongst them a high ranking officer from the Military Academy, who was always on the lookout for likely candidates for officer training. He recommended the nine year old Jozsef to the Academy and his military career began at that early age.

The Military Academy was a rather rigid task-master that did not allow its student officers to marry until the day of their commissioning.

When that day came Maria and Jozsef married and in 1932 they were blessed with Joe. Their joy turned into grief when their first daughter, Marika suddenly passed away half way to her first birthday. Maria always prayed for another blond little girl with blue eyes and as the years passed Jozsef Buja rose in rank and in 1936 Maria's prayers were answered: Rozsa arrived and made them happier than ever before.

Life was good to the Buja's: members of the family loved each other; friends and neighbors respected the officer, the gentleman whose honor, honesty, ability and loyalty was questioned by none. They lived in Budapest, the capital of Hungary and when the weekends came the family strolled together the beautiful esplanades of that magnificent city. They walked many times to the ancient Parliament building; visited the museums that dotted the city; looked down from the Fishermen's Castle at their beloved river, the Danube where Jozsef fished whenever time permitted. Their happiness was complete, in spite of the gathering storm-clouds of the Second World War.

November 20, 1940, when Hungary signed a Military agreement with Germany, Italy and Japan, Jozsef watched his country's decision with great sadness. His sadness turned to anger when on June 26, 1941 the Hungarian Cabinet of Ministers declared war on the Soviet Union. Jozsef's sadness and anger fought against his honor and loyalty. In his mind and heart the battle raged, and then his initial reaction was vindicated on December 7, 1941, the date England declared war against his homeland. He was a well trained military engineer, holding the rank of Captain by this time and he knew that no power, not even the mighty Germans could win a war fighting on two fronts.

When his orders came to embark to the Eastern front his honor and loyalty allowed him no other option than to embrace his wife and his two children; to say a tearful farewell to those he loved; to promise that he will return to them and to their nicely appointed apartment, on the second floor of a villa, on Csillag mountain, located in Buda, on the west side of the Danube.

Weeks grew into months; months stretched into three years and only Jozsef's infrequent letters gave hope to the three Bujas.

"Your father promised to return. He always kept his word," Maria Buja said to her children time and time again. She assured them at home; she repeated her assurance as they sat in bomb-shelters while the bombs fell, devastating their city.

She was preparing for Christmas of 1944, hoping that at least on Christmas Day the bombers will take a rest. She baked a cake with her last flour and eggs; she decorated a Christmas tree with 'szalon candy' she saved from previous years; she wrapped two presents, one for each of her children, gifts that at any other time would have looked deficient. But this was a war-time Christmas, where shortage of food was common place, where consumer goods were almost nonexistent. Rationing became a way of life long ago. With tears in her eyes she surveyed her preparations for the coming of little Jesus and knew that her children will be disappointed.

Then she heard the door open, sun-light streamed around the large man blocking her door. She was blinded for a moment, her eyes could not identify the stranger, but her heart knew the truth. In a split second they were in each others' arms. They could taste each other's tears as they kissed; their arms shook with excitement as they held each other, then the children burst into the room, flew into their father's arms. The night's sky darkened as the four Buja's rejoiced; the stars appeared and the happiest ever Holy Night beckoned them to the decorated Christmas tree.

I saw tears lurking in the corners of their eyes as they told me about that special event and as I listened to Jozsef's voice I found out how that miracle came to be.

Captain Buja and his remaining men were ordered to retreat to Budapest and to defend the city against the Soviet Army to the last man. The war was lost, it was lost from the very beginning, Jozsef knew and dead were many of his men, but he could not face losing one more, could not allow one more family to lose a father or a husband, so he called them together and quietly urged them to disperse, to discard their uniform and guns, to head for their homes and to dedicate their lives to the families they left behind, so long ago.

His soldiers respected him; considered him a wise man and after saying their farewells they obeyed his instructions. Their parting was final, they knew; the bond of friendships they forged in battle had to be broken; their families needed them desperately and the hope of seeing them, a hope that faded with each skirmish, suddenly was rekindled by their Captain. They obeyed him before in everything he ordered them to do and now their Captain obeyed the highest duty an officer ever had: to save his men.

When all of his men dispersed, Jozsef began his journey and two days later he was home. Once the Buja family celebrated the miracle of that Christmas long enough, Jozsef's pragmatic mind turned to the things he had to do. While fighting in the Soviet Union he learned much about the people of that vast country and even more about its plundering Red Army. Whenever the Hungarian Army gathered intelligence from civilians who came in contact with Red Army soldiers, Jozsef filed away all the information and now he was ready to act.

His uniform he exchanged for old, worn, civilian clothing. He took his uniform to the back yard and behind a few bushes he watched the flames consume the garments with their insignia. He was saddened by what he did, but his family's safety was paramount in his mind.

While on the Eastern front he sent money to his family, whenever he could, but not in letters that would be opened. He always used a trusted soldier or officer who was given the opportunity to go to Budapest to recuperate from injuries. Those occasions did not come often, thus the money he was unable to send home he accumulated and now he was ready to use.

Maria knew where the wine cellars were located. Was acquainted with the vendors of that special commodity, who were not unwilling to raise their price daily for the precious substance. Jozsef used much of his money to obtain as many bottles as he could. He carefully lowered his treasure of survival into the holes he dug in the back-yard. He marked each hidden reserve of wine bottles, but only in his engineer's mind and prepared his family for the coming of the Russians.

Maria he instructed not to wear clothing that made her look attractive. He ordered her, but not unkindly, to use no make-up, to keep her hair uncombed, to appear unkempt, but never spoke about the source of his fears; the stories of rape of old and young alike, he heard so much about. He instructed her to put away as much food as she could and when the enemy arrives to treat them like long lost friends. Show them the famous Hungarian hospitality.

He instructed Rozsa to make herself look even younger than her eight years. He took great pains to teach Joe obedience to the coming masters; ordered him to curb his desire to roam. When he couldn't think of any more to do, he listened for the sounds of the coming Red Army.

His wait was less than two weeks when from the Pest side the Germans retreated under heavy fire. The fighting raged on for days on the eastern shore of the Danube between the invaders and the remnants of the German Army that were unable to cross the vast river, its seven bridges destroyed, some of them by the Allied bombers, long ago and the remaining bridges by the retreating Germans, who in their confusion, in the heat of the bloody battles left some of their units stranded. As the weeks passed, the fighting shifted from Pest to the bombardment of Buda.

"They must have crossed the river...," Jozsef told his family late in January. "I can hear the unmistakable sounds of street-fighting just block away." They listened with fear to the sound of explosions that rocked their neighborhood; they saw the flames that painted red the night skies over Buda Castle on the night of January 24. When the bombardment died down he expected the impending arrival of those who were his enemies for three years, but not anymore.

He looked at his wife, glanced at his daughter and knew that they obeyed his every wish. Maria was no longer the attractive woman he loved with all his heart. She became a worn, old hag who might not be desired. Rozsa looked different too: her dress was that of a simple, younger child, even her facial expression made her look a lot younger. Then he gazed at Joe and hoped that even he would remember to behave as he was told.

When the three Russian soldiers broke into their house they commanded them to stand in the middle of their living room, while two of them searched their apartment for Germans, for weapons, for any sign of threat and when they found none they looked them over. The Buja family never knew why the Russians ignored the females. It may have been their exhaustion or their decency that existed even amongst the Russians or perhaps Maria's fast action.

She signaled the Russians without words that she wanted to go to the pantry. One Russian escorted her and within seconds she carried the large pot of chicken paprikas to the kitchen, she prepared it two days ago for just such an occasion. She placed the pot on the stove, began to warm it and while the food began to simmer, while its aroma filled the place; she put three place settings on the kitchen table. She pointed to the three chairs, then to each of the Russians, making them understand. The Russians looked at each other; one that appeared to be the leader uttered a single sound: 'Da'.

The three soldiers sat down on the chairs, never let go of their machine guns with the round magazines and seemed to relax a bit as she heaped the home made food on all of their plates.

One of them motioned to indicate their thirst and this time Jozsef sprang into action. He took out the only two bottles of red wine that he hid in the house, uncorked both bottles and filled their glasses.

The Russians fell upon the steaming food like hungry wolves; they drank like camels upon reaching an oasis. Before their plates emptied Maria filled them again. The soldiers gave her appreciative glances not of carnal desire, but glances that were filled with gratitude. Jozsef saw this and his fear began to dissolve. He waved to one of the soldiers and pointed to the empty wine bottles, then to the door, making them understand that he had two more bottles elsewhere.

The leader grunted his agreement and spoke a single word: 'Karasho'. Even Jozsef's limited Russian vocabulary allowed him to understand that it was all right for him to leave the apartment.

In less than ten minutes he returned with two full bottles and found himself facing one of the machine guns. The Russians filled with good food and partially satiated with good wine, became once again cautious; remembered that anyone could be their enemy, so they made him remove the cork from both bottles and prompted him to take a swallow from each in turn. Once he obeyed their commands he saw a wide smile spread over the soldiers' faces and they began to drink.

Before the fourth bottle became empty one of the Russian soldiers began to hum, the other two picked up the embryonic tune and their voices filled the room. They sang an unfamiliar, nostalgic, even heart-wrenching song, something about Volga and Mother, Jozsef guessed. When the first song was finished they sang another and several more.

"They were not at all what I feared them to be," Jozsef told us in one of our conversations. "Once I discovered the truth I gave a silent thank you to the Lord that delivered us to hands that did not belong to evil. They were not so different from my own former soldiers. They must have longed for their families; desired nothing more than to end the war, to return to their home-land; they had needs like all human beings and once the basic needs were satisfied they were calm and no longer threatening as they were before."

The three soldiers passed a couple of evening hours eating, drinking and singing, probably about their homeland and sweet-hearts they left behind. Then the leader must have remembered the call of duty. He stood up gave an order to the youngest Russian, that none of the Bujas understood and when the soldier appeared to obey the order, when he lay down on the chesterfield in the living room, Jozsef grabbed the advantage.

He concluded that these three soldiers were anxious to take up residence at their home; that one will rest while the others carried out their duties and no doubt they would alternate as his own soldiers were made to do during the long war.

Jozsef reached for the hand of the young soldier, shaking his head in disagreement. The soldier rose, a quick puzzled look crossed his face, and then he followed Jozsef to the bedroom that belonged to Joe and Rozsa. There Jozsef pointed to the bed and he used the word he heard before: 'Karasho'.

The soldier examined the soft bed, touched the fluffy pillow, ran his hand over the feather bedding, and his 'Karasho, Karasho' sang out conveying happiness.

The two other soldiers have left and the next three days bore the truth of Jozsef's guess. The other two soldiers returned from time to time. They never came empty handed: a hen, a ham, a goose, loafs of bread they brought with a smile. They always handed these precious items to Maria and pointed to the stove. She prepared many meals willingly, while Jozsef disappeared and returned with a few more bottles.

On the third day of this daily routine Maria set the table for three, but the oldest Russian shook his head, his gestures indicated clearly that seven places she was to set. From that time on the three Russians and the four members of the Buja family sat at the same table, ate the same food, sipped at the wine sparingly not to deplete the hidden treasures too fast. Whenever the Russians had their fill two of them left and a different one occupied the large double bed that no longer belonged to Joe and Rozsa.

Thus the days passed and when the Russian High Command gave the order to have the forty-eight hours of looting begin many families found themselves in deadly peril. Their meager possessions were taken by the intoxicated Russian soldiers; mothers and daughters were gang raped in front of their husbands or fathers who just stared into the muzzle of the guns held to their heads to prevent resistance. Some resisted in spite of the deadly threat and lost their lives in trying to prevent what could not be prevented.

On several occasions the Buja family faced the same danger, but each time the resident Russian made his presence known by stepping out on the balcony and letting loose a bursts into the air from the machine gun.

On February 13, 1945 all fighting ceased in the capital of Hungary; it moved to the west and so did the Buja's protectors.

Jozsef Buja reported to the Russian High Command, presented his credentials and was put to work. For months he was in charge of building pontoon bridges across the Danube. When his skills were no longer needed to carry out these tasks, he was assigned to a river patrol unit to free the Danube from the thousands of mines that prevented shipping. All the tasks he was given he carried out conscientiously and when that job was completed he was sent to Baja, as Captain of the Danube River Police. For some time, after their relocation, the family lived in an apartment above Jozsef's office, they faced shortages as others have; survived the raging inflation that followed the war and when late in the summer of 1946 the back of inflation was broken by the issue of new currency, named Forint, the Buja family began to save and in two years time they were able to realize their dream: the purchase of a home, across from mine.

***

As the months passed the mild fall moved aside making space for winter. The snow began to fall; its large flakes glistened on Rozsa's unblemished cheeks, on our way to the movie-house. This was the second time that Rozsa's parents gave me their trust, that her home-room teacher rewarded the superb student, and she honored me to be her companion. I remember even today the large, fluffy flakes drifting toward her, seeking to touch her beauty. Snow covered her red, knitted bonnet; the flakes swirled around us and descended on her horse-hair blanket coat. She reached for my arm, probably to make her footing surer and I accepted her gift gladly.

We walked arm-in-arm to the cinema and back to her home.

"Did you enjoy the movie? Was this the best you ever saw Laszlo?" she turned her face toward me; her eyes sparkled as she asked the questions, reminding me of what I said about our last movie.

"I am happy we went, but no I did not enjoy the movie."

"Do you mean that you are happy we were there, but you did not care for the movie?"

"Exactly that..," I began. Then I looked into her sweet face and couldn't stop. "I am happy whenever we are together. The place really does not matter, nor does the movie we happen to see."

"It is strange you would say that. Whenever I went to see a movie and saw a film that wasn't any good I always felt cheated, but today it really didn't matter," she spoke the words rather slowly, carefully, all the while watching my face for any reaction.

I envied the snowflakes that landed on her cheeks; I most begrudged those fortunate few that kissed her lips. I tightened my arm around hers and choked out the words boldly: "Your words made me truly happy."

"A little happiness never hurts. That movie was so full of misery," the strong wind carried her words behind us and the young man walking on our heels in the gentle snow-storm, the man we didn't notice before, picked up her words and made a statement. I remember his words clearly, although I didn't know who he was, nor did I ever see him again.

"It is so sad that people have to live the way they live in America," the young man stated. "Exploitation, degradation, poverty and lack of trust are miseries indeed. That is what that movie wanted us to understand. The title <u>Hope Turned Despair</u> was truly appropriate. You are a foolish young lady, who doesn't want to see how people live in a capitalist country. Maybe you are an enemy of this nation? Some day you will understand, us Communist will teach you."

I turned around, ready to defend Rozsa and her point-of-view, but our instructor rounded a corner and in the swirling snow disappeared.

"Do you believe Laszlo what that man said?"

"I doubt his words, as I doubt the story of the movie, for two reasons. For over two years I have had letters from my pen-pal, who lived in the United States. His father is a coal miner. They live in a nice house, they eat good food, wear nice clothing and they have freedom. If I didn't believe all he wrote then there is my first cousin, Erzsi, who has relatives in America. They send her parcels and letters, not infrequently. The parcels' contents speak for themselves. The sweets and chocolates are far better than any I have ever tasted; the clothes are far superior to what is available in Hungary; the occasional toys in those parcels, speaks of pride of workmanship and imagination; the pictures they send do not show hovels, but homes that are splendid; the letters they write speak of freedom and boast of plenty." I was happy to speak about a topic that spoke not about love. I was truly afraid to frighten Rozsa with out-pouring of my feelings. So I continued to speak about Erzsi; then about her Mother, Tercsi, my father's sister, whose first husband's sister immigrated to the United States, in the early twenties. Erzsi wasn't even born when her paternal aunt left her home-land. Yet her aunt knew about Erzsi's entry into the world, she was also notified when Erzsi's father passed away and ever since then the parcels came bimonthly to remind Erzsi that she is not alone. When I got this far in my story Rozsa stopped in her tracks, turned toward me and with eyes wide she asked her question.

"Erzsi you said? Are you speaking about Erzsi Angermayer?"

"Yes, that is the name of my cousin, but only since her adoption. Her name was Erzsi Zilahy. Do you know her Rozsa?"

"Erzsi and I are friends. Come to think of it, it is really strange. She is my friend and she doesn't know that you and I..." she began to say, but I never found out what were the precious words she left unsaid.

"Nor did I know that the two of you are friends. I never saw her at your place," I stated.

"She is not allowed out in the evenings. Pista, her adoptive father, is rather strict. So she and I meet on the way to school and back. Now and then she comes over, but only in the afternoons. She was at our place, at least five times, when you and Joe worked in the back. Yes, I am absolutely sure now...She came in, looked around and I sensed her disappointment. When I asked her what was wrong, she just shook her head, a sad shadow crossed her face, and then she asked if I wanted to play. I think now that she was hoping to see Joe. Yes, that is the case I am sure. Whenever she sees him she changes completely: she becomes a lot more mature; she shyly hides the doll we play with; she chooses her words more carefully than before. What do you think makes her do that?" she asked and I didn't know if Rozsa was so young, so innocent that she couldn't fathom the meaning of love or if she was setting for me a trap. So this time I cautiously approached a subject I knew was dangerous to speak about.

"Erzsi is two years older than you Rozsa, maybe she fell in love. Or is that impossible at her age?"

"I really do not think so. People fall in love even at an earlier age." she stated without hesitation and I clamped my lips together; forced my tongue to remain idle; shoved my questions into the most hidden part of my mind, the questions that scorched my soul: "Did you fall in love my beloved? Am I the one you love?"

A silence descended upon us; I felt a strange tension that Rozsa signaled by removing her arm from mine and walked the rest of the way to her home totally unaided.

I felt suddenly lonely, sad and troubled. In my mind I have recalled each word we spoke; tried to find out the reason behind her sudden coolness, but my mind refused to grant me an instant explanation. We were almost at her house's gate when I unexpectedly cheered up. For years I have played chess, not too well and not too badly, so it was not unusual for my gray cells to examine each and every possibility and to settle on the one that promised the greatest advantage.

"She offered you her arm and you didn't know the reason. You suspected that in the slippery snow she needed your support, if that was true then she would not have walked the last few hundred yards on her own. She wanted your touch, it is that simple," I heard the voice of my brain and its consolation made me smile. "Do you want to know why she drew back? When you walk on ice, when you sense its thinness what do you do Laszlo? You step back, your feet search for solid support. When you two talked about Erzsi and the love she must have for Joe, Rozsa drew back for that topic held some danger. Remember that at her age that topic may create nothing but conflicting emotions, confusion and may be some panic," my brain reasoned and I promised myself once again to be very patient, to bide my time until Rozsa becomes comfortable with my love and adoration.

When we reached her gate her words were cool: "Thank you..," she said and something she saw on my face made her brighten.

"It is not even eight o'clock. Would you like to come in Laszlo?"

My face must have lit up with the happiness her words caused and not trusting my voice I nodded my head. We entered her kitchen, the only entrance into their apartment, and found Rozsa's Mother and father sitting at the kitchen table.

"So how was the movie?" Mr. Buja asked.

I still couldn't trust my vocal cords, so I waited for Rozsa to answer.

"It was terrible."

"What did you see Laszlo?" Mrs. Buja forced me to speak.

"A Russian movie: <u>Hope Turned Despair.</u>" I offered no more.

"What was it all about?" Mr. Buja asked, not prying, just trying to make conversation.

I listened with reverence to Rozsa's words that painted an accurate picture of the Mexicans' hope to enter the United States; their struggle to cross the border; their joyful arrival to the land of plenty where they found nothing but slavery, poverty, desolation, wretchedness and despair. When she finished describing the story-line her father posed a question.

"Did you say it was a Russian movie?"

"It was, with Hungarian sub-titles," Rozsa replied.

"What is the relationship between Russia and the United States, Laszlo?"

Did he try to draw me into the conversation or did he just want me to display my lack of knowledge of world history? I did not know, but by then I knew better than to remain silent when Mr. Buja asked a question.

"During the Second World War they were allies. The Americans supplied the Soviet Union with weapons, war materials and civilian goods. After the end of the war they became bitter enemies. Communism and Capitalism are in a terrible struggle."

"Right you are Laszlo. Now tell me what do you expect enemies to do?"

"I don't understand your question," I was truly baffled.

"I see...My question covered too wide a topic, so let me rephrase it. If you were an American, an enemy of the Russians, and you were about to write a story about Russia, would you write about the good things or would you try to stress, to exaggerate all that is wicked about them?"

"I would amplify everything that is adverse about them," I replied and tried to avoid using the exact words Mr. Buja used.

"I would think so. So what do you expect from the Russians?"

"I would anticipate them doing the same."

"Right you are again. So what does all this mean to you Rozsa? I mean about the movie you saw."

"The movie avoided everything that is good and enlarged everything that is bad in America," Rozsa offered.

"I am pleased to hear that you understand my dear little girl," with great care Mr. Buja placed emphasis on the last two words of his statement. 'Little girl', were the words I was meant to hear, to heed, to understand. "You see my child; movies are used to make propaganda. The Germans did it during the war; the Americans do it now, but with much more skill and the Russians do it, but very crudely."

"But Dad, how could that be? I saw the Hunchback of Notre Dame not long ago and it was nothing like that," Rozsa spoke matter-of-factly.

"Well my earlier statement was incomplete. The Americans and others make movies to entertain, their propaganda rarely takes the upper hand, but the Russians do not even attempt to pretend. They are not interested in entertaining the masses. Their interest lies elsewhere. They try to educate the masses, at least that is what they claim, but I call it something else."

"What do you call it Mr. Buja?" I asked almost sheepishly.

"Before I answer your question Laszlo I must speak about something else. We allow you to come to our house. We know all about the way you help. We appreciate that, but that is not enough. No...wait, let me finish," he ordered firmly, sensing that I was ready to give words to what I thought. "I didn't mean to be rude, Laszlo. I just want you to understand. Rozsa is not even thirteen years old. We let you come and see her; we allow you to take her to a movie, now and then. We do this because your parents are our friends, because we trust you Laszlo. Trust is a sacred thing, so do not ever disappoint me!" his words left no doubt as to what he meant. "Since I trust you, we trust you, now I am ready to answer your question. What the Russians do I call brain-washing. Dangerous words to use, I know. So never repeat what I said.

"I have served on the eastern front during the war; I saw how the Russians lived. If those Mexicans of that movie were able to get to Russia, instead of the United States, they would be horrified. They would find themselves in Siberia, in Stalin's prison camps. They would not be the only ones there: there are tens of thousands of German, Hungarian, Polish soldiers in Siberia. I think you know that Laszlo. Isn't your uncle amongst them?" Mr. Buja waited for an answer and took a sip of wine.

"My poor uncle, Jozsef Santa, was captured by the Russians at the end of the war. He was on his way home. They brought him with thousands of others to Baja, the city where his wife, Gizella, waited for his return. My father tried to have him released, after all he was captured in civilian clothing, after the war ended, but all his efforts were fruitless. Uncle Jozsef was loaded into cattle cars, with thousands of others, and shipped to a Siberian prison camp. We got a few letters from him. He is alive, he was alive, but we know little else."

"I know my boy from your father all that happened to your uncle Jozsef. I know how close you were to him and how in your pain you blamed your father. I know it hurts, but either his return or time will heal that. You are very young and the young heal more easily." There it was again, but this time it was my youth that was stressed, not that of Rozsa. "Do you know what else I have learned?" Mr. Buja didn't wait for an answer. "I have learned that Stalin was no kinder to his own people: the victorious Russian soldiers were sent to Siberia as well. Stalin couldn't risk being exposed as a bungling military idiot whose soldiers were driven to victory by political hacks who stood behind the fighting Russians with loaded machine guns, who drove the vodka drunk soldiers toward the west. When the soldiers were thus condemned then it was the political officers turn; so they were made to join the soldiers of many nations and the 'kulaks' of the Soviet Union.

"Do you know who the 'kulaks' were? I am sure you don't Laszlo," his words became more forceful, his telling betrayed his bitterness. "During the early years, that followed the Great Russian Revolution, Lenin and Stalin confiscated all larger land-holdings and gave small, few acre plots to the land-starved Russian peasants. A few years later, after Lenin's death, Stalin made his underlings force the small farmers to give up their land, to join collective farms of thousands of acres. Those very peasants, who praised Stalin, who included his name in their prayers, loved the land and were loath to give it up. Anyone who resisted in any way became a 'kulak', so millions of 'kulaks' were sent to the

Siberian prison camps. They were followed by everyone who opposed Stalin and when opposition completely disappeared, when the high death-rate in those camps demanded fresh laborers, Stalin continued his insane condemnations. Everyone who displeased him, everyone who uttered a wrong word, everyone Stalin considered his enemy, found themselves in Siberia. I told you these things because I trust you and because I want you to understand." Mr. Buja stopped and I couldn't miss his sadness.

"May I ask you a question Mr. Buja?" momentarily I must have forgotten Rozsa's presence, if that was possible, and my hatred for the Russians made me bold. I never told them until this night that I witnessed a Russian officer violating my aunt Gizella. This time the dam of my silence broke, and I described how the Russian mob broke into our school, drank off the formaldehyde straight from the jars that covered frogs, snakes and other preserved animals in our biology lab. I repeated the stories I heard about the atrocities members of the Russian Army committed. I described in great detail how the women in my own family escaped rape only by keeping two Russians as guard-dogs and offering our protectors the two willing gypsy prostitutes, who lived in our house, thanks to my mother's foresight who offered them a free room, just weeks before the arrival of the occupying army. Then I asked my question: "The Russians are Communist Mr. Buja. Are they not?"

"The Russian leadership is Communist, but the average Russian is no different from us," came his reply, dictated by his fairness.

"The Russian leadership created the Hungarian Communist Party. Is that correct?"

"I do admit," came his reply and he must have begun to see where I was headed.

"And you Mr. Buja belong to the Communist Party, as does my poor father. So why is that?"

"I take no offense; I guess your question wasn't designed to give any. Let me explain. I came home from the war and shortly after I have joined the Social Democratic Party, as did your father. Both of us hoped to create a just society and prosperity for our people. Stalin had other plans. He sent back to Hungary his hench-man, Matyas Rakosi. That Communist wormed his way into our political structure and he became the most powerful minister in the coalition government. His 'salami tactic' slowly demoralized the other parties, and there were many. By the beginning of this year only the Social Democratic Party and the Communist Party existed. Without our support, without the approval of our party's membership, on June 12, 1948 the Social Democratic Party and the Communist Party joined and formed the Hungarian Workers' Party, an alias for the Communists. All former members of both parties automatically became that of the new one. Your father and I contemplated to leave the new party, but there was great danger in that, not only for me, but for your father as well. He and I talked about the right course of action, many times and the conclusions we have reached I want you to understand.

"Let me begin with your father. I am sure you know that for some old political crime, he committed as a young man, he was condemned during the war to be a slave laborer. Before the Germans began their great retreat from the Russian-Hungarian border, they forced their slave-workers, at gun-point, to dig their own graves. They made them stand in front of the long trenches facing the German guns. When the machine guns began to bark and he fell unhurt into the trench, covered by the dead bodies of his friends, when he crawled out after the Germans retreated and began his dangerous, two week long trek to reach his home, he vowed to better the future of this nation. As time passed he established himself as the owner of a shoe-making factory, he provided employment to the heads of thirteen families and to yours as well. He was free to leave the new party, but he was warned, just as I was. If he were to leave the party, he would lose his factory license and fourteen families would become destitute. What would you have done Laszlo in your father's place?"

"I do not know," I replied, unwilling to confess my tendency to do as my father did.

"I do not think you are being honest," Mr. Buja scolded me for the first time and I instantly regretted my answer. "Your father, at the age of eleven, lost his father and was made to fend for himself. He had six brothers and sisters, all in the same boat, around 1930, I understand. Two of his brothers died in Russia while fighting the enemy. Out of the four remaining brothers and sisters he lost one sister during the bombing of Budapest, two other of his brothers just disappeared during the war. He saw how their families suffered without bread-winners, a suffering that not even his generous help was able to completely ease. Now it is only your aunt, Tercsi, and your father who have the means to help the less fortunate members of your family. He is not like you Laszlo. He knows that a man's duty first and foremost is to his family. If it wasn't for your youth I think I would be forced to condemn you for your answer. Family must always come first, that you must understand."

"I do! I am sorry for my earlier answer. Maybe I was too hasty in my reply. Thank you for making me see things as I should have seen them on my own," I tried to redeem myself; I tried to erase my earlier mistake.

"Very well, young man. You have a long way to go before you are mature enough to be the head of a family. Being that requires sacrifices," Mr. Buja stopped, letting me think of what he said, then after a few seconds he continued.

"This much about your father should be sufficient. Now let me explain my decision. I was a Captain in the Hungarian Army; fought against the Russians as my oath commanded; when I was ordered to have my unit defend our capital to the last man I had a big decision to make. My honor, my oath, my training, my knowledge of Russia urged me to fight to the last breath, but my obligation to my family and to that of my men weighed heavily on my soul and in the end I urged my men to desert, as I was about to do. In my heart and soul I created a gaping hole, but I did that for Maria, Joe and Rozsa. A few months after the war ended I became the Captain of the River Police, as you know. Should I have given up even that? Should I have sacrificed my family's welfare for the sake of my pride? I don't think so. Rakosi and his followers began the persecution of their former enemies. They started with the highest ranking military officers and the top politicians of the former regime. It will not take them very long before they are ready to replace all of us. Should I have given them an excuse to eliminate me? What do you think would happen to Rozsa?" Mr. Buja's gaze bore into my eyes, he used its portals to see into my soul and heart and before I spoke he must have known my answer.

"Sorry I ever asked you about the Communist Party. I do understand."

"I am glad Laszlo. If you didn't I would be forced to ask you never to come again to the house of a Communist Party member," his words tore into my heart, created havoc in my mind, gripped me with fear of understanding.

"Thank you Mr. Buja for trusting me, for letting me see my father in a different light. Thank you for not casting me out for my foolishness," my words trailed off, knowing not what else to say. Rozsa and her Mother listened to our exchange and when it ended my love came to my rescue.

"Dad, may I say something?"

"I am always willing to listen to my angel."

"I didn't understand it either, not until today. Are you in any danger? What you said seemed to indicate that."

"This is not the first time I have to face danger, my daughter. When the time comes that the regime discards me I will still provide for all of you."

"But what if they do not let you?"

"As long as I live, as long as I have my health, I will take any job, nothing is beneath me."

"But if they will not let you do anything, what will happen then?" Rozsa persisted.

"What you are saying my dear requires a complex answer, an answer that I cannot give."

I was relieved how Rozsa shifted the focus from my earlier foolish question and I have recovered from the scolding I took.

"On the way home I told Rozsa about my first cousin, Erzsi and her relatives in the states," after those introductory remarks I detailed carefully all I said about the United States. "Would it be possible for your family and mine to go there, instead of waiting for the Communist to punish you and maybe even my father?" I posed the last question with all the eagerness of my youth.

"Many people have left their home-land before the war ended. They escaped before the Russians' arrival. They are somewhere in the west, homeless, friendless, probably pining for everyone they left behind. To leave the place where we were born; to desert our homeland; to leave our beloved relatives behind is not my choice. I am proud to be a Hungarian. Throughout our history many were sent into exile. One of them was Lajos Kossuth, a freedom fighter a century ago. He composed his most famous poem, somewhere on the shore of the Adriatic. Either of you Laszlo or Rozsa remember what it said?"

"I listen alone to the murmuring of the ocean..," Rozsa's clear voice sang out the first line of that painful poem.

"Yes, my lovely, that is what Kossuth wrote. His poem spoke with so much feeling of the pain an exiled person has. There is not much difference between self-imposed exile and the exile of Kossuth. That option, Laszlo, is not an option for either families, yours or mine. Enough said, look at the time, it is almost midnight. Laszlo you better scoot home or your parents will be worried. Rozsa off you go to bed."

***

That night I lay in my bed, unable to sleep. I thought about the joy, the ecstasy I have experienced while I held Rozsa's arm; I thought about our long conversation; the mistake I have made; Mr. Buja's patience in explaining his and my father's position. I tossed and turned, and before I drifted off to sleep, I promised myself never again to judge the conduct of those whose motivation I do not understand; never to get involved in the dirty game of politics; never to divert my energy from the only thing that mattered: to make that sweet little girl feel love for me as deep, as true, as limitless as my love is for Rozsa.

After that sleepless night I went to school expecting nothing unusual. My home-work was done; my studies were completed. I was called front of the class by my history teacher, probably to ask me a question, when the knock came and our vice-principal entered. He whispered something to my teacher, who pointed at me and to my surprise I was asked to step out of the classroom.

My vice-principal closed the door, turned to me and his words set fear in my heart. "The principal wants to see you." With those few words he turned on his heels and I had no choice but to follow him to the office all the students dreaded to enter.

"Come in Laszlo...This is a comrade who wants to speak to you," she pointed at the stranger, did not reveal his name or status, then added: "Comrade I will leave the two of you alone. Use my office as long as you like."

"What is your name boy?"

"I am Laszlo Lichter."

"Are you a Communist?"

"I have no political belief," I announced remembering my sleepless night's resolve.

"You are either for us or against us! There is no middle of the road," the official declared and the next question truly surprised me. "Are you a friend or an enemy? I demand an answer."

"I do not know you. How could I give you an answer?" I looked at him, challenged him, tried to force him to tell me who he was.

"Very well. I understand your hesitation. I will tell you what you want to know, but after that you must decide. I am an officer of State Security. My job is to ferret out enemies of our nation. So Laszlo, are you a friend or an enemy?"

"I am not an enemy, I assure you."

"Why is it so difficult to declare yourself to be a friend?"

"I don't make friends that easily."

"But you have friends amongst your classmates?"

"Yes I do. But we have attended school together for over two years and I met you only minutes ago."

"Oh, I see. I didn't ask you to be my friend, just a friend of our nation. Are you that?"

"I am a true Hungarian."

"Very well. We are getting somewhere. Do you ever help your friends?"

"I do."

"How do you help them?"

"In any way I can."

"Good. Are you willing to help Hungary, in any way you can?" he appeared to take pleasure in taunting me.

"Yes I am willing to help my country. But young boys like me are rarely able to do that."

"Nobody is too young to protect the security of our nation. Besides, I know you have some talents," he spoke the words and winked at me knowingly. He must have talked with my principal about my academic record, he must have found out that I am not a terribly poor student; I perceived and decided to ask him what he meant.

"What talents do I have that would be of use to you?"

"Not to me, but to the cause I serve. Get one thing straight comrade, I am the one who asks the questions," he spat the words at me, baited me and in my inexperience I gave him the upper hand.

"I am not a comrade, I want you to know," I threw back the word he used.

"You do not have your priorities straight Laszlo. You declared yourself to be a friend and our friends are our comrades. Or did you lie to me?"

"My mistake..." I gave in. "So what do you want friend, comrade," I imitated him in return.

"Right now just a few minutes of your time. Some information about you. Perhaps later there will be more. Is this your third year in this school?"

"Yes, I began my studies here in 46."

"Why did you choose this school, rather than another?"

"Before I finished grade eight in the public school system, I had to apply for admission at three different schools, if I wanted to continue my studies. This was the only one that accepted me."

"Why do you think this one accepted you, but not the others?"

"I do not know."

"Were your marks good when you finished grade eight?"

"All of them were over eighty-five percent," I stated not without pride.

"Those marks are really good. I never ever made marks like those when I finished my schooling. You wouldn't know how I wanted to study, but the son of a factory worker was lucky to finish public school. We were not wanted in schools like this before the war. Consider yourself lucky Laszlo. You are here thanks to our liberators, the Soviet Union.

This is a new era when even the offspring of a shoe-maker is given the opportunity to study, to become a man of learning. Don't you agree?"

"I know about the previous regime. Not too many workers' children were given the privilege to study," I admitted reluctantly the truth; noted that he checked my background, he even knew my father's occupation and I ignored the remark about our liberators; 'some liberators', I thought.

"Those who are given freedom, like you were given, owe a great deal to the state. Are you willing to show gratitude?"

"I am not the ungrateful kind. What do you want me to do?" I was weary of the game he played.

"Nothing, I told you before. Just a simple conversation. So in 46 you entered this school. Were you allowed to choose your subjects?"

"I was allowed to choose only one. In this school the rest of the subjects are compulsory."

"What are the compulsory subjects?" he pretended not to know.

"Hungarian language, mathematics, chemistry, physics, biology, shorthand, typing, book-keeping, economics, history are all compulsory." I listed all those subjects without hesitation.

"And what were you allowed to choose?"

"Only one from the foreign language group."

"What were the choices you were offered?"

"One from German, Russian, French or English were the choices in 46."

"You seem to stress 46. Why is that?"

"By the beginning of the 48/49 school year I had no choice at all."

"I am not sure I understand. Will you make yourself clear?"

"What I meant is very simple: in 46 we were able to choose one of four foreign languages, but in 48 Russian became compulsory and German, French, English were no longer offered."

"You seem to be bitter about that. Or is it just my imagination?"

"I don't feel bitter at all. If you imagined something surely it is not my fault." I didn't see where the conversation was going, in spite of the twenty minutes that elapsed since my arrival and was somewhat irritated by his meandering questions.

"We can agree on that. My imagination is free to roam, but for such roaming I should not blame you. So you are studying the Russian language since the beginning of this school year?"

"That is so."

"And you studied English for two school years. Am I correct?"

"I thought it was simple enough to understand."

"Now you are being sarcastic comrade...I have no doubt of that, but I forgive you...After all you are only sixteen...half my age...and you posses not even one tenth of my wisdom," he spoke the words slowly, insultingly, probably trying to invite my anger.

"Sarcasm is not my forte...my age is not my fault...my lack of wisdom will be remedied," I imitated his pattern of speech and perceived that for the first time I got under his skin.

"Cooperation is not your..., what was that strange word you used? I think it was something like fort?"

"Forte..," I corrected the ignorant, uneducated, security agent. I wasn't wise enough to know that one cannot mess with power; I was not mature enough to avoid speaking words that would do no good; I wasn't experienced enough to know the nature of man; in short, I was no less reckless during this meeting than I was the night before.

"You are just like the upper class of the former regime. They were always willing and ready to correct my uneducated speech, they gave no heed to the fact that it was them who kept me ignorant. All this has changed my boy. No one should dare to mock me, to correct me, to shame me, to embarrass me, for now I have the power. You better remember that," white foam appeared at the corners of his mouth, his face was completely contorted, his flashing eyes betrayed insanity as he spit the words out, firing them at me like so many bullets.

"I am sorry...I didn't mean..," I began rather feebly, but he was not going to accept an apology. He reached into his pocket, removed a revolver, with hooded eyes examined the gun, clicked off the safety, checked the magazine to make sure it was fully loaded. He looked at me once again, placed the gun between us on my principal's table and his voice thundered.

"If I wasn't a good man I could shoot you for the insult. Who do you think you are? You are a young punk; you just began to wear long pants; you are nothing; less than nothing. You are the son of a capitalist. If I shot you, here and now, who do you think would question me? Who do you think would condemn me for killing an enemy of our Russian brothers; an enemy of the Communist Party? Do you think you would be the first one?" his raving continued for several minutes; each statement more insane than the one before. For the first time in my life I felt helpless. I didn't know then that his behavior was standard practice, designed to create havoc, confusion and fear. All the things that I felt then.

As suddenly as his tirade began he calmed down and gave me a strange smile.

"Did I frighten you Laszlo? I didn't think you frighten so easily. I thought you were used to the ravings of your history teacher or to the shouting of your former English teacher. Or is my information incorrect?"

"Not at all. My history teacher does yell a lot. My former English teacher has a strange habit: he puts one cheek of his face on his table top, his head kind of tilted. He peers at us over his black-rimmed glasses, and shouts at the top of his lungs: 'Sheep herd.' But his insults no longer frighten me, I am used to them. At least my teacher does not try to frighten us with a gun."

"I frightened you. I am sorry about that. I had no intention to frighten a little, stupid boy, whose only strength lies in using words like 'forte'. If I ever decide to really frighten you, you'd be the first to know. Now let's get to the end of all this nonsense. I gave you too much credit trying to have an intelligent conversation with the likes of you. You are not worthy, you are nothing, you are not even a scholar of foreign languages. You almost flunked Russian the last term and I doubt you did any better with your English." I knew I should not have reacted to his taunting, but nature endowed me with a fast tongue and I rarely missed an opportunity to give words to what I thought.

"I was far from flunking Russian and my English marks were always excellent. Even my pen-pal praised me for my grammatically correct letters."

"Indeed? I didn't know. In only two school years you have learned enough to write in that language? That is really worthy of praise," his voice became gentle as he said that; his face became almost friendly and suddenly my intuition warned me to be cautious.

"Thank you," I stated insincerely, but offered nothing further.

"You must have been the best English student amongst all your class-mates," his statement sounded like a question and I was in no mood to boast, nor did I have the right to usurp the distinction a class-mate of mine held.

"There were a few who were a lot better..."

"Now that comes as a surprise. I hope you are not trying to mislead this uneducated fool," his words still contained a hurt, but they contained something else. I searched my mind for that elusive something, but I had little experience with conniving, so I fell into his trap.

"Karoly Titkos is a lot better than I. Was in English, is what I meant to say."

"Was only?"

"He still is."

"How would you know? You two no longer take that subject?"

I fell for him again. I was truly stupid. "Karoly and I study it together. We do it on our own," I announced proudly. I do not know why I wanted his praise, his approval. I do not even know if I just wanted to brag.

"You only study together, nothing more?"

"I am not sure I understand what you mean."

"Did he have a pen-pal as well?"

"Yes."

"You are lying, comrade."

"I am not lying, that is the truth."

"The truth does not lie in the past, it resides in the present. He has, not had a pen-pal and so do you."

"Yes we both do," I saw no harm in admitting. The letters we wrote to two boys, both in Pennsylvania, in the USA, we always mailed at our post-office, without any thought of trying to make our correspondence a secret.

"Your pen-pals live in America. Am I correct?"

"In Pennsylvania, in the USA." I almost spelled out the name of the state for him and clarified that it was the USA and not simply America.

"There you go again. You correct all my mistakes and it appears I do make many. I hope you can be this correct in all you do."

"I try," my mouth formed the words before my brain could take control.

"You shall try indeed. You will try to be at this address, seven o'clock this evening." He handed to me a piece of paper. "You will try to satisfy my every whim. You will try to be silent about everything that we said in this office. You will try to avoid answering truthfully all your class-mates' inquires about why you were called to the principal's office. You will try to keep our secret. I know you will not fail in any of these things. No relative of prisoner Santa could afford to be a failure."

I sat in the principal's office for a few minutes after the official left. Fear gripped my heart; sweat poured off my forehead. I remembered last night's conversation about my uncle Jozsef; about the cruelty of Stalin and his henchmen. What seemed to be just conversation, less than sixteen hours ago, now became my personal nightmare, a nightmare from which there was no waking.

***

I returned to my class-room in a daze. Those who sat nearest to my seat whispered their questions and I remained silent, just as silent as I was later, when during recess my class-mates bombarded me with their questions. I resisted all their attempts and perhaps the first time in my life, my brain worked frantically while my lips rested.

The rest of my day was totally empty: my classmates didn't exist; my parents I barely noticed; my brother's questions, concerning my obvious distress, I didn't answer; my love that day I didn't see.

I sat in my room during the late afternoon, my books and scribblers in front of me, yet I wasn't reading, wasn't writing, just stared into space, when George approached me.

"I do not see any marks, so you didn't get a beating. Then what is it Laszlo?, my brother asked and probably recalled the many times I came home with a bloody nose, or with scratches on my face or with scraped knuckles. "Tell me if anyone bothered you and I will beat the shit out of him," he offered, as he did many times before. He was three and a half years younger than I was, but neither his youth nor his small body, no doubt inherited from our father, ever made him run from his oversized opponents. What he lacked in stature he made up in courage; he compensated for his not fully developed muscles by using skill that he acquired in the not infrequent fights he engaged in. When all his prodding failed; when his questions remained unanswered; when he realized that I wanted to be alone, he shook his head and left me to brood.

I ate with my family the supper my Mother cooked; kept my sullen silence, broken only by the thank you I always offered after every meal.

"After supper I have chores for you Laszlo," my Mother announced before she cleared the table. I glanced at her, then at our alarm clock, noting the time to be five thirty and without words I had indicated my willingness to do the chores.

My Mother began to list them and before she got to the end of her rather lengthy list I voiced my objection.

"It will take me hours to do all that."

"So what if it does?" she dared me to say another word.

"I have only an hour, Mother. After that I have something to do."

"Now I have heard everything. In this house you are not as willing to do things as you are over there," she pointed in the direction of Rozsa's house. "Why don't you go over there now and ask them if you are permitted to help your Mother?" she raised her voice and not even my father missed the sarcasm her words contained.

"Leave him alone, Ilona. George and I will do all that needs to be done, let Laszlo be."

"You always give in to Laszlo. Tell me why is that? Is he something special? Is he too educated to do the chores? You treat him as if he was the youngest. Let him do the work and then he can go see his Rozsa for all I care."

"I am not planning to see Rozsa," I announced foolishly and my Mother pounced on me instantly.

"That'll be the day when you will not see her. Ever since they moved into that house nothing and nobody matters to you. Aren't you too young to pester that girl constantly? Isn't she even younger? If I were in her parents place I would take the broom to you," she poured out her scorn and I was devastated. I faced today the secret policeman; now I had to face my Mother; then back to that cursed agent, all without the comfort of seeing, even for one minute, the girl I loved.

I choked back the tears that stood ready to invade my eyes, rushed out of the kitchen to bring water, to feed the pigs, clean the pig-sty, to split some wood and before I finished the list of tasks I saw that the time was nearing seven. I left our yard, making sure that my Mother wouldn't see me, ran over the uneven, broken sidewalks to reach the address the agent gave me.

I reached the dilapidated, hundred years old, two story brick building, stepped into its dark stairwell, and I stopped for a moment to compose myself. Three minutes later I stood on the second floor, front of the room that displayed the right number. I knocked once, then once more and the door opened.

A tall, skinny man with sandy, sparse hair, sporting a bulbous nose slightly twisted to the right, his muscled arm revealed by the rolled up shirt sleeves, opened the door. I saw his mustache, still stained by some unknown food he had eaten; pungent odor of garlic assaulted my nose, but not half as much as did his words.

"You are late, you young punk. You were supposed to be here at seven. I am really not happy." I heard his words and judged him to be even more crude than the other.

"My watch shows only seven. I am not late at all."

"Come in and do not argue. This is not a place where such tone of voice is tolerated. Others who are invited here, or brought here are a lot more humble, but you will get your lesson young man."

He led me to an inner room, offered me a seat across from his, at the table. I saw bread crumbs on top of the table. I watched with amazement one ant that paid no heed to the presence of a member of State Security, an ant that busied itself rolling a large crumb. I saw the empty skin that stood in the ant's way, a skin that must have come from a piece of salami. I watched the ant skirt around that piece of crap and I almost opened my mouth to let the official know that the pig sty I finished cleaning a little while ago was a palace compared to this place of power. I thought better than to utter one word, so I set there, my uneasiness making me shake slightly.

A door opened behind me, I heard the man burp before I saw him. The chair legs scraped on the dirty floor and my visitor lowered his bulk at the end of the table. I couldn't help but compare the two: Both of them with wide, cruel faces; one sporting a red mustache, the other clean shaven; one with sandy, sparse hair, the other almost bald, with a few tufts of his former red hair showing; on one face the bulbous nose, on the other a beak like an outgrowth. In my mind I named the one who opened the door 'Sandy'; the other one I decided to call 'Forte', in memory of our earlier conversation.

"I am glad you made it Laszlo. You made the right first step," Forte began and suddenly he turned on the charm. I didn't think he possessed any. "I am terribly sorry for having called your father a Capitalist during our conversation. I sincerely hope you accept my apology," he didn't wait for my answer, instead he pushed on. "When I saw you last I didn't know that your father was a member of the Communist Party. Sons of party members we always treat gently. Look, I will put my gun aside, with you I don't need that," he tossed his gun on the small, blanket covered cot that stood in the corner. "You do the same comrade," he pointed to Sandy, who obeyed him instantly, allowing me to believe that Forte was his superior. "We will treat Comrade Laszlo with respect. He is a scholar, a future Communist, he surely deserves that."

By then I knew better than to object to the word 'comrade' or to my being a 'future young Communist'. The only word I dared to latch on to was the 'scholar'. "I am only a student, far from being a scholar," I said and I was truly puzzled.

Forte was far more polite than he was at the school. He seemed to have acquired compassion, understanding and his new personality clashed with his squalorly surroundings. "Was he putting on an act at the school or is he acting now?" I wondered and decided not to pass judgment, until we come to the end of this clandestine assignment.

"I said he is a scholar, he even writes, reads and speaks English. How many people do you know comrade who do that?" his sly look, cast in the direction of Sandy, made me wonder. "He even corresponds with a pen-pal, somewhere in the United States. Can you believe that?"

"I believe that when I see it. Let's put him to a test," Sandy stated and produced a piece of paper from the desk's drawer. He handed it to me and I held it in my hand. The simple English words stared me in the face, as did the two agents. "Now comrade we will see if you are as good as I was told. Read it to us," Sandy ordered.

I began to read the neat handwriting rather slowly, then as I warmed to my task I gathered speed and finished reading the one page letter, that contained neither address nor the name of the writer.

"Well that sounded good. Don't you think comrade?" Forte chuckled.

"It was fluent enough reading, that much I admit, but what do we know? Neither of us understood a word of what he read. Let's continue with the test. You translate what you have read comrade. This time you will not be able to fool us, if that is your intent." He pulled open the drawer once more, removed two sheets of paper, handed one to Forte and held the other one in his hand. "Begin translating," Sandy barked out the order and I no longer knew which one of the agents was in charge. My new guess was that they were equal and wanted to remain nameless, perhaps that is why they used no other title than 'comrade' whenever they addressed each other.

"It has been some time since I was able to write to you..," I began my careful translating, wanting to make no mistakes, wanted to impress my hosts. Five minutes later, having finished translating the page, I placed the paper carefully on the table, but only after I pushed aside a few crumbs.

"So what do you think comrade?" Sandy popped the question.

"I think he will do well. He has the skill, we might as well begin. Give him the letter comrade."

The drawer was pulled out once more, this time a properly addressed envelope, with the sender's name blanked out and three handwritten sheets were placed front of me. I glanced at the first page, flipped it over, scanned the second sheet and turned that over. I saw the signature of the sender was blanked out as well.

"Is there something wrong Laszlo?" this time it was Forte who appeared to take charge.

"Nothing," I lied and tried to cover my surprise, hoping that they bought what I said. The handwriting was that of Karoly Titkos, my friend and classmate. "What do you want me to do?"

"You were looking for the name of the writer. Don't worry about that. It is none of your business. Begin to translate, but do it accurately. Mistakes we do not tolerate, I assure you," the voice gurgled out from under the bulbous nose.

"Dear Robert," the letter began and with great care I translated into Hungarian all it said. When I finished my relief was great. "I was asked to do nothing that would hurt my friend. Anyone could have translated that letter, as someone did the other page. But why did they ask me?" these thoughts ran through my mind, but only what followed allowed me to get a glimpse of the answer.

"You did quite well translating exactly what the letter said, now we want you to tell us what each sentence really means."

"I do not understand. What else could it mean than what it says?" I almost shouted the question at the state's defenders.

"Do you take us to be fools?" Sandy raised his voice just an octave above my own. "A Hungarian writes a letter to the enemy of our beloved Soviet Union. He praises our brothers to the east; he tells his friend how well we live; he writes about the many freedoms he enjoys; he even speaks highly about our leaders. Why would he do that?"

"Do you object to that comrades?" I threw my question at them like a bone.

"No, we do not object to that, if the writer is sincere, but how could that be? He was identified a year ago as an enemy of this country. His letters have been monitored ever since. The one you read is only one of many, and all of those letters were full of praise. Does that make any sense?" Forte explained, displaying great patience.

"It makes sense if the writer was mistakenly identified as an enemy. Judging from this letter, he is more likely a patriot," I tried to defend my friend Titkos.

"The way you speak seem to indicate two things Laszlo: First you brand us as idiots, by telling us that the writer was mistakenly identified as an enemy. We don't make mistakes, you better learn that. Second, you try to defend a stranger. Can you explain why you would do that?"

"I am defending nobody. The letter speaks for itself."

"Do you know Laszlo that it is a crime to send confidential information to anyone? It is even greater a crime to send such information to the enemy. The only greater crime is to aid the traitor." Sandy's hooded eyes bore into mine and his voice became even harsher as he continued. "Why do you put yourself in danger? Why do you cover for your friend? Is it possible that you write similar letters to other people in the States? Is that your reason for trying to mislead us?"

I didn't know which way to turn; I had no idea which question should I address. So I began with what I guessed to be the least harmful.

"I am misleading nobody. I told you..," I turned my head toward Forte, "I told you comrade that I have a pen-pal. Yes, I write to him a few times a year and he always replies. Do you want me to bring to you all his letters?"

"No. We are not interested in you. We are only interested in the traitor, whose letter you translated."

"But there is nothing in that letter that would indicate treason."

"Isn't there? You are truly naive Laszlo. Look at the address."

I picked up the envelope, stared at the address and saw nothing that I didn't see before.

"What do you want me to look at?"

"Look at the name to whom it is addressed." Sandy ordered.

"Master Robert Willett..," I read aloud.

"Now look at the last two digits of the postal code," Sandy issued his next order.

"Those are 6 and 9," I informed him.

"Do you see the code?" Forte shouted.

"What code? I do not see any."

"You are a young fool or maybe a falsifier. Look at the second last digit."

"It is six."

"Now look at the last."

"That is nine."

"Do you still insist that you cannot see it?"

"I see it, but I do not understand."

"You declared yourself to be a friend. You promised to help us and instead you are obstinate. Is it because you know the writer?"

"How would I know that? The sender's name is blanked out and so is the final salutation." I lied again, but this time I couldn't convince even myself.

"Who else in your class did you say writes to the States?" Forte reminded me of the mistake I had made in the principal's office.

"I told you before, Karoly Titkos also has a pen-pal."

"So you said. Are you happy Laszlo when you receive a reply from your pen-pal?"

"I am."

"And you share your happiness with another. Isn't that the truth?"

I recalled how I cherished receiving a letter from my friend, so far away; how I read and re-read his letters; how I showed it to Karoly on the first opportunity I had; how Karoly lamented when he had to wait a longer time for a reply than I had; how overjoyed he was when he received a reply from Robert; how he let me read it, as I had allowed him to read all of mine; and I also remembered that all the other classmates, who also used to correspond with someone in the States, stopped doing that when we were no longer allowed to study English. Having recalled this I couldn't find refuge in a lie.

"Yes I do, but surely that is not a crime?"

"Don't misunderstand me. We accuse you of nothing, but that doesn't apply to your friend," Sandy leaned toward me and I didn't dare to wipe his spittle from my face.

"What friend are you talking about?"

"Look at the letter again. Do you see the peculiar way the 't's are crossed? Do you see the way the dot above the letter 'i' is not a dot, but a circle? Have you seen this kind of peculiar handwriting anywhere before?" Forte pressed.

"I cannot remember."

"Is it not true that you once asked Karoly Titkos why does he cross his 't's that way; why does he use a circle above the 'i's?" Forte continued.

"I forgot that a long time ago," I tried to extricate myself from the lies I told.

"But now you remember?" Forte urged me, this time gently.

"I do..," I could hardly speak the words.

"And from the very beginning you knew that the letter you were translating was written by your friend!" Sandy's triumphant announcement came.

"I didn't know at the beginning. I began to suspect later, but I thought there might be others who write in that manner."

"Very well you young fool. Lucky for you that your father is one of us. But I told you that before, didn't I? I think it is time that you level with us. Is it possible that the letter was written by Titkos?"

"Yes, but you knew that before you blanked out those parts you didn't want me to see."

"We knew that, but we had to find out whether or not you are a friend. You wasted a lot of our time, so waste no more. Take this piece of paper and that pencil. Now write the number six on it," Forte issued the order and I obeyed him without hesitation. "Now turn the paper around and tell me what number do you see."

"Nine," I said, not very calmly.

"So the numbers 6 and 9 are the inverse of each other?"

"Yes they are." I still couldn't see what they were after.

"Could those two numbers instruct the reader to believe the inverse of what the letter says?"

"How could it? Those numbers are just a part of the postal code and neither of them appear in the letter."

"Take a good look at the address and then the letter itself. What names do you see?"

"Robert Willett on the envelope. Five times Robby and twice Robert in the letter itself."

"Very good Laszlo. You are becoming quite observant. Now tell me is it possible that the six stands for Robert and the nine for Robby?"

"I suppose that is possible, but it is far-fetched."

"Is it indeed? Read quietly over the letter and pay attention to the paragraphs that begin with a name."

I did as I was told and for the life of me I couldn't make a connection. "I finished," I said.

"So what did you discover?" Sandy asked the question.

"Nothing at all."

"You are not the scholar I thought you were. Now you can see why we work for State Security, in spite of our lack of skill with fancy words," Forte spoke and allowed me to see his resentment for my sarcasm in the principal's office. "Now let me explain: six stands for Robert and nine stands for Robby, for that is the order in which the numbers and the names were used. The suggestion to the reader is very simple. When Titkos uses Robert he writes the truth. He does this each time he speaks about his marks, his playing soccer, when he describes the weather, but when he starts to write about politics, the conditions in our country, he switches to Robbie, suggesting to the reader that he should invert the information. What do you think of that Laszlo?"

"I never would have thought of that."

"I guess you wouldn't. Even us in State Security missed that for several months, but now we know. Do you believe that what I said is not only possible, but rather likely?"

"I cannot deny the possibility. I am not prepared to argue against two professionals. You comrades work for State Security, not I," I replied and began to fear for my friend, Titkos.

"As long as you are not willing to argue with us we ought to be satisfied with your help," Sandy offered and rushed on to prove his point. "Some day this evidence maybe given in court. We might call you to testify that what we say is quite possible. Are you willing to testify? Or do you need more proof?"

"I have never been asked to do that before. I must think about all this. If you have more proof, let me see that," I struggled against making a commitment; I hoped for a miracle, for my friend's sake and for mine.

Forte stood up, began to pace, then he stopped, leaned over the table, his foul breath almost made me gag, his eyes only inches from mine, as he spoke.

"Have it your way. We will go and get more proof. For a patriot what we showed you, what we told you, should have been enough, but you are a young fascist, just like your friend. Very well. You will wait as long as it takes, but not in here. You will stand outside this door until we return. In the meantime remember this: You were never here; you were never questioned; you will not warn your friend; you will not tell what happened today, not even to your girl-friend. Do I make myself clear?" each phrase Forte uttered came out louder; with each of his words my face moistened more, but his spittle I could no more wipe away than I could wipe away my fear.

***

They led me into the dingy hallway, illuminated by a single light-bulb, hanging on a cord from the ceiling. They locked the door. Forte checked his watch, without addressing anyone he announced that it was nine-thirty.

"You may have a long wait fascist," Sandy smirked, distorting his tilting nose even more.

His words died away, then their foot-steps and I was alone. I couldn't remember a time when I felt more lonely. My only companions were my many thoughts.

"Will I be made to testify, thus condemn my friend? Will I be strong enough to deny them? Should I tell my father all that had transpired? Would he, a member of the Communist Party, be able to help? Would I be better off if I told everything to Rozsa's father? If I do not cooperate will they be able to punish my uncle Santa? Did they bring up his name to frighten me? Dear God what is this all about? Why is it a crime to correspond with someone in the west? Why do they sow the seed of mistrust? Why do they look for enemies where there is none? What is my country becoming? Why thugs like these two are given so much power? Is Rakosi no better than Stalin? Why can't nations live in peace? Why did two great nations, who fought and won the war together turned against each other, making us their pawns in a struggle we do not even understand?" My thoughts swirled around in my head as I waited.

My questions I could not number and my answers were very few: "Karoly Titkos was in danger...Somehow I must make him stop sending any more letters, but I cannot tell him anything, I do not want to put him in any more danger...I will never write another letter to my pen-pal. I will not involve my father, nor will I endanger Mr. Buja..," I stood by the wall of the hallway, beside that cursed door. My legs became tired; my heart was far too heavy; my mind was clouded with all that happened. Slowly, reluctantly I lowered myself toward the worn, unwashed, linoleum covered floor and sat down, leaning my aching back against the wall. From time to time I looked at the cord that held the bulb, but hanging myself was not an option.

"My whole life just began when I met Rozsa. She will learn to love me; we will marry; have at least two children," I began to tell myself and with those happy thoughts I chased away the shadows of my soul. From time to time I checked my cheap watch that my aunt, Gizella, gave me last Christmas and as the minutes passed by, as they grew into three hours without my prosecutors' arrival, I stood up. I took one more look at the door that Sandy opened, hours and hours ago; listened for sounds of approaching foot-steps and hearing none, I descended to the bottom floor. I opened the door that led to the street; looked in every direction. I saw the completely deserted, late night street and began my slow, fearful walk to the sanctuary of my home.

Chapter 2

For the first time the shadow of oppression fell upon me; I felt the heavy hand of the totalitarian state upon my shoulders. Before my dreadful experience, my days were happy, although they passed slowly.

When at school I never thought the school day would end and I would see my Rozsa. When at home, studying or doing chores, the minutes dragged on slowly as if they were held back by an invisible restrainer. It didn't matter how many times I glanced at my watch, how I prayed for a faster passage of time, it stood still. Then ages later-at least that is what the passing of a few hours seemed to me-I was able to cross the street; I was finally able to open the gate, behind which my dream-girl lived. Once I sat beside her; once she began to talk, I was torn between conflicting wishes: I wanted the days, the weeks, the months, the years to move with rapidity, so that she and I would be older; yet I wanted our moments together never to end.

That was before...I seemed to have entered a new phase of my life: I feared the passage of the moments, in case they bring forth my pursuers. Even in the presence of Rozsa, I felt totally alone. My secret locked in my head, my knowledge festered within me and I was unable to talk to anyone, after all they warned me not to do that. Yet in spite of my dread, time marched on and not even the passing of three weeks brought any sign of my interrogators.

"Could they have forgotten me? Did they find more urgent tasks that needed doing? Did my Father's membership in the party made them reconsider? Are they trying to lull me into false security? Will they strike when I least expect it?" my mind searched for answers, day after day, but my heart hoped to be able to ask the same questions as long as I lived. I stopped writing to my pen-pal. Whenever I found it possible I stayed away from Karoly Titkos.

"You no longer want to talk to me!?" he half stated behind the wood-shack, in the yard of our school, where he found me, as I puffed on my fake cigarette, made from corn-silk and newspaper.

"There isn't much to talk about Karoly. I am busy with my school work, I have many chores..."

"And you are courting someone," Karoly added to my list of excuses.

"Yes, Karoly I am courting a very sweet girl."

"Am I the only one you put to the side?" Karoly asked and reached out for one of my cigarettes.

"No...I am neglecting my family; I am neglecting all my former friends, not that there were many," I stated the truth and grasped the opportunity to warn him, yet not inform him. "I am even neglecting my pen-pal."

"You no longer write to him," Karoly didn't sound surprised. "You loved to do that. You waited anxiously for each of his letters, no less than I did for mine. Yet you stopped, you gave it up? Why is that?"

"I was a child when I began. I was an English student when I got his address. There is really no point to struggle with that language. Maybe I shall look for a Russian pen-pal," I lied between puffs.

I saw Karoly inhale deeply, let out the acrid smoke through his nostrils-something I tried many times, but was never able to master-before he began: "I have known you Laszlo for over two years. We have been friends. Do you think you can fool me?"

"I don't know what you are talking about," I stated when the school-bell rang to indicate the end of recess. "We better go Karoly, I don't want to be late." I sought to escape him and the desire to tell him all that had happened.

"We could cut this class. I think we should have a long talk, we could help each other," Karoly tried to convince me.

"I have never cut a class before. They will find us and punish us. Maybe even send us to the principal's office. I don't want to risk that," I tried to disengage myself from the dangerous conversation.

"Not if we play it smart. Do you see these loose boards?" he pointed to two boards of the shack, boards I have never noticed before. "If we hide in this shack and speak quietly, they will never find us." Karoly's offer was tempting and I was desperate to end my isolation.

A minute later we were inside the windowless, pad-locked hiding place and Karoly began to whisper.

"Have we not gone to many movies together Laszlo?" I was surprised by his question, but decided to play along.

"We have seen a few, whenever we got permission, during the last few years."

"We saw western movies; we watched many movies about the war and so many others. Do you remember our favorite comedy actors?" Karoly juggled my memory and I was sure his question served a purpose

"Laurel and Hardy...," my lips spilled out the name of the bumbling idiots, whose antics brought laughter to both of us, at least on three occasions.

"Well I met both of them during the course of the last few months," Karoly began to tell his secret. "My real live Laurel and Hardy look different from that of the movies. They have wide, cruel faces; Laurel has a red mustache, Hardy is clean shaven; the first one has sandy, sparse hair; the second is almost bald, with a few tufts of red hair showing; the first one has a bulbous nose, the other one was blessed with an ugly beak. Have you ever met them?" Karoly described the agents of my fear and I had no doubt that they were Sandy and Forte, as I named them.

I wasn't able to voice my objection, so I remained silent, hung my head, looked at the shack's floor.

"You are afraid Laszlo!?" Karoly continued to whisper and put a finger front of his lips to silence me. Someone walked around the shack, we could hear the foot-steps, then the rattling of the lock.

"They are not around here...The shack is locked. They couldn't be inside." We recognized one custodian's voice and heard the reply of the other. "Let's go back. We will tell Szepes that we couldn't find them." We listened to their receding steps and I could picture our home-room teacher roaring at us: 'sheep herd, sheep herd'.

"Don't worry Laszlo. Szepes is not our concern now, it is Laurel and Hardy we must speak about," Karoly spoke when he was sure we could not be over-heard. "Laurel was the first one to approach me. He came to my home one night, I think this was eight weeks ago. He identified himself as a State Security agent and wanted to see the letters I received from my pen-pal. I showed them to him and after he glanced at the letters, he obviously was unable to read, he informed me that he will take them. I didn't argue, he reminded me so much of Laurel of our movie. He was clumsy, a half-wit at the best, a self-important fool. He informed me where and when I can get the letters back. I went to the building when the appointed time came two weeks later, the building just behind our City Hall. Climbed to the second floor office, where I met Laurel's partner, Hardy.

"The two buffoons warned me to never reveal to anyone their existence; they questioned me in their inept ways; they even asked questions about you Laszlo and made me translate a copy of a letter you wrote to your pen-pal." I looked at my friend's face as his lips revealed the surprising news and I saw no fear in his eyes, no hesitation in his telling.

"They explained to me their idiotic suspicions about some stupid code you used to convey secret information. I just laughed at them, made them angry, taunted them and before they let me go I gave my word to watch the only spy they will ever have the ability to catch and that is you."

It was obvious that he made light of his encounter with Sandy and Forte, unlike I, but now I was a lot bolder, having heard something of his encounter with the agents, so I began.

"I gave them different names, Karoly. The guy you call Laurel, I named Forte, the other one I call Sandy". Then I told him about what happened in the principal's office and in great detail I described all that happened on the night, when my fear began. I did all this in whispers, fearing that we may be discovered by the custodians and fearing even more the consequences of having repeated what Sandy and Forte said. When I finished my story, when Karoly saw my unmistakable fear, he burst out laughing, almost betraying our hiding place and I covered his mouth with my hands to stifle the uproar his laughter produced.

"I will be more careful..," he whispered and crossed his heart. "Are you afraid of them Laszlo?"

"I am. I cannot help it. They are evil. Yet there was something about them that I didn't understand. You are right Karoly, the names you gave them are far more fitting, than those I coined. Laurel and Hardy are just entertainers, harmless creatures, never to be taken seriously. Should I not be afraid of them?"

"I will tell you something that may put my Father and his friend in danger. Can I trust you Laszlo?"

"How can you ask that after telling me about your Laurel and Hardy and after I told you about Sandy and Forte? Neither of us would have said a word if our mutual trust didn't exist."

"Yes, of course. I am truly sorry. I should have never asked that. My Father has a friend who is a high ranking State Security agent, yet a decent man. Their friendship goes all the way back to their early child-hood. I told my Father everything, soon after the comedians came into my life. Although he did not worry about my corresponding with my US friend, he promised me that he will check things out. That he did and learned a great deal from his friend."

"What did he learn, I mean your Father? Can you tell me Karoly?" I spoke the words and held my breath.

"I give you the whole scoop. It is rather funny. My Father's friend I will not name, not because I do not trust you, but he was a skillful agent of Horthy, whose skills the new regime could not afford to go without. He heads up the Department of the Internal Security in our county, at least for now. He employs many, who have skills, but many more like Laurel and Hardy. The likes of these two are forced upon him by the Communist Party, so he accepts them, knowing full well that some of them can neither read nor write, that all of them are without much education. They lack common sense, knowledge and finesse agents require. So my Father's friend assigns them to meaningless tasks, tasks that are totally unimportant.

"He assigns those who can read, Laurel and Hardy among them, to steaming open all letters addressed to the west; he told them to watch out for possible traitors; he gave them permission to frighten the subjects of their investigations, but limits them to two contacts only. Once they have made the second contact with any individual, they are to hand the case file over to him. My Father's friend saw my name among those Laurel and Hardy investigated and he saw yours as well. Our files he buried deeply. Our comic characters will never bother us again, they are too preoccupied with reading the multitude of meaningless letters and with other useless tasks they were given. Was I able to reduce your fear Laszlo?"

"That you did and I kick myself for not having come to you, for avoiding you, but everything Sandy and Forte, no wait, I shall call them Laurel and Hardy. Everything they said and did frightened me greatly."

"I knew that the minute you told me that you stopped corresponding with your pen-pal, Laszlo. What are you going to do now? Will you pick up your correspondence?"

"I will not do that. My Father was called a capitalist by them, although Laurel offered his apology. I do not want to cause any trouble for my Father, nor do I want to put Mr. Buja in any danger."

"Who is Mr. Buja?"

"He is the man whose daughter I truly love." I corrected the oversight of speaking about someone I thought Karoly didn't know.

"I think you made the right decision. Mr. Buja may be in danger. Our Captain of the River Police was an officer in the Hungarian Army, if I am not mistaken. According to my Father's friend former officers, agents, even high ranking civil servants of the previous regime will be eliminated. His guess is that none of them have more than three years before the ax will fall."

"I don't understand. Your Father's friend is among the marked men, if I understood you correctly."

"He knows that. He is prepared for that, but his plan he wouldn't even share with my Father. That is not important really. My advice to you is to level with your Father and even with Mr. Buja. If either of them is in any danger, they will be better off knowing what happened to you. Don't be afraid of Laurel and Hardy, just hope that neither of us will give cause to be investigated by someone else."

I thanked Karoly for all the information; urged him to stop writing those dangerous letters; pumped his hand with gratitude and when I thought there was nothing more to say, when I was ready to leave, he put his hand on my shoulder and whispered a few instructions in my ear.

***

Szepes came into our classroom to take the attendance for the afternoon. He read aloud the first name of the class roster. When he heard the mandatory 'present' being shouted out by the name's owner, he moved down the list, each time tilting his head down, letting his glasses slide to the front of his large nose, peering over his glasses, looking toward the assigned seat of the boy whose name he read.

I sat in my seat, making myself even smaller than I was, waiting for my name being called, hoping to avoid Szepes' anger.

"Laszlo Lichter," he called out my name.

"Present," I whimpered.

"So you have honored us with your presence? Aren't we lucky? Are you sure you can afford the time to be with us? You are a sheep, you are worse than sheep, you make up a sheep herd all by yourself!" he screamed in my direction, yet suddenly I was no longer afraid of him, not after I have overcome my fear of Laurel and Hardy.

"I am here and I don't need the insults," even I couldn't believe that I spoke the words.

"What was that? Did I hear right?"

I reveled in my new found courage and just to make sure that I was the one who spoke those words, I spoke them again.

"I am here and I don't need the insults," this time I spoke the words even more loudly.

"I want to hear from the sheep-herd. If you agree with Lichter's statement say 'baaa'," Szepes instructed, expecting to hear not a sound.

I think it was Karoly Titkos who bellowed the first 'baaa', and as he continued to make that sheep cry others joined him, until not one single class-mate of mine remained silent.

"Baaa..," came from all three isles, where we were seated, two at a desk; "Baaa..," came from the back of the class room, where the tallest, the strongest were seated.

Szepes looked at all thirty-two of us, then he must have searched for a way out of his unexpected dilemma and having found it, he grinned and spoke words to indicated his superior intellect.

"I always knew you were a sheep herd. This time I tricked you good. Didn't all of you make the sheep sound? Well that proves my point. I will cease calling the roll. It is obvious that all my sheep are present. Go to your next class! Class is dismissed!"

Karoly Titkos was right when he whispered in my ear: "This afternoon Szepes will call the roll. Your name begins with 'L', so he will get to you before me. Stand up to him...Shake him...Divert his attention from our skipping...Hurt his pride...Do anything you can to make him angry...I will have the class support you...Trust me Laszlo," and he was right. Szepes never questioned us about the class we skipped and I have promised myself to remember the lessons I have learned: "I will always stand up and be counted. I will never ever allow myself to be abused. I will always display courage, the only thing cowards run from."

***

That night I didn't go over to the Buja's; remained home and waited for my Father's arrival. I waited until he ate his supper; I watched him as his black hair glistened under the light bulb, as he tossed back a glass of red wine diluted with soda water; I admired his black mustache; I no longer feared his stern eyes, that were always ready to register his displeasure and when I saw that he was relaxed, I plunged in.

"May I talk with you, Dad, in private?" Before he could give his reply, George spoke up.

"Something has been eating at my brother. What it is he wouldn't tell me." I didn't know if George was complaining or he was just anxious to warn my Father, but it really didn't matter. My Father stood up, waved to me to follow him to the front room that faced the street, which also served as their bedroom. There he sat down in his favorite leather chair by the warm stove and began to speak.

"You know Laszlo where I keep the chocolates. Take two for yourself and bring me a glass of my favorite peach brandy. Then we can talk." He knew that as a young child I always lit up at the mention of getting a treat.

I opened the large cabinet, removed two pieces of the rare chocolates we were given only on Sundays and returned to where my Father sat, handing him the drink he always enjoyed.

"Now let's talk. Was your brother right? Something is eating you Laszlo?" no preliminaries, no small talk, just plunging right to the heart of the matter. That was my Father's way on those rare occasions when he was willing to talk. He firmly believed, as many Hungarian parents did, that children were to be seen, but not heard. In his eyes I was a child when I was born; I remained a child all through my sixteen years; and even now when I began to understand the injustices of life, when I tasted the bitter-sweet feeling of loving a wonderful girl, but not knowing if I was loved, I was nothing more in his eyes than a child.

"Maybe I am making a mistake?" I asked myself, but it was too late. My Father granted me an audience and wouldn't allow me to bail out. "Where should I begin?" I wondered and I remembered Sandy's insult.

"A few weeks ago someone called you a capitalist. He later apologized. He didn't know that you were a member of the Communist Party, at least that was his excuse." I stopped not knowing how to continue.

"So which one bothered you more: Your Father being called a capitalist or the fact that I am a member of the Communist Party?"

"You misunderstood me Dad. Mr. Buja explained to me why the two of you belong to that party. That I understand..," he didn't let me finish. His eyes flashed with anger, he looked at me rather strangely.

"Does it bother you that I belong to the party?"

"It did, but no more. Mr. Buja explained it all."

"My son goes to Mr. Buja for an explanation? He does not trust his own Father? Laszlo doesn't come to me with his questions, but goes to another man, requesting an explanation? Jozsef Buja is a friend of mine, that is true, but I am your Father. Don't you think you should have come to me if you had trouble with my political affiliation?" his words, his tone did not indicate anger, but his eyes betrayed how he felt.

"We were just talking about this and that and the topic came up..," I tried to explain.

"If you want to give me an explanation then you better tell me everything that was said," he ordered firmly.

I spoke about the movie Rozsa and I saw; about our walk home; the stranger's attack on Rozsa's statement; the details of the conversation that followed in my beloved girl's kitchen. When I finished giving an exact account of all that was said, I stopped.

"I see. It would have been better if you came to me. I am your Father, not Mr. Buja," there was bitterness, jealousy in his voice. "All that my friend told you is true and accurate, but there is a lot more to be said. When my Father died my Mother had too many mouths to feed and little income..," he began to tell his story.

"I was only eleven years old. An uncle took pity on me; took me in; made me live in a rat infested storage room. I became his shoe-maker apprentice; I had no hope of ever returning to school and all my eleven years I dreamed of becoming a doctor. That dream no longer existed. I began to learn a trade; I have worked for a pittance before and after I married your Mother. When you arrived we were no better off. Nor did our circumstances improve when George was born. So I suffered in silence; resented being exploited and exploited by a relative at that. I saw no way out. What I have earned during my twelve hour workdays, from Monday to Saturday was less than enough, so on Sundays I went fishing. As I have learned more and more about our beloved river, the Danube and the many fishes that called it their home, I began to harvest the river and caught enough to feed all of you and sold the surplus.

"Then the war came. I was drafted as a slave-laborer. I escaped death when my friends perished; I walked home, having faced many dangers on the way. My uncle died during the war and I lost others, but those I loved. I had no job, no hope, no prospects, just my skill of making shoes. I began to do that at the back of the house, in that small room where I left my work-bench, as a constant reminder. Then one day a Russian officer heard about me and at gun-point he ordered me to repair a truck-load of Russian boots. He gave me one week, or else.

"What was I to do? I went in search of shoe-makers who could help me; I found a place that lent itself to set up shop for thirteen workers. I thought I was going out of my mind when day after day we were forced by the Russians to meet almost impossible deadlines. My misfortune, or what I considered misfortune then, turned into a windfall, when that terrible inflation came. I convinced the Russians to pay us in lard, flour, salt and other staples, instead of Hungarian Pengos, that no longer had any value. I joined the Social Democratic Party and hoped to be able to help create a new order. I didn't want a single human being to be exploited as I was. I didn't want anyone ever to experience a war like the one that raged in our country for several years. I didn't want anyone to ever experience shortages, starvation and other kinds of sufferings. My plan seemed to have worked, conditions steadily improved and my workers and I began to make shoes for the populace, when the Russians' demands waned. Then came the merging of the two parties and your Father found himself a member of the Communist Party. Should I now leave and give up all I have accomplished? Should I condemn my workers to being unemployed? Should I give up my hope of you and George receiving an education? Should I give up the opportunity to help the surviving members of my family?" my Father's words poured out like the waters of the Danube, when in full flood, all the while hoping for my approval.

"No Dad. I am not urging you to do any of that. I understand all you have said. In your place I would have done exactly what you did," I assured him, remembering Mr. Buja's question and the stupid answer I gave then.

"I don't know son why we have never talked like this. Maybe I was afraid..," his voice trailed off, explaining not what he feared.

"So was I Dad. I was afraid to talk to you freely, but no more, I promise you that."

"I am glad my Son, this talk was long overdue. You had your sixteenth birthday, months ago. I should have grasped long ago that I cannot expect you to get an education, yet remain a child forever. We, Hungarian fathers are strange creatures. We maintain that children are just that, until the death of their parents."

"I can get all the education I am able to get; I can age many years more, but you will always be my Father and I will always be your child Dad," I offered him the only comfort I could.

"Thank you Laszlo, but it seems that in my eagerness to make you understand me, I strayed. It was you who wanted to talk; it was you who was troubled, yet it is I who is being comforted. Let's try to go back. Who called me a capitalist?"

It was my turn to dive into my story. I told him everything, concerning Laurel and Hardy. I spoke about my friend, Karoly Titkos. The only thing I couldn't tell him was Karoly's source of information.

"You had quite a scare son. How long ago did this happen?"

"Three weeks have passed since I was called to the principal's office. Not even a day passed since my fear ceased to exist."

"Well son, let's take things one at a time. First, did I understand you correctly that you stopped corresponding with your pen-pal?"

"I stopped Dad."

"Very well then. I really don't think that anyone should curtail your freedom to correspond with anyone, but these are changing times, such activities may hold some danger. I am glad that danger no longer exists. Second, did I understand you correctly that neither of the two agents made contact with you in the last three weeks?"

"Not since the initial contact and not since my forced visit to that office."

"Maybe the information you received, concerning how the agents are assigned to useless tasks, is correct. But just to be on the safe side, I ask you to tell me if you are ever bothered again by them or by anyone else. I really want to know. I have friends who may be willing to help, if such help is ever needed."

"I will come to you Father. I promise you that."

"Now the last item I want to speak about takes me to the point where you begun. Laurel, or whatever you called him, called me a capitalist. Is that correct?"

"That is what he said, but I told you..."

"Never mind to go back to that apology. You may compare him to Laurel, the funny actor, but remember that not him, nor any others are as harmless. He had good reason for using that term."

"What reason Dad? You employ thirteen people; you provide their families with a means of survival; you shouldn't be called names for that."

"Shouldn't is an interesting word Laszlo. I shouldn't have been exploited by my uncle; I shouldn't have been drafted as a slave laborer; I shouldn't have lived while my friends died; I shouldn't have served the Russians; I shouldn't have been so remote from you and from my family. There are millions of things that shouldn't be, yet they are. The new government shouldn't have nationalized all factories that employed over one hundred workers. Did you know that this is what they did on March 24, 1948?"

"I didn't know Dad. I don't bother reading the newspapers and you never..," I stopped what I was going to say to him. The last thing I wanted to do is to hurt him.

"Why didn't you say what you were about to tell me? Shall I say it for you Laszlo? I never spoke to you as an adult, before today. Is that what you were about to say?"

"Yes Dad, but I didn't want to hurt you."

"I promise son that will change. From now on you will be treated as an adult, at least by me. Your Mother, well she will never change. She will ride you for helping the Bujas; she will ridicule you for being in love, at your age; she will load you up with chores, but never when you have time on your hands. She will wait until you are ready to go to see Rozsa, then she will strike, but that cannot be helped. Anyway, how did I get here? We were talking about nationalization...Do you know what that means?"

"Individuals lost their factories, businesses if they had more than one hundred workers?"

"That is exactly what happened, almost nine months ago. Those owners were not compensated. One day they were rich and the next day they were paupers. They were branded as capitalists, enemies of the country. Now what I tell you Laszlo must remain just between us. I don't want your Mother or brother to worry. Last March it was those capitalists' turn to be nationalized; soon it will be those who have over fifty workers; and they will work that number down, until everything is owned by the State. All of us capitalists, as we will be called, will be just like the 'kulaks' of the Soviet Union."

"Don't say that Dad. Surely the leaders of this country will not do what Mr. Buja told me about the kulaks?"

"They will do it Laszlo, they have already begun. They have divided up the large parcels of land; they have given a few acres to each Hungarian peasant, who wanted to be a land-owner, but they have also created a plan. Each peasant is told what to grow, what his harvest of each crop must be. For getting the land the peasants must show gratitude, must give to the government one half of the calculated harvest. When the crop fails, regardless what the reason is for such failure-there can be many: floods, draught, hailstorms, too much rain, infestation by pests...-that is not the government's fault, so the farmer owes the state the same. In the end they will have little choice, they will beg to be allowed to join the collectives, that have already began to pop up here and there."

"Dad you are speaking about farmers, but said nothing about you and your factory."

"You are correct. They have not announced a date for nationalization of small factories like ours, but the signs are there. Since April I had more and more difficulties to obtain raw materials. Most suppliers of leather and of other goods I need were businesses with over one hundred employees. Once they became state owned their production, operation deteriorated and they are no longer able or willing to supply us with all we need."

"But Dad, you are still operating."

"I have many friends and very few enemies. For the time owners of smaller firms take me to the back of their stores and show me what they have. I bought up all I could. It is not unusual that a friend of mine warns me about a coming price increase and I buy up even more. Your Mother is quite angry with me for putting so much money in the business. She sure lets me know quite often."

"But if you can see Dad what is coming why don't you give it up and salvage what you can?"

"Not yet Laszlo. I have urged my workers, my friends to seek employment elsewhere. Neither my concern for them, nor the law allows me to dismiss them. They just laughed at the suggestion. They are almost like co-owners in the factory and not my urging, not my begging, not my forecast for the future made them change their minds. They want to stick with me as long as they can. So what am I to do? I will operate the factory, as long as I can. Your Mother doesn't understand this, no matter how I tried to explain my reasons. At least you son understand me."

"I do indeed. If there is anything I can do, you just need to ask me," I told my Father. He nodded his head and my first ever, adult conversation with him was at an end.

I was pleased with all I have accomplished on that day: I have overcome my fear of the Security agents; I have restored my friendship with Karoly Titkos; I had a fine conversation with my Father and I was ready to walk next door, to say hello to Rozsa and her parents.

***

The days began to get warmer as we turned a page of the calendar to the month of March. I missed the snow. Rozsa no longer reached for my arm, but I consoled myself with the frequent walks we took. We sauntered the city's 'Korzo', as we called the promenade around Trinity square; we strolled on the bank of the Sugovica, the man made canal that carried water to the Danube; always leaving the best to last, the city park of Dery.

The large, rectangular, well appointed, pleasant park was donated to the city by one of its richest citizens, many years ago. The six ornamental iron gates, set in the high brick fence, that surrounded the park, were always open during the day, allowing the population of Baja to seek the shades of the parks many trees. The old poplars reached for the skies; the ancient weeping willows spread themselves, like huge tents, over the wooden benches, where parents sat, while their children ran around on the curving, graveled paths.

Before I met Rozsa we went to the park, mainly on Sundays, but this spring I no longer went there with my parents. It was Rozsa who walked by me; it was my love who pointed to the colorful flower beds, admiring the colors that burst out in the early spring in every color of the rainbow.

My dearest and I stood by the granite monument, at the upper end of the park that was recently erected in memory of our liberators. A white granite square served as a pedestal, above which an elongated pyramid stood. At the very top of it a huge, red star dominated the landscape, its five, sharp points stood as a reminder. The designer and his words wanted us to remember our fallen liberators, the Red Army, but what we remembered was the drunken Russian soldiers; rapists of women; plunderers of our homes, stores and factories. The inscription that described the fallen soldiers as our dead, who died for our freedom, failed to invoke in me the proper emotions. Every time I read it I remembered the terrible night when a Russian officer raped my aunt, Gizella. Brought back the memories of her screaming, the soldier's grunting and my bold action. I saw myself rushing into the room of the despicable act, grabbing the heavy, glass ashtray and in spite of my youth and my lack of courage, pounding that soldier's head, drawing his blood, but causing far less damage than I intended. I pictured him, once again, stopping the act, jumping off the bed, grabbing his pistol. I heard my aunt's cries and her words that somehow hoped to save me. I saw the officer hesitate and then for a reason I didn't understand, he prodded me with his gun to leave the room. I stood outside, my tears soaking my face and my shirt front, but I no longer had the courage to attempt to re-enter that room of doom.

I turned away from the monument, seeing behind me the nine granite steps that led to the lower park, separated by a steep, grassed, well kept slope. The green, four foot high hedge ran left and right, as far as we could see, providing a decorative border to the slope's upper and lower edge.

My beloved looked at me, when I turned, her sweet smile appeared to indicate that she understood the turmoil I felt front of the hated obelisk.

"Have these Russians really died for our freedom?" she asked me, as we began to descend the steps.

"They died, but it was not for our freedom. You heard your Father Rozsa, freedom we have less and less."

"Yes I heard him..," she said it, maybe only to herself and she reached for my hand, perhaps wanting to chase away the demons of my memory she have sensed.

I felt the warmth of her hand, her gentle squeezing and the Russian soldiers no longer mattered. I have learned, sometime before, to create compartments in my mind. Rozsa belonged to the largest, the richest, the most important compartment, whose door I happily opened and I slammed shut the doors of all the other compartments. My studies no longer mattered; my interrogators vanished; my Father's dilemma became forgotten; the memories of the war were locked away securely.

I held her hand, as we navigated the nine steps; I stood beside her when she stopped below the lower hedge. I still remember her beautiful, blond hair blowing lightly in the breeze; I see her well shaped, round face with her tiny, pointed nose. Even then she was an inch or so taller than I, so I had to tilt my head up slightly to look into her beautiful, blue eyes. I saw her tiny ears, the skin of her neck that her white dress, with the embroidered edges did not cover. My heart beat like a loud drum. I have never felt happier than during those moments when we stood there, her hand in mine. The Russians' monument stood behind us and the most splendid part of the park of Dery spread out front of our eyes, inviting us to explore. We began to walk toward the park's other end and her hand remained in mine; I hoped that it will be this way forever.

We sat down on a bench, under a huge weeping willow, that covered us like a tent, hid us from everyone else. We were truly alone. I stood up just for a moment, walked ten feet to the flower patch, picked two yellow daisies, but not before I looked around to assure that no one would see me. I gave one of them to my pretty, young companion and kept the other one for the game that was sure to come.

Rozsa looked at me, but asked no questions. She was willing to play the game that Hungarians played for as long as I can remember.

She pulled out one of the daisy's many petals, she said something silently to herself. Then she continued pulling out the rest of the petals, one at a time, each time asking herself the silent question. When only one more petal was left, when she separated the delicate green petal from its Mother, she looked downhearted not like before.

"It is your turn Laszlo," she whispered and I began to pick off the petals, one by one.

"She loves me..," I told myself when the first petal was removed and "She loves me not..," with the next. I continued until the small flower was almost denuded and my fear of the outcome of the game mounted, as much as my hope did, should the last petal tell me what I desired.

"She loves me not..," I almost prayed when I separated the second last petal and even though I knew the outcome of the foolish game, I reached reverently for the last remaining petal. "She loves me..," in my excitement I must have spoken out loud, as I removed it and my heart skipped a beat as her voice sang out ever so gently.

"She really does."

I sat stunned under that old weeping willow and I held back the tears of happiness that gathered behind my eyeballs.

"So she loves me!? That is what she meant when we spoke about Erzsi's age and her probable love for Joe. I told her then that 'Erzsi is two years older than you Rozsa, maybe she fell in love. Or is that impossible at her age?' Her reply remained with me ever since: 'I really do not think so. People fall in love even at an earlier age", that is what she said then and her statement then and now, combined into one, made me doubt no longer.

I was ready to pour out my soul; to speak words I have never spoken to anyone; to declare my love for Rozsa; to reach for her sweet face and to kiss her lips, but Mr. Buja's words intruded, they came like something spoken years ago: "Rozsa is not even thirteen years old…We let you come and see her; we allow you to take her to a movie, now and then…We do this because your parents are our friends, because we trust you Laszlo…Trust is a sacred thing, so do not ever disappoint me!"

The magic moment passed and Mr. Buja's words stopped me, as they stopped me a few times after.

I stood up. I couldn't stay beside her, under that weeping willow. I had to escape if I didn't want to betray her Father's trust. Rozsa seemed to look surprised; she stood up; ran her hand over her linen dress, maybe to straighten out its creases. She looked at me. Behind her blue eyes I sensed disappointment, but I didn't know the cause.

We walked away in silence from the place of my joy and from her place of misery. She did not offer her hand and I didn't dare to reach for it. Her strides became more purposeful. She walked, a step ahead of me, toward the iron gate that we always used to exit the magic kingdom of Dery, the gate that was closest to our home.

We walked in silence toward the lowest part of the park. We didn't stop by the pond of the many gold fish that swam around in circles, delighting all that watched them, as they jumped for the bread-crumbs offered. We exited my paradise, her place of disappointment. We made the long walk home in complete silence and when we reached her gate her farewell was icy.

***

March turned into April, the temperature climbed steadily higher, but the coolness I received from Rozsa was far worse than the chill of our fiercest winter.

I tried to find out from Joe what bothered his sister, but he didn't know. I remembered that Rozsa and my first cousin, Erzsi, were friends, so I approached her.

I didn't know how to begin, how to confess to Erzsi my confusion. She was blessed with female intuition and a directness that suited the petite, dark haired girl.

"You want to talk to me about Rozsa. Just go ahead," Erzsi broke the ice and the dam of my emotions.

I told her about our last walk in the garden of Dery. I described my happiness when we finished playing with the daisies. I told her, for the first time ever, how much I loved my angel. I repeated the words Rozsa spoke: 'She really does.' Then I described how I felt, what I wanted to do, how I was held back by the words Mr. Buja spoke to me. She had no difficulty sensing my misery as I described our silent walk home; her icy farewell and her coolness toward me, ever since that day.

"I really do not understand her. I do not understand women," I announced to Erzsi what I thought, with the solemnity of a grown man.

"You can say that again," Erzsi burst out laughing.

"You wouldn't laugh at me, if you knew how miserable I became."

"You should be miserable. All of you men should be that."

"I do not understand you," she chuckled even more, upon hearing my words.

"Please help me Erzsi. If you know how I offended my love, tell me and I will change," I begged her.

"Very well...But what I tell you must remain our secret."

"You have my word," I declared.

"You probably didn't know that I had a crush on Rozsa's brother."

"I didn't know, but I suspected," I didn't want to lie.

"Yes I had, but when I discovered his interest in an older woman. In that girl who lives in their house, the one who works at Kozponti, as a cinema ticket-taker. I was cured fast when I discovered Joe seeking and receiving her lustful favors. My infatuation lasted only two months, then I met a boy and I really fell in love." Thus far I listened patiently, but my poise lasted no longer.

"Are you going to tell me about Rozsa? Or are you going to prattle on about things that don't concern me?"

"Don't be so impatient. You do not understand girls. So let me tell you my story and when I finish you shall have your answer."

I must have looked quite sheepish, I judged from Erzsi's mirth.

"You are quite a sight Laszlo. I am glad you cannot look in a mirror. You would truly frighten yourself," Erzsi giggled, as we spoke in her back-yard.

"I know...I know...But could we get back to..."

"I told you, you do not understand us, girls. We have to tell our story our way..," Erzsi seemed to drag out the conversation.

"Maybe she enjoys my suffering," I thought and decided not to press her any harder.

"Now where was I? Oh, yes, I remember. I fell in love with someone. I have waited for weeks to have him tell me that he loved me. We went to movies; we went to dances; we walked on the Korzo and in Dery Park. We even kissed each other, first very chastely, but that didn't last. Our kisses, our embraces became a lot more ardent and one day, one foolish moment I couldn't wait any longer. 'I love you', I told him, between kisses, but his reply never came. I hated myself; I despised myself. It is the male who is expected to do the courting; it is the male who should speak those words. Girls can wait only so long and if we don't hear the words we desire, we either lose interest or we offer a cold shoulder. So for weeks I didn't allow him to kiss me. I didn't invite him to my house; I didn't accept his invitation to a movie, or to a dance. In short I had made him suffer, until he came to me, he told me he loved me. He begged me to return his love. Since that day we have experienced nothing but bliss. Do you understand Laszlo what I am trying to say?"

"I do and I don't. Everything you said centered around you and your boy-friend, but you told me nothing about Rozsa?"

"Do you remember those moments Laszlo when you two sat under the weeping willow? Do you recall what you two did with the daisies? Do you remember what Rozsa said?"

"I remember everything. Do you think I could ever forget? When I picked the last petal off the flower, I must have said out loud: 'She loves me...' and I heard her words: 'She really does...'"

"And what did you do Laszlo? What did you say to the girl, who, in her own way, confessed her love?"

"I did nothing. I said nothing. I remembered Mr. Buja's words about his trust and I was afraid I might betray him."

"So you stood up without another word?"

"That is what I did."

"So how do you think Rozsa felt?"

"I am not a mind reader."

"That you are not, I assure you. Rozsa and I talked, shortly after that event."

"What did she say?" I asked and held my breath.

"She told me all that happened, but that is not important. What is important though is the question she asked, as she tore off the daisy's petals. 'He loves me...He loves me not', were her thoughts as well. But in her case the last petal came off when she got to 'He loves me not.' Rozsa knew it was only a game, the outcome couldn't be trusted. This is why she confirmed your finding by saying to you: 'She really does.' She did not dare to say: 'I love you Laszlo.' That would have been too direct, yet she said just as much. It was then up to you to chase away the negative answer she got, but you remained silent. You allowed her to believe the outcome of her game: 'He loves me not...'

"That is what made her so icy. That is what bothered her ever since," Erzsi finished, expecting me to confirm my understanding.

"Does she really love me?"

"She told you that Laszlo, just as she told me."

"I know that now, I thank God for that. I did hear her precious words, but what followed crushed the joy I felt."

"She did only what females have done for ages. When we don't hear what we want to hear, you men catch our wrath."

"So what am I to do now?" I wanted to know.

"If you still don't know Laszlo, then you are dumber than I thought. I better go now, we have a lot of walnuts to shell," her words rang in my ears long after she left me and entered her apartment.

***

I walked the short distance to my home and on the way I have decided to go over to see Rozsa.

"Where are you going?" I heard my Mother's voice, just as I opened our back gate.

"Just next door and only for a few minutes," I shouted to my Mother, who stood in our kitchen's door, some twenty feet away.

"Not before you do all the chores," came her stern command.

I rushed around to complete the chores with more speed than ever before. I practiced front of our two pigs what I wanted to say to my darling: "I love you Rozsa." I went to get two buckets of water and while I pumped the handle of the communal well, to bring to the surface water that the well gave up grudgingly, I practiced saying that precious sentence with each down-stoke: "I love you Rozsa." I must have repeated it a hundred times, before the two buckets filled. I walked back to our house, as fast as my burden allowed me. I picked up the ax and began to split the wood. With each swing of the ax I repeated that wonderful sentence: "I love you Rozsa."

Then the moment came to walk across the street, to seek out Rozsa and with each step that carried me closer to my destination I practiced even more...

I found her in the kitchen, all alone. Her eyes looked red; her delicate right hand held a handkerchief, soaked with her salty tears. She just sat there when I entered and never moved.

"Hi Rozsa," I whispered the greeting.

"Hi..," was all she said.

"I came over to tell you something..," I began lamely, but I couldn't continue. Her whole body heaved with deep sobs; her handkerchief traveled to cover her magnificent eyes, to hide her tears.

"Is something wrong?" I forced out the words.

"Something is..," came Mr. Buja's voice from the door, as he pulled aside the blanket that hung over the door-frame to keep the heat and flies out.

"Something is very wrong..," Mrs. Buja spoke, who stood beside her husband.

"Will you tell me? Can you tell me?" my voice shook with fear.

"Let us all sit down Laszlo. Then we shall talk."

I sat down on the wooden chair, as close to Rozsa as I dared. Mrs. Buja sat across from her daughter and Mr. Buja across from me.

"We have talked many times before Laszlo and I have told you much about my past. Those things I don't need to repeat," Mr. Buja's words came slowly; his tone full of sadness. "In one of our conversations I told you, here in our kitchen, front of Rozsa and my Maria, that 'Rakosi and his followers began the persecution of their former enemies. They started with the highest ranking military officers and the top politicians of the former regime. It will not take them very long before they are ready to replace all of us.' Do you remember those words of mine?"

"I do Mr. Buja," I didn't dare to call him Jozsef.

"Well the time came, but not as I expected."

"I do not understand."

"You will Laszlo, once I finish what I have to tell. I expected the Communists to replace me, but I thought it will be many months or even years, before they are ready to do that. I expected them to give me the boot, but I have misjudged their conniving. They transferred me instead," his voice died down for a moment.

"But being transferred is not so bad..," I foolishly stated. My mind wasn't working fast enough to realize that Rozsa and I will be separated. I could only think of the relief I felt upon hearing the news that Mr. Buja wasn't fired.

"No, being transferred is not so bad, but the way they did it; the reason behind it, makes it dreadful. When I first got my appointment, I became the Captain of a poor bunch of police-men. I have worked hard; I faced many problems; even one big tragedy, the sinking of the cross-river ferry. It took me a long time to forgive myself for the death of fifty-six men, women and children, although God knows I have taken every precaution, a prudent man could. As the months passed, as I have gained the trust of my men, my rag-tag police force became the envy of the country. They trust me, respect me, but no more that I trust and respect them. We became friends, we became a team. Now they ready to take away my command and give it to an untrained Communist, I found out.

"They didn't tell me, but I know what is going on. They didn't dare to fire me, to eliminate me, for they fear the reaction of my men. Instead they transferred me to a new post, far away from here and there, I suspect, they will bring things to an end."

"Maybe they just want to have you create another superb team? This country needs your talents," I tried to offer some reassurance, but not my words, not my tone could hide the misery I felt.

"Thank you Laszlo. Your words are appreciated, but I know the truth. Our life was going uphill, ever since I became a soldier; we have reached the zenith of our hill. There is nothing on the other side, but a steep descent."

"Could you not resign Mr. Buja? You have so many skills ... To get another job would be easy. Maybe my Father could help?"

"I have offered my resignation, it was flatly refused. They want to uproot us, punish me, and everything they do must be on their terms, their way, I assume."

"So what will you do now?" I stammered out the question.

"I was given three weeks to pull up roots. I am to work with the new commander all that time, to show him the ropes. I am to sell the house; in fact, they brought to me a buyer. I am to take my family and move all our belongings to Szob."

"Isn't Szob somewhere in the north of Hungary?" I tried to picture our country's map.

"It is Laszlo. At least two hundred fifty kilometers north of here, on the Danube, close to the Slovakian border."

Mrs. Buja and Rozsa followed our conversation; must have decided to say nothing until Mr. Buja finished. Rozsa kept wiping her diminishing tears; her Mother reached out one hand for that of her daughter and the other one she placed on top of the table to make it possible for her husband to touch whenever he needed.

"When will you leave?" my heart almost shattered as I asked the question.

"We must be there before Easter," Mr. Buja hung his head.

"We will be there before Easter and we will be together, remember that," Mrs. Buja spoke up, her face beaming encouragement at her husband.

"I am sorry if I caused any of you pain, but it can't be helped," Mr. Buja stated, his words came more calmly than before. "Now if you two don't mind I want to have a word with Laszlo. I will go with him to the gate."

"But I wanted to speak to Rozsa. I wanted to declare my love," I lamented, but only in the most hidden part of my mind. I stood up and the two of us walked to the gate.

Mr. Buja closed the gate when we stepped out on the street. He faced me, towered over me and his words came out quietly and calmly.

"You must have seen my sweet daughter cry." I didn't know whether it was a statement or a question.

"I saw that and it broke my heart."

"I know Laszlo how you feel, but both of you are too young to have such intense feelings. The years will pass and who knows what the future will bring. You will find someone else."

"Never!" my denial came out as a shout and Mr. Buja put his hand on my shoulder.

"Never is a long time Laszlo. Study hard and try to forget our daughter."

"I will study hard, that is all I will promise," my words carried such conviction that Mr. Buja dropped that subject.

"The real reason for this private conversation is this. My policemen will give us a special send-off. They want to surprise my family. Next Sunday we will go by boat to a very special place. Your whole family is invited. Tell your parents to be at Turr, by the Danube, next Sunday morning at nine. They should bring nothing, food and drinks will be provided. Tell not a word to Rozsa, let it be a nice surprise."

***

Six miserable days followed. I informed my Father, who received Mr. Buja's transfer with a great deal of sadness and the invitation gladly. I have visited Rozsa daily, counting the days, the hours, the minutes left before our parting. I asked her to go for a walk, or to a movie, but each time I did that she shook her head.

"I have to pack...I have so much to do...I don't think I can," came her excuses and from time to time she tried to smother her tears.

I suffered in silence; shed my own tears where no one saw me, just our pigs. Then Sunday came and we stood by the Turr, on the bank of the Danube. I looked at the river whose treacherous currents took so many unwilling victims and I remembered others who gave their lives to this majestic water-way not unwillingly, but eagerly to escape famine, to end their misery or to terminate their great disappointments.

"That is what I should do when they leave. Life is not worth living," I told myself as I stood there waiting. Then the Buja family arrived; I saw Rozsa and her presence chased away the earlier dark thoughts.

The wooden boat stood ready to receive the nine of us, four Bujas, four Lichters and the policeman who was to operate the outboard motor.

"Here we come, Rezert!" shouted Mr. Buja trying to cheer all of us.

"What are we going to do there?" Mrs. Buja inquired.

"You shall see," Mr. Buja replied, as the motor coughed, sputtered and started on the fifth pull of the rope.

Our boat began to move against the heavy current, fighting for each foot of progress, moving to the north. We were above the demolished bridge, where only the piers were untouched by the American bombers, when we heard the crack. All of us who faced to the front, suddenly looked back and were shocked by what happened.

Our driver looked behind him, shook his head in frustration and before we have comprehended the enormity of our misadventure, he shouted: "I lost the motor! Stay put! The current is driving us against the pier!"

Mr. Buja grabbed an oar, my Father grabbed another and they began to row frantically to avoid the collision. We missed the pier only by inches; we drifted and turned in the treacherous current, below the bridge, for what seemed an eternity. Then we saw the large boat, flying a Russian flag, that came down the river and we began to wave and shout.

The Russian vessel approached us. Helping hands reached for our boat, for the nine passengers, pulling us all aboard.

"What happened?" asked a Russian officer in halting Hungarian.

Our excited words, spoken by almost everyone he couldn't understand.

"Captain Buja please quiet them down. You are safe now. You tell us what happened," the Russian officer spoke again to the Captain he knew quite well.

"We lost our motor. It is down there somewhere," Mr. Buja shook his head.

"Very well. You all make yourself at home. I will have a diver search for your motor," he announced calmly.

Many minutes have passed before the diver surfaced, shook his head, indicating, without words, that the motor must have been carried away by the strong current.

"Where were you going?" the Russian officer asked.

"To Rezert. The third dead branch of the old Danube on the west side," Mr. Buja explained.

"Very well. We will take you there, then we come back and search for your motor."

"I appreciate your offer, but I have my own diver. Tomorrow we will do that. You need not bother. We thank you for your kindness. If you take us to Rezert, I want you all to be our guests," Mr. Buja offered, his resentment of the Russian liberators momentarily forgotten.

"We accept your invitation," the Russian officer stated and in Russian he gave his order. Within fifteen minutes we turned to the right, crossed the river and entered the dead branch of the Danube that was a coveted fishing place for carp, white fish, cat fish and sundry others.

Another few minutes of navigating the narrow water-way made the boat take the sharp curve and we saw the commercial fishermen's camp. We also saw twenty or so men and a few women waiting on shore for our arrival.

"Over there," Mr. Buja pointed at the camp's landing and before we reached shore we heard a chorus of voices break into the song: "For he is a jolly good fellow, for he is a jolly good fellow, which nobody can deny."

Captain Buja's policemen sang their hearts out; the fishermen bellowed their agreement; the three gypsies broke into a lively Hungarian tune and the surprise party began.

Several cauldrons of fish cooked on open fires; the many bottles of red wine, beer and palinka were passed form hand to hand. Hungarian songs alternated with that of Russians and the old feelings between foes seemed to have disappeared.

I was caught up in the jubilant celebration only for a few moments before I realized that I didn't see Rozsa. She wasn't on shore, she wasn't in the huts, she was nowhere to be seen. I began to search the Russian boat, that I believed to be empty, and in one of the small cabins I found her. She sat on a bunk-bed, her tears flowing freely.

I could help myself no more.

"I love you Rozsa. I love you more than life itself."

She looked at me, her tearful eyes cleared, a sweet smile appeared on her face, her lips parted and I kissed her for the first time ever.

***

I tasted her sweet lips even days after. I could never forget those priceless moments, in the Russian boat's cabin. I lived off that sweet memory until we stood at the railway station, before the train was to take her away.

My parents were there, shaking hands with the Bujas, wishing them well, urging them to come and see us. I stood beside them, holding back the tears that Rozsa bravely managed to hide until the last moment. Then the conductor gave a shout: "All aboard..." and my life was about to end.

I reached out for Rozsa's hand, felt its warmth once more. I have already said good-bye to the others. I couldn't let her hand go; I couldn't allow her to leave me.

"We just found each other. How can you be so cruel Lord?" I spoke to none but myself.

Rozsa's parents climbed aboard, I still held her hand and her tears and mine could no longer be constrained. I became bold, I became careless. My lips found hers, just before she was forced to pull away and I tasted her salty tears that mingled with mine. I found her sweet lips, just for one moment.

She took one step away from me, her hand reached for the railing of the steps. Her hand was grabbed by Mr. Buja, who pulled her up and away from me.

The train's whistle blew, the wheels made their screeching noise, those on the platform shouted their last farewells, then I heard my beloved's voice:

"Don't ever forget me. Come and see me," were her words that kept echoing in my ears, as the train and my happiness disappeared together.

***

I no longer remember how long I stared after the train; how long I stood on the empty platform. My heart was in complete control and my mind obeyed it, transported me to the train. I imagined sitting beside Rozsa, holding her hands, hearing her tear stained, sweet voice, examining each and every word she kept repeating.

"Don't ever forget me..," I heard her say it again and I knew that I would never do that.

"She was my morning Sun; she was the breeze that caressed my body; she was my setting Sun and my rising Moon; she was all the stars in the heavens; she was my only purpose for living and she will always remain all that and so much more," I told myself. A resolution to write to her daily, I made right there and then. Then I realized that I cannot put in the letters all I feel and desire, so I vowed to begin to keep a diary.

"'Come and see me...," her words echoed in my mind. "I will my love! I will take the diary with me. Then I will read it to you and we will be happy again, together."

I was reluctant to leave the platform of our parting. I touched my still burning lips, where the taste of her kiss lingered, and warned myself foolishly never to wash them, just in case the sweet taste, the memory would disappear. I imagined still holding her hand, as I stood there, but the warmth of her skin, degree by degree, began to vanish.

I turned away from the train-tracks, took a few tentative steps away from the rails, but something made me turn. I thought I heard her crying; I imagined hearing her scream my name, but it was nothing more than the wind's shrieking and the moaning of my soul.

I ordered my feet to obey me. They carried me out of the station, across the paved road, down the steps that led to the station's park. I walked by the swing sets where children shouted with joy, as their adult companions pushed them high in the air.

"Mother brought us here when we were little. She pushed both swings, allowing George and I to try to surpass each other." I remembered the joy I felt whenever the swing was pushed to make me fly, but then I have realized that all that was long ago. There was no joy now, just agony. There was no more flying through the air, just a great void of despair and miserable desolation. I cannot recall how I got home, yet somehow I was about to enter our gate. I looked across the street, at the house where I felt so much joy and a new wave of loneliness hit me.

"She is not there! She is gone!" my mind suggested, but my heart wanted not to believe that. I walked across the street, I entered Rozsa's former home, but this time nothing looked the same. The flowers in her yard appeared to be wilted; the house was devoid of her laughter. I went to the back-yard, sat down on the wood-pile that I cut and split and piled for their next winter.

"It will be not my love who will be warmed by this wood's fire," I almost screamed the words and in my anguish I pushed over the neatly piled rows, I kicked at the scattered pieces until I spent my fury. It took me some time to grasp that I became a trespasser and when that realization hit me, I rushed across the yard and slammed the gate of that house for good.

***

I set in my room, pen in hand, paper on my small table and began to write the first letter, of over one hundred, to my love, Rozsa.

My Dear Rozsa,

I cannot describe the pain I felt when you were taken from me. I blame the Communists for that. I hate them, I will never forgive them. I wish I was wiser while we were together, so much time I have wasted. Had you been a little older, I would have told you a million times how much I love you, but your Father's trust kept me from doing that, until that boat trip on the Danube.

I will never forget that day. Those moments were more than precious. Why is it that I can sit down and write down my most secret thoughts, yet couldn't speak them, share them, even with you, until now? Your train couldn't be more than sixty miles from here, as I sit in my room, writing to you my first letter. I imagine your sweet face looking out the train's window. Do you see the farms, the fields, the herds of cattle, or are you blind like I am and see nothing other than the face of the one you love? On my walk home I felt misery like I have never felt before. I could see nobody and nothing other than you and your tears. I can still taste your sweet kiss and wonder if mine is long forgotten? I must not believe that...'Don't ever forget me...Come and see me.' were your last words.

How could I ever forget the girl I love? How could I ever forget the person I want to marry? How could I ever forget the mother of my future children? Please don't be offended by my words. The first day I saw you these are the things I told someone. From the first moment I laid eyes on you, I knew you were meant for me.

I hope my letter will convey how I feel. I hope your reply will do the same. You told me to go and visit you. Did you really mean that? If you did, I will grow wings; I will learn to fly. Of course I am only joking. I will save up all I can and when I have the money I need, when I have your permission and that of your parents, I will go to you my love.

In the meantime my misery will be eased by my daily letters. I know there are things I cannot yet say, even to you, so I will begin to keep a diary and when you are ready I will read it to you.

Now I must say good-bye. You know I have to study and have many chores to do. I hope you will like your new home. Give my best to your parents and Joe too. Until tomorrow, my Dear Rozsa I say farewell.

Don't ever forget the boy across the street. He loves you so...

Your Laszlo

***

Three weeks have passed since I said good-bye to the one I loved and each and every day brought with it more misery.

I couldn't keep my mind on my studies, no matter how hard I tried. I had no desire to spend time with any of my friends. I rarely spoke to my parents or to George.

Each evening when the Sun began to set, I walked to our back-yard, sought out our two pigs and while feeding them I spoke to them as they slurped their food.

"I came to you, my only friends for three weeks. How many times have I told you that I love that girl? I know I said that a thousand times, just as I told you that I wrote to her every day," the two pigs heard what I said, as they continued their feeding, their beady eyes glanced at me from time to time, but never disturbed by my confession.

"Three weeks have passed since I have sent her my first letter, yet I haven't received a single reply. I never told you before my friends that each day as I walk home I count my steps from the gate of the school to our door, but not in numbers," I continued confessing what I dared not tell anyone. "When I take the first step I always say 'A letter is waiting...," with the next one 'There will be no letter from my love...' As I get close to our gate, I always make sure to adjust my steps. My last whispered statement, that matches my last step, is always the same: 'A letter is waiting...', but I fool only myself.

"Has she forgotten me already? Is she too busy to write to me? Were her parents offended by the kiss I gave her at the station? Did they forbid her to write to me?" I asked these questions and many more from our pigs. Now and then they grunted, as if in reply, and I allowed my imagination to translate their answers: "She will never forget you!" grunted the smaller one. "She has much to do in their new home..," came the answer from the fat one. "Her parents understood. They will never forbid their daughter to experience the joy of love," the two of them grunted together and I was consoled greatly.

When I left my pigs I went to my room. When no one saw me I reached into the hiding place, removed the hard covered diary, I bought on the first day of my never ending torment. I opened the book with great reverence, read over the first twenty entries and after entering carefully the exact date and time, I began my written confessions.

"My dear diary. Twenty one days have passed since I lost my Rozsa," my first line always began with a count of those days of unbearable agony. "While she was with me I was foolish. I should have kissed her a million times. I should have touched her even more. I should have done so many things, but I was a coward. I should have made her know the enormity of my love. Today I went to talk to my pigs, once again. I asked them many questions and they seemed to have replied. They assured me that she loves me! Or was it only I who assured myself? Am I going insane? Am I unable to face the truth? Tomorrow I will write to her again and I will wait, I will be patient, I will never give up hope."

That night when I went to bed, after I said my never changing prayer, asking God to make Rozsa love me, I fell asleep and in my dream we were together.

My dream was no longer a dream, but reality. Rozsa and I sat, side by side, in a strange kitchen, on a narrow couch. Her hand in mine, her silky hair tickling my face as she teased me. I sought her lips, kissed her a thousand times, in spite of the sounds of disapproval her Father made, somewhere in the adjacent room. Our kisses became more ardent with the passing of each minute. My feverish mind urged me to continue, to seal her lips with mine, to deny her even a second of freedom to inhale some air.

I saw her flushed face, her eyes that sparkled in the dark, she seemed so much older and I lost my mind, I became bold, I was ready to ask her to be mine, to marry me, but suddenly I heard a knock, then hushed voices and a shout: "No more!"

I didn't know if I was still dreaming or awake. "Was it Mr. Buja whose knock and shout tried to stop me?" I asked myself and as the fog of sleep cleared from my mind, I have realized that the voices came from our kitchen, that one of them belonged to my Father.

I tried to tear myself away from the reality of waking. I wanted to be back in that kitchen, on that couch; I wanted to continue to kiss Rozsa; I wanted that dream to never end. I shut my eyes and ears, trying to resurrect my happiness, to banish the misery I felt whenever I woke. My efforts have failed and one by one the voices from the kitchen destroyed all possibility of continuing the dream.

I heard my Mother's sobbing; my Father's anguished voice, whenever he replied to that of Peter Berkovitch. I rose from my resting place, dressed slowly, savoring the memory of my dream and when I could no longer deny my concern for my parents, I entered the kitchen.

My Father sat beside the table, he held his head in both hands, shaking it from side to side, either from rage or from sadness, I didn't know. Peter, his partner, who helped him run the shoe-making factory, stood beside him, his face drawn, his hands on my Father's shoulders, trying to calm him. My Mother sat by the stove, her tears running down her face, as she tried to resurrect last night's fire.

I glanced at the three of them, noticed George's absence, who was still asleep in our room and when I could no longer remain silent, when the adults proved reluctant to speak, I found my voice.

"What is wrong Dad?"

I must have caught my Father by surprise. He dropped his hands, looked at me. His eyes softened, although his face displayed anger, tinged with sad resignation. He was about to say something when my Mother began her lament.

"I told your Father a thousand times not to put money in his cursed factory. He wouldn't listen...I am a stupid woman, he always thought, but now he knows better," her fury grew with each word. "Didn't I ask you Ferenc to buy me new furniture? Didn't I beg you to get me a new stove? Didn't I tell you to put us first and your factory, your workers, your foolish pride last? You deserve all you got..," she didn't get any further.

"That is enough Ilona! Not another word or I don't know what I do," my Father raised his voice and my rarely quiet Mother fell suddenly silent.

"Leave us alone Ilona. Peter, Laszlo and I have a lot to talk about."

"But I have to get the breakfast ready..."

"Very well. Make the breakfast. We will go to the front room. Come with me," he waved at Peter and I and we left my Mother alone. We could hear her muttering something under her breath, but my Father wasn't in the mood to reprimand her in his usual way.

"Sit down Peter, sit down Laszlo. Peter you tell Laszlo what you told me," my Father stated and he fell silent.

"Early this morning, I think it was around four o'clock or so, a neighbor knocked on my window. She lives beside the factory and sleeps with her windows open. She heard noises around two, looked out, from behind her curtain and saw four men load a truck. First it was boxes of shoes that they loaded and thinking nothing of the unusual time of the activity, she went back to bed. The noises continued and another truck arrived, even before the first one left. She got up again and peeked out at the men, who began to load large bundles of leather, then tools and sundry other items.

"She found it strange, but didn't know what to do. Then she heard one of the workers say something that raised her curiosity even more: 'Those bastards will never make another pair of shoes.'

"She didn't dare to leave her apartment until the truck pulled away. Then she rushed over to my home, knocked on my window and told me all she witnessed.

"I dressed quickly and rushed over to our factory. What I saw there broke my heart. All the shoes we made for Stellner, the big retail store, were gone. Three hundred pairs of shoes vanished. Then I discovered that all our raw materials were also taken, so were all our tools," Peter finished telling all he knew.

"I don't understand..," I could think of nothing else to say.

"I think I do," my Father took over. "We were robbed Laszlo...I suspect it is really worse than that. Those words the woman overheard seem to indicate a lot more. 'The bastards will never make another pair of shoes', is what she heard, what she repeated to Peter. Simple criminals, and God knows we have many, would commit the crime, would take all the shoes, but not the tools, not the materials. They would leave those behind, hoping that we will make more shoes, set ourselves up for the next plunder. Criminals of that kind would never make that comment."

"Your Father is right. Someone is out to ruin us," Peter revealed.

"Why would anyone do that?" I was still too young, too naive to fathom the real motive behind what happened.

"Not long ago we had a frank conversation. Do you remember that Laszlo?"

"I remember every word we said."

"I told you then that last March nationalization began and the Communists will not rest until everything is owned by the State. I told you that since April I had more and more difficulties to obtain raw materials. I told you that I have many friends who take me to the back of their stores and show me what they have. I told you that I bought up all I could. I also told you that I have urged my workers, my friends to seek employment elsewhere. They just laughed at the suggestion. I also told you that I have decided to operate the factory, as long as I can. It seems that is not what the Communists expected, so last night they struck. They finished us for good!" my Father stopped.

"Wouldn't it have been easier for them to nationalize everyone, if that is what they wanted?"

"You still do not understand. If they rushed into complete nationalization, the population would revolt. On the other hand, if they can demonstrate that private enterprise cannot succeed in this country, nationalization becomes an accepted necessity. So they robbed us of our means of production. Who will blame the Government for a simple robbery, apparently committed by criminals?" my Father's question hung in mid-air, making Peter and I search for a solution.

"I got an idea..," Peter began. "Let's pretend that we believe the act was committed by criminals, after all that is what they want us to believe. What would you do Laszlo if you were robbed?"

"I would go to the police."

"Right you are," Peter continued. "Ferenc we will go to the police. We shall demand an investigation."

"And they would pretend to do that. They would come up empty handed," my Father shared his thoughts.

"Yes, I agree, but we would be free to attempt to appeal to the Government for raw materials, for tools to provide the population with needed shoes. If we do that, one of two things might happen. Either we are wrong in our assumptions and the Government will help us, or they will drag their feet; maybe deny their help and we will know the truth."

I remained silent for the rest of the conversation, allowing the two adults to make their plans.

***

Several weeks later my Father called me into his room and told me all that had transpired.

My Father and Peter reported to the police the robbery. For two weeks or so the authorities pretended to carry out an investigation. At the beginning of the third week my Father and Peter were summoned to the Police Station. There they were told that the robbery was more than a simple crime. They were informed about the existence of roving gangs, who worked for the Americans, who were on the pay-roll of the CIA. One of these gangs robbed my Father's factory, they were told in confidence and warned not to say a word to anyone about the successful sabotage these gangs perpetrated.

If conditions in our country were different from what existed, the two shoe-makers would have laughed at everything the Police Chief said. He was an uneducated, untrained cretin. He began his career as a brick-layer; during the war he was a member of the Hungarian Fascist Party, known as the Arrow Cross; after the Russian's arrival he joined the Communist Party and rose in importance; held important positions, and now he was the Police Chief of Baja. He was not swift of thought, but an obedient tool of the regime. All this was widely known about the man. Yet now he had the power, so my Father's request to assist him in replacing the stolen tools, to help him obtain the raw materials needed to re-open the factory, did not seem out of order.

"I have to think about that," the Chief's words tried to hide his confusion.

"What is there to think about Comrade Chief? If you cannot find the Americans' stooges, if you cannot recover all that was stolen, then the enemies of this country win. Surely you don't want our enemies to be the winners?" my Father strung him along.

"No, that I don't want. Rest assured we will get you on your feet. You will be dealt with fairly." The Chief's last words were repeated by my Father.

"I found out all about his fairness. For several days I heard nothing from the Chief, then yesterday a police man came to see me.

"'The Chief sent you a message Lichter.' No comrade, no Mister, just Lichter, is what he said."

"So what was the message?"

"'He sends his regret for not being able to help you,' was all he said. I wasn't really surprised, that message and what followed confirmed my suspicions. I approached my friends for materials, for tools. They didn't dare to look me in the eye. None of them took me to the back of their store. They just shook their heads. 'We have no materials, no tools to sell you', they lied and I did not press them. They had their orders too."

"What are you going to do Dad?" I finally asked him.

"I have closed the door of the factory. All the heavy machinery the rascals didn't take I left there. My workers have left me. They understand what really happened. The small supply of raw materials, Peter stored in his home, he gave to me. In the back room, where I used to work, I still have my old tools. My two hands still possess the skills needed to make shoes, my knowledge they can never take from me. What am I going to do? I will keep on being a shoe-maker. I will work alone and I will provide for my family. Your Mother will not be happy, but she was never happy anyway. She gave her hand to a simple shoe-maker, after her Father stabbed her Mother to death in a drunken fit and she was unhappy with her lot. When I was drafted, during the war, she had to work as a house-keeper to provide for you and George. She was un-happy then, knowing not if I was ever to come home. When I got home, just before the war ended, I thought she was overjoyed, but that didn't last. I began to build up my business, my factory; put everything into that enterprise and that made her quite unhappy too. Now I have completed life's circle, I am back where I was years ago."

Those were the last words my Father spoke about his misfortune and from that day on he rarely left the house. Some of his friends supplied him with small amounts of materials, in secret of course. His old customers wanted shoes from no one else. His earnings diminished; he no longer threw lavish parties; he saved his money like he never did before.

I watched this victim of the Communist party and wondered, in silence, about Mr. Buja.

"They have finished my Father, just as Mr. Buja predicted. Will they do him in as well?" I asked myself and when my despair of not getting any letters from my beloved Rozsa for over seven weeks, climbed, life dealt me a surprise that caused me joy.

***

I was on my way home from school, after finishing two written exams. I still played the foolish, immature game of using my footsteps to predict the arrival of Rozsa's letter, perhaps out of habit only and not real hope or expectation of a letter's arrival.

I stepped up to our gate, with my last step uttering the words: 'A letter came from my Rozsa.' A few weeks ago I have stopped asking my Mother: 'Did the mail-man bring me anything?', I did not want to hear her unsympathetic, usual answer: 'Who would ever write to you?' I avoided going to the kitchen, where my Mother resided, instead I sneaked into the back, where my Father worked.

I didn't hear the sound of his hammer, which was somewhat unusual. I entered his kingdom, his refuge from the world and when he saw me his face began to beam.

"I got the most splendid news Laszlo. I hope your Mother didn't tell you. I wanted to see your face when you heard it. I wanted to share in your happiness."

"What good news Dad?" I could hardly voice the words. My hope of receiving a letter from my Rozsa was instantly resurrected. My desire to end my doubt, to terminate my waiting became terribly urgent.

"Laszlo you are almost seventeen, a few weeks and you will be that. You are old enough to have a drink with me. We will do that and then I tell you the news," he rose, from a drawer he produced a bottle of palinka, poured some into two small glasses and handed one to me.

"From the time you were a toddler every Sunday I gave you a little wine with lots of soda water. As you grew older I put more wine into the glass, but I have never ever offered you this strong essence of plums. Plum palinka is reserved for men only. You are a man Laszlo and you should be fortified before you hear the news. So drink up my boy, swallow it in one gulp as a man should."

I drank the searing liquid, but never noticed its taste. My hands wanted to throw away the glass and reach out for my letter. I shook and shivered with anticipation, thinking of nothing and no one, except the letter and Rozsa.

My Father must have noticed my impatience, at least his words seemed to indicate that.

"Yes you are almost seventeen Laszlo, but there are things for you to learn. Bad news grows wings and flies straight to the receiver, casting his heart into the pit of Hell. It takes almost no time to achieve that, but good news is something totally different. It travels ever so slowly; it loses itself on its way; it makes everybody wait, but when it arrives it should be cherished. That is what I used to do when I received a letter during the war, which was rather rare. I used to put the letter in my tunic's inside pocket, just to know that it was there. That made me happy for a whole day. Next day I opened the letter and looked only at the signature, it was always your Mother's, I knew, yet I spent the whole second day just treasuring that thought. On the third day I allowed myself to read just one section and one more each and every day. I know it was foolish to keep from myself most of what the letter told, but that was my way of survival. Others grabbed their letters the moment of their arrival. In their haste they tore not only the envelope, but even the paper.

They gobbled up the words in a few minutes and when they were done they were broken hearted. Letters came so rarely and for the next letter their wait was long. But not me my boy...I had one section saved for each day and when I was lucky a new one came, even before I finished the first. Do you know what I am trying to say to you?" I heard his words, understood his wisdom, was sure that a letter came from Rozsa. In my impatience I wanted that precious letter right away; I wanted to see her writing; I wanted to read her words of love. I didn't want to act like my Father, I was like all the others, he spoke about.

"Please give me the news Father..," I begged him without success.

"I tell you what Son. We have one more drink, then we shall rejoice," his speech revealed that he did some drinking even before my arrival.

"Why would he celebrate the arrival of a letter from my love?" I asked myself and I began to fear, with the passing of each moment, that my assumption was really wrong.

"Fine, Dad. I have one more drink with you, but after that I must have the news," I slurped my drink in a hurry and both, the anticipation and the alcohol I consumed, made my heart beat very strangely.

"You better sit down. Are you ready?" I nodded my head, as I sat down on the three legged shoe-maker's stool.

"Do you remember when you rushed into the factory, all out of breath, back in 45? You were crying and screaming for my help."

"Dad you promised to tell me the news and here you go again dragging things out, making me wait."

"Is that what I am doing Laszlo?"

"Yes! You are almost like Mother. You make me suffer even more. Please give me the news."

"I know how you feel Laszlo...But you have waited ever since 1945, by now you should be used to waiting."

"Rozsa left only before Easter...It is since then that I have waited for her letter," I blurted out and the realization dawned on me that I misunderstood my Father.

"I am so sorry Laszlo. I had no intention of misleading you. It is a letter from Rozsa you were thinking about and I, in my stupidity, mislead you. It is much better than a letter that I speak about," his words dropped on me like a bomb; it detonated in my mind and my heart was shattered.

"I am the fool Dad. I thought the world revolved around the letter that never came. Forget it Dad and so shall I."

"Do you want me to go on Laszlo or is your pain so great that there is no place in your heart for joy?"

"Go on Dad...Joy I could really use."

"Very well then. Let's go back to 1945, to the time when you rushed into the factory, begging me to save your Uncle Jozsef from the Russian prison camp. Do you remember Laszlo that day and all the things I have tried and how I failed?"

"I have never forgotten those days. You promised to save Uncle Jozsef and you truly tried. Don't blame yourself Dad. I stopped blaming you a long time ago."

"I wish you have told me that. It would have been so much easier to bear that failure, had I known."

"I couldn't tell you Dad that when the Russians took Uncle Jozsef to Siberia I was broken hearted. Later we drifted apart, we rarely talked."

"I know that Laszlo and you must know about my regret. I was foolish to promise you something that wasn't within my power."

"Everybody makes promises they may not be able to keep. Rozsa promised to always love me; never to forget me and in all these weeks she never wrote me a letter," my words spilled out without control; my pain, my burden proved to be too great to carry alone.

"She is very young Laszlo. Give her time. Life has a strange way of working things out. If you were truly meant for each other, you will meet again and you will be happy. In the meantime pay attention to your studies...Make something of yourself...Acquire all the knowledge you are capable of acquiring. Go after only those riches that no one can take away from you, as they took mine, save my skill of making shoes."

"I will do that, but you have a strange way of straying from the topic. You began to speak about Uncle Jozsef. Is there any news from him?"

"You are quite right Laszlo. I stray a lot...Particularly when I had a few drinks. I had my share today. After I have received the good news I couldn't pick up my tools, I couldn't force myself to work, so I began to celebrate, to drink alone, until you came."

"The good news Dad...That is what I want to hear."

"Oh. Yes, the good news. After you went to school this morning someone began to bang on our door. I went to open the gate and there he stood. I threw my arms around him; I led him into our kitchen; I couldn't take my eyes off of him. To have him return, after four years in Siberian prison camps, to see him home was the greatest miracle I have ever seen," my Father reached for the bottle, once more.

"Are you talking about Uncle Jozsef? Had he come home? Is that what you are saying?" my excitement rose with each word I spoke, my disappointment of not receiving a letter from Rozsa I have forgotten.

"Didn't I tell you? I must be farther gone than I thought. Of course it is your Uncle Jozsef who returned. He came so unexpectedly, without any warning, that I had difficulty believing his arrival. He is well Laszlo. Lost a great deal of weight, but he is well. He is home...Isn't that splendid?"

"You are telling me the truth? I couldn't stand another disappointment," I stated foolishly.

"I would never ever joke about something like that. I am not that drunk Laszlo. He came home and when he found out that Gizella moved from her apartment he came to us to find out where she lived. I wanted to keep him here, to see him, to be able to believe his miraculous return. I wanted to celebrate with him. I wanted to hear all his stories. I wanted to rejoice in his good fortune, but he naturally wanted to see his wife, so we have parted, after I gave him her new address. I wanted to go with him, but he insisted to go alone. So I came here and began my private celebration. Your Uncle Jozsef is home Laszlo, he is home for good, "my Father's words tumbled out, repeating himself time and time again, perhaps to reassure me and himself.

"I am so happy Dad...Uncle Jozsef's return from Stalin's hell is something I gave up on long ago."

"Me too my Son, but I was wrong to do that. One must always keep up hope; without hope life is not worth living," his last few words wiped away my new, enormous joy and my despair returned. His words echoed in my ears: 'Without hope life is not worth living.'

"Why should I live then?" I asked myself and thought of ending my misery, but then I remembered the splendid news and did not allow myself to spoil that joy.

***

That night, after supper, all four of us descended on my Uncle Jozsef and Aunt Gizella. They anticipated our arrival. Their always clean, small apartment sparkled even more. Their kitchen table was set with the finest of food and drinks.

Gizella and Jozsef sat close to each other, their hands touched and never let go during the entire evening. I tried to forget Aunt Gizella's adulterous betrayals that I knew so much about and rejoiced in my Uncle Jozsef's happiness.

We ate and drank. The adults swapped stories, but not one of them spoke about sad things. Disappointments, lost relatives, sufferings, betrayals, hopelessness were left for other times; this evening was a time for only joy.

At midnight we left them, but not before a great deal of kissing, hugging, touching, all designed to assure ourselves that this event was real and not a dream.

***

In spite of the late hour, after George went to sleep, after my parents went to their own room, I fished out my diary from its hiding place, took it to the kitchen where I read the forty-nine entries, some brief, some more lengthy and I began to write:

"Fifty days have passed since I began to confide in you, my diary. You are my true friend, who knows all my secrets. For all these days I have waited with less and less hope for that letter from my dearest. My Uncle Jozsef unexpectedly arrived from Siberia, my joy is great. I have waited for this day for over four years. That wait of mine is now over. I hope Gizella and Jozsef will find a new happiness, fate gave them another chance. Will it give me the same? I really do not know. My hopes have been dashed with the passing of each day without a letter. My Father told me that 'Without hope life is not worth living.' What should I do? Keep hoping and experience, day after day, a bitter disappointment? Or should I end it all? I couldn't do that...Now that my parents were given joy, among so much disappointment, I shouldn't commit a foolish act; I must not hand them another blow. No, that would be selfish and stupid. I will visit my Uncle, as often I can. I will look up one friend, I have neglected so long, Joska Lazar. Maybe that will ease my pain?

"A few years ago I have read something, that just popped in my head. It was all about life's happiness and misery. I no longer remember the name of the writer. He wrote, I am sure he was a male, that at birth we are all created equal. We are given a life-line, something like a straight line on a graph and our Maker ordained that each person experience happiness and joy during the life he lives. Those splendid occasions are recorded as peaks above the straight line. To balance things out the Almighty also ordained misery and suffering that we all must experience and those events are recorded as chasms below the straight line. When our Maker is planning to take us, He examines our graphs. If he finds that we have had too many peaks that deviate from the straight line we are given a few more miseries like sicknesses, before He summons us to Him. If His finding is the opposite, He blesses us with a few extra days of happiness, before he strikes. He created all humans equal and before the end He keeps His promise.

"Do you think my diary that it is so? If it is, the joy I was given today, having my Uncle returned to me, put a big peak on my chart. Does that mean that I should be prepared for a chasm? If that is so I ask my Maker to make me blind; to strike me dumb; to cripple me if that is His wish, but not to disappoint me in my love.

"Oh, one other thing my diary… Ever since Rozsa left I have been saving my coins. I have taken on odd jobs to earn a few Forints; I have gone to my Aunt Manci, who is always so kind and generous. She gave me not only all the money she could spare, but a few old, broken rings, earrings and even one small medallion. I think I have almost enough money to buy a return train-ticket to Szob and maybe even a small gift for Rozsa. I don't know what to do…I need a letter from Rozsa; just a few words, a single clue, to help me make my decision. I better go to bed now, get some rest before I write my next exams. I have only five left, then all the orals and the school year will be over. The day after school closes I want to go to her; I want to hold her; I want to kiss her, but none of that can happen, if she remains silent"

***

I stared at the exam paper for a few minutes, regretting that in the excitement of my Uncle's return I have neglected to study. I felt tired, my mind was reluctant to function, but I forced my gray matter to recall all I have learned during every day of this third school year and to my surprise my mind worked out the answers, my pen recorded all I knew.

Algebra wasn't an easy subject, yet problem after problem the solutions came, and the checking methods we have learned from our teacher, as well as those I have invented for myself, all indicated that I was able to solve all the problems correctly.

"My dearest Rozsa would be so proud of me," I thought of her for just one second, as I finished my exam paper. A smile must have crossed my face, I must have looked too relaxed, thus my teacher pounced on me.

"Get back to work..," his voice was quiet, yet so firm that I got frightened.

"I finished Sir," I whispered my explanation.

"Thirty minutes more before the end. You are not finished Laszlo," his voice barely audible to the others.

"I am finished. I have all the answers."

"Check them; then check them again and when you have finished checking them, start checking them again. No minute of exam time should be wasted. Am I understood?"

"Yes Sir," I replied obediently and did as I was told.

When the bell finally rang, when our teacher collected the papers, when he left us, the excited voices of my class-mates intruded.

"It was the toughest exam I ever saw," said Karoly.

"That fifth problem was a real ball-breaker," someone complained among the boys.

I grew tired of their crabbiness. I picked up my small leather case and left the building. On my way home I recalled each and every math problem our teacher set for us, challenged us to solve. For the life of me I couldn't see what was so difficult about them and realizing how well I must have done I was greatly cheered. I was about to enter Sip Street, when I recalled that my Uncle was home, so I turned in my tracks and walked the short distance to his home.

They lived in a very large house, owned by a printer, Tibor somebody, his name I can no longer recall, but I will never forget the large, fortified gate, through which I have entered the well kept yard. I headed to the third apartment in the back, where, until yesterday, my Aunt Gizella lived alone. I knocked on the door and Uncle Jozsef with a wide smile on his face, beaming his pleasure upon seeing me, opened it. He extended his hand to grasp mine and for whatever reason I began to stammer.

"I couldn't go home...I had to make sure...You are really here."

"I know how you feel Laszlo. Last night I woke up a thousand times, I think. I had to turn on the light to make sure I wasn't dreaming. I looked at your Aunt, as she slept peacefully beside me, and gave a silent thank to God for his mercy."

"I am so glad. I was devastated when in 1945 I saw you among the prisoners. I rushed to Father to have him pull strings to make them release you, but there wasn't enough string to pull. He wasn't as powerful as I have believed."

"I know Laszlo that he did a lot, but never expect the impossible. In truth I have never expected to be released. I was really lucky, but that is a long story, a story I will tell you some other time. Now I want to know all about you. Do you still play soccer?"

"I gave it up. I wasn't any good."

"Have you made any new friends?"

"One, Joska Lazar, the son of a tailor, but I haven't seen him for almost a year."

"Friends are to be treasured Laszlo, true friends that is. Was he a true friend of yours?"

"I never had a better friend, except you Uncle, if you don't mind me calling you a friend."

"I am proud to be your friend, I assure you. You will never know how much I thought about our precious days before the war. Do you remember me teaching you to play soccer? Do you recall the long talks we had? The many times we went to the movies and how, upon our return home, I made you tell the story of each movie to your Aunt?"

"I remember all that...I will never forget those things. It was so good to have someone treat me as an adult, only you Uncle Jozsef did that."

"I did that, that is true, but now that you have grown up...What are you now, seventeen? I will really treat you as a mature adult. We will have many talks; I will share with you all I have experienced during those four years. We will play pool and cards together; we will go to the movies again; you will tell the story lines to Aunt Gizella, it will be even better than the old days," he spoke with such exuberance, such joy that my heart was filled with the kind of love that should have really belonged to my parents.

"I am so happy you are back and that they didn't change you."

"I have changed Laszlo, make no mistake about that, but those changes will never impact on our friendship. I will always be looking out for you; take care of you; teach you all I know. Well enough of that...Let's start your first lesson. Before you go home you will go and see your friend. What was his name? Joska Lizar?"

"Joska Lazar," I made the correction.

"You go now Laszlo, see Joska. Rekindle that friendship, I hope you can. Then come to me tomorrow, I will be home. I will not seek a job just yet. Then we shall talk. I need some rest."

***

Even if I didn't respect my Uncle as much as I did, if I didn't love him like a Father, even if I did not consider his word to be law, I would have been unable to resist seeing Joska. I was more miserable than I can describe. Before I have met Rozsa, before my world began to revolve only around her, Joska's and my friendship prospered.

***

We met by chance, watching a soccer game on a Sunday, years ago. We happened to sit side by side on the elevated wooden bench. When I shouted, urged my team on to victory, so did he and after the game was over, our team defeated, nothing seemed more natural than to enter into a conversation. We lamented about our team's defeat, then spoke about the skill of the other team. Our conversation drifted from sport to the school we attended and we have discovered to our surprise that Joska and I studied at the same public school, that he was also in grade seven, although in another class, just one year from graduation. When we left the topic of school, when we finished speaking about my plan of becoming a chemist and his plan of becoming an electrical engineer, he squinted at the high Sun and his words surprised me.

"Why don't you come with me and meet my parents? I know they would be happy to meet my only friend."

"He called me his 'only friend', just after two hours of conversation. Nobody ever did that to me. He must be as lonely as I am," I thought and gladly accepted his invitation.

Joska's Father-whose pride in his Son was so great that he named him after himself, with the usual Junior designation front of his name, to be able to distinguish which Lazar people spoke about-was a tailor, I had learned later.

In one room of their small apartment, he plied his trade with great skill. When we entered my nose picked up scents that floated around their apartment: freshly baked bread gave out one aroma; onion and spices announced their presence; a faint tang of something, I couldn't identify, filled the air and the strongest of all came from the charcoal iron that Senior Lazar used, even on Sundays, to press the creases of newly made pants, until he was satisfied with their sharpness.

When Joska introduced me, his parents smiled.

"We knew your Father. What is he doing now?" Senior Lazar stated and asked. An impish look spread on his wide face; his completely bald head he tilted to one side, expecting my answer.

"He is away. He was drafted," I said it with a trace of sadness.

"A real shame. They took away a useful man to fight a useless war. Look, this is my favorite pair of shoes, not that I have many, we are poor people," he pointed at the pair of brown shoes he wore. "Your Father made this, he is a skilled shoe-maker, but no more skilled than I am in making suits, blazers and pants. I just finished this one. Take a look at the fine material. Put your nose here. It smells of sheep and of the green fields where the sheep grazed. I can even smell the clover. I love the smell of wool, maybe more than that of cotton. Did you know that every material has its own smell?" he spoke on and on, displaying great pride in his creations and I have listened with growing envy.

"I have never heard my Father speak like that. Was he not proud of his creations?" I wondered and then I noticed that Senior Lazar expected an answer. In my reverie about my Father I never heard his question.

"I beg your pardon, could you repeat that?"

"You are just like Joska. One minute he is here, the next minute he is far away. I can see now why he came to like you."

"I am sorry, I just didn't hear your question."

"I don't mind that...You were thinking about something else. Maybe a bright future? A girl perhaps? Or about fishing? I know Joska thinks about all these things and America. Yeah, America is his passion. He hopes to go there some day. That has been his dream, ever since he was a small boy. Do you have any dreams Laszlo? Young boys should have dreams and hopes..," his torrent of words continued and I felt an even greater envy than before.

"How lucky Joska is. He grew up with a Father, who hides no thoughts, who talks to his son constantly, who understands him," I thought, but this time I heard Mr. Lazar's question.

"I asked you if you've heard from your Father?"

"He writes sometimes, but his letters come rarely."

"The war will come to an end Laszlo. He will come home and he will make fine shoes again. As long as a man uses his God given talent, as long as he applies his skills, as long as he doesn't give up, he is never defeated. What did he do for relaxation, when he was home?"

I thought about that for a minute. I recalled the occasions when he drank, but that fact I didn't want to share, I didn't want to judge him unfairly. I knew he was not an alcoholic, just a man who had to submerge his sorrow or to boost his joy.

"He used to go fishing every Sunday. In season that is."

"Well, he is a man after my own heart. Did Joska tell you how I love to fish?"

"We just met today."

"Well you will come to see us often, I hope and we shall talk about making suits, fishing and all kinds of other things." Mr. Lazar would have spoken on for the rest of my first visit, but his wife found her voice.

"You can even come for meals. I love to cook and bake. It would be nice to have a second Son. I had two Sons, long ago. I loved both of them equally, with all my heart, but Joska's brother, when he was five, passed away. God took him from me for some sin I must have committed, but what that sin was I do not even know."

"Hush Mrs. Lazar, that was long ago. You cannot mourn forever," Senior Lazar spoke up, trying to put an end to his wife's obvious misery.

She must have gotten used to her husband's desire not to be reminded of that tragedy, so she changed the subject.

"Stay for supper. I am sure we would enjoy that. We rarely have any company, just the clients who bring my husband endless work. They do not stay. He looks at their materials, if they bring any; he offers them some fine tweed, if they came empty handed; he measures them for size; they agree on a price and then they are gone. So why don't you stay?"

I thanked her sincerely, but that first time I refused her invitation, I knew my Mother must have been concerned about me.

***

After that first, joyous experience, Joska's home became mine; his quiet, small, simple Mother became a second Mother to me. His Father filled the void I always felt over my Father's and Uncle Jozsef's absence. I went to their place, almost daily. I ate Mrs. Lazar's cooking, almost as often as I ate what my Mother provided. We have had many congenial talks; some fishing trips to Senior Lazar's favorite fishing holes and the three of us went to see a soccer game every Sunday.

As time passed we became like a family. I was so pleased that Joska's Father was never drafted. I worried about his heart condition, as one would worry about that of a Father. Then a few months before the end of the war came, my Father escaped the army, he arrived home and our family was whole again. We celebrated the great event in our humble home and next day we celebrated that with Joska's family.

"I told you Laszlo that he will come home. Do you remember me saying that?"

"I will never forget it. Whenever I felt despair you chased away the shadows Mr. Lazar. Whenever I felt hungry, and even when I didn't, you fed me Mrs. Lazar. You three were really good to me."

"And why shouldn't we be good to our own son," Mrs. Lazar announced for the hundredth time and I knew that everything they did during the years of 43 and 44 was a testimony to what she said.

By the time the spring of 45 arrived, my Father and Mr. Lazar became friends too. They began to fish together those rich tributaries of the Danube that were full of carp and cat-fish. They talked and drank together; played cards and exchanged stories. Their friendship paralleled ours and the Lazars and Lichters were, at least for the time being, truly happy.

Joska and I were asked to help our Fathers to spin the fishing lines from black threads, to wax them, to prepare them for the season. We were sent to the Danube to cut branches that they carefully cleared of bark, branches that they dried and shaped and strengthened, until those were strong enough to become their fishing poles for the season. We were given the important job of killing frogs, skewering them on long branches, placing them in the marshes that were plentiful around Baja and when the leaches found their victims, it was our job to pluck them out from the frogs' innards, to place them into glass jars, covered tightly with strong cloth. We were given the job of digging big, fat worms in the muck that lay close to the marshes and all the tasks they gave us Joska and I carried out together.

When Joska and I have reached the ripe old age of fourteen we were finally allowed to use their precious wooden boats, my Father and Mr. Lazar built together, the boats they have tarred early in the spring to prevent the rotting of the wood. They kept their boats by the old bridge, securely chained and locked to the wooden pilings on the north shore of the canal that flowed into the Danube, just above the ruined bridge.

I will never forget the first time when Joska and I walked to my Father's boat, unlocked the padlock, pulled out the chain from the eye-hook, and left the safety of the canal. The sun was shining, a few high, white clouds drifted over the Danube, as we headed north, just far enough, across and above the entry to the old Danube. There we changed course, began to paddle across the river's strong current, that pushed us south, just far enough to enter the old branch, where the water warmed early in the year, where the large sand-bar hid. The two of us paddled while singing rowdy songs, not even noticing the coming change in the weather. When we began our first, exciting journey the winds were calm; when we entered the dead branch of the wide river, we were sheltered and never noticed the dreaded south wind that began to blow.

By early afternoon we have cut more than enough branches for our Fathers to choose from to make their fishing poles. It was then that the heavens opened up, dumping their wet load on us, helpless, inexperienced boys. We became soaked to our skins within minutes. Our boat, tied to a small, flimsy jetty, bobbed up and down in the roaring wind and it began to fill fast with water.

I grabbed a paddle, while Joska used the wooden spoon to bail out the water. His efforts were slightly more successful than mine. I was hardly able to drive the boat any distance, while Joska was keeping us afloat, in spite of the pounding rain.

Perhaps we should have stayed where we were, but our inexperience and our fright made us push on and three hours later we had reached the three-quarter mile wide Danube, the water we had to cross. Our beloved river was in full rage; its surface was whipped into one huge cauldron of white foam by the strong south wind that began to lash us. The rain let up, allowing Joska to pick up a paddle. The wind raged on, stole my voice and that of Joska, whenever we tried to span the four foot distance between us to shout scared instructions and encouragements to each other. Our progress was slow, our hope of survival even smaller.

We could not see far with our stinging eyes that were full of tears of fright, our exhaustion blurred our vision, thus we never saw the two frantic men rushing up and down the eastern shore.

We must have fought the elements for two hours before we realized that we had succeeded robbing the river, whose hungry mouth opened up many times, trying to swallow us and our small boat. A few hundred feet above the canal, from where we began our journey, about eight hours earlier, we had reached the shore. Our ears rang from exertion; our eyes were blind from fatigue, but neither deafness nor blindness prevented us from hearing our Fathers' tongue lashing, seeing their angry faces.

"You God damn fools..," shouted my Father.

"You stupid ass-holes..," screamed Mr. Lazar.

"We just, we just wanted..," Joska had no energy to finish his explanation. He fell into his Father's arms, just seconds before my Father embraced me.

"Thank God you are safe Laszlo and you too, Joska. Thank God the river didn't take you. When we allowed you two to take the boat, we never suspected the coming of the storm, otherwise no begging, no crying would have softened our hearts."

"Your Dad is right. In a storm like this, no sane men would ever attempt to cross the Danube. There were some who tried years ago, some on a dare, others out of necessity, but none succeeded. So many have drowned, so many perished. The south wind is our enemy, far more dangerous than the Russian Army," Mr. Lazar spoke on and on, but his voice and that of my Father began to soften with relief.

***

These were the memories and some others that rushed through my mind after I had left my Uncle and began my short walk to where the Lazar family resided. I must have walked very slowly, either to enable myself to bring forth all these memories or perhaps out of fear of how my second set of parents and my friend will receive me after almost a year of absence.

I need not have worried about that at all. When I entered their apartment, they greeted me like a lost son. Mr. Lazar shook my hand so vigorously that I felt my shoulder blade ready to separate. Mrs. Lazar patted my face that she hasn't seen so long, all the while telling me about the fresh bread I must taste, fresh cookies that she baked just hours ago and about the fried chicken that we will have for supper.

Joska stayed in the background, just for a few minutes, and when his parents exuberant welcome began to wane, he came to me and all my fears dissolved. I ate with them an early supper; enjoyed the fresh bread and even had some cookies. When we were satiated by the food Mrs. Lazar provided, Mr. Lazar turned to me.

"I am so sorry Laszlo. The news about your Father shook me greatly."

Momentarily I forgot what he was referring to, just as I forgot, for the first time, my ache for Rozsa.

"News about my Father?"

"The robbery is what I am talking about. I understand that he closed his factory, lost all his workers after that tragic event. I haven't seen him anywhere: he must have stopped fishing; he is no longer seen in the city. What is he doing now?"

"He began to make shoes at home. He is back where he was before the war," I gave him the information.

"I thought of going to see him, but I understood from friends that he wishes to see no one," Mr. Lazar explained his absence.

"He became a loner, that much is true. He suffers in silence and when he can no longer stand the setback he finds solace in solitary drinking." I saw no harm in revealing the truth.

"Well I don't care about what he wants, I will go and see him. Do you think he would throw me out?"

"He wouldn't do that. He needs friends now more than ever before."

"You and your Father Laszlo both need a friend. I want you and Joska to go to his room and catch up on all the things that happened during your absence."

***

For the next hour Joska and I huddled in his room. That is where I told him all about Rozsa, that is where he told me about how he met a girl and we both rejoiced. Two young men in love had a great deal to share: he shared his happiness that his girl-friend brought into his life and I shared my pain that Rozsa's absence, her silence caused.

Before I left Joska and the Lazar family's flat we swore to each other never again to neglect our friendship. Even now I can recall his words of parting.

"To be in love is the most magnificent feeling, but such joy needs sharing. Promise me that you will come and see me, at least every second day and if you do not keep your promise I will park on your doorstep. Now go home and don't ever give up on the one you love. That Rozsa of yours must be quite a gal."

***

I walked home, my heart brimming with the feeling of love and friendship. This time I didn't fear my Mother's scolding for having missed supper and I didn't count my footsteps.

"It is high time you have honored me with your presence. You should have been home hours ago...Your Father decided not to wait. He went back to his shop and probably to his bottle, he doesn't think I know. George was too impatient to wait, he went to bed," my Mother lamented, as soon as I have entered the kitchen. I saw one place setting waiting for me on the table. "For weeks you rushed home right after school, almost always asking the same question, although you haven't asked me lately," she reminded me of my long wait for a letter. "But today of all days you come home almost six hours late and you don't even ask. May I ask Laszlo if you no longer care about that letter?" she seemed to have finished her scolding, that was more like a tease and I noticed that her fingers touched something in her apron's pocket.

"I care Mother, but I stopped asking."

"Well maybe today is the day when you should ask," her teasing continued.

"Very well, I am asking. Did the postman bring me anything?" I asked and in spite of her hand reaching into her pocket, I expected nothing other than her usual, unkind answer.

"Only these..," she removed three envelopes from her pocket, raised them above her head and before she handed to me the precious papers, letters that were to make me rejoice or send me into despair, she demanded that I give her a kiss.

I hugged my Mother and planted a fervent kiss on her cheek, holding back my tears of joy.

"Well that is much better. You haven't done this since you met Rozsa and that was some time ago. Mothers don't get any more kisses once their sons are able to dispense them to someone else," she explained what bothered her for the last year. Her words tumbled out and so did a single tear. "Now you sit there and eat your supper. After that you can have your letters."

"I already ate..," I began to say, but I realized the futility of refusing the meal she prepared. I recalled the many times I have set beside this table, with meals front of me that I was loath to eat; how she made me sit there for hours; how she supervised my stubborn refusals. On those many occasions when she had no work to attend to, she just hovered over me or sat beside me, letting me know that she will win. During those occasions her will and mine, neither of them weak, always clashed and when it was over she was victorious and I was always defeated.

Knowing the outcome of the contest, I submitted to my Mother's will. I polished off the large meal faster than ever before, I thought my small stomach was going to burst, but for those three letters I would have done anything.

"Now drink your milk Laci!" she issued the order, using the diminutive of Laszlo, which she always used when she demanded that I behave like a little boy. Although she knew how I gagged and sometimes lost my supper when she made me drink the hated, boiled milk with the curdled, crusty layer it received from being boiled, she still insisted.

"Please don't make me do that. You know how my stomach rejects the milk."

"I don't care about your stomach. Do you care about these letters?" she announced and with those few words she settled the issue.

I forced down the hated fluid; gagged a couple of times, as it slid down my throat toward its destination; my stomach heaved ready to expel its contents, but I banished all memories of my second supper and I concentrated on thoughts of the letters Rozsa wrote.

"You see Laszlo the milk didn't kill you. It is good not to be so stubborn. Here are your letters, read them here, I will go to bed."

***

My fingers burned with the touch of those precious papers. I spread them out on the table and from the post-marks I have determined that they were mailed in different months. One bore an April postmark, the other May and the last one June.

I saw the sender was indeed my Rozsa, who carefully penned the return address. Her beautifully shaped letters, like pearls arranged on a straight string, spelled out my name and our address. I picked up a knife and with shaking fingers slid open all three envelopes, but dared not remove their contents.

"Was it the postal service that was so tardy? Or was it something else? No, my

Mother couldn't do that...Why would she want to make me suffer? It really matters no longer. I would have died just for one letter from my darling and now I have three! What shall I do? Read them as fast as I can or should I follow in my Father's footsteps? He rationed my Mother's letter, one paragraph for each day. What should I do?" I was torn between the alternatives, but neither my mind nor my heart was patient.

I removed the April letter, unfolded the white paper that was covered with her neat handwriting and began to read.

"My Dear Laci,

"It has been three weeks since I was torn away from you. I cried for the first two hours while the distance grew between us. Neither my Father's comforting words; nor my Mother's touch on my shoulder eased the pain I felt.

"After six hours and one transfer we have arrived to Szob. Our flat is in the building occupied by the River Police, it is kind of nice, but I will not compare it with what we had across from you. Two days later our furniture arrived. I tried to find the time to write you, but my parents needed my help and my new school kept me busy.

"Whenever your daily letters arrived I locked myself in my room. I have my own room. I no longer sleep where Joe does. There I have read your letter and your words of love brought tears to my eyes. Why have we wasted all the time we had? I shall never forget that trip on the Danube...I treasure that memory as much as you do. We shall see each other again, I really believe that. Will you come and see us when the school year is over? I hope with all my heart you will do.

"Until then please take care of yourself...Give my regards to your family and give yourself a big hug from me.

"Your loving Rozsa."

I finished the first letter, its warmth touched my heart, brought tears to my eyes. It comforted me; made up for all the days of my agony and when I reached for the one she wrote in May I began to think.

"Maybe my Father gave me the right advice. I should keep the remaining two letters for a time when I need to ease my suffering," I urged myself and I didn't read the other two.

I placed the three treasures under my pillow, said my prayers and thanked the Almighty for the gift of love and friendship. Within minutes, after my head hit the pillow, I fell asleep. An hour later I came awake with a start. I must have had a bad dream I couldn't remember. My pajama was soaked with sweat, my heart trembled with unexplainable fear. I sought the comfort of Rozsa's letters, clutched them in my fingers, held them over my heart, hoping to fall asleep. I must have dosed off, for I began to dream.

I traveled on a train; walked from the station to a house; knocked on the door that was opened by Rozsa. I stood front of her, my arm extended for an embrace. She just stood there like a statue, her sweet face displayed no smile of pleasure, her arms remained by her side.

"You asked me to come..," I spoke, feeling more the misery of her rejection, than the fatigue of the journey.

"That was before..," all she said and once more I woke. I jumped out of bed, rushed into the kitchen, turned the light on and spread out her letters on the table. I have re-read the one that caused me joy and I began to devour the others.

"Dear Laci,

"I guess it is time that I write again, almost a month has passed since I wrote the last one. You must be angry with me for my infrequent letters, although yours come daily. I have been terribly busy and each and every day I have something new to do. I do my school work and prepare for the year-end play in which I will be the leading lady. I take long walks in the hills, close to our home. We pick flowers and admire nature's beauty.

"I read your letter, mostly on the same day, when it arrives, but I must confess that to do that every day is too much. You must have better things to do. Do not neglect your work and friends, because of me.

"Do you still plan to come to see us? It would be nice. I would introduce you to our new friends, there are many. Just one more thing: Your letters come but never speak about mine. Did you receive it?

"Take care of yourself...My regards to your family and to you.

"Rozsa."

I placed the April and May letters side by side. I compared their length, by counting the words and my heart trembled upon finding that the second letter contained only one-hundred-sixty-seven words.

"That is sixty-five words less than the first one," I told myself and searched for an excuse. "She is busy with school work, the play, and her friends." Then I turned my attention to the two salutations. The first one 'My Dear Laci' and the second, 'Dear Laci' only. "Is that only an oversight? Or a sign of Rozsa changing?" I tormented myself in the middle of the night and the more I re-read the two letters, the stronger my suffering became.

"She no longer locks herself in the room when my letter arrives. She no longer expresses a fervent wish to see me. She doesn't seem to miss me any longer. She sent her regards to my family and only the same to me. It is only her regards that I deserved in May. I shudder to think about the third letter that she wrote a month later," I told myself, tortured myself and slipped the last letter from its envelope.

My worst fears came true. Her salutation appeared to be cold; her words that spoke about not love, but endless tasks she had to perform, conveyed no warmth. Those words could have been written to a stranger. Just after she finished her letter, with regards to my parents, but none to me, she added a few more words.

"P.S.: If you still wish to come to see Joe and my family, please write to my parents. It is their permission you should seek."

I just stared at the last letter in disbelief.

"Could such a short time and the distance blunt her love so much? Did I frighten her with all my declarations about my undying love? That is what must have happened. Stupid me. After one kiss on that Russian boat and another at the station made me bold, careless and unthinking. Have her parents taken offense at the station? I am sure that is what happened. I have betrayed her Father's trust. She still wants to see me, I am convinced, but I need her parents' approval. That is what my love wants me to do! This very day I will write to them; beg them to allow me to make a visit. They will not refuse; they are kind, understanding people. When my school year ends I will go to Szob; I will resurrect our love if that is what is needed," with that last thought I went back to bed and during the rest of the sleepless night I convinced my mind to conclude what my heart wanted to believe.

Chapter 3

Rozsa's first letter lay flat against my heart, in my jacket's inner pocket, as I began to write one of the two exams that remained. Her other two letters, those I didn't want to remember, lay hidden in the back of my diary.

I was always in the habit of pre-planning all I had to do. On this day, after I finished my exams, I planned to write to Rozsa's parents.

I set by my table, pen in hand, paper at the ready and after I wrote down: "Dear Mr. & Mrs. Buja..," I didn't know how to continue. I had no difficulty to write school exams; I had no trouble expressing my feelings to my diary; I have always found it a joy to write to my darling Rozsa.

"This letter and the reply, if I receive any, will determine my fate. I must choose my words with great care. I must touch their hearts, force them to agree," I warned myself and after ten drafts and two hours of constant struggle, I have read the last draft over.

"Dear Mr. & Mrs. Buja,

"Many weeks ago you lived across the street, but now all of you are far away. How I cherish the memory of our conversations! How I recall all the words you spoke Mr. Buja. Your wisdom I shall never forget. Your predictions came true, the Communists finished my Father. I do not have the heart to write down all the details, but maybe I will have an opportunity to tell you everything that happened, if you two will be kind enough to allow me to pay you a visit. My Father has been devastated; he is devoid of hope and friends, he has become a recluse.

"I have almost finished all my exams and I did rather well. School will close in less than two weeks. My parents and all my relatives have been very kind. They have given me what little money they could spare and I have their permission to undertake the journey to Szob.

"If your friendship with my parents wasn't so strong I know they would have never granted their permission. Mr. Buja do you remember that farewell party at Rezert? People we know still talk about that; how we lost the motor; how it was recovered, but most of all they talk about your kindness and your caring. I am not the only one who misses you all, but I may be the only fortunate creature who will have the opportunity to see you soon.

"Please give my best to Joe and Rozsa, I miss them too.

"I will look for your letter daily and when your reply comes I will be the happiest boy in Baja. Should you be kind enough to invite me I wouldn't overstay my welcome. Five days is all I would be able to stay or maybe even less.

"Greetings and best wishes from my parents. Many thanks for all your kindness. Best wishes to all of you.

"Laszlo."

I have read and re-read this last draft and when I could think of no more modifications I went to see my two friends.

***

I told Uncle Jozsef about my visit to the Lazars and the happiness I have experienced on being received not like an ungrateful, forgetful, negligent friend, but as a beloved member of their family.

"I am glad you went Laszlo. When one is given a true friend, one should cherish that great gift, one should never neglect him. In Siberia, in one of the prison camps, I became the friend of the Commandant and he proved himself to be a friend indeed. Without his help I would not be home. May God bless that kind, unfortunate man. Well I will not say more about him, not yet that is. What I would like to know is why have you neglected your friend for almost a year?"

So I began to tell him my story, with as much care as I always used when I told Aunt Gizella the story-line of a movie. I left out not a single detail. By the time I have finished my lengthy narration, Uncle Jozsef knew about the first day I saw my darling Rozsa; he knew all about my strenuous attempts to befriend Joe; he followed us on our lovely walks around the city; he shared with us the joy of our frequent visits to the park of Dery; he was with us when occasionally we were allowed to go to a cinema. He was able to share my excitement whenever I was able to link my arm with Rozsa's; whenever we held hands. Then I spoke about the many conversations we have had with the Bujas; I made him share the fear Mr. Buja felt and made him understand the predictions that wise man made about the future. I spoke about Mr. Buja's transfer; the farewell party we attended; the first kiss I have ever given a girl and the second at the station. I spoke about my constant waiting for Rozsa's letters and then I told him what I thought my Mother did."

"You are wrong about your Mother. She would never confiscate your letters Laszlo. If you thought even for one moment that she did that, you owe her an apology," were the first words Uncle Jozsef spoke, since I began my long story.

"How else can I explain the arrival of three letters on the same day, when two of them were written months ago?"

"Be happy the letters came. Life is so full of mysteries. Happy are the men who accept what fate brings them and miserable are those who constantly search for explanations. Had I done that in Siberia I would have gone crazy. There I have learned to take one day at a time; I have learned to take the good things with the bad. Your parents love you Laszlo, in their own way, I do admit. You must never forget that. Love is the most mysterious feeling. I love Gizella. I loved her from the first moment I saw her, when your Father introduced us, much the same way you began to love Rozsa. Does your Aunt Gizella love me? I am sure she does, even if she betrayed me..," his sudden shift of topic and tone almost made me blurt out all I knew, but his need for love, his desire to receive affirmation of the love he cherished, made me modify what I was about to say.

"I have lived with Aunt Gizella most of the time while you were away. Her love for you was always constant," I lied and was caught up in my desire to offer him what comfort I could. "There wasn't a day she didn't cry. There was never a time that she doubted your return. She could never speak to me about anything else. I wish I could be that sure of Rozsa's love for me."

"To be sure of one's love is not that easy. Yet we must force ourselves to be convinced, that is essential for our survival. How far is Szob from here?"

"Maybe two hundred fifty kilometers."

"Six or seven hours by train?" Uncle Jozsef asked, leading me on.

"It is probably no more than that."

"And how far is Siberia? What do you think?"

"Two, three days away?" I asked displaying my ignorance.

"It took me two weeks to come home by train. Even if the Russian trains ran on time, it would have taken me a whole week. Can you imagine Laszlo four years away from home? The doubts I had to chase away? Can you imagine two weeks on a train? All the while thinking about not only what I shall find upon my arrival, but even more about whether I shall arrive at all. At least you will have only a short train-trip and once you are there your heart will rejoice."

"I do not even know if they will allow me a visit. In her June letter Rozsa urged me to seek her parents' permission."

"Do it then friend, do not hesitate."

"I wrote a letter...I fear it might not do."

"I know you Laszlo well enough. Your letter will be answered."

"I wish I was as certain as you are Uncle Jozsef."

"Have you mailed the letter yet?"

"I brought it with me...Maybe you could?" I hesitated to make my request.

"Sure I will read it. I will read it gladly." He fished out his spectacles, just before I handed him the letter, almost ready for mailing.

His brow wrinkled in concentration as he deciphered my hand-writing and when he finished, he placed it on the table.

"So what do you think Uncle Jozsef?"

"I think you must have spent a great deal of time and effort to find the right words, the right phrases."

"Have I found them?"

"Well it is hard to know. I do not know the Bujas, but I know this. If I have received a letter like this, so full of kind words and reminders about their friendship with your parents, I couldn't resist. You skillfully gave them news about your Father, yet held back all the details. What could they do, but invite you? And why wouldn't they do that? Your letter speaks not about your love for Rozsa, about your burning desire to see her, instead it places emphasis on seeing them all. They will assume that your love has cooled, as you assume that Rozsa's did too. They will read your letter, they will think about its content and after a few days of thinking, they will send you an invitation."

"Is there anything I should change?" I asked him and waited for his answer.

"Not a single thing Laszlo. Mail it as it is."

***

A short time later it was my friend Joska, who held the letter in his hand and read it carefully, while I waited for his opinion.

"So what do you think?" I finally asked him.

"I think you are a rascal. Do you love Rozsa as much as before?"

"That much and even more. My love for her is like the Danube's current, it cannot help itself, its currents cannot diminish."

"Yet you hide that love in your letter. I think you are wise to do that. Parents are strange, especially parents of a girl who is loved. Their first instinct is to protect their daughter from someone else's love, as long as they can. I know that my girl's parents behave that way, whenever I get near her. They don't seem to understand that loving someone will never change how my Magdi feels about them. Mail it Laszlo. Isn't that what your Uncle urged you to do?"

"I told you that Joska, but what do you think?"

"I think they will be delighted to receive news by word of mouth from their former city. They will invite you, if for no other reason than for that."

***

After I left Joska's home, I sealed the letter, walked to the post-office, bought the stamps needed and after a few whispered, impassioned words to the Almighty, I deposited it in the mail-box.

The next few days I spent finishing my oral exams; attended the closing ceremonies of the school year. I visited my Uncle and the Lazars daily. In my heart's and mind's hidden recesses I held on to the hope of the letter's coming, but as the days passed, as no letter came, I have suffered and waited.

When our school closed, when summer vacation finally began, two weeks after I mailed my "letter of hope', as I called it, I intercepted our mail-man daily, but for several days his reply never varied. "I am sorry, but there is no mail addressed to Laszlo Lichter."

If I didn't have Joska for a friend; if I did not have Uncle Jozsef to talk to, I would have despaired, but neither Joska, nor my Uncle, allowed me to give up hope. Their words, their stories, their constant encouragements were designed to cheer me and then the day came when our mail-men gave me a different answer.

"Is this the letter you have been waiting for?" with those words he handed me an envelope from Mr. Buja.

I put the un-opened letter in my trousers' pocket. Carried it to my room, where I found George reading; I carried it to the kitchen where my Mother busied herself with her cooking; I did not even consider entering the front-room that was out of bounds to kids, except by invitation. The only place left, where I could be assured privacy for the tears that were sure to come, if I was rejected, was by the pig-pen.

The two pigs grunted their usual greeting. "A letter came from Mr. Buja," I shared the news with my companions and with fingers that shook with excitement, I opened the flap and removed the single sheet of paper.

I began to read Mr. Buja's neat hand-writing and as I read paragraph after paragraph what he wrote, I felt the cold hand of despair tearing at my heart, I felt his words tearing at my soul.

"Dear Laszlo,

"We have received your letter, just a week ago and after much discussion I am finally ready to send our reply. I have been nominated by members of my family to write to you.

"Each and every member of our family felt great sorrow about your Father. The bad news surprised us greatly, and it pained us to be informed that 'the Communists finished him'. What does it really mean? He is alive, thank God. That much we know from your letter, but not much more. Will you please describe the details in your next letter to Rozsa, we would really like to know. I wish we were a lot closer. Then I could talk to him, maybe I could help him realize that a man with as many friends as he had is never alone.

"Yes, I do remember our many conversations Laszlo and truly miss them, but that can't be helped. Fate took us away and unless another surprise awaits us I don't think we shall see each other." I couldn't read any further.

"Joska was wrong! So was my Uncle! My letter did accomplish nothing. The Bujas do not want to see me," my bitter protests poured out and my tears I couldn't control. "Should I even bother reading the rest?" I asked myself in trepidation, but my heart wouldn't give in, expecting a miracle it just wouldn't give up hope.

"Thanks for your kind words Laszlo. That trip to Rezert we will always remember and we will remember those good people of Baja you wrote about.

"Here we have made many new friends, but assure you that we have not forgotten any of those we left behind. You are counted among them Laszlo, as is your whole family. The four of us, Maria, Joe, Rozsa and I speak about you quite often. We remember you not only for your help, but for your understanding. I have asked you to never betray my trust and as far as I know you did that only once. But that was a very emotional occasion, caused by my transfer and our moving. Well we don't hold that against you, young people sometimes forget, Mrs. Buja and I understand that.

"Before I close this hastily written letter there is one last thing..," I stopped reading once again. My tearful eyes did not dare to see the rest; my agitated mind imagined the coming of the refusal; my breaking heart didn't dare take any more.

"Should I read the two remaining lines and be cast into Hell? Or should I dream on and still expect a miracle? I think Mr. Buja made it quite clear that he did not forget my betrayal. But it was only one kiss at the station. A simple kiss for me to remember forever and for Rozsa to take on the long journey. Surely Mr. Buja couldn't be that cruel? He must remember his youth and how he loved?" My debate, my anguish would have continued, had I not been interrupted by my Mother's shouting.

"Where are you Laszlo? I need your help! You better come out from wherever you are hiding!"

I knew that my Mother wasn't the patient sort, so I read the last few lines in a great hurry.

" and that is a favor I want to ask you. Will you go to the Gomoris, tell Margit that her sister and her family are well. When we have time we will send them a letter. Thank you Laszlo and farewell.

The letter was signed simply: "On behalf of your friends, Jozsef Buja."

In my grief I forgot my Mother, whose calling subsided and re-read the letter once again.

"There is not a word about an invitation. No refusal and no permission either. Did Mr. Buja forget my request? He surely couldn't do that...More likely he just side-stepped the issue. He didn't want to hurt me by a refusal and he didn't want me to get close to Rozsa. For that one kiss, he knew about, he made me pay dearly." I wiped my tears, ready to obey my Mother, with aching heart I looked at his signature and noticed the small sign tucked in the letter's lower, right hand corner.

My heart began to race; the unexpected, almost unnoticeable command to turn over the page made me shiver.

"P.S. I am sorry, in my haste I almost forgot. You asked about a visit to Szob. We have the space and the inclination to hear all about your family, so do not write...Hop on the train, but let us know about your arrival."

"The miracle happened. my heart was right. Thank you God for granting me my wish. Thank you Mr. Buja for being so understanding. Thank you Mrs. Buja for your kindness. Thank you Rozsa for whatever you did to change your Father's mind. Thank you Joe for whatever help you gave me. Thank you my pigs for not laughing at this fool," my mind sang, my heart was ecstatic, my legs trembled as they obeyed my Mother's earlier order. My lips and tongue shouted the joyous news.

"The letter came! I was invited! I am going to see Rozsa."

***

My feverish preparations began when I ran to the railway station, two hours and many chores later.

"Go find out when the train is going. And don't forget to find out the cost," my Mother gave in grudgingly when I completed the chores.

I ran the one mile like a sprinter. I didn't notice the children on the swings or the passers-by, who looked at me strangely. I took the steps by twos and flew into the station.

"I want to go to Szob. When is the train leaving?" my raised voice, my eagerness must have surprised the ticket seller, behind his window covered with brass bars.

"Judging from your demeanor young man I don't think you can wait for the next one. The train for Budapest left hours ago. That is where you have to catch your connection to get to Szob."

"I am sorry I have misled you. I want to go to Szob two weeks from now."

"Well that is better. Do you plan to wait here or do you plan to come back then?" the old man squinted at me, not even trying to hide his amusement.

"I will come back; I have a lot to do."

"And so do I. So walk over to that board and check the schedule. That is what you should do," chuckled the civil servant and pointed to the large boards that covered the wall to his right.

"Could you tell me how much it will cost?" I suddenly remembered my Mother's order.

"That board will tell you everything you need to know." I was dismissed and began to study the board just a minute later.

I searched the departure board for 'Baja to Budapest', hesitated in making my choice, then I settled on the earliest train, wanting to get there as early as possible. On my piece of paper I noted carefully the time of departure and the estimated arrival to Budapest. Then I searched for the connection from 'Budapest to Szob' and I wrote down that as well. I was never more happy, just seeing the name of Szob seemed to convert my plan, my hope into reality. Our reunion with Rozsa loomed on the horizon as a fact.

I turned around, danced out of the station when I have realized that the fare I didn't note. I rushed back, searched for the information and with great relief I saw that it cost far less than my savings.

My next trip took me into the heart of the city, to a jewelry store. In the first one I couldn't find what I desired; in the second the choices were even less. In the last one I found the gold signet ring I wanted to buy for Rozsa.

"May I see that ring?" I asked the clerk and when she handed it to me with a smile, I began to ask my rehearsed questions.

"How many carats is this ring?"

"Fourteen..," she replied, still smiling.

"And the price please?"

"Three hundred Forints," I heard her say and the realization hit me.

"I have only a hundred fifty left after I pay for the tickets. And I will have no pocket money," but to the clerk I wasn't willing to disclose my financial situation.

"And how much would it cost with engraving?"

"Depends on where and what you want us to inscribe."

"Just a few words: 'R and L forever," I gave her the information.

"Well that will be an extra fifty."

"Do you think you could...What I mean is this the best price you can give me?" I was embarrassed about my dickering.

"Well that ring and the engraving will cost you no less. I am sorry. Is this ring for your sweetheart? Are you getting engaged young man?" her smile broadened and I felt my face on fire.

"This ring is a gift to a girl I know." I wasn't willing to share my happiness, my love, my adoration with a stranger.

"Lucky girl, I am sure, but if you cannot afford it may be we can find something cheaper."

"No! This is the ring I must have."

"Very well then. It will be three hundred fifty Forints and the engraving will be done by tomorrow. Do you think you could pay half of that in advance?"

I just stood there, front of the counter, reached into my trousers' pocket, removed the tissue paper that hid my treasures and one by one I offered them to the sales-lady.

"I have a broken gold ring here. Do you think I could use this as part of the payment?"

She examined the scrap gold with her magnifying glass and nodded her head in answer.

"With this the price will be fifty Forints less."

"I have a single earring too..," I could hardly utter the words.

"Another twenty five off," came her reply.

"And here is a gold medallion. I know it is scratched, but maybe it is worth almost a hundred?"

"Eighty I can allow for that, but no more."

"Three hundred fifty-minus a hundred fifty five for the three pieces comes to one hundred ninety five Forints. I am still short..," I calculated. "This ring must be Rozsa's!" I have made my decision and made my offer to the lady.

"I give you those three pieces. That is one hundred and fifty-five Forints and here is twenty Forints cash. That satisfies the down-payment, does it not?"

"Very well...I think you have made the right choice. Any girl would be more than happy to receive this magnificent gift of love. Come back tomorrow and bring the rest of the money. By the way do you want us to size it?"

"What do you mean?"

"Well I need the size of her finger; otherwise she might not be able to wear it."

I tried to picture Rozsa's lovely hand. I could see her slender fingers, but I was helpless when I tried to figure out what size it may be.

"I really do not know what size to pick," I announced dejectedly and found her fingers in my hand.

"Are her fingers anything like mine?" the young girl asked and waited.

"Nobody's fingers are like hers. They are far more slender and shapely. When God created her He took great care in creating beauty," I thought and almost voiced my opinion, but not wanting to offend I pointed to one of her fingers.

"I think her finger is the size of this one." I pointed to her pinkie.

"Are you sure? That one is too small, unless she is very young. How old is she?"

"Only thirteen, she was last month."

"Thirteen? Well she sure started early," the sales-lady couldn't hide her amusement and I couldn't hide how much I was annoyed.

"Just size it as I told you. Get the engraving done and tomorrow I will be back."

***

Before I was ready to inform the Buja's about the time of my arrival, I had to find a way to cover my financial shortfall.

When I told my Uncle Jozsef about my predicament, his generosity got me a step closer to realizing my dream, but he wasn't the only one who was eager to help. My Father gave me some money, my Mother shoved a twenty Forint bill into my pocket and by the time I have touched the hearts and pockets of all my relatives I was rich like never before.

My letter to Mr. Buja was rather short. It contained nothing more than my thanks and the day and time of my arrival.

The days that remained before my dream-trip I spent reading my diary, trying to decide whether I should take it to Rozsa, but in the end I decided against that; I kept visiting my Uncle Jozsef and my friend, Joska. Both of them celebrated my good fortune; wished me the best of luck, much success and the realization of my most secret dreams. Each and every night, before I went to bed, I looked at the signet ring in its black, velvet box and when my eyes became heavy with sleep I kissed the small, oval surface where the inscription stood.

"'R es L orokke' stands for 'Rozsa and Laszlo forever', I know my beloved will know that," I whispered in the semi-darkness and before I closed the velvet box I kissed the ring of love once more.

"How fortunate you are little ring. You will encircle her slender finger; you will be her constant companion; you will share with her all the days of her life and you will be her constant reminder about me and my undying love."

***

The night before my journey my family had gathered at our home to give me a proper send-off. All of them slipped a few more Forints into my hand and filled my head with endless suggestions.

"Make sure you will be polite and eat everything they give you," my Mother instructed.

"Give my regards to the Bujas, but don't burden them with too many details of my story," my Father suggested.

"Girls like to know that they are loved, remember that," Aunt Gizella shared her knowledge.

"Be happy Laszlo that you will see her. Don't frighten her by being too forward," Uncle Jozsef cautioned me quietly when my Aunt turned her attention to someone else.

"Tell her I love her. We will be friends forever," Erzsi whispered in my ear.

I was there, for a while I have even heard them, but my heart and mind were many miles away. The cacophony of their voices faded and when they have realized that I was tired they began to leave. I followed them to our gate, thanked them for their kindness, listened to their last bit of advice and when our place emptied, I said good-night to my parents and George, before I retired.

I finished my prayer of thanks to the Lord, who created Rozsa, and before I fell asleep my mind imagined the joys of the next five days and nights will have for me.

"I will be under the same roof that covers the girl I adore. When we eat we shall sit at the same table; when we talk we will be within hearing distance; when we walk we shall walk side by side; we will breath the same air; share the Sun's rays; if it will rain we will be under the same umbrella; when we retire we will be just a few feet away from each other; when we get up her face will be the first I will see. Five days we will have together, seventy hours and sixty times that many minutes. I will slow time down, will make my joy last for an eternity," the joyous thoughts enveloped me and I fell into a blissful sleep.

Early next morning, on July 10th, Joska Lazar waited by our gate and we began to walk to the station. I carried the one small suitcase that hid my precious gift and the few pieces of clothing needed. The five a.m. departure of the train prevented my family from coming with us and I was truly relieved.

"The last thing I need is more advice from well meaning adults, but advice I could use from Joska," I thought and turned to him.

"We had one great journey together Joska. Do you recall the day we almost perished?"

"Neither of us will ever forget that. Nor will our Fathers." Joska knew that I referred to our dangerous trip on the Danube.

"Whenever I recall that adventure my fear returns, but that fear is dwarfed by what I feel now that I am facing this journey," I shared what I felt in the day-light that contained none of last night's joy.

"You always fear something Laszlo. You feared you will never get a letter from Rozsa, but when those fears disappeared you replaced it with that other fear of not getting an invitation. Then when you had no reason to feel either of those fears, you create a new one. What do you fear now?"

"I fear of getting there and finding that Rozsa has changed. I fear her rejection; I fear...Oh I don't really know what."

"When we began to cross the fuming Danube you felt the same fear I did, but you said nothing, you didn't stop your paddling, you just forged ahead. Why did you do that Laszlo?"

"There was nothing else to do...We had to make that crossing, we had to find out if we were strong enough," I replied without thinking.

"Right you are. We found out we were strong enough. Are you now any weaker?"

"I don't know."

"You will get on that train and you will be with Rozsa. If she loves you-I don't see why she wouldn't-you will know that. If, on the other hand, she had changed toward you, then you will be strong. You will not show her your disappointment; you will not cry, you will act like a man. If your worst fears come through you will face them like you faced our river and when you return I will be here to help. There is nothing we cannot tackle together, we are friends," his words echoed in my head when the train's whistle sounded, when the locomotive began to pull and even when I could see no longer Joska waving.

***

I sat on the hard wooden bench, being flanked by many strangers, but I was totally alone. I submitted to the rocking motion of the train; looked at my watch; estimated our speed and when I judged that we have traveled at least ten miles, my heart and the metal train wheels began to sing.

"Ten miles closer...Ten miles closer..."

"We are scheduled to arrive to Budapest shortly after ten in the morning. There I will have a two hour wait. By three o'clock we will pull into Szob. She will be there, she will be waiting. Will she be alone? Should I hug her? Should I kiss her? Should I shower her with words of love? But what if she is not alone? If Joe comes with her to the station and I kiss her, will he tell? What if her parents are also waiting? I must not give Mr. Buja regret for his invitation. I will have to play it cool. I will just shake their hands, including Rozsa's. Yes that is the way I must greet them. I will feel her warm little hand. Maybe she will clasp her fingers around mine; she will give me a sign of love. It will be heaven to be near her," my thoughts, my plans, my hopes occupied me for a long time. I noticed not the many stops the train made. I paid no attention to the country-side we sped by, my mind, my heart and even my eyes were filled only with Rozsa.

I imagined her the way I first saw her. Then I thought about all the joyous moments we spent together. My mind recalled our tearful farewell at the station, almost four months ago.

"Four months is a long time, so many things could happen," I thought with fear that was resurrected, then I thought about my Uncle Jozsef's four years of waiting for his return and my fear dissolved.

"If Uncle Jozsef could wait that long and never give up hope, then what do I have to fear?" I asked myself and just to end my torture I turned my mind to one of my Uncle's stories.

***

The first story about Siberia he told me weeks ago. He was called to the camp Commandant's office in the middle of the night. They talked like equals, while he offered him food and drinks. The man appeared to be lonely, needed someone he could trust and for a reason, he made clear only much later, it was Jozsef he selected.

After a week of nightly visits, the Commandant confessed the kinship he felt and the trust he was ready to bestow on my Uncle. His name was Resnic, my Uncle told me as he warmed to his story.

The camp, Resnic commanded, was his fifth assignment since 1940. At each and every place he studied the dossiers of prisoners and to pass his sleepless nights, he had picked people he thought he could trust. He had them brought to his office, just like he summoned my Uncle and each time they talked freely...The Commandant assured Jozsef that he never betrayed anyone who was brought to his office, at his request. He met many prisoners in this manner: professors from the best Universities, former Government officials, simple tradesmen, peasants and former officers of the Red Army. They were imprisoned for the same crime: Posing an imagined danger to their beloved Father Stalin.

Commandant Resnic was the son of Communist parents...He wasn't physically fit to fight during the Patriotic War, but not unfit to join the Communist Party. Then one day he was told to take a course and when he finished, he was promoted to the rank of Sergeant and within months, out of the blue, they jumped his rank to that of Captain. His first assignment, after receiving his present rank, was Camp Assistant Commander.

He arrived to his first post and was devastated by what happened there. He knew that Uncle Joseph will be amazed by what he was about to tell him, but he explained that he had to talk to someone to ease his pain. He couldn't trust the camp guards who were barbarians from the darkest corners of Asia. He couldn't trust his fellow officers either. No two Russians could trust each other, Father Stalin saw to that.

After those confidences Resnic plunged into his first story.

"I reached my destination at the Kuznets Coal Basin, where my first camp stood. I forgot its number, but not the cruelty I saw. The officer in command was a beast. He had an endless supply of prisoners, so to accommodate them upon their arrival, he devised a plan.

"The working hours in the mines he made much longer, the prisoners' rations he cut in half, and when the arrival of two hundred new, fresh prisoners was signaled, he activated the first step of his secret plan.

"I will never forget the sight of prisoners lined up," Resnic's voice filled the night with images of horror, as he re-lived the unthinkable act. "They stood in the middle of the night, by moon-light and by search lights, front of the barracks. 'Sound out one, start the count...' The commandant of that cursed camp ordered the first exhausted men, at the head of the long line. Then he ordered all of them to follow the first prisoner's example: 'Sound out two, you next miserable traitor and every one of you, dregs of our society, go on like that, until you reach the end.'

"The first one shouted 'One!' the second 'Two!' and the counting continued in this manner until the last one shouted: 'Four hundred.'

"The Commander stood front of them all the time, knowing that the barracks he emptied must contain exactly that number.

"Then the Commander shouted: 'Is there a professor of mathematics amongst you?' When an old, skeletal creature stepped front of him, Ivanovich shouted.

"'Are you that?'

"'Yes, I was.'

"'Where and when?'

"'Until 1938 I was the head of Moscow's most famous University's mathematics department.'

"'What happened then?' Ivanovich pretended interest.

"'I saw Stalin's projection of the grain crops for 39 and I knew the arable acreage our home-land possessed. It did not take a genius to calculate that our yield would have had to be twenty times greater than the average of the last twenty years. So I expressed my doubt about the accuracy of Stalin's prognostication. I was sent to Siberia, to camps like this and for the last nine years I have been what I am.'

"'Professor I will let you practice your old profession. Tell me, what is your number?'

"'Two hundred sixty-four... '

"'Do you prefer even or odd numbers Professor?' the Commander inquired.

"'I really do not know.'

"'Don't waste my time prisoner. Give me the answer.'

"'Maybe even numbers I prefer. My beloved wife was born...,' the prisoner began, but Ivanovich cut him short.

"'Even numbers it is. Thank you Professor. Now hear this. All of you who announced an even number step out,' Ivanovich ordered and when two hundred prisoners stepped front of the others, he continued.

"'Stalin has decreed an amnesty. You men of odd numbers will return to your barracks, when told to do so. Wish your cohorts the best of luck, they are the recipients of the amnesty. Now return to your barracks.'

"The lucky possessors of even numbers stood, their legs rooted to the ground, their hearts beat faster, they couldn't believe their good fortune.

"Then the Commander gave the information: 'Each of you will be given two Rubles, a loaf of bread, a canteen of water. Our transportation system is dismal, I regret to say. You will have a day's walk through the forest, behind our camp. Head to the east, always east and you shall reach the railway station. Now go, you are free men and on your own. May you find peace at the end of your destination.'

"The prisoners were bewildered, but no more than I was and the guards. The men just stood, looked at each other, knowing not what to do. Then a young man, still in the prime of his life, gullible and naive, shouted: 'Where do we get our money and the stuff?'

"'Close to the camp's gate there are tables. Line up and take what you were promised.'

"'Let's go! We are free.' Shouted the young prisoner and their feet began to move toward the gate of freedom and picked up what they were given.

"I saw the camp-gate swing open, the two hundred prisoners approached it slowly, but once they stepped outside the gate their hidden energy surfaced and they broke into a run.

"I was glad for them. In my heart I wished them a good journey. Then I heard the Commander: 'Officers and guards follow me.' We entered the miserable meeting hall and waited.

"'Twenty volunteers I need,' Ivanovich announced and he selected twenty from among them. 'The rest of you may go,' he announced. "Resnic you stay," he added.

"The twenty-one of us stood and waited. Our wait wasn't long, but our surprise and my shock was colossal.

"'Resnic you are in charge of this most important task. You shall remain in camp and await the return of the guards. When they return they are to give you four hundred Rubles.'

"'Commander where will they get that much money?' I asked.

"'That is where the fun begins...,' we heard him, still unaware of his plan.

"'What fun?' I inquired with mounting fear.

"'The twenty guards who volunteered will have twenty-four hours for the hunt. I do not want any animals, just every one of the two hundred prisoners. Not one must reach the station. When you kill one, you take the two Rubles from the dead. When you come back, the sum you hand over to Resnic must not be short of four hundred Rubles. For every two Rubles missing one of you will die. This way you do not need to build new compounds for the fresh arrivals. You have your orders, go and have a successful hunt. I only wish I was young enough to partake in the fun.'

"'Commander comrade, you cannot be serious," I made my mistake.

"'Not one word from you Resnic. If you say one more word I will make sure that the money will be two Rubles short when I count it and you will be the first to perish.' I heard his threat and knew his power.

"The twenty guards left the room and within twenty hours straggled back to where I waited.

"They began to hand over the Rubles that I counted carefully and when I have realized, just five minutes before the deadline, the shortage of six Rubles, I turned away, and surreptitiously added from my pocket the missing sum.

"I was heartbroken. I sought a transfer to another camp. My Commander did not mind, I was capable of interfering with his sport. When I submitted my request for the transfer, he looked at me and without flinching he gave his consent.

"'You will get your transfer, but remember one thing. You will not find any camp to your liking. You are weak, you are a fool, you are nothing. If you ever reveal what happened here...Well I know you will not do that, I took out some insurance against that possibility', he said and I was dismissed.

"I knew in my heart that he had the skill and power. I wondered what he will do to account for the missing two hundred and soon I got my answer.

"'How do you spell that sickness, typos or something?' The Commander's clerk asked me when I picked up my transfer papers.

"'How would I know?' I stated, pretending disinterest.

"'I understand you are well educated, so why can't you help me with my report?'

"'All right, you spell it this way: 't y p h u s,' I suggested.

"'Thank you, the Chief of Camps will be pleased. Only two hundred died in the epidemic."

When Resnic finished his story he turned to Jozsef.

"I hope now you understand the evil men are willing to do to their fellow men and you understand also why I have to unburden my soul."

This was the first horror story Uncle Jozsef shared with me and when I recalled his exact words, I was no less troubled than I was upon the first hearing.

"I have learned during my short life that men were always capable to do evil against each other. Ever since our occupation, my hatred for the Russians grew by degrees and since the Communist took power in 48, I began to hate them too. When I heard my Uncle's first story I had to modify how I felt. There was no reason to hate Resnic, who was a Russian and for a time even a Communist. I remembered the Russian who raped my Aunt, but his memory and my hatred of him, was balanced by my gratitude to Resnic, who freed my Uncle. I hated the Communists who allowed the incompetent Laurel and Hardy to make my life miserable, although it lasted only for a short time; I hated the top ranking Communist who transferred Mr. Buja and by that act he took away my darling Rozsa; and I hated those communist robbers who destroyed my Father. I hated Stalin and his Hungarian hench-man, Rakosi, most of all.

"But hatred always destroys the hater," my Uncle's wise words came back to haunt me. "Am I doing the wrong thing by nurturing hatred? Should I not devote all my energies to only love? I love my family, my relatives, the Lazars, the Buja's, but all that love rolled into one doesn't come near to how I love Rozsa. I will soon see her, hear her sweet voice..," I told myself and before I could continue to blank out my hatred with the intensity of my love, I heard the conductor's voice.

"Five minutes to Budapest...Get ready to embark."

***

The rest of my journey I fought against recalling stories about Siberia. It was love and not misery I wanted to think about.

"How long before my arrival? It was one hundred-sixty kilometers to Budapest. There could be no more than ninety left," I told myself and closed my eyes, trying to picture Rozsa's sweet face, trying to see her every lovely feature.

I saw her as she sat beside me under the weeping willow; I saw her pluck the petals from the daisy; I saw her sitting in the Russian boat by Rezert; I saw her lips as I gave her my first kiss; I saw her at the station where we parted. When I have re-lived our moments together, my cursed mind shoved her letters front of me and my happiness began to fade, fear invaded my mind, my heart began to ache.

"What if all the things I remember she has long forgotten? Didn't her letters seem to indicate that?" My doubt grew and for the first time I reflected on the wisdom of my visit.

"Should I have tried to forget her? Should I have never gotten on this train? If I was to turn around; if I didn't continue my journey, I could go home, make myself believe that nothing changed. I could tell myself that she still loves me; I could wait for her letters, I could live on the memories of those precious days we had in Baja. If I continue my trip and find that she fell out of love, what will I do? Will I begin to hate her, like I hate so many others? No, that will never happen, my love for Rozsa is far too strong," I forced my mind to stop, to put an end to my torment and forced myself to look out the train's window.

I saw that the Great Plain that stood between the Danube and the second large river of Hungary, the Tisza, has disappeared. In its place stood the Duna, on my left, in all her majesty and on the right, mountains-peaks rose toward the heavens.

The sights I saw held me in awe. Steamers and small water-crafts plied the Danube, covering its smooth surface with waves as they passed. When the waves settled down the smooth surface of the regal river glistened under the summer Sun. Its blue waters reminded me of Rozsa's eyes. The steep mountains, covered in the splendor of green forests, towered over me as did our love.

I watched the splendors that sped by me, as they calmed my troubled soul and my trepidation was replaced by wonder. With each new sight I had to marvel. The birds that soared above the mountain-peaks, I have never seen before. The towering, huge ever-greens that stood like sentinels on the mountain-sides were strangers to the Great Plain where my home town stood. The towering peaks reached toward the heavens, not unlike two hands placed palm by palm, in silent prayer. Two hours have passed before I heard the conductor again.

"Our last stop in Hungary is coming up. We will be in Szob in five minutes."

I picked up my small suit-case; combed my hair in the reflection of a window and positioned myself by the door.

***

The train's breaks screeched, the long snake began to slow down and when it came to a full stop I stood on the top step, scanning the platform of the small station.

"There she is...My beloved Rozsa came to meet me." I filled my eyes with her small figure; I searched her face for a sign, any sing that would announce her love for me and I noticed happily that she was alone.

I jumped off the trains steps, rushed toward where she stood and when I almost reached her, when I was ready to throw my arms around her, to kiss her sweet, cherry lips I saw Joe emerge from the station with two other boys. I hid my disappointment and took control of my emotions.

"Hello Rozsa...Hi Joe..," I extended my hand toward Rozsa. She held mine, but very briefly and her hands felt ever so cold. I missed her warm fingers that held mine, at another station, several months ago.

"I am glad you came, Laszlo," it was Joe who voiced the welcome. "Our parents were unable to come. We brought two of our friends, this is Robert and this is Andy," he introduced the two boys, and our handshakes were even cooler.

Rarely before have I felt a pang of jealousy, but seeing those two giants, who towered over me, who were clearly handsome lads, that feeling overwhelmed me.

"It is only a short walk to our home," Rozsa finally spoke up and I listened to the cadence of her voice, her words and felt her closeness.

"I will take your suit-case, I am stronger than you..," Robert turned to me and without my agreement he took my small burden, replacing it with one far more heavy. He immediately stepped to Rozsa's right, while Andy flanked her on the left and the three of them began to walk.

Joe and I have followed. I quietly, feeling the magnitude of Rozsa's rejection and Joe loudly, asking many questions. He inquired about the friends he had in Baja; about my parents; about my life and I had to force my mind to comprehend his questions, urge my lips to give him my brief answers.

I couldn't tear my eyes away from Rozsa, seeing only her back; her shapely legs, as she walked; her missing pig-tails; her cascading hair that made her look so much more mature and the two boys beside her, both of them closer than I to the girl I loved.

"She is even more beautiful than she was. She has grown, her body holds the promise of becoming a gorgeous woman," I observed with aching heart. "I fell in love with this angel. Does Andy and Robert feel for her love like I do? Nobody could love her that deeply". I resumed to torture myself, then I saw her head turn toward me and listened to her words.

"Over there, that two story building is where we live. On the first floor is my Father's office and on the second awaits my Mother." Her words sounded kinder than those few she spoke before.

"Beautiful," I said to her, not remarking about the drab, gray building. She turned her head, ever so slightly and her sweet smile indicated that she knew what I spoke about.

That one smile, directed at me, set my heart on fire and I knew that her reserve will melt once we find ourselves alone.

We were about to enter the building when her Father appeared front of his office. He extended his hand to shake mine and offered his words of welcome.

"I am so glad to see you Laszlo. Welcome to Szob. Mrs. Buja awaits you. By supper time I will be with you and we shall talk. I hope you will enjoy your visit."

We walked up to the second floor and entered Rozsa's home. Mrs. Buja welcomed me like one would welcome a lost son.

"So you finally arrived. I am truly happy. Some of us were worried that you may change your mind, but not I. I knew you would come. We will have supper in a few hours, in the mean-time you may want to rest. Joe show Laszlo to his room. There is also a small bathroom, you may want to wash up. Rozsa you come and help me. Andy and Robert it was nice to see you," Mrs. Buja's words poured out, setting all of us in motion.

Joe led me to my room, then he led me to the bathroom, two doors away. I marveled at the indoor plumbing and Joe must have read my mind.

"No more digging holes for the out-house. Do you remember that fiasco Laszlo?"

"I will never forget Joe. I can still see your face when you and I stood in that new hole. I can see myself jumping on the ladder when the separating wall broke between the old hole and the new. I can picture you as you stood up to your neck in that sewage."

"So can I and sometimes I can even smell it. Which reminds me, I should let you wash up and when you are finished come to the living room and there we shall swap some more stories."

I stood in the neat, clean bathroom, watched my reflection in the large mirror and even though I had no desire to compare myself to Andy and Robert, I did just that. They were several inches taller than my five feet four inches. Their arms bulged with muscles, not like mine that were skinny. Their bodies appeared to be solid, unlike mine that was lean, that wouldn't be envied even by a starved cat.

"How could I compete with those boys?" I asked myself and shook my head. "I wish Mrs. Buja asked Rozsa to show me my room. She must know how I waited for this moment. Perhaps that is why she chose Joe? Mrs. Buja is good-hearted, welcomed me with more warmth than I deserved. Did she notice how I looked at those two strange boys? Is that why she dismissed them so abruptly?" I spent more time sorting out my thoughts, speculating on things that I couldn't answer. I washed my face, combed my hair, changed my shirt and joined Joe in the living room.

"Well you look a lot better...That was a long train-trip. Sit down on that sofa, rest your bones. How are your parents? What happened to your Father? Your letter said so much and yet so little," Mrs. Buja was putting me at ease and solicited my answers.

I was about to satisfy her curiosity when Joe spoke up.

"Father will be home for supper, he will want to hear all of Laszlo's stories. Don't you think Mother we should wait until all of us are together?"

"Yes, you are absolutely right, Joe. We will wait for your Father and for Rozsa's return. I sent her to the store for a few items. You two chat and I will continue to prepare the supper."

Joe and I began to talk about all kinds of things and all the time I kept my eyes on the curved entrance that separated the hall where we sat.

"Was Rozsa sent to the store for needed items or was she simply sent away from me?" I wondered and decided that Mrs. Buja wouldn't do that. Then another unpleasant thought invaded my mind and I couldn't help, but pump Joe for information.

"Can you tell me Joe where Rozsa went? Was it the store or perhaps something else?" My words, my eyes begged for a true answer.

"Will you promise me that you will keep this a secret?"

I made my promise and began to fear his answer. "Maybe I should have left things alone," I scolded myself, a second before Joe's words hit me badly.

"Robert is...Robert isn't my friend," Joe stammered.

"I am not sure I understand you," I lied, hoping against hope that somehow I misunderstood.

"He is Rozsa's friend. I don't want to hurt you, but you should know that they spend a great deal of time together. When Robert left the two of them went for a walk."

I heard his words like they were coming from nowhere. As he spoke them they came at me like daggers piercing my heart, destroying my soul, condemning me to hell. I must have done a poor job hiding how I felt.

"Your paleness betrays you. Try to put it out of your mind, I never said a thing."

"I heard you, but you are right, you never said a thing," I groaned and I was devastated.

"Have a good time and try to understand women. I know..., I know Rozsa is not that yet. But she is a female and females are my specialty. You remember what was her name? That ticket taker who worked at the cinema? Well never mind, neither of us can recall her name and why should we? To you she was nothing and to me she was just a teacher, if you get my meaning. I had a few teachers before and a few since we left Baja. If Rozsa wasn't my sister, if she wasn't so young I would urge you to treat her like I treat my women. Take what you can, like a honey-bee takes from a flower. Once the nectar is gone, fly to another and taste her sweetness. 'Give nothing and take everything...', that is my motto. When you leave here forget Rozsa, she is nice, but no girl is worth five minutes of suffering. Find others, take what they offer and discard them. If you follow my advice Laszlo, you will no longer suffer. Joy will be the only thing you will experience."

"I know you mean well Joe, but I am not like you. I can love only one and that one I love with such intensity that my heart is closed to all others. That is the way I feel about Rozsa. How can I ever forget her? How can I look for someone else? We were destined to love each other. I came all this way to remind her; to reaffirm my love; to give her this ring," my words poured out and from my pocket I removed the velvet covered box that contained my gift of love.

"It is nice...It is even inscribed. 'R and L forever'. Well I don't know what to say."

"Say that I should give her the ring. Say that she will accept it. Say that she will be proud to wear it. Say that she will be truly happy."

"Well a few more lies are nothing to me. I say all you have asked Laszlo and I say one more thing. There is nothing worse than a sentimental fool, who is willing to deceive himself. Have it your way my foolish friend, but make sure that when you give her the ring you two will be alone and you will be strong."

"I have less than five days to find the opportunity. Do you think you could help me?"

"You helped me a thousand times Laszlo when we lived across the street. Now it is my turn to extend the help. What do you want me to do?"

"Give me some time alone with Rozsa."

"I will do that, I promise you, but you may have to wait."

"I have a few days and a great deal of patience. I have waited for months for this trip; I suppose I can wait until you succeed."

***

Half an hour later Rozsa graced the alcove with her presence and I stood up to extend my hand.

"I am so happy to be here, to see all of you," I spoke the words and held on to her hand as long as she let me.

"I am happy too, but for a different reason," she spoke softly, mysteriously and slowly she withdrew her hand.

I stood in the middle of the room, confused, hurt. For several moments I didn't know what to say, then I decided to switch to a safer topic.

"A few minutes before your arrival, Joe and I recalled the day when the two of us dug a new hole for the outhouse, when the wall collapsed and he was badly soaked. Do you remember that Rozsa?"

"I will never forget it. We grabbed you as you jumped on the ladder, but Joe we couldn't reach." Rozsa's voice, her recollection thrilled me and finding the topic safe, I continued.

"You remember what we said?"

"Oh yes! I will never forget that either. 'A man who steps into sewage will be lucky.' That is the old adage we recalled and considering the amount of sewage that covered Joe we predicted that he will experience immense luck."

The three of us began to laugh at our recollections and for a very brief moment we were younger, we were back in Baja and Rozsa and I were still in love.

"I seem to recall that some of that sewage touched my shoes. It brought me luck." I steered the conversation to what I really wanted to speak about.

"I am glad you consider yourself lucky Laszlo." Rozsa's words were music to my ears and I grabbed the opening she gave me.

"Yes I am lucky indeed. I have received three letters from you. I got your Father's permission to come for a visit. I am here and we..," I got no further when Joe interrupted.

"I just remembered that my home-work is not completed. If the two of you will excuse me I will go and finish it before supper."

"I love Joe. He kept his word and so soon," I thought and turned back to Rozsa who sat at the other end of the sofa.

"What have you two cooked up? Joe rushing to do his homework is a new experience to me."

"I don't blame you for being suspicious. Is it not possible that Joe has changed?"

"People change Laszlo, I hope you do understand that, but Joe changing, I really doubt it."

"I haven't changed at all Rozsa..," I was ready to pour out my soul, to declare my undying love, to give her the gift.

"From your letters I judged that you changed Laszlo. You became bold; maybe too outspoken. You wrote about things we never dared to speak about while we were together."

"I am sorry if my letters offended you, if they scared you. That wasn't my intent."

"I know that, I understand that, but the intensity of your words; the overt discussion of your feelings would scare even a grown woman. I am not even fourteen yet. How can I deal with that?"

"Was that your reason for writing so rarely?"

"That was one of them, but there were others. My school work, helping my Mother, the school play, in which I had a leading role, all ate into my free time. That left no time for frequent letters."

"Thank you Rozsa. At least now I understand. I was afraid it was something else." Before she could answer, before I could fully utilize the time Joe so kindly provided, Mr. Buja's booming voice came from the kitchen.

"So where did you hide our guest Maria?" he asked and in a split second he entered.

"So there you are Laszlo and my sweet little girl. A handshake for you my boy, just so that you know you are welcome and a kiss for my sweet little angel." He grabbed my hand, planted a kiss on Rozsa's cheek and sat down between us.

"Now where should we begin? We left Baja early in April, over three months ago and from your letters I judge that a lot has happened since. Let's talk about your Father first of all."

"I will be glad to do that later. Please don't misunderstand me...Mrs. Buja and Joe suggested that we wait for your and Rozsa's arrival. The two of you are here, but Mrs. Buja wants to know too. I was shown your apartment, I really like it. Maybe you could tell me about your new job?"

"Much like the old one, but with fewer friends and more headaches. Most of my police-men are Communists, who no doubt report to someone every mistake I make." Mr. Buja's hesitated and then he pushed on.

Before we were called for supper I have learned that his duties included some he didn't have in Baja. Szob was a border town by the Danube. His police force was to control the fishing activities; to regulate and check on the cross Danube travel; to search for bodies that the river took. All of these activities were much the same as at his previous posting, but there was one, far more dangerous task that he and his men had to perform. Some Hungarians and Czechoslovakians have practiced the art of smuggling for generations and that illegal trade the Hungarian Government wanted to curb most of all. It was Mr. Buja's task to stem the flow of illegal goods coming into the country and to intercept those Hungarians who were foolish enough to try to smuggle out much needed Hungarian commodities. Both groups were armed and didn't take kindly to interference in their lucrative trade.

On one occasion, a Hungarian smuggler opened fire on the River Police. He was shot to death during the pursuit and when his body was recovered from the Danube, when he was identified as a high ranking Communist party official, his crime was forgotten, his greed forgiven and Captain Buja was severely reprimanded.

"How could they do that, when you were not even present, when you had no way to know the identity of the man?" I asked naively.

"When they transferred me I suspected their reason. I think I even told you. They wanted to separate me from the men who trusted me. They wanted me in a new situation where they could blame me for whatever I do. When they have someone who could replace me, they will dig out that reprimand and some others and I will be finished much like your Father Laszlo...I think we are being called for supper, we better go."

***

During supper we talked little, but once we have consumed all Mrs. Buja prepared, it was my turn to speak about my Father.

Rozsa set across the table from me and I saw her eyes become moist with tears as she heard the details of how my Father's factory was robbed, how he lost everything. When I finished my rather long story, Mr. Buja shook his head and began to speak.

"I know I speak for all of us when I say that we are truly sorry. Your poor Father suffered so much...But that I don't need to tell you. Then he began to prosper, devoted his life to his factory and to his workers and the thanks he got must be hard to take. Such is life in a Communist country. May God curse the Russians for their evil deeds."

"That is the way I felt, until I heard my Uncle Jozsef's story," I commented on what he said.

"Did I hear you right? Are you speaking about the Uncle your Father tried to free? The one who was taken to Siberia?"

"Yes...He was released and came home not long after you left Baja."

"I am truly happy Laszlo...Very few are fortunate to return from that hell. How did it happen? What story were you talking about?"

Slowly I began to tell the story that I recalled on the train and as I noticed their rapt attention I warmed to its telling. As I finished the first one, as they urged me to tell even more, I plunged into the next one, recalling it word for word.

***

"After Commander Resnic unburdened his soul with the story of the hunt organized by Ivanovich, he pulled out Uncle Jozsef from the labor-gang and his long, torturous hours of work ended.

"'Make a list Jozsef, you will need some special tools and materials to rewire all the buildings', Resnic told my Uncle. 'I am putting you in charge of the re-wiring project. You will need men to help you. Pick anyone you wish.'

"My Uncle thanked him and asked Resnic to explain something Jozsef wondered about.

"'How is it that you speak Hungarian so well?' my Uncle asked the Russian Commandant.

"'I told you a great deal about myself Jozsef, but one thing I have omitted. As you know now I have joined the party a long time ago. There I met a family of Hungarians. We became friends, really good friends...Their daughter, a shapely young lady, I have courted relentlessly. His brother, Dani, resented my attempts, watched me constantly. I think he despised us, Russians.'

"'It did not take us long. Julia and I fell in love. Life was beautiful. We walked the streets of our city, hand in hand. As darkness fell we hid in the recessed gates of houses and kissed ardently. Her lips were like fresh rose-buds, her body melted into mine.'

"'On one of these occasions I have asked for her hand. Megkerem a kezedet. Leszel a felesegem? As she heard my Hungarian words, asking her to marry me, she burst out laughing. Her laughter tinkled in the dark of night and I was devastated.'

"'Are you laughing at my proposal?' I asked her, fearing her answer.

"'Not that my darling, not that...,' I heard her say.

"'You did not give me an answer.' I reminded her and she raised herself on her toes, whispered her answer in my ear and we sealed our agreement with a kiss.

"Then I remembered her laughter and probed.

"'Oh it was just your Hungarian I laughed about. I did not know you were trying to learn my language.' Julia said with an impish smile.

"'I have loved you from the first moment I saw you...So I tried to learn your language. I wanted to ask for your hand properly', I said.

"'Well you have a lot more to learn my fiancé.' She cooed. 'I am quite willing to be your teacher.'

"From that day on we played a game...Each time I learned a new word in her Mother tongue, she kissed me and I became the fastest learner on earth. By the time we got her parents' agreement, by the time we set the date of our wedding, I was quite proficient. Then tragedy struck. Her parents were arrested...What their crime was, if any, we never found out. They just disappeared. Julia cried for weeks and Dani became even more morose. Within two weeks Dani had disappeared. I never again set eyes upon him or his parents.

"Julia and I became inseparable. We spent all our time together, went everywhere, hand in hand. Our love blossomed even more than before. We were determined to wed on the appointed day. Slowly she accepted what could not be changed and we began to plan for our life together.

"Back in those days my parents were still members of the Communists party, as was Julia and I. So it was only natural that we went to that cursed meeting. One by one we were called to the podium to exercise self-criticism, and when my parents were applauded, when I received the membership's approval, when Julia's name was called out, I suspected nothing.

"Julia walked to the podium and in her sweet voice she gave what was expected.

"'My parents suffered in Hungary under that cursed regime. They emigrated to the Soviet Union and brought my brother and I to this great country.'

"I have listened to her silky voice and understood what she was doing. By then she spoke perfect Russian and was able to reveal clearly what the comrades wanted to hear and she hid her pain and hatred.

"When she finished, I was greatly relieved and waited for the customary applause. But that never came, instead a gruff voice shouted.

"'You lied to us! Your parents came to this country to spy against us!'

"'Not true!' she replied.

"'Were they not arrested?'

"'Yes they were...But so were many others,' Julia made a dreadful mistake.

"'Are you accusing our beloved Stalin? Are you saying that he orders the arrest of innocent people? Do you know that nothing happens in our country without Comrade Stalin's knowledge?' the accuser shouted.

"I heard others join in the blood-sport and my fear intensified. I jumped up, ran to the podium and tried to save her.

"'You know me comrades. I am a true Communist, so are my parents.' I stood beside her, as I challenged her accusers. 'This is my fiancé you are torturing. Is it not enough that her parents were arrested? That her brother disappeared?'

"The Party Secretary, who remained quiet all this time, stood up and spoke: 'For the time being I will overlook your interference Comrade Resnic. You prevented your fiancé from answering the charges. She will do that now, and you shall remain quiet!'

"Julia stared at her accuser, pushed my reaching hand aside, her voice boomed out with contempt: 'I do not accuse only Stalin, I accuse every one of you. God will be the judge of his action and yours too comrades. Innocent or not does not seem to matter in this country! Yes Stalin is all knowing, he is omnipotent, many fools believe that. Have I answered all your questions?' Julia asked and her fate was sealed.

"I had made one more desperate attempt to save her: 'She is distraught as you can see. Her parents gone, her brother disappeared and now her own party is torturing her.' I began to say, but my Father jumped up and sought permission to speak.

"'My Son forgot himself comrades, forgive his words. We have been good Communists, that you all know. He fell in love, the foolish boy, with the wrong person. Love is blind, you all know that. We have objected to this marriage from the very beginning and if you give him one moment to collect his thoughts, I know my Son will do the right thing.' I heard his words, my mind in turmoil.

"'Can I save Julia and lose my Father?' I asked myself and without thinking I moved aside from where she stood.

"Julia must have noticed my struggle, she must have noticed the one step I took away from her and in spite of her youth, she understood. She jumped off the platform, ran through the meeting hall and she disappeared.

"I just stood there like a fool. I tried to convince myself that what I was doing was to save her and I spoke. 'She made a dreadful mistake comrades...Her attitude will be corrected, when we wed.'

"'Is it your intent to marry an enemy of the state?' the Party Secretary inquired and I had no choice, but to try to satisfy him.

"'An enemy of the state will not be my wife.' I tried to deceive them and made my plan. I have decided that we will move to another part of the country, we will marry there. I will love her, hold her, erase her memories and we shall be happy. That is what I planned to do, but I fooled only myself.

"What a fool I was! I never saw her again, after that meeting. I accepted the congratulations of my parents, and that of the members of the party: 'You did the honorable thing. You denounced her and by doing so you embraced our beloved Father, Stalin.' I heard their voices, but my heart bled, and its wound never healed. My futile search for her never produced a scrap of information, she just vanished.

"'Do you see Joseph what I have become? What we Russians have become? Stalin and his hench-men turned us into uncaring animals. We love, but that love is turned into hatred, at their command. We treasure life, but take the life of anyone, when demanded. We pretend to trust and trust no one. We praise our leaders loudly and curse them under our breath. Spouse betrays spouse, child the parents, friend a friend, relative a relative, stranger betrays a stranger, that is our way. Why do we do that? Wouldn't it be easier just to end it all? No my friend, that we cannot do. We hang on to this cursed life always hoping that the day will come when we no longer need to pretend, to shout slogans we do not believe, to stick with an ideology that has been subverted. So I go on, guilt-ridden by all my deeds.'

"'I think you understand now Jozsef why I said that I cannot trust any of my officers, or my guards. Yet someone I have to trust...I did that elsewhere and I had no regrets, as I will not regret trusting you. I am grateful to fate for having allowed me to meet you. I will do all I can to assure your survival. Somehow I will make it possible for you to return to your home-land, to your wife. When you do that, remember me with kind thoughts and comments, then I will have atoned for my sins.' This was the second story Resnic shared with uncle Jozsef." I finished the telling and allowed a deep sigh to escape me.

"This story holds many lessons for us, Laszlo. What happened to Resnic and his love could have happened only in the Soviet Union, but that is no longer true," Mr. Buja spoke with great contemplation. "Slowly we are becoming just like them. Well the hour is late...I think we should all retire. I am looking forward to tomorrow night and to your next story."

***

The next day we spent exploring first the small town and after lunch the meadows covered with wild-flowers, at the bottom of splendid mountains. I bent down, whenever I saw a particularly beautiful flower, tore it from the soil that nurtured it, and then I reached for one after another, until I had collected a large bouquet.

"Joe must have gotten tired. He fell far behind us. Or did he do that just to keep his promise? It really doesn't matter...We are almost alone. Thank God Robert and Andy didn't join us," I told myself and after a brief hesitation I reached for Rozsa's hand.

"I picked this bouquet for you. Please accept it. They pale beside your beauty," I told her, holding her hand and blessing Joe for his kindness.

"Thank you Laszlo...I really don't deserve them," she stated, removed her hand from mine, held the bouquet to her chest with both hands, buried her fetching nose to inhale their intoxicating fragrance.

"Nobody deserves them more than you Rozsa," I declared and the intensity of my words made her shudder.

"I think we better wait for Joe...We could sit down and let him catch up, don't you think?"

I spread my jacket on the grass, offered her to sit on it and I sat down beside her.

"Do I have enough time to offer her my gift?" I wondered and glanced downhill to judge the time Joe gave me. I saw him take a few steps toward where we sat, then I saw him lower his body to take a rest.

"Rozsa, I have to tell you something. I have something I brought you from Baja," I began. She must have sensed the pleading in my voice and nodded her head in agreement.

"I love you more than anyone has ever loved. I have waited for this visit..," she was ready to say something. I saw her lips beginning to form the words, but I rushed on, giving her no chance to speak. "'Don't ever forget me. Come and see me.' Isn't that what you said before we parted?"

She lowered her eyes in agreement and I was encouraged by her silence.

"I could never ever forget you. Every night, when the skies are clear and the stars are out, I looked up at the heavens and knew that those stars existed ever since God created the Universe. Yet my love for you seems to be older than any of those stars; it is vaster than the heavens; deeper than the deepest crater; everlasting like that mountain above us. I have never forgotten you, as you see. Ever since the train took you away from me only your words sustained me: 'Come and see me.' I am here Rozsa. I did as you asked me. I am truly happy. If you do not want me to hold your hand I will hold all of you in my eyes and in my heart; if you do not let me kiss you I kiss the air that surrounds you. If you do not wish to be near me I will be with you from far away.

"Here, I brought this for you. Let this gift be with you day and night; let it feel the warmth of your finger; let it be your constant companion, please accept it. Please do not refuse me," I held the box front of Rozsa while I spoke those words, while I entreated her not to destroy me.

She looked at the small, blue velvet covered box and then she looked at me and her blue eyes swam with tears.

"The words you spoke Laszlo are just like your letters. They touch my heart, yet make me afraid. I am too young; the distance between us is too great; are we foolhardy?"

"We would be that if we refused God's greatest gift. To love and to be loved is what He decreed. You have my love, nothing can change that and you have my gift."

She reached out for the small box, held it in her hands. Slowly, hesitantly, she opened the cover and saw the ring. Her lips parted, ever so slightly, her eyes sought mine, then they broke contact.

"It must have cost a fortune..," she gasped the words and raised the ring closer to her eyes to read the inscription. I remained silent.

"R and L forever," she read the engraving and with a sad smile she put the ring back into the box, handing it to me.

"I wish I could accept it, but that is not possible Laszlo."

"If you refuse to accept it, you refuse not only me. This is a gift from almost every member of my family, including Erzsi. They all gave me some money and pieces of gold jewelry, so that you would have this gift."

"I don't want to reject their gift or yours Laszlo. But I have no choice. You asked me to keep it with me day and night; to let it feel the warmth of my finger; to let it be my constant companion. I cannot do as you wish. My parents would be upset; my friends would mock me. So please take it back. Keep it until you find someone who truly deserves it."

"It is yours Rozsa. I want you to have it. Keep it somewhere where only you will see it. Once a day look at it and please remember the one who gave it to you with all his love."

"Do you really want me to do that?"

"I do and we will keep it our secret. When I leave at least I will have that." I accepted what I couldn't change and having made a decision, I got up and began to walk to where Joe rested.

***

Just before supper time the three of us walked into the kitchen.

"Did you get lost?" Mrs. Buja asked us and the only one who could have answered in the affirmative was I, the guest.

Once we have finished our supper, Mr. Buja asked for the other story.

***

I hid the way I felt, the rejection I suffered in the afternoon and if for no other reason than to forget my suffering, I began to tell the next story

"Early winter came to the tundra and the prisoners' suffering have reached never seen proportions. The temperature plummeted, day after day, until it reached minus sixty Centigrade. The prisoners, in spite of the cold, the unmerciful winds, the hard, frozen earth, which they were to dig with blunted shovels, were made to walk, rags covering their bodies, to the open pit they mined for years," I repeated Uncle Jozsef's words, once again with as much accuracy as I could muster.

"Now and then a prisoner stumbled, fell and never rose. The unmerciful cold claimed another victim. When fourteen hours later they returned to the camp, when their guards made another attempt, to count them, as they stood front of their barracks, they felt nothing any more. The cold numbed their senses, wiped out all their desires, save those for food or shelter.

"The guards tried again and again, but the count was short. They conferred with each other: 'There were two hundred of them when we left the camp. Now there are only one hundred eighty-eight,' said one of the guards.

"'One hundred eighty-eight and the six that fell on the way to work, those that froze where they fell, makes one ninety-four. So six others are missing', determined another of the guards.

"'What about the two we shot, when they refused to begin to work?' asked someone else.

"'Now that makes one hundred ninety-six...We are still four short, I think', spoke the first.

"'Let me count them...', offered another guard and he began.

"'I counted one hundred ninety-five...', the new counter announced proudly.

"'You are dumb, comrade. You cannot count. One hundred ninety-five, six that froze and two we shot, makes two hundred and three. So where did we get the extra three?' asked the lead guard.

"As the guards argued, as they began another count, Resnic stepped into the square, felt pity for the poor prisoners and contempt for the ignorant guards.

"'I will count them', he offered and tried to complete the task with speed.

"'The count is exactly one hundred ninety-two. Get them in their barracks, see that they are fed, make sure their stoves have plenty of wood. When all that is completed the guard in charge will come to me.'

"Resnic turned on his heels and cursed under his breath. He was seated by his desk when the soldier appeared.

"'So you were eight prisoners short. How do you account for that?'

"'Commander some of these rotten prisoners do not want to work. On the way out six of them lay down and wouldn't move. We left them behind, they probably froze.'

"'Didn't I order to have all of them brought back? Even the bodies', Resnic fumed.

"'We tried, but on the way back we lost our way. We did not see the bodies', offered the hapless soldier.

"'What idiots you all are? You didn't see the bodies? How do you know they are dead?'

"'They must be Commander. In this cursed cold no one would survive resting on the ground as those did. I know, otherwise I would have shot them like those two others, who refused to work at the mine.'

"'You shot two prisoners?'

"'What else could we do? We ordered them to work, but they just stared at us, wouldn't pick up their tools. So we wasted no time.'

"'Wasted no time? You wasted two human beings, instead.'

"'Not human beings Commander, just two enemies of our beloved Stalin', came the stock reply.

"'I suppose that I cannot change. But the bodies must be brought back to camp. Go and do not return until you have all eight of those poor men.'

"'I will get enough prisoners to do what you commanded.'

"You will do no such thing. Get your fellow guards. You and only you, guards, will search for your victims. You and only you will bring them back', Resnic issued the risky order and with a wave of his hand dismissed the incredulous killer.

"Next day the chief cook and clerk stood front of Resnic.

"'You shall prepare a meal for two. It must be ready by midnight. You, my clerk, will summon Prisoner Santa to my quarters at the same time', he announced and as they left he began to prepare the list and documents needed.

"'You asked for me again', Jozsef stated when he entered the office. His eyes fell on the food-laden table, saw the bottle of wine, and a grin spread over his face.

"'Surely this is not Stalin's birthday. So why the celebration?'

"'All in good time my friend. This is not the birthday of Stalin, at least not for a few days yet, in that you are right, otherwise it would be dry bread and water for us. Nor is this the day of his death, which I would gladly celebrate. This spread is for you and I and for the eight fallen prisoners. God curse my guards. Eight prisoners died yesterday. Ten the day before and who knows how many tomorrow? In spite of my orders to keep them from harm, my blood-thirsty guards go on killing, if not by gun, then they take advantage of this cursed cold. I fear for your life Jozsef, although I think you are safe.'

"'Each time I hear about the death of another prisoner Alex I feel an enormous guilt. You have given me a special job, which we completed today. That saved me from working outside, spared me from the elements of nature, yet I carry this guilt of not being with them, not sharing their suffering.'

"'Do not be so gloomy Jozsef, this is a special night.'

"'Is that the reason for the spread?'

"'Yes my friend. This is a special night. Now eat and drink. When you and I had our fill, then and only then, will I tell you the reason for this banquet.'

"So the two friends ate what they could, drank almost all they had and when they were finished, Resnic began to speak.

"'Some time ago I have helped you to survive. I have even promised that I will try to help you to return to your wife. I asked you to remember me with kind thoughts and comments. Do you remember that, Jozsef?'

"'I remember well. You not only helped me to survive, but provided me with the means of survival. Six months have passed, each and every day I have heard rumors of a coming amnesty, but that never came', Jozsef shared what he heard daily from hopeful, rumor spreading prisoners.

"'Until today Jozsef.'

"'What do you mean?'

"'Let me read to you the order I have received.'

"'To all Commanders of Siberian Camps,'

"'You are hereby ordered to prepare a list of ten prisoners. This list must not contain political criminals, must not include trouble-makers. The list you are commanded to prepare should contain men whose crimes are minor, preferably petty thieves or prisoners-of war.'

"'This amnesty has been granted by our magnanimous Father Stalin to show the camps' population that his generosity knows no bounds, his mercy has no limits, his kindness is bottomless. It is HIS wish to have all camps celebrate his sixty-eight birthday on December 21st.'

"'You are ordered to cut all necessary documents before that day, to prepare the receivers of amnesty for release.'

"'Long live Iosif Vissarionovich Dzhugasvili, known by his loving comrades as Joseph Stalin', Resnic finished reading the order and looked at Jozsef kindly.

"'I cannot believe, an amnesty for some, finally.'

"'Yes Jozsef an amnesty for some, but who should they be? I became very fond of you. Each time, when I began to prepare the list, each time when I was ready to add your name, my heart pulled me one way and my promise in another direction. Tonight is a truly special night. Do you know what day this is, Jozsef?'

"'I really don't.'

"'It was exactly six months ago that we sat and talked for the first time. So you might say this is a kind of semi-anniversary of our friendship.'

"'God bless that day...,' Jozsef stated and waited with anticipation.

"'Do you want this to be our last celebration, Jozsef?'

"'I do not want that...Yet, I hope you will understand. I want to return to my Gizella and to others of my family. I wish to step on the soil of my country.'

"'And that you shall Jozsef. Here are your papers, these will make you free. On that cursed birth-day you and nine others shall be transported to the station. The journey will be long, but you will be home long before spring, I am sure of that.'

"Jozsef sat where he was, his thoughts in turmoil, his heart beating faster, his breathing labored and as he looked at Alex Resnic, he felt an enormous pity for his friend.

"'He has the power to release me, but not the power ever to release himself. He has suffered more than I can imagine, yet he will remain in this frozen wasteland. There are no parents to ever welcome him, there is no Julia to embrace him, his life is empty', my Uncle Jozsef thought, almost refused the undeserved treatment, when Alex sensed his thoughts and with a smile playing around his lips he diverted Jozsef's attention.

"'When I read the order did you note the name of the generous man who ordered the amnesty?'

"'It was Stalin...Wasn't it?' Jozsef replied.

"'Yes it was the man of steel, as he calls himself, but did you notice his real name, that long one?'

"'I did, but I am sure I couldn't recall.'

"'Well his real name is Iosif Vissarionovich Dzhugasvili. All Russians are grateful to him. Do you know why?'

"'That I truly doubt.'

"'Never doubt what I say. We are grateful to him for having changed his name to Stalin.'

"'And why is that?'

"'Can you imagine us cursing Iosif Vissarionovich Dzhugasvili? That would be rather straining, so the villain unknowingly made it easier for all of us. So Jozsef lets take advantage of his folly, there is one more drink left, so here is my toast.'

"'May you find your Gizella in good health, may you rejoin those you love, may your life be blessed with plenty, may you remember not the Russian killers, but men like me. May our beloved leader of the short name be welcomed by the Devil into his Kingdom, and may that time come soon." I finished the story Uncle Jozsef told me and waited for Mr. Buja's comment.

"So that is how your Uncle was delivered from hell? I think his deliverance deserves a toast. Maria please give us some wine."

A glass of wine Mr. Buja held in his hand and the rest of us raised our glasses that contained a smaller measure.

"May your Uncle Jozsef prosper, may Stalin be taken soon by his partner, the Devil himself," and with those words he emptied his glass and turned to me.

"Thank you Laszlo for accepting my invitation. Your stories thought us a lot. We all suffer in our own way, but our suffering is great only when we become selfish and consider not those who suffer so much more. This is not the first time I heard about life in Russia, but never before was I given the opportunity to hear authentic stories about those Siberian prison camps. All of us owe you a lot. The hour is getting late. Maybe we should retire and look forward to tomorrow night's story telling."

"I would be happy to tell you more, there are many more stories Uncle Jozsef told me, but unfortunately I will not be here. This is my last night and I thank you for your kindness. Tomorrow morning I will take the train, go home and never forget you." I announced my painful decision, a decision I made as we walked home from the flower laden meadow.

I saw the Buja's glance at each other; I saw their disappointment, but hearing no objections, noticing their quiet acceptance, made me stand up and rushed to my room to hide all I felt.

***

After a sleepless, miserable last night at Szob, I joined the Buja's in their kitchen. I hardly touched my breakfast.

"Last night you gave us a nasty surprise Laszlo..," Mr. Buja was hesitant to continue, then he looked me squarely in the eyes and spoke briefly.

"Have we offended you in some way?"

"Please don't think that...I really enjoyed my visit, your hospitality couldn't have been greater."

"Then why have you decided to cut your visit short?" Mrs. Buja asked.

"I thought I might stay for five days or less, as I said in my letter. I planned so much to tell you and misjudged the time it might take. I have told you all I wanted; I have accomplished all I wanted to achieve. It was nice to see you all, but last night, when I spoke about my Uncle Jozsef, I began to miss him and my family," I lied and didn't dare to look at Rozsa.

"You are welcome to stay. We really enjoy your company. Are you sure you won't re-consider?" Mrs. Buja offered and I couldn't utter a word, just shook my head.

***

An hour later the three of us stood on the station's platform, waiting for the boarding call. Having said good-bye to Rozsa's parents, before we left the house, only one painful task remained.

"How shall I say my final good-bye to Rozsa?" I searched my mind, my heart, my soul for an answer. "The last time we parted at a railway-station we kissed each other and that gave me hope. Her single sweet kiss sustained me for months, but this parting will give me nothing to remember."

"All aboard!" we heard the announcement and it was Joe who sprang into action. He shook my hand vigorously, then changed his mind and embraced me. Then he turned to Rozsa.

"Give him a kiss. I will not tell anyone," he whispered in her ear and gently pulled Rozsa in my direction.

She offered her lips that trembled, either from anticipation or from anger. When our lips met, I tasted her breath, the sweetness of her kiss and I almost changed my decision.

"Should I stay at least for one more day? Maybe that time would be enough to resurrect her love? What would her parents say? What would Rozsa think? They probably would consider me a fool. I must leave now and remember only this precious moment." I picked up my suitcase with one hand, with the other one I touched Rozsa's beautiful face, just for one instant, and then I was on the train, by the open window, turning my head to wipe away my tears, hiding it from the girl I loved.

The train's whistle sounded; from the innards of the locomotive's a gush of steam poured out, hiding Rozsa from me for an instant, then revealing her once again. The train began to move, to gather speed. My eyes were fastened on my lost love and then I saw her reach into her purse, remove something and slip it on her finger; with one hand she waved after me and with the other she touched her lips and blew a kiss in my direction.

Chapter 4

I sat on the train, bewildered, unaware of my surroundings. Before I changed trains at Budapest, I stood on the platform and my eyes stared toward the north where I parted from that sweet girl, whose existence warmed my heart; whose love I had cherished; whose rejection, if that is what it was, hurled me into the crater of despondency, into the pit of doom. Yet my heart hung on to hope.

"Did I see right in that last moment? Did she put my ring on her finger? Did she blow me a parting kiss? Did she suffer when we parted? Did her sadness match my own?" I searched, but found not a single answer.

I arrived home, my soul aching, my mind in total confusion, my heart empty.

"You came home rather early," my Mother observed plainly, but she must have sensed my sadness, guessed my defeat and said no more.

"It is good to have you home," my Father greeted me, when I entered his small shop, where his hammer played its usual rhythm. He busied himself with finishing a pair of shoes and between the strikes of his hammer asked a few questions about his friends, the Bujas.

I have given him my answers and avoided to make any mention of Rozsa.

"Poor Captain Buja. It seems likely that he will follow me, he will be the next victim of the Communists," my Father stated morosely, and when he asked me no more questions I went to see Joska.

"So how did it go Laszlo?" Joska asked and I hesitated. On my long train trip from Szob to Baja I vowed never to share with anyone the set-backs I have suffered.

"Are we not friends?" I heard Joska and his simple question, his genuine concern for me eroded my earlier resolve.

I began to tell him all that happened and when I finished, with tears lurking behind my eyelids, he put his arms around my shoulders and began to speak.

"Do you remember when we finished grade eight together, back three years ago? Do you recall my dream of becoming an electrical engineer? Do you recollect how we waited for answers to our applications to continue our studies? Do you remember the day the letters came? You were accepted for further study and I was refused. I was devastated, back then I had only one love, one dream: to become an electrical engineer. When my disappointment reached its zenith, you comforted me Laszlo. We are both young and we haven't learned yet to accept life's heartbreaks and disappointments, my Father told me often and he was right. While you were at Szob I have received a letter, asking me if I would be interested in a new program that would allow me to realize my dream after four years of study. They offered me a full scholarship and I can begin this September. When I have read that letter I jumped from joy. I have to leave Magdi and that pains me, but our future is more important. I don't know what changed their decision, after three years, but I really do not care. I am telling you this not to brag, but to show you that things do change. What happens in the end is all that matters. Let's be happy Laszlo that we both are allowed to study; let's make the best of it. As time passes your pain will disappear. A few years from now we will be men of learning. Think about Rozsa, if you must. Love her if that is what you desire. Keep your hope alive if that makes you happy, but never ever allow your bitterness to destroy your destiny."

"I thank you for your kindness, Joska, and most of all for your understanding. I value your opinion my dear friend. I will try to follow the advice you gave me. What I have experienced at Szob has put the deepest of chasm on my life's chart and your surprising, good news added one significant peak. I am truly happy for you, please believe me."

***

Two days later I found Uncle Jozsef home and I had no more desire to hide details of my trip to Szob.

"I am sorry, Laszlo, I am truly sorry. It would have been nicer to have you experience nothing but happiness, but life is not like that. So what will you do now? Become a monk?"

"A monk? No, I will become a chemist. I will study harder than ever. Next school year is my last, before I enter university. In the meantime I will hope and pray for a miracle, but I will stop writing to Rozsa."

"You should write one more letter."

"I cannot. I won't know what to say."

"I didn't mean to Rozsa. Your letter should be addressed to Mr. and Mrs. Buja. Just thank them for their hospitality; wish them health, prosperity and happiness. Make them believe that you really enjoyed your visit. Common courtesy dictates that."

That same day I followed my Uncle's advice and when I have mailed the letter, I thought I broke all my ties with them and Rozsa.

***

During the remainder of the summer I have helped one of my class-mates prepare for his supplementary exam. When the summer heat abated, when the heat wave no longer drove Joska and I to the Sugovica to take a swim in the canal's refreshing water; when September came Joska and I said our farewells. When the train took him away, when I began to feel my loss, I turned to my neglected diary, that lay in its hiding place, and against my better judgment I read over all the entries.

My first entry began the day Rozsa and her family left for Szob. The last entry was dated July 9, the day before I began my trip to the north. I have read everything I wrote and the echoes of my old feelings tore at my heart, yet somehow it seemed that all those words I never wrote.

My Father continued to work at home; my Mother never changed. George fought his fights as he fought them for ages. Erzsi tried to talk to me about Rozsa and I began to avoid her, I wanted no reminders, I didn't want to resurrect my pain. My Uncle Jozsef was assigned to a new job, about sixty kilometers from Baja and his frequent absences pained me. My Aunt Gizella refused to move, probably enjoying her new found freedom, and I avoided visiting her, except on Sundays, when my Uncle was home.

***

A few days after Joska left, I have begun my last year of study at the Gymnasium. The work-load was quite heavy during the previous three years, but none of us could believe our ears, when our home-room teacher, Mr. Szepes, described the conditions set for our matriculation.

"Well, well my sheep-herd is back again. I hoped you grazed well during the summer, for you there will be no more grazing. Your six school days, each and every week, will begin eight in the morning; you will have a short recess around eleven o'clock and my job will be finished when you hear the two o'clock bell, but yours will just begin.

"The thirteen subjects you must take will give you hours of home-work, which you must do if you want to graduate. During the last three years you have enjoyed my company and when the year came to its end you wrote your exams and took your orals. This year will be the same, but with one big difference that will not be to your liking.

"Anything we have studied during the last four years, all the books we made you read will be part of your exams," Szepes finished his initiation speech, pushed the spectacles over his eye-brows, lowered and tilted his head toward the table, laid one cheek on its surface, in his customary manner, his stony eyes searched our faces, his lips dared us to react.

"Now my sheep I give you just one opportunity to ask your questions. After this day you will be my slaves, you will speak only when addressed."

My seat-mate nudged me and I sprang into action.

"Mr. Szepes..," I lost my voice.

"Well you are my favorite sheep, have you forgotten how to bay?" his sarcastic remark must have been designed to stop me, but it had the opposite effect.

"Mr. Szepes..," I threw caution to the wind. "How can we be expected to recall what we have learned so long ago?"

"I do not expect you to recall anything. I am sure you have long forgotten that episode of a year ago. Or do I misjudge you?"

"My memory is not exactly faulty...Try me and you will know." My class-mates looked in my direction, enjoying not only what I said, but more so the challenge I dared to issue to our master.

"Very well my sheep...A year ago I met you in town. Your arm was linked with that of a young lady. I stopped you two and corrected your behavior. Do you recall what I said?"

"A gentleman always links his right arm with a lady. Only a sheep doesn't know that". I repeated the insult he made, front of my dear Rozsa, and my face flushed in anger reborn.

"Well my sheep did remember...And where did that comportment originate? Do you remember that as well?"

"In the middle ages. That is how the knights protected their ladies," I repeated Szepes' words of long ago.

"If you can recall something as insignificant as that fact then you should have no trouble recalling everything else we have taught you." Szepes left no doubt that our conversation was over.

"Any of my other sheep dare to pose any more questions?"

I sat in silence, waiting for my class-mates to match my daring, to have them support me, but that never came.

"This school day I will cut short. Go and enjoy your last day of freedom," Szepes dismissed us and I rushed out of the class-room, out of the school-yard, not wanting to hear my class-mates excuses for their betrayal.

"They put me up to it. They urged me to challenge Szepes. They promised to follow me into the battle, but they have deceived me, like others did."

***

I sat in my room re-living Szepes' past insult.

"He shamed me in front of Rozsa and I was helpless. Our teachers know no limit, their powers are endless, not even confined to the class-rooms. They are a collection of peculiar creatures. Though they are knowledgeable and dedicated. Maybe that is the reason why with the passage of time we have learned to love them, to respect them and to appreciate them the way we did?"

***

Our history teacher was in the habit of asking one of us to come to the front of the class-room, where the victim was made to stand waiting. When the confused student asked what he should speak about, our teacher berated him for his folly.

"If you were smart at all you wouldn't have asked me. You would have started to speak about any topic of your choosing. Only a moron would ask for a task that he might not be able to carry out. Very well then, give us a lecture about a tooth-brush that is capable of climbing a vertical wall and you better not stop for five minutes. Your fluency will be judged," the history teacher issued the challenge, during the first class we had with him.

The unfortunate student stood, his shuffling feet, his shaking limbs betraying his confusion, but his lips remained silent.

"You are a moron...You cannot put two words together. I will mark in my book that you have failed. I need a witness...Lichter come here...Watch me engrave a big, fat zero."

I stood up, went to where my teacher sat. His mark-book opened at the right page, he placed his pen beside the name of his first victim and there he placed a zero.

"Now tell the class what I did."

"Jancsi Titkos received a zero in history on the date of September 2nd, 1946," I made my announcement.

"Now hold my shaking hands. Pin them to the desk. You must prevent me from killing that stupid oaf."

I obeyed him and held down his hands on top of his desk until his pretended rage passed. After a few moments of silence, he spoke again.

"You did that quite well Lichter, for this you receive a seven." He turned the pages until he found my name and there he placed the highest mark I was ever to receive in that subject.

"So what have you learned from what just happened?"

My class-mates and I sat silently, uncomprehending and when our teacher was unable to wait any longer, he lunged into his first lesson.

"Four years from now, when I finish with you, all of you will have the talent to speak fluently about any topic. Fluency, no hesitation, daring will be the skills I will teach you and the hell with the history curriculum. Who cares about dates? Any imbecile can memorize them. It is skills to live life fully what you need boys and those things you will learn from me."

After that first lesson not one of us has ever waited for our teacher's question; we began to speak fluently about any topic that popped into our heads; we spoke without hesitation and slowly we came to the realization that our self-confidence began to grow, and now and then we have even learned something about what happened ages ago.

Our other teachers were not unlike Eszterhazy...From our math teacher we have learned never to accept the conventional methods of solving a problem.

"Always innovate, look for new ways" was his motto.

Our Hungarian language teacher, an attractive, slim brunette, in spite of her many idiosyncrasies, made us become discriminating readers and writers who enjoyed that craft.

Our teacher of book-keeping screamed at us his demands, but as time passed we have begun to understand the secrets of creative book-keeping.

Our teacher of economics, who hated the Communists with all his heart and admired the Americans even more, lectured to us endlessly about the Communist's five year plan. He heaped so much praise on the Communist's wisdom, over-rated their non-existent accomplishments that we learned to doubt.

"The Americans think they have it good. Most of them own a house and a car and many other material goods, but the fools will be left behind. For each American who owns a car there will be a hundred Hungarians who will own two vehicles by the end of the great Plan," he announced loudly, time and time again, varying the coveted items he spoke about. If one of us was inclined to inform the authorities about his treason, he would have thirty witnesses to back him, to prove that he had nothing, but praise for the system. In his own, conniving way he turned almost all of us into discriminating doubters.

***

I broke my reverie about my teachers and began to map out my plan for Szepes' challenge.

"This school year I will work daily, even more than before. I will be well prepared for all my exams. When I matriculate I will be among the top five. I will make my parents proud; I will make uncle Jozsef happy; I will assure my entry to a university and I will make, at least, one of my dreams come true: I will become a famous chemist."

I should have felt great happiness, for I could see no obstacles to carrying out all my plans, yet I felt a vast emptiness. To fill the void I unlocked my heart's secret compartment where Rozsa dwelt.

I knew that I will never be able to love another...I have dated one girl since I left Szob. When Rozsa sat beside me in the cinema the poorest of pictures brought nothing but joy. Whenever I took another girl to a movie, even the best of films I couldn't enjoy. I have paddled on the Sugovica with Agi, a young girl, I have known for ages. As our boat glided over the tranquil water and Agi looked deeply into my eyes, seated two feet away from me, it wasn't her I saw, but my lost love Rozsa.

Now and then I spent some time playing chess, a game I loved, but whenever I made my moves that brought me victory, I could think of nothing, but the game of love I lost.

Then September turned into October and slowly winter approached. In the middle of November, just when I almost gave up hope of ever seeing Rozsa, Agi Boros waited for me front of my school.

"I would like to talk with you Laszlo," she began.

"What would you like to talk about?"

"Us!," her words said much and meant nothing to me.

"What about us? Whatever do you mean? I have a lot of work to do. I cannot neglect my studies."

"Let's meet after supper. Please come to my Father's candy store, I will wait for you there. Maybe we could go for a walk and have a talk? What do you think?"

"I will meet you there. Would six o'clock be too early?" I gave in reluctantly.

"I cannot pine for Rozsa forever. She is beyond my reach. Agi is a nice girl, but not like Rozsa. She is two inches shorter than I. A bit chubby, yet she is kind, she is understanding..," on my way home I tried to justify my decision to meet her, yet I felt enormously guilty.

***

"It is high time you got home Laszlo," my Mother greeted me, as soon as I entered.

"I am home so tell me what do you want me to do, before I sit down to study."

"Nothing at all. Well may be one thing, if you can afford the time?"

"I always have time to help you," I declared the truth.

"What would you say if I told you that it is I who can help you this time and not the other way around?"

"Help me how?"

"By having a talk."

"You and I Mother rarely talk about anything other than chores."

"Maybe it is time to change that?"

"If that is what you want." I gave in and sat down by the kitchen table.

"How long ago did you go to Szob?" her question surprised me.

"Over four months ago."

"And how do you feel about Rozsa?"

"Mother...Do you really care?"

"If I didn't care would I ask you?"

"I really do not know."

"If you don't then you are a greater fool than your Father. Why are men so insensitive? Why do they think that we have no feelings? When you returned from Szob I didn't pry, I didn't probe, I knew you were hurt and I thought that with time you will recover. I hear you in the dead of night crying your eyes out. I see you staring into space sitting at our table. I notice your eyes cloud over whenever we speak about the Bujas. I watched you suffer in total silence and I know that you find no joy in anyone's company. It's no use hiding the truth from me, so I will ask you once more. How do you feel about Rozsa?"

"Why is it suddenly so important?"

"Once you tell me, you may be able to see."

I hesitated to open my heart, to tell things to my Mother I never told her before. Then for some unexplainable reason my hesitation disappeared, the dam of my emotions crumbled and the torrent of my words found their freedom.

"I loved her from the first moment I saw her. I believed that we were meant for each other. I knew that I could never ever experience happiness without her. When she was taken away from me I was desperate, but not without hope. I knew that I will go to see her and that hope sustained me. Then I went on that journey of hope and two days later I undertook the return journey, the journey of despair.

"I locked away her memory in my mind's and my heart's most secret compartment. I thought I threw away the key, but I couldn't have been more mistaken. When I am in our yard I imagine her next door; when I walk on the streets she is beside me; when I go to a movie it is her who sits with me; when I am awake she is always in my thoughts; when I seek escape in sleep, when I hunger for oblivion, she comes to me in my dreams and I am immensely happy, then I come awake and my despair returns, my tears begin to flow.

"Now you know Mother how I feel. Why did you force me to reveal all that?"

"I have my reason, rest assured. I had an unexpected visitor today. We had a long, frank talk about you and Rozsa." She wasn't ready to continue and I just stared at her wondering who the visitor could have been.

"Are you not interested to know who came to see me?"

"Was it Kate, your old friend? Nobody else comes to see you. Why would she talk about us?"

"It wasn't Kate. It was someone else."

"Please do not torture me any longer. Tell me what you have to tell me," I begged her and my confusion grew.

"Am I torturing my own Son? Is that what I am doing? Shouldn't a Mother know how her Son feels before she makes her decision? A decision that may change your life and only God knows how?"

"You are more melodramatic Mother than I have ever known you to be."

"Call it what you will, your big words do not hurt me. I hope Mrs. Buja's visit will not hurt either."

"Mrs. Buja came to see you? How could it be?"

"Her husband got the ax, much like your Father. They moved in with her sister Eta and her family. They are destitute, they have lost everything. Rozsa is without friends and she pines for you. Mrs. Buja came to ask me to have me talk to you, to maybe convince you to pay Rozsa a visit."

I couldn't believe my Mother's revelations; I couldn't fathom what I was to do. I thanked her like I have never ever thanked her before, when I was ready to leave her I planted a fervent kiss on her cheek.

"So what will my Son do now?" she inquired and I knew not what answer to give.

***

I tried to study until supper, but neither my eyes, nor my mind could turn away from the enormous news. I felt sorry for Mr. Buja, yet I couldn't help but rejoice over the card fate has dealt me. I hated the Communists before for taking from me my dear Rozsa, by transferring her Father, but I hated them now even more.

"Why have they cast out that good man? Why have they made them destitute? Have they, the Communists, obeyed a higher power? Have they unwittingly acted in my best interest? Is it our fate to rekindle our love? Should I go and see her? Could I withstand another blow, another disappointment? Mrs. Buja urged my Mother to convince me to pay Rozsa a visit. She wouldn't do that if Rozsa didn't want to see me. What about Agi? I promised to meet her. I must keep my promise. Maybe I could talk to her about Rozsa? Should I tell her how I feel, like I told my Mother? Would she be disappointed? Would I hurt her like I was hurt at Szob? That couldn't be. We never spoke about love, just friendship. We never kissed, never held hands, love between us never existed." I finally convinced myself and after supper I went to meet Agi.

***

We walked aimlessly in silence. We went by the City Hall; skirted around the park of Dery. When we have reached the City Hospital, Agi couldn't stand my silence any more.

"You are with me Laszlo, yet you seem far away. Is there something you want to tell me?"

"Nothing at all. I thought you wanted to talk to me?"

"Yes Laszlo. I wanted to talk to you. My family has been asking about you a lot. 'What is he to you?' is their usual question and I don't know what answer to give." Agi looked at me eagerly, her eyes pleading for an honest answer.

"We are friends Agi, we are good friends, that much I know."

"Are you telling me that you treasure our friendship, but nothing more?"

"I want to be honest with you. I always had trouble making friends and your friendship I consider a gift from God. I have loved once, a lovely girl, but I haven't seen her for four months. I think of her very often, with great sadness, I must admit. I tried to forget her, to banish her memory, but I failed to succeed."

"I thank you Laszlo for being so honest. Your friendship I treasure, I assure you, and I am willing to settle with what I have," her voice died away when we have reached the cemetery of Calvaria.

While we walked and talked my feet received their command from my heart, my mind wasn't consulted and when we stopped beyond the cemetery, I realized that we were just two blocks away from where Rozsa lived.

"We should part here Agi. I think that would be for the best." I surprised myself with my sudden, intense, eager desire to approach that house, to knock on the gate, to look at Rozsa's sweet face, at least once more.

"Is there something you want to do Laszlo? Am I in your way?" her simple, honest questions startled me for a moment and then I thought about the pain Rozsa's rejection caused me and shook my head.

"I just want to check on an old friend. Their house is only two blocks away. You could walk with me a little further. You could wait for me by that corner..," I pointed ahead toward the house and made a promise: "I would be back in less than ten minutes."

"I am willing to wait for you a lot longer," she declared softly and her words, her voice, her eyes left no doubt as to her meaning.

***

I knew the house quite well where Rozsa's maternal Aunt, Eta lived. Rozsa and I visited the three Maurnyis on several occasions. Her Aunt Eta was always kind to me; her first cousin, Klara, was always pleased to see me; her Uncle Andor paid as much attention to me as he paid to his own family. I hoped not to find him home. His frequent abuse of his wife and daughter I knew about and I had no desire to exchange unpleasant words with that cantankerous being.

I ascertained that I was at the right house. The three windows were shut tightly, the gate locked, forcing me to bang on it with my fist.

I stood in the recessed gate, still not knowing if I was doing the right thing; still afraid of a cool reception; fearful of feeling the pain of being slighted. I have listened for someone's footsteps in answer to my pounding, but nobody appeared.

"Maybe nobody is home," I thought with a bit of relief and then I heard the voice of my angel.

"Is somebody there? Please come to the window."

I stepped back into the street, took a few steps toward the angelic voice's owner and then I saw my Rozsa.

She stood by the parted curtains, held apart with her lovely hands. The open window revealed a vision and both of us were speechless. We stood, facing each other. The brick wall separated us, but allowed me to feast on her never forgotten face. Recognition dawned on me slowly. It was my Rozsa, there was no doubt about that, yet she looked different in some strange way. Her cheeks and jaw were badly swollen; her face was ravaged by a strange fire, her voice was rasping.

"It is you Laszlo. I wish you didn't come to see me."

A scream was about to escape me.

"I should have forgotten you long ago! I should have been wiser than to come! I am stupid. A love-sick oaf, that is what I am." My mind cursed me and I was ready to turn, to return to Agi, but I couldn't do that without hurting her as she hurt me.

"You are not the only one who wishes that, Rozsa. I wish I didn't come. I made a terrible mistake, but rest assured this was the last time I was stupid enough to do that."My words were harsh, my tone icy, my pain intense.

"Please wait. You totally misunderstood. This afternoon I began to swell up. My

Mother took me to the doctor. I got the mumps; it is contagious. I did want to see you, I want you to be close, I missed you so much. And now that you are here; now that we could be together, I am burning up with fever, my head is pounding and I am a mess. In nine days I should be better, the doctor told us. Wait until then and please come back to me." I listened to her words and I soared up from the deepest pit of hell to the highest pinnacle of joy.

I extended my hand to touch her, but she withdrew, fearing that I might catch her illness. She told me ten days later and waved to me from her window allowing me to see her ring finger.

I danced all the way to the corner where Agi waited. My new found joy, my enormous happiness, my changed being must have been noticed by Agi and I heard her words before she turned and walked away.

"Your friend sure made you happy. For us Laszlo there is nothing left."

***

Nine days I have waited; nine long days and nine dream-filled nights. I was intoxicated with Rozsa's words. Day after day I repeated what she said and I had no more doubts, no more regrets, no more fears about our future.

"She will be my darling wife and we will have two children. That day when I last played soccer, when I first saw her I knew my fate and I was a fool to ever doubt it," I told myself, while I sat in my classroom; I repeated the same words on my walk home; I thought about them while I sat and studied. The words echoed in my mind while I ate. I thanked God while saying my prayer and when I fell asleep my dreams were filled with Rozsa.

I had learned a great deal about life during those nine days: "Events shape our lives and we, unknowingly, shape those events. Had Agi not come to me, ask me to go on a walk, I would have sat in my room trying to decide what to do and in my fear of another disappointment I probably would have avoided visiting Rozsa. But Agi did ask, we did go on that walk and my heart, my feet made their own decisions, they led me to that sweet girl of love.

"Had I not replied to Rozsa so angrily, had I just turned around and disappeared, everything between us would have been over. But she spoke and those few words changed everything.

"Is life a succession of events that lead us in some unknown direction? Yes, that is all it is. One thing leads to another, and that carries us one step further...If that is so then we are never in control. I think that is true. We are like a big boulder sitting on the top of a snow covered, steep slope. One loud shout, one falling rock, one careless human being makes that boulder change its center of gravity and it tumbles, making the deep, immense snow-field move, first slowly, then it begins to gather speed and the avalanche begins," I have analyzed all that happened, I was like the boulder whose center of gravity has shifted, and my life's avalanche did begin.

***

The tenth day of my waiting fell on Sunday. When early afternoon has finally arrived, I looked one last time in my small mirror, combed back my black hair, and it was not Uncle Jozsef I went to visit, but my Rozsa.

She unlocked the gate within seconds after my knock. I handed her the box of chocolates and she offered me her lips in return. When our lips decided to part, we stood back and surveyed each other. Her eyes were filled with love and joy; my eyes were filled with the sense of wonder. I must have stared at her for several minutes.

Her sweet features returned to normal. Her cheeks and glands were no longer swollen; her face was not ravaged by the fever of illness, instead it burned with the intensity of her love.

"We have waited for you since early afternoon. We knew you will come today," she broke the spell and extended her hand to lead me to where her parents waited.

Hand in hand we have entered the small cluttered room and after Mr. Buja shook my hand, Mrs. Buja embraced me.

"We are so happy you came Laszlo...The day I saw your Mother I did not expect Rozsa to get the mumps. She told us all about your last visit. After Szob I was afraid you might be cross, you might resent us, but that was long ago. You are here now and Rozsa is really happy. Aren't you my dove?"

"I am happier than I have ever been," she spoke the words and reached for my hand, made me sit beside her on the sofa. This time her Father did not sit between us, but sat down in a chair, just a few feet from me.

"My job is gone. Szob is far behind us..," Mr. Buja's words came slowly. "Although I knew what was coming, bad things are never easy to accept."

"How could they do this to you?" I asked and he began his story.

"A week after you had cut your visit short, which surprised us greatly, we received your letter of thank you. While I read it I had recalled your stories about Siberia and the inhumanity of men. Then I remembered what I told you: 'When they have someone who could replace me, they will dig out that reprimand and some others and I will be finished much like your Father Laszlo.' I figured that may take them a year or more, but I was wrong. Six weeks after you had left us an official arrived from Budapest. He identified himself as a representative of the Ministry of Interior and without any ceremony I was stripped of my rank, lost my job and I was ordered to vacate the apartment within twenty-four hours, then he left.

"We were lucky to find a small apartment in that short time and we have moved, but our luck ended there. I searched for a new job, for any job, but found none. I turned to those I considered friends and found them either unwilling or unable to help. Our small savings ran out in less than a month and if it wasn't for my Maria we would have starved. She noticed that there were many unused bicycles with flat tires and she hit on the idea of concocting a solution that could be used to patch up the tires' inner tubes. We made up bottles of this solution and began to sell it on the open market. We prospered for a few weeks and even saved a few Forints, but that didn't last. The Communists didn't want us to survive, so they somehow managed to shut down our raw rubber supplier.

"Maria wouldn't give in. She began to sell her own clothing, then that of Rozsa. Next came the many doilies she made, the needle-point pictures and the rest. In two months we had only the beds we slept in and Maria's favorite China cabinet and when she was ready to sell even that cherished item, I put my foot down and have decided to move back to Baja. Our relatives were more than kind when they sent their reply to my letter. They have invited us to stay with them and we decided on staying with Eta. Her husband, Andor, is away most of the time and they had a spare room, we knew. So we are here while I search for a job. All our worldly possessions are in this room and even some of what you see belongs to Eta."

"I am so sorry, I only wish there was something I could do."

"You did what you could. You came to see us and that makes all of us happy," Mrs. Buja spoke softly and to my surprise she began to speak about Joe.

"You are not like our Son, Joe. He is almost eighteen. He could probably find a job and help support the family. Oh he goes and says he looked, but he never finds anything to his liking. Yet he complains constantly. He is not satisfied with this cramped room; he is fed up with not being given fine foods. He no longer attends school either. He doesn't even want to learn a trade."

"Maybe I could talk to him? Maybe I could convince him to help?" I offered and the two adults just shook their heads.

After several hours of talking, all the while holding Rozsa's hand, I said good-by to the Buja's and at the gate I once again tasted Rozsa's cherry lips.

***

I visited Rozsa daily and when I returned home, late at night, I finished my homework that I had no time to complete before. Christmas of 1949 came and went. My small, insignificant gifts to every member of the Buja family were almost all truly appreciated. Rozsa loved the silver necklace; Mr. Buja puffed on a cigarette; Mrs. Buja admired the silk, embroidered scarf and Joe looked at the book I gave him, which he tossed aside promptly.

Two months have passed, the bitter cold made the Buja's suffer, before their sun began to shine again.

"I got a job. A real job. My engineering training came really handy," Mr. Buja announced during one of my March visits.

"That is great!" I shared his joy.

"The High Rise Development Company hired me and my salary beats that of a Captain. We have found an apartment we can rent, so next week we will move," Mr. Buja's announcement gladdened my heart and I shook his hand in congratulation, kissed Mrs. Buja on the cheek and Rozsa a lot more fervently. When I offered my hand to Joe, I saw a strange expression on his face.

"Aren't you glad?" I asked him frankly.

"Easy for you to be happy. You do not have to toil daily."

"But I study...I do my chores...I don't understand what makes you so unhappy."

"If your Father wasted no time to put you to work, would you be happy?"

"If my family needed my help I would be happy to do anything."

"Well Dad got a job, he could provide for all of us, as you heard, but that is not good enough for him. He asked his new boss if he could hire me and in two days from now I will be a slave."

***

Mr. Buja loved his job. Joe resented all he had to do. Mrs. Buja began to furnish their apartment, that each day improved, took on a new look and three of the Bujas were truly happy. Spring came, Rozsa and I began our joyous walks. We have returned to our favorite place, that was closed during the winter, and walked on its lovely curved paths, admired the thousands of blooming flowers, sat under the weeping willows.

"Do you remember Laszlo when we sat here, when you brought us two daisies?"

"I will never forget that event," I whispered in her ear and offered her a kiss.

"My daisy told me that you do not love me. It sure was wrong."

"We were children than. We pretended to believe the daisy's petals. We tore off one petal and whispered 'Loves me...', then we tore off another and switched to 'Loves me not...' We played the game and believed its outcome. We should have been as wise as we have become. We should have just asked each other, as I ask you now. Do you love me Rozsa?"

"I do with all my heart! Do you love me Laszlo?" It was her turn to ask the question and my turn to reaffirm my love.

"Do parents love their children? Does the moon circle the earth? Do the stars come out on a clear night? Do flowers bloom in the spring? Do fish spawn in our rivers? Does snow fall in the winter? Do the seasons follow each other? Do the days pass and yesterday never returns? Each of these questions request a 'yes'. To your single question Rozsa one 'yes' would be insufficient. With God's blessing we may live sixty more years, before we pass on. We may live almost twenty-two thousand days. On each day of our lives ask me one hundred times the same question and that many times I will declare my love. In those sixty years, I spoke about, you will hear my declaration over two million times and my 'yes' will never vary. I love you Rozsa now and that will never change."

"Hearing the intense affirmation of your love makes me truly happy. I think we should do something very special to commemorate this event. Let's find a tree, a young weeping willow. We will carve a heart, and our initials, on its bark. That tree will grow as time passes and our carved heart will grow with it, just like our love. We will return to it as often as we can and when we have grown old together, we shall sit under that huge tree and remember this day of love."

We had searched the park for a suitable tree and when we found one, with a bench front of its skinny trunk, we had glanced at each other and nodded our heads in agreement. I had removed my pen-knife from my pocket, carefully carved a small heart, level with the back of the bench, and inside it I have carved the letters: 'RB & LL'.

Rozsa sat down on the bench that stood front of our tree. She pulled me beside her and the two of us turned our heads to admire the heart and the names that were joined forever: 'Rozsa Buja & Laszlo Lichter.'

I offered my lips to seal the act and an old woman, who just passed by, smiled at us and shook her head.

***

We have returned to our tree almost daily and examined our memento.

"I think it grew," Rozsa observed.

"It did indeed...I carved it level with the top of the bench and now it has moved a little higher."

"And the heart seems to be larger," my love spoke again.

"Just one month and our tree grew, much like our love."

"How much higher would it grow by next year? What do you think Laszlo?"

"It will grow, but not as much as our love will, in spite of the distance," I broached the subject I was reluctant to speak about before.

"What distance are you talking about?"

"As you have known I want to become a chemist. When we marry I want you to be the wife of a man of substance. I am doing very well in school and a few days ago I have made applications to two universities. I didn't want to say anything, just in case I wasn't accepted, which is not likely. Veszprem and Szeged have good universities, not like Baja. If they take me, I will have to be away for four years. Just the thought of being away from you makes me shudder, but our future, our life together means more to me than those years of absence. I will write to you daily, I will come to visit you whenever I could and maybe you could come and see me. What do you think Rozsa?"

"I feared the day I knew was coming, but your dreams are mine. We will stick by each other. I am finishing my eighth grade this year and I have applied for admission to one of our gymnasiums. If they accept me I will live home, do my studies and when you finish I will have my matriculation. Then we will fulfill our dream, will get married, I promise you," she made her pledge and we were both truly happy.

***

For one more month we enjoyed our bliss. Our growing tree grew much slower than our love. We rejoiced over Rozsa's Father's success; we enjoyed our frequent outings, but not as much as we enjoyed sitting in Rozsa's kitchen, after her parents retired.

My Father recovered slowly from his disappointments and welcomed his old friends' visits. Mr. Lazar went with him fishing; Mr. Buja's stories, he told while my

Father hammered away, cheered him greatly, while my Mother and Mrs. Buja chatted in the front room.

All was well with our little world, although the Communists had all the power. None of us bothered too much with their lies, with their conniving; with their never ending bravado. We have subscribed to the main newspaper, not so much for its content, the paper we didn't read, but more so for the simple fact that toilet-paper didn't exist.

Almost daily the front page was decorated with the picture of one of our beloved leaders and simple men like us took pleasure in simple things.

"The front page is mine..," George claimed with glee and carried the precious sheet to the outhouse to honor Stalin in a most deserving way.

"Today it's mine..," I grabbed the paper and Rakosi joined his brother. Thus the pictures of our beloved leaders served a purpose and each time I committed the act a grin spread over my face. I have bested all our precious masters and forced them to keep each other's company.

***

Early June I have received two letters, they came two days apart. One from the University of Veszprem, inviting me for an interview five days thereafter and another from the Science University of Szeged, informing me that their decision will be delayed.

I rushed to see my Father; I went to see Uncle Jozsef; I carried the letter proudly to the Bujas, all on the day of the letter's arrival and the next day I showed it to my classmates, who congratulated me no less warmly than all the others.

"I didn't know you applied too," Ferko Horvath, one of my classmates, informed me.

"You did that too?" I asked him and hoped that he got the same answer.

"Here, look at their reply."

"They want you to go for an interview and on the same day as I. I think that is splendid. I hope we will both succeed, we could even become room-mates and four years from now we will graduate together. Wouldn't that be great?" In my exuberance, I almost missed Ferko's sadness.

"I got my letter two days ago. I showed it to my Father. Do you know what he said? 'I am a poor farmer, forget about all this nonsense. Stay home and work the land.' When I tried to plead with him, to make him understand my desire, he just gave me a stern look and made his announcement. 'If you want to go for the interview you better start walking now. I will not give you a single Forint for the trip.' So what choice did I have, but to accept his edict. You will be there alone Laszlo. I will not be your room-mate, nor will I ever become a chemist..," his voice faltered with the pain of shattered dreams.

"I will talk to someone my friend. Maybe we can find a solution. Tomorrow we shall talk again."

***

That night I approached my Father.

"Come with me to the front room. There we shall talk," he extended the invitation and within minutes we were seated in the room, its windows open, but covered by heavy blankets in a futile attempt to keep out the June heat, yet I shivered from fear.

"Will he help me or will he act like Mr. Horvath?" I wondered and began to speak. "Dad when I showed you the letter from the University of Veszprem you congratulated me, as did others, but there it ended."

"You might as well speak your mind Son. What has ended?"

"Veszprem is well over three hundred kilometers from Baja. How will I get there? What do you think?"

"You will not get on a train, nor will I allow you to travel by bus," he announced his decision, yet offered no solution to my dilemma.

"Do you want me to walk there? Are you like Mr. Horvath?"

"Walk there? You must be out of your mind Laszlo. By the way, who is Mr. Horvath?"

I told my Father about my class-mate and his dilemma.

"Mr. Horvath is a stupid fool. To make a talented son work the land is more than a crime. To deny him an education is a sin indeed. I have urged you many a times to seek not material riches, but to reach out for knowledge. The first is taken from us by the whim of men, but the other remains yours forever. Mr. Horvath should understand that; his son should be allowed to pursue his dream. Now here is what I have arranged and what I want you to do.

"When I still had my factory, I had a small car, as you well know. We had some good times, didn't we? Parties at the 'Csarda," I am sure you remember that beautiful place; the superb food; the fine drinks; the gypsy playing. Well those good times are gone, but not the car. The day after the robbery I gave it to Egervary, my trusted worker and my chauffeur. Ever since then the car was registered as his, with one condition only. Should I ever need the car I would get it back, should I ever want to take a trip, he would be at my disposal.

"So now back to your question. 'Do you want me to walk there?', you asked Laszlo. Did you think I would let you do that? If I had to give up my last Forints, you would have the finest transportation. I had a dream long ago, I wanted to become a doctor. My dream was just a dream, but your dream of becoming a chemist will become a reality. You will be the first in our family to get a university education. You will fulfill my dream Son. Egervary will drive us to Veszprem and back. So what do you think of that?"

"I think I am really lucky to have you for a Father and not Mr. Horvath," I judged the moment right to keep my promise to my class-mate. "I am so pleased to have you come with me on my journey. Can the three of us fit in your car? I mean into Egervary's."

"We sure will and one seat will be empty," my Father gave me a sly wink, guessing what was coming, but allowing me my small victory.

"Do you think we could fill that empty seat?"

"The car wouldn't even notice. So should we take your Mother with us?" he played with me.

"Well she probably wouldn't want to come; it was someone else I thought of."

"Very well then. Tell Rozsa I will be delighted to have her company."

I was flabbergasted by what my Father's said. I admonished myself for not having thought of Rozsa. I was about to accept my Father's suggestion when the disappointed face of my class-mate intruded.

"I promised him to talk to someone about his dilemma. His whole future rides on this trip. I am sure Rozsa would understand." I thought it over and when my decision was made, I announced it to my Father.

"Rozsa would love to come and I would love to have her with me, but to her it would be no more than a trip. To Ferko Horvath this trip would be a God-sent; it could decide his future. Do you think we could take him?"

"Isn't that what you planned on doing, from the moment you heard there was an empty seat?"

"Is it a crime to help someone? Is it a sin to care for others? He and I could become friends; maybe even room-mates and we could receive our degrees together. He is a very good student, I know he would succeed."

"When you get a bee in your bonnet my boy, you are no less stubborn than your old man. I am proud of what you allowed me to see. A selfish boy would have chosen Rozsa, but you chose right, instead."

Next day I have laid out everything that happened to Ferko, save the true owner of the car, as the two of us huddled in the school-yard, when classes ended.

"Can I go against my Father's wish?" Ferko asked.

"You will not go against his wish if you play your cards right. Go and tell him that you were offered a free trip to Veszprem. Convince him that a farmer's son is not likely to be accepted. Induce him to let you go, to find out for yourself. Let him see that once you are rejected you will be content to become a farmer. I think he will give his permission. It will cost him nothing and for years after he will praise his own wisdom."

"You may be right...I will have to trick him to gain his consent. But what shall I do if they accept me? I would want to accomplish my dream and would destroy him in the process."

"I do not see it that way. You live in the small village of Gara. Almost everyone knows your Father, if I am not mistaken."

"They know him and respect him, that is true, but what that got to do with anything?"

"Well, let me see. If you were accepted by the university, upon your return to your village you could bump into people before you go home and tell them what you have achieved. Avoid your Father for a few hours and a change in him you will see."

"I could do what you said Laszlo, but what purpose would it serve, that is what I cannot see."

"In a small village news travels faster that wild-fire. A number of the men would rush to your Father and would say things to him that would force his hand. 'Imagine that. One from our village goes to university. Why that is splendid', some would say and others will express their regret. 'If only I had a son, as smart as yours Mr. Horvath.' 'Wouldn't I be proud to clink glasses in the pub with many, to toast my son, to drink to his success.' 'To have a chemist in the family and not a farmer, that is beyond my wildest dream.' They would speak to your Father words like these and neither his pride, nor his new-found fame, would allow him to return to his old plan. He would push you out of his house; he would force you to attend university; he would kill you if you resisted. So what do you think of that?"

"Laszlo you should become an attorney. You can twist words; you can argue soundly and me you did convince."

"Do what I said and on Sunday you will sleep at my house. Early Monday morning we shall begin our trip."

***

The horn sounded, just once, in the dead of the night to urge us to get ready. Within minutes we began our six hour trip and on the way Ferko and I dozed, then came awake.

Mr. Egervary drove on, stopping only once to accommodate our bladders. Pieces of bread with a few slices of salami were handed to us in the back-seat and we ate and listened to our elders.

"I want my Son to get an education," I heard my Father say.

"I feel the same way about my three daughters. No sacrifice is too great to make," the driver replied.

"We live for our children and for no one else. They will fulfill our dreams," my Father's voice droned on and once again I fell asleep.

***

"Is your appointment at nine thirty?" my Father asked me for the fifth time, since we sat down on the wooden bench, waiting for someone to call my name. "And yours Ferko just an hour later? They are running late." He couldn't hide his excitement, his impatience.

"Laszlo Lichter, is he here? Come with me..," I heard the voice and as I stood up, as I began to follow the small man, I saw my Father cross his fingers and Ferko's thumb sticking up in the air.

"Sit down here," the man commanded and took a seat on the opposite side of the table. He was flanked by two others, who exchanged a glance and the chairman nodded his agreement.

"I have your application front of me young man. I see that you want to become a chemist. Is that correct?"

"Yes comrade," I spoke, as my Father instructed me.

"Your marks from the gymnasium are not bad. You have been recommended by your home-room teacher and even by your principal, I see. Comrades do you have any questions to ask this aspiring chemist?"

The bespectacled man on the chairman's right began to speak.

"We can admit fifty one students. Four years from now our country expects us to provide it with that many chemists. Do you think you would succeed?"

"I am a hard worker. I have never neglected my studies. I will succeed," I announced without hesitation and saw my questioner place a check-mark on his paper.

"You are sure of yourself comrade, aren't you?" the third man spoke up.

"I am indeed."

"And why is that?"

"I do not understand the question."

"Well let me ask you one that you will understand. What does your Father do for a living?"

"He is a very good shoe-maker."

"I see. Was he always a shoe-maker?"

"He was ever since he finished his apprenticeship."

"And he always worked alone?" the chairman took over and glanced at a paper, attached to my application.

"He worked with others for a short period of time," I gave my answer.

"Do you think you will make a good chemist?" my interrogator continued.

"I do believe that."

"A chemist is a special person, who deals with facts. Do you agree?"

"I do agree."

"Yet you avoided one fact when you answered my earlier question."

"I simply answered your question."

"Very well, have it your way. Your Father didn't work with others, you tried to mislead us. They worked for him."

"Well that is true, but he had the license and the others have received very good pay."

"How many of them worked for him?"

"That I cannot remember."

"A future chemist requires excellent recall. Your recall seems to be lacking. Was it one, or five, or even more?" I saw him glance, once again, at the paper and looked at me expectantly.

"It was thirteen," I gave in.

"So he is a capitalist."

"He is not and never was. He closed his factory several months ago," I tried to control my anger.

"And in the process he broke the law," the chairman's condemnation of my Father incensed me.

"The God-damn robbers who destroyed him broke the law, not my Father." I no longer cared to be admitted to this den of inequity; I felt no more fear from the three Communist clones of Laurel and Hardy, but most of all I didn't care to follow my Fathers advice.

"Answer all their questions and do it politely. Call them Comrades, regardless how you feel. Your future will hang in the balance, always remember that," he told me the night before we began our trip.

"The law is clear. No employee is permitted to fire his workers. That is what your Father did," the chairman's voice was stern, without a trace of compassion.

"Was it my Father who applied to this university? Is it my Father's dream to become a chemist? Have you no sense of justice?" I screamed at them, unable to think clearly.

"It was you who applied, that we know. It is you who is rejected. Our quota has been filled. You are dismissed!"

***

We sat in the car and waited for Ferko's coming, whom we left in the ante-room to wait for his interview.

"Laszlo I am dying to know what happened. You haven't said a word, since you came out of that room. Your face was drawn, your eyes blazed with fire, I sensed your anger, so I waited, but I will wait no more," my Father made me talk.

I lounged into my story, left not a word out of what has happened and when I finished my Father jumped out of the car, shouting.

"I am going in there...I will tell those bastards what I think. I will kill them with my bare hands, the rotten Communists."

It took Egervary and I several minutes to calm my Father, to make him sit in the car, where he brooded, without another word, until Ferko's arrival.

"I got accepted. I cannot believe it! Thank you Mr. Lichter. Thank you Laszlo and you, Mr. Egervary. I have never been so happy in my entire life. We will become the chemists we want to be," Ferko pumped my hand, never noticing the deadly silence, the lack of our jubilation.

"You will become a chemist. I wasn't accepted," I mumbled under my breath.

"I do not understand. You were not accepted? How could that be?"

"They had their quota filled before I was even interviewed, that is what they told me." I had no desire to repeat my painful story.

"They lied to you...Maybe they made a mistake? They did not even mention a quota to me. They praised my marks, which were not as good as yours. They praised the valiant efforts of my farmer Father. They spoke about our leaders' desire to educate children of workers and farmers, to make us a part of this country's glorious future. You are the son of a worker, not unlike I. Were you nervous Laszlo? Did you say something to offend them? Let's go back. Make your apology."

"Enough of that Ferko! Just let it be. Laszlo will become a chemist, but it will not happen here. Congratulations Ferko and make the best of it," my Father spoke for the last time during our six hour journey and the rest of us didn't dare to speak.

***

Within one week everyone dear to me knew my story. The Bujas have learned from me what has happened.

"Curse the Communists dogs for what they have done to you," Mr. Buja's face became red, as he spoke the words.

"May God punish the heathens. They finished your Father; next came my dear husband and then it was you," Mrs. Buja spoke softly.

"Cheer up Laszlo...Don't forget about Szeged. Maybe that university will take you?" Rozsa consoled me, as she held my hand.

When my Uncle Jozsef returned home, I told him the story.

"I wish it was otherwise Laszlo. Our country has learned a great deal from the Russians, it is sad to say. They punish children for sins their fathers never committed. They condemn parents on a whim. Resnik was right, I should have never doubted his story," even before Uncle Jozsef lunged into another episode about life in the Soviet Union, I understood his intent.

"He wants to divert my attention from my own loss. He wants me to understand that life's disappointments are to be viewed relatively," I thought and began to listen.

"During one night, in that Siberian prison camp, Resnik offered me food and drink. 'I thank you for the food, but I dare not have a drink. Over two years since I had one. God only knows if my stomach could take it.', I told the Commander.

"'We can take a lot...More than we have ever expected. Some time ago I sat with my Commander at another camp, that was a few months after the hunt that made me ask for a transfer. We sipped some vodka and as we drank to this leader and that, as we discussed life in general, as we proceeded to get drunk, he became bold.

"'Do you want to have some fun?' he asked Resnik and when he tried to find out what kind of fun he had in mind, he explained.

"'From time to time I invite two prisoners to join me for dinner. First I introduce them to each other, not using numbers, but their real names. I make them sit and watch me eat and drink. I let their mouths water, their thirst increase. Then I offer them a small portion of what is on my table, but before they take it, I pop my question. Who should be next?, I always ask them. Right away they do not comprehend. They know not what I talk about. Who should be next in our weekly sport? I ask them again and watch them pale.'

"'Give me the name and I will give you food and drink. I announce my request and watch them and wonder. Which one will sacrifice a camp mate for a scrap of food? When they are slow to offer a name I urge them with words like this: Only the first one that gives me a name will be rewarded, the other shall remain hungry. Now will you answer my question? I ask them and it rarely fails. They trip over each other to be first, to be rewarded and nine out of ten times the smarter one will offer his dinner companion's name, just to assure his silence. You see the name of one spoken at my table is always shot next morning, as an example to the rest. Oh we do say that the prisoner tried to escape during the night, or fabricate some other story, but the end is always the same. So what do you think, are you up to a bit of sport?' the commander asked Resnik.

"Of course he tried to decline the offer, but the Commander wouldn't hear if it. He called his clerk, asked for the roster and scanned it. Then with booming voice he announced: 'Get me prisoner number 458934, now.'

"'Only one this time Commander?' the clerk inquired.

"'Oh this is such a special occasion...I think one will do', came his chuckled reply and Resnik suspected nothing.

"Within five minutes an old prisoner, cap in hand, 458934 on his tunic, entered. The face lined with creases, his body skeletal, his bent back made him appear even shorter than he was.

"'Sit there 458934 and watch us eat. If you behave well you may even get a share of this chicken, you can wash it down with beer, laced with good vodka. Would you like that?' the Commander tortured the man and watched Resnik with a beaming face.

"'Yes comrade I would like that...,' came his reply and he began to drool. In his embarrassment he wiped his mouth with the sleeve of his tunic, without taking his eyes off the food and drink.

"Twenty or so minutes have passed since the old prisoner entered, before the Commander asked his question: 'Who should be next in our weekly sport?' Resnik should have suspected the trap. The prisoner's reply came too fast, but Resnik chalked it up to his hunger.

"'235689 does deserve it. Can I have my food and drink?'

"'That you shall have, here enjoy it and then disappear', the Commander handed him a drum-stick and a tankard of beer containing a drop of vodka.

"'I always keep my word, just like your previous Commander did', came the cryptic announcement and Resnik felt an unease about being reminded.

"'Clerk bring in 235689. By the way what is that prisoner's name?' the Commander pretended curiosity.

"'Let me see...,' the clerk replied, scanned the roster and announced: 'It is Misha Resnik, comrade.'

"'What a coincidence? Resnik indeed? I hope he is no relative of yours. That would be funny', the Commander chuckled with amusement.

"When the prisoner entered Resnik first could not see his face clearly. As he came closer and the light shined on the beloved face of his Father, Resnik nearly screamed. The old, broken man, raised his eyebrows, commanding his Son's silence, as he always did when he was a child, and Resnik obeyed.

"'Well prisoner 235689, I understand that your name is Resnik. The same name this officer is known by. You two wouldn't just happen to be related?' he asked and when the old man shook his head Resnik's heart broke, yet he remained silent.

"'What could I have done? What should I have done?' Resnik asked me when he got to this part of his story.

"'I do not know. Your Father wanted to spare you, he did not want to put his Son in any danger', I told my friend.

"'You are right. He did not want to do that, but he was given no choice.'

"The Commander gave a laugh and made Resnik's Father stand beside him. 'Look at each other...Even I can see the resemblance. So why do you lie?' he screamed at them.

"Resnik couldn't stand denying his Father, so he shouted: 'He is my Father!' and the old man just shook his head sadly.

"'He is more than just your Father. Much more, I assure you', the Commander spit out the words.

"'I don't know what you mean', Resnik matched his tone.

"'I will explain to you gladly...But that will have to wait. Now old man start telling your Son what brought you here.'

"'He is no Son of mine!' announced Resnik's Father and his heart went out to him.

"'You know I believe you...But just to make sure let me explain. You were picked for tomorrow's shooting, so your life is over old man. But I am not without compassion. I have the power to spare your life...And I shall do just that. One Resnik or another shot for escaping is no big deal. So this is what I will do: Offer your Son to take your place and spare your life in that manner. What do you say?'

"'I beg you to shoot me commander. In the name of God...No, in the name of our beloved Father, Stalin, I beg you to shoot me, not him...He is my Son', Resnik heard his Father's pleading and he was ready to jump, to grab his Commander's scrawny neck, to choke him, demolish him, to slaughter him, but his Father embraced him and whispered in his ear: 'I have lived my life Son, just let it be.'

"'How touching...,' the Commander stated. 'Now will you start telling your Son what brought you here?'

"Resnik's Father began to tell his story: 'Four weeks ago I came home, greeted my wife of many years. Had our supper and went to bed. In the dead of night I heard a crash and our door was torn off its hinges. The officers ordered us to dress; their guns stuck in our faces, and led us out of our apartment to two waiting cars. There they shoved your Mother into one and I just stood there, watched her disappear. My heart shattered as I glimpsed her lovely face for the last time, as she turned and waved her farewell through the car's rear window. I was put into the other car, then came prison, the interrogations, and finally my confession.'

"'What was your crime? What did you confess?' the Commander asked him.

"'My crimes...I poisoned my Son's mind with hatred for our Father, Stalin. I spied for the Americans. I hoarded food-stuffs, while others starved. I aided the Germans during the war...The rest of my crimes I do not even remember', Resnik's Father recited the long list.

"'Those are grave crimes against our country. So you deserve to be shot. Tomorrow that will happen.'

"Resnik couldn't stand it any longer. He screamed at him, he begged him, he dropped to his knees front of him and offered his life to save his Father's.

"'No I cannot take your life in place of his...You we need, but you have to learn to obey the state. Will you do that?' Resnik heard him say.

"In his desperation he promised everything that a man could promise to save his Father's life.

"The words the Commander spoke next surprised Resnik greatly: 'Well there is a way, I think. Your Father's life I may be able to spare...It is your choice really.'

"'I will do anything to save him,' Resnik promised rashly.

"'Tomorrow one prisoner must be shot, our weekly show I cannot cancel. If your Father's life is to be saved then we must pick a victim and an executioner. Resnik you pick the victim and I pick the executioner. Do we have a deal?'

"Resnik was ready to do as asked, but his Father intervened: 'Do not do that my Son. Allow me to die...'

"He couldn't let that happen. So he cursed himself and began to think. 'Who should die? Is there anyone who deserves this?' he agonized over his dilemma and suddenly he remembered the old prisoner who gave his Father's number and by doing so condemned him without hesitation.

"'God should have struck me dumb, He should have destroyed me, but in his Mercy he allowed me to utter the number and thus condemned me an eternal Hell.', Resnik told me Laszlo.

"'It should be prisoner number 458934', Resnik heard his disembodied voice announce and his self-hate began.

"'A splendid choice Resnik,' the Commander offered his congratulation, then continued: 'Now if I can do as well as you did, we will be all set. Let me see...The executioner I pick should be someone who owes me a favor. Don't you agree?' he asked the younger man.

"In his stupidity, in his confusion, in his still innocent mind Resnik searched for an answer to his Commander's question and in the end he just nodded his head.

"'Splendid!' the Commander announced, 'It is you I have picked. You owe me your Father's life.'

"'Son do not do this...,' Resnik's Father cried out, but the Commander screamed at him.

"'I had enough! The matter is settled. Unless you both wish to die?'

"'Let him live...Let my Son live...,' the older Resnik begged.

"'I gave you my decision. Will you do as I commanded?'

"Resnik whispered his feeble promise and his Father averted his eyes, turned his back on the traitor, who was no longer his Son.

"'Thank you comrade. Prisoner leave us', the Commander ordered and when the prisoner left without another glance, without a word to his former Son, Resnik's life has also ended.

"'Now that this issue is settled let me set the time. You will do it at 6:00 o'clock tomorrow morning. Now let me go back to what I promised earlier, you see I always keep my promises. He is more than just your Father, I said before and I promised to explain.'

"'The old fool does not know the real reason for his arrest. He thinks he may be guilty. It is not him who committed the crime...It is you Resnik and that is why he is where he is. That is why your Mother rots in another prison camp.'

"'What are you talking about? What crime did I commit?' Resnik asked him and felt even more miserable than before.

"'Do you remember the hunt? Do you remember how you tried to object to Ivanovich's ingenious way of making space for the new prisoners? Do you remember him demanding your silence? Do you recall Ivanovich promising you that he will take out some insurance to guarantee your silence? Well my boy this is a small world indeed. Ivanovich's cousin is a Secret Police officer, so he did what was needed. I am a friend of Ivanovich, so it was no accident that you were transferred to me, that you met your Father here. Just in case you did not know, I tell you now, that some of us are superb planners. If you doubt my word then think how well all this has worked out. If it eases your conscience I tell you that prisoner 458934 was already dead before he gave your Father's number, which by the way he did on my orders. I said that prisoner was already dead...Let me explain.'

"'Before you joined me for supper I sat with that prisoner and another, I played my little game. I asked the two prisoners who shall it be this time and the younger of the two prisoners had the presence of mind to read off the number of his supper companion. That way he was condemned', the Commander explained and Resnik noticed that he was getting tired of the sport.

"'What guarantee do I have that you will not execute my Father?' Resnik asked and feared.

"'Oh that. You have my word. Is that not enough? I guess not. Well let me explain to you what you should have figured out for yourself. Ivanovich needed insurance to silence you. Your Father or Mother would be no insurance at all, if they were dead. I had never any intention to destroy our assets, you fool. They will remain prisoners. Your Father will write to you once a month, just to let you know that he is alive. Those letters will be sent to your next camp, just to assure your cooperation. You cannot remain here, that would be impossible, with your Father here, and all that...You will be transferred once again. If I had the power to deal with you differently, you would be dead. Now get out of my sight, pack, here are your transfer papers, as you can see everything has been planned. Tomorrow after you pull the trigger you will go. May your next Commander be less compassionate.'

"By 5:55, next morning, all the prisoners were lined up to witness the execution. The night before Resnik prayed to a God he did not know; he made his peace with the Almighty he has never believed in and he was ready to take one life to save two.

"The prisoner was made to kneel in the dust, no blind-fold, no last request, just a brief reading of his crime by the Commandant.

"'Prisoner 458934 tried to escape in the dead of the night. His punishment is death. Proceed Comrade Resnik'

"Resnik stepped behind the kneeling man, cocked his revolver, placed the muzzle at the back of the condemned man's head and he heard him whisper: 'Don't be afraid Son, I forgive you,' then Resnik squeezed the trigger. 'He forgave me, but I could never forgive myself.' That is how he ended his story.

"I think Laszlo the loss of not being accepted by the university you can suffer far more easily than Resnik suffered all that happened to him. His Father was executed two days later, although Resnik didn't know for over a year. He kept receiving post cards from him. He found out later that all of them were written at one time and were post-dated."

I thanked my Uncle for the touching story; I knew that my trials were far less than that of other men, yet that knowledge, that understanding didn't do anything to diminish the pain I felt.

***

During the remaining days of June I have concentrated on my exams. Thirteen exams I had to write and thirteen times I have faced the panel.

Two teachers and one man from the Ministry of Education grilled me for fifteen minutes to determine how well I have prepared myself in the Russian language. Then came the next subject with two different teachers, but the one man from the Capital was always present. When I have faced the last grueling trio, when I have answered all their questions, I was finally free.

I rushed to meet Rozsa at Dery, at the usual hour of our rendezvous, at the bench where our tree grew, to give her the news of my success, but before I was able to utter a single word, I saw her beautiful face shaded with sadness, saw that her magnificent blue eyes were encircled in red.

"Did something happen to you my love?"

"I got a letter. They decided to treat me just like you Laszlo," her tears began to reappear.

"Who decided? What do you mean?"

"My application was rejected. The writer has made it quite clear that the daughter of an officer of the former regime is not entitled to any further education."

"But they cannot do that to you," in my stupidity I tried to assure her.

"Why am I different from you Laszlo? They can do anything they want. Isn't that clear?"

"I am sorry my darling, but do not grieve. Maybe we will not have to wait four years to get married? I got a job for this summer. Perhaps I should give up my hope of going to university? I may be able to earn a living with the education I got?"

"I do not want you to do that. Try to get accepted by Szeged. Do not let the Communists win."

"If that is what you desire Rozsa I will do whatever I can. Why don't you try another school?"

"I will my love, never fear. I will not let them defeat me."

***

Two weeks later we have followed the route of our traditional graduation walk, that began at our home-room, continued through the long corridor of our school, out the door, into the street, circled the City Hall and ended in our school's meeting hall.

We wore the traditional black suits, mourning the passing of our child-hood; wore neckties to signal our maturity; on our jackets' left lapel we had our Mothers, or our girl-friends, pin a single red rose to indicate our eternal gratitude to those who taught us, guided us during the last four years.

We have listened to endless speeches given by the Communist Party Secretary, then by our Principal, who was followed by Szepes, our home-room teacher for those four years.

To the first speech I have paid no attention; to the second I have paid some heed and when Szepes began to speak I marveled at his humanity.

"My dear students; my beloved former sheep,

"For four long years I may have abused you; for that many years I bruised your egos; when you lagged in your studies I bullied you. Well all that no longer matters, you have achieved. Today I stand here proudly and proclaim to the world the truth. You have risen to my challenge and you have become the men I wanted you to be.

"I have been one of your teachers for all these years. I have taught you many subjects, but that is the least of my achievements. You have learned to suffer abuse in silence; you have learned that life is not unlike I, rough and cruel and demanding, but full of love and caring. Now that you have reached this milestone in your life, I wish you success. Remember me."

The applause has thundered from every corner of the meeting hall and we, Szepes' students, began to shout.

"Hurrah Szepes, hurrah Szepes, hurrah Szepes, thanks from us, no longer sheep."

Then came three other home-room teachers, who spoke not unlike Szepes did. Every single member of my family, and even a few friends, stood with me, while we waited for the long line of graduates to snake their way to the stage to receive their diplomas. When they began to call those whose names began with 'k', I became tense. When my name was announced my steps were unstable, but I made it to the stage. I stood there while my Principal announced my achievement.

"This young man has received an average of six point seven out of a possible seven over his four years of study. He is also the recipient of three awards," I heard and in my excitement I missed what she said, but not my diploma and the three envelopes that were handed to me.

"I am so proud of you Laszlo," Rozsa whispered in my ear, as did others, including my Mother, but I heard only one voice that really mattered.

"I did it for us my beloved, as I will do everything, as long as I live."

***

When I was able to tear myself away from Rozsa, when my family and I have arrived home, my Father made us all sit by the kitchen table.

"Congratulations Laszlo, your graduation is a first step. Ilona bring us some palinka, we have two great reasons to celebrate."

"I am glad I have succeeded, yet I have failed, but I thank you Dad for your congratulation."

"Enough of this...Let's have a drink, let's clink our glasses. Then I will continue," my Father raised his glass in salute and so did my Mother and George. Then we have placed the empty glasses on the table and my Father began to speak.

"When I jumped out of the car in Veszprem, ready to go and kill the bastards, you calmed me my Son and just as well. All the way home I ruminated over the injustice of life and that of the Communist Party. I know Laszlo, just keep quiet...I am a dues paying member of that party, not active, but a member nevertheless. The first thought that came to me when we drove away from that place of disappointment was to rush to Party Headquarters, upon our arrival to Baja, to spit in the face of the Party Secretary, to tear up my red book and leave them forever, but that action would not help Laszlo, I eventually concluded.

"I sat glumly in that car all the way home and after a sleepless night, I went to see someone. He and I go back a long way, we have suffered together during the war and his life I saved. 'He has power and he owes me a debt.' I told myself and decided to call in my marker, I think he paid.

"This is a letter for you my Son. It is your name that is written on the envelope, it is you who should find out," with those words my Father handed me the letter that came from the Science University of Szeged.

My fingers trembled as I was about to open it and I hesitated.

"If they reject me too my misery will be much greater. If they accept me I will have to leave Rozsa." I seesawed between the alternatives and no longer knew what I really desired.

"Are you going to open it or do you want to kill me with suspense?" my Father ended my hesitation.

"Comrade Laszlo Lichter," I began to read aloud.

"Your application for study here has been approved." I didn't get any farther. My Father jumped up, hugged me, kissed me in jubilation. My Mother began to cry the tears of joy. George began to pound my shoulder.

"You are in...You will be a chemist...What did I say Laszlo in the car when I silenced Ferko? 'Laszlo will become a chemist, but it will not happen here.' That is what I said then and this time I kept my promise. Read on Laszlo. What else are they saying?"

"Unfortunately we are unable to offer you a scholarship; however there will be no tuition to pay.

"You are to register with us on September first and your classes will begin on September second. It will be your responsibility to find accommodation, to purchase your books and everything else you need.

"Welcome to our university," the letter ended with the signature of the registrar I couldn't read.

"My Son is in!" my Father shouted, blinded by his own achievement.

"And how will he live?" my Mother's pragmatic question made him stop.

"He pays no tuition. Didn't you hear?"

"And he will live on the street and eat with the rats, that is what I think."

"Not my Son! Not ever...I won't permit that. He will have the best of accommodations and he will have fine food to eat," my Father must have forgotten his financial situation and my Mother pounced on him again.

"And Ferenc will have his factory operating. Ferenc will be rich and maybe, just maybe, he will be given wisdom too. He will not squander his money on buying useless machinery, instead he will spend it on his family. He will help Laszlo," the venom of my Mother's words poured out with such intensity that my Father was dumfounded.

"Laszlo is better off staying home; taking a job and he should forget that foolish dream," my Mother concluded.

"Not on your life! Laszlo will go Szeged. He will continue his study and I will work day and night to support him!" my Father stood up, ending the evening and I no longer dared to even contemplate any other alternative.

Chapter 5

The rest of the summer I toiled at a government office, taking dictations, typing letters, sharpening my book-keeping skills. When the end of the work-day came, I rushed home, did what was needed and the joyous part of my life was about to begin.

Each and every day of that lovely summer, Rozsa and I met at our tree in Dery. During one of these occasions, she shared her splendid news with me: "The secretarial school accepted me for a two year study. Thank God there are a few private schools still in existence. Just to spite the Communists, two years from now I will not be without useful skills."

On other days we went to the Sugovica. We sat side by side on its sandy bank; swam in its warm water; declared our love time and time again.

When the day came to say good-by, my heart was heavy, yet my anticipation of arriving to Szeged, of beginning the last phase of my studies eased my pain.

My Father had made all the necessary arrangements: I was to board with a family in New-Szeged, on the east side of the treacherous river, Tisza, that was well known for its flash-floods and dreaded by those who were not protected by at least five meters of concrete embankments. I was to travel for fifteen minutes to reach the university by a tram-car. I was to receive breakfast and supper at my lodging, but for lunch I was on my own. He told me all about the arrangements; he prepaid the cost of my first month's boarding; he handed me the money for my books and a crisp, twenty Forint bill, which was my monthly allowance.

"Dad can you really afford this?" I asked him before we parted.

"Do you see these hands Laszlo? They could make a pair of shoes even when I am asleep. That is the skill that will support you. When you will finish your studies your skills will reside elsewhere. Over there..," he pointed at my head and smiled at me. "When I have no orders to make shoes, I will resort to something else. I will go fishing, that is what I will do Son. When the fish refuse to bite I will speak to them. I will tell them I need their cooperation; I will beg them to take my bait; I will persuade them to become mine and when I arrive home with my bounty, I will sell them and you shall have the money. Now go Son and make us proud again."

Before I have left the house, carrying my meager wardrobe, in my battered old suitcase, my Mother wished me luck and slipped a ten Forint bill into my pocket. Then it was George's turn and when he shook my hand, I was five Forints richer than before.

I have said farewell to everyone else the day before. I wanted not a single relative or friend at the station and they have respected my unspoken wish to be alone with Rozsa during the last minutes of our parting.

She waited for me at the station, as had promised and the last few minutes we spent together in serious conversation.

"Twice before we have stood at a station, parting from each other. Do you remember my love?" I asked her and she nodded. "Once it was here when you moved to Szob. Do you remember what you asked me?"

"'Don't ever forget me. Come and see me,' I do recall."

"Those were your words my dearest love. I did obey them. I have never forgotten you and I went to see you. It was at Szob when we parted once again. That was a painful leaving, I think you know that Rozsa. But before I lost sight of you, I saw you put my ring on your finger and wore it ever since. Promise me you will not remove it. Promise me that you will answer my letters. Promise me that you will wait for me and I will promise you whatever you wish."

"I promise you those things Laszlo. And you promise me this: Study hard and return to me."

We sealed our promises with one tender kiss and I was on the train, stood at the window, drinking in her beauty, her lovely face, her waving hand, until there was nothing more to see.

***

The distance between Baja and Szeged was only one hundred kilometers, yet that really didn't matter. A hundred feet from Rozsa was unbearable to think about; one hundred kilometers without an affordable mode of transportation was a sad prospect indeed.

"I cannot afford a train ticket, not even once a week. How will I survive for weeks upon weeks without seeing her? How will I endure her absence? Four long years without her, from September to the end of June, will be terrible, but then we will have glorious summers together," the thoughts that ran through my mind almost forced me to leave the train at the next station, to return to my love in Baja and to give up my dream. Then I saw her face at the station and heard the words she spoke to me: "'You promise me this: Study hard and return to me.' She wants me to become a scholar and that is what I must be."

I sat in the dirty, crowded train compartment, wedged in between sweating, strange bodies, feeling the hard wooden seat, but that discomfort was nothing to me.

"Four long years...Almost fifteen hundred days I must be away. How will I endure that?" my thoughts' torture I could stand no longer, so I forced myself to divert my attention, I began to take notice of people around me.

Three of us were seated side by side, another three across the narrow gap between seats that faced each other. Another six sat across the aisle. At the beginning of my journey I took no notice of anyone, but now their voices intruded.

"Where are you going my friend?" a civilian asked a young burly man.

"To Debrecen, far away."

"And where do you come from?"

"Kaposvar, that is where I live."

The two strangers carried on their conversation for over an hour, stopped only to share the food and drinks they brought for the trip. When they lowered their voices, I began to listen more intently.

"The old farmer was blessed with a new neighbor. In the dead of night he went to a tree, where he began to dig. He looked around shrewdly to assure that nobody observed his activity, then he went back to bed," the older of the two began to tell a joke.

"Two hours later the Secret Police dragged him out of bed. They accused him of hoarding food. The farmer denied everything, so they have led him to the very spot where he dug earlier.

"'What is hidden here, you dirty scoundrel?' one of the armed men demanded.

"'Nothing comrade, I assure you.'

"'Well, we shall see...Dig here, and pray that you told the truth. Five years in prison is not an unheard sentence for hoarding food. Dig away old man,' they urged him until his shovel hit a metal container.

"The Secret Policemen sprung into action. They dug around the round, metal container and lifted it from the ground.

"'Is this nothing?' asked the one in charge.

"'It is nothing comrade...,' I told you before.

"Once the cover was removed, in the light of his torch the policemen saw nothing but garbage. 'You stupid fool why did you bury that?' shouted the leader.

"'I wanted to know the nature of my new neighbors, there was no better way.'"

The two men broke out in hearty laughter, after the punch-line of the joke and the younger one decided to reciprocate.

"Have you heard about Stalin and the President of the United States taking a trip in a plane over Russia?" he inquired and when the older man shook his head, he continued his risky story.

I had no more desire to listen to the two strangers, instead I recalled what my Uncle told me, over a year ago, before I went to Szob.

"Whenever you travel on a train, be very careful. Speak to nobody, trust not a single soul. There are many employed by the State to induce tired, bored passengers to tell risky stories. They strike up a conversation, usually with a strong, young man. They offer him food and drinks and pepper their conversations with funny jokes. They know the nature of Hungarians, who love to engage in conversation, who love jokes and when they are told a good one they are inclined to serve up one joke that is even better.

"Political jokes are what these bastards want to hear and slowly they lead their victim in that direction. Our jokes fall into several categories: two year jokes, five year ones and some even in the ten year category. I don't mean Laszlo how old the joke is. I speak about the prison sentence handed out for a single telling. After the war there was easy picking. Soldiers, deserters, simple criminals filled the labor camps to provide free labor, but those times have changed. Now the agents use the trains to find their victims and for each arrest that follows the telling of a political joke they have one new inmate for the camps. I have seen it happen Laszlo, so be aware."

"I hope that older man is not one of the agents. I hope this young man shall remain free." I prayed silently for his safety and when the train pulled into the station at Szeged, I left the train, never to find out how that conversation ended.

***

Within two days I have completed my registration at the Science University of Szeged. I have received my lecture schedule and a lengthy instruction sheet. When I have finished reading all of it, what I have learned shook me badly.

"I will write to my beloved Rozsa," I had decided and began to write my second letter to my angel, so far away.

In my letter I have described my distress of not being with her. I wrote about the love I felt and after some hesitation I wrote about my great disappointment.

"I don't mind my darling the heavy schedule I have to carry. Six days of lectures from eight in the morning until four. I have a great deal to study and so little time, so I do as much as I can on the weekdays and even a lot more on Sundays. All this I wouldn't mind, but there is something that really pains me.

"I hoped with all my heart to spend our summers together, but that dream now is beyond my reach. All of my summers, while I am at university, I must spend in the army. I don't know how will I be able to stand that? Maybe it would be better to quit now, to rush to you and enjoy our days? Should I really do that? Or should I suffer without you, as you must suffer without me?"

I continued writing my pain-filled letter and when I was no longer able to add anything, I kissed the paper and the envelope that bore her precious name.

***

My first three weeks at the university proved far more arduous, yet less interesting than I have ever expected. My science and mathematics courses I didn't mind, those were a joy to study, but two half days a week spent in political science and military training was not at all to my liking.

Communist Party hacks, with little more education than grade six and eight weeks of quick up-grading, were our political science instructors. They held their so called lectures in the amphitheater of the university, where over six hundred of us gathered to hear their pearls of wisdom. It was some time later that we have found out that their words were written by someone in Budapest and was disseminated weekly to the almost illiterate 'professors', who faced us from their podium, exhorting their stupefied students.

"Before I finish the year you will understand, you will believe and you shall know the might of the Soviet Union; the greatness of our beloved Father, Stalin; the brilliance of that deity; the ingeniousness of our Soviet brothers and sisters; their generosity in helping us to rebuild our devastated country. We will teach you to love them, to adore them and despise the Capitalist, war-mongering herds, led by the Imperialist Americans, whose only aim is to destroy everything that is decent; to exploit the masses for their own profit, to feed their greed. The enslavers of millions in the west...," thus spoke our first lecturer of political science and I was perplexed by the lack of quality in his reading.

My attention shifted from the words of that man, who would not have survived a single day at my former school, to that of the greatness of my former teachers.

"They did not read to us from notes, as this man does. They were far too intelligent to try to snow us. They were teachers indeed," I thought and I began to wonder if I was the only one who noticed the sham. I glanced to my right, then to my left and my eyes traveled to the back of the heads of students, who sat in the row, below me. I saw a blond head bent in concentration, as she appeared to take notes and I wondered why anybody would do that. Then she turned to her right, ever so slightly, whispered something to the brunette beside her and I saw.

The paper front of her wasn't covered with pearls of wisdom, instead it revealed a caricature of a blood-thirsty Stalin. I saw those bushy, severe eye-brows, the wide, black mustache, and his plain tunic. I saw his two hands extended front of him holding two blood-dripping severed heads.

"Hide it, cover it, destroy it," I whispered to the girl and when she turned the paper over I was relieved.

One week later we sat in our assigned seats and it was not our lecturer who stood by the podium, it was a far more fluent man. His severe countenance conveyed a threat, even before he began to speak.

"The two students assigned to the following seats are to come to the front. Three hundred ten and three hundred eleven," his voice thundered and then he waited.

I glanced at my seat number, three-hundred sixty and I noticed the two girls stand up, descend slowly, reluctantly toward the harsh, unknown man.

"You two, stand right here, beside me. A week ago an unspeakable act was committed. These two enemies of our beloved Father Stalin were the perpetrators. I called them here to confess their crime; to make their apologies for that terrible act. Tell all of us what you did," his condemnation, his order thundered at the shaken girls.

"I do not know what you mean," the blond replied.

"I do not understand," the brunette moaned and paled badly.

"To compound your crime by denial will make your punishment even more severe."

"But what have I done?" the brunette asked.

"A week ago the only act I can recall is taking copious notes on the lecture," the blond asserted.

"You two are liars. You are conniving bitches. Do you think a high ranking agent of State Security will accept your flimsy explanations?"

"Comrade, I am telling you the truth. I can show you my note-book. You can see for yourself that I spoke nothing but the truth."

"Can you also show me that piece of paper? I am sure you can't. You were seen to destroy it."

"I did no such thing!" she almost screamed.

"You were seen by our vigilant comrades. They saw the cartoon, which I will not describe. It was Comrade Stalin, wasn't it?"

"It is true I drew a picture of Comrade Stalin, but it was not a cartoon I assure you."

"What was it then?"

"It was not unlike the hundreds of posters we see daily. Look over there, that is the picture of our glorious leader that I tried to copy. I tried to chisel that beloved face into my mind. I drew it not only on my paper, but also in my heart that is full of gratitude," the blond tried to convince her accuser, tried to extricate herself from the peril her drawing created.

"And what about you? Is that what you saw you sly brunette?"

"I saw nothing comrade, I was too intent to listen to our professor."

"You are lying. You were seen to look at that cartoon. It was then that you giggled."

"I did no such thing."

"Have it your way you rotten bitch! Your punishment will not be less severe."

"And what if I make a clean breast of it?"

"Do that my dove...Do that and we shall see."

"I made a mistake comrade...I did glance at the cartoon, ever so briefly. I giggled too, but not at what I saw, only at the stupidity of my friend here," she threw herself at the mercy of the man and betrayed the other human being.

"And what did you see?"

"It was a cartoon she drew and it wasn't complementary."

"Whose caricature was it?"

"It was Comrade Stalin, our beloved Father."

"And what did he hold in his two hands?"

"Two bloody heads is what I saw. I was revolted, I quickly turned my head."

"And you didn't report it!" came the agent's statement.

"I was confused and terribly afraid. I have made a grave mistake comrade," the brunette moaned.

"And so did we. We have allowed two enemies of the state to further their education. Errors must be corrected. You, the creator of that traitorous piece of garbage, are hereby expelled from this university without right of appeal. In addition you are barred forever from all institutions of higher learning in our country. Let this be a lesson to all traitors," the judge and jury of condemnation paused for effect, then he continued.

"You, my little brunette conspirator, in spite of your cooperation, is hereby expelled from this university without appeal. In addition you are barred for ten years from all institutions of higher learning in our country. As you can see cooperation deserves a measure of mercy. Now the two of you will be drummed out of here. While they go all of you are to pound your table, to show contempt for their crime and approval for the punishment they have received."

The two girls hung their heads to hide their tears and walked out of the amphitheater, our pounding reverberating in their ears.

***

Our military instructors possessed no great knowledge either. Sons of farmers and that of workers were rushed through a brief indoctrination course and those who couldn't read or write became officers in the army, while others, whose talent exceeded that of the former group, became professors at our universities.

They lectured from pre-prepared notes, received weekly from the Ministry of Defense. Their halting readings droned on for hours, almost inducing sleep in the more intelligent students, yet when the end of a lecture came we were forced, by fear, to join those dupes who gave the officer a standing ovation.

***

The political lectures, coupled with the military exhortations created such boredom that I have decided to spend some of my scant saving to go to a movie. I was always fond of operas and Il Trovatore was playing. I sat in the cinema, recalling those precious hours that I spent the same way with my Rozsa. The haunting music, the touching story, my Rozsa's absence joined together and made me even more lonely than I was before. When the movie ended and I stepped outside, I felt a hand on my shoulder.

"I can't believe it. It is you Laszlo," Ocsi Parej grabbed my hand. "I knew you were studying in this city, but I didn't know how to find you. Let's go and have a beer. I am buying."

I hesitated, but only for a moment. "The hell with study; the hell with political indoctrination, the hell with military training, the hell with this everlasting loneliness..." I told myself and within minutes we were seated at a nearby pub.

Our conversation led us back to the school we both attended at Baja; to the teachers we shared for four years; to Ocsi's struggle to graduate; to his good luck of being accepted by the Teachers' University of Szeged.

"I couldn't believe it Laszlo when I got the letter of acceptance. No tuition, a scholarship of three hundred Forints a month and a little help from my parents were almost too much to believe. I started the second of September. As you well know I am not a scholar, but with luck and some help, I might become a teacher. Now what about you Laszlo?" Ocsi's exuberance made me speak.

I spoke about my eternal love for Rozsa; my bitter experience at Veszprem; my Father's intervention that got me here. Then I mentioned the distress I felt about my financial struggle, without a scholar-ship; my disappointment with our political and military instructors; the cruel expulsion of those two unfortunate girls; and I ended with confessing my loneliness.

"I know how you feel Laszlo. The political and military instructors are no different at my university, but all the other things are really to my liking. No financial worries, thanks to the scholarship and the superb professors I have, especially the one for chemistry."

"I didn't know you are studying that subject. That is my major, but I don't know if I will be able to fulfill my dream."

"Is it chemistry you wanted to study Laszlo?"

"Ever since I was a tiny tot," I confided.

"Do you want to study chemistry and become a chemist? Or would you settle with anything less?"

"I am not sure I get your drift?"

"You could study chemistry at my institution, but it would be a teacher you would become. Is being a teacher of chemistry any less that being a chemist? That is what I want to know."

"Even if I was willing to become a teacher, don't you think I missed the boat? The university year is a month old."

"I don't think it would bother anyone. There is a desperate shortage of teachers, Dr. Kobor told us the first day. There are many spaces, even in my faculty, that are still vacant. I want you to meet Professor Kobor. I think you would really like the man. Maybe you could switch over? There is even space in our subsidized dormitory. The more I think about it the more I want you with me. So what do you think?"

"I have to think about that. Give me your address and I will look you up, maybe in a week."

"Don't wait too long; opportunity like this may never knock again."

***

For three long days I pondered the possibilities and on the forth I went to see Ocsi.

"Come in, come and meet the other boys," he ushered me into the small, narrow room with a skinny, long table and six chairs, wedged in between three double bunk-beds and six small lockers.

"This is Peter Veres, he studies chemistry; this here is Alfie Kovacs, the lady killer, who is in the literature department; this guy is Jeno Kiss, a future teacher of biology. All of you meet my friend, Laszlo Lichter. As you can see two beds are empty. One of them is waiting for you! Have you decided?"

"I thought about things a great deal since we met, but I have not decided. One minute I want to jump at what you suggested, another minute I don't know what to do," I told Ocsi and the other boys.

"Think of the fun we could have together," Alfie stated, resting on one of the upper beds..

"We would become friends, I am sure of that," Peter followed.

"If you cannot make a decision Laszlo, you need some help," Jeno offered.

"And who would be able to help me?" I asked.

"Dr. Kobor is the man," Ocsi settled the issue and insisted on arranging an appointment.

***

Another two days passed before Dr. Kobor was able to see me.

"Come in and perch on one of the stools. If you don't mind I will keep on working". Professor Kobor stood on no ceremony, his white lab coat-covered with a thousand stains-flapped as he moved around, lighting three Bunsen burners. "While these concoctions come to the boiling point we should talk. If I have to jump up, never mind it. I am preparing these solutions for titration. Parej told me that I should meet you. So just sit here and we will talk. Did I get it right? Your name is Laszlo?"

"Laszlo Lichter," I was stiffly formal.

"Thaw out a bit and call me Jeno. All my students call me that."

"I am not really your student," I objected, rather meekly.

"But you will be...You will not be able to resist my charm, nor the scholarship I could offer you, if what Parej told me is true. Is it Laszlo?"

"I do not know what he told you."

"You had a matriculation average of six point seven. Isn't that true?"

"Yes it is."

"And you are really interested in chemistry, the science I love and teach. Is that correct?"

"I was interested in that subject from grade seven on."

"Ocsi told me that you have no scholarship at that other institution," he spoke about the university I was attending with a great deal of derision."

"It is so."

"Then why are you still there? Are your professors perhaps better than I? Are they any more knowledgeable? More devoted to their students?"

"It is not that Dr. Kobor."

"Jeno, you mean. So why not join us? I have twenty-six students; a few of those wear that label poorly. They major in chemistry and minor in math, thank God it is not the other way around. I couldn't stand that. So why not become my student?"

"Well I don't know enough about this university to make such a big decision."

"Fair enough. Let me just attend to my concoctions, before they boil over." Jeno jumped from table to table, moving a test tube here, adjusting the flames on all Bunsen burners, clamping a retort in a tripod and when he returned, he wiped his brow and apprised me.

"This is the Teachers' University of Szeged. Our sacred task is to turn out as many teachers as possible, in as short a time as we can. Before the war it took four years to complete the task. Many teachers have perished during that conflict, some retired and many more have left this honorable calling. By 1949 we have begun to experience a dreadful shortage. We cut the length of study to three years; we have added a good practice teaching facility to our campus; we have obtained funds to offer everyone a scholarship, but all this is not enough. Few young men and women are willing to make the sacrifice and in our country to become a teacher is a great sacrifice indeed," he stopped for a few moments to attend to some tasks, then he returned and looked me in the eyes.

"I do not want to fool you. I do not want to mislead you. I am a Doctor of Chemistry. In industry my knowledge would fetch a tidy sum and here I am paid a pittance. If you become a teacher you will probably earn less than what you would be paid if you took a job now. Yet I am proud to be what I am and you should be proud to join our ilk. Others produce things, we shape young minds. The products become useless in a short time, but what we, teachers, accomplish lasts a lifetime. Now and then one of my former students comes to see me and we talk about what he accomplished. You should see how their faces shine; you should listen to their words of joy. Rarely do they complain about their meager remuneration, never do they express regret.

"They work with youngster and that gives them eternal youth. They shape young minds; they challenge young human beings to reach their capacity; they convey the love for knowing. Our maker made men out of clay, until his creation was to his liking. Educators are next to God, we take raw materials the Almighty created and add our own touch. Could there be a more noble profession? Is there anything worth doing more? I do not think so," his rapid fire questions, his enthusiasm for his profession had a profound effect on me.

"I think you are right. I recall some of my former teachers and I can now see what they did. Yet I hesitate to make the change."

"Years from now when you review your life, before you meet your Maker, you will ask yourself a few questions. That is what I will do. My questions will be simple: Did I make the world a better place? Will my brief presence be remembered by anyone? The answers must be yes to both, if I did not waste my time the good Lord gave me. A doctor will be remembered by some of his patients; a teacher by a few of his students; a politician by rarely anyone and a chemist by no one at all, unless he achieved greatness. Do you recall any of your teachers with fondness?"

"I do, more than one."

"Be like them then. Join us Laszlo. I am authorized to grant you a full scholarship. Three hundred Forints is not a large sum, but you will manage. For two years you will study with me and practice teach, beginning in January. When you finish your second year you will be given one year to further sharpen your skills at a public school. You will return to write your State examinations at the end of that year and you will receive your degrees. You will be a full-fledged teacher. Think about that Laszlo and make your decision, you must not hesitate." After those words, he dismissed me.

***

For days after my meeting with Dr. Kobor I thought about all he said, yet I vacillated. One minute I was ready to jump at the opportunity, then I thought of my Father's effort to get me to where I was and I have decided not to make the change. My decision lasted a few minutes and I have teeter-tottered for many days. Five days later fate decreed what I shall be.

Late Friday afternoon the brief, scary, disturbing telegraph came.

"Laszlo,

"You are needed at home, Egervary will explain.

"George."

The cryptic text disturbed me.

"What could be wrong? Something must have happened to my Father. Please dear Lord, do not make him sick again. Why didn't he send the wire? Maybe he is dead. George didn't make himself clear at all. What has happened I do not know. Should I grab a train and go home right away or should I wait for clearer instructions? Why will Egervary tell me all about the trouble? When and where and how will he do that?" I searched for answers and then I knew.

"Egervary drove us to Veszprem. He must be coming for me with the car. My Father must be alive, only he could have asked Egervary. I will wait six hours. If he doesn't come by then I will grab a train," I had decided. Counted my few Forints that was just enough for the train-fare and tortured myself for four long hours with dark thoughts of a hundred different possible tragedies and unexpectedly I felt joy.

"Less than a half day and I will be able to see my dear, beloved Rozsa. My wait of at least two months will be cut short. It will be so nice to see her; to hold her hand; to talk with her; to tell her about my loneliness; to have her help me make my big decision," I almost forgot the telegraph, the trouble it seemed to signal, I was so wrapped up in my selfish joy. Then came the sound of a car's horn and I rushed to the street.

The small, beaten, old car was parked by the edge of the pavement and Egervary alighted.

"Grab your things Laszlo...Say good-bye to your landlord...We must be on our way." He gave his rapid orders and my heart broke with the realization.

"I am through with my studies...My dream is over."

Five minutes later I threw all my possessions in the back of the car and we began our journey.

"I am sorry I had to rush you, but I was rushed too, when George came to me..," he was about to say more, but I interrupted him.

"My Father, is...he...dead?"

"No! I should have told you. He is neither dead nor sick. Just allow me to tell you the story."

"I am sorry Mr. Egervary. When the telegraph came it said so little and made me think the worst."

"I understand. Very early this morning George came to me and told me all that happened. He informed me that he will send you a wire and, on behalf of your Father, he asked me to come to fetch you. The car needed a bit of repair, before I was able to get under way." Egervary had a habit to remain quiet when in the company of more than one, and to speak on endlessly when he had only one for an audience. He was also notoriously slow to sort out what was important from all the peripherals.

"Please could you tell me why I was ordered home?"

"I was just about to tell you. Well let me see where should I begin? Back in 48 our revered Government began the process of nationalization, I am sure you recall all that followed. Your Father was unable to get raw materials needed to make shoes, but he managed to operate the factory in a limited manner. Did you know Laszlo that he went to the officials, even to the Communist Party Secretary and asked to have them nationalize his factory?"

"I didn't know that, he never told me."

"Well he did and they just laughed at him. 'Do you employ a hundred workers?' they asked him mockingly and denied his request. Later came that cursed robbery and after he closed his factory. It seems now that he didn't do the right thing. In this country, under this regime who knows what is right? They begin to travel down a particular road and when we think we know where they are heading, they turn sharply in a different direction. Not even the most devout, top Communists know what to do. Over a year ago, I think it was in June, Rakosi cooked up a plot against other Communists who may have conspired against him. He had Rajk, Palffy, Szonyi and Szalai executed; he had Justus sentenced to life imprisonment and many other Communists received long prison terms."

"Mr. Egervary, please..."

"I know, I know. Youth and impatience go hand in hand, but if you wish to understand what has happened then you must allow me to tell it my way or would you rather wait until we reach Baja? You just have to tell me what do you prefer and if need be I will remain silent," he waited for my answer, obviously offended.

"I am willing to listen, please continue."

"I told you this so that you will understand that nobody is safe in this country. Communist or not does not really matter. So your Father sat in that small room and hammered out a few pairs of shoes, while his expensive machinery stood idle in his former factory. The nationalization process touched those establishments that had over a hundred employees, that was in 48, but I told you that before. In 49 they dropped the number twice and in 50, just two weeks ago, that number was dropped to over ten.

"That is when your Father's real trouble began. The day before last he was summoned to the Communist Party's emergency meeting. I am sure you know that he has remained a member of the party, in spite of all he suffered at their hands."

"I knew that, but he only paid his dues, he did not go to the meetings. He thought of getting out when you were driving us from Veszprem to Baja, but decided against doing that. He did so for me."

"I know. Your Father told me. And he also told me what happened at the emergency meeting he had to attend. He was called to the podium where he was questioned by the party Secretary.

"'You were a capitalist Lichter. Can you deny that?' the party Secretary addressed your Father.

"He told the assembled two hundred or so how the Russians brought truck-loads of boots to him; how they threatened him at gun-point to repair them; how he found shoe-makers to help him; how he found the old, abandoned Jewish school-house to set up a repair facility. He led them step by step through the years of inflation; tried to explain to them how his workers earned not useless Pengos, but commodities that assured their survival. He told them that he was the only one who had a license from the Government to carry on the trade; how well he treated his friends, who worked with him; how the repair facility became a factory to produce shoes for the general public. Then he told them about the first law that was created to start nationalization; spoke about the shortage of materials and finally the robbery that brought him to his present state. When he finished telling them all that happened, he turned to the party Secretary and challenged him.

"'I described my life from the end of the war to the present day. All of you know that I spoke the truth. Can you still call me a capitalist?' Your Father was sure that the accusation will be retracted, but he was shocked by what followed.

"'You are worst than a capitalist Lichter. You exploited thirteen workers, but that is the least of your long list of crimes. You have dismissed those unfortunate, exploited, abused men in 49. You closed down your factory and deprived our people of needed shoes. Then you have compounded your crimes by neglecting your expensive machinery for well over a year. Your factory was nationalized a week ago, by a decree of our Father, Rakosi. And what have the citizens of this country inherited from you? A rust heap...Machinery that are unusable...That is sabotage Lichter. That is a ghastly crime indeed. Then there is one more, but that will be corrected. You hid amongst us, pretended to be a Communist', the party Secretary screamed at your Father his revolting accusations.

"You know your Father Laszlo. I think you can even guess his reaction."

"He must have quit," I spoke slowly, picturing him hurt, devastated, yet proud, and angry.

"Yes he did that, but how did he do it is what matters. He turned to those good citizens of Baja. 'Most of you have known me. Two of you escaped starvation when you worked for me and I paid you with commodities, while others labored for Pengos that bought nothing. I have lived in this city all my life; we have played cards together; we drank together; some of you ate at my table. Let's see who is willing to show his gratitude. Stand up and support me', were his exact words. He tried to look into the averted eyes of his former friends; he tried to make at least one person to stand with him and when he grasped the futility of his waiting, he reached into his pocket, took out his red, party book and raised it above his head.

"'This is what I think of this party, this is what I think of all of you', he raged and tore the book into shreds, letting the pieces fall where he stood. Then he walked the length of the meeting room in total silence and came to me."

"I have listened to you Mr. Egervary for the last thirty kilometers, but I am no wiser than before." I did not want to hurt him, yet I cried out, wanted to know if my Father was in any great danger.

"I am coming to the end of my story...Have patience Laszlo. That is what you need, if you wish to help your Father."

"Help him how? He did what he had to do! Wait a second...There must be more.

He wouldn't have ordered me home, because he quit the party. Something more dreadful must have happened."

"There is more, but you keep interrupting me..."

"I am sorry...Please continue."

"So he came to me and told me everything. He seemed to be fearless and relieved that all was now in the open. Before he left me he told me he was proud of himself for having told those scoundrels how he felt. I haven't seen him since. Then early this morning George came to me, as I told you before."

"'Please go get Laszlo from Szeged, he must come home at once', he said. When I asked him what has happened, his words confused me.

"'They got him...Broke down the door...Took him from us...It was still dark, maybe three in the morning...His last words were to have me come to you and to do what I said.'

"I asked him to compose himself; not to rattle on , but to start at the beginning. 'Who came for your Father? What did they say? Where did they take him?' I asked my leading questions and George composed himself.

"'We woke to the sounds of our gate crashing in. Then four uniformed policemen dragged Father from his bed. By then I was awake. 'Get dressed at once...Hurry up...You are under arrest...,' that is what they said.

"'What crime have I committed?' your Father asked them, but the policemen remained silent. George dressed in a hurry, while your Mother screamed at the cruel men. When they left the house with your Father, George followed them as far as he dared and watched them take your Father inside the city's prison, after that he came to me."

"Dear God! He is under arrest? I cannot believe that. Will his suffering never end?" I moaned in distress.

"Now you have heard the story. I hope you forgive me for dragging it out, but all of these things had to be said."

"There is nothing I need to forgive you and there is a lot I can never forgive or forget."

***

I thanked Mr. Egervary as we reached Baja and rushed into our home to console my grieving Mother, to comfort my younger brother.

"I am glad he wanted me home. Now I have to figure out what to do."

"They took your Father and even more," my Mother lamented.

"What more could they have taken?" I asked in a daze.

"They took the short-wave radio he bought two years ago. They confiscated his remaining tools. They searched the house and took the little money we had," my Mother wailed.

"I don't care about all those things. It is Father I care about."

"Do you think I do not care about him?" her voice was sharp. "He is the one who ordered me to tell you what they took; to urge you to get his things back. 'Laszlo will know what to do', that is what he said. He needs his tools when he comes home. He loves that radio, as you well know. And the money I need desperately and you too Laszlo. Without money your education is at an end."

I was stunned by all the events, and foolishly I made a promise.

"My education can go to hell. I will get back everything, if that is the last thing I ever do."

***

That night I sat in the Buja's kitchen, repeating everything that I could.

"I am truly sorry Laszlo," Mr. Buja spoke.

"I hate them more than ever before," Mrs. Buja spoke up next.

"Don't give up hope Laszlo," Rozsa urged me.

"My studies are over. My Father is in prison. What hope can I have?" I shook my head in resignation.

"The rotten tyrants," Mr. Buja spit out the words and suddenly I remembered.

"Thank you Mr. Buja," I cheered greatly.

"What did I do?" he asked me bewildered.

"You made me remember something my Father said a year ago. I know now what he meant."

"I sure do not follow you..," was Mr. Buja's next statement.

"I know, I know, but it is rather complicated." I began to explain my thoughts, my memories and my half formed plan.

"You may be right Laszlo. That might work, but you should be cautious," Mr. Buja endorsed my plan.

I stood up and walked to the street, my heart gladdened not only by the prospect of succeeding, but more so by Rozsa's presence. We stood for one moment in the recessed gate, touched hands for the first time since my arrival and then we gave each other a kiss.

"Be very careful Laszlo. I couldn't stand losing you. Remember we have life-long plans."

***

I lay in bed, thinking about my precious Rozsa; then I forced myself to formulate details of my plan.

"There are small tyrants and there are tyrants above them. Our new society was built on fear. Imagine a long ladder with many rungs. On each rung sits a group of tyrants, but there are other tyrants above them. On the very top sits Rakosi, but the ladder doesn't end there. It continues in the Soviet Union and on top of that enormous ladder sits Stalin himself. The ladder shakes and swings endlessly, but it is not the one at the very top who fears the fall. That fear exists in reverse order.

"'Will I be able to climb any higher? Or will the one above me cause my fall?', they ask themselves constantly and keep wary eyes on all above them," my Father's story came back to me far more clearly than it did at Buja's and I saw precisely what Father meant.

"I must begin my actions immediately. Shake those on the bottom of the ladder; make them believe that those above them are not really happy; imply things that are not really true, yet make them think about dreadful possibilities. Yes, that is what my Father must have thought of, that is what he must have meant; that is why he assured my Mother: 'Laszlo will know what to do.'"

***

The following day, late in the afternoon, I went to the city prison, seeking permission to visit my Father. Permission was denied promptly, as I expected, by the administrator of the old, worn, brick facility that stood at the corner of Pesti Street and by the statue of Andras Jelky. Legend had it that the Hungarian hobo, born in Baja, traveled around the globe, became the King of an African country. So the people of Baja sprang into action: from donations, solicited from far and wide, they erected a huge statue, fashioned its pedestal like a globe, and placed on its top an eight meter tall, walking Jelky. The courage and achievement of the statue's owner cheered me, reduced my fear.

"May I have your refusal in writing, comrade?" I made my first move, modulated my voice to display extreme courtesy and a hidden threat.

"May I ask comrade why do you need that?" he asked and adjusted his tie.

"I wish I could tell you comrade, but the reason even I do not know."

"Who are you trying to fool? You do not know the reason, yet you ask for my written statement. Even you must find it strange."

"I do indeed..," I strung the corpulent official along, watched his cruel face, his slightly slanted eyes and saw him adjust his tie again. "When I spoke to other men of authority, all of them advised me to do that. They gave me not their reasons. They simply told me to demand that," I lied with ease and recalled how I spent my morning.

First I went to the Communist Party headquarters; entered the building; inquired from the janitor where could I find the office of the Party Secretary; climbed the two flights of stairs; entered the ante-room and there asked about the whereabouts of the Head of Internal Security. I was promptly informed that I am at the wrong place. I shook my head and stated that I was summoned to see that high official, at this address. Once again I was told that I have made a mistake. I declared with the certainty of youth that I, Laszlo Lichter, do not make a mistake and left.

Next I have entered the building that housed the Police Department; declared that I was looking for the Communist Party Secretary and the same conversation was repeated, although slightly modified, and then they set me straight. I dropped my name, once again and went to two more places.

"If this bottom rung dweller does not know yet about my four visits, he will soon find out and will begin to fear those who roost just one rung above him," I assured myself and enjoyed my game.

"Maybe you should tell me who advised you in that manner?"

"I am afraid comrade to betray their trust. They told me never to mention their names or their positions. They also told me that if I do otherwise, they will deny that I have ever saw them," my lies came more smoothly as I progressed with my plan.

"Can you tell me how many of them did you see?"

"I see no harm in that comrade. Let me see..," I began to count on my fingers, then I gave him the information. "Four of them...or maybe five...Sorry, I had such a busy morning."

"So… maybe the fifth or sixth you came to see? If you wanted to see your Father why didn't you just come to me?"

"I am not sure I dare to tell you that?"

"You should have come to me first. I am in charge of your Father."

"I know that comrade, I know that far too well. If I dare to tell you what I know, I may face your anger and put myself in danger."

"I assure you no harm will come to you, if you tell me."

"Very well then. I have heard during the last two years that you are a man of great ability, intelligent, even benevolent on rare occasions, but all these qualities put together do not reach the magnitude of your ambition. Some officials suspect that you covet their positions, so they speak about you in a derogatory manner. I heard someone say that 'our prison administrator should be cut down to size.' Someone else complained that 'he treats prisoners so cruelly that they and their families become enemies of the state forever.' Another statement I picked up lately: 'He is getting too big for his breeches...Maybe it is time to purge him.' I am sorry you made me tell. I can only imagine how you must feel hearing these terrible things from a young man. I hope you forgive me for what I repeated."

"Who cares about wagging tongues?" the prison chief spoke, but his action betrayed him, he grabbed his tie, adjusted it, unable to hide his nervous tension.

"May I see my Father now?" I asked him and watched his vacillation.

"I am not sure it would be wise. I have to think about that. Come back tomorrow, nine in the morning and you shall have my final answer.

***

I sat down on one of the benches that faced the walking Jelky. I thought about the hobo who lived in this city, so long ago. Who dared to leave his birthplace, walked across the border into another country and never stopped his journey, forged on until he crossed border after border.

"He must have been a daring young man. Am I like him? I have no life experience, yet I have embarked on a great journey. Am I putting myself and perhaps my Father in jeopardy? Should I give up my quest? Should I cease what I began to do before I cause an avalanche?" thus ran my thoughts, but my eyes did not idle. I saw the prison administrator step through the small, brown, metal gate and watched him walk toward the center of the city.

When he was a safe distance away, I followed him surreptitiously, until I saw him enter the building of the Communist Party.

"Exactly what I have expected," I acknowledged not without satisfaction, turned on my heels to go home and wait until late afternoon, to carry out the next phase of my plan.

***

"I am here to see the Chief of Police," I announced to the secretary.

"Do you have an appointment?"

"I don't have that..."

"Who shall I say wants to see him?"

"Laszlo Lichter...Tell him I have information," by adding the last words I assured my success.

"Come in young man," the Chief stood by his office door and waved a hand.

"I came to see you as soon as I could, I have some important information."

"I am all ears. So tell me what brought you here. Rarely does anyone come to see me, unless brought to me by my policemen," he snickered with amusement.

"First may I ask you a question?"

"Go ahead..."

"If I came to tell you that I stole something, what would be your reaction?"

"Is that what you did?"

"Well it was only a hypothetical question."

"So you want to know what I would do. I would have a confession prepared; I would have you sign it and when that is done I would have you front of a Magistrate."

"And if it was someone else who committed the deed, what would you do then?"

"I would follow standard police procedures. The culprit would be arrested, tried and if found guilty he would be sentenced."

"Regardless who it is?"

"I think this has gone far enough. You are a young fool. Nobody should dare to question my impartiality."

"I am not the one who is doing the testing," I announced without hesitation.

"Did I hear you right? Someone put you up to asking these questions?"

"Did I say that? If I did, I let the cat out of the bag."

"You speak in riddles...Wait just one second. Your name sounds familiar. Laszlo Lichter, isn't that what you said?"

"That is my name and my Father's is Ferenc Lichter. He should be well-known by you."

"Is that so, well let me see..." he picked up one of the folders that lay on his desk and studied its contents. "Now I see what brought you here...Your Father was arrested almost two days ago, for crimes against the state. Is that why you came to me?"

"That and something else. If my Father committed a crime, for which he was arrested, a judge will deal with him and with the issue of confiscation," I stated clearly.

"Confiscation of what? There was no such thing."

"How many policemen did you send to arrest my Father?"

"Four, the documents state."

"So four of them shared the money. Two hundred Forints for each of them is not a bad pay for an hour's work," I stated the amount of money they took, hoping that he will take the bait.

I saw him glance at the folder once more and saw him pale.

"And how will they share the Telefunken radio? Or will they sell that, along with the tools?" I judged the time right to ask those questions.

"You are dead wrong...Only the tools were taken. Those tools belong to the nation as a result of nationalization," the Chief's anger surfaced slightly.

"If that is the case then I have mistakenly reported the action of your policemen," my bold statement found its target.

"Reported? Who would pay any attention to a mere boy? The audacity of your accusations wouldn't be believed by anyone."

"The men I saw felt otherwise." I took a calculated risk, firmly believing that the Chief knew something about my morning's activities and kept a vigilant eye on all those eminent people who perched on the next rung of the Communist ladder.

"You saw no one besides the administrator of the prison," he slipped, allowed me to know that my calculations were correct.

"Is that what he told you?" my bold words made him wipe sweat from his balding head. "Did he also share with you our entire conversation? I am sure he did. Very well then. I see I am getting nowhere, thanks for the time you gave me." I stood and left.

Three hours later a policeman entered our house. Under one arm he carried my Father's radio, which he placed on our kitchen table.

"Our Chief of Police sent his apologies. One enemy of the state will face disciplinary action. The radio was found in his home...The money that scoundrel took from you has also been recovered. Here...Count it..," he handed the crumpled Forint bills to my Mother, who was totally bewildered.

"It is all here...Eight hundred Forints is what I counted," she announced and looked at me in amazement.

"The tools cannot be returned, those are confiscated until the trial. There is one more thing left to do...You must sign this paper."

"And what am I to sign?" my Mother asked boldly.

"Just a simple statement, confirming that the radio and money were returned to you."

"I want to read it." My Mother snatched the document from the hand of the policeman and she read it aloud.

"The undersigned acknowledges that a Telefunken radio and eight hundred

Forints, taken in error by one of the policemen, has been returned.

"The undersigned also agrees to withdraw all complaints against the arresting officers.

"Signed by Ilona Lichter: _____

"Dated: October 20, 1950"

"So it was only a mistake...And was my husband's arrest a mistake too?" my Mother screamed at her target.

"I am not authorized to say any more," the policeman fidgeted and offered his pen.

"What should I do Laszlo? Should I put my name to a pack of lies? Calling theft a mistake? Withdrawing all complaints while your Father is still in prison?"

"Sign it Mother and say no more," I commanded and for the first time ever I took charge, trying to hide my exultation.

***

Promptly at nine the next morning I entered the city prison and without any explanation I was led to my Father's cell. We held each other for at least two minutes and when we have separated I sat with him on his hard bed.

"I am sorry Laszlo I had to drag you back, but what choice did I have? Your Mother is a hot-head, your brother is too young to take any action. Did Egervary go for you? Did your Mother tell you what I have requested?"

"It is fine Dad. Egervary brought me home the day before yesterday. Since then I was rather busy..," I told him all I did and informed him about our success. I was greatly surprised that no guard supervised us, nobody watched us and even by the length of our half an hour visit.

"You understood my message, thank God for that."

"I understood and acted as you have hoped I would. What will happen to you now Dad?"

"Do not worry about me. My expulsion from the party bothers me not. My arrest is only a sham."

"Some sham it is. You are innocent Dad," I proclaimed and I felt my intensified hatred. "How I despise them! They harassed me; they destroyed your factory; they put you in prison; they persecuted Mr. Buja; they denied me entry to the University of Veszprem; they refused Rozsa an opportunity to receive higher education. What they have done to Uncle Jozsef in Siberia and the stories he told me make things even worse..," I would have gone on, but my Father commanded silence.

"Slow down Laszlo. You better temper your judgment. They just want to set an example. I let the machinery rust at my former factory, so they want others to know that sabotage will not be tolerated. Maybe a trial? Probably a suspended sentence? They treat me well, I assure you. Two of the guards have been my friends for many years. They will allow your Mother to visit. They will even allow her to bring me food, whenever she wishes to do that. Do not worry about me Laszlo. I fret about something else."

"All of us will be fine, you need not fret."

"Your Mother will manage...She did that during the war. George will be looked after, but it is you I am concerned about."

"Don't do that Dad. I will apply for a job with the office where I worked during the summer and I will help. I will come and visit you whenever I can."

"You will do no such thing! You must return to Szeged! Your education must not end. In that you must not disobey me, promise me that."

I was inclined to describe to him the financial difficulties I have faced during the last five weeks; to tell him that without his fiscal support I cannot survive at the university, but seeing my brave, broken, innocent Father; sensing the despair he really felt, commanded me to falsify a few facts.

"I will continue my education, I make that promise. I will become a learned man." I made my pledge and we stood up, embraced once more and he, the devastated man, spoke up, pretending levity.

"Now go Laszlo. Don't worry about me. This place is far safer than the Danube; a lot less colder than my boat in early spring; they treat me far more kindly than I was treated during the war. Tell your Mother I would enjoy some of her fried chicken and maybe a good bottle of red wine. When Christmas comes come home for a visit, long before then I shall be free."

***

Before I returned to Szeged I informed my Mother about details of my visit. Then I went to meet Rozsa, at the place that belonged to only us, at our tree where we were always happy. I told her about my actions, which in retrospect I considered reckless. I spoke about the boldness with which I have acted. Now that all that was behind me, I saw my stupidity of taking on men of power. I saw myself as an irresponsible youth, who got carried away by the distorted image of his invulnerability. I glimpsed the risks I have created for those close to me and suddenly I tasted fear, fear that I should have felt all along. Then I shared with my beloved the conversation I had with my Father.

"Without a scholarship and your parents' support how can you survive my dearest?" she asked with concern.

It was then that I told her all about Ocsi Parej, Dr. Kobor and the offer they made to me. When I finished my long story, I looked into her sweet face and asked her the most important question.

"If I do not become a chemist will you still want to marry me?"

"When you fell in love with me Laszlo, did you fall in love with the girl I was or with a woman I someday might be?"

"I fell in love with your blue eyes, your pony tails, your tiny nose, your shapely ears, your lovely lips, with the intelligence you possess, with the young girl who walked by me on the day I first saw you," I spoke the words in adoration.

"It was no different with me, although it didn't happen on that first day. First I began to appreciate your willingness to help; then recognized the depth of your shyness; your loneliness really touched me. Your shiny black hair; your commanding, yet begging eyes; your small stature; your love of books; your willingness to learn, I came to appreciate quite a bit later. My love for you grew by degrees. Yes, it is the boy I love Laszlo, not the chemist you want to be. Our future together you must never doubt. Rich or a pauper; a man of stature or a man of no importance, makes no difference to me. Become what you can; reach for whatever you want, but please always reach for me," when she completed her affirmation I gave her a kiss and my solemn promise.

"I will return to Szeged and switch universities. After two years of study I will begin to teach. The shorter time, we will be away from each other, delights me. Wait for me my love and I promise you we will be happy."

An hour later we have parted. The train began to move and my heart was heavy, yet with my improved prospects I was ready to face my new destiny.

***

Two days later I became a student of Professor Kobor and a class-mate, room-mate and friend of Ocsi.

Slowly I began to warm to the other boys, who shared our tiny room; who bent over the long table, even in the middle of the night, to try to complete our never ending assignments.

For a month I studied arduously. Chemistry, Hungarian language, pedagogy, I loved; mathematics and educational psychology I battled constantly; physics and biology were not to my liking; Russian, political science, physical training and shop training I detested intensely. Regardless how I felt about any of my subjects, I did not neglect a single one, pushed on relentlessly to satisfy all course requirements, then I was ready to relish the most precious moments of my daily life.

I picked up my pen to write a letter to my dearest Rozsa. When my hands were exhausted from writing, when my eyes could no longer remain open, when my mind could take no more, I climbed to the top bunk and lay down to get a few hours of sleep. In the dark of night, listening to the snoring of my room-mates, I had no choice but to face reality. My Father was still in prison without a trial; help from home completely dried up; the huge amount of scholarship money, I have received upon my enrollment, seemed to just disappear.

Three hundred Forints first appeared to be a large sum before I paid out one hundred, each month, for the dormitory space I occupied: one of six bunk-beds, one sixth of a not too large table; a simple, uncomfortable chair and the roof above my head. One hundred -fifty Forints for fifteen meal tickets that permitted me to eat fifteen dinners at the university's shabby dining room. The remaining fifty Forints I had the luxury to spend any which way I preferred: stamps to mail my letters to my beloved Rozsa or for tickets on the tram cars that would take me to my university over two miles away. I bought the stamps and commanded my feet to walk, whenever weather permitted. My fifteen cooked meals a month, a slice of bread with lard spread over it, well salted and sprinkled with paprika was my breakfast and the same fare repeated in the evenings, made my stomach rebel. So it frequently grumbled, but not as loudly, nor as often as Alfie's did.

The tall, lanky, blond lady killer sprang from the loins of a sugar-beet farmer. His anticipated package from home came usually at the end of the month and it contained nothing, but a few pounds of cubed sugar. His parents had nothing else to give. Alfie, an aspiring writer, studied life, rather than his subjects. He spent money not the way I did. When he received his scholarship the first of the month, his first stop was the tavern, close to our dormitory, by the railway station. He made the wine flow; his Forints induced the gypsies to play, but the girls he never paid, yet they surrounded the fair young man, nibbled on his ears, invited him to their beds and two days after he came back to us, completely broke.

By the fourth day, after his money evaporated, he had no energy to climb down from the top bunk bed. We brought him left-overs from the dining room, but never sufficient quantity to restore his strength. Day after day he remained where he was, pencil in hand, paper resting on his bony knees. When we have returned from our classes he accepted gratefully what little food we brought and in gratitude he enthralled us with his poems born in pain or stunned us with the dangerous stories he wrote.

The girls came, stood under our second floor window, called out for Alfie, urged him to join them and one of us was always asked to inform them: "This is not the first day of the month yet. When that day arrives come back and we shall rejoice."

***

The interminable days dragged on slowly, as it always does in our youth. The tree-lined boulevards of Szeged were littered with the leaves that rustled under our feet, as the four of us strolled the city's streets on Sunday afternoons. The ancient oaks, elms, poplars cast off their green ornaments, no longer hiding the stone carved statutes that adorned many of the famous, ancient buildings.

Ocsi, Peter, Jeno and I took time out from our studies to admire the Opera House with its stone cherubs, carved window sills and dozens of art pieces created by the hands of master carvers. We looked in awe at the magnificent Cathedral, flanked by the outdoor theater, where concerts were given on every Sunday. We sat down on its elevated stone benches and listened to the inspiring music of great composers.

Our Sunday walk took us to the shore of the Tisza, where we stood at the top of the high, concrete wall, looking down on the twisting river, ten meters below us, whose inevitable floods threatened the city in early spring and during the dying fall.

When we were filled with the old city's beauty, we headed toward the Glory gate, its arches guarded by statues of fallen soldiers, passed under their watchful eyes and headed to our dormitory.

The cold winds of December impeded our progress, tore at our coats, combed our hair, pelted us with flying leaves, yet we were happy until we reached our dormitory, where Alfie lay on top of his bed. His happiness existed only once a month. In spite of our begging not to squander his scholarship money on booze, gypsies and his energy on women, Alfie's life remained on course. For two days, at the beginning of the month, he was the undisputed king of the nearby tavern and for the rest of the time he was the starving, talented pauper of his bunk.

We feared for his health; we dreaded the possibility of his expulsion; and each Sunday, after our return, we sat around or lay on our beds, listening to his touching stories.

His first story depicted a childhood of misery. He rose four o'clock in the morning, toiled with his entire family until dark, on his Father's small plot of land, to grow sugar beets. When the green shoots poked their heads above the ground the entire family celebrated; when the hail-storms destroyed the plants they grieved together and eyes averted from each other, thought about the coming suffering. They starved until their fortunes changed and when it didn't they starved some more.

Slowly his stories changed from their own misfortunes to that of the entire country and Alfie's writings became more dangerous. His words cried out against the Russian oppressors, against the injustices of the Communist Party. He boldly predicted a bloody revolution. As his body wasted away, as his soul suffered his self-imposed torture, as his mind became more feverish, his words took on the brilliance of polished precious stones.

Two weeks before the beginning of our Christmas vacation, that by now was officially called the 'Holiday of Father Winter', the four of us appealed to the university.

"Alfie Kovacs is starving himself to death. You must do something..," I told the Director of Students Services.

"He will die unless you help..," Peter Veres joined my call for help.

"He is totally disillusioned..," Jeno Kiss let it slip and we saw the flicker of first interest in the eyes of the Director.

"What does he do with his scholarship money?"

"Two days after he receives it, he has none left," Ocsi Parej shared the truth.

"Three hundred Forints is what you boys receive. Does Alfie get any less?"

"It is not that. His family is poor, they are sugar-beet farmers. He sends them most of what he gets and the rest of the month he starves with them," I tried to salvage the situation.

"I understand and will examine your friend's state of affairs," he dismissed us, his words may have contained a promise, but sounded more like a threat.

***

Two days later Alfie received one hundred Forints and we had a new room-mate to occupy the sixth bed.

Bela Gero was a skinny, shifty-eyed extrovert. He tried to befriend all of us with his open smile, his ribald jokes, but he succeeded only with Alfie.

"Get out of bed you lazy bum. Teach me to have a good time. I have the money," Bela urged Alfie a week after his arrival and waved under his nose the bills he held.

"Is it really money I see? That much could make us happy for three days at least," Alfie announced and he found strength to climb down from his castle.

"This money my parents sent me. Where would you like to go Alfie?"

"We will go to my favorite tavern. The booze will flow, the gypsies will play gladly and the women I know…Well that you will see," Alfie promised and the two of them left our dormitory.

***

Three days later the worn out Alfie and the jubilant Bela, returned to our room. Alfie climbed back to where he truly resided and Bela didn't hide his exultation.

"What a time we had you will never know," Bela announced to the four of us, while Alfie slumbered.

Not one of us was in the mood to ask any questions, so we have turned to our books, pretended disinterest.

"That Alfie is some guy I tell you. He can drink like a fish and when others fall under the table he drinks some more. The gypsies like him. Have you ever see him dance on top of a table? Have you ever heard him sing like a skylark? His voice is sweet, his lips are even sweeter, his ability as a lover is totally endless, at least that is what everyone of his four paramours told us when he brought them back, one by one, from wherever those girls were taken. Too bad Alfie has no other talents," Bela stopped and waited for our reaction.

"You saw only those things that do not count Bela. Anyone can drink, sing with the gypsies, be with a girl, but only Alfie can write beautiful stories," Ocsi broke our silence.

"He never mentioned that to me. Are you telling me the truth?" Bela inquired.

"He sits, day after day, on his bunk-bed and he writes fantastic stories. On Sunday evenings, when we return from our weekly walks, he reads them to us and we are truly awed," Peter spoke up.

"Sundays you said? But that couldn't be…You must be kidding me. I was here last Sunday. The room was quiet like a church, there was no reading, just some snoring and the sounds of stealthy movements," Bela described the unusual Sunday that followed his arrival.

I remembered well that Sunday. The four of us decided to persuade Bela to go on the usual Sunday walk and I was to stay behind to warn Alfie.

"Alfie, could I speak to you for a moment?"

He held up his wasted hand, that held the pencil and with a look he commanded me to remain silent. Ten minutes later he lowered his writing tablet, turned toward where I sat and made his apology.

"Sorry Laszlo I was rude. Do you know anything about writing?"

"I am not in the literature department."

"You are irritated Laszlo. That I can understand. You are used to being answered when you ask a question; you demand undivided attention when you speak, but when I write, I must focus all my attention. Writing is a most difficult process. One must be inspired; one must develop the idea, the writer must search for the perfect words, for the right emotional context. Only when I have a section completed can I turn my attention to other things. I am driven Laszlo by some inner compulsion, I admit I do not know exactly what it is. Only my dreams, my dreadful nightmares, give me some indication. Frequently I dream about an early death. When I come awake I am all sweaty, I shiver with fear that I will not be granted enough time to create the stories that I am compelled to tell.

"You and your friends think that I am a lazy bum, I neglect my studies, I do not attend my classes, I just live for those two days of carousing at the beginning of each month. You are all wrong! I have a God given talent...Don't judge me for my conceit, for that is not what it is. When I was a young child I have learned to read and write on my own. Before I have entered middle school, I have read many books and wrote many stories. When I worked our land my mind was spinning out stories, not cultivating sugar-beats, like my Father. Each seed I put in the ground was the germ of a tale; each harvest, when there was a harvest, I imagined seeing my crop, a published book. I want to be a famous writer, a teller of eternal truth," Alfie stopped his monologue.

"I know Alfie that you have a great talent. You have entertained us on a few Sundays; you have illuminated our minds; made us learn what life is all about. We all appreciate that, but your stories hold a great deal of danger. That is what I want to talk to you about. The boys asked me to stay behind and to warn you about the danger."

"Danger exists only in your minds, as stories exist in mine."

"You are a fool. For the things you have read to us you could be imprisoned, your life could be cut short. You must face political reality...Bela may be a nice boy or he could be a plant," I delivered my warning.

"So what do you suggest I do?"

"Tonight please do not read to us. That is what we have decided to ask you, we are terribly concerned."

"Deny you all the only pleasure I can give? Deny myself the gratification of reading my stories? A writer cannot do that."

"Just for tonight and maybe a few more Sundays, please do as we ask. Later on, when we grow to trust Bela, if we will ever trust him, you can return to your readings," I begged my friend.

"Have it your way Laszlo...I will keep my stories to myself."

I was relieved by having Alfie's promise and that Sunday he remained absolutely silent.

He broke his silence, on the first Sunday, after the three day frolic Bela financed. That night, when all of us sought our bed, Bela began to grumble.

"We sure had fun Alfie, a few days ago. We spent my money, which I didn't mind; we had good booze; splendid music and those women must have enjoyed your talents. You have never told me what happened when you sneaked out with the blond, then with the brunette and later with those two others. Did you take your pleasure with them? Did you make them listen to your stories?"

"I please women the way I should. I read only to my friends," Alfie announced and I sensed his fleeting hesitation.

"Am I not a friend of yours? Did I not prove that?" Bela spoke and Alfie's hesitation vanished. He propped up the pillows behind his head, he reached for the sheets of papers and his melodious voice filled the room.

He read his master-piece's title, then he continued with the sad, tragic story. We have listened silently to the struggle of two farmers, who pined for owning land, who were exploited by their masters, the large landholders. We rejoiced when the new Government, around 48, gave both of them a parcel of land. We toiled with them from day-break to dawn, from planting to the time of harvest. One of them was a devoted member of the Communist party; the other devoid of any political persuasion. The first one had a bountiful harvest, but the second, who lived a hundred kilometers to the north, had his crops destroyed by the flooding Tisza. The first one falsely claimed flood damage and he was exempted from all his obligations; the second one was less fortunate. The authorities demanded delivery to the government's store-house tons of wheat, barley and corn. When he was unable to meet their demands, he was imprisoned and there he met his self-inflicted death.

When Alfie read the last few pages, his voice thundered with indignation; his soul cried out against the injustice. When he read about the unfortunate farmer's death, his voice quivered and then he became silent.

Four of us gave him our usual, well deserved applause, but spoke not a word. Bela, who did not clap, spoke instead.

"Alfie I think you should stop writing, you do a lot better when you dance on top of tables, when you drink, when you sing and probably when you make love to your women. You should apply your talents to things that are appreciated."

"I take it that you didn't like my story?"

"I don't want to talk about it anymore. I am tired, I will grab some sleep."

***

Early next morning we woke to the sound of thunder, the heavens cracked their whip. Flash of lightening illuminated our room with greater and greater frequency and the rain began to pelt the roof-tops. Not even the portentous elements kept four of us from attending classes, but Alfie remained in bed and Bela refused to join us.

Early in the evening, one by one, we have arrived to our empty room. No sign of Bela, which did not disturb us. Alfie's empty bed concerned us.

"What do you think happened to Alfie?" I asked my three room-mates.

"I am sure he did not go to classes," Peter announced.

"He couldn't have any money this is the wrong time of the month," Ocsi stated.

"Maybe Bela induced him to repeat their last performance?" Jeno speculated.

Having thought of no other logical explanation for the duo's disappearance, the four of us turned to our studies. We have waited that night, but they did not appear. We had two more days of futile waiting, before I got an idea.

"Maybe we should break open Alfie's locker? Search his belonging?" I suggested and the four of us sprang into action.

A few pieces of clothing hung in Alfie's locker, but neither in that place, nor in any other could we find Alfie's stories.

"Maybe he was expelled from the university and went home?" Peter speculated.

"He wouldn't leave us without a word. He would have taken all of his belongings," I suggested.

"Maybe we should check for Bela's belongings. Don't you think?" Jeno didn't wait for us, instead he broke open the totally empty locker.

"He is gone too. What are we to think?" Jeno lamented.

"Tomorrow we shall check at the university. Peter you check on Bela. Does any of you know in which department did he do his studies?" I asked and before any of them had time to reply, I cursed myself.

"I was stupid. Bela never mentioned what he studied. I should have noticed that. Did he tell any of you what were his courses?"

"He never spoke about his courses," Jeno declared.

"Come to think of it he never mentioned any of his professors," Ocsi added.

"What if he wasn't a student?" Peter's words set fear in my heart.

"We should have been a lot more careful. Bela was not unlike my Laurel and Hardy of long ago," I whispered in consternation and the boys knew what I was talking about. I kept no secrets from them.

"I will check with the registrar about Bela and you Laszlo should go to the literature department. There is nothing more we can do today," Peter settled the issue.

That night I lay on my bunk-bed, and before I fell asleep I thought about Laurel and Hardy and the many misdeeds of the Communists.

"They have investigated my former friend for the letter he wrote to the United States; they have drilled me about the non-existent code in his letter. They have ruined my Father; first they robbed him, and then imprisoned him for no crime at all. They have demoted, cast out Mr. Buja, my beloved Rozsa's Father, for being an officer and gentleman, who received his commission before the war. They have dragged my Uncle Jozsef from his home-land and from his family to Siberia. They have expelled those two girls from all universities for a simple cartoon, one of them drew. They have spies everywhere, they know everything. They must have known about Alfie's writing."

***

We came back to our room around five thirty, the following afternoon and shared the results of our investigations.

"Alfie was not expelled," I informed them. "The Literature Department Head was very kind. He hasn't seen him for a long time, but recognized Alfie's talent and closed his eyes over his non-attendance. He checked with the local police and found out that Alfie was not involved in an accident; he was not arrested, at least not by them. He contacted the police of Mako, that is where Alfie lived and hours later he was informed that Alfie never returned to his family. I am afraid Alfie vanished."

"The picture is getting clearer by the minute," Peter took over. "I spoke with the Registrar, a decent man. He searched the roster of the university, but found no Bela Gero. Then he recalled the disappearance of another student, six months ago...Guess who was one of his room-mates? None other than Bela Gero. I hate to tell you what I suspect. Bela Gero was a plant, a member of Internal Security"

Day after day we have waited for Alfie's return. We recalled his memorable stories; spoke about the affection we all felt for that dear friend. Before our Christmas vacation began I ran through my mind the list of those who suffered at the hands of the Communists and added Alfie Kovacs' name to my list of grievance.

***

The Christmas of 1950 I recall as a bitter-sweet event. During my ten days of break I was allowed to visit my Father in prison on two occasions. Both times he tried to cheer me; to urge me to continue my studies and he held out hope for his eventual release.

"You know I am not guilty and my accusers know that as well. My lawyer, my friend is optimistic. I will soon be released, he constantly tells me. Once I get out I will look for a job. I will earn money and support the family, even send money to you Laszlo. I am glad you didn't quit. You will be the chemist you want to be..," he repeated his hopes and promises and I had no heart to tell him what I didn't tell anyone, except Rozsa.

I have listened to his words, to his false hopes. I saw his broken heart, that he couldn't hide from me and gave him my brief agreements.

"You are not guilty Father. I know you will be released. I know you will find a good job. All of us will be happy again. I love my studies and I was granted a scholarship, so I will become a man of learning. Don't you worry about me..," I put as much conviction into my words as I could muster and to avoid an outburst of my bitterness that lurked just below the surface I thought about my sweet, beloved Rozsa.

When the prison gate closed behind me, I rushed to her. When she came to open the gate I kissed her briefly and the two of us joined her family.

Mr. Buja wanted to know all about my Father. Mrs. Buja inquired about my health and that of my family. Joe asked about my adventures in my new city. Rozsa's blue eyes displayed her happiness about being together and pain upon hearing my stories.

I told them about my prison visits; I spoke about my Mother's constant tears and George's hatred for the authorities. I described the dedication of my professors. I gave details of what happened to those two unfortunate girls who were expelled from all universities of our country. I made them see our dormitory and my friends who lived there with me. But most of all I spoke about Alfie, his remarkable stories and his dreadful disappearance.

"I have received many letters from you Laszlo, yet you never wrote me about these sad things. Why did you not share with me your burden?" Rozsa's eyes sparkled, her beautiful face shone with love, as she asked her question.

"I was tempted to pour out my soul, to describe all that had happened, but something urged me not to do that."

"And you were right Laszlo!" Mr. Buja came to my rescue. "There are things one can write down. The weather for example or how you feel, but never ever your feelings about the Communist Party, or the Soviet Union, or conditions in our country. Those things, in the wrong hands, could do great harm. There are few people one can trust, as your story about Alfred illustrated. All of us must exercise great caution in this cursed country."

Mr. Buja's condemnation of our home-land surprised me. He was always a patriot; a man dedicated to his country of birth. Over two years ago Mr. Buja said something when I asked him a question. I searched my mind, as I sat there, trying to recall what we spoke about.

Slowly the memory of that long ago conversation came back to me. Mr. Buja spoke about his past and gave a gloomy picture of what he could expect. It was then that I asked him: "'Would it be possible for your family and mine to leave this country, instead of waiting for the Communists to punish you and maybe even my Father?'"

His reply came back to me clearly: "'Many people have left their home-land before the war ended. They escaped before the Russians' arrival. They are somewhere in the west, homeless, friendless, probably pining for everyone they left behind. To leave the place where we were born; to desert our homeland; to leave our beloved relatives behind is not my choice. I am proud to be a Hungarian.'"

That is what he said then and now, more than two years later he used the words: 'cursed country'. I had no need to ask him for an explanation. He had experienced many disappointments, not unlike my Father, not unlike me.

My daily visits with Rozsa; my two visits with my Father; my occasional conversations with my Mother and George; my one, long visit with Uncle Jozsef and Aunt Gizella; a brief visit with my surrogate parents, the Lazars; and Christmas Eve, which I spent with my precious sweetheart, filled my ten, brief days and the time of saying farewell came far too soon.

Once again we stood on the train-station's platform, the black, hissing snake almost ready to take me, when Rozsa spoke.

"How many more times do we have to part? How many more tears must I shed? When you go away Laszlo my days are empty...," she wiped her tears.

"Just one year and six months my darling. I know it is a long time, but it is no better for me. My days are filled with my studies, but when the lights go out I dream about only you," with those words we have parted and the train whisked me away.

Chapter 6

Alfred's disappearance; the harshness of the winter that came in February; the increasing demands of my studies; my constant hunger; the chill of our poorly heated room; my Father's lasting imprisonment, made me think about terminating my education. But not one of them; not even all of them put together, were sufficient for me to make such a big decision, until I added one that outweighed all the others. I wanted to see, each and every day of my life, my adored Rozsa; I desired to hear her voice, to touch her hand, to steal a kiss from her sweet lips, to talk with her, to walk with her, to be reassured that she still loved me.

"I have no choice, but to quit..," I announced to my three friends, early in February, my reluctantly reached decision.

"Why would you do that?" Peter asked me.

"There are several reasons..," I was loath to continue.

"Give me just one," Ocsi demanded.

"I don't even know where to begin. Well let me see...For the last few weeks I have been depressed over Alfred's disappearance."

"Do you think you are the only one? Do you think we don't miss him?" Jeno's accusing tone made me shiver.

"And this cursed cold room; the constant studying while my stomach rumbles with the pain of hunger; my Father's lasting imprisonment. How many more reasons do I have to give you?" The dam of my complaints broke, my difficulties gushed out.

"Stop your foolishness Laszlo. You will quit over our dead bodies. You complain about studying, yet you succeed with far less effort than I ever could," Ocsi grumbled.

"Do you think we love the cold any more than you do?" Peter goaded me.

"Would your Father's imprisonment be eased by your leaving? How would he feel if you did that?" Jeno made me think.

"All of you got a point. But what about the hunger?"

"We are hungry too!" Ocsi announced calmly. "So why don't we do something about that?"

"What can we do? Not one of us has any money from home...Not one of us will survive long on the few cooked meals we can afford," I argued with my friends.

"So we will survive on more..." Ocsi's broad, smiling face, his impish look seemed to suggest a solution.

"Whatever do you mean?" Jeno inquired and all three of us looked at him for his answer.

"Well let's sit down and carry out a small experiment..," Ocsi commanded.

We watched him arrange his dining-room ticket, an eraser and a small round piece of paper front of him, like a magician ready to perform a trick.

"Yesterday when I went to have my meal, I presented my ticket to be punched, but this time I did that with one small difference. I held my palm under the ticket to capture the punch-out. The small piece of round paper, you see here, I hid in the palm of my hand and now I will put it to good use."

Ocsi placed the ticket on the top of the table, carefully inserted the punch-out in the last hole and began to work his magic with the eraser. When he was finished, he insisted that all of us inspect his creation.

"You take a look at it Laszlo. Yesterday I ate my third meal out of fifteen. How many holes do you see?"

"Two holes I see," I announced and began to perceive what Ocsi was trying to accomplish.

"Yet I had three meals so far and thirteen more to go. Now if I do that five times each month, I will have twenty meals for the price of fifteen. What do you think of that?"

"They will notice it and Alfred's crime will pale in significance. To do this is cheating. They will surely expel you if they ever discover."

"And who shall we cheat, pray tell me? Whose food is it we will be stealing? The State owns everything and the State is the Communists Party. I thought you hate them Laszlo. Wouldn't you love to have a small victory, any victory over the hated? Have you not listed to us all the crimes they have committed against you? Should I list them for you? They have investigated you; they have robbed, ruined and imprisoned your Father; they have demoted, cast out your beloved Rozsa's Father; they have dragged your Uncle Jozsef from his home-land and from his family to Siberia; they have expelled those two girls from all universities for drawing a simple cartoon. Did I get your list of grievances right Laszlo? Are you a coward or a fighter? Sure they will expel us if we cheat them, but first they must catch us in the act. Are you ready to pay back the bastards or will you run with your tail between your legs without even trying? In some ways you are smart, but if you quit now you are nothing but a coward and a dummy. Don't you think, my dear friends, that we should at least give it a try?" Ocsi argued and when he heard the answers, he became triumphant.

"I will try it!" Jeno declared.

"I will do it," Peter announced. Their eyes, their ears awaited my answer.

"I don't know..," I mumbled under my breath.

"You will do it Laszlo, once I detail my plan. Each day one of us will fix the ticket. We will wait at the dining-room until there is a line-up. The four of us will stand in the following sequence: three good ticket holders, followed by the owner of the one we doctored. There are four of us, we shall alternate daily. Each of us will be one third less hungry and we will beat the Communists twenty times each month. To assure our success, the first three of us will grumble about the long waiting. That will make the attendants somewhat less observant. We will try this out tomorrow. I will go first and my failure or success will determine Laszlo's future. If I fail he can leave, he can quit, he can throw in the towel without any argument from any of us. Do we have a deal?"

Jeno and Peter both agreed and I-having nothing to lose, but a portion of my hunger-acceded.

***

My heartbeat quickened as I stood in the long line, Jeno behind me, followed by Peter and then Ocsi.

"The line is moving too slowly," I complained, my voice shaking, as I neared the ticket handler.

"I am hungry, blast this line-up," Jeno grumbled, after me.

"Maybe only members of the Communist Party should be given the job to punch the tickets. I am sure they would be a lot more efficient," Peter announced boldly.

My ticket was closely examined, then punched and I took a step forward, anticipating nothing but the coming calamity. Jeno's ticket was punched out next and he captured the needed punch-out. Peter's ticket was hardly looked at, as the checker tried to be more proficient. Then the crucial moment arrived.

"Hurry up man, you are holding up the line..," the official urged Ocsi, as he processed his doctored ticket.

The four of us sat down by an empty table; gave each other a knowing look and I broke out in a rare smile, nodded my head to concede Ocsi's victory.

Day after day we alternated holding the modified meal ticket and when each of us had tasted victory at least on five occasions, we congratulated Ocsi.

"I am staying...We beat the bastards twenty times," I sang out in jubilation.

"The four of us are formidable," Peter announced proudly.

"Ocsi you are a genius..," Jeno proclaimed loudly, as we sat around in our tiny room.

"Thank you guys for having given my plan a chance. We have eliminated some of our hunger; we have beaten the Communists."

***

Time has passed and the arrival of the early spring; the balmy, warm days that greeted us the middle of March, gave us cause to rejoice. Our hunger eased; we no longer suffered from the chill of winter; our studies were no less demanding, yet far more bearable than before. The cold winter, that was behind us; the daily, small victory, we have created at the dining room, strengthened the bonds of our friendship. The four of us became brothers. A good examination result was hailed by all of us. A poor mark received brought comments of encouragement to the recipient and help from the one whose strength lay in that subject. The occasional, small parcels of food that came from one home or another we shared without hesitation. Letters, any of us received, were read out loud, with a few exceptions. When the news was good we shared our joy; when it was bad we shared our sorrows.

Two weeks before Easter, I have received another letter and when my hesitation to open it was noticed by my three friends they began to chide me.

"Now I have seen everything! At other times you fell on Rozsa's letters like a hungry wolf. And now you dilly-dally," Ocsi hooted.

"How long do we have to wait? I want to know if she still loves you," Jeno cried out.

"Don't be such a chicken...Open that letter...Let us hear those lovely words of your intended," Peter teased me.

"If it was a letter from my beloved do you think I would wait?" I revealed my trepidation.

"So who else did write to you, if it is not from your worshipped Rozsa?" Peter's question came more soberly.

"That is what puzzles me...It is not my beloved's writing, but more like that of my Father."

"So open it and let's hear the news."

I tore the flap open, removed the single sheet and began to read. My three friends watched me with anxiety. They knew about my Father's unjust, long, trial-less imprisonment and granted me their silent waiting. Even when they heard my shout of 'How can I believe this?'; even when they saw my tears appear; when they saw me read it once more silently, they did not raise their voices, they just looked at me in watchful expectation. After the third silent reading I wiped away my tears of joy and began to speak.

"My Father wrote this letter...He wrote it from home...He was released. His imprisonment was a mistake, the authorities admitted. Almost six months he was in prison. My dear, innocent Father sat in prison since October for a crime he never committed. What am I to make of a political system that imprisons people; never gives them a trial and then declare their own deed a simple mistake?" I moaned in misery that spoiled the joyous news.

"They are swine..," Ocsi condemned them.

"They are unjust, treacherous, crude and unrepenting Communists pigs," Peter stated.

"All that we cannot change, but the good news we should celebrate," Jeno, the level headed, declared and waved at us his remaining Forints. "Let's go over to the tavern and I will buy all of you a beer."

**

We began our celebration. My first sip of beer made me brighten; the second one loosened my tongue and the third one made me smile even at strangers.

"You boys seem to be in a good mood...I feel kind of lonely. Do you mind if I join you and buy each of you a beer?" The stranger spoke up and without waiting for our invitation, he pulled his chair to our table. "And what are you young men celebrating?"

Each of us looked at the bearded man, who must have been in his mid-thirties. My three friends appeared ready to confide in our benefactor, but I remembered Bela Gero's perfidy, Alfie Kovacs's disappearance and placed a finger across my lips to command them to remain silent.

"We are celebrating nothing. We are students at one of the universities and we have neither the money nor the inclination to engage in revelry. We are here to enjoy a quiet beer." My cautious remarks received my friends' approval.

"Laszlo is right. But thanks for your offer anyway," Ocsi spoke.

"Are you refusing my offer? Are you university students too high and mighty to accept a beer from a simple truck driver?"

"Never do we refuse such a magnificent offer from anyone." Jeno's sensible comment made the stranger place the order for five tankards of beer.

"Well even if you have no reason to celebrate, do you mind if I do that? I have delivered a load of goods from Baja and made a tidy sum of money."

"You came from Baja?" I couldn't help asking.

"That is where I came from, that is where I live."

"So does Laszlo and so do I," Ocsi stated.

"Well this is a small world indeed...Maybe I should introduce myself. My name is Bandi Kemeny. Now let's enjoy our drink."

"I am Ocsi Parej and this here is Laszlo Lichter. The others are Peter Kovacs and Jeno Kiss. Thanks for the drinks Mr. Kemeny."

"You are welcome, I assure you. A minute ago I drank with strangers, but now I will order another round for my new friends. By the way I am not too old to be called Bandi by all of you and I shall reciprocate. I know your Father Ocsi and even yours Laszlo. Baja is a small city, not like Szeged. Ocsi's Father is a mailman and Laszlo's used to be the best shoe-maker in our city. That poor man can no longer make shoes...Unless he does it in prison."

"But he was released. I had a letter from him just today. We lied to you, I am sorry Bandi. It is my Father's release we are celebrating." My resistance broke down and I began to weigh the possibilities. "I haven't seen my Father since last Christmas. I haven't spoken to my beloved Rozsa, since then. I haven't held my darling's hand for almost three months. I have almost forgotten the sweetness of her rare kisses." I tortured myself and my desire to quit the university overwhelmed me.

"Well that is splendid news. Your Father is finally free. I knew he was innocent, but that rarely matters nowadays. Can I be candid with you boys? I have spent some time in prison for selling on the black-market, but they kept me for two weeks only. They recognized my talents early and put them to use. Now I deliver needed goods, but only for the Communist bosses and that way I make a lot of money and I face no danger at all."

"Is that what you are doing in Szeged?" I asked Bandi boldly.

"I was given a truck to use after my release from prison. From Baja I brought a load of furniture to furnish the homes of the mighty. On my return trip I will take a load of world famous salami, made in this great city, for the commies of Baja to enjoy. My truck is being loaded as we speak. Early tomorrow morning I will be rolling again."

"You said earlier that you are lonely. That is why you have joined us. Are you lonely during your trips?"

"Not if I can help it. Sometimes I pick up someone on the road. Sometimes I get lucky and have company all the way. I hate being alone..."

"Maybe I could give you company tomorrow morning?" I popped the question, alarming my friends with the possibilities.

"You are welcome to join me. It would be my pleasure indeed. I could pick you up anywhere, but it would have to be before six."

Before I could answer him my friends pounced on me.

"You cannot do that Laszlo. You will be finished if you leave," Ocsi tried to sway me.

Then it was Jeno's turn to offer his arguments: "Hunger almost made you quit, but Ocsi solved that problem; the winter's cold you have survived; you have no trouble with your studies; your Father is finally free, so why do such a foolish thing?"

Next came Peter and I have listened to his arguments, as I have listened to all the others, but my heart beat faster with the thought of seeing Rozsa and her cherished face, her beautiful blue eyes, her every feature beaconed to me, urged me to end our suffering.

"Let's go home boys, I have packing to do. Bandi please pick me up at the railway station. I will be there long before six." I stood up and marched out, preventing any further debate.

***

"What are you doing home?" My Father's first words didn't stop me from throwing my arms around him.

"I was so happy to get your letter. I had to see that you are really free."

"I wanted to see you too, I do admit, and I hope you have received permission for this visit?" His voice was stern, his eyes blazed with their usual fire.

"I had no time to seek permission from the university. I got a truck-ride home, quite unexpectedly."

"You threw away your future just to see me? I really doubt that! Surely you can give me a more believable reason?"

"I did this for many reasons!" I became indignant.

"You better begin to list them," came my Father's command.

I began to tell him my whole story, rather slowly, but as he listened to me patiently, as he nodded his head in understanding, at various stages of my narrative, the pace of my telling picked up and during the next half hour I have made a clean breast of it.

"I am sorry I wasn't able to help you when you most needed it. Life is a strange thing. An honest man works all his life to support his family. He never shirks his duty; never neglects those he loves and keeps a keen eye on every honest opportunity. He reaches out for success that promises plenty and with some luck the day comes when he sits at the top of his small world. Then his fortunes shift. What appeared to be his limitless, clear sky, suddenly clouds over. His fortunes fail; his friends desert him; he is accused falsely and even the means of making a living is taken from him. Joy and hope and success are replaced by bitterness and hopelessness and failure. All these things had happened to me.

"Had I not experienced life's traps and surprises, I wouldn't understand your decision Laszlo. I would condemn you for selling out your future for a plate of lentils, but I will not do that. Your switching universities does not trouble me. Whether you become a chemist or a teacher I will be equally proud of you. The hunger you felt for food I have felt during the war; the cold that made you shiver is no stranger to me; the hardship of your studies are no different from the things I have experienced; the bitterness you feel against the system is my bitterness too. The love you feel for Rozsa is the love I felt as a young man. My love for your Mother made me work so much harder. No sacrifice was too large; no loneliness was too intense to bear; no desire was too overwhelming; no obligation was too heavy to stop me from forging ahead. Now let me ask you a simple question: Do you love your Rozsa less than I loved your Mother?"

"I love her more than any man has ever loved...I adore her like no one was ever adored...That is why I have left the university," my answers poured out.

"You thought of only yourself Laszlo, that is a sin. If you love her as much as you stated than you must find a way to be reinstated!"

***

We were alone. My darling sat beside me listening to my monologue that detailed my experiences in Szeged; the reasons for my return and the conversation my Father and I had, just hours ago.

I feasted my eyes on my beloved. I drank in her beauty as I spoke; I immersed myself in being close to her. My friends, the university became fading memories, yet I was troubled. My mind searched for a solution to do what my Father commanded.

"What will you do now Laszlo?" My beloved spoke when she realized that I have stopped moments ago.

"I really do not know...What would you like me to do?"

"I love to have you with me. I missed you no less than you missed me. These things you ought to know. If you look for a job… If you find one, I will be content. If you find a way to return to the university, to complete your study, to become a teacher, my contentment will be replaced with happiness. When you were denied admission to Veszprem you were devastated. Years from now, when you look back on what you gave up for me, you may begin to hate me." Her voice revealed warmth; her words conveyed her sincerity; the way she held my hand, the way she trembled, the warm kiss she gave me spoke ever so clearly.

"You are mistaken, for I could never hate you. How could I go back my love? I left without their permission...They will never tolerate that."

"You will find a way, just use your imagination."

***

The next two days I have spent reflecting on my deed and when the Sun began to set, when dusk was about to arrive, I headed to see my beloved. The distance between our homes was over two and one half miles, a long walk, permitting me to search for a solution.

When the idea finally came I was almost ready to reject it. Later when I saw Rozsa, when I looked deep into her blue eyes; when I imagined our future together, I no longer hesitated.

"Let's go for a walk my dearest." I asked her and she walked beside me silently, unaware of my intention.

I led her in the direction of our city's only hospital, where I stopped at the gate that led to the emergency department. For one moment I hesitated. I dreaded the thought of being a patient, submitting myself to the care of any doctor, but my Father's words mingled with that of my love and I found new strength to carry out my unspoken resolution.

"Please wait me for my dearest...I must see someone," I asked her and without waiting for her agreement, I let go of her hand, entered the emergency department. When I made my request, the doctor looked at me strangely. Once his brief examination was completed, he announced his decision.

"I can do it tomorrow morning at nine o'clock, but you must check in tonight before seven. And just one other thing...We require all our patients to bring their own pillow."

I returned to Rozsa without any explanation and we have continued our walk toward where I lived.

"It is nice to see you Rozsa. When Laszlo is away you never come to see me." My Mother gave her a half-hearted greeting.

"May I have a pillow Mother?" I surprised both females with the unusual request.

"And what will you do with a pillow?" my Mother asked me, while Rozsa remained silent. Both of them stared at me in concern, but neither of them made any further inquiry.

"Please don't ask me any more questions. A pillow is what I need and I have no time to explain things."

"No time for me...Never any time for me... Well take this pillow and do whatever foolish thing you set your mind to doing. Now go, you seem to be in a great hurry."

Rozsa and I began our return walk, following the same route we took earlier. I hoped she wasn't going to press me for any explanation. I hoped with all my heart that she would not try to push me. I knew quite well that she would try to change my mind, once she knew my intention. I also knew that I wouldn't be able to resist her, that her slightest attempt to persuade me to abandon my plan would meet with success.

When we neared the entrance that led to the emergency ward, I stopped, faced her, looked into her beautiful eyes.

"What I am about to do will assure our future. Promise my love that you will not try to dissuade me."

"I promise you that, rather reluctantly. Ever since you went in to the emergency department I have been uneasy. When you asked your Mother for a pillow I began to suspect your intention. Are you planning to fake some illness? Are you trying to fool the doctors to obtain a medical certificate? Is that the solution you spoke about?"

"You are close to the truth my dear Rozsa, but I am not trying to fool anyone."

"Then what are you planning to do?"

"Tomorrow morning I will undergo an operation..."

"What? An operation? Have you gone insane Laszlo? You fear doctors...You hate hospitals...But most of all you have always dreaded the thought of being cut. What operation are you contemplating?"

"Everything you said my darling is very true. Yet I could find no other solution. As a child I have suffered with my tonsils. I had fevers, the chills, sore throat, on a few occasions I had experienced pain swallowing. My tonsils became enlarged, the doctor found and he is willing to do a tonsillectomy. Tomorrow morning at nine o'clock he will remove them."

"Dear God in Heaven...You are willing to do this for me?"

"For you my dearest and for my Father. I will be sick for a few days; I will recuperate for another week, but I will have a medical certificate for the university, explaining my absence."

"Are you certain Laszlo? Do you really want to do this?"

"You promised me Rozsa that you will not try to dissuade me."

"I promised that, but I had no idea..."

"I want to go back to the university; I want to become a teacher. I want you to be the wife of a learned man. You must agree to my stupid plan and you must help me."

"I will not argue; I will not beg you to change your mind. Tell me what can I do Laszlo?"

"You can come and visit me daily...And you could let my parents know."

"I will go and see them tomorrow morning. I will be here...I will sit with you and hold your hand...I will ease your pain...And I will love you even more." Her words wiped away my fears, her love that made her face radiant reinforced my resolution.

***

"Open wide!" The doctor ordered as I sat with my hands strapped to the arms of the chair. I was ready to scream when I have grasped the full nature of my operation. No general anesthetic, just a spray where he was to cut. Before the medication could freeze my tonsils, the doctor began to cut, to scrape, to cause pain and constant gagging. I began to retch. Had my arms been free I would have grabbed the doctor's probing hands; I would have stopped him from hurting me, but I was unable to do so...I closed my eyes, choked back my tears, controlled my rage, cursed my stupidity.

When the procedure was over, when the effect of the drug wore out, I felt the soreness, the painful fire that nested where my tonsils used to be. For four days I lay on my bed or sat in the sunlit yard of the institution. The frequent cones of ice-cream eased my pain only slightly, but when Rozsa came to visit me, when we looked into each other's eyes, when we held hands my pain departed.

She came to see me twice a day and when we were together the operation no longer mattered. I was truly happy. Once I was discharged from the hospital-clutching the priceless medical excuse in my hand-I returned the pillow to my Mother.

"You did a foolish thing Laszlo," she scolded me.

"I did what was necessary."

"The doctor advised us when you were barely seven to have your tonsils removed. When I told you, you screamed and kicked and fought against the idea, until I gave up on ever having your tonsillectomy. Later on your tonsils rarely bothered you, I seem to recall, yet you go and have it removed without ever telling me. Will I ever understand you?" She would have gone on chastising me had I stayed around, but I escaped her and went to see my Father.

"I must admit that I was angry. You never told us what you were planning. Rozsa had to come to inform us. You hurt your Mother, you hurt me badly. I hope you understand why we never went to see you?"

"I understand your anger Dad, but you must learn to understand me. You must recall the words you spoke to me, several days ago: 'You thought of only yourself Laszlo, that is a sin. If you love her as much as you stated than you must find a way to be reinstated!' This is what you said then and after two days of searching and finding a solution, after having the courage to carry out my painful plan, you berate me. I have this paper. The university will accept it and after Easter I will be back at Szeged to continue my studies. I thought you would be happy?"

"You know me well Laszlo. I am proud and stubborn. I rarely make an apology.

This is one of those times when I do so. I spoke those words, that much is true, but I have never ever dreamt what those words will cause you to do."

"Please don't apologize to me. You were right in what you said and I was wrong to leave the university. I may be hungry and cold and disgusted again; I most surely will be lonely, but never again will I abandon my studies. When the urge to do that grabs me hard I will touch the spot where my tonsils used to be and the memory of the operation will stop me."

"You did something very brave Laszlo. You have proved your respect for me and more than that, you have proved the depth of your love for Rozsa. That kind of love is rare. That magnitude of devotion is worth remembering."

***

A few days later, on Saturday, before Easter, my family joined the Buja's to watch the Resurrection parade. In spite of the covert attempts of the Communists the citizens of Baja lined the main street and rejoiced in the religious ceremony. As the priests walked by the crowd, hundreds of us fell behind them and joined the devout populace that dared to challenge the authorities.

When the parade reached the Priests' Church, entered its vestibule to celebrate the Holiest of all Masses, the church bells of our city rang out, filled our hearts and rolled over the far reaches of our community.

An hour later the Bujas said farewell to my parents and the two families separated. It took me only a moment's of hesitation to decide which family I should join and I fell in beside Rozsa.

"Where do you think you are going?" my Mother challenged.

"Leave Laszlo alone!" my Father hissed, his eyes flashed their warning and I was grateful to my Father for his acceptance, for his understanding.

***

Having finished the Easter Monday dinner, Rozsa and I sat in their yard, behind the closed gate, front of the picket fence that separated the yard from their vegetable garden.

"Does it still hurt?" she asked me kindly.

"I can barely remember..," I fibbed smoothly. "I am glad you didn't stop me."

"I wanted to...I couldn't stand the thought of you suffering, yet I dared not after you made me promise."

"I am grateful...For over two days I struggled to find a solution and the strength to carry it out once I found it. When I came home I never thought I would return to Szeged, but my Father's words and what you said gave me a lot to ponder. I did some calculating: I left the university two weeks before the beginning of our one week Easter break. I had three days home before the operation, five days in the hospital, six days home recuperating. These days account for the two weeks I was away from the university. When I present my medical document they will find no excuse to expel me. I am certain I will be readmitted." My voice trailed off and I began to think about another painful parting.

"You calculated very well Laszlo, yet you seem to be in distress. Are you thinking about our next parting?"

"That I am not looking forward to...Another parting at the station...Over two months of loneliness without you. Then five days at home. Five glorious days with you my Rozsa and then two months of service in the army. I already regret what I have done. I should have stuck with my original decision, that way we would enjoy daily each other's company."

"Don't talk like that ever Laszlo. Such foolish talk will solve nothing. We will take whatever comes our way and when you finish, our being away from each other will be only a fading memory."

"Yes it will be that. There is another thing I did not consider before."

"What is it that popped into your head Laszlo?"

"The compulsory military service is what I almost forgot. What a fool I was. Blinded by my love for you and hungering for seeing you, I left the university to be with you forever. I lost sight of all reality. University students are made to serve the military during the summer months, thus getting exemption from the draft. Others, who are drafted, are made to serve two or three years in the army. My years at university, with a lot of privileges, I almost exchanged for years of military service, with no privileges at all. I can't believe how foolish I was not thinking of that."

"Do not blame yourself any more Laszlo...You made it all right, even if the method you used was rather outlandish. We will say our good-byes at the train station this time and many more times before you return to me for good. We will suffer our parting in silence; we will endure our lonely days; we will dream about each other every night; we will write letters very often and the time will pass away."

***

The day before classes began I have returned to Szeged; entered the dormitory and poked my head into our tiny room.

"I don't believe my eyes...," Ocsi shouted, jumped up and embraced me.

"Laszlo is back. He changed his mind!" Peter followed Ocsi's example.

"I am also glad to see you..," Jeno spoke; his greeting contained less warmth than the others'.

"What is wrong Jeno?" I asked. "You have no wish to embrace me?"

"Maybe we should all sit down...I am happy you changed your mind, but your return to the university concerns me."

"I don't know what you mean," I blurted out.

"And I wish I didn't have to tell you. You were expelled for your absence, just one week after you left. A friend of mine works at the Registrar's office and she informed me."

I listened to Jeno patiently with a knowing smile crossing my face, but instead of telling them my story I began to play a game.

"Could they expel a student for being sick?"

"And what sickness did you have Laszlo? Love sickness may not be sufficient." Jeno remonstrated.

"Just answer my question. You have a friend in the Registrar's office, so based on the conversations you had with her, do you think they would expel someone who was absent due to being sick?"

"Not if the student notified them before his absence." His reply made sense.

"What if he was too sick to give notification?" I pressed on.

"He should have had someone designated."

"Designated to do what?" Ocsi asked and gave me a wink.

"To notify the Registrar's office."

"Well all of you must remember how sick Laszlo got that night when we came home from the tavern. What was your problem Laszlo? I seem to forget." Ocsi's devilishness wasn't missed by the others.

"My tonsils gave me a terrible time," I almost chuckled.

"Yes I remember now...You could hardly swallow the last bit of beer. You gagged on it; got sick to your stomach. You complained about intense pain and fever, when we came home and then you got the idea," Ocsi invented as he spoke.

"What idea? What pain? What are you talking about? Was I too drunk to remember any of this?" Jeno asked, but by that time Peter saw what Ocsi was trying to accomplish.

"I was sober and I remember clearly." Peter entered the conversation. "Laszlo got the idea to go home with that truck-driver and to have his Mother take care of him while he was sick."

"And he asked us, his friends, to notify the Registrar's office. You must recall Jeno that you were supposed to tell your girl-friend and she was to record Laszlo's illness. Either you forgot to do that or she was very sloppy," Ocsi continued.

"In your dreams boys. Are you trying to get her in trouble just to help Laszlo?"

"The four of us have cheated the system; we have become inseparable; we swore to help out each other. Or have you forgotten Jeno?" Ocsi pushed harder than before.

"I haven't forgotten a thing. To cause that girl that kind of trouble would mean the end of my relationship with her. Come to think of it that is not a bad idea...She has become rather demanding lately. Let's say I back up your story, I lie for Laszlo's sake. Would it make any difference really?" Jeno gave in.

"It would help some, but may be not enough." Peter was thinking out loud. "He could have gone home sick; he could have asked us to give notification of his illness, which Jeno gave, but got lost in the shuffle. Wouldn't they argue that Laszlo should have gone to see a doctor; should have gotten a medical excuse to cover his absence?"

When Peter finished, when Ocsi and Jeno nodded their heads in agreement, when the three of them looked at me sadly, my triumphant moment came.

First I waved the doctor's certificate above my head. Then I handed it to Peter. He read it, passed it to Ocsi, who handed it to Jeno.

"You crafty bastard," Jeno broke out laughing. "You had your tonsils removed? You have never told us a thing."

"You are not the only one I didn't inform. My Mother and Father are still bitter."

"Now I have seen everything...Your tonsils removed for a few days with your Rozsa. What next?" Jeno burst out laughing and then holding his belly, that shook with his laughter, he sputtered the words: "Don't you ever give in to another urge Laszlo. Your tonsils are gone and voluntary castration will not be to your liking."

***

The following day the four of us appeared in the Registrar's office.

"My name is Laszlo Lichter. I like to see the Registrar." I made my request and within moments I sat across from the skinny, short-sighted, old man.

"What can I do for you?"

"I was told I must see you after I return from my illness."

He searched for my file for several minutes. When he found it he squinted at its contents, then at me.

"You were expelled two weeks ago."

"You must be kidding. I got deathly sick; I sought immediate medical attention comrade and for that you expelled me?"

"We have our rules young man. You should have notified us in advance."

"Before I got sick I should have notified you about my illness? Is that what you are saying?"

"Well not exactly. You should have notified us when you became sick."

"I see...I should have gotten your permission comrade to begin my illness?"

"You come to me to seek a favor and you get cheeky with me. That is most unusual. You should have had someone notify us, after you became sick, if you were too ill to do that. Am I making myself clear?"

"You did and I will reciprocate. I got very sick; I was immediately transported to the city where my parents live. One of my room-mates notified one of your clerks and if you were running this office as efficiently as our beloved Communist Government expects it, you would have known, you wouldn't have expelled me." I saw him pale, as I spoke those threatening words.

"Oh I see. It was not I who was notified, but one of my clerks. They are humans, make mistakes. I am not prepared to carry out a witch-hunt. If you were indeed sick you would have a medical certificate, which I do not see."

"Is it a medical certificate that is needed? If I had one you would re-admit me?"

"You are absolutely right...But, since you haven't produced one, your expulsion shall remain."

I touched my throat, cleared it slowly, pretended to speak with a new-born difficulty.

"Is...this...what you need...comrade?"

He raised the paper, I handed him, close to his thick glasses; read it slowly, while his color took on the hue of a fully formed red rose, then he slowly placed the document in my file.

"I cannot make a sick boy pay for a mistake that was made in this office. I hope you have fully recovered to continue your studies. I hope you will forget the mistake that was made. The mistake wasn't yours it belongs to another. I will immediately notify your department." The Registrar rose, extended his hand and I was fully reinstated.

That night the four of us celebrated my success and the bond of our friendship became even stronger.

***

We always ate breakfast together, when we had something to eat. We went our separate ways when our classes so demanded. When Thursdays came we waited for each other and walked together to the huge lecture hall to receive our political indoctrination.

We were no longer bothered by the stupidity of the buffoons who read the lecture notes. They read with some difficulty, rarely deviating from the type-written text, but when they strayed they added tidbits of personal trivia from their own lives, probably to increase their own importance, thus they have revealed pride in coming from the mines, the fields or from the factories; they bragged about their lack of education and declared their love for the Communist Party, their benefactor, responsible for elevating them to their undeserved status. The four of us always sat together, passed snide notes to each other, unable to resist the temptation of daring the State, cheating the prying eyes, yet never forgetting the fate that awaited us, if we were ever discovered.

No political lecture was ever delivered without the raised voice of our lecturer announcing that "Our beloved Father, Stalin, who learned at the feet of the all knowing

Lenin, who is adored by millions, upon millions of people around the globe, will unite all destitute Nations; will free the enslaved multitudes; will wipe off the face of the earth the power hungry, greedy, exploiting capitalists. Everything will belong to the State, to the people. All will work according to their abilities! All will share in the Global Nation's wealth, according to their needs! Peace will reign over the world and happiness will be known by the enslaved, as it is known by all of you, fortunate citizens of Hungary."

Each and every Thursday night we talked and laughed and mocked our 'professors of Thursday mornings'-as we called our political instructors. We discussed earnestly the Leninist doctrines.

"Everyone will work according to their ability! Isn't that what our 'Professor' shouted again? By now I have heard it so many times that I will surely get an 'A' in the subject of Marxism-Leninism." Ocsi spoke up Thursday night, after we locked our door, after we assured complete privacy.

"That is what he shouted and in his enthusiasm his face took on the color of his red hair. He looked like an idiot on fire. Yet some of the students bought into their doctrine. Some fell for the lies. Gobbled up his every word. Why did God ever create morons?" Peter asked in stupefaction.

"They want to get ahead. Those guys and gals joined the party. They play at being Communists, just like their Fathers and Mothers did," Jeno observed wryly.

"That is not their only purpose..." I began to explain what I believed. "They want power. 'Everyone will work according to their ability.' Didn't Lenin say so? But who is to determine a human being's ability? Those in power will have that luxury. You and I, my dear friends, will be found to have great abilities to slave. Just as we are made to slave now. On how many Sundays did they make us give up our Sunday walk or a soccer game? How many times did they herd us to the trains, took us into some field of a collective farm and made us slave with no pay at all?"

"Laszlo is right... That is why they have joined the party. They want the advantages of having power," Ocsi spoke.

"But that is not all. Lenin also declared that 'All will share in the Global Nation's wealth, according to their needs!' And who will determine what the need of an individual is? Those who get their hands on power. They are already doing it. While we slave and wipe our brows from the sweat of labor where are the Communists? When we are made to dig for potatoes, they supervise us, sitting at the edge of the field, gorging themselves on fresh bread, fat salamis, drinking beer or wine, while we crave for a sip of water. The cotton we pick is turned into suits by other slaves. Not us, nor them had the means to buy a new piece of garment, only the rotten Communists could afford such luxury. While we are made to look for potato bugs, allegedly dropped by the planes of the imperialists, what do they do? They are holding a seminar of young Communists. They are putting their heads together to dream up another scheme. 'The imperialists are hell bent to destroy our potato crop...,' they announce and we are made to search the potato fields for Colorado bugs. 'The enemies of Communism are planning to burn down our grain elevators...,' they dream up another threat and we are to spend some of our nights in the highest church steeples as fire wards. Our abilities are great, so we are made to do everything; our needs are almost non-existent, so our share of the Nation's wealth is almost nil." I finished my dissertation and in one night destroyed almost everything accomplished by our political indoctrination.

So the four of us learned from each other and to wipe away our occasional miseries we laughed and mocked and scorned and despised the young Communists.

Then a Thursday morning came when Ocsi still felt the illness that came upon him the night before. We urged him to stay in bed, not to attend his classes, but he insisted to climb out of bed, to get himself ready and the three of us waited.

"We will be late..," Jeno muttered.

"Better late than not attending," Peter stated.

"Do you guys think we should go ahead?" I questioned, somewhat shyly.

"Not on your life! The four of us will go together." Peter stated and half an hour later we opened the door, poked our heads into the crowded lecture hall, climbed the twenty or so stairs to the top row and took our usual seats, while the lecturer paused, shook his head and after a brief hesitation he continued.

"...as I was saying before we were interrupted, the Americans experience recession after recession, while our economy proceeds in an orderly manner. Our Five Year Plan, not unlike that of our beloved, magnificent ally, the Soviet Union, created the climate where nothing is left to chance. Our Plan sets out the amount of seeds that are to be planted and the tons of produce that will be our harvest. Our Plan is built on study, research and the wisdom of our leaders. Our leaders know the needs of our people, thus they determine what we must produce. Let me give you an example: During the next five years we shall need seventy-five thousand apartments. Each apartment will consist of two rooms of equal size. Then we calculate how many square feet of wall needs to be built. The number of bricks that are needed.

"We know that even the Americans try to imitate us, but they are fools, they know nothing. They try to smuggle spies into our country to find out the secrets of our success. Sometimes they do succeed, but to no avail. Their work force and ours are totally unlike. Their workers are lazy, where ours are enthusiastic. Their workers demand double pay for work on Sunday. Our workers volunteer their day freely. With songs on their lips they march to their factories, to their fields, to their place of labor on more and more free Sundays. They want to reach the end of the long road. Picture this comrades: the first road sign they ever saw, 'Fascism', made their hearts bleed. The next one, 'Liberation', made them rejoice. The sign, 'The First Three Year Plan', put food in their stomachs and hope in their souls. The sign that followed, 'The First Five Year Plan', allowed them to see the glorious future planned by our worshipped Father, Stalin. Now they look far ahead and they see two more signs: 'Socialism', followed by 'Communism's' and they can hardly wait for the end." Our digressing lecturer stopped, took a sip of water and I palmed my scribbled note, placed it front of Ocsi.

"Aren't we all waiting for the end?" my note stated and Ocsi smiled at me, nodding his head.

"Well I got carried away...Back to the example I began to give you." Our 'professor of Thursday morning' announced and continued.

"As I said we know the number of apartments needed, the total wall space and the number of bricks. Our brick makers and our brick layers have great skills, but they are not as good as those craftsmen of the Soviet Union. The Soviet artisans come to our country and give their time freely to teach their brothers how to make bricks faster, how to lay them with even more skill. We learn from them; we establish a new hourly quota and we know that our Five Year Plan will be reached in four years or less.

"We experience no vandalism like they do in capitalist countries. We have no sabotage any more, like we had in the beginning. Nobody malingers any more. Slackers are not tolerated by the workers..." Our lecturer paused for effect and dropped his bombshell.

"But there are still a very few, and I assure you they are among us, who are playing into the imperialists' hands. They are the late-comers to this lecture...They sit up there, in the top row. Stand up, you boys!" He pointed at us, ordered us and we stood reluctantly.

"You are the enemy of this Nation. You are the betrayers of our Soviet brothers. You are not worthy to be among us. Your lateness betrayed your traitorous nature." He would have continued to berate us, I was certain, but the shrill bell stopped him and surprised me, almost as much as did his denunciation.

***

I left the lecture hall in a daze. It was time to have our dinner, but my appetite was replaced by fear. I parted from my friends of treason, headed to my afternoon classes and until the coming of the evening, felt nothing but apprehension.

"Will they banish us? Will they treat us like they treated those two innocent girls? Had I undergone the operation to regain my place at the university for nothing? Am I going to be forced to give up my dream? They cannot do that...They will not do that...After all what crime have I committed? We were ten minutes late to a lecture...Surely that is no crime at all. Why did our professor make our lateness into such a big issue? He called us traitors, malingerers, supporters of the imperialists, betrayers of our Soviet brothers! Are they planning to set another example?" My thoughts rolled on like thunder clouds, preventing me from listening to Professor Kobor, whose chemistry lectures never failed to fascinate me. I sat in my seat, my mind in turmoil and to end my seemingly endless worries I forced myself to think of pleasant thoughts.

"If they expel me I will be able to see my darling Rozsa. I will explain to her what has happened. Her Father received unfair treatment too, she will understand. She may even be happy. My Father will not blame me. Was he not imprisoned unjustly? Was he not robbed by the Communists? His experience with our present rulers will make him see." My earlier apprehensions were replaced by joy.

"I quit before. I left the university to be with my beloved. By doing so I gave up my entire future, or so I believed...Now, they will make that choice for me." I espoused this last thought, almost as warmly as I imagined the wonderful moment when I will be able to embrace my Rozsa. I have imagined seeing her within days; kissing her upon my arrival, holding her ever so tightly, never ever having to leave her again.

***

I barely entered our tiny room, when Ocsi spoke up. "Well that was some display of true stupidity."

"What can we expect?" Jeno asked and continued. "When students do not show up for political lectures-I am sure all of you have noticed the empty seats-nobody says a word, but when we are late, well that is a different story."

"Have you ever seen anybody coming in late?" Peter queried.

"Now that you mention it, I cannot recall," I replied, still hopefully happy.

"We were more than stupid," Jeno announced.

"What do you mean?" I popped the question.

"I have never seen anybody coming in late, but the empty seats did not escape me. Yet I have never put two and two together. The others, whose interest in political indoctrination couldn't possibly exceed ours, had it figured out a long time ago...If you cannot get there on time, don't get there at all. That is what they must have been doing. That is what we shall do in the future."

"What future? They will surely expel us," I announced, unable to hide my hope.

"You would really like that Laszlo? You would rush home, embrace your Rozsa, hoping never to leave her again. I know that is what you think, but once again the draft you have forgotten." Ocsi's statement sobered me greatly.

"How can we avoid the consequences of our deed?" I asked and the return of my fear, of my sanity, shook me.

"We will wait and see what comes tomorrow. I have reason to believe that our 'professor of Thursday' was only blowing steam," Jeno announced and his certainty eased my reborn fear.

"What did you guys think of his impromptu example concerning our glorious building activities?" Ocsi tried to divert my attention from my disquiet.

Before I could give my opinion Peter spoke up. "I nearly laughed...With each lecture he becomes more daring...The red-headed idiot. He digresses from the prepared lecture and wonders into areas that creates nothing but dissatisfaction. Speaking about increased quotas; the happiness of our people and the Soviets, who come into our country to show our workers how to increase their productivity, are touchy topics with the masses. If he tries to push for our expulsion, I know exactly what to do."

"And what is that?" I spoke again.

"Rakosi is concerned about the growing dissatisfaction of his subjects. He wouldn't take kindly to professors who do not follow the Communist Party's ideological twists and turns." Peter winked at us knowingly. "I think a report signed by the four of us, attesting to the misdeeds of the red-head, would cause his expulsion and not ours."

"And what would the report say?" Ocsi inquired.

"Our professor does not stick to the prepared lectures...Maybe he does that for a purpose? He calls attention to the ever growing production quotas, thus he creates dissension. He takes every opportunity to reduce the number of his students, by recommending expulsions. Wasn't he the one who had those two girls expelled for a loving caricature of Stalin? He never saw that master-piece, as I recall it was never found. He is probably an enemy of the Nation. If we state these accusations, in writing...If we sign it and may be get a few more signatures, Rakosi will probably throw him to the dogs, just to satisfy us and other disenchanted citizens of the country." Peter laid out his plan, convinced us that it had a chance to work.

"I think Peter is right...Rakosi is always looking for scapegoats, particularly now," Jeno suggested.

"And why is that Jeno?" I asked softly.

"Do you not read the papers Laszlo? Have you not read Rakosi's last speech?"

"I use the papers in a different manner..," I didn't need to elaborate.

"Well it wouldn't hurt you to read some of the articles. The pictures you use and the way you use them may give you some satisfaction, but little enlightenment." Jeno chuckled, no doubt conjuring up my activities in the outhouse, while at my home, and in the bath-room where I had the extra satisfaction of flushing away our beloved leaders. "In his last speech Rakosi said something that caught my eyes: 'You Hungarians complain constantly that our *zsemle* is becoming smaller...It is not the buns that are getting smaller, it is your mouth that is becoming bigger.' That is what he said and you know what that means. He recognizes the restlessness of his people and he is ready to sacrifice a few Communists. That is his usual method of satisfying his people."

"If he wants to please us he should do away with the quotas," Ocsi stated.

"Oh the quotas...Well I should know something about that." Peter launched into a story. "My Father works in a factory, where they manufacture parts for tractors. He is a lathe operator. A few months ago they brought in a modern piece of Soviet machinery, placed it beside the ancient machines my Father and his co-workers toil on. Then a Soviet *Stachanovitch*-an expert lathe operator-arrived, he worked on that superb piece of equipment for thirty minutes and produced five splendid parts.

"Next the factory manager called a meeting of all lathe operators. This is what he told them: 'You have seen what our Soviet brother was able to accomplish. He manufactured five precision pieces of parts in thirty minutes. You comrades have eight hours each day and what do you produce? Sixteen pieces in eight hours! That is two pieces an hour only. Less than one half of what our Soviet brother was able to make. Starting today your quota is raised to forty pieces, each and every work day. I know you will produce even more. This is why we have decided to give a bonus to every one of you for every piece above the norm. I know you will earn a lot more; you will fulfill your quota enthusiastically. However there are still a few slackers among you. Would it not be fair to punish them for sabotaging the Five Year Plan? Sure it would! If we reward with extra wages those of you who excel, we should do something about the shirkers. For each piece produced under forty their pay packets will contain less.'

"My Father tried to do his best with the antediluvian machinery...He really tried and when he failed, his pay packet was cut by twenty-five percent. My family starved on his previous wage and thanks to the Soviet experts, the *Stachanovitchs*, my family became experts in the art of starving."

"Those Soviet *Stachanovitchs* are something else...," I recalled what I heard from my Uncle Pista and decided to tell his story.

"My Uncle, I will call him Pista, is a waiter. He has the opportunity to hear many stories from the inebriated. I know that Pista hates the Russians with all his heart, that he killed many Russian soldiers during the war, when he served as a paratrooper. So the many anti-Russian stories he bombarded me with I have no desire to repeat, but the one I am about to tell you came from his brother, Pal, who to this date is employed as a special brick-layer. His story is about two Soviet *Stahanovitchs*, who came into Hungary and traveled around demonstrating their fantastic skills. They have moved from town to town, from city to city to build brick walls, while being timed. Pal was made to travel with them and his job he was sworn never to reveal.

"In each place, the two Soviets visited, they had built five meter long, two meter high brick walls. Their fantastic achievement was timed each time. They never spent more time than one hour and forty minutes to achieve their feat. So the brick-layers quotas were raised to match that of their Soviet brothers. Each demonstration was followed by a five minute address by the local Communist boss and then the spectators and the Soviets were ushered away to celebrate.

"Pal was the only one left behind. His task was simple. Brick by brick, he was to take down the hastily built wall. People were told that the task was necessary to save the bricks. Pal knew better. Those brick walls were held by little mortar, had no strength at all, a year or two all of them would collapse.

"'A scam it is…Nothing, but a rotten scam. Their flimsy wall would not stand long, yet the speed record the Soviets set had to be matched by everyone, if they were to receive a bonus and not a penalty instead. Those criminals, the Communist bosses, have no concern for the safety of those who will dwell within those walls. Their desires to raise the quota; to fulfill it; to report the glorious achievements to the higher authorities are the only things they care about.' He confided to trusted family members the misery he felt, but after each of his confessions he urged us never to reveal what he said. Whenever we begged him to leave that cursed job, he just shook his head sadly. 'I have signed that foolish contract for five years, before I knew the exact nature of my job. I have tried to get out a few times, but each time the specter of Siberia was raised and I did not crave to enter the hell Jozsef returned from. Pal was referring to another Uncle of mine who was captured by the Russians in 1945 and was taken to Siberia. 'I too have a family. To me they are most important..' Pal closed the subject and still serves in the same capacity."

"What a country we live in..," Jeno lamented.

"We probably should have been born long ago, or maybe not at all," Ocsi stated.

We had talked, swapped stories late into that night. I had the distinct feeling that they were like I, willing to talk about anything; keen to dredge up all the injustices the Communist regime perpetrated, thus avoiding the topic that really bothered us: the coming day and the consequences of our great crime of lateness.

***

When the first rays of the sun began to fill our room, the four of us rose, wiped the night's sleep or sleeplessness from our eyes, according to our needs and sat down by our table. The one, small loaf of bread we shared. We spread goose fat on the slices from Ocsi's small bottle. We ate in absolute silence, each of us occupied, like I was, with our own thoughts, fears and apprehensions. The plan and stories of the previous night were momentarily forgotten.

Without word we have cleaned bread-crumbs from the table; grabbed our notebooks and left our room. Our walk took us by the custodian's small office. We were about to pass by the large bulletin board laden with various announcements, when Ocsi's eyes fell on the largest, newest poster.

"Look at this...Can you believe it?" His whispered words captured our attention, as did the caricature and the letter below it.

"It is us...I must be the short one; you, Jeno the lanky lad; Peter with his prematurely balding head and Ocsi with that exaggerated, beaky nose." I whispered at my companions. "Look at the American flag we are waving. See the Hungarian and Soviet flags trampled under our feet?"

""Let's read the letter..," Ocsi urged us and all four of us began to read.

"Dear Peter Veres, Jeno Kiss, Ocsi Parej and Laszlo Lichter,

"No doubt you will be surprised to receive this letter from the President of the United States. I was moved to write to you to tell you how much your support is appreciated.

"Any enemy of Communism is a true friend of mine, I am certain you know that. Sabotage is what we love; saboteurs of any Communist country are truly cherished. Keep up the good work my dear friends.

"Your mentor, your guide, your devoted supporter...

"Harry S. Truman

"President of the United States." The letter ended.

"What imagination these young Communists have. They must have wrecked their stupid brains to come up with this nonsense," Ocsi stated.

"They are willing to do anything to cast others in unfavorable light and to ingratiate themselves," Jeno moaned in misery.

"If this is the only poster, maybe we should remove it," I suggested meekly.

"That is exactly what they want. We will leave it here; let the bastards have their way," Peter announced firmly and the four of us moved on to find at least one poster in every one of the university departments, not unlike the one in our dormitory. The caricatures varied slightly, indicating different authors, but the letters were all the same.

During that day and for weeks after we were condemned by many publicly, but the reactions, given in private, by students who never knew us, coupled with no action indicating expulsion, were truly gratifying.

"'I am honored to have a friend of President Truman in my class...' I shared the comment-made by Professor Kobor, in the privacy of his office-with my friends and conspirators that night.

"That is nothing...Just listen to what happened to me." Ocsi smirked with pleasure as he spoke up. "You know that I am not attractive to the opposite sex. My big nose and my other features don't exactly turn females on, but my fate has changed, thanks to those posters. A beautiful blond approached me. 'Could I have a word with you Ocsi Parej? I have recognized you from the caricature.' She announced, led me to an isolated spot on campus, planted a small kiss on my ugly mug and asked me for a date, with the following words: 'Would you care to spend an evening with a commoner? I would enjoy the company of a friend of Mr. Truman.' You can imagine how gladly I accepted her bold invitation."

"Those stupid Communist bastards sure played into our hands," Peter smiled, before he began to share with us what happened to him. "I went to the dining-room at noon, hoping to find you guys, but I became somewhat impatient. So I have joined the line and as we were admitted, I sat down by a table. When I have finished my meal I was still hungry, but not much longer. Without a word a piece of meat was placed on my plate by a young lady; followed by a slice of cake from a boy, who sat across from me. They spoke not a word; they just smiled at me as they stood up and left me to enjoy my banquet."

"Maybe we should be late more often," Jeno suggested and gave us his nicest smile to indicate that he was being facetious.

"Never again will I be late to our political indoctrination." I promised solemnly and from that time on President Truman's friends were never late, but rarely attended.

***

Our popularity slowly vanished, new events have replaced the old and final examinations loomed on the horizon. Those of us, who studied constantly, continued our practice, while others began to cram. Rarely did we find time to chat and when we did all our talks centered on our more difficult subjects.

"The first set of exams we have all survived, two of you with flying colors." Ocsi moaned, bleary eyed from his hours of study.

"It will be no more difficult this time..," I tried to assure him.

"No more difficult for you Laszlo and for Peter. God gave you brains, but what about me?"

"Don't underestimate yourself Ocsi," Peter tried to calm him.

"I never do that as you well know, but if I fail even one subject I will be out. No supplementaries are permitted," Ocsi replied.

"That is true, but not one of us will fail. We will help each other," Peter promised and I offered my help as well.

For two solid weeks, at the end of June, we have gone our separate ways either to write one exam or another and when that task was over we began to face the ordeal of oral examinations.

The day I was to appear front of the Russian Language Department's Examination Committee, even I felt some trepidation.

"My knowledge of that language is almost non-existent," I admitted, but only to myself and the fear of failure engulfed me.

During the year we had studied fifty-two units, as they called them. The first five were quite simple, but the others were more complicated. I dreaded the coming ordeal and weighed my chances of failure or success.

I remembered the hundreds of curse words I have learned from members of the occupying army, knowing full well that those words wouldn't help me. I remembered hardly any Russian we were exposed to during the last two years at the Gymnasium. I recalled even less of what little Russian my professor half-heartedly attempted to beat into our heads.

All of these things ran through my head as I walked toward the university to face my examiners, yet each time when I was about to lose all hope of passing another memory intruded.

***

Late in May I have made a dreadful mistake. The professor asked me a question, of course in Russian, something about a mother. Before I could think clearly, I have utilized a choice phrase the Russian soldiers were in the habit of using frequently. I was summoned to the professor's office, where he reprimanded me for my rich, four letter vocabulary. He seemed to be in a pensive mood, appeared reluctant to dismiss me, so I sat there and waited. Then he began to speak and I learned about his background.

Before the war he was a professor of languages. He had full command of German, French and English. He was eager and happy to teach keen, young men and women the language they chose freely. Then the war came and he was drafted; in 44 he was captured by the Soviet Army and sent to a concentration camp in Siberia. When I heard that, I told him about my Uncle Jozsef, whose fate was no different from that of his and I got carried away, repeating stories my Uncle told me. He listened to me, from time to time nodded his head in agreement, and as I finished my second-hand stories, he displayed his trust that truly surprised me.

"They released me in 1949, after five years in that living hell. The condition of my release was simple. I was to teach in this university the Russian language I have learned and truly abhor. Each time I enter the class, each time I begin to teach, mostly unwilling students, like you Laszlo, my memories of the camp flood my mind and my lack of enthusiasm pains me. Had you been given a choice what language would you have chosen?" He asked me candidly.

Without hesitation I replied, "I would have chosen English. Learning that language gave me joy."

"And how long did you study the language I most love?"

"Two years...Then I was forced to switch to Russian."

"What a tragedy. When one loses the freedom of choice, one loses a part of himself."

It was after his statement that I couldn't resist and told him almost everything that happened to me and to those I loved. I spoke about Laurel and Hardy; my correspondence with my pen-pal; my Father's tragic life. I spoke about my beloved Rozsa and the injustices her family had suffered. I have described what happened to Alfie Kovacs; the two girls who were expelled and I ended my rather long monologue with the posters and the letter from the American President.

"I saw those posters...I knew you were one of them...Had you not been declared a friend of President Truman I would have reprimanded you today and that is where our conversation would have ended" he admitted and allowed himself a small chuckle.

"It is strange how things evolve. When the posters first appeared I was sure we will be expelled, but as it turned out our lateness turned into a blessing." It was my turn to smile at the recollection of that event.

"A blessing indeed, no thanks to your political instructor. When he demanded the expulsion of those two young ladies, the university's President gave his consent. Shortly after we have formed a professors' committee and managed to get to vote on all important issues, including all proposed expulsions. Our President was greatly relieved, the last thing he wanted to do was to take full responsibility for decisions made, without being able to hide behind a committee. Thus it happened that by the time your expulsion was recommended and that of your three friends, that decision was to be made by the five of us. Your staunchest supporter was Professor Kobor, I don't mind to tell you. He was furious with your accuser and in his anger he attacked him.

"'For one single occasion of lateness you would have four young men give up their dream of becoming teachers?' he asked the Communist.

"'My party demands nothing less, but the expulsion of all enemies of the Nation.' Your accuser shouted at Professor Kobor.

"'Are you saying that a student being late to one of your classes makes him the enemy of the Nation?' Kobor pressed.

"'That is exactly how I view the event. And I am not the only one. Have you seen the posters and the letter the students created? Have you noticed their anger?'

"'I have indeed. Were they any less angry some five months ago when someone else was late?' Kobor spit out the words.

"'I cannot recall that particular event, but I can assure you they must have been just as angry.'

"'And in their anger have they demanded expulsion? Or should I use the word *resignation*?' Kobor persisted.

"'What is your point Professor Kobor? Make it...' Our President could no longer remain quiet.

"'Very well then, I will make my point. Five months ago six hundred students sat and waited for over two hours for the late appearance of this comrade. When the four students were ten minutes late, a total of forty minutes were lost from political indoctrination and that is called sabotage, but what about the twelve hundred hours those six hundred students lost? That is far more than sabotage, I think. Lets expel these four young men, I am all for it and lets demand this comrade's resignation for the crime he has committed.' Kobor played his cards right and the rest of us enjoyed the accusing comrade's silence, his pasty expression.

"'I think we should vote, but only on the expulsion of those four young men. The comrade's lateness is to be judged only by the Communist party.' The President announced and when he called for the question there were five 'nays' for your expulsion."

"We have wondered as to what had happened," I finally spoke up.

"Well you know now...The hour is getting late, you have a lot of studying to do for your examinations. I enjoyed our conversation and I would appreciate your discretion."

"I thank you too for trusting me. What you told me will never be repeated. You are right I have a lot to study, especially in your subject, Russian."

"If I were you I wouldn't worry too much. The last thing I want to do is fail any of my students." He sounded reassuring, but it wasn't him I feared.

"You may not want to fail anyone, but the others on the committee..."

"I see now what bothers you Laszlo. Well to put you at ease I tell you a secret. My students don't know much Russian, my committee members know even less. When you come in for your oral remember this: Always raise your eyes to the heavens and always look for the right choice."

His mysterious words meant nothing to me then and whenever his words came to mind I tried to ponder their significance, as I did now, standing in the corridor with many other students before we were to face the examination committee.

"What did my professor mean? 'Always raise your eyes to the heavens and always look for the right choice.' Was he being philosophic or am I to take his words literally?" I asked myself, time and time again, and watched as a student entered the examination room and some twenty minutes later, when he reappeared.

"How was it?" Several of us asked in unison.

"Dreadful...I don't think I have ever seen anything like this," came his reply and a strong fear gripped me.

"Can you tell us more?" I asked, but his reply was too late for the unfortunate student who was next to enter.

"We had covered during the year fifty-two units of study. There were fifty-two cards on the table, all of them face down. Four rows of thirteen cards. The professor rearranged them, and then he asked me to select one. After I did, the committee members turned their note-books to the unit I picked and began to ask their questions. I wasn't really lucky. The unit I picked dealt with Russian writers, with a number of poems and the most convoluted topics of grammar. Even what little I knew I suddenly have forgotten." He gave us the information, hung his head and left.

"I will have to choose a card...If only I could pick the right one," I thought and the professor's words echoed in my mind. 'Always raise your eyes to the heavens and always look for the right choice.' Did he give me a hint? Was he suggesting how to pick a card? If that is what he did the words 'heaven' and 'right' must have great significance. What could they mean? Could *heaven* mean the top and could *right* mean the direction? How could that be? He shuffles the card before I could take one..." I struggled with the puzzling idea and then it was my turn to enter.

***

"Sit down Comrade Lichter. We shall begin as soon as we are ready," my professor addressed me and looked at his two committee members, who signaled their agreement to begin.

"The cards you see front of you represent each unit of our study. When you pick one you will show us what you got and all our questions will relate to the topics of that unit and nothing else. These are the rules of this committee." He announced and smiled at me encouragingly, while he very slowly, carefully moved the cards around and rested one hand on the top, right card just for a fraction of a second.

I have noticed not only his smile, but his slight hesitation and the words he spoke rushed at me once again, making me reach out for the card that was in the top right corner. Before I dared to look at what I picked I showed it to my examiners.

"You may want to pick another one...Unit number one is not exactly complicated." One of the committee members spoke up and I shook my head.

"No, unit number one is not really a challenge, but we have our rules. He picked that card and he need not exchange it." My professor made his ruling.

"But that is not fair...," the other member of the committee began to argue.

"Well I will make it fairer...If Comrade Lichter wants to stay with his pick the highest mark we will give him will be a 'B', even if his answers are all perfect. Will that satisfy all of you?"

"I does me..," said one, somewhat reluctantly.

"The same goes for me..," announced the other.

"It is fine with me..," I blurted out my relief.

Ten minutes later I stepped outside, felt like I have just graduated from kindergarten. I was asked to conjugate the simplest verbs; I was told to recite a childish poem; I was ordered to translate sentences that only a five year old child would utter. Having done well all the basic things they asked me, my guilt battled with my happiness.

On my way home it finally hit me: my professor and I, two haters of everything Russian, scored our own kind of victory.

***

On July second the four of us stood in line to pick up our 'record books' and when I have finally held in my hand the black book bearing my name and picture, I have turned to the seventh and ninth pages where my marks were recorded:

"I can't believe it..." I turned to Ocsi, Jeno and Peter. "Five is the highest mark and I have received that in Political Science, Hungarian Literature, General and Inorganic Chemistry, Laboratory Practice, Military Theory and Pedagogy. Only a four in Psychology, Russian Language, General Science, Algebra, Higher Mathematics. Geometry and Physical Education were the lowest, but that is no surprise, I am lucky I even got three in those subjects." I wasn't trying to brag, but my happiness over having survived and succeeded my first year of university gave me such joy that all considerations escaped me.

"What is your average for the year?" Peter asked and I gave him the figure proudly.

"Four point five out of five."

"You did me proud...But you didn't beat me. One tenth of a point is not much of a difference, I do admit."

Peter and I were safe, but we waited and hoped until Ocsi and Jeno received their black book. Then the moment came when the two of them were handed those precious documents and the four of us had great reasons to rejoice.

Jeno and Ocsi passed all their subjects, although their average marks were almost a point below ours. Each of us was given a military card that commanded us to report, in six days, to four different units of the army. We would have dearly loved to spend our summer service together, to be able to support each other, to ease whatever trials and tribulations were coming, but that was out of the realm of possibility, so we consoled each other with the arrangements we have made for the following year of study.

"I will see all of you in September. Thank God we acted early enough to be roommates for another year," Peter stated and we pumped each others' hands, pounded each others' shoulders and with tears in our eyes we parted.

***

Within an hour I sat on the train. The pain of separation from my friends was fast receding. I had a few hours of travel to contemplate my next five days of joy, the long, eight weeks of military training and my constant change of love and hate for my mode of transportation.

"Those five days will be precious...I will spend every minute with my beloved Rozsa." I promised myself, but as soon as I have made that promise I was forced to modify it. "I must spend some time with my parents and with my brother, George-there goes half a day at least. I have neglected so many of my relatives and my few friends during my rare and short visits home. I must see Uncle Jozsef and Aunt Gizella-a few hours at least. I must look up Mr. and Mrs. Lazar too and particularly my friend, Joska. He will be home on vacation. We should spend a half day together at least. But that will leave me less than four days with my darling. Oh why do I have to bother with the army? What will it be like to be in boot-camp? Will I survive the horrible things the second year students spoke about? I will do whatever I must...I will endure anything and when it is over maybe I will have a few more days in the company of the girl I love?" My thoughts meandered here and there, but the joy I felt on this trip was too intense, was too precious to spoil with anticipating anything other than Rozsa's sweet face, her lovely eyes, her ruby lips, her cascading hair, her charming presence.

"When I last saw her was at the train station and when I could no longer see her I cursed the train that carried me away. It is really strange...The train I cursed then is the instrument that takes me to my love now. Move on dear train...Go much faster...Each minute you are late will shorten my bliss," I spoke to myself and to the train that pulled into the station.

***

The five free days that were at my disposal sped by in a blur and when it was over, nothing eased the pain of our parting.

I saw every member of my family. I learned with great happiness that my Father had a new job with the military. I went to see my Uncle Jozsef and Aunt Gizella and we had a long, sincere talk. I had a pleasant, long visit with the Lazars. We had many precious hours with my darling Rozsa. I tasted a few of her sweet kisses. I shook with the memory of our occasional embraces. I cherished her congratulations on my success. I never forgot a single word of love we spoke. I felt the pressure, the warmth of her hand as we took many walks.

Then the day came when my five days of happiness was over. It passed away like a fleeting moment and Rozsa stood beside me, once again, at the train station.

"When will I see you again my darling?" She held on to my hand and was reluctant to let it go.

"I wish I knew… No visitors are allowed, the other boys told us. Maybe they are wrong. Maybe you would be allowed to come and see me." I tried to ease our pain, but I have never succeeded.

"When it is over will you be able to return to me?" she asked softly.

"When they discharge us we will have three beautiful days together," I told her and the train's whistle ended our conversation.

One sweet kiss and a warm embrace later I jumped on the train that was to carry me to Tapolca and as I hung on to the train's railing, standing on the train's steps, holding my small, battered suitcase, I saw her throwing me a farewell kiss. The train's steam hissed, hid her just for a moment and when it dissipated I saw her tears, heard her sobs and my heart broke with the pain of parting.

Laszlo S. Lichter

Chapter 7

The train came to a halt at the station of Tapolca and the shouted, crude words of uniformed men hailed my arrival and that of many others.

"The bastards from the universities are to line up here..," the soldiers shouted and the train's younger passengers, all of them boys, about my age, obeyed the orders.

I felt my stomach rumble, my weariness made itself known and in my impatience I dared to address one of the uniformed man.

"How long are we to wait here comrade?"

"Shut your trap you bloody traitor!"

I was taken by surprise. "How could he know who I am?" My astonishment didn't last long, within minutes inquiries made by others met the same fate, expressed in words that hurt me, cut deep into my soul and I began to feel much greater fear than I have ever known before.

"Shut up you enemy of our Nation," shouted one of the soldiers, sporting the single stripe that indicated the rank of a Corporal.

"Speak when you are spoken to..," screamed his order another.

"You will stand there as long as I want you to..," I heard another soldier's reply to the boy who stood beside me.

I tried to speak to my companion, hoped to receive his assurance that we were in the wrong place. "Maybe they expected the arrival of a bunch of prisoners and they mistook us for the dregs of our society?"

Before I was able to utter two words, the shouted orders poured out.

"You will not speak to each other...You will remain silent...You are the class enemy...You will be treated accordingly..."

So I stood there, as did all the others, silent, cowed, not even daring to be indignant.

Our wait was long, for some unexplainable reason and two hours later, when my hunger complained loudly, another train arrived and from it poured out another bunch of unfortunate creatures.

They were treated no more kindly than we were before. The soldiers focused on the new arrivals and I was able to whisper to my nearest companion.

"What is going on? What do you think?"

"I am as puzzled as you are. I came from Budapest. Where are you from?"

"I am from Baja, but attend university at Szeged. I am studying to become a teacher. What about you?"

"I will become a doctor when I finish my studies."

"And I will become an engineer," spoke up another lad.

"If we ever survive this," piped up someone and hearing his words of truth we all became silent.

Four hours had passed; the sun disappeared behind the horizon and the chill of the coming night, the hunger of the long wait began to take its toll.

I looked around me, saw at least three hundred boys, all standing, looking miserable and tired; I decided to sit down on my suitcase.

"What the hell do you think you are doing? Get up and stand at attention until I tell you to do otherwise." A lowly officer gave the order and turned his attention to some others, who began to follow my example.

Around ten o'clock in the evening, finally they began to march us.

"At last...We will be taken to the barracks. I hope it is not too far, that we will be fed and get a good night's rest." I thought, but as the miles melted away behind us, as my feet almost gave out, as my heart began to labor, my foolish hopes slowly diminished.

I have estimated that we must have marched over six miles when I began to see the lights in the far distance.

"We are getting there...Maybe it will not be as bad as it first seemed," I tried to tell myself, but the hope my heart harbored, my mind readily rejected.

"These soldiers are totally uneducated. They treat us as if we were criminals. Surely, once the higher ranked officers find out about their actions they will reprimand our reception committee." I still tried to convince myself as we neared the gate, as I noticed the guard towers, the search-lights that swept around us and the barbed wire fence that seemed to surround the compound.

The gravel crunched under our tired feet, that were no longer lifted, but rather dragged and when our escorts called a halt to our seemingly endless march, I dropped my suitcase, afraid, yet no longer caring about being reproached for my small act of defiance.

We were made to face a large podium that stood at the side of the wide, graveled boulevard-later I have learned its name *the Minister's Road.* There we waited, but this time our wait was short. A high ranking officer appeared on the elevated platform, flanked by two other officers of lower rank. I should have been able to identify their ranks, but my mind was too exhausted to recall what I have learned ages ago, at the university, from my military instructors.

It was in the wee hours of the morning, around two o'clock, that the highest ranking officer addressed us.

"Listen up men, if that is what you are. We shall see in the coming weeks. You are here to learn to defend our beloved country from the imperialist hordes that are hell bent on its destruction.

"We know defending our regime is the farthest thing from your minds, after all you are members of the *intelligentsia,* you are *the class enemy.* Your officers, including myself, are members of the working class. The struggle of this class against all other classes has been going on, ever since our liberation by our beloved Soviet brothers and sisters. Here that struggle will continue. You will obey all our orders. You do otherwise and will find yourself front of a court-martial. Now your guards will take you to the dining hall, there you will be given food and after that you will be taken to the supply depot to be outfitted. Tonight you will sleep under the stars and tomorrow you will dig your home. The coming weeks will be hard you soft bastards, but we will transform you all into fighting machines.

"Each time you are asked a question you will reply by using the word *comrade*, followed by the rank of your questioner. Am I making myself clear?"

"Yes, Comrade Major General," some of the others recognized his rank and they shouted.

"Very good. You already know my rank. These officers at my side are both colonels. The one on my right is our political officer and the other is the security officer. You are privates...When you meet any of us you will salute us, as you will all others, but in our case you will do even more: you will begin to walk in goose-steps, at least twenty paces before you reach us and twenty paces after you passed us. Did you get that?"

"Yes, Comrade Major General." This time all of us shouted and I have recalled the manner of that hated walk. "Right foot kicked out high toward the front, slammed to the earth with forceful vigor, followed by the left foot, imitating its brother..." The words of my military instructors echoed in my mind; I could see them demonstrating the art of that peculiar walk, many months ago.

"We are finished with you, at least for now. Officers take charge!" the Major General commanded.

We were fed, if anyone wanted to overstate what happened next. Someone shoved into my hand a *csajka*, the square, tin can; an old, bent, aluminum fork and a spoon that sported years of abuse. Some slop was splashed into the *csajka*, that reminded me of dishwater I gave my pigs. My hunger suddenly disappeared upon taking the first sip of that tasteless concoction. It made my stomach heave, ready to give up the remnants of fine food my Mother prepared for my long journey. That revulsion I never forgot, I had to fight it three times a day, that is on the rare days when we were kindly treated.

It was a relief when we were ordered to stand and line up to be outfitted.

A pair of rubberized, canvas boots; three sets of *kapca*-the rags we were to wind around our feet-in place of socks; one pair of pants; two pairs of undergarment; a tunic; a leather belt; a peaked cap with its hated red star; a single horse blanket; an empty straw bag, to use as a mattress; a short spade, that we were to fasten to our belt. Once we were outfitted, we were lead to a section of a field where we were to spend the rest of the night, until the bugle sounded.

I spread out the empty straw bag, laid my exhausted body on it; placed my head on the bundle I fashioned out of the pants and tunic; covered myself with the scanty blanket and for the rest of the short night I stared at the stars that shone upon my dearest Rozsa.

"I am far away from you my darling. If I survive this night-mare I will return to you." The chill that intensified with the breaking dawn found me still awake and my self-pity began to mount.

"I was never strong...As a child I have suffered more than my share of illnesses. I will never survive this...There will be no return to my adored Rozsa...I might as well expire now and save myself the weeks of miseries," I thought sadly and suddenly my stubbornness, inherited from my Father, took command.

"I will do whatever I must; these bastards will never beat me." My resolution slew my self pity.

***

Had I been less stubborn I would have screamed when at five o'clock the bugle sounded.

"You will begin to dig your home..." Our unit of twenty-four was assigned a Corporal, as were all other units. Our minder was a towering giant, his muscles, developed on the field of some farm, bulged under his uniform. In a booming voice he told us what we were to accomplish in the wee hour of the morning. He divided us into four groups of six. "Each group is to dig a hole, deep enough to accommodate a six foot man. The sides must be straight, the steps leading to the surface must be perfect. When you have that task completed you will be fed, that is if you are finished in the allotted two hours, otherwise you will go hungry." We heard the orders and our feverish bodies fell on the task, dreading another bout of hunger.

My group of six barely managed to complete the task in time and when I heard the next set of orders I was ready to scream, to rebel, to disobey.

"You will come with me to pick up your metal bunk-beds. Then you will stuff your bags with straw and you better make it perfectly rectangular...Then you will be given a tent which you shall erect promptly. You will make your hovel habitable. You will wait for my inspection of your new home and don't forget to square your bed as you were thought at your university. You do all this well and you can have your breakfast." As I listened to the hours of work laid out by the class enemy, words rushed to my lips to protest, but my earlier resolution, my stubbornness and the taste of the slop that still lingered in my mouth stifled my words of protest.

Three hours later our new home passed inspection and we were led to the open, uncovered dining hall, where I fell upon the rotten food, checked my revulsion and ate everything.

We were back in hour underground hovel, where we were to change into our uniforms and to place our civilian clothing into the bags our masters provided. I began the task of changing. The underwear fit me nicely, but the pants were far too large, even after I made them stay on with the help of the belt, which I pulled around me as tightly as the holes permitted. The tunic hung loosely on my upper body. Next came the task of carefully winding the *kapca* on my feet. When I slipped on my boots I have discovered to my horror that they were at least two sizes too large, but my shock increased greatly when I saw one of my companions fully dressed.

"Look at your uniform...It is that of a Russian," I told the young man.

"And so is yours, in case you didn't notice," came his reply.

We have inspected each other and then another companion spoke up.

"We look just like our liberators."

"But that must be a mistake...We are in the Hungarian army." I barely hid my hatred.

"There was a Hungarian army, but no more I suspect," spoke up another and I felt shame at my vanishing identity.

When the bugle sounded, a few minutes later, we have obeyed the command its tune conveyed.

"You look quite good. Finally you look like our beloved Soviet brothers. Why you have been given the honor to be the first so outfitted I will never know." Our Corporal spoke, as we stood at attention front of our abodes, and his words made me angry.

"Comrade Corporal may I speak?"

"Be my guest, I cannot refuse a soldier wearing a Russian uniform." He gave his reply, laced with a good dose of cynicism.

"I would like to change my pants which are too large, my tunic too, but most of all my boots that do not fit me."

"And you would like to be promoted while we are at it. Is that what you want?"

"I beg your pardon Comrade Corporal, but I can barely walk in these boots."

"Don't give it another thought...You will rarely have to walk." His reply surprised me, but only for a short while. From that moment on we rarely had to walk, in that he told the truth. Everywhere we went we had to step lively, many times we were made to run, except when they announced that our rest time was to be used for *cultural activity*.

Across the road a reserve battalion was located, we found out during our first *cultural activity*. They were provided with better food; they were given free time to use as they saw fit; they were denied only one thing: the use of a latrine. They were ordered to deposit their feces behind our dug-outs, whenever they felt nature's call and the narrow field, the large expanse of woods, behind us, became dotted with their deposits.

Each evening, when other soldiers were given free time to write letters, to listen to radios, to read or simply to rest, the university battalion was formed up and with our short spades we were to engage in our *cultural activity*. We were taken behind our mansions and ordered to scoop up the human waste with our spades. Once our spades could hold no more of its precious cargo, we were to goose-step to the far-away latrine and there the reservist's feces were to be added to our own products. The flies had joined us; followed us; buzzed around our heads, probably laughing at the learned young men earnestly putting to use their high education. When our spades were finally empty, we were to run back to the mind-field of shit and to repeat our activity, all the while listening to the shouted exhortations.

"Be happy we allow our class enemy to serve the workers! Take pride in your work comrades and hope that the reservists don't get constipated! Should that ever happen we will make you carry your own stinking feces, you rotten intelligentsia."

It took no more than two days before the *bunched up kapcas* began to take their toll on my feet. On both of my heels blisters appeared and when those blisters opened up, the blood, the crippling pain, my constant limping made me seek medical attention.

"Comrade Corporal may I go to the infirmary?" I asked him after three days of constant suffering.

"So what is your problem soldier?"

"My feet are killing me; they are full of blisters; they are bloody raw. I am in constant pain." I described my situation.

"I told you not to give it another thought."

"But how can I do that?" I moaned in my misery.

"Learn to wind your *kapca* properly and give it time. In a few weeks your feet will be so callused that you will never feel anything."

"But in the meantime..," I began to continue, but he cut me off sharply.

"No more complaints from any member of the class enemy. Do you understand me? We were warned about the likes of you university students. You are soft, lazy with a mind on malingering. The infirmary is out of bounds to the likes of you. Now shut your mouth and don't ever dare to speak about pain or any other problems. The more you suffer the more you will appreciate the meaning of class struggle."

I was amazed how fluently he was able to put me in my place; how cruelly he disregarded my medical problem. At the same time I knew that he had his orders, like thousands upon thousands in our country and that his political indoctrination, his few weeks of brain-washing made him what he became.

After that day I ran when I was so ordered; I goose-stepped my way from the woods to the latrine and rushed back to scoop up more and my indignity started to disappear.

When our escorts had discovered that our frowns were replaced with barely concealed smiles, they came up with a new variation on our *cultural activity*.

"You seem to enjoy your job comrades. You sure know how to put your vast knowledge to good use. From now on you will not carry the precious loads in total silence. I want to hear songs about our beloved Stalin. I am sure you have learned a few at your universities. Now start to sing and anyone who stops singing will get double cultural duty." The announcement came with a chuckle and our submission came instantly.

One of the boys began to sing; his strong, sweet, cultivated voice rang out, almost with sincerity. The rest of us picked up his tune and from that day on the Stalinist songs filled the woods, whenever we were made to honor two kinds of feces.

***

After two weeks of early rising; endless drills; political lectures; mock attacks from the imperialists, that came always around two in the morning; nightly cultural activities, we were given a special treat.

"You have done such a fine job that I have decided to give you a break. Tonight you will not be allowed to clear the field, instead you will be given free time to write letters to your loved ones." I heard the unexpected announcement and felt a pang of guilt.

I have thought about my dear Rozsa each and every moment of the last fourteen days, but I have never had the time to write her a single letter. I fished out my only pen and the few pieces of papers in my possession and sat on the bunk-bed of our hole. My words rushed out and the pages began to fill. I wrote her at length about my pains, disappointments. Detailed our senseless activities. Compared our feasting at the university to the starving in the people's army. I wrote to her about my never ending love, about my hope to return to her. When I scribbled my salutation and was ready to seal the envelope, I felt an inner alarm, a fear that made me think.

"When Rozsa gets my letter what will she think? Will my beloved worry about me? Will this letter cause her suffering?" I asked myself many questions and before I could provide the answers, my fingers reacted. The small pieces of the torn letter fell on the wet, muddy bottom of our pit. I picked them up, carried them behind our tent, and made all my complaints go up in smoke.

I had one sheet of paper left and I began again. This time I forced myself to write only about our love, our coming re-union and sent her family and mine a warm greeting.

The sheet of paper I placed in the envelope, which I addressed with great relief. When finished I sat for a few more minutes on my bunk-bed, until the bugle sounded.

"I hope you enjoyed the special treat." Our Corporal was almost kindly. "Now let me have the letters you wrote...We will post them right-away."

We fished our letters out of our pockets, handed them to our leader and I hoped that within days my cherished angel will be able to read my words of love and devotion.

Three days have passed with hum-drum activities before we were all ordered to line up on the *Minister's Road*. As we stood there, front of the same podium where we were so graciously received on the night of our arrival, I was surprised to see the coming of the reservists and other units of the regular army. An ominous silence descended and I felt fear once more that nibbled at the edges of my nerves before I tore up my longer letter.

"Comrades we have something very important to announce. This time it will be our political officer and our security officer who will speak. Comrade Colonel, please proceed."

"You know my rank, my name is not important," the political officer announced and continued. "I have been with this army for over four years...I am the son of a worker who was exploited by the Horthy regime. When our beloved country was liberated by the Soviet Red Army my Father and his entire family rejoiced. It was indeed a great event and I wasted no time to volunteer to serve this country. Ever since that time I have given my great talent to enlighten young minds with our glorious ideology. Day after day, more and more Hungarian youngsters have become devoted to our cause, but there remain a few who refuse to embrace our doctrine, no matter how kindly they are treated, how many opportunities they are given. Those are traitors and I denounce them. Thanks to the vigilance of Comrade Colonel, our security officer, we have identified one of those renegades. I will let him produce the dastardly traitor. Comrade Colonel please proceed."

We stood there awe-struck, waiting. A young man in civilian clothing was brought to the podium. He was white as a sheet. He was shaken. His hands, front of his frail body, in a pair of hand-cuffs.

"This loathsome creature betrayed all of us to the American imperialists. I wanted all of you to see him, to face him, to denounce him, before he is taken to the capital, where he will be punished for his crime in a well deserved manner. His destination is Fo Street, where all such scum rightfully belong. His crime you will want to know, but it will not be I, but him who will enlighten you. He will speak to you about a letter he wrote and the confidential information he tried to send out of here, three days ago. I tell you now that traitors are not tolerated. Eternal caution we have learned from our Soviet brothers, that vigilance I practice every minute of every day. Beware all of you from now on, if you wish to avoid this filthy creature's fate." The security officer screamed at us the last statement, then shoved the unfortunate creature front of the microphone and whispered something in his ear.

"I am not allowed to tell you my name, but my crime I gladly confess," the frail creature began to speak. I seemed to sense his act was preceded my many rehearsals for his words came without hesitation and were quite well enunciated.

"I was hired as a paid spy by the American imperialists, who are hell bent on destroying our beloved country, the Communist Party and everything the Soviets had achieved. I was to send them information vital to timing their attack. I was to use a code that my runner provided. Three days ago I wrote a letter to my Mother, but the true recipient was not her, but my handler. In that letter I had given them vital information: The day when our fighting unit is at its lowest point of preparedness. Had they gotten my letter our Hungarian army would have been attacked by the Americans and their filthy allies on an early Saturday morning. How did I give them this information? I am sure you wish to know. I wrote about many things and among those innocent lines I hid the ultimate information.

"'Every Friday we are fed slop.' That is all I needed to say. My meaning was clear to those American intelligence officers: 'Attack on Saturday morning for that is the day when we are most hungry, when our fighting spirit is at its lowest ebb. I regret what I have done! I confess my treason freely and without coercion! I am relieved that I was caught before I have caused the destruction of tens of thousands of young men like you! I praise our officers' vigilance! I am ready to accept my fate! I have made a dreadful mistake! May our leaders live long and show their mercy!"

I marveled at his smooth delivery. Felt sorry for the young student whose only crime was that of not tearing up his letter like I did.

"He is no more guilty than I am," I told myself and my pity deepened. "Whenever the Communists want to sow fear in their subjects they put on a show like this. He is no different from those two girls who were expelled from my university. He committed no greater crime than my lateness to political indoctrination. He is no more a traitor than Mr. Buja. He is as innocent as my Father. Yet the Communists need victims, always more victims. I am sad for him and grateful for my life experience that allowed me to avoid his fate. From now on, if I am allowed to write to my angel, my letters will be guarded." I pondered what I have almost done; felt great sadness for the lad as he was led away. Then some thought began to form at the edge of my mind and suddenly I glimpsed the possibility of another interpretation.

"I have never seen that lad before…I will quietly check with other students to try to find out if anyone knew him. His confession was far too smooth, even with many rehearsals. Maybe be he was not an innocent letter writer, but a plant?" I asked myself and the more I pondered the possibility, the more I believed that I was on the right track. "Whether a plant or an innocent victim the outcome is the same: Our letters will be free of factual information; our obedience will increase in direct proportion to our fear; we will never dare to trust each other; we will never be able to forge alliances while in the army, not like at the university." There ended my thoughts and I turned my attention to our commander, who began to speak once again.

"Regular army units and the reservists are to be dismissed. Now that all of you have seen what happens to traitors, I want to speak with the class enemy alone." Our Major General waited until the other units were led away, then he continued. "Just in case another traitor got the information to the Americans we increase our level of alertness. You may have wondered why you have not received weapons of any sort. We had our reasons, I assure you, but this event had changed them. You will be issued machine pistols, our Soviet brothers so generously provided, but live ammunitions you will receive only when you are on the firing range or in case of an actual attack. You will take care with those priceless guns! You will care for them like you care for your lovers. Never a rust spot or you will be tried for neglect. I have referred to you as the class enemy and so did others. It's time you learn our reason.

"The workers and peasants of many countries have been subjugated by the upper classes and the *intelligentsia*. The Glorious Russian Revolution put an end to that in the great Soviet Union and after the Second World War in Hungary as well. Thanks to Stalin, the wise, the mighty, the benevolent.

"Ever since we have been liberated the lackeys of the former regime have tried in vain to block our efforts and they were always supported by the so called learned men. You will be a new breed of intellectuals, but until you prove worthy of our trust, you will be treated like the enemy. Earn our trust and you will be able to take your place in our new society; betray us and you shall find no mercy. You are dismissed!"

***

Within two days we had our guns and our instructions on how to care for our new lovers. For a whole week we have spent all the time our keepers gave us to take the machine pistols apart, to clean them, oil them, reassemble them with great care and when we were finished we were driven to resume our *cultural activity*.

My short spade and my machine pistol, with its round magazine that sat below the black, perforated jacket with the short barrel hidden inside it, became my most precious possessions. With the former I put to eternal rest the workers'/peasants' body-waste and with the latter I was ready to defend their freedom.

It was around the fourth week of our servitude that we were led to the firing range by a Sergeant and several armed soldiers. Ten of us were selected to stand by the wooden firing pads, to face the targets and not to move a muscle until we received our orders.

"I will explain what you are to do! You better pay attention. One mistake, one mistake, doesn't matter how small, will cost you your life. The soldiers behind you have orders to shoot, if you provoke them." Hearing my Sergeant's words made me glance behind my back and I was pounced upon instantly.

"You there...," the Sergeant shouted. "You who turned your head. Turn around and face me. Are you stupid? Do you want to die? Did I not tell you not to provoke your guards? Had you turned your head after the live ammunition was passed out you would have been shot. That would have been the last mistake of your young life. Remember that! Now turn your ugly mug toward the enemy soldier and follow all our orders."

I turned around, every muscle in my body trembled and my thoughts raced.

"The Major General called us the 'class-enemy'. He sure wasn't joking. They don't trust us; they fear us; they would waste us without hesitation. I must follow their every order, otherwise I will never see my Rozsa...Just the thought of never seeing her slim body; never holding her hand, never looking into her loving eyes; never to taste her sweet lips, to touch her hair, to admire her rare beauty causes me unendurable pain. I will obey them. I will assure my survival." I chased away my disturbing thoughts and listened to the Sergeant's explanations.

"Front of you, three hundred yards away, stands your enemy. Those are American killers. They are ready to destroy you; they will spoil your sweethearts; rape your mothers; kill your fathers; rob you of all your possessions, enslave you. Now you lie down on the firing pads! Pick out the target that faces you. Sight your weapon at the heart of your hated enemy. Work on your hate...Make it glow like hell's fire...Make your soul scream for the death of the bastard. Now hold your breath and slowly, very slowly squeeze the trigger...Imagine hearing the report of your gun...Conjure up the image of your enemy falling dead with the bullet that pierced his heart. Pull the trigger again, but do it slowly and put another bullet in his foul body." The orders came and I clutched my empty gun.

"The stupid bastards want us to kill the enemy with an empty gun. Even now, lying in this prone position, they don't trust us with a single bullet. They are afraid we will shoot them instead of the wooden targets." I allowed myself a hidden smirk and took joy from the fear of our masters.

"Now you will receive two bullets each. Once you loaded your gun you must remain on the firing pad. Never turn around. Never dare to swing your weapon away from the target. After you fired two shots at your enemy, you must place your gun beside the pad, no more than two inches away, and on my command you will stand up. Your gun will be checked by a guard to assure that it is empty. On my order you will run to the target and bring back the poster for my inspection. I want to see two holes in your enemy and those better not be flash wounds either."

One soldier walked behind us and placed two shells in the palm of my right hand. The command came and I resolved to follow his orders precisely.

"Load...Aim...Hold your breath...Squeeze the trigger...Fire..." The shouted orders came and my ears were deafened by the reverberating cracks of gun-fire.

"Guns down...Remain in your prone position...Guard check the guns..."

"All guns are empty!"

"Begin to run to your dead enemy!"

I reached my target many seconds after the others did. My feet still hurt, although the blisters were gone, there was no more bleeding. I removed the paper target and imagined the American's eyes mocking me. I carried the unmarked target back to where the Sergeant stood and waited for his inspection.

"Superb! One shot in the heart and the other smashed his skull," the Sergeant announced his first observation.

"Not bad either. The imperialist is dead. Our people can rest easy."

"What is this? You shot off his balls. Where is the other hole? Our factory workers volunteer to work a free Sunday and you squander what they produce. Get out of my sight you imbecile."

I stood in line, listening to the achievements or failures of the boys ahead of me, then my turn came and with a shaking hand I held out my target. The wind suddenly swirled and grabbed the paper out of my fingers, rolling it, blowing it on the ground, away from me.

"You clumsy idiot...Run! Retrieve it."

I made a mad dash for it, but my slowness and my aching feet impeded my progress. When I almost caught up with the paper, the wind gave another teasing puff and I was forced to throw myself on the ground, hoping to arrest its flight, but success eluded me. I ran and hopped and finally I was able to carry out my Sergeant's order.

"The Americans have nothing to fear from blockheads like you. You shouldn't be in the army." This was the first statement that I had agreed with since I was torn away from my darling and I, just for a single moment, sent a fervent, short prayer to the Almighty.

"Please Lord make his wish come true. Let me survive this ordeal and never again allow them to draft me."

"What did I tell you? All of you soldiers gather around me. Look at this target. The American is untouched, not a single hole in his body. Not even a puncture in the entire target. Where were you aiming you stupid bastard?"

"I aimed at his heart..." I tried to convince my torturer, but he would have none of that.

"You aimed at the sky! You aimed at thin air! You are a lackey of the enemy. You are a traitor! You should be sent to Fo Street to join that other traitor. His crime was writing a letter; spying on our country, but you are much worse than that. You have refused my order. You hate not them, but us, you rotten trash, you rubbish, you filthy bastard."

I was about to protest, to tell him what I felt, to explain to him the mediocre training they gave me, but his scorn remained unchecked and my rage I stifled, hung my head and waited.

"You will get back to your firing pad. You will be the only shooter. You will be given two more bullets and you will not waste a single one, or I will fire one in the back of your head!"

I heard the threat and my limbs began to shake. I didn't dare to pray, in case the good Lord was too busy to listen to my supplication. In my mind and heart I said a silent farewell to my beloved Rozsa and then I fired.

A few minutes later I have reached the target and I was astonished. Two big holes punctured the chest of my enemy. I forgot the pain of my injured heels; I ran with unbelievable speed to the Sergeant, whose pistol was drawn, whose face displayed his murderous determination.

He gazed at the paper, his bushy, black eye-brows drawn in concentration. He looked at me, then back to the target, all the while his head shaking.

"You proved that you are a traitor. Had you missed again I would have chalked it up to your natural inability to handle a weapon. But now I am forced to think differently. The first time around you had no desire to hit your friends, your allies. You used your skill in the service of your country only when I threatened your life. Anyone who does that is truly our enemy." In spite of his words he holstered his pistol and instead of relief I felt only hatred.

"These rotten Communists twist everything we say or do. If we make even a small mistake our life is in danger; if luck allows us to satisfy their order, they find a way to twist our motives and we are marked again as traitors. This country is cursed. This life holds no hope, except at the western border." I recalled Joska Lazar's childhood dream of escaping from Hungary and I now had many more reasons to feel like he did, to acknowledge my friend's wisdom.

***

My days in the Peoples' Army, as it was proudly named by the Communist leaders, were not unlike what I have imagined Hell to be, but I was wrong. Once we have learned to shoot at the enemy, once we had minimal skills to defend our country, the late night alarms began to sound. My personal Hell took on new dimensions when, in the dead of night, our masters began to march us.

Twenty to thirty kilometer treks were the norm. Had we been able to dictate our own pace, perhaps we would have survived these events without too much suffering, but our leaders had other ideas. The weight of our back-packs was increased greatly by loading them with the heaviest of objects.

When the marches began we were given our instructions.

"If you hear the command to trot you will pick up your pace and keep up with your platoon leaders!" We were told and I looked at the well fed, strong, revolver toting officers, all of them without back-packs and I knew that to keep up with them will be next to impossible.

"Whether you walk, or ordered to run, you will sing to show your enthusiasm!" we were told not one kilometer into our track and I knew that I will barely have the energy to draw a breath and that without singing.

"When you hear us announce the presence of high flying planes, you will throw yourselves on the ground and cover all parts of your weapons that could give off a glint." I heard the order and I doubted that I will ever be able to get up, to find my feet.

"If we signal low flying planes you will drop to the ground facing the enemy. You will fire at them, make their cursed planes crash and kill the pilots." I almost laughed upon hearing this command and contemplated the great damage we shall cause with our guns that were still empty.

So we marched and sang and ran and dropped to the ground in various positions and those of us who could no longer stand the pace, those of us who stopped singing were chastised severely during our infrequent short breaks. We were made to remain standing at attention. We were denied food the others received and we were to stand there without a single sip of water. Our leaders rested their bodies on the ground, where they lounged, ate and drank, all the while cursing us for our crimes, for being their enemy and the friends of the imperialist, chain rattling dogs, who flew the non-existent planes, who were the real cause of our sufferings.

When our marches ended, when we got back to our camp and hoped for the briefest of rest we were ordered to form up and once again commence our *cultural activity*.

When darkness fell, when we could no longer distinguish feces from any other objects we were fed the usual slop and our day has ended.

***

Two weeks remained from our *summer vacation* and I began to contemplate my possible return to Baja.

"I will be with my darling Rozsa, it will be a few days in Heaven. We will hold hands and talk about our eight weeks of lonely existence. We will steal a few sweet kisses. I will borrow my Fathers bike and Rozsa will sit on the handle bar as I drive her to the shore of the Danube. There we shall swim, frolic in the refreshing water. This summer and all I have experienced I will shut away in my mind's most hidden compartment. I will be immensely happy." I dreamed sweet dreams without sleeping and for a few hours I forgot the fatigue that never left my body.

Then my thoughts suddenly turned in a different direction. I have recalled the first time we were marched through a small village where the Hungarians mistook us for a bunch of Russians. On this occasion we were ordered not to sing, but to remain absolutely silent. I found this order strange, but much easier to obey than some others. We have marched through the village and endured the shouted, derogatory remarks our countrymen heaped on us.

"Look at these Russians, our *liberators*," said one man, as he sat at the side of the road, firmly believing that we spoke no Hungarian.

"Liberators indeed...rapists, plunderers, killers, enslavers. That is what they are." His partner added and expressed his disgust by letting his spittle fly.

Then the two of them got even bolder and began to taunt us.

"Why don't you go home boys where you belong? Why don't you f... your mothers? Better yet, why don't you f...yourselves?" The two men began to laugh at their own boldness and I glanced uneasily at our platoon leader, who pretended not to understand the insults.

As these memories rushed through my head I began to understand why we were made to wear Russian uniforms.

"A day will come when Hungarian soldiers will be indistinguishable from that of the Red Army. Probably the Poles, the Checks, the Romanians and other Soviet satellite countries will force their soldiers to wear the same hated uniforms too. When war comes, if it ever does, we will all look alike. The Soviets will send us into the front lines, will offer us as cannon fodder to the enemy, as they did in the Second World War their Asiatic brothers. We will be sacrificed." My thoughts meandered aimlessly during the sleepless night and as I explored the Soviet's motives another thought came to me.

"They must be some talented men, these stupid Russians. The boots they designed and made us wear, even the Devil would be proud of. The rubberized canvas heats up under the Sun, cooking first the *kapca*, then our feet. When the chill of night arrives the canvas contracts and acts as a vice. Ingenious indeed! Their achievement doesn't end there...They did an equally fine job with the pants and tunic. The materials they chose is rough canvas. They soak up our sweat and become like rocks. Neither pants, nor tunic dry for hours after a downpour. The course fabric chafes our skin, turns it into a bloody pulp. A few weeks wearing these uniforms had make the healthiest man turn sickly. They are clever, I do admit. They know how to torture our souls and how to devastate our bodies." I must have fallen asleep, but my slumber was brief and around three the bugle sounded.

***

"The Americans attacked our country. The Third World War began just minutes ago. Fascists, imperialist paratroopers landed all over our country. Two hundred rounds of live ammunition will be issued to every one of you. You will be marched to face the enemy. Contain them! Destroy them! Make our leaders proud! Die if you must with Stalin's name on your lips! Take no prisoners! Kill all of them or perish in trying." The loud-speakers exhorted us, repeating their awful announcements while we stood, clutching our weapons. Some time later we have received two loaded, round magazines and one half day's ration of food and water.

For almost seven weeks we rarely spoke to each other, but the fearful news, the fright we felt, the semi-darkness of the night, the apparent confusion, the fear of facing death, the ensuing chaos all joined together and loosened our tongues. We no longer feared to trust each other.

"Is this really happening?" I asked someone.

"It must be the truth," his reply came.

"Could this be an exercise? A drill?" I wanted to hear affirmative answers.

"What is in your round magazines?" someone asked, but didn't wait for an answer. "We all got live ammunition." The speaker said no more.

A babble of voices joined ours.

"They never ever trusted us, but now they are desperate."

"They fear death no less than I do."

"They are shitting their pants."

"They have more to fear than the American invaders. I am ready to get even..."

The voices came from all around me, the speakers using the cover of semi darkness.

"What am I going to do?" I began to question myself. "If I hold an American in my gun-sight will I be able to shoot him? Are they really my enemies? Have they made me suffer like my own country-men did? What if in the night I find one of my officers standing ahead of me? Will my hatred for the Communists overwhelm me? Will I kill a friend or rather shoot a foe? I cannot kill another human being. People are flesh and blood...God gave all of us one life and one life only. Once that life is taken it is all over. I cannot break God's commandment...I will not kill. But what will happen if they fire at me? Will I be able to fight for my own survival?" I would have struggled with my conflicting emotions God knows how long, but the loud speakers stopped me.

"The nearest attacking unit has been pin-pointed twenty-five miles east of here. The university brigade is given the honor to wipe out that unit. Get ready to march out! Remember your sweet-hearts, defend your family. Make us proud and keep us free!"

The forced march began, but this time without singing.

"Be prepared for the fight of your life! Make sure your safety is on. We want no accidents, nor an accidental warning shot." One of our officers walked beside us and he repeated his message time and time again. I seemed to hear the timber of his voice shaking and my fear increased greatly.

Then another officer issued a whispered order at the head of the column that reached me a few minutes later and our predicament became clearer as the night sky began to recede.

"Pass it on...No talking in loud voices. We must take the enemy by surprise."

About two hours later our officers stopped our forced march and told us to take a well deserved rest. The battalion's political officer approached group after group and when he reached mine the kindness of his words, the smile on his face, his sincerity almost touched me.

"I don't want you boys to be overly concerned, this is why I tell you that Hungarian planes attacked the enemy units. They are pounding the hell out of them. If we are lucky they will leave us a few to kill. Rest now, eat and drink, reinforce your bodies. The field kitchens are just behind us. You will receive hot, nourishing food, as soon as possible. I must go and inform the others..." He turned on his heels, but before he could take another step one of the soldiers stood up and shouted.

"Stop right there you rotten commie!"

The officer turned in surprise and all of us turned in his direction.

"For almost eight weeks we were the class enemy. You treated us like shit...You abused us...You never trusted us, but now you expect us to fall on our knees with gratitude for your kind treatment." The desperation in the boy's voice could not be mistaken, nor could we miss the threatening move he made with his gun. A hush fell on our group, I couldn't believe the soldier's boldness. My fear was no longer centered around my safety.

"It was just part of your training...It was done in jest." The officer's words betrayed no fear as he faced the gun. "What do you plan to do? Shoot a Hungarian my dear boy? Go ahead...pull the trigger...put a gaping hole in my chest. What will that prove? Is it revenge you want? Or are you itching to fire your gun? Why don't you wait until you face the enemy? Lower your gun my dear friend...You made a mistake, but nobody will ever recall that. We are comrades...We are Hungarians...Let's face the enemy together..." His voice stopped, he locked eyes with his would be executioner.

"You scum...You tortured us for all these weeks. You made us pick shit and you called that *cultural activity*...You have sent my best friend to Fo Street for a letter he wrote. He was no spy. He was an innocent boy in the prime of his life, but you destroyed him." The soldier's gun did not waver.

"You are truly gullible my dear boy. Your friend was recruited to make that confession. Then he was transferred to another unit to repeat the act. He loves acting and we gave him his life's biggest role." The officer's words wiped away my conflicting thoughts about that condemned boy and his words made the soldier hesitate. The machine pistol was slowly turned away from his chest, his attacker hung his head to hide his tears.

"Keep your gun, son! Spare your ammunition for the real enemy. We will never again speak about this incident. I hope you all get my meaning," were his last words and we have nodded our heads in agreement.

***

Three more times we were given time to rest. Officers came with various bits of information and in the intense heat created by the merciless August Sun we welcomed the shade of the acacia trees.

When we reached the foot of the unknown mountain range, we saw our officers gather. Their comportment appeared to be too calm, too peaceful at a time when we were about to face the deadly enemy. Yet I gave no thought to the possibility of an error or to the probability of being mislead. I saw two of them study intensely a map...I watched them as they seemed to argue over the compass that sat on the spread out map.

Then the highest ranking officer appeared to assert his authority and pointed toward one of the highest peaks and we were formed up to begin our ascend.

Sweat came off my body in rivulets. My pants, tunic and boots were soaking wet within moments of our climb toward the far away mountain peak. My feet cooked; my body was tortured by the roughness of my uniform. I put one aching foot ahead of the other, felt the newly formed blisters and dragged its brother after it with an effort that sapped all my energies. I began to stumble, almost fell, but one of the boys caught me and whispered in my ears.

"Don't give up now...It's almost over."

"Thanks for helping me." I felt obliged to reward his kindness and as the evening came, as the stars began to shine above our heads we were stopped and ordered to dig fox holes.

"The enemy is within a few hundred yards. Work fast to hide your bodies...Do it silently. Be alert, but do not fire until ordered."

Our ration was gone hours ago. Our canteens were empty. Hunger gnawed at my stomach. My throat was parched, my lips cracked from thirst and fear. There was no sign of the field kitchen that was supposed to catch up with us long before night-fall and there was no sound of the enemy.

I cowered in my shallow fox-hole, hid as much of my body as I could.

"If only I could become smaller..." That thought amused me for a few moments. All my life I have bemoaned my fate of having a Lilliputian frame and in that fox-hole I felt myself to stick out like a giant. With the last few ounces of my energy I began to deepen the hole of my salvation and as I dug myself deeper and deeper into the rocky earth of the pine forest I prayed to God to grant me enough time to finish the home that will save my life, that will hide me from the enemy.

The hunger, the thirst, the fatigue began to take its toll. One of the boys close by began to mumble. His words made no sense, they carried no meaning.

"He is sick. He is ravaged by fever," came a voice from the adjacent hole.

Suddenly the feverish boy jumped up, began to scream. The night was shattered by his shrill voice as he cracked under the strain of the past several weeks. He began to take a few teetering steps away from the defense line when he was accosted by the battalion's security officer.

"Get back to your fox-hole soldier or I will have you placed under arrest!"

"You are the devil...You make me burn...I feel your heat...," came out the slurred statements and suddenly, in the breaking dawn, we saw him raise his gun, just inches from the officer's chest and the crack of the shot surprised me.

I expected the officer to fall, to have his body torn by the impact, to see his blood pouring out on the pine needle covered forest floor, but those things were not to be. He remained standing, not even a drop of blood poured out of his body, his evil face he thrust into his assassin's face and he screamed at the feverish boy.

"We have fooled all of you...The bullets you have received are all blanks, made to look like the real things. There was no attack by the Americans. There is no war. We the workers deceived our learned class enemies. We wanted to make you suffer; to bring you to your breaking point. Two traitors we have flushed out! One imagined that he killed me; the other raised his weapon to our political officer. Both of them will be tried like that other one, the spy was, and their punishments will be death...The bullets they will receive will be real."

I couldn't believe my ears. "It was all a game to these morons. How cruel can they be? I almost wish the Americans came and wiped them out, even if that meant my own death. Curse them for their perfidy."

***

A few hours later the news began to circulate.

"We will not be fed until we get back," someone announced in a whisper and when he saw our astonishment, he explained. "I overheard the officers as they argued. They have misread the compass. Made a mistake with the map. They brought us to the wrong mountain top, while the field-kitchen and cooks were taken to the foot-hills of another mountain...They are many miles away."

"But how could that be?" someone asked and we gathered around the soldier, who was not only willing, but eager to share information.

"These officers were given six weeks of training. They are almost fresh out of factories and farmers' fields. I heard them blame each other for this calamity. The language they used I could hardly believe. They cursed each other...They called each other some terrible names, but the brunt of their anger was directed at the security officer, whose action gave the game away." As I listened to the dreadful news my mind conjured up Rozsa's Father's kind face. "Knowledgeable officers like him were purged from the new army to be replaced by the likes of these..." I almost missed the questions asked by one of the soldiers.

"What will happen now? What do you think?"

"Well, after they cooled off they began to look for a solution. They didn't know that I was made to work behind their tent and couldn't miss their conversation, even if I didn't want to hear. They have decided to falsify the records...To change the facts...They will all testify that we were led to the designated place and if needed they will offer proof."

"That is nonsense. These fox holes are going to betray them," announced a skeptical soldier. "You made all this up."

"Everything I told you is true, so help me God. And there is more..."

"Then tell us...We want to know," another soldier urged him.

"They will make us fill in the fox-holes and cover the signs of fresh diggings with pine needles. Then they will march us to the right mountain where we will dig new holes."

"What if we don't cooperate?" I asked with apprehension.

"We will, I assure you. They have decided to bribe us for our silence." The speaker smirked as he spoke.

"Bribe us with what?" we asked him, but he refused to answer our question.

"Wait and see," he stated and said no more.

***

We have sat on the ground, rested our tired bodies, prepared ourselves for the next ordeal, until two officers approached us, about an hour later.

The political officer was the first to speak.

"We have received new orders comrades. You are to fill in all these holes. No sign of our presence must remain. Cover the fresh diggings with pine needles. Pick up every piece of garbage. No one must ever know that we were here. Another hill we will have to conquer. There we shall dig a few fox-holes and after that we will take a leisurely walk back to our camp. This second climb is our real destination; the first one was only a test of your skills. All I said and our presence here are now classified information. Do I make myself clear comrades?"

Our less than enthusiastic replies made him look at the security officer, who nodded his head.

"Your silence is most important...And so is ours about the two incidents that never happened. The soldier who pointed his gun at me and the other who fired the blank will remain free...Those incidents must be forgotten, if they are to live. What do you say men?"

A lanky red head was the first to speak.

"Leave it to me comrades...I will persuade my fellow students." He gave his assurance.

"Very well friends...Those incidents never happened, but just to assure your silence I will tell you this. We are powerful men, not like the other officers. We hold the lives of those two students in the palms of our hands. We have the ability, the cunning and the will to punish anyone who gives away a state secret." The speaker turned and the two of them walked away.

The red-head asked us to gather around him and when he was satisfied that all of us were within hearing distance, he began to speak.

"Did any of you say anything to anyone about those two incidents?"

"We spoke to no one..."

"The others were far away from us..."

"Nobody knows, but us, unless the officers passed on the information," came the replies from various students.

"I doubt that very much. These officers are ashamed of how the exercise was bungled and their pride would not allow them to speak about how they were attacked." Stated someone and all of us agreed that his statement made sense.

"Fine. Now I must ask for your word to remain silent. Surely saving two lives deserves that."

We have made our promises one by one and like a young bunch of boys pledging eternal brotherhood, we shook hands with each other.

***

We marched; climbed the other mountain; had our first hot meal in two days. When we finished digging new fox-holes, we began our descent and when we reached the vineyards covered foot-hills someone began to sing. The old love songs left our lips, swirled in the slight breeze and were picked up by the other units. The officers looked at each other, perhaps contemplating to order us to change our tune, but they have remained silent.

***

In spite of the long march, back to camp, I felt less exhausted, my heart was no longer heavy, even the despised, uncomfortable uniform bothered me less than before.

"I was part of our little group...There was no war...I did not have to kill anyone, instead I played a small part of saving those two boys whose desperation pushed them beyond the limit of their endurance, before I was about to crack. I will be able to return to my Rozsa...Only a few days and I will be heading home." The joyous thoughts brought a rare, involuntary smile to my face and a boy beside me spoke up for the first time on our return journey.

"You seem to be in a happy mood. Almost eight weeks have passed since we came to serve our time and I have never seen you crack a smile before."

"Did we have anything to smile about?"

"Not much. Maybe nothing at all, I guess, but we are alive...We didn't have to face the enemy."

"The enemies were all around us," my words slipped out.

"I know that well." He stated in a whisper. His four simple words contained so much warmth, such sincerity that I couldn't remain quiet. For almost eight weeks I felt totally alone; I have never dared to trust anyone, but there on the dusty road, under the scorching Sun, I felt a sudden, desperate need to touch just one soul, to experience the warmth of sharing.

"The Americans are not the real enemy. They are not evil. They didn't rape our women; they did not invade our country."

"I grant you that...It was seven Russian soldiers who raped my Mother and my little Sister, seven years ago. My dear Mother and my sweet Sister, may they rest in peace, took their own lives after the Russians left them bleeding. I was a young, helpless boy watching their suffering...My tears came in rivulets...I begged the pigs to leave them alone, but the drunken animals paid no heed to me," he almost sobbed as he shared his recollections.

"I am sorry...I didn't know."

"There is so much we don't know about each other. The Communists are very skillful in making us keep our silence. All of us are forced to suffer alone."

"I know that well, but now and then we must trust someone. I have three friends at the university and we share our secrets; we carry each others' burdens; we partake in each others' joys."

"It is no different with me...But here we have forgotten how to create bonds of friendship." He spoke about what I had missed during the entire summer.

"It is never too late," I stated boldly and for a long time I spoke to him like I would have talked to a trusted, life-long friend.

"You didn't have it easy either," he acknowledged and lounged into his own story.

The rape of his Mother and Sister and their suicides were the first blows that young boy had experienced. The poor orphan was reared by his Father for three long, lonely, painful years. When his only remaining parent was arrested; when his Father was sentenced to death for conspiring against the Communists, he was only sixteen years old.

He spent a year in an orphanage; then they enrolled him at a university to become an engineer. His joining of the Communist Party was the price commanded for receiving his higher education. He paid the price and kept his silence; locked his hatred in his heart and waited for his opportunity to take vengeance.

When he finished unloading the burden of his soul, he made one more statement.

"A few years from now there will be a revolution."

Once I heard the dangerous word, once that word was spoken my fear reared its ugly head and a tremor shook my body.

"Have I gone too far trusting this stranger? Have I put myself in mortal danger? Did I ruin my chances of being free, of being able to return to my dear Rozsa? If he is real and not a plant, I have shared my deepest secrets with a plotter. If they ever nab him; if he then confesses; if he would implicate me as part of his scheme, I would be finished." I thought in misery and cursed my stupidity for ever having started this conversation.

"I know what you are thinking. I had similar thoughts many times before. You fear that I may betray you. Have no fear my dear friend. I do not know your name and you do not know mine. We will leave it that way...In two days we will go our separate ways and probably we will never see each other. I ask one thing only from you: when the revolution breaks out remember what I told you. I will pick up a weapon and make sure that it is loaded with real bullets. For each rapist I will take one life and when I am finished there will be seven Russians less." His words were somber, his face set in stony resolution, his tall frame was bent with the weight of his agonies resurrected by our conversation.

We never spoke another word again to each other. An hour later we have reached our compound and stood on the Minister's Road, waiting to be addressed.

"Stand at ease, soldiers. In the name of our beloved Stalin, on behalf of our great leader, Rakosi, I congratulate you. Words of your success have reached us long before your return. The attack you have carried out without a single misstep. Your almost eight weeks of training have enabled you to force back the enemy. The fascist, imperialist bands retreated in fear...They dared not face you...They ran before you...I congratulate you on your magnificent success. They will never dare to attack us as long as we have a skillful, well trained, superbly equipped army. Continue to defend our peace! Remain as vigilant as you were during these last few days and they will never dare to invade us," our Major General spoke at length, puffed out his chest with pride of our false achievements and beamed at the Colonels, who stood proudly beside him.

"Now you will be given a day of well deserved rest. You will receive food, normally reserved for heroes...The beer that will be issued, a huge tankard for each of you, will be to your liking. The day after tomorrow you will return your uniforms, your weapons and everything else that belongs to the army. You will don your civilian garments, I think quite reluctantly and you will return to your universities. It makes us sad to see you go, but ten months is not a long time...Be patient, time will pass, and you will be allowed to rejoin us at the end of your university year. You have done a fine job! You are dismissed!"

***

The steam locomotive began to cross the Danube on the newly built bridge and the steel structure shook and I shivered with anticipation.

"Just ten more minutes and I will be in Baja. I don't expect anyone to meet me. I will rush home; great my parents and George; catch up on all the news I have missed out on for eight weeks; then the greatest moment of my life will arrive. I will rush down to Lokert Row, where the Buja family lives. I had only one letter from Rozsa all these weeks, but that letter spoke about nothing other than our love, her loneliness, her hope for my return and her successful finish of her secretarial studies. She will get a job she assured me. Her hard work, her excellent results, cut the length of her studies almost in half and she became a fully qualified secretary at the young age of fifteen. I hope she is well...I hope she still loves me...I hope for three days of absolute happiness." I thought about her and my next three days in heaven and the train finally pulled into the station.

Each and every day of my service in the army seemed to last for an eternity, but once I entered Baja; once the clock began to tick off the minutes of my three days' stay, the passage of time shifted from slow to great rapidity.

I tried to slow the passage of time, but my watch kept indicating my desire's futility. The few hours I have spent with my family flew by like a brief moment, but it was long enough to learn that my Father still had his job in the army; that my Mother was well and so was George. My Uncle Jozsef and Aunt Gizella lived a quiet, happy life. The rest of my relatives fared well during the hot, sweltering summer.

When there was no more news to listen to, I glanced at my watch and my heart began to beat a lot faster.

"It is five o'clock already. I can begin to walk to the Buja's. By the time I arrive to their home they will have finished supper. Rozsa will be home...She will be surprised and truly happy."

Thirty minutes later I knocked on the wooden gate and with my heart in my throat I have waited. No answer came to even my second knocking and then a window opened at the next house and a woman shouted.

"Stop your knocking...Can't you see that they are away?"

I walked up and down the street; glanced at my watch from time to time and felt a dread that made me terribly unhappy.

"Seventy-two hours is all I have. No, that is wrong. Three hours of that I had spent with my family and by walking here. Sixty-nine hours are left only, or maybe even less. Where could they be? Had they gone to visit someone? Maybe the Gomorys?" I ran the length of Lokert Row, down the long street of St. Antal, renamed by the Communists to honor one of their own, Szamuelly. Before I reached the squalid, brick house, owned by Rozsa's maternal Aunt's family, I began to think fearful thoughts.

"Did something happen to my beloved Rozsa? My parents said nothing about her. Were they silent about my beloved to spare me from pain? Is it possible that Rozsa's parents have learned the news of my arrival and for some unknown reason they are trying to prevent her from seeing me? That is stupid! I must stop this nonsense. Why do I always imagine the worst? Curse my nature..." Thank God I have reached the home of the Gomorys' before my imagination had time to dwell more on millions of possibilities.

I banged on the huge, wooden gate, while I kept my finger on the bell's push-button. In my mind's eye I could see the long yard, almost every square inch of it covered with many different flowers. I picked up the sweet perfume of roses, the fragrance of carnations. I could see the long hallway where the large family always gathered to celebrate birthdays, anniversaries, name-days or the killing of a pig. I knew that the hallway's outside wall was always covered with heavy bunches of grapes Rozsa's Uncle cultivated with loving care. The same care he lavished on countless carrier pigeons that now fluttered high above the house. I loved that house and all the people who occupied it. I loved to sit there with Rozsa and to talk with her relatives.

Her maternal Grand-Mother was always kind and wise and understanding. When she looked at the two of us, she of all people best understood the depth, the strength, the reality of our love. Whenever she could, she provided us with a few moments of privacy, but not without her kindly warning: "You be good kids...You be good."

Rozsa's Uncle Sandor, Aunt Margit and their only son, Sana, were just as kind, but less understanding. Sana loved to tease the two of us; Sandor demanded a share of my time by insisting to have me play cards with them, even when I would have loved to spend every minute of my time with my darling Rozsa. Margit was endlessly plying us with food, sometimes suggesting that people cannot survive just on love.

I stood there and waited for one of these kind people to come to the gate to admit me. The slow response to my bell ringing, knocking and to my silently screaming soul surprised me, but when I was about to give up, I heard the key turn in the large lock and Sana's round, twenty-four year old, beaming face appeared.

"What are you doing here Laszlo? I thought you were in the army, defending our country, protecting our peace, like a good Hungarian boy should." He was joshing me of course, but since he served his two years in the army, he had little use for anyone who was able to avoid the two or three year long draft.

"I finished my summer service. I just came home, but couldn't find Rozsa. I hoped to find her here."

"Her Father and Mother are here...So is her brother...Well let me think. Did she come with them or did she go somewhere with a boy-friend?" He would have teased me, tortured me longer, but my patience evaporated.

"For God's sake, Sana, don't waste my time. I had enough of that in the army. If she is here tell me now. If she is not, I want to know."

"Aren't we impatient? Well never mind, come in, have a drink, maybe even a card game?" His eyes twinkled, as he kept up his torment, threw back his sand colored hair with a shake of his head and led me into the glassed-in hallway.

In the fading sunlight of the evening I searched the long, wide, enclosed hallway for the one person that meant the world to me. I saw the three Gomorys, Grandmother Pestalits, the three Bujas, but for her I searched in vain. While I shook hands with everyone, while I have listened to their warm words of welcome, my mind raced and my heart began its irregular beat.

"Was Sana right? Did my Rozsa go somewhere with a boy friend? How could that be?"

I was made to sit down. I sipped the red wine from the tall glass, provided by the older Mr. Gomory. I answered all their questions that came from various speakers, but all the while my eyes flitted from door to door, hoping, wishing for my angel to appear.

"How long will you be home?" Mr. Buja asked me.

"I had seventy-two hours when I have arrived home, but that time is fast disappearing." My lament wasn't wasted on Mrs. Pestalits.

"You must be looking for my Grand-daughter, if I am not mistaken." She didn't wait for my answer, instead she tried to ease my misery. "She should be back any minute...We sent her to the vine-yard with two large, empty *demizsons*. Our customers love our wine and we almost ran out. She must have filled the *demizsons* by now...She must be on Sana's bike, driving home. Soon she will be here."

I imagined my darling sitting on the old bike; I could see on the bike's handle-bars the two full, three gallon glass jars-tightly covered with woven reeds to protect the precious content-hanging; her lovely feet pushing the paddles, reducing the distance, coming to me.

I could picture not only her, but the vine-yard with its press-house, where she and

I have spent many pleasant hours. The few acres of sandy plot with its neat, long rows of grapes I could see clearly. The press house, built from mud and straw, with its thatched roof, provided us with a few, occasional moments of privacy. Whenever we spent some time at that lovely place we admired the many tall poplars, that stood in a long row, pointing their countless branches toward heaven. That sight never failed to move us. The press-house we never entered without being tempted to steal a sweet kiss, whenever we were alone.

I imagined the large, concrete, cylindrical tank that stood in the middle of the vine-yard, where Sana and his Father, two or three times a year, had mixed the spray that was to protect the young grapes from any and all disease. I have re-lived that hot, sunny afternoon when Rozsa and I went there, so long ago. We wore our swim-wear under our clothing...The concrete tank was full of inviting, cooling water and the two of us were urged by Sana to take a dip. Rozsa and I climbed into the refreshing fluid, that came up to our necks and her nearness, the occasional, accidental touch of her thighs even now made me tremble, but not as much as we both did a few hours after our foolish adventure.

Sana knew that the water contained trace chemicals, but he never suspected how much damage that could do. For weeks after our dip, I had suffered itchy rashes that attacked my most tender parts. When I complained to Sana, when I blamed him, he burst out laughing. I could hear even now his words of mocking.

"I thought love made you strong Laszlo...Those precious moments you spent in the water, so close to each other, surely was worth the cost," he continued laughing and Rozsa and I began to blush.

"So I was right...The two of you were real close in the tank. The rash will disappear with time, but your memories of those moments will live for ever," he shouted at us, as Rozsa chased him playfully with a broom-stick.

My thoughts meandered around the past and then the doorbell rang.

"It must be Rozsa!" Sana announced and went to the gate and I, without thinking, jumped up, rushed after him, unable to wait a single moment.

She was slightly flushed from the four mile bike trip...Her face was even more beautiful than I had remembered. Her hair sparkled, took on a reddish halo from the kisses the rays of the setting Sun gave her and I had envied even the Sun for being able to touch my darling. Her wonderful blue eyes shone with excitement and in their depths I saw a glint of sadness, a trace of fatigue. Her lips opened slightly as she began to speak.

"When did you get home Laszlo?"

"A few hours ago."

"How long can you stay?"

"Only three days and some of that I have already wasted." She understood what I have meant and so did Mrs. Pestalits, who joined us.

"Well...Why waste any more? Rozsa you take the *demizsons* into the pantry. Fill all the empty bottles you can. Laszlo go with her, she could use your help. Sana you come with me." She issued the orders. Two of us were ready to obey her, but Sana had other ideas.

"I go where I want to. Laszlo and Rozsa will need my help."

"When we needed two *demizsons* of wine, did you or Joe volunteer? No, it was Rozsa. She is kind, willing to work, a sweet little girl...She and Laszlo will work in the pantry and you will come with me." She raised her voice and Sana's defiance ceased to exist.

Rozsa and I entered the pantry, closed the door and my words rushed out.

"I missed you so much my dearest, my darling."

"I missed you too Laszlo."

"Eight weeks without you was more than I thought I can endure. It was living hell just to be away from you, but what they have put us through made it a lot worse. It was so bad that you can never imagine."

"You are back Laszlo, that is all that matters. We have only a few moments before someone will come in..." She took one step toward me and I stood there for one moment, not daring to accept her inviting lips.

She took one more step, I picked up her sweet scent and my hesitation disappeared. The one, long, sweet kiss wiped out eight weeks of suffering and my misery abated.

"I love you dearly...," I told her when our lips have reluctantly parted.

"And I love you even more," she declared, just before the door opened.

"How is the job coming?" Mrs. Pestalits inquired and a smile played around her lips. "Now fill the bottles and be quick about it. I don't want my daughter or my son-in-law to become impatient. They gave you a hard enough time Rozsa...Didn't they urge you to forget Laszlo? Don't misunderstand my dear boy what I revealed. They think Rozsa is too young to love, but that is only half of the story. They think you are sickly...Will be unable to provide for Rozsa...They fret about how serious your love for each other became."

"But that is not so...I will be a teacher in a year. I will make a living...I will provide for Rozsa...I will make her really happy!"

"You will fill those bottles, that is what you will do. Then you two will come out and spend time with them and remember to behave." She stepped out of the pantry, pulled the door in behind her and I paled with what she had revealed.

"I thought they liked me..."

"They do Laszlo, but they are my parents. Is it so unnatural for parents to fear the loss of a daughter?"

"That I understand, but they will never lose you even when we marry."

"That is not the way they see it. Have patience my love...And now please help me, we wasted enough time already."

'Wasted enough time...', her words echoed in my mind, as we hurriedly filled the bottles. 'Wasted enough time...' I recalled her words as we sat down in the hall-way. 'Wasted enough time...', those three words circled around in my head as I tried to listen to the adults' conversation.

Rozsa and I set in the two corners of a divan, a vast gulf between us, that I didn't dare to bridge. 'Remember to behave...Remember to behave...Remember to behave...', the warning of Rozsa's Grandmother echoed in my mind and I didn't dare to move closer to Rozsa; I barely dared to open my mouth, in case my feelings rushed to my lips; I looked in her direction only when the adults wouldn't notice and I nursed my pain.

Almost two hours later the Bujas said good-bye to their relatives and the five of us began to walk toward their home. Rozsa and I front of her parents, flanked by Joe, who peppered me with questions about life in the army. I gave him curt answers, still smarting from Rozsa's words of 'wasted enough time.' Still trying to understand what Mrs. Pestalits said about Rozsa's parents and their fear for their daughter's future.

When we reached their gate, when they were about to enter, I hoped to receive an invitation, but that never came.

"May I come in for a little while?" My voice must have sounded sheepish, it certainly sounded to me and I hoped to be allowed in; to be able to sit with Rozsa on the cot in the kitchen, where we sat so many times before. I hoped with all my heart that her parents will go to bed, that Joe will somehow disappear and that Rozsa and I will have time to talk and by so doing the blow of her unusual words would be softened. I didn't want to say good-night, not yet. I didn't want to part her without another kiss.

"It may be better if you do not come in. It is almost eleven o'clock and Rozsa needs to rest," Mr. Buja delivered the devastating injunction and three of them entered the house, leaving the two of us alone.

"I am so sorry Laszlo...," Rozsa said.

"I understand...You had a long bicycle ride and it is quite late..." I tried to hide my misery and reached for her hand.

One small peck on her cheek was all I dared, one touch of her warm palm and slim fingers was all I managed, before she was about to disappear.

"Will I see you Rozsa?" I asked her in the dark street, and the night's shadows, I hoped were deep enough to hide my agony.

"Yes Laszlo...At the usual time and place."

***

I sat on the bench, behind which our tree grew almost two feet, since I carved the heart with our initials.

"R. B. stands for Rozsa Buja, the girl I love, the girl who loves me. Will she be strong enough to withstand her parents' urging or will she be weak and forsake me?" I asked myself and as six o'clock approached I did not doubt that my fist assumption was correct. Then as the minutes ticked by, as the appointed time slipped by and Rozsa didn't arrive I began to fear that her parents already succeeded.

Suddenly I felt two hands covering my eyes and my heart jumped, my spirits lifted. I didn't see her approach me, I didn't hear her footfalls, she just appeared.

"I feared my darling that you will not come," I whispered to her as she sat beside me, this time close enough to have our legs touch, to have me feel her body heat.

"I promised you Laszlo my everlasting love. Why do you doubt that?"

My heart beat even faster, but my tongue wouldn't obey me.

"Say something Laszlo...Tell me what you feel."

"I feel a terrible thing...How shall I describe it?"

"You were never lost for words before..."

"That was before...Your parents Rozsa...The things your Grandmother said...Are they really against me?"

"No, that is not so...They are against anyone who might take me away from them."

"Maybe I should tell them how much I love you? Maybe I should explain to them that you are my life, my hope, my dream. You are everything I have ever desired!"

"Maybe you shouldn't do that...Wait till you finish university. Once you begin to teach we will explain things to them together." Her urging, her words made sense and I changed the subject.

"I am sorry my darling for not having congratulated you before on having finished all your courses in half the time. I am so proud of you...Congratulations my dearest."

"Thank you Laszlo...Last night I didn't have a chance to tell you that this morning I was going for a job interview."

"I hope you were successful."

"I will not know for a few days, but they were impressed with my speed of typing and my short-hand came very handy. One of the officers dictated a letter and he barely finished a sentence when I had it down on paper. When I typed up all he dictated there wasn't a single mistake in the letter."

"Did you say an officer? You didn't send an application to the army?"

"I sent out two. One to the local office of the National Health Service and the other to the Defense Ministry. I haven't had a reply yet from the former, but the army was quite prompt, within a week they wanted to see me."

Had it been any other time, maybe I wouldn't have objected, but after my eight weeks of association with those magnificent, well trained, unscrupulous bastards I feared to have Rozsa work with men like those and my objections spilled out.

"Please do not accept a job with those rotten Communists. You have no idea what scoundrels they are...What hideous creatures they can be," I begged her trying to control my anger.

"We are not even married and you are ready to control me. My Father may be right... He told me you will object."

"I am not trying to control you...I am trying to save you from a fate that no girl of your talent, no woman of your charm, no lady of your beauty should need to tolerate."

"So what fate do you fear Laszlo?"

"I had eight weeks of being their class enemy. They used us, abused us, made us suffer all kinds of indignities..." All the things I have tried to forget, things I tried to lock away in my mind's hidden compartments spilled out of my mouth, but before I could continue Rozsa stopped me.

"I am not trying to join the army...I will be a civilian secretary, if they have me."

"They will have you, I have no doubt of that. They will force you, they will violate you, they will destroy your innocence...They may even rape you." I knew I went too far, having used that word that was not to be uttered in the presence of a lady.

"I see! My Mother was right too. She told me you are the jealous kind, who will not be able to trust me."

"I love you Rozsa...I cannot stand the thought of anyone being near you...You belong to me," I uttered the foolish statements; I confirmed her Mother's findings.

"How am I ever to take a job? How am I to earn a living, with what you have just told me?"

"I am sorry. Please forgive me...I didn't mean to hurt you...I came home from that living hell. Counted the hours we will be together...I was looking forward to seventy-two beautiful hours. I have wasted a few with my family, I have wasted a few more, last night, while I have waited for you at the Gomorys. I have lost several hours when your parents refused to invite me in. All this day I walked around the city, pining for you and counting the hours I was losing and now that we are finally together I was stupid, started a fight...Please forgive me!"

"Very well...We will waste not another minute. Let's go to a movie." Her peace offering I accepted gladly. I bought the tickets to the upper most row of the gallery and there we sat in the darkness, nobody behind us, in total privacy. She allowed me to hold her hand, my hurting words probably forgotten and when the movie ended I didn't even remember the title, I was oblivious of the story line, I have not even seen the screen. In the flickering light of the projector I watched her beautiful face, her slightly pointed nose, her rosy cheeks, her tiny ears, her silken skin, her graceful neck, her cascading hair and I filled my mind, my heart, my soul with her being.

***

On the third day of my short stay Rozsa and I decided to spend the day together. I borrowed my Father's bicycle and his short, wooden *csickly*.

When we left our house Rozsa sat on the cross-bar and I began to drive us toward the Danube, where we wanted to have a picnic.

With great care I drove the bicycle, trying to avoid the road ruts, trying to assure her safety.

"I will not let this wonderful day be spoiled by anything," I promised myself. My jealousy I tried to fight; my fear of her parents' disapproval I tried to forget. Her closeness to me; her beauty; her sweet voice I found quite distracting and for just one second I lost my concentration and we took a spill.

"Dear God...Please forgive me...Are you all right? Are you hurt? Should I take you home? I am sorry I was so clumsy." My questions tumbled out almost without end; my apologies were sincere, all the while fearing that my stupidity ruined our precious day.

"I am all right Laszlo. Just a bruise on my leg, but it doesn't really matter. I don't want to go home. Let's just continue."

We resumed our journey, but this time we walked beside the bicycle. I felt utterly foolish. We reached the Danube, just above the new bridge, where my Father's *csikly* was chained to the boat landing.

"There it is Rozsa." I pointed at the three meter long, narrow, wooden boat and I rushed to pick up a paddle, to unlock the pad-lock that secured the small boat.

When Rozsa stepped into the boat I held her hand, stabilized the flimsy craft and made her sit. I took up my place at the squared, rear-end of the boat, facing her and pushed it away from the shore of the Danube's tributary. I pointed to the mouth of the small river and explained my plan to my beloved.

"We will turn up-stream when we reach the Danube...I will paddle three miles or so against the current. Upstream there is a lovely, sandy island. That will be our destination."

"Isn't that too far Laszlo?" I wasn't sure if she doubted my ability, my stamina to paddle that far, but her voice, her words indicated concern.

Just to demonstrate that I am not an invalid I picked up the tempo of my strokes.

"I had paddled this boat many times before, even across the Danube..." I assured myself and never gave a thought to the fact that on every one of those occasion Joska Lazar was with me and even with his help the task of traveling on this river wasn't easy.

For one mile I have paddled and Rozsa chatted on about the beauty of our river. She pointed in excitement at the ducks that flew near-by. Her laughter rang out when an occasional wave reached over the side of the boat and a few drops of water kissed her bare, shapely legs, or wet her lovely shoulder, where her short-sleeve blouse didn't cover.

She rocked with the waves of a passing streamer; she let the sun-rays caress her up-lifted face; she allowed the slight breeze to hug her gorgeous body; she moistened her lips with her tiny, pink tongue. I watched her every action, basked in the joy of having my love with me.

I was so absorbed by the sights, the sounds of my beloved that I almost missed noticing the first rock pile that jutted out from shore, far into the Danube to direct the current into the shipping-lanes. The rocks were just below the surface; the water rushed above them making our small boat slip and spin. My paddle strokes changed the boat's direction, away from shore, seeking the tip of the rock-pile, hoping to navigate above it.

My first attempt failed and our *csikly* was driven south. I have spent too much energy during the first mile of our trip and suddenly I felt myself weak and helpless.

Rozsa became silent. She looked around for a second paddle and when she had found none she had paled. Her body became rigid, maybe she became frightened, but her words remained kind and understanding.

"We don't really need to go to that island. It is too far away and the current is too strong. Maybe we should turn back. There are lots of nice places over there..." She pointed toward the shore.

I said nothing...I slipped our boat under the rock pile and made three more, futile attempts. Sweat poured off my body. My exhaustion made my breathing raspy. My arms could barely lift the paddle. When finally I have succumbed to being a weakling, I turned the boat toward the shore and tied it to the trunk of a huge tree.

"I am sorry Rozsa...Your parents are right...I am not strong. I am sickly. I am no good for anything."

She gave me one of her sweetest smiles, sat down under the huge weeping willow and patted the ground beside her, inviting me to sit.

"You are strong in your own way. You are not sickly. You are good...for me."

I had reached for her bare shoulders, pulled her just a little closer and when our lips met the world began to spin. I was dizzy with happiness; I was weak with consuming desire; I was exhausted from my fight with the Danube and I was immensely thankful for her understanding.

"I promised to take you to that island, but I failed to do that. I promised to drive you to the Danube, but I have dumped you instead." Suddenly I remembered the red welt just below her knee and I couldn't help myself. My lips had a mind of their own and they found the injured spot, touched it to make it better.

I would have liked nothing more than to kiss the rest of her lovely leg, to smother

her entire body with endless kisses. My heart desired one thing, but my mind intervened.

"I scared her about the officers of the army and here I am ready to prove that I am no better," my mind screamed and commanded me to tear my lips away from her injured leg. I shifted my position to put some distance between us and when she spoke I was truly glad.

"Thank you Laszlo...For a moment you made me afraid."

"Please Rozsa, never fear me. I will wait until we wed."

For a few hours we ate and drank and marveled at the Danube. We spoke about a thousand things and when it was time to turn toward home, to catch my late afternoon train, I looked deep into Rozsa's blue eyes and I saw the depth of her love, the strength of her commitment.

Chapter 8

The joy of seeing my friends again brought new hope and after three nights' of sharing our army experiences we have exhausted the subject. Our full attention was turned to our courses and all four of us began to get excited about our first practice teaching.

I was given a week to make my preparations and when the time came to enter the class, to face my pupils, I thought of my beloved Rozsa, screwed up my courage and plunged into the lesson I have worked on for several days.

Those eager faces followed my every move; their alert eyes watched the experiments I chose to demonstrate; their keen ears have tuned in to every word I spoke and when it was over they rewarded me with an splendid ovation.

My twenty-seven classmates witnessed my performance, as did Professor Kobor and the pupils' regular teacher.

When Professor Kobor faced us, in his lecture room, he began to speak.

"Laszlo had his first taste of teaching and he did quite well, I am pleased to say, but I am not the only judge...Their regular teacher will evaluate his performance, then his class-mates will do the same." I was alarmed by hearing Kobor's announcement, but I picked up my pen, ready to take notes, so that next time I could do even better. I thought of how proud I would make my dear Rozsa; how I would satisfy my critics' every whim.

The regular teacher spoke at length about my good lesson plan that was carried out rather poorly; my class-mates followed his example. They did not pull any punches. One after another they have found fault with something I said, with something I did, with the way I moved, with the timber of my voice, with my stern facial expressions and when they fell silent I had good reasons to feel devastated. Until later I was unable to understand what made them disregard Professor Kobor's praise, what motivated them to accentuate the negatives.

"Today I was the victim of their words, but tomorrow and the days after they will be the teachers and I will be called upon to criticize them. Why were they so outspoken? Why were they so stingy with their praise?" I asked myself these questions and many more, after I have retired for the night. I began to see, very slowly, the explanations for their cruelty, for that is what I considered their deeds to be.

"In our society it is expected from everyone to pay lip-service to excellence and even when a feat is attained the critics are expected to demand always greater achievements. My fellow students have learned to tow the party line, at least in public and they expect nothing less from me. Criticism of self and of others became a necessary ingredient of our daily lives, without it we were the enemy." I comforted myself by analyzing our political system's quirks and promised myself that all my lessons I shall prepare with more painstaking care than I have prepared the last one.

Before my next opportunity came to teach a class, before winter was about to dump its first load of snow, I have received a letter from my brother with the shattering news.

Our Father was arrested just days ago, once again put in prison for some crime I was sure he has never committed. His lawyer was still unable to find out what his crime was and I was ordered to remain at the university. George wrote about our Father's command, issued before he was taken from his family.

"Tell Laszlo to remain at the university. I will not tolerate him quitting...He is not to come home to try to visit me. When the charges are known, when a trial date is set, then and only then will he be permitted to return to Baja," George wrote and I could see my Father once again sitting in the city's prison; once again facing an uncertain future. Had I dared, I would have rushed home to visit him, to console him, to tell him that I believe in his innocence, to share with him the stories about other Hungarian men and women who were also condemned falsely by the political masters, but I dared not defy his orders. My friends tried to console me when I told them the terrible news, but none of their words, none of their actions eased my pain, a pain that began to take its toll.

I didn't allow my studies to flag, but my feeling of hatred for our leaders was coming to a boiling point as inevitably as day follows night, as winter comes after fall, as days march one after another. My hate kept filling up my heart, in spite of my never ending fight against that self-destructive feeling, but love resided there as well. Love for my far-away Rozsa; hope for a long, happy life together; desire to see her soon; to hold her hand; to feast my eyes upon her beautiful face, slowly pushed aside the hate and my happiness took center stage, surrounded by hidden ugly feelings.

In that confused state I have attended my many classes, carried out the required laboratory work, prepared my many assignments and warmed to the children whom I was to teach, once a week. Slowly my professor, the real teacher of those students and even my classmates found less and less grounds to chastise me and when they began to give their guarded praises on my improved practice teaching my spirits lifted and the process of healing began anew. Hate was shoved aside by love; bitterness was replaced by hope and satisfaction of a job well done took over.

My Father was still in prison when November began to dump its first cold rains, down-pours that cut through my flimsy rain-coat, chilling me to the bone and our once again cold dormitory offered some refuge, but little warmth. My moments of solace came from Rozsa's letters that spoke of her undying love; spoke about the job she has taken with the National Health Department of Baja, where she became the personal secretary to the Director, after her first month on the job. I was deliriously with happiness when I have learned that my love wasn't working for the hated Hungarian Army. Whether she chose to reject them or the other way around mattered not the least to me.

We have exchanged letters regularly, ever since our wonderful three days together, and neither of us had ever failed to reaffirm our love that with the passing of each day grew immensely. Her last letter came in the middle of November and when I have read it my heart rejoiced.

The rains became more frequent, but the chill that insidiously worked on my body couldn't penetrate to where my love warmed me, protected me, sustained me. Not until the dreadful day when another letter arrived, not from her, but from her Father, Mr. Buja.

"Laszlo," I stared at the single word. Didn't want to believe the absence of endearing adjectives. For a few minutes I didn't dare to continue my reading. I happened to be alone in the room and shook with fear, shivered with dread, as I forced myself to continue my reading.

"Ever since your last visit home Maria and I have given a lot of thought to what I am about to do. Please do not take it as a personal attack on you Laszlo...It is not that, but our parental love for Rozsa forced us to reach this conclusion.

"Rozsa is far too young to have a boy-friend whose intentions are as serious as yours. She has a job and barely passed fifteen. With her whole life ahead of her she should meet other people, make something of her life, go to dances, have many dates, enjoy life, be given time to mature.

"When she reaches the age of twenty, she should be still single and wise enough to make a choice. That choice she is not permitted to make now. Before you become a teacher; before you come to us to ask for her hand, as we know you will do soon; before you force her to ruin her life by becoming a far too young married woman we decided to act.

"We have forbidden her to see you again. She is an obedient girl, we know that, but we also know that she thinks she loves you and on your request she probably would disobey us. Thus we have no choice, but to appeal to you as a friend. If you truly love her you will let her be free. If you respect us you will stay away from our daughter. If you defy us you will incur our wrath.

"Find someone older to love and leave our daughter alone."

"With best wishes, Jozsef Buja."

I stared at the letter with my heart in a million pieces. I have re-read it several times, each time feeling a dagger plunge deeper into my heart and I felt the futility of life invade my soul, cry out for release. I was unable to face my friends, to remain in the room one moment longer. I rushed out into the rainy evening, feeling not the chill of the cold wetness. Stumbled along streets that I knew well, yet no longer recognized. I passed by many others, who shivered in the frigid weather, in spite of their heavy coats and umbrellas that provided them with a measure of protection.

I must have walked for hours-aimlessly, daring not to think about the girl I loved, about that dreadful edict-before my friends came upon me.

The bed did not provide warmth, the blankets did not thaw out my frozen soul, the hot soup, my friends tried to force into me, made me gag. Then some time later I have begun to shake and shiver and felt intense heat that replaced the cold and oblivion enveloped me.

***

"Three days you have been out...Oblivious to everything. Thank God you are out of danger." I heard Ocsi's voice, but his face was blurred, distorted.

"Say something Laszlo; for God's sake tell us what happened." Jeno's voice intruded and I have realized with deep regret that I was alive, I was only sick. I wanted to die; I wanted to escape the memory of that letter and all the other injustices, all the sufferings, so I just lay in my bed and remained silent.

"Is it your Father Laszlo? Did something more happen to him?" Peter asked me and I had no desire to even shake my head.

"He is unable to talk...The doctor told us this may happen. The meningitis must have affected his brain. Please God do not let him die, please help our friend." I heard Jeno's words and prayer, yet it seemed he was far, far away.

"Should we contact Laszlo's parents?" Ocsi wondered out loud and I was puzzled. During the days of my delirium I thought I saw my Father sitting beside me, holding my hand, while my Mother was wiping my sweaty brow with a wet, cool towel. Rozsa stood beside them, touching my feverish cheeks, showering my face, my lips with her healing kisses. All through the ordeal the three people I loved most made reassuring promises, offered encouragements.

"You will get better, never mind what the doctor said..." my Mother's voice came back to me.

"You are like me, Son...You are stubborn, you will use that stubbornness, that is what will make you live," my Father told me.

"You will live Laszlo...You will get well...I cannot live without you...I love you...Never mind that letter...My Father didn't mean to send it...Please my darling, get well for me." I heard Rozsa's sweet voice, repeating those words, day and night, and the three of them never left my side, they fought for me, they urged me to recover, yet they were not really present, they were far away, unaware of my illness.

"No...We shouldn't bother Laszlo's parents. His Father is in prison, his Mother has more than enough to worry about," Peter suggested.

"And what about his sweetheart?" Ocsi groped for any course of action.

It was at that point that they began to search my book-bag; they picked up my pants and coat and looked in all the pockets. My first reaction was to stop them; to prevent them from finding the letter, but my weakness overtook me and my protests died before my lips could have obeyed me.

The darkness that came I welcomed with my shattered heart. The oblivion may have lasted for only a fraction of a second or for hours, I never found out. Then their voices once again intruded.

"After the letter Rozsa's Father wrote to Laszlo we shouldn't do that either." I heard Peter's startling revelation and I wondered how did they know, but I was too weak to search for an answer.

The old doctor came every second day with his black case that he placed beside my feet and sat with me for many moments.

"How do you feel today Laszlo?" he asked me on the eight day of my illness, as he did during each visit, but this time I heard his question clearly. I just stared at the bottom of the upper bunk-bed, wishing for nothing less than death. Wanting nothing less than an end to my misery.

"Is there anything we can do for him?" Ocsi asked the doctor.

"Feed him. Keep him warm and find a way to restore his will to live," the doctor replied and Ocsi's statement startled me.

"We have force-fed him all these days; we kept him warm, but his spirit cannot be mended."

"What do you mean? Tell me everything, if you want your friend to recover," the doctor's face turned to Ocsi, expecting an honest answer.

"For over three years Laszlo has been in love with a sweet girl. Her name is Rozsa. That name is the only one that crossed his lips during his illness. In his feverish dreams he screamed her name; with tears rolling down his cheeks he beseeched her to keep on loving him."

"Well, there is your answer. Write to the girl. Tell her about Laszlo's condition. Convince her to come to see him...That may be the only way to save your friend." The old doctor held out new hope that Ocsi dashed with a single statement.

"Here is a letter Laszlo has received just before he fell ill. Please read it and once you did, you will understand why we cannot do as you suggested."

I watched the doctor reading the letter, dropping his old, wrinkled hands into his lap with a shake of his head.

"Why do parents do these things to their offsprings? Kids are born and grow up to be young adults, whose fate, whose right is to leave the nest. We understand that, yet we try to hold on to them. The hell with the stupidity of my generation. Her Father is no more important than this boy lying here. Do as I told you! She is the one to keep him alive...My medical knowledge; my medicines can do far less."

***

Two weeks later a letter came from Rozsa.

"My Dearest Laszlo," I have read with disbelieving eyes, with my last ounce of energy, the first line of her life saving letter and I felt a surge of hope, a new-born vitality. I didn't notice then that the letter was already open when Peter held it front of my eyes and ordered me to begin to read. I wasn't aware that I wasn't the first reader. My friends opened it, read it, I found out much later, to protect me from any further disappointment.

I became hungry, but not for food. I was ravenous for her neat handwriting, for her dear words, but most of all for her declaration of love.

"I have received a letter from your friends, Jeno, Ocsi and Peter. Thank God you have friends like them, whose every word beseeched me.

"I am sorry I didn't write to you sooner. I love my parents; all my life I had obeyed them. My love for you and my respect for them fought daily and had I not received your friends' letter, perhaps the latter would have proved to be strong enough to keep my silence, but no more of that. Love like ours happens only once in a life time...I know that now and I know about your illness. Please live Laszlo...Please get well...I cannot live without you...I love you...Never mind that letter...My Father didn't mean to send it...Please my darling, get well for me." I stopped my reading, my heart full of love and joy. Her last few words were not unlike what I imagined hearing during the first three days of my illness.

"Could it be that our love is so strong that not even the distance was able to hide from her what happened to me? Did she sense my almost fatal illness? Did I only imagine those lovely words or did she really reach out for me in my feverish dreams?" I wondered, but it no longer mattered. I turned back to continue reading her most precious letter.

"When you are able to travel please come home and I will meet you at our usual place. You name the day and the time and I will run to you with my arms open. Some day even my parents will forgive me.

"Now I must stop for my heart bleeds knowing that you, my precious, are in danger. Please get well...I pray for you daily. May the Good Lord help you and convince you about my love, as I will when you return to me.

"Your loving Rozsa."

I have re-read the letter three times and each time I felt a lot stronger. I sat up in my bed; swung my legs over the edge and to my friends' great amazement I stood up, teetering only slightly and began to speak.

"Thank you my friends...Your kindness will never be forgotten."

"This is a miracle...," Peter shouted.

"A miracle of the power of love," Ocsi declared with great solemnity.

"Miracle or not I think Laszlo you should see the doctor. That old man was truly concerned about you."

***

Within an hour I sat in the doctor's examination room and when I have answered all his questions; when he was satisfied with the results of his probing, he shook his head and uttered a few words.

"Now I have seen everything."

I sat there not quite sure what to say or what to do, but his silence didn't last long.

"The first time I saw you I was certain you will not survive. Meningitis is a very serious illness. Do you know what it is?"

"I know it is an illness." My stupid answer made him smile and he launched into his explanation.

"The brain of a human being is encased in a lining. Whatever causes meningitis inflames that lining. High fever, weakness, heart palpitations and inflammation of the cortex follow. I have lost more patients to this dreaded illness than I care to remember. You had all the classic symptoms of the killer disease and each time I went to see you I have expected the need to call a priest. Maybe I should have sent you to a hospital, but I figured you will get much better care from your room-mates than at any of our institutions. So I left you where you were and thank God that proved to be the right choice. When someone gets that illness, any serious illness that is, no medicine, no care, nothing in the whole world can replace the will to live. You had none of that precious commodity when I saw you last, yet you are here. How did this miracle come about really beats me."

I have listened to the doctor's lengthy description of my illness and I felt grateful for all he did.

"It was you doctor who saved me..."

"It wasn't I...Or if it was, I sure don't know how I did it."

"You told my friends what to do and their action restored my will to live."

"I see...The girl you love has responded?"

"She wrote to me."

"One letter, a few kind words, maybe a declaration of love and death was cheated." The old doctor made the simple statement and I nodded my head in agreement.

"I am happy...You have survived that terrible illness, you are on your way to a full recovery. What happened to you my boy gives me hope for the next time I have the misfortune to diagnose that illness. Now you must take care of yourself. You must eat well...Eat lots of honey. You must not catch a chill. Your heart has been weakened by your illness, so whenever you have to climb stairs be very careful. Take frequent rests, avoid all stress. These things are most important and at the slightest sign of any further trouble come back to see me. Now here is a note for the university...Three weeks you were ill and for two more weeks you are to take it easy. No more physical education classes for you young man and it wouldn't hurt if you could avoid the army." We shook hands before we parted and that was the last time I ever saw the old man.

***

I caught the first train to Baja and within two hours of my arrival I wrote my brief note to my beloved Rozsa. Elisabeth, one of my first cousins, poked her head into our kitchen, where I sat with my Mother, who was still wiping her tears, remembering what I told her about my illness.

"Laszlo just told me how sick he was..." My Mother's voice faded away after those few words and her renewed sobs made me regret that I told her anything.

"What was wrong with you Laszlo? You seem well, although too pale for my liking," Elisabeth inquired.

"Maybe I will tell you another time, but now I need to ask you a favor." I held my letter ready and I was about to ask her to deliver it.

"Well...You deny your first cousin the story of your illness, but you don't mind to ask her to do you a favor?"

"Don't argue Elisabeth...Take Laszlo's letter to your friend, Rozsa. She saved his life...That darling girl. If it wasn't for her Laszlo would probably be dead." She choked out the words and her crying infected Elisabeth.

"What are you crying about?" I asked her gently.

"You almost died. My favorite cousin almost died and I am not even allowed to cry?"

"Very well then...Cry a little Elisabeth, but do not take too much time. My letter must be taken to Rozsa."

My Mother and Elisabeth shed their tears; made comments about my dreadful illness; about my miraculous recovery; about that angel who saved my life and when they had no tears left, Elisabeth began her journey.

***

I have imagined my dear Rozsa receiving my letter; preparing herself for our six o'clock meeting in the garden of Dery, by our bench, front of our growing tree and that gave me so much solace that I dared to ask about my Father.

"Tell me about Father," I asked my Mother.

"Your Father is in prison, but that you know. Surely you had received George's letter?"

"I did Mother, a long time ago. Have they charged him yet? Have they set a date for his trial?"

"They sure did, the conniving bastards. You should go and visit him. He will tell you what you want to know."

"Will he not be angry? He ordered me not to come home."

"If he gets angry I will give him a piece of my mind when he is released. He will wish then that he was still in prison. You tell him that. Besides, once he knows how sick you were he will be glad to have his Son back."

"I will rather not tell him about my illness. He has enough to worry about."

"He worries, no mistake about that, but for some reason they treat him well. He is even allowed to play cards with other inmates. You know how he loves to play cards, maybe he will want to stay there?" My Mother prattled on, but didn't fool me. Her heart bled for my Father's loss of freedom, but not to put me under any stress she made light of his situation. "We are even allowed to take him food at the time of our weekly visit. We were given passes we can use. George and I alternate. This week neither of us has seen him yet, so here is the pass...Go see your Father."

***

I entered the visitors' room, not even a screen between us. He looked quite well, but his sharp eyes noticed immediately the unmistakable signs of my illness.

"You look like hell, Laszlo. What happened to you?"

I was tempted not to tell him about my illness, but his commanding eyes, his demanding words left me no choice, so I told him all that happened.

"I knew that something was wrong with you Laszlo. For weeks I wasn't able to sleep and when I did I had night-mares. I was truly worried about you, but why I couldn't fathom. I thank God for that old doctor...I thank your dear friends also...And your beloved Rozsa I shall never forget. Well enough of that my dear boy. You are a fool...No, I take that back. You are a love-sick fool and that Mr. Buja will someday have to face me. I will give him a piece of my mind. My Son is not good enough for his daughter?"

"That is not what he said in his letter. Please don't say anything to him ever. Promise me that you will not meddle."

"So now my own Son accuses me of meddling? Why am I always accused of things I didn't do?" His words revealed his bitterness.

"What are their accusations?"

"Where shall I begin? I got that job in the army...It wasn't much of a job, but it paid the rent. I was to serve in the army store as a sales-clerk and I did the best I could.

"'Run and get me a dozen bottles of beer.' Or 'I want two packs of cigarettes.' The soldiers' requests came and I served on them as fast as I could. Everything went fine until the political officer came into the store one afternoon.

"'Two bottles of beer, two packs of cigarettes, five chocolate bars and twenty decagrams of candy.' That was his order and I have assembled all he asked, but when I presented him with the bill, he declined to pay. 'You will get your money when I see you next, if I have it.' That is what he said and I defied his rank, his authority.

"'And you will get the goods when you have the money,' I announced boldly.

"He looked at me with eyes that couldn't believe my audacity and gave me one more chance. 'Just hand over the goods and I will forget your defiance.'

"'I have to account for every *filler*, my books must balance at the end of the day. So you either pay me now or make your purchase elsewhere.' He turned on his heels, but not before he put one finger to his temple and imitated the unmistakable sound of a gun discharging."

"And that is your crime Father? I cannot believe that even in this country someone would be put in prison for something like that."

"This is not even half of my story," my Father continued. "Two months have passed and we were ordered to go to summer camp. In our make-shift store we served soldiers, then when they have gone on long exercises we followed them and set up a tent. During their short breaks they rushed to get something to drink, something to eat and I and my helper served them as fast as we could. Sometimes in our hurry we have made mistakes in making change; at other times we have forgotten to return to them the few *fillers* of bottle deposits. Our books, that we have closed around mid-night every day, obviously didn't balance. One *Forint* doesn't buy much, one hundredths of a *Forint*, a *filler*, buys even less. Some nights we were out by a few *Forints*, other times only by a few *fillers*. During the whole summer we were out by less than one hundredths of one per cent. I gave not a thought to our great misdeeds, until I was arrested late this fall.

"The civilian policemen, who came for me, wouldn't or couldn't tell me anything. My jailers knew even less. My lawyer ran into a brick wall, until recently. The charges and the date of the trial were announced at the same time. I will be tried by Judge Tarnay."

"So what are the charges? When is the trial?"

"I am charged with profiteering; inflating government sanctioned prices; embezzlement and being the class enemy." He rattled off the charges and I was totally flabbergasted.

"Now it is my Father who is the class enemy. A simple shoe-maker who had no opportunity to get a decent education; one who earned his bread with the sweat of his labor. Class enemy indeed! These scoundrels use that label very freely. All the university students; all the learned men and women; all the people who ever crossed a cursed commie were labeled thus and their lives were turned up-side-down; their images were forever tarnished." The bitter thoughts brought back memories of my summer, but I took no time to dwell on that.

"Those are fabricated charges, Dad. During the trial you will be exonerated."

"That is what my lawyer tells me, but February 20th is still far away. That is the trial date, my Son, and until then I am a menace to society."

"I will come home for your trial. I will be in that court-room, so help me God!"

"And I will be pleased to know that you are there. Now how is your Mother and how is George?"

"They are well, Dad. They do manage."

"I am allowed to see one of them once a week."

"I am happy to know how lenient the Communists became."

"What choice did they have after your last visit? Do you remember the irritation you caused? After my first imprisonment you set fear in the hearts of minor officials and I guess the prison warden this time took the easy out."

"I did nothing special even then. A few fake visits to the bosses of the warden was all that was needed."

"Your mentioning the word 'visit' Laszlo forces me to ask a question. Will you see that dear girl, Rozsa? If you will and I can't imagine you without her, give her my thanks for saving you."

"I cannot do otherwise Dad. I sent her a note with Elisabeth. I must see her…I must be with her…I must face Mr. Buja's wrath."

"I understand, but will the Bujas do?"

"I have no choice. I told you before how much I love Rozsa. I could sooner stop breathing than give her up."

"I am not suggesting that Laszlo, but you must be circumspect. See her; love her; be with her whenever you can, but make certain that her parents do not know. Time has a way of changing things. When you finish your studies, when you will be a full fledged teacher, their attitude toward you will soften and you will be ready to face them. Now go my Son…Our time together has slipped by too fast. Give my best to your Mother and to George. Come and see me once more if you can."

As I shook my Father's hand, as I said good-bye to the tortured man, I saw him turn away his face, probably trying to hide his tears and I was no longer able to disguise my hatred.

"Some day I will make them suffer for what they have done to you," I muttered and my Father shook his head.

"Do not do this to yourself, Laszlo. Hate never ever solved a thing. Fill your heart with love for your beloved Rozsa, leave no space for anything else."

***

For two short weeks I did as my Father commanded. Rozsa and I have met every day at six o'clock in the garden of Dery, the park that was kept open in spite of the approaching winter. We talked and walked and went to the movies. We kissed, we hugged, we held hands when no prying eyes could witness our actions. We have agreed to keep our meetings a secret from her parents. We didn't dare to visit the Gomorys, in case they would inform Mr. Buja.

When the first snow-fall came we marveled at the huge flakes that covered our heads, fell gently from the gray skies above. My strength, nurtured by the delight of being with the girl I loved, began to return. My cheeks slowly lost their deathly pallor; my body began to regain much of what it lost during my illness and my heart's shattered pieces began to find each other to re-form the whole heart, filled with nothing but love.

The two glorious weeks have slipped by without another visit to see my Father. My Mother wasn't willing to give up her chance of seeing her husband and I didn't argue. The little time I didn't spend with Rozsa, I devoted to rest, to a few visits to my Uncle Jozsef and Aunt Gizella.

When the day came to part from my beloved I felt no reluctance; experienced no regret. She had taken time from work to be with me. She has reported ill to her office to give us a few extra hours of joy. She was everything I have ever wanted. She was my savior; she was my redeemer; she was my healer; she was my joy.

***

The days, the weeks, the next two months I have spent in pursuit of my studies. My illness was far behind me, a fading memory. My visit with my Father-who was still in prison, waiting for his trial-was a painful reminder of the depravity of the Communists. Rozsa's frequent letters, so full of love, so much alive with the promise of a happy, long life together, sustained me, until February arrived and I was once again close to my angel, Rozsa.

***

Her parents were totally unaware of our secret meetings, she informed me the minute I returned. She stole time at her office to write to me all her letters; she even went to a few dances, escorted by her parents. Had a few dances with the always present young, army officers, just to fool her parents. I have learned all this soon after my return and had my mind, my heart, my soul not been fully occupied with my Father's up-coming trial my jealousy would have bloomed, but there was no time for that during this visit.

The trial lasted only a few hours.

"Ferenc Lichter, you are charged with profiteering; inflating government sanctioned prices and embezzlement," Tarnay read the charges and asked the mandatory question: "How do you plead?"

"Not guilty, your honor."

"You are guilty. If nothing else, you are guilty of using words from the old regime. *Your honor* is no longer permitted. *Comrade* is the only word you are allowed to use when you refer to me." The judge, about thirty years old, sat on his bench in a rumpled suit, cigarette hanging from his lips, the smoke curling toward the high ceiling, his look totally bored, stared at my Father, who set in the docket, beside his lawyer.

One row behind him I sat with my Mother and my brother, George. I suddenly recalled a movie about an American trial and I was struck by the vast difference between that and what I was witnessing.

In this trial there was no jury. There wasn't even a prosecutor, only Tarnay who was my Father's prosecutor, his jury, his judge and the executioner.

"I ask you once again: How do you plead?"

"Not guilty, Comrade."

"In that case the trial shall begin. Too bad you do not have the decency to save this court the time and money by pleading guilty, which you no doubt are. I suppose that cannot be helped...You are a stubborn man, Lichter. Not even several months in prison made you see the light; made you realize the enormity of your crime; made you ready to confess." The judge spoke and I couldn't believe what I heard. "A judge is to judge, but only after hearing all the evidence. Yet this man, this flunky of the Communists doesn't even try to hide the fact that he is ready to find my Father guilty," I thought and had I been able to kill anyone by one simple look, Judge Tarnay would have keeled over, dead.

"I call the first witness. In order to protect the vigilant defender of the State, he shall remain nameless and he will enter through the back door and sit behind that screen."

"You have reported Ferenc Lichter to the authorities for profiteering; for inflating government sanctioned prices and for embezzlement. Is that correct?"

"Yes, Comrade Judge."

"Now answer my questions as briefly as you can. Did Lichter profiteer?"

"He most certainly did!" I saw my Father whisper something to his lawyer, who placed one comforting hand on my Father's shoulder and nodded his head in agreement.

"Did Lichter inflate government sanctioned prices?"

"He did that many times."

"Did the prisoner commit embezzlement?"

"He stole from the soldiers. He cheated the defenders of our country. He is swine...A class enemy of our nation."

"Thank you for your testimony. You may step..."

At that point my Father's lawyer intervened.

"I object, Comrade Judge...Is it not our beloved leader's, Rakosi's wish that all the crimes of guilty parties be exposed to the fullest?"

"So what is the nature of your objection?"

"If you dismiss that witness now the details of my client's crimes will never be revealed fully. I object to his dismissal. I wish to have the opportunity to ask him a few simple questions."

"The witness will remain where he is. He will answer all your questions, unless I decide otherwise. Proceed."

"But Comrade Judge....," the voice came from behind the partition. "You promised..."

"Keep quiet and do what I said," the judge reprimanded the no longer enthusiastic witness.

"Proceed Comrade Counselor."

"Thank you Comrade Judge. I direct my question to the hidden Private behind the screen."

"You are a fool lawyer. I am a high ranking officer of the Hungarian army. Do not insult me by calling me a Private."

"My sincere apologies. Had I known your rank I wouldn't have called you a private." I heard my Father's lawyer; detected a trace of taunting in his voice and I sat up straight trying to capture the drama that was about to unfold. "This must be the political officer my Father told me about...He must have identified him to his lawyer." I thought and my heart began to beat faster.

"So how do you wish to be addressed?" the lawyer asked.

"Just call me Comrade Officer."

"Very well. Comrade Officer, I assume you have never ever purchased anything in the store where my client served. Am I correct?"

"You are wrong! I most certainly have made many purchases where that criminal committed his crimes."

"Let me get this straight. The officers, and you are an officer, have their own store where they can purchase everything at cheaper prices. Is that not correct?"

"That is the case," came the reply from behind the screen, relinquishing not an iota of his cockiness.

"Yet you have frequented the store sat up for enlisted men?"

"I did!"

"Tell us why did you do that?"

"Political officers have a duty to practice vigilance. It is our job to ferret out all those who commit crimes against the State."

"So you went there several times and found out my client's crimes?"

"Yes I did."

"How many times did my client serve you?"

"Many times."

"Ten times? Five times? How many times?"

"I cannot remember the exact number."

"Can you remember if you wore your uniform whenever you entered the place of my client's crimes?"

"I always did."

"You always wore your uniform? Is that what you are stating?"

"You heard me right."

"How many stars are there on your uniform?"

"I will not answer that question Comrade Judge!"

"You don't need to answer that."

"Well the exact number of stars is not important. It is sufficient that there was a star at least on your uniform. Is that correct?"

"You got it right lawyer." The accuser's cockiness did not diminish.

"Did anybody ask for your name when you tried to make a purchase?"

"They never did."

"Were you aware that the two clerks had to record the rank of all officers shopping in their store?"

"Why would they ever do that?" came the first sign of surprise from behind the screen.

"Because they followed all orders they were given. Now that you know about this practice do you still maintain that you went there many times?"

"How can I remember something as unimportant as that?"

"The number of visits you made are unimportant to you, but not the crimes you have discovered. Let me see what were those crimes? I seem to recall that you reported Comrade Lichter for profiteering; for inflating government sanctioned prices and for embezzlement. Did I get all the charges right?"

"You most certainly have."

"So let me see...On your first visit which crime did you uncover?"

"It was profiteering."

"What about your second visit?"

"Inflating government sanctioned prices."

"And on the third occasion?"

"Embezzlement."

"Now please enlighten us. How did you discover the first crime?"

"Well, let me see...I went in there...That guy with the mustache served me. I wanted to buy some candy. When I pointed out the kind of candy I always buy for my little boy I found the price too high and left. Later I checked the prices in three stores in Baja and everywhere it was cheaper."

"Do you remember the price my client gave you?"

"I most certainly do."

"Then share it with us...Surely that is not a State secret."

"You better watch your words counselor. I will not tolerate sarcasm in my court." The judge intervened and didn't hide his annoyance.

"Sorry Comrade Judge. I shall rephrase the question. Please give us the price you were quoted by my client and the prices given to you in those three other stores."

"I will be happy to do so. Two Forints for ten decagrams of that candy your client quoted. In the three stores, where I had inquired, ten decagrams cost only one *Forint* and twenty *Fillers*."

"So my client inflated the price of the candy your little boy loves so much?"

"That he did."

"Now if I am not mistaken that is inflating government sanctioned prices, but you were giving testimony not to that, but to profiteering."

"The two of them are the same!"

"Now you succeeded to confuse me. Have you not reported my client for profiteering and for inflating government sanctioned prices?"

"That is what I did."

"So you demanded that my client be charged with those two crimes, yet you consider them to be the same?"

"Comrade Judge, please don't allow the lawyer to twist everything I say," the first pleading came from behind the screen and my spirits lifted.

"Counselor don't badger the witness!"

"I am sorry Comrade Judge. The last thing I wished to do is to badger, to accuse anyone. I will try again. So you went to buy candy and on that one occasion you have found that my client was charging a higher price, thus he broke the law. Am I correct?"

"That he did!"

"And on the same occasion he was about to profit from the deed. Is that what you have suspected?"

"Had I paid him the two Forints he would have made a profit. That is correct."

"Now have you seen him put eighty *Fillers* in his own pocket? Is that what you meant by reporting embezzlement?"

"No I didn't see him do that. I was far too smart for that conniving bastard. I left without making a purchase."

"That was wise. I would have done the same thing. So he inflated the price of the candy...He would have made a profit and he would have embezzled the sum of eighty *Fillers*? Did I understand you correctly?"

"You most certainly did. If it wasn't for my vigilance this criminal would have gotten away with this."

"But he didn't get away with those crimes? Thanks to your cautious nature this man was unable to commit those crimes. Am I correct?"

"That one time he didn't commit the crime, but he has served on thousands of gullible soldiers. He over charged them, he pocketed the extra money and he is guilty as sin."

"Well we shall see about that. Comrade Judge, I would love to know if there will be other witnesses. If it is so I will not take up much more time with this officer."

"There will be only one more witness, who will also prove your client's guilt."

"In that case I will have only a few more questions to this witness. I had the opportunity to search the records from the day my client got his employment to the day he was arrested. The record shows that only one officer tried to purchase anything during that period of time. The record also shows that the officer asked for two bottles of beer, two packs of cigarettes, five chocolate bars and twenty decagrams of candy. Is it possible Comrade Officer that you were the one whose rank is recorded, whose order consisted of everything I have mentioned?"

"It is possible I guess!"

"Since there is no other recorded visit by any officer, is it possible that you went there only once?"

"It is conceivable...I have more important things to do than to recall such minor details."

"I suppose it is also unimportant what you said to my client and what he said to you on that single occasion?"

"I most certainly wouldn't recall anything a mere clerk may have said!"

"A mere clerk? Is that how you have referred to my client?"

"A mere clerk! You got it correct."

"I beg your pardon Comrade Officer...You are no doubt a Communist and I praise you for that, but in a country where laborers are held in high esteem, where justice, equality and fairness are held in high regard, how can someone like you belittle another human being?"

"I am sorry, I have made a mistake." The first cracks in the accuser's armor began to appear.

"You made a mistake in calling him a mere clerk...You made a mistake in the number of times you went to the store where he worked...You made a mistake testifying that on the first visit you caught him profiteering; on the second you found out that he was inflating government sanctioned prices and on the third you identified him as an embezzler. How many more mistakes have you made, Comrade Officer?"

"None I assure you!" This time the officer's voice came in a whimper.

The lawyer bent his head toward my Father. Their whispered conference was short and ended when the judge became impatient.

"Either you ask for a recess, which I shall deny promptly or proceed Counselor. There are many more criminals I must try today."

My Father kept urging his lawyer to do something, but obviously his urging fell on deaf ears. His lawyer turned back to the witness.

"Comrade Judge, I am almost finished with this witness, but there is one more thing I must do. I have a bag of assorted candies in my possession. Would you allow me to pass the bag to you. I respectfully request that the officer pick out his son's favorite candy, if that kind is in the assortment. Will you permit me to do that?"

"I see no harm in what you request, unless the witness proves to be reluctant. What do you say Comrade Officer? Are you willing to pick out your son's favorite candy?"

"I will be pleased to cooperate!"

The bag of candy was passed to the judge, and then it disappeared behind the screen. The large, ornate wall clock ticked as it recorded the passage of time and two minutes later the bag and one single candy was handed by the clerk to the judge.

"Am I holding your Son's favorite candy, Comrade Officer?" the judge asked gently, his sympathy clearly on the side of the accuser.

"You do Comrade Judge...You most certainly do..."

"Very well then. Clerk, pass this single candy to the counselor."

Within seconds my Father's lawyer whispered something into my Father's ear, gave my Mother one, single, triumphant smile and continued to press his witness.

"Is this your son's favorite candy?"

"It is, but I said that before."

"Is this the candy the accused tried to sell you at the price of two *Forints* for ten decagrams?"

"You got that right too!" came the impudent answer.

"Is this the candy you have priced in three different stores?"

"That is the one!"

"Please remind us what prices were you quoted."

"In all three stores the price of this candy was only one *Forint* and twenty *Fillers*."

"Are you absolutely certain?"

"I am...Otherwise I would not have brought charges against your client!"

"Comrade Judge. I gave you that bag of candy. Now I want to hand over to you the detailed receipt I have received from the store where I bought the assortment. Please note that there are fifteen different sorts of candy listed on the receipt and there were fifteen different kinds of candies in that bag. The accuser has identified the one that he claims was offered to him at an inflated price, thus the charge of profiteering, charging inflated prices and embezzlement. Please note that not one single kind of candy sells for less than two *Forints* for ten decagrams." The lawyer stopped talking, handed the receipt to the clerk and waited for the judge's examination.

"The lowest price listed here is indeed two *Forints*. All the other prices are higher. Maybe, Comrade Officer, you have an explanation."

"I must have made a mistake...May I look again? I am sure I can find the right one." The requests came in a moan.

"And how do you propose to do that? Do you expect to find one that sells for less than two *Forints* when there isn't any such thing on this receipt?" The judge seemed to be perturbed and highly disappointed.

"Maybe I could look again. That receipt proves nothing! What about the money the accused pocketed when bottle refunds were not returned to the soldiers? What about the times when many soldiers were short-changed? Why do I have to prove everything? He is the class enemy...He deserves to be punished," the officer's distraught remarks gushed out, but before he could make things even worse the judge decided to speak.

"Counselor I hope you are finished! I have every intention to dismiss this witness."

"I am finished and so is he!" The lawyer allowed himself the pleasure of one final cynical remark to end the farce created by the accuser.

***

The second prosecution witness wasn't accorded the court's protection. The Private sat on the slightly elevated witness stand and waited. On his ruddy, flat face I saw his slanted eyes and bulbous nose. His lips were thick and slightly parted, making him look like a caricature of a simpleton, probably the butt of many crude jokes.

"You heard the charges against the prisoner Comrade Private, so I will not repeat them. Can you tell us if you had any occasion to observe the accused committing those crimes?"

"I had Comrade Judger."

"It is not Judger, but Judge," the witness was corrected.

"Yes, Comrade Judge...I am not used to speak here."

"I can see that, but that is not important. Describe what you witnessed."

"Last summer, I think, it must have been summer. It was hot and humid and we sweated a lot. The officers worked us hard, very hard Judge. You are lucky..." The witness would have rambled on, but the judge became very impatient.

"Spare us the details comrade. I have no time for trivialities."

"What was that word, Judge? Trivi...something?"

"Forget it, just give your evidence."

"If I don't know what that tri...means how can I avoid it. Besides Comrade Judge you used another word I don't rightly understand. Evident or something."

"All I want from you is what you have witnessed."

"You don't want me to tell you everything the political officer told me to tell?"

"Forget that...Tell me what you saw."

"When Judge?"

"Are you trying to be a hostile witness?"

"Host...what?"

"Never mind. I will lead you. Did you buy stuff in the canteen where the accused worked?"

"I got stuff there."

"You mean you bought stuff there!"

"I did."

"And what did you buy?"

"Once a chocolate bar, but I didn't like the worms in it." The few spectators burst out laughing.

"What else did you buy?"

"Well it is not easy to recollect. Beer? Candy? Cigarettes?"

"Are you asking me private?" the judge's face was set in stony anger. I guessed he must have regretted to call this witness more than he regretted the political officer's poor performance.

"I am not asking you, Judge. You weren't there. Miska was and Joska and Pisti, I think, but not you Judge."

"Stick to the point, Private. Did you buy beer?"

"I did."

"What did you pay for a bottle of beer?"

"I didn't buy a bottle, I always bought more."

"That is nice. But I asked you what did you pay for one bottle of beer."

"Let me see...I had once ten *Forints,* a ten *Forint* bill. I haven't had ten Forints for a long time, not in one bill, but I had change. My reckoning is not very good...I always got poor marks in grade four. My teacher figured me for a fool..." At this point the judge must have decided that his witness was hopeless; that no intervention on his part would ever remedy that, so he just sat back, trying to hide his disdain for the prattling imbecile. "As I said my reckoning is not good, but I think for that bill I got nine bottles of beer. So I must have paid one Forint and ten Fillers for a bottle of beer. Yes that is right...That is what the officer told me."

"I am not interested in anything anyone told you! You are the worst, the most stupid witness I ever had in my court!" The judge's poise cracked, his eyes flashed in annoyance, his irritation he no longer tried to hide.

"So you paid one Forint and ten Fillers for one bottle of beer?"

"I sure did, but sometimes I even paid more."

"Now we are getting somewhere...Tell us about that."

"Well once I bought twenty bottles of beer. Not for me, but for all my friends. That is when I paid more."

"I see...," the judge became more cautious. "What is the government sanctioned price for a bottle of beer?"

"It is too expensive."

"All right...A bottle of beer is too expensive, you say. But was it more expensive in that canteen than elsewhere?"

"It sure is. I have a friend who runs a pub and he used to give me beer for half as much."

"Private we are getting nowhere...Did the accused charge you more for a bottle of beer than he should have?"

"He did many times...He should have given it to me cheaper."

"You mean he over-charged you?"

"Yes, that is the word I was looking for. The political officer made me repeat that word a hundred times, but I am not smart like you, Judge, so I couldn't recollect."

"Fine...You were made to pay inflated prices for beer. What about other items?"

"Everything was dear...I don't recognize that word, influted or something."

"Well the word is inflated. It means a higher price than what the price should be."

"In that case everything was inflated, as you said, Judge."

"Now just one more question. Did the accused make you pay a bottle deposit?"

"He did, but he called it something else. Let me think...Yeah, I got it...He said and I tell you word for word, I am quite good now remembering. He said: 'This bottle cost you ten *Fillers*, if you bring it back I will give your money back.' That is what he said."

"Did you take the bottle back?"

"I did, Judge."

"Did you get your money back?"

"No...He wanted to give me only ten *Fillers*, but only sometimes."

"Can you clarify that?"

"I try, if I got your drift right. I wanted my money back, but that guy wouldn't give it to me. He said: 'You drank the beer, so you get back ten *Fillers*.' and I said: 'You told me you give my money back.' And he said: 'But only for the bottle.''

"Did he always give your deposit back?"

"No...Twice he didn't."

"Did he explain why?"

"He sure did, Judge. He said: 'This bottle is cracked.' And I said: 'It is only a small crack. We almost got into a fight, but he is puny so I just walked away."

"All right, Private. I thank you for your testimony, I think." Then he turned to my Father's lawyer. "Comrade Counselor, do you care to ask any questions from the witness?"

"I do, Comrade Judge."

"Then proceed..."

"Well, Private, you sure had a hard time in this court. I will try to make my questions simple. Are you rich?"

"I am poor like a church mouse."

"How much money do you get from the army?"

"When?"

"Did you get any when you were drafted?"

"None."

"When did you get your first pay?"

"At the end of the month I reckon."

"How much did you get?"

"Twenty *Forints*, but only at the end of the month. Barely enough for a few packs of smokes."

"And you never had any other money, so how could you make all those purchases in the canteen?"

"I got other money..."

"From the officer?"

"Yeah, he is a friend of mine. He gave me money after each lesson, but he told me not to let on to anyone."

"What were those lessons all about?"

"He was teaching me how to behave in here and tried to teach me what to say. I guess he will be quite angry. I figure I didn't do too well. Did I, Judge?"

The judge pretended not to hear his question, so no reply came from him.

"How do you plan to give the money back to the political officer?"

"He didn't say I had to give it back and it wasn't much anyway."

"Would you have testified without being paid?"

"I didn't want to come here in the first place. He kept chewing my ears and offered money, so I came."

"Are you telling this court that you are a paid witness?"

"I was paid to say a few things, that is so."

"How do you feel about it?"

"What do you mean?"

"You were told to say things that may send an innocent man to prison. How do you feel about that?"

"The officer never told me that someone will go to prison. Am I in trouble, Judge?"

"You are not in any trouble...," the judge stated.

"I thank the Good Lord for that."

"You will not invoke the name of the Lord in my court-room."

"We did that in church, Judge...My Father always said, may he rest in peace, that the church and the court-room are special places. If you don't want me to say 'Lord' then how shall I refer to the Almighty?"

"You will refrain from saying any more! You are dismissed!"

My Father's lawyer turned toward us and his wide smile conveyed encouragement.

***

The judge announced a ten minute recess and when re returned from his chamber he was ready to render his judgment.

"Ferenc Lichter, stand up and face the court. You have been found guilty on all counts." Had I not been seated I would have collapsed.

"I am not without mercy...Although you have been found guilty; your sentence will be light. You have spent four months in prison. I consider that confinement sufficient punishment for the crimes you have committed. You are now free!" The judge rose, gathered up his papers and walked out from the hall of justice where he performed his State assigned duty, where he proved nothing other than his loyalty to his Communist masters.

***

The family gathered around my Father and his lawyer in the corridor of the city's court-house.

"You are free my darling," my Mother cupped my Father's face in her hand, offered her lips to welcome back her man.

"You heard Judge Tarnay...I may be free, but I am a branded man."

I spoke not a single word, just stood beside my innocent Father and touched his hand.

"You let me down." My Father's words were directed at his lawyer.

"I couldn't do what you had demanded. Please understand that, Ferenc."

"You could have told the judge what motivated my accuser."

"Had I told him that he asked for credit and you had refused, that officer would have denied it."

"But that is what he did! He tried to use his rank, his position to obtain goods without ever paying."

"It would have been your word against his. Who do you think the judge would have believed?"

"Does that really matter? People in the court-room would have heard it...They would have known the truth."

"That is true and you would have been charged once again, but this time with defamation of character. Did you really want to spend another four months in prison, waiting for another trial? You know that is what would have happened!"

"Enough of this nonsense. What is past cannot be helped." My Mother cut the debate short, grabbed my Father's hand and began to drag him away from the place I, from that moment on, considered not the hall of justice, but a theater.

"I knew you will be free...I knew you will be coming home. I prepared a feast for the entire family. So, tonight, we will have a celebration," my Mother announced loudly and not even my Father dared to deny her the pleasure of welcoming home the innocent, yet guilty man.

***

The relatives arrived by seven o'clock. As they entered our small, humble apartment my Mother urged them to sample all the food, to grab a glass of wine or if so inclined a tumbler of strong spirit.

Istvan Tobias, my Mother's brother-in-law, needed little encouragement. With one hand he clasped my Father's hand, shook it vigorously, while with the other he lifted a tumbler of palinka, the strongest of drinks, and trying to avoid spilling any of the precious fluid, he drank the tumbler's content, smacking his lips in satisfaction.

Aunt Manci, my Mother's sister, cast disapproving glances at her husband, while with one arm she pulled my Father's head to her own level and planted a big, loving kiss on his forehead.

Aunt Tercsi entered with her husband and daughter, Elisabeth. The three of them rushed, like hungry wolves, but not at the food, not at the drinks, but at my Father.

"I knew my brother that you are innocent!" She held him with one of her pudgy hands, while she tried to control her tears by gnawing at her own knuckle. "My dear brother is an innocent man! I will shout this at everyone at the market. That rotten judge should rot in hell!" She would have held my Father all evening long, but the new arrivals propelled her aside, making space to stand beside my Father.

Aunt Gizella blew him a kiss, and then looked around the room with an air of superiority, trying to gain center stage on this momentous occasion. Her husband, Jozsef, shy as he was, moved to my Father's side, but only when all others began to eat and drink. He held out his hand to his brother-in-law and whispered something in his ear.

I stood in the corner quietly observing everything. The trial, the injustice, the lying witnesses, the absence of my beloved Rozsa, the pushing, shoving, milling, eating, and drinking relatives and my enormous disappointment almost made me scream.

"How can you eat? How can you drink? How can you celebrate on a day like this? Don't you know what has happened? My Father was arrested, not because a crime he committed, but because he is not a Communist. Can you not understand that he has become a marked man? All his life he will be hounded, persecuted. Will always be denied a moment of peace. For him and for the likes of him there is no life, no hope, no future in this cursed country. Those of you who did not come to his trial will never really know what has happened. The accuser and the only witness were caught in a hundred lies, yet Judge Tarnay found him guilty. He knew from the moment my Father was arrested the outcome of his case, maybe he knew it even before. Four months of imprisonment someone must have decided before the police came to take him away. The trial, that farce, that comedy was only for the record...Another Hungarian was found guilty and hundreds learned to fear the Communists' power.

"In any civilized country a person is innocent until proven guilty, but the Red Army liberated us from all forms of civilization. You go into prison if that is what they want...You rot in jail if that is their desire...You are given a kind of trial...Not a trial where evidence is weighed seriously, but one where the outcome has been decided, well in advance. How many good men and women are in our jails? How many have been executed? How much blood will they spill to satisfy their Soviet masters? I fear that bit-by-bit my great love will be consumed by hatred. No, I will not let that happen! I will always love that lovely girl. I still pine for her; plan a happy life with her; hope to have her give us at least two children. Am I a fool? Is it a sin to bring children into this world, into this country?"

My misery grew with the passing of each moment. It was quite late when I have realized that what began as a family gathering turned into a boisterous, drunken party. Uncle Istvan's deep, booming, inebriated words broke into my gloomy thoughts and brought me back to my senses.

"F...the Russians. F...the rotten commies. During the war I killed many...I made my machine pistol chatter...Mowed them down...Had I killed all of them Ferenc wouldn't have never tasted prison food. F...Judge Tarnay...His day will come...When the revolution breaks out...," Istvan shouted at the top of his lungs and suddenly my Father's voice intruded.

"That is enough Istvan…I will not tolerate such language in my home. You are reckless, putting all of us in danger. You are drunk and a fool. All of you go home! The party is over!"

One by one the relatives wished my family good-night and our apartment began to empty.

"It is time to go to bed…Tomorrow I will have to look for a new job," was all my Father said when the four of us found ourselves alone. We fell into each other's arms without any words and the day of the glorious trial ended.

***

That night I lay in my bed, thinking about what Istvan said.

"He spoke dangerous words about a revolution. There was only one other who uttered those words in my presence. Who was he?" I asked myself.

"Not my room-mates at the university. Not my Father. Not Mr. Buja. Not anyone I can remember. But I did hear that word from someone. Who was he?" I searched for an answer and as morning came, as my tired mind struggled with the puzzle, I saw the boy, wearing a Russian uniform, but his face was blank.

"Yes I remember now. It was that nameless, faceless soldier, whose Mother and Sister were raped, whose Father was executed. So Istvan is not alone. How many other nameless, faceless Hungarians speak cautiously about a revolution? How many others feel the misery caused by our oppressors? Only six years have passed since the Russians occupied us and we became a nation of slaves. Six long years may not be enough to bring us to the boiling point. The Turks occupied our country for one-hundred-fifty years, before this nation rose. Do we have to wait a hundred-forty-four years before we rise again? Can we stand oppression of this magnitude for that many years? Long before that they will kill us all." With that last bitter thought, I fell asleep.

***

Rozsa and I were to meet three in the afternoon. The appointed hour came very slowly, but when it arrived my love replaced all the hatred. Rozsa and I met at our usual place and when she agreed to come to my home my heart filled up with joy. No more doubts; no more hatred; no more trial; no more betrayal; no more thoughts of injustice; no more sadness existed any longer, just the joy of being with my dearest Rozsa.

We sat on my sofa, in my tiny room. Our hands touched, our lips sought each other and for the first time our kisses became ardent. Nothing existed except our love...Had my Mother not arrive home perhaps we would have lost our heads, but her footsteps, as she passed by my window, brought back duty, honor and reality.

"Hello Rozsa...It is nice to see you. Did Laszlo tell you what happened yesterday?"

"We just arrived...," I lied to my Mother and to cover my confusion I started to tell the story.

A few hours later the two of us walked to the rail-way station and there we once again parted.

Chapter 9

Exactly six weeks after I left my sweetheart, for the first time ever a letter arrived from my Father. While Rozsa's letters almost always contained news that warmed my heart, caused me pleasure; while her letters I always tore open without waiting; this letter I opened slowly, approached reading it with great trepidation.

"My Dear Son, Laszlo..." my father wrote.

"Whenever you received bad news your brother was asked to write the letter, because I wasn't free, but this time the news is good, glorious is more likely the word I am looking for.

"When you were home, when that cursed trial took place, I was despondent. I do not mind to admit it. The day you left I began to look for a new job and I kept doing it for several weeks. Each time I was rejected; each time a door was slammed into my face, I felt like a real criminal, without hope, without a future. When the constant rejections cast me into the deepest hell, I met an old friend of mine, Lajos Klein, who is in a powerful position.

"Lajos knew me when I was a simple shoe-maker. He was one of my best customers. He watched me, but from a distance, when I became a capitalist and later he grieved over the loss of my factory. He lost track of me when I began to work in the army and then, he read a brief article in the local paper about my criminal activities that earned me that four months sentence.

"Had I not been so desperate, I wouldn't have gone to the pub, I would not have met Lajos. Life is so full of twists and turns, it is so full of surprises that I no longer dare to make predictions. Thus I would have never predicted that all my visits to stores, to factories, to other work places would leave me jobless and my single visit to a pub would land me the splendid job it did.

"But I am slightly ahead of my story...I sat in the pub and ordered a beer. Interestingly enough I paid more for that bottle of suds than any of my soldiers ever paid me. There I sat nursing the only bottle I could afford, when I felt a heavy hand on my shoulder.

"Lajos Klein stood behind me, but only for a moment. He ordered a couple of beers and sat down facing me. He let me drink my second bottle before he began to inquire about my arrest, my imprisonment and the trial.

"It felt good to speak to someone. Many of my former friends began to shun me. So I began to tell him my story, which I ended with the futility of my long search for employment.

"It was at that point that Lajos asked me: 'If you were rich, if you didn't need to toil for a living, where would to spend your time?'

"'On my beloved Danube.' My reply even surprised me.

"His next words stunned me. 'Well do that, Ferenc!'

"'Easy for you to say Lajos. Here I am jobless, desperate, a branded man and you take the time to jive me.' I was ready to get up and leave him, I made my hesitant move, but he reached over the table and with one hand restrained me.

"'I am not bullshitting you my friend...Maybe you do not know what I became, what happened to me.' He began to tell his story and when it ended I looked at him with a measure of envy. After the Communist party took full power in '48, Lajos was a long time, loyal member of that party and he was rewarded accordingly. He became the undisputed boss of a State owned organization that was charged with the control of the Danube. His many ships, his two barges, his draggers and his over five hundred men were always busy. They dredged the Danube to keep the shipping lanes open; they built up the dikes to protect us from flooding; they erected huge stone walls, reaching like probing fingers deep into the strong currents of the river to direct it where it was needed. They worked like ants on the shores, on the ships and some even under water. The strenuous jobs took their toll, so he had a sizable turnover.

"'I come here often...' Lajos stated after he finished his life's story. 'I come here in search of new workers. There really is no better place to find desperate men, down on their luck. It is easy to push empty wheel-barrows down to the shore from my ships, but to push them up, when fully loaded, with heavy rocks, takes real muscle-men. They do that eight hours a day for a pittance and when one ship is filled they start a new one. How would you like to do that Ferenc?' Lajos asked me.

"'I don't mind hard work...I am a good worker...'

"'Then it's settled. Tomorrow morning you come and see me!' He stated, rose and pumped my hand.

"Well, next morning I went to see him. I was received by him like a long lost relative. 'My dear Ferenc...I wasn't sure you will accept my challenge. But you are here! Are you ready to sign for your wheel-barrow? Are you prepared to break your back? Now watch out for the scoundrels. They will trip you on the gang-plank. They do this to all new workers. The unfortunate, tripped creature always receives that treatment when his wheel-barrow is fully loaded, while he struggles to push it up on the gang plank. The wheel-barrow, laden with its burden and the man fall into our beloved river. I saw that done many times. When the victim comes to the surface, he curses his tormentors. During the summer the victim soon comes to his senses and he becomes even grateful for what has happened. The kind river's water cools them, they soon realize that and learn to trip themselves, but during the winter...Well that is another story. So what do you say? Are you ready?'

"I saw a mischievous grin on Lajos' face, but what came next I never expected. 'I am ready...Where do I go to get my equipment?'

"'Don't be in such a big hurry...You will get your uniform and your first pay-packet, after we had a drink.'

"'I don't understand...A uniform to push a wheel-barrow? And to be paid before a week's work?'

"'Well...It may sound strange to you, but all my helms-men are required to wear a uniform and my friends and their families I don't allow to remain hungry. Now drain your drink and I will be glad to enlighten you.'

"We had our drink, and another one, followed by a few more. As you know Son I was never hesitant to imbibe when I had the opportunity. So there we sat in Lajos' sumptuous office and when neither of us could take another drink, he began to giggle.

"'Last night when I met you in the pub I had a great problem. One of my helms-men died and I needed a new one. I reserve those good jobs only for my real friends. Ferenc you are one of them. You are a decent man I can trust. I toyed with you, I admit that, when I enticed you to become my coolie. But you were willing and I was glad. You passed the test and now you will be one of my few trusted officers. Your pay will be good, have no doubt about that.'

"'But you will be in trouble with the party...You will be chastised for hiring a criminal.' I stated lamely and Lajos began to roar.

"'F...the party! Do you think I fear any of them? They stay away from me...They no longer question my loyalty. Once, just once, a high official of the party came to my office; insisted on inspecting my operation. I took him on the inspection tour. It happened during last winter and when he was about to climb the unsteady gang-plank, it took only a nod of my head to have one of my loyal men do my bidding. The party official was in the cold, icy water of our Danube and when I pulled him out, when I saved his life he became my slave for ever. They will not question me...You will have the job I gave you...You will be safe for ever.'

"'But I know nothing about steering a ship,' I lamented.

"'Nonsense my friend. You know this river better than anybody. You have traveled her every inch. Besides you will get the hang of it. Now we shall go or should I say stagger to pick up your uniform and the money.' Lajos settled the issue and I thanked him, I thanked my lucky stars, I thanked the good Lord and your Father became a happy man.

"So my Son, I am now an officer on a ship. From this day on I will be able to help you. The enclosed Forints are the first of many more you shall receive.

"With my best wishes, your loving Father." I stared at the letter for many moments and when I found no reason to disbelief its veracity I was truly happy.

***

Two days later another letter came, but this one from my beloved Rozsa. The small, black and white picture fell out of the envelope and I feasted my eyes on her splendid beauty.

As she tilted her chin, at a haughty angle, it threw slight shadows on her silky neck. Her smooth, round face beamed with pleasure. Her lips were moist, inviting; slightly parted, allowing me to see her lovely, even white teeth. Her brownish hair, pulled tight by a ribbon behind her left ear, cascaded over her right shoulder, while on the left it fell way down around her other shoulder, exposing one, well shaped ear, her long neck, which was adorned with a pearl necklace. Her blue eyes sparkled with a promise of new maturity.

The picture was a true likeness of my beloved, yet it was no longer a girl who stared at me, smiled at me, but an eager, desirous, inviting woman of great beauty.

I turned the picture around to read the inscription, but to my greatest disappointment it was empty. I raised the picture to my lips and gave it a kiss, felt the same thrill I felt when our lips last touched and then I began to read her letter.

She described her lonely days that were filled with hundreds of tasks her job demanded. She wrote about her parents. Her Father was still working as an engineer and her Brother, Joe, had also begun to work for the same building company. He was responsible for some office work and with the more tempting job of delivering the weekly pay envelopes to distant job sites. Rozsa's Mother was also doing well. Her letter was filled with many news items, but the one that caught my eyes was her recent visit to a photographer. She informed me that her Aunt Margit wanted her to have a picture. So she went to see a professional. The man tried her in many poses, but finally he settled on one that he liked most, not even asking for the opinion of Rozsa. When the picture was finished, a week later, she went to pick it up and to pay for the photographer's services. The man wouldn't accept her money, she told me in her letter and my jealousy was immediately ignited.

"What was the bastard trying to do? Was he after the girl I love?" The questions popped in my mind and my doubts suddenly fell upon me. My doubts slowly evaporated as I read the rest of her loving letter.

She informed me that the artist liked her picture so much that he offered her a deal. If she allowed him to display her picture for advertising purposes, she didn't need to pay. She saw no harm in that and accepted his offer.

The last part of her letter spoke about the time we were together last, about my Father's trial and about his new job, Rozsa learned of from my Mother during one of her visits.

Her letter was so full of love; so enriched by her loving words that the pain caused by the missing inscription faded from my mind. Her letter and her precious picture I placed close to my heart for many days and under my pillow for all the nights that followed. Thus passed my happy days.

***

Rozsa's letter and her picture were in my jacket's left, inside pocket. My thoughts drifted back to the day the heart-warming items arrived and I almost missed the second lecture as well.

The tall, gaunt military officer cleared his throat, as he replaced the previous lecturer, whose words never penetrated my mind that day-dreamed about my beloved. I tore my mind away from her letter; I shut my eyes just for a second to enable them to see something else than the face of my beloved Rozsa and I began to pay attention to the coming lecture. Having studied chemistry for almost six years, my interest peaked when I heard the words: 'Chemical weapons'.

Our military lecturers always read the typewritten text, provided by the Ministry of Defense and they rarely deviated. This officer was about to follow the same practice. The early heat wave that came that spring made the room most uncomfortable. That must have been the officer's reason for putting down the neatly stacked sheets on his lectern. He took a few steps to open one of the windows, not expecting the sudden gust, not anticipating the calamity.

The wind rushed into the small lecture room, kissed our faces with its cooling kindness and blew off most of the sheets from the lectern. I was one of the few students who rushed to the officers aid to pick up what he needed. As I picked up two sheets, as I handed them to the officer, I glanced at them and I became excited.

"The sheets are not even numbered. He will have a hell of a time to make sense from any of these." I thought not without a measure of satisfaction and suddenly I saw the young boy who was taken to Fo Street from our military camp; I heard the voice of my unknown comrade who spoke about the revolution; I was reminded of our officers' cruelty, their conniving; their lack of education and I have decided to latch on to his every word, to grab any opportunity for a small revolution.

"I was delayed by that blasted wind. I better close the window. You don't mind the stifling, hot air, I am sure." He moved to the window once again, but this time to close it with one hand, while his lecture sheets he clasped tightly with the other.

"The title of today's lecture is Chemical Weapons." He began his halting reading, never taking his eyes off the notes, giving my nearest class-mate a chance to whisper in my ear.

"Now we shall be truly enlightened."

I gave him a smile and picked up my pen, poised to jot down any word that may give me an opportunity.

After fifteen minutes of dull reading about the Imperialists' great desires to wipe us off the face of the earth; about our leaders' heroic efforts to wreck the enemy's plans; about the shield the Soviet Union provided to her allies, our lecturer raised his eyes to scan his audience and announced boldly: "We are ready to defend our beloved homeland. Our chemical weapons will now be listed."

A few minutes he spent on mustard gas, praising the Soviets who claimed credit for creating it, as they have claimed credit for everything that was ever invented. Then he moved on to other chemicals created by the same Communists. When he reached the topic of carbon monoxide and read a few words about that, he turned to the next page and with a slight shake of his head, with one fleeting second of puzzlement, he continued his reading.

"Our delivery system consists of shells, fired from big cannons, aimed at the enemy. The devastation caused by this weapon leaves no soldiers alive." At that point my pen became active.

The officer continued his reading for several more minutes and when he placed the last sheet on the lectern, my classmates turned to me. Their whispers urged me to exploit the officer's mistake; their words, their elbows fueled my desire to fight my enemy.

"Now that I have finished describing our level of preparedness in case of enemy attacks, I will be glad to answer all your questions. Don't be shy! Inquiring minds are appreciated."

I stood up and the silence that preceded my words was full of tension.

"Comrade Officer, as you know all of us major in chemistry," I began my probing.

"I am well aware of that," came his reply.

"Within a few months we will be front of many students. If those students are to become knowledgeable citizens of our beloved country then we have an obligation to enlighten them. In order to achieve that we have to know. You spoke about a chemical weapon, carbon monoxide, you called it, if I am not mistaken." I strung him along and he nodded his head.

"Ask away, don't be shy..." He urged me to continue.

"Well, I and my class-mates, know little about that weapon, carbon monoxide." I sensed my class-mates' anticipation. "So, we would really appreciate you giving us a lot more information."

"You would? Would you now?" The officer obviously knew nothing about that common chemical, that posed no danger except in confined spaces.

"Yes, we truly would comrade," I insisted.

"We have a Hungarian saying: 'Curiosity killed the cat.' Have any of you heard that one before?"

"We have Comrade Officer, but that doesn't answer my question." I became even bolder and watched with joy the beads of sweat that began to run off his fore-head.

"Some of you may think that I try to evade the question. That is not the case, I assure you. How old are you Comrade Lichter?" He asked me after he consulted his seating plan.

"I am almost twenty," I announced.

"Do you want to reach twenty-one?"

"I most certainly do." I gave my reply and gave him no chance to escape my inquiry. "I want to live until a ripe old age. I want to teach the youth of this nation and I want to able to answer all their questions. Maybe comrade you should do the same."

"Very well then, that is exactly what I will do. If you want to live to the ripe age of twenty-one then you better not pry into state secrets!"

"I am sorry Comrade Officer. Had I known that all information on carbon monoxide is classified I would not have probed." I felt the tension build and waited for the officer's reaction.

"Very well...Your apology is accepted. Carbon monoxide is our secret weapon...Even I know nothing more about it then what I shared with you. You and I are not alone. Our Soviet brothers, the inventors of this terrible weapon, are the guardians of this secret. Not even our Minister of Home Defense knows much about the nature of this dreadful weapon."

As he spoke these last few words; as he revealed his and his Minister's ignorance, my class-mates' chuckles escaped slowly, then grew into hilarious, uncontrollable laughter until the walls reverberated.

The lecturer made a few futile attempts to curb our merriment, but my class-mates were like I, young, knowledgeable about that chemical, superior to this buffoon and even to the great Minister. So our laughter did not die away, not even when the officer rushed out to seek escape.

"Did you see him run out of here with his tail between his legs?" someone shouted.

"The fool. The stupid bumpkin tried to bluff his way out of this. Laszlo did well...He played him like a fish. Well done, Laszlo."

"I have pined for revenge for what these bastards did to us during the summer and Laszlo gave me the sweet taste of that.' Shouted some-one else and the hullabaloo would have continued, had it not been for the entry of two uniformed men.

***

In spite of my class-mates courageous protests, I was lead away and within ten minutes I faced the university's highest ranking officer.

"As you know Lichter I am the Commander here and you, young punk, you are the accused."

"What am I accused of, may I ask?"

"Shut up you fool, you have caused quite a commotion."

"I have caused nothing comrade," I pleaded and all the hilarity, all the joy of taking revenge, all the hopes for my future suddenly began to fade.

"Do you deny prying into state secrets?"

"If carbon monoxide is a secret than the writers of all chemistry books are to be tried for treason," I announced, believing that I gained the upper hand.

"So you are not as smart as you thought? You knew about that chemical! You knew it is not a weapon! Yet you tried to ridicule your lecturer, but you have not succeeded. It is us who will claim victory, but not you Lichter. Let me explain: The lecture was designed to flush out all traitors...It was a well calculated move...At other lecture halls, by many lecturers, the same notes were read the same way. Many traitors fell for it.

We wanted to know who is with us and wanted to learn who wants to make us look ridiculous. You are one of those Lichter...Do you have anything to say?"

"I lost my head comrade. I didn't think clearly."

"You can say that again. Once you were almost expelled from this university. At least that is what your file states. This time we may not be able to avoid that!"

"But comrade...I had a very serious illness. I have suffered from meningitis. It affected my brain. You can ask my doctor and my room-mates."

"Your brain was most certainly affected, but not by meningitis. You hate us Communists! You hate all officers of the army! Do you dare to deny that?"

My desperate situation I could no longer ignore. "My audacity, my lack of thinking; my desire for revenge got me into all this trouble," I thought sadly and made my appeal.

"I am truly sorry. I am not even twenty, as I told the officer. I do not hate anyone. Please give me another chance."

"Your fate will be decided in due course."

***

The days and nights that followed my folly were full of fearful anticipation. I was certain of my expulsion from the university, yet I was not summoned by the Registrar's office. It would not have surprised me to be arrested by the military police, but as the weeks passed, as I have attended the military lectures, without ever asking another question, I began to hope that the unfortunate episode will be forgotten.

When the one week long Easter vacation finally arrived, I jumped on the train to return to Baja, to my Rozsa and as I put miles behind me and the scene of my enormous crime, my fears receded.

I bought a small gift for my darling within an hour of my arrival. I wrapped up the beautiful, hand-painted, Easter egg with great care. I pictured Rozsa's happy smile as she unwrapped my present. I could taste the sweetness of her loving kiss; I could feel her grateful hug; her warm hand holding mine and I have rejoiced over a week of togetherness.

It was still too early in the afternoon to go to the meeting place, so I walked around our ancient city, admired its many old buildings; stared in the windows of our two cinemas, picking out the few movies Rozsa and I might go to see. My feet carried me aimlessly around the streets and I found myself by the corner of the City Hall and of Main Street, where I looked into the window of a jewelry store.

Two old women stood not far from me and I could hear their conversation. I couldn't see what they were looking at, but their words peaked my curiosity.

"Isn't it nice to see such love?" asked one of them and the other cleared her throat.

"When I was young, I knew love like that. A boy looked at me with the same adoration. Look at those two: The officer, in the left corner, staring down at the girl he loves. And slightly below and to the right, that girl is a real angel. Her up-tilted face, her lovely eyes are enchantingly inviting. What a nice married couple these two will make!"

I waited until the two women walked away and slowly, reluctantly, with a feeling of foreboding, I approached the spot where they stood and looked at the pictures that were the focus of their attention. The large display cabinet was fastened to the wall and from behind the glass two, large pictures stared at me.

In the lower, right corner, a larger version of the picture, that warmed my heart ever since its arrival, was displayed. The picture was that of my beloved Rozsa. Up on the left an officer's picture stood. I recalled the words the women spoke and my world collapsed.

"That cannot be! Rozsa loves me, not that stranger. She is my girl, my beloved. How could this happen? How could anyone mislead people in this manner? How could she allow this to happen? I know she couldn't have meant it. She probably never thought of the consequences, but her picture is here. Everyone who sees them will be convinced of their love. When I have received her picture, I felt it belonged only to me, but now what am I to think? How can I share her with thousands of others?" I tortured myself and raised my fist. I was ready to smash the glass; to snatch her picture from its display case. Before I committed the act my heart dictated, my hasty act with the military lecturer suddenly popped in my mind and I hesitated.

"I have caused enough trouble already. I better not commit another thoughtless act. I will speak to Rozsa. We will go to the photographer and demand her picture's removal. Yes, that is a much better solution," I decided and forced myself to move away, before my impulsive nature gained the upper hand.

I stood at the opposite corner, still watching the display case and those who stopped by to admire that couple, seemingly in love. I reached into my jacket's pocket and brought out the picture Rozsa sent me.

"You my darling belong to me only," I declared silently and I looked at her tilted chin that now appeared quite provoking. "Her silky neck; her smooth, round face; her moist, slightly parted lips; her inviting look; her lovely, even white teeth; her brownish hair, cascading over her shoulders; her long, smooth neck; her sparkling blue eyes were offered to that officer and their love became public property!" I almost screamed in anguish, having made this terrible discovery and my running feet carried me to the display case. This time there was no hesitation, no weighing of consequences. My fist was raised; the glass was ready to shatter.

A heavy hand I felt on my shoulder and Joska Lazar's voice brought me back from the brink.

"If I didn't know my friend Laszlo, I would think I am touching a mad man." His words, his touch, his closeness made me drop my hand.

"What are you doing here Laszlo? Admiring your beloved? Don't you have your own picture of her?" Joska asked me.

"I do..." I mumbled and reached into my pocket to offer him proof of my statement.

"Then don't stand here like a moron. Do come with me."

I went with him blindly, my pain unabated.

"Now show me your bench; show me your tree and there we will talk."

"I have never seen you as agitated as you were when I found you." Joska began, after he inspected the growing heart with our initials, after he took a seat beside me. "What brought that rage on? Do you want to tell me?"

I needed little urging. I was happy to unburden my soul, to spill my guts. When I finished Joska tried to help me.

"Rozsa loves you. Do you doubt that?"

"No...I could never doubt my beloved."

"I am glad to hear that. But you don't seem to perceive the contradiction Laszlo. She loves you, of that you are convinced, yet you think that she loves that other man? Now how could that be?"

"I don't rightly know, but you saw their pictures. Who put them there? What do you think?"

"The photographer...Who else?" I spoke in misery.

"Yes my friend...The photographer and he must be a real artist. He made your beloved Rozsa pose and no doubt selected an officer's picture to display with your beloved. He created the illusion of love between them."

"Do you think that is what happened, Joska?"

"What else could it be? Now let me tell you how you should feel. You should look at those two pictures and laugh at that unfortunate officer, who is condemned to admire Rozsa's beauty without ever being able to get closer to that lovely creature. You should tell yourself that those who stare at her picture are truly unlucky, for the love that shines on her beautiful face shines only for me. You should tell yourself that those who admire your beloved are being cheated. They are the ones who should feel envy. It is your initials Laszlo that are carved beside hers and will grow bigger each and every day. True love comes in each life only once. You are fortunate that you found yours, unlike me."

Hearing my dear friend's words wiped away my anxiety and our conversation began to change its course. We spoke about his years at the university; his military service that was not unlike what I have experienced and as we warmed to our topic I told him all that happened to me.

We lost track of time and when in the distance I saw Rozsa approaching, I stood up, glanced in her direction and my friend took his leave.

***

Our reunion, after the many weeks of my absence, was warm and delightful. My hand touched hers, but only for a moment, for on this warm, wonderful April day the garden of Dery gave us little privacy. I thought of asking her to come to my home, but I recalled the last time we were alone there and I began to fear the intensity of my love, the depth of my desire and I desisted.

We spoke about each and every member of our families. We spoke briefly about Joska, whom Rozsa saw, just before he disappeared. Then I handed her the modest present and after she unwrapped it, after she stared at it, she turned to me and gave me a brushing kiss.

"I am sorry I have nothing to give you Laszlo," she stated sadly and to make her feel better I brought us almost to the brink, thanks to my stupidity.

"But you did, my beloved."

"Did I? And what did I give you?"

"You sent to me this beautiful picture." I took it out of my pocket and when my eyes fell upon it, my misery, my anger, my confusion came upon me.

"Oh that is what you meant. I am happy that you like it. When I sent it to you I hoped that it will make you happy. You know that I love you!"

I should have accepted what she said. I should have changed the topic, but my miserable nature didn't allow me.

"If you truly loved me you would have written something on the back."

"Didn't I?" she asked and I turned the picture to expose its blankness.

"You see you didn't!" My words betrayed the pain I felt.

"Well, I am sorry. I must have forgotten."

"The absence of an inscription really pained me, but that pain is nothing compared to that other. How could you do that Rozsa?"

"What are you talking about Laszlo?"

"That disgraceful display of your picture with that officer, for everyone to see." Joska's wise words were forgotten.

"You might as well spell it out, because I don't know what you are talking about."

"You gave permission to the photographer to use your picture for advertising purposes! You had your picture taken with that cursed officer. You look at him adoringly" I shouted the string of accusations.

"I did allow him to use my picture, that much is true, but I told you that in my letter."

"You didn't tell me that you love someone else. You kept from me that every Jack and John will have as much opportunity to look at your lovely face as I have. I kept your picture with me every moment of every day and even at night I placed it under my pillow, believing that I was the only one who could feast his eyes on your lovely features. Then I come home and find it displayed at a street corner. Did you want me to see the two of you together? Perhaps you didn't dare to tell me?"

"You are insane Laszlo. One more word of such nasty accusations and we are finished." Her voice shook as she spoke and I knew that I had gone too far, that I had to salvage the situation.

"I love you Rozsa, please believe me. How can I not feel enormous jealousy?"

"By trusting me; by loving me; by remembering all our happy moments together."

I reached for her hand and spoke words that would allow her to know that my whole world revolved around her; that my life meant nothing without her; that somehow I will overcome my terrible nature.

She looked deep into my eyes, with her chin raised slightly and when I heard her words the garden's flowers suddenly blossomed, the trees swayed gently, the setting Sun became a thousand times brighter and in the whole universe no happier creature existed.

"My love belongs to only one and that one is you, Laszlo. Remember this and we will always be happy. Forget it and your life and mine will come to nothing, but ruins; everything will be in shambles."

I raised both of her hands to my trembling lips and showered them with gentle kisses. Then we rose and, without another word, we began our usual journey. The huge oaks, that lined the street of Szamuelly, leaned over us, their canopies blotted out the rays of the setting sun and before we were half way to her far away home darkness descended. Now and then I slowed our walk, wanting this night to last forever. When her hand was held by mine I felt warmth, peace and contentment. When my lips found hers, just for a brief moment, I felt the passion of her love.

Since her Father's letter we always separated at the end of the long Avenue, where Lokert Row began, but this time I could not leave my darling.

"Do you think I could walk with you just a little further?" I asked her and she nodded her head in the deepening darkness.

Her street was deserted, so I dared to hold her hand, expecting not to be seen by anyone. I was so absorbed by my happy thoughts, by the pleasure of feeling Rozsa's fingers that I missed noticing our arrival.

"I think you better turn around now Laszlo. I don't want my parents to discover..." Rozsa quietly called my attention to the possible danger.

"I think it's too late for that," her Father's voice boomed out of the darkness.

"It's too late indeed," her Mother joined in.

"Well never mind it. It's best if both of you go into the house," Mr. Buja issued the order and the two of us no longer touched, entered the house and our fearful waiting began.

"I hope you do not think we were spying..." Mr. Buja was the first to speak after they entered. "We just tried to enjoy the warm evening, sitting under the acacia tree, never expecting to see you Laszlo."

"I am so sorry...Please understand that I couldn't stay away." I was barely able to force out my words of apology.

"Have you stayed away from our daughter after my letter?"

"No Sir!" I decided to be truthful.

"Have you disobeyed us Rozsa?" It was Mrs. Buja's turn.

"I did Mother, but I am almost sixteen..."

"And does that give you the right to disobey me and your Mother?" Mr. Buja asked not unkindly.

"It was my fault. I am the guilty party." I tried to help Rozsa.

"No, Laszlo. It was my fault too...You Dad loved my Mom for a long time. The two of you know the meaning of true love and that is what Laszlo and I feel for each other." She tried to exonerate me.

"I see now that we have made a mistake my children." I heard Mr. Buja and I couldn't believe what he called me. "I am sorry Laszlo for having written that letter. When we heard about your illness I should have written to you. From now on you can see Rozsa whenever the two of you wish to be together. We will never again try to separate you. Am I right Maria?"

"You are my husband, your word is the law around here, but there is one thing I want to say. Great love like yours must remain pure...We trust our daughter and we trust you Laszlo. From now on you are welcome in our home. What we have we share with you: eat with us, drink with us, laugh with us, talk with us, enjoy Rozsa's company, but until the two of you are married you both must be on your best behavior."

After those words the four of us talked late into the night and when we parted, close to midnight, I danced the length of Lokert Row; then I flew over the remaining streets and when I fell into my own bed I have reviewed this remarkable day.

The joy of my home coming; the disappointment of seeing Rozsa's picture displayed in the center of the city; Joska's words and my foolishness of not heeding them; the ruin I almost created; Rozsa's forgiveness for my stupidity and the crowning event of the day: her parents accepting me. All of these things rushed through my mind and my lips began my prayer.

"Thank you dear Lord for Your Mercy! Thank You for that dear girl's love! Thank You for all Your gifts!" I whispered into the room's darkness and I fell asleep.

***

A glorious week followed: I have visited the Bujas daily. We no longer had to hide, to meet in secret. We went to gather weeds to feed the pigs; we climbed to the attic, where the dry corn was stored to feed the live-stock and there we dared to steal a kiss. We had long walks and talks and visits with our beloved relatives and when the day came to walk to the train station we talked about the rest of April, the month of May and my return when in June I was to graduate.

"This time there will be no tears Rozsa!" I declared bravely. "April will slip by fast; May will go as April did. In June I will write all my exams and I will rush back to you my darling. After that there will be no more parting. As soon as I start teaching I will go to your parents and ask for your hand. By the time we will wed I think you will be almost seventeen." As soon as I spoke those words the ugly specter of military service intruded, but I was loath to mention that likely possibility.

"We parted with a gentle kiss. We were on our best behavior and as the train began to move, as Rozsa's kiss throwing hand receded, I sat down and took out her picture.

"This dear girl is mine...She was given to me by the Lord and her parents. Let that street corner, with her picture, remain as is, it does nothing less than declare my incredible victory." My thoughts on this trip gave me no pain, just an overwhelming joy, quiet peace and gratitude for the good things that happened to me.

***

We were nearing the last month of our studies. My friends and I were exhausted by our intense preparations for the coming exams. The four of us needed a break badly.

"How long can we keep this pace up?" Ocsi moaned late one evening, around the end of May.

"If I don't get a drink I am sure I will perish," Jeno lamented.

"If only we had any money." Peter stated with a knowing wink at me. He knew about my Father's second letter and the two hundred Forint bills he sent me.

"I know what all of you are thinking about. I know what you three desire." It was up to me to display generosity. "Pack up your books you thirsty creatures. I will pay for an evening's entertainment."

"Now that is more like it. The three of us were convinced that you will horde your money." Ocsi taunted me with his remark and when I carefully removed from my billfold those two bills, the three of them began to take my offer seriously.

"Where shall we go?" Peter asked us, when we began to walk toward the city's center.

"Pannonia is my choice!" Ocsi shouted.

"Pannonia it is!" I declared reluctantly. The large, expensive hotel stood close to the bank of the Tisza, the winding, capricious river that terrorized the city. Throughout the ages she sent her surging waters to demolish homes, to destroy lives, to wipe out livestocks, but by the time of our night on the town, the city fathers had a ten meter high, concrete bank erected to protect the most populated sections of the city.

It took us half an hour to reach the park, where the old hotel stood, where in its basement the pub dispensed everything we needed.

"We will start with a glass of palinka and chase it with a mug of beer. How does that sound to you my friends?"

"As long we don't stop there, it is fine with me," Jeno declared and I placed the order.

"Now I want to propose a toast." Ocsi raised his voice in the crowded pub. "Here is to Laszlo. May he be the greatest teacher at Bacsbokod. May he find love and happiness with his Rozsa. May they give life to many happy, healthy children. May all of us enjoy a bright future!"

We drained our drinks, smacked our lips, enjoyed the break from our constant studies and as the minutes slipped by, as I have ordered another round, we began to chat about the government's strange way of operating.

"When I enrolled at the university to become a teacher..." Ocsi took the lead. "I first didn't think I will ever succeed, but now, that I was assigned to teach at Gara, even I have hope of succeeding, unless I flunk my examinations."

"They need teachers very badly, so I doubt they shall fail anyone," Jeno announced.

"Are you saying that I will not earn my degree? Are you implying that it will just be given to me?" Ocsi began to quarrel.

"I beg your pardon, my dear Ocsi. I implied no such thing. For the last two years the professors drove us without mercy. They wanted us to study, they wanted to avoid the need of failing anyone. That is what made them so ruthless...They fear the Minister of education more than anyone. That high and mighty official had his staff determine how many teachers will be needed in the school year of 1952/53 and all the professors worked us hard to assure the proper number's delivery." Jeno gave his explanation.

"Is that why the Minister informed all of us about next year's teaching assignments?" Ocsi asked.

"Next year's teaching assignment? I think you didn't read that edict clearly." Peter stated. "Let me highlight the main points of the Minister's order: First, I was assigned to a small village school to begin my teaching career in August of 52. Second, I am to serve there for thirty-five years, unless the nation's need demands otherwise. Three, I will be paid the magnificent sum of eight hundred Forints each and every month, with ten Forints increase after each year, until I reach the fantastic salary of eleven hundred and fifty Forints, but that will be thirty-five years from now. Four, I will be required to teach six days every week and to engage in cultural activity every Sunday. Five, I will be given two months of summer vacation each year, with full pay, but in exchange I will have to volunteer four weeks of that to supervise children. Now that sounds to me more than next year's teaching assignment." Peter stuck in the air an extended finger each time, as he added another condition. "I am certain your orders listed all those points."

"Mine did and only the place where I shall teach will be different." I confirmed Peter's statements.

"And so did mine," Jeno added.

"So we are all in the same boat...Had we been given a prison sentence it could not have been harsher!" Jeno announced and asked for another drink.

"What could they do if I decided to quit?" Ocsi raised the question.

"Wow! A few minutes ago Ocsi expressed his earlier doubts about becoming a teacher and now he is talking about quitting." Peter smiled and punched Ocsi in the shoulder.

"Don't be like that. I asked only a hypothetical question," Ocsi hit him back.

"And now let me tell you about the sixth condition, in case you guys forgot that one: Anyone who leaves his position without the Minister's approval will have to pay back all scholarship money with a hefty interest." Peter lifted up one more finger.

"During the last two years we each have received around six thousand Forints!" Ocsi counted on fingers, the alcohol reverting him to his early childhood.

"And that sum, my friends, is almost as much as we earn in a whole year of teaching. So how could any of us afford to quit?" I asked them and they began to chuckle.

"So we have sold our bodies and souls for the privilege of becoming underpaid teachers," said one.

"Just like prostitutes...," said another.

"We were fools, I do admit," spoke up the third one.

"We may have been all those things, but just think my friends, we will be teachers. We will shape the minds of young people...We will guide them...We will teach them...We will prepare them for the future." I repeated the words I have been told by professor Kobor.

"Enough complaining... Let's have another drink," Jeno stated.

"My money is fast evaporating," I announced.

"One more round wouldn't exactly ruin you. Would it?" Ocsi announced and I ordered another round of drinks. We no longer desired to speak about serious matters, so someone began to tell a joke. The stories came fast, each of us trying to outdo the other. When we ran dry, not able to recall another joke, Ocsi began to sing. We sang gentle songs about love, about mothers, about tearful farewells and then Jeno's hand called for silence.

"Enough of your foolish sentimental songs, let me teach you a lewd one."

"I may have been sixteen and a half..." Jeno began to sing about a fallen young girl, who unexpectedly became pregnant. The time has passed and we have proved to be good students of several naughty songs.

Before midnight the place began to empty and when the clock began to chime the hour of twelve the four of us were ushered out.

***

We staggered out of the pub and our uncertain steps carried us many feet into the park. At a small, metal building, which I recognized as a transformer shack, we leaned against the trees and tried to clear our heads.

"I got an idea, let's have a contest," Ocsi's slurred words captured my friends' attention.

"So what...brilliant idea...popped into your head...Ocsi?" Jeno could hardly make himself understood.

"Are you willing to contribute ten Forints Laszlo?" Ocsi asked.

"Have I not paid for the drinks? Have I not spent enough already?" Not even the alcohol fumes could change my frugal nature.

"You did Laszlo, but would another ten hurt your pocket?" Ocsi urged me.

I reached into my pocket reluctantly and gave Ocsi a ten Forint bill.

"Here...Have your fun, but leave me out of it." I sulked and supported myself by holding on to a metal lever, that was fastened to my tree.

"All right...Jeno, Peter and I will line up behind this building. Come on...Now unbutton your pants, take out what the good Lord gave you. Ten Forint says I can piss higher than either of you." Ocsi issued the challenge and without waiting he hit the building close to the window that was at least four feet above where his legs parted. I watched the three of them struggle to surpass each other and when Jeno dropped his pants and squatted down I became frightened.

"What the hell do you think you are doing?"

"Having a shit...Don't you ever do that?" He laughed wildly.

"Let's see who can produce a bigger pile? Do you have another ten to spare Laszlo?" Ocsi dropped his pants and I turned away, not interested in witnessing their drunken antics.

As I turned I stumbled and tried to hang on to the lever. The simple metal rod slipped down, just very slightly and in that second my intoxication had disappeared. My experience of the next few seconds was not unlike that of a man dying. Images, news items, rumors and facts ran through my head and what I remembered terrified me.

Several months before, a huge statue of Stalin was erected in the center of this park. I saw it on the day when workers, teachers, students in the thousands were ordered to attend the statue's unveiling. I didn't listen to the speeches, I almost missed what followed when the white sheet was slowly lowered to the ground, but thank God I did not miss the finale. Stalin sat in that huge chair, just as the sculptor's hands fashioned him, but his face was smeared with feces, on his lap stood a huge basket, exuding the unmistakable odor of foul things. Around his chest the white ribbon proclaimed his deed: "You took everything else from us you bastard, so now you take our shit!"

The crowd roared its approval not to praise the original artist, but those masters who in the dead of night sabotaged the unveiling.

Rumor had it that the anti-Communist underground movement was responsible for that act. Within minutes the crowd was dispersed and the manhunt began with no success. Two days later huge spot-lights were erected to illuminate that dark being and a twenty-four hour honor guard was created to protect the Communists' Almighty.

These thoughts rushed at me, sobered me, improved my vision to recognize what I did. As my hand pulled down that lever, to my left, far behind the trees I discerned lights being extinguished. When I tried to correct my mistake by pushing the lever back to its rightful position, I kept my eyes on the far away darkness and my mind and that statue simultaneously became illuminated.

"Run!" I shouted and after a moment's hesitation my three friends melted into the dense vegetation. I stood there trying to follow my own order, but my feet wouldn't obey me. I was benumbed with fear, but there was no time to contemplate my future.

Finally my feet began to move, but I wasn't fast enough for the running guards.

"Stop!" came the order from a few feet away.

"Stop or we shoot!" thundered a deeper voice and the two of them appeared.

I was rooted to where I stood. My heart was racing. My mind searched furiously for some kind of credible explanation.

"Put your hands up!" I obeyed the order instantly and felt the muzzles of guns pushed against my back.

"Comrades...," I found my voice and helplessly pointed at the lever, a few feet away from me.

"Well, are you trying to confess your crime? Is that why you are pointing at the lever that controls the spot lights?" asked one of them, his voice harsh, without mercy.

"I didn't know what that was...I had a few drinks that is all. I came here to rest and to have a leak."

"I smell shit," said the other and began to make wider and wider circles around me. He must have stepped into one of the piles.

"God damn it! Now I will have to clean my boots and I almost destroyed the evidence," he muttered and came back to me.

"You are a f...-ing bastard! You are the enemy. Now we know who was responsible for desecrating Stalin's monument. You tried to repeat the act, no doubt. You are finished. Keep your hands up in the air. Follow my comrade...Don't try to pull anything funny or you will die instantly."

"But comrade, it is a mistake...I wouldn't do such a terrible thing."

"Shut up and do as I told you."

One of the guards led the way out of the park and across the wide boulevard, toward a big, white building.

"That is the Communist Party's Headquarters." I recognized the building. "Maybe they will hand me over to a party official? Maybe I can talk my way out of this?" I screwed up my courage and those thoughts slightly cheered me.

The wide, main door of the white building was flanked by two others. One of the guards opened that small door with a key, and in the dim light of the Moon I could see the sloping concrete floor as I was pushed inside by the guard behind me.

"I take it from here. You go and guard the monument. When I am finished I will relieve you." The one behind me spoke and the other guard disappeared. My guard flicked on a light switch. I could see the concrete floor and walls surround me.

I felt the first punch in my back and turned in surprise.

"But comrade..." The next punch caught me squarely on my chin. I fell to the concrete floor. I lay there curled up, nursing my aching chin.

"Get up you bastard. Get up right now or I will use my feet."

Before I could decide what to do, his boot kicked at my chest. I smelled the shit he stepped into, but the stench of my own fear was far more persuasive. I raised myself on one knee, then tried to stand up, but my fear, coupled with the punches and the kick made me weak.

"Get up right now or you are a dead man."

I struggled to my feet and stood there dejectedly.

"That is better. Tell me who your friends are!"

"I was alone."

"You are a lying son of a bitch. There were others with you, I know."

"Comrade, please believe me."

"Don't call me comrade, you scum. Tell me what I want to know!"

"I was alone. I just told you."

One punch; the floor; one kick and I was standing again.

"Now tell me!" He held me by my shirt close to him and his spittle hit me.

"I was alone," I kept insisting.

"You don't want to cooperate with me. Very well then. I will report the incident to the Security Forces. They will make you spill your guts. The judge will not exercise mercy. Hand over your identification card."

With a shaking hand I removed my identification booklet and handed it to him.

"Your name is Laszlo Lichter?"

"Yes," I groaned.

"And you are a university student?"

"Yes," I replied.

"That is what we have suspected. You bastards are given an education by the State and even a scholarship and that is the gratitude we receive. To desecrate our beloved Father's monument; to cover Stalin's face with shit, will fetch you a life time in Siberia. You and your friends can rot there and all of you deserve it."

"I was alone...," I still insisted.

"Have it you way. I don't give a shit."

Punch; floor; kick and another struggle to get to my feet.

He must have tired of his sport. He took out a pen and a small booklet.

"I will fill in your name; your address; the time and nature of your crime. Tomorrow morning I will have to prepare a detailed report. Do you see what you have done you fatherless scum? If it wasn't for you I could have walked around that monument for two more hours and go home to my family. But no such thing now...I will have a lot to do. Thanks to you, you f...-ing bastard."

He finished writing, closed his booklet, placed it in his inside pocket. Unexpectedly his open palm met my face and I saw drops of my blood splatter on the floor. I was enraged.

"You report me! You do that! And I will report you for your abuse, for your action," I screamed at him, trying to stem the bleeding.

"Maybe I should have shot you? Well it is too late for that. Now get out of here...Do not dare to leave the city...They will find you! This you will not escape."

**

I staggered home in the dark night, contemplating the coming days.

"They will arrest me...They will blame me for what happened to that monument...They will make me talk...I will not have the strength to shield my friends...I will never be able to teach...I will never see my family again...Nor my beloved Rozsa. Why have I agreed to a night on the town? Why did I have so much to drink? Why did I not remember the presence of that monument in the park? Why did I get myself into this mess? What should I do now? There is only one solution: suicide! Am I strong enough to commit that act? My friends will miss me...My family will be devastated...My beloved Rozsa will never understand...I must warn my friends first! I must give them a chance to disappear. Then I will do away with myself! I will be strong. I dare not face this enemy."

Having resolved what I was to do, I walked to my dormitory and to my surprise I found our room empty. I have waited for well over two hours, thinking about all the things that happened, about my resolution and I began to waver.

"Maybe I need not kill myself? Maybe I can convince them of my innocence?" I asked myself, but then I recalled my Father's unjust imprisonments, my Uncle Jozsef's stories about the Siberian prison camps and I no longer tried to deceive myself.

Peter was the first to arrive. He was followed by Ocsi and Jeno.

"Thank God Laszlo the guard told us the truth," Ocsi spoke up.

"What do you mean?"

"I let Peter tell you the story."

Peter cleared his throat and began the telling.

"Our story will sound incredible to you Laszlo. But so help me God what I am about to tell you is true. We heard your shout and before we have realized what we were doing we ran, hid behind the dense hedges and watched what was happening to you. One of the guards almost found us, but he fortunately stepped into one of the land mines.

"We heard him curse under his breath. We watched them talk to you, take you away. We followed them until you entered that building and one of the guards returned to his post, while the other followed you in. At that point we could only guess what was happening inside that building. Slowly we worked our way toward the bank of the Tisza and from there we watched the guard, who kept walking around the monument.

"Later on your arresting officer appeared and relieved the other guard.

"I told Jeno and Ocsi what I planned to do and they agreed with me. The guard came around the monument, with Ocsi already in position. Jeno and I grabbed the guard, stifled his coming scream and I whistled. Ocsi did his task, the spot lights were extinguished and I whispered in our captive's ear: 'What did you do with our friend?'

"'Nothing,'" came his muffled reply.

"'I don't believe you!' I told him and he was quite frightened, but not as much as he became when we lifted him over the parapet.

"'I know you cannot see where you are, but you must feel your feet dangling. Ten meters below you is the concrete covered bank of Tisza. If we drop you, you will break your neck; if you are lucky you will die."

"'Please...I have a family...' He was pleading.

"'What did you do to our friend?' I asked him once more.

"'I...just punched him a few times...,' came his admission.

"'What else, you bastard?'

"'I gave him a kick or two...,' his moaning became more frantic.

"At that point I whispered to Jeno: 'I cannot hold him much longer.' The guard heard my statement and began to sob.

"'Please pull me up...I don't want to die...I will do anything.'

"At that point Ocsi returned to where we stood and his harsh voice commanded: 'Drop the God damn commie...Let him die.'

"'Have mercy...I have released your friend, he is free...He is all right.'

"'He is a lying son of a bitch. Don't believe a word he says!' Ocsi stated.

"'I can offer you proof...I have it in my inside pocket.' The guard moaned and for good measure I let go of his hand, but not before I made Ocsi hold on to the back of his jacket.

"'What proof do you have?' I asked him.

"'I took his name, his address, wrote the time and nature of his crime in my book.' The guard's words were slurred, yet sounded convincing.

"'We will pull you up. Don't make a sound.' I told him in the dark, silent night and we pulled him up, held on to his gun and stuffed into his mouth my handkerchief.

"'Nod your head if you can hear me,' I ordered him and he nodded.

"'I will search your pockets now...Remain still.' I ordered him and in a second I had the small book in my hand.

"I couldn't read a thing in the darkness, but we had already spent too much time with him. I feared the appearance of another guard, so I had to act fast. 'Did you beat him?'

"He nodded his head.

"'If I think for a moment that you are lying, you will die. Do you understand?'

"Another nod came, but that one came much faster.

"'When you released him was he able to walk?'

"He indicated his agreement.

"'Did you report the incident to anyone?'

"He shook his head.

"'We will empty his gun of all ammunition...We will take the report book with us...We will let him live.' I told the others and pulled out the handkerchief. 'You shall remain silent, unless we ask you a question,' I commanded.

"His nod came fast.

"'You heard what I told my friends.'

"Another nod indicated that he did.

"'Now tell me if you can get another book to replace this one?'

"'I can.'

"'Your bullets will rest on the bottom of Tisza, be glad we don't make you join them. Can you replace those bullets as well?'

"'Yes,' he replied.

"'What about your comrade? How will you handle him?'

"'Leave that to me...'

"'Now listen to me carefully. Your life will depend on how you react. If you come after our friend, if your report him, he and us will end up in Siberia. But before we do we shall talk. We will confess that we surprised you, while you dosed on duty. We will tell the

Security Forces that we have disarmed you. We will tell them where your bullets are scattered. Have no doubt the divers will find them. We will offer your book as proof of your dereliction of duty, of your inability to protect the great Stalin. Do you believe me?

"'I do.' He didn't need to say anything more.

"'You tell whatever you want to tell your comrade, but make absolutely certain that he will remain silent. Will you do that?'

"'I will for the sake of our families.'

"The three of us had little choice, but to accept his promise and to issue a last warning.

"'For ten minutes you will not make a sound or we will be captured and we will talk. After that you shall go and replace your bullets and your report book. Then you will guard this monument as if nothing happened. You lie down on the ground and count off those ten minutes.'

"We watched him as he lay down, we watched him begin counting and then we took to our heels. Now you can understand Laszlo why Ocsi exclaimed when he entered: 'Thank God Laszlo the guard told us the truth.'" Peter finished his incredible story.

"Now think hard Laszlo...Was the guard's story accurate in every way?" Ocsi demanded.

"I got a few more punches, a bloody nose, one more kick, but otherwise everything he told you appears to be true." I assured them. "You guys are something else. I thought you deserted me. I can't believe the chance you took."

"Listen to me Laszlo..." Peter spoke once again. "If they kept you; if you were handed over to the Security Police, you wouldn't have lasted a day. You would have spilled your guts, as we would have under the same circumstances. All of us would have been arrested and sent to Siberia. So what did we have to lose? We had to gamble, to take a calculated risk."

Thus ended the evening of our near tragedy, but not the fear, not the worry, not the constant anticipation.

Whenever a knock came on our door we were relieved to find that it was only another student. When a professor called my name I was unable to give a coherent answer, for it was not a question I anticipated, but a summons from the authorities. When I heard footsteps behind me, I slowed my walk and imagined being handcuffed and led away.

The last few weeks of my last year of study dragged on slowly and when the postman delivered three letters, all addressed to my three friends, they were stunned, and so was I. Their reluctance to tear open the envelopes disturbed me.

"Please open them. Open them fast," I begged them. "It couldn't be what you fear. The agents of the Secret Police wouldn't just write you a letter. They would come in the dead of night and besides it would be I they would come for, not you guys, not until a day or two later."

All three letters were suddenly open; all three of my friends read them and their paleness disappeared.

"What is it? Please tell me!" I asked and Ocsi spoke up.

"Nothing much, just my marching orders. I am to report on July third to Veszprem, for machine gun training."

"And so am I but to another city," Jeno announced.

"Me too…On the same date, but I will have to do it here," Peter stated.

I was dumbfounded. "And I got no invitation. What do you think of that?"

"Don't complain Laszlo. A day or two and you too will receive your order." Ocsi wasn't exactly trying to cheer me.

***

The days have passed and I alternated between my fear of being arrested and my dread of being called up to serve in the military. Then our examinations began and I shoved fear and dread in the background, I concentrated on what was most important.

When the results were announced the four of us rejoiced. We waved our certificates proudly and the letter that was attached.

"I am a teacher! I have succeeded!" Ocsi shouted his jubilation.

"And so did I!" Our shouts alternated.

"You didn't notice that letter. Did you my friends?" Jeno asked and we stared at him like three morons.

"Well we will be only practice teachers. When the year is up we will have to return here and take our State examinations. Then we will be full fledged teachers, if we performed well at our schools; if we studied hard for a whole year and if we didn't forget anything we have learned," Jeno enlightened us.

"But, but, I thought it was only a formality," Ocsi almost stuttered.

"Formality, my foot. I spoke to students who finished their studies a year ago. They came back to take this 'formality', as you called it Ocsi. Well it was a lot worse than that. One out of every four were flunked. They are out of teaching and they must repay their scholarship money."

"But that is a lie...Just a scare tactic...That couldn't be true. Didn't someone say that there is a quota our professors fear not to fulfill?"

"Yes that was said, but the State examinations are not conducted by our professors." Jeno continued and he succeeded to scare only Ocsi.

"Who in hell is qualified to do that?" Ocsi asked.

"Some committee from the Education Department undertakes that task and if what I hear is correct, then by failing many they terrorize the professors and the students into applying themselves to a much greater degree."

"It seems to me that our life is a never ending saga. I should have taken a job after I graduated from high school. My pay would have been better; my sentence would have been lighter; my cross would have been easier to bear." Ocsi continued his complaining.

"Well look on the positive side Ocsi. All four of us are healthy...Not like poor Eva." I spoke about one of my class-mates, who suffered from a terrible heart disorder, who was assigned to teach in a small settlement that didn't even have a doctor.

"I feel sorry for Eva. But what could anybody do? Professor Kobor asked the Minister of Education to consider her plight, but even that didn't move that rotten man of unlimited power." Ocsi repeated what they heard from me, just a week ago.

"Didn't Professor Kobor promise your class that Eva will be re-assigned?" Jeno asked.

"Yes, that he did, but even Kobor, that decent, good, caring man lacks the power to influence the high and mighty." I stated the fact and Jeno added.

"In a year, when we are to return, we shall see."

***

The day of our parting arrived fast and the four of us decided not to stick around for the formalities. Our small suitcases packed, our train tickets in our hands, we spoke about those two years; about our struggles; our adventures and our miraculous survival. When there was nothing more to say, we hugged each other, shook hands and parted.

Our friendship, forged during the last two years, was strong, so we never suspected that most of us will never see each other again.

Ocsi and I lived in the same city. Our train was the first one to pull out from the station and this time it was Jeno and Peter who waved farewell to the two of us. We waved back to them and when I lost sight of them, I felt a great void, a terrible loss and enormous gratitude to the boys, my dear friends who saved me.

***

At the station of Baja, Ocsi and I said our farewells and promised to visit each other often. Had we known the demands of the coming school year we would have made no futile promises.

Minutes after we have parted I rushed to my home and when evening fell to my beloved Rozsa.

"I am finished. You are looking at a teacher my dearest," I announced proudly upon my arrival.

"Congratulations Laszlo." It was Mr. Buja who repeated my Father's words, my Mother's words, that of George and those precious words of all my relatives, who came to our home to congratulate me. All the congratulations I have received that day added together meant far less than the words Mr. Buja spoke.

"All of us are proud of you! We knew you will make it. Now tell us where do you go from here?"

"I was assigned to teach at Bacsbokod. I will have to report there on August first."

"And what about your military service?" Mrs. Buja asked and I saw my darling Rozsa's face covered with a shadow of sadness.

"I wasn't called up. I have all of July to enjoy." I almost burst with joy as I watched Rozsa break out in a sweet smile and I touched her hand to convey my feeling.

"Laszlo, just hold on for a minute. Did I get this clearly? Last summer you became a Corporal? After this summer's service all of you were due to be promoted to the rank of Sub-Lieutenant?"

"That was my understanding," I replied quickly.

"I smell a rat. I hate to tell you, but I know a few things about the military," Mr. Buja pushed on and I wasn't going to allow him to spoil our summer.

"There is nothing strange about that. They must have spoken to my doctor. The meningitis I had many months ago probably made me unfit." I offered the only explanation I was able to find during many sleepless nights after my friends received their notices.

"May be...," Mr. Buja said and it appeared that he was about to continue, when I saw his eyes fall on the happy, sweet face of her daughter and he changed the subject.

"So what are you going to do with a whole month?" Mr. Buja asked and I almost gave him an honest answer.

"I will spend every minute with your sweet daughter. I will shout from the rooftops how much I love Rozsa. I will take her to swim with me; to boat with me; to walk with me and we shall talk about our future." Before the dangerous words spilled out, I caught myself and decided to disguise my true intentions.

"Well, I will spend some time at Bacsbokod, just to get acquainted with the village, with my school and I will also look for a place of lodging. I may even try to get a job for the month. I will visit my relatives and friends and whenever you allow me I will come to see you and Rozsa."

"Your plan seems sensible enough, but surely you can find some time to come fishing with me?" Mr. Buja extended his invitation for the first time ever and I knew the honor he bestowed upon me.

"I would like nothing more. Thank you for the invitation."

"I am sure Laszlo that you are not totally sincere." He winked at me and the next day the two of us went fishing.

***

I truly enjoyed being with Mr. Buja, in spite of the long bicycle journey. We paddled on the dike that skirted the Danube, past the bridge, heading north. When we reached the third break-water, that reached at least a hundred meters into the body of the splendid river of Danube, Mr. Buja pointed at the far tip of it.

"That is our destination. We will climb over the rocks and when we get there we be ready to try our luck."

He and I carefully navigated over the moss covered rocks and boulders, our fishing box and fishing poles in our hands, now and then Mr. Buja calling my attention to danger.

"Be careful Laszlo! The rocks here are slippery...Watch out! Some of the rocks are tipping...Make sure you don't fall...We are almost there."

When we reached the very last rocks, he placed his equipment on a flat one and pointed to another where I was to fish.

"Well we have made it this far. It was a perilous journey, not unlike life, but if you take all your steps with great care, never losing sight of your destination then you have a good chance of succeeding." He began to prepare his three fishing rods.

I had many conversations before with the man I hoped will become my future Father-in-law, but this time I sensed that his words conveyed more warmth and caring.

"First we shall try for an hour or so to land a carp. Have you ever fished for carp Laszlo?"

"I did on one or two occasions with my Father and many times with Joska Lazar."

"Your Father is a great fisherman. Fish seems to feed wherever he goes. Let's hope we will be that lucky. How come you fished with him so rarely?" He baited his hook with a single eye of cooked corn and allowed his hook to drift with the current. He repeated his action twice more with the other fishing poles, but on the third hook he put a good sized piece of *csusza*. "Do you know what this is?" Mr. Buja asked before he offered it to the fish.

"I saw my Father mixing flour, corn-meal and paprika and when he was satisfied with the consistency, he rolled it into round, long pieces before he cooked it. That is the way he makes his *csusza*," I told my fishing partner.

"My method of preparing this bait is not much different from your Father's, but every fisherman guards his recipe. Come to think of it you didn't answer my earlier question: 'How come you fished with him so rarely.'"

"When I was a small boy and he went fishing, I always begged him to take me with him. 'You are too young...You will chase away the fish...I am staying for two whole days, so you better stay with your Mother.' He always found an excuse and when he began to walk to his boat, I used to follow him for a mile or so. I cried all the way, I wanted to be with him so badly, but he often lost his patience and when that happened I turned around,

ran all the way home and continued to cry somewhere where none would see me." I re-lived those heart breaking events, I was a little boy once again. "Twice he softened and allowed me to go with him. On one of those occasions I even caught a fish."

"What did you catch Laszlo?"

"I caught a huge pike perch, my Father couldn't believe the size of it when he took it in. It was as long as his wooden fish container."

"That is fantastic Laszlo. Pike perch are prized fish and the big ones are rare indeed..." He was about to say something more, but his attention was riveted on one of his rods. I saw his quill begin to sink slowly, then suddenly it jumped up and lay flat. That is when he jerked his rod. The line went tout, the fish began to run in semi-circles and he slowly, carefully reached for his long handled net. He played the fish for at least five minutes and when he led it close to the rock pile he gently dipped the net under it.
The carp was at least two kilos and I hooted my joy. Mr. Buja placed one finger front of his lips and I stopped my noise making.

"Well, Maria will be happy. All members of my family love fish...This carp will give us a feast."

"I am really happy. Do you think there are more where this carp came from?"

"Laszlo you see the end of this rock-pile and the way the water rushes by it. Then the water turns back on itself creating an eddy. New feed is washed into that eddy every minute and the fish stay close-by ready to feed. Carp will take nothing other than corn or csusza; cat fish will eat worms, grub and even leeches; for pike, pike perch and other fish you need live minnows." He began to teach me and an hour later we each had one additional carp in his container.

"Now let's try to catch a few cat-fish. A mixture of at least two kinds of fish make the soup taste a lot better. Grab a worm Laszlo and thread it on your hook, leave a little bit hanging. But be careful, fishing for cat fish needs a different technique. Carp is a very cautious fish...It will swim around the corn, once or twice it will flick at it with its tail and if the fisherman is wise enough, patient enough not to react to the first touching, the carp will suck in the corn and that is when you must hook it. But not so with cat fish. They are greedy...They gobble up the worm in one single swallow and if you miss to hook it at that instant it is gone, his long, black whiskers shaking, no doubt laughing at the flabbergasted fisherman. Give it a try; let's see if you are a good study."

Mr. Buja treated me like I was his son and my happiness I couldn't hide.

"You haven't had a cat fish bite yet, but you seem to be over-joyed Laszlo. Can you tell me why is that?"

"I am happy...A few weeks ago I was ready to commit suicide..." It just slipped out, I never even told my dear Rozsa.

"What? Are you crazy? Did I hear right?" He was in a shock and when his rod jerked, he didn't have the presence of mind to set the hook, he just stared at me.

Many minutes later I finished my story about Stalin's monument and Mr. Buja pulled in his lines, came over and sat down beside me.

"Rozsa is the apple of my eye. Do you realize Laszlo what your suicide would have done to her?"

"What was I to think? I couldn't face imprisonment. I couldn't survive Siberia. I was in a desperate situation."

"Nothing ever should drive a man to suicide, that escape route is reserved for cowards. Promise me now, right beside the river we both love, that you will never ever again even contemplate that possibility. If you cannot promise me that then you should never again see Rozsa."

I was afraid to make an empty promise, but the prospect of losing Rozsa terrified me.

"What can I do? Life under the Communists sometimes becomes terrifying. There may be times when nothing other than suicide makes sense."

"First you make that promise Laszlo, then I will tell you some things." His voice was gentle, yet commanding.

"I promise!"

"You promise what?"

"I promise never again to contemplate suicide."

"Do you swear Laszlo?"

"I swear on the life of the one who is dearest to me."

"Always remember this place Laszlo. Look up and memorize the skies under which you swore. Look at our beloved river and think of it when desperation grabs you. It will take time, but I will begin to teach you. This river comes from Germany, its source is somewhere in the Black Forest. When she is about to enter our ancient land, to her right she sees a fence. I call that fence the border of hope. This side of it I call the fence of despair. Whenever you feel despair, as I have felt that many times, think of that structure and a new life beyond it. Recently I had reasons to think about crossing it, but not yet. Now when someone pushes me I yield a bit, but never enough to hurt anyone, to compromise values I hold dear. I suggest you do the same. I study the Communists' weaknesses, and God knows they were blessed in that department, and I exploit their inabilities. I let them believe that they are superior to me. That warms their black hearts; that gives me time; that gives me breathing space. When they become too strong for me; when their demands become too great to bear, it will not be suicide I will contemplate. I will find a way to approach my border of hope and with my family I shall cross it. When we put the fence of despair behind us, we will kneel down, kiss the ground and we will be free.

"Remember everything I told you, but never repeat them to anyone. Just thinking about escape is a grave crime in this country. I put my life in your hands Laszlo just by speaking the way I did."

"Mr. Buja you can trust me. I recall a conversation we had years ago. Back then you scolded me for raising the possibility of our families escaping. What changed your mind?"

"Yes, I too remember that occasion. I was loath to leave my home-land, but things have changed."

"But back then there was no fence of despair." I didn't need to elaborate.

"You are right, Laszlo. Back then there were no guard towers, no guard dogs, no mine fields, no barbed wire fence and there were few informers." Mr. Buja described what separated hope from despair.

"Yes, back then it would have been easy."

"It is never easy to leave our home-land. But when they force one to betray anyone, especially his best friend, then what choice do we have?"

"Is this what they are trying to do to you, Mr. Buja?"

"The picture is not that clear yet Laszlo, but I think that is where things are heading. Now we better head home, I think, or it will be too late for a banquet."

We walked the treacherous rock pile, carried the day's catch and we reached the Rozsa's home before darkness descended.

***

"I will clean the fish Maria." Mr. Buja proudly diplayed our catch. "Laszlo is quite a good student, he caught this carp. Isn't that a beauty?"

"It sure is, but once I prepare all this fish they will look even better," Mrs. Buja stated and suddenly the adults became busy.

Rozsa and I sat in the yard, not too far from each other. We talked about our fishing trip, about her Father's kindness and many other things until we were called to the supper table.

The dish prepared by Mrs. Buja tasted better than anything I have ever tasted.

"My Father is one of the best fish cooks," I thought. "But his fish never tasted this good. Why is that?" I searched for an answer and then I found it. "It is being close to my beloved; it is being trusted by Mr. Buja; it is his patient teaching how to fish; it is his candid talk; it is his caring; it is the new hope that he gave me. All of these things and the fish I tasted."

***

That special day was followed by many others. Thirty days is not a long time, yet it gave me time for many fishing trips with Mr. Buja; it allowed me to enjoy Rozsa's sweet company. I bicycled to the village of Bacsbokod, where I saw the large, old, brick, two story school, right beside the Roman Catholic Church, that stood in a small park with a statue of Virgin Mary front of it. The school was deserted...The church was empty...I stopped strangers to make an inquiry and a little later I met the old couple. His name was Pista and hers was Maris. They proved to be very kind people.

"So it is lodging that you require?" Maris asked me and I nodded in agreement.

"Well, we have one room that could be used for that purpose, I guess...What do you think my precious?" The old man asked his wife. The endearing term, the naked love of that one word, coming from a man who was clearly over seventy surprised me.

"I wouldn't mind to have a teacher for a boarder," came Maris' reply and we struck a deal. My trip back to Baja seemed shorter than the distance of eighteen kilometers and when I arrived I have decided to go straight to Rozsa.

"The school is ancient, but I am delighted. There is a nice church close to it my darling," I bubbled with joy like the waters of a swiftly running stream. "I found an old, charming couple, who will give me room and board. They will charge me only three hundred Forints each month. You must meet them Rozsa. They both look like they had a hard life. Their faces are wrinkled, but their eyes dance constantly. And the way they address each other. He called her 'my precious' and she calls him 'my darling'. I hope we will grow that old together. I know we will love each other no less than that old couple. I know my darling that no matter what will happen we will always be happy."

Chapter 10

On the first day of August I made the trip to Bacsbokod, not on my bicycle, but by train. I couldn't risk reporting to my principal late. I was to appear eight in the morning, sharp. At least that is what my principal's terse letter stated.

The steam powered locomotive stood front of the station and at five thirty I climbed aboard with many other passengers, anticipating our imminent departure. The trip would have taken less than thirty minutes, if the train maintained its schedule, but on this occasion it pulled out from the station over an hour late and I reached my destination shortly after seven.

I walked the two kilometers to my school, as fast as my feet permitted. My watch showed seven thirty when I entered the brick building through the large door, climbed the stairs to the principal's office and walked up and down, waiting for the man's arrival.

Eight o'clock came and went. When nine o'clock arrived, without anyone appearing, I became impatient.

"I am surely at the right place," I told myself and dug out my principal's letter. "It is indeed eight o'clock and this is his office." I determined from the letter and began to walk around the building. As I went around one of the corners I almost got tripped by the broom of a stranger.

"And who might you be?" he asked.

I gave my name, told him I was a new teacher and shook his hand. He almost dropped his broom in surprise.

"You are the first teacher who did that. I am only the janitor around here. Would you like me to show you around?"

"That would be nice." I was glad to make the first human contact.

"These are the classrooms. Let's step in here. I show you this one, the others are all the same."

I stood with him inside a classroom. Three rows of simple wooden desks filled most of the class-room, each seat was built to accommodate two students. A large, scratched, pitted black-board was fastened to the wall, front of which stood an ancient, battered desk. In the back corner I saw the soot covered, pot-bellied stove and I stared at it.

"I see, you are surprised."

"Well, in the city..." Before finishing the sentence, I stopped, not wishing to offend him.

"Well we are not in the city. Bacsbokod is a village of six thousand people, so we get little money to refurbish things. That stove in the winter will come really handy, but only when we have some wood to start a fire and coal to keep it going. Each morning when the temperature drops way below the freezing point each teacher is given a small bundle of wood and one bucket of coal. When that time comes you better be ready."

"I am sorry, but I don't follow you."

"You should come dressed warmly, that is what I meant. Otherwise you will freeze here in the winter."

"But what about the children?" I became concerned.

"Well the children are used to it. They come in winter coats, if they have any. They wear scarves and even gloves and when the Minister decides that it is far too cold for them to sit here, he gives them a two weak coal vacation, rather than wood and coal."

"But how do they get an education?"

"That to me is a mystery. Now let me show you another part of the building." He led me through a strange connecting door. "These were cells a few years ago." He pointed to his left, where several small doors could be seen.

"Cells?" I asked, not believing.

"This is where the nuns used to live. This school belonged to the Roman Catholic Church until nineteen-fifty, then the State took it over and the nuns were all deported. Now we better turn around, the rest of the building you are not allowed to visit. That wing over there..," he pointed to the next connecting door,"...used to be the residence of the Mother Superior, but now it is Pallosy who lives there."

"Pallosy is the principal...I almost forgot that I must see him."

"So when is your appointment?"

"It was supposed to be at eight o'clock, but there was nobody at the office." He heard my words and burst out laughing.

"I probably shouldn't say this, but you shook my hand, you are decent. Pallosy rarely gets up before ten, that is during the summer. When school starts he changes his habit. By seven thirty he stands in the main doorway to assure that none of his teachers come in late. Then he sneaks back into bed. That man is cruel and lazy."

"Thanks for the information." I could hardly believe my ears.

"You are welcome young man. If you need advice come to me. When winter comes I might even be able to double your coal ration."

"What should I do until ten?"

"Well, the staff-room is closed, until Pallosy opens it. You might want to go to the recreation room; there you may find a few kids."

I entered the former classroom that sported a table tennis table. It was otherwise totally empty. I picked up one of the white balls, bounced it on the table, then I reached for a paddle and it came back to me.

"I used to like this game...I wasn't very good at it, but on a few, rare occasions I even had a win. All that was before I fell in love with my angel, since then I had no interest to play again." I mused about my almost forgotten fondness for that activity.

"Hello there!" A young boy entered and came to me. He was taller than I, by several inches, and his muscles bulged below his short shirt sleeves. "My name is Janos Karaj...What is yours?"

"Laszlo Lichter," I stammered out my name.

"I am glad to meet you Laszlo. I will be in grade eight this year. Will you be in the same grade?"

I hesitated just for one moment, then I gave my answer: "In grade eight I will be." I didn't know why I have phrased my answer the way I did, but when he shook my hand, when he gave words to express his delight that I will be his class-mate, I was about to clear up the misunderstanding.

"I am sorry I mislead..." I didn't get any further.

"Which one of you is Laszlo Lichter?" A giant of a man stood by the door, his red face betrayed anger; his blemished, huge nose attested to copious drinking; he wore his black hair like a mane that rarely saw a comb; his black mustache was stained with whatever he ate for breakfast. The wrinkled, ill fitting suit hung on his large frame, sported many stains. But what surprised me most was his deep baritone that came from deep down inside his belly.

"I am not used to my teachers being late. Come with me." He turned and his beefy legs carried him away from the place where I made my teaching career's first mistake.

"You are a bloody teacher...You lied to me...You will pay for this!" Janos Karaj hissed at me.

***

"My name is Joska Pallosy, but you know that," my principal began, after he led me through the small staff room into his large, comfortable office. The two rooms were separated only by a French door, the inside of which was covered by a large curtain.

He was seated, while I stood front of his desk. After my train journey and my walk to the school I wouldn't have minded to rest my legs, but that comfort he did not offer, instead he laid down the law and I listened.

"Here you will teach two classes of grade seven Mathematics, two classes of grade eight chemistry and mathematics. Five periods of each every week, that makes thirty periods. We keep our school open from eight in the morning until one in the afternoon. Each period lasts fifty minutes, followed by a ten minute break. You and the students eat, but only during the breaks. Eating in the class-rooms I do not tolerate. Nor do I tolerate any lack of discipline from any of our students. And I tolerate that even less from my teachers. Am I understood?"

"Yes, Sir," I answered him.

"You better not use that word! 'Sir' is not permitted. That went out with the Horthy regime. You will address me 'Comrade Pallosy', but only when I speak to you...I cannot be bothered with teachers coming to me, bitching, complaining, and always asking for extra privileges. Now back to your duties young man. Every second day you will be on yard duty during every recess. I do not permit my students to fight, if there is a fight, while you are on duty, you will have to answer to me. If you are within the borders of this village after school hours I expect you to appear at Government House and volunteer your services. On every second Sunday you are expected to conduct student activities. Now look out this window. What do you see?"

"A church, I think it serves us Roman Catholics."

"You will never enter that church or any other, while you teach here. I will not have any of my teachers disgrace me."

"I see...," I broke into his thoughts.

"You don't see...I haven't finished telling you your duties. Do not ever disturb my line of thought. Now where was I before I was so rudely interrupted?"

I remained silent, I wasn't willing to tell him that his last words were to 'disgrace me'.

"Yes, I spoke about teachers disgracing me...It is a disgrace to have my teachers come in late or to leave early. Which reminds me, did I not order you to appear eight o'clock this morning?"

"You did Comrade Pallosy and I was here."

"The hell you were. When I arrived you were not standing by my door. I had to search for you. I had to go and get you. I am not used to such disrespect."

"But I had waited by your door for over an hour." I wasn't going to let him blame me.

"Did I not tell you to speak when I ask you? No teacher ever dares to argue with me. You better learn that you puny, stupid creature. Do you think your university education entitles you to argue with your superior?" He didn't wait for my answer, which by now I wouldn't have dared to give. "You will learn, I assure you. Now one more thing then I am finished. You will arrive to school no later than seven thirty; you will always enter by the front door; you will always leave the same way. Your last class ends at one in the afternoon. You will supervise an orderly dismissal and when all your students have left the building, you may leave, except when I call a staff meeting. Now have you understood everything I said? I would hate to repeat anything."

"I do Comrade Pallosy. Since there are no classes to teach when am I permitted to leave the school?"

"I told you already. One o'clock and not before."

"But the afternoon train leaves at one and the station is two kilometers away." I tried to change his mind. "If there is no one in the school am I permitted to leave early?"

"Until one o'clock there will always be someone here. You and three other teachers, all of you from Baja. I hate that place."

"But that means the four of us will not be able to go home until the next train, which is at nine thirty," I complained.

"So much the better...The four of you will be able to provide a lot of volunteer service. The chairman of the village council will be delighted."

***

Tery Egervary, the daughter of my Father's old friend, arrived first, followed by Margit Jeges and Jancsi Takacs. It took us little time to get acquainted and since we had the school to ourselves in the absence of students, the four of us put our heads together and talked a great deal.

"The hell with Pallosy. I will keep on leaving on time to catch the one o'clock train," Jancsi announced and the two girls agreed.

"But he will be angry. Didn't he give you the same orders he gave me?" I asked hoping to find a solution to my predicament.

"Pallosy did that two years ago, when we came on staff. For two, long years, we have defied his orders. The man is stupid. He barks a lot, but his bite is toothless. You are welcome to become a part of our defiant band of renegades," Jancsi announced.

"What do I have to do?" I asked him.

"Each day one of us will use the front door, while the others will sneak out through the back gate. We will alternate daily. Are you interested?"

I thought about my beloved Rozsa, whom I wanted to see desperately and welcomed the first glimmer of hope out of my dilemma.

"I am with you...Now let me hear the details."

"Well, it is rather simple...One of us goes to the main door, twenty minutes before one o'clock. We give our students work to do and they will be quiet. They hate Pallosy as much as we do, so they will never betray us to that mad man. Pallosy always stands by the main door and intercepts the teacher trying. Sends him or her back to the class and waves his finger, pretending to be angry, but he is jubilant. He captured the one daring soul and never knows that three others have succeeded. This way three out of four will reach Baja early in the afternoon, and only one of us is delayed. The three of us worked this system quite well during the last two years. So are you with us Laszlo?"

"I am, but only during August."

"Only August? And why is that?" Margit asked me.

"From September on I will live at my boarding place."

"Now that is stupid." Terry tore into me. "Pallosy will make you volunteer your services every day."

"What can I do? I have made the arrangements already. I cannot go back on my word. I couldn't hurt that old couple who were so kind to me. But wait a second...Pallosy must know that we are not here. While your method is being used the government office gets only one volunteer."

"So you think we didn't think of that? You are wrong Laszlo. Let me tell you how we avoid being found out. The one who stays behind goes to the Government House and volunteers our services. He tells the official that there are four volunteer teachers, but the other three are finishing some work at school. They take the four names and give out forty questionnaires. Many of them ask general questions of no significance; a few others are live-stock surveys. The first batch contains no names. We are to go to random households, where we ask a few simple questions: 'Are you satisfied with your living conditions?' 'Do you have any difficulty to raise the quota of your crops?' 'How do you rate the local Government's decrees?' And other questions like these. The first few times we have gone to ask those questions we have found that no one dared to give honest answers. They have always expressed satisfaction with everything. So we have decided to fill out those questionnaires ourselves without asking anyone and the government officials are always happy to receive the positive feedback. The livestock survey we carry out with due diligence. We count the number of pigs, the chickens, the geese and all other animals, as demanded and whenever Government officials check our tally they express total satisfaction. So what do you think of that?"

"You three had it figured out well. I am amazed." I spoke words of admiration.

"In this country my friend the key word is 'survival' and survive we shall." Jancsi closed the conversation and for the month of August three working days out of four I was able to see my darling Rozsa.

***

During my ill gained free time I spent with my beloved and when her Father asked me to go fishing I gladly joined that kind man. We revisited the break-water on the Danube and we talked.

"And how are you doing at Bacsbokod?" was Mr. Buja's first question.

In reply I told him everything.

"Be very careful Laszlo! The game the four of you play may work for now, but once they catch on, there will be hell to pay."

"This month only and then my game is over. I will board at Bacsbokod," I assured him and we became silent.

When we rode home with our catch; when Mr. Buja finished cleaning all the fish; while Rozsa's Mother busied herself with preparing another banquet, Rozsa, her Father and I sat in the enclosed yard. He brought out a large book, seated us beside him and began to speak.

"This book I got from Lajos Miklos, a distant relative. You know him Rozsa and you may know of him Laszlo."

"Doesn't he have a bicycle store by the statue of Jelky?" I asked and Mr. Buja replied.

"The very same. Lajos got this book from abroad…He pines for riches and he is determined to reach his aim. Now look at this Sears' catalogue. It is full of items, we Hungarians, have never ever seen. And look at those low prices…All these things are readily available in the U.S.A. That is where Miklos hopes to go…That is where he will become rich."

The three of us turned the pages; stared at the goods and I began to dream.

"Some day I will get my love one of these washing machines…She will have a refrigerator and all kind of nice clothing. I will buy her everything she ever desires…Oh, my God, what is this? I have never heard of such a thing. A Television?" I turned to Mr. Buja.

"What is this thing here?" I pointed at the strange contraption the screen of which displayed a picture.

"That is a television Laszlo. Miklos told me that the Americans can even see movies on this thing."

"But how is that possible? In Hungary there is no such thing."

"Nor is there any in Russia. This is a totally new invention," Mr. Buja explained to us.

"I thought the Russians were first in everything. Didn't they invent the radio, the telephone and all sorts of other things?" my love questioned.

"The Russians are great in inventing lies; they are the creators of deceit." Mr. Buja touched Rozsa's arm. "Some day my pet we will go to America. We will place our orders from catalogues like this. Your Mother will be a happy woman and you Rozsa, will have everything."

I didn't want to ruin the promise Mr. Buja made to my beloved, so I kept my silence until the next fishing trip.

***

This time our trip was very short. We stood by the bank of Sugovica, where one could fish in the shallow waters that rolled gently over the sand bars.

"This is where the white fish live. I cast my hook out to the edge of the sand bar and from the deeper water the fish will attack my bait." Mr. Buja hardly got the words out when he jerked his rod and two minutes later the white fish was beached.

"Wouldn't it be nice if all our plans were this easy to fulfill?" I cautiously approached the subject I didn't want to talk about front of Rozsa.

"Yes it would. What were you thinking about Laszlo?"

"About that Sears catalogue and the hope you created for Rozsa."

"Day after day I have more reasons to plan an escape." Mr. Buja made sure that no one could hear us and when he was satisfied that we were alone, he began to share his grief.

"I was called to my boss' office where I was introduced to a man. He took me out to dinner; he plied me with drinks; he praised my achievements, but I had my own suspicions of who he might be. I didn't have to wait long before he began to inquire about details of how our company operated. He asked me to prepare a report on our construction activities. When I appeared to be somewhat reluctant, he dangled front of me a big bait. I was supposed to grab it like that white fish did mine." He pointed at the fish in his draw net. "I asked him for time to think about his request and he told me he was not in a hurry. He gave me one month to think, after which he expects to see me again. This was last week and I haven't seen him since."

"Is there any harm in doing what he asked?" I inquired.

"No, there is no harm in that, but once I do it he will ask me to do something else. Each time his demands will become greater and some day he will ask me to betray someone dear to me. That is the way they operate. I mean members of the Secret Police."

"Can he do that? I mean to force you."

"Laszlo I thought you knew that they can do anything."

"So what is the answer? What can you do?"

"I will be like a cagey fish. I will approach his bait and almost suck it in, but in the last minute I will veer away. I will let him hope that next time I will take the bait. In the meantime I will talk with Miklos and we will explore the possibility of our escape."

"How soon do you think you will be ready?" I asked and my fear of losing my sweet Rozsa became very real.

"It may be a number of years yet." I heard his answer with great relief.

***

The month of August slipped by. There was no time for more fishing trips with Mr. Buja and precious little time to spend with Rozsa. I moved into my boarding place at Bacsbokod. My lonely room contained a bed with huge pillows; a huge, down filled comforter covered the bed during the day and my body when I crawled under it, thinking, pining after the girl I cherished. A wash basin sat in one of the corners, with a bar of soap and a pitcher of water. My only suit hung against the wall on one of four pegs. A round, old, wooden table stood in the middle of the room, beside it a hard wooden chair. There I prepared my lessons to teach my over two hundred students.

The night before my first day of school I went to bed, and there I took one more glance at the curriculum for all my classes. These came in the mail from the Department of Education and so did the stern warning: "No deviation from the curriculum will be tolerated. Our inspection teams must find everything in good order."

Each time I looked at the lengthy document my reaction was one of amazement.

"There must be thousands of schools in Hungary and many times more grade seven and eight students. Each and every day, each and every period, the same lessons will be thought all over the country to all the students. This may be an advantage when, on a rare occasion, a student transfers, but the disadvantages are far too many. To disregard the students' rate of learning will bring about misunderstandings and confusion. The State demands uniformity, rigidity, regimentation. Why are they so foolhardy?" I asked myself and the answer came easily.

"Elimination of all traces of individualism is what they desire. Everyone in this country must march to the same tune, in the same direction. We are like an army of ants...We start here...We go there...We do this...We do that...and at the end of our lives we can look back at nothing, have no fond memories, just that of a disheartening existence." Had I continued to allow my mind to dwell on these morbid thoughts I would have had no desire to continue living, so I placed the documents on the floor, beside my bed and reached under my pillow to gaze at the picture of Rozsa.

"That is not so...This sweet girl came into my drab life, her love brought with it illumination. Her existence makes my life bright; her love creates warmth and joy and contentment. When I am away from her these are the things I must think about and when I am with her I must forget everything." These thoughts warmed me more than my comforter and after I kissed her sweet face, admired her beauty, hugged it to my chest, I drifted off to dream land.

***

The staff room was packed with teachers, but I knew only my three conspirators. During the month of August each of us went to the front door six times only to be turned back by Pallosy. Each of us enjoyed an early arrival to Baja on eighteen days and Pallosy never got wise to our absence.

The principal stood front of us, glanced at his watch and at eight o'clock began to speak. I counted thirty-two teachers, sixteen on each side of the long table. At the head of the table, by the window, Pallosy stood and the morning Sun sneaked into the room, its rays surrounded him with an undeserved halo.

"Good morning comrades..." A few of the old hands returned his greeting, while the rest sat in sullen silence.

"This day there will be no students present; I hope you didn't forget that. Today I will teach you! There is a lot to do, so I will make this as short as I can.

"Congratulations...All of you arrived on time. That is the way it must be every day of the school year. Lateness I will not tolerate. And there is something else I will not sanction...Going there!" He turned toward the window and pointed outside, in the direction where the church stood, its steeple, crowned by the gold covered cross pointing to heaven.

"Comrades Koch, you have been with me a few years, but you never seem to learn. I forbade you to enter that church, yet you disobeyed me. You and your wife are a disgrace to this school. Stand up you two, let the other teachers see the traitors."

I saw the old, frail, white haired woman stand up, beside the tall, wrinkled, bent, old man, who was her husband. I saw her giving his hand a slight caress. They stood together, bent with age, broken by disappointment. Later I found out that they were Roman Catholics who never began their day without attending the early morning mass. I also found out that Pallosy watched them and took great joy in humiliating them.

"What do I have to do to reform you? What can I say to make you see the light? Is this the kind of example any of my teachers should set for our students? If you weren't so close to retirement; if you weren't too old, I would kick both of you in your rear end." Pallosy worked himself up into a frenzy and then came the first of many displays of his total ignorance. He lifted his right leg, tilted slightly to the right and gave voice to his fecundity by farting.

"Well I feel a lot better now. Enemies of my beloved country give me gas, they give me plenty. They are stinkers; they befoul our society far more than I do by letting you smell my anger." He shouted those words and repeated the act.

"Now that this is out of my system...," Pallosy grinned at his own sense of humor, "...I will conduct the rest of the meeting from my chair." He planted himself in his arm chair and gave a sigh of contentment.

"Let this be a warning to you all...Comrade Koch and Mrs. Koch you may be seated. I wouldn't want your Jesus to take you to his bosom while you stand. Fine...Everyone relax...There will be no more need to blast anyone, if you follow all my orders. So here we go..." He consulted his notes and belched.

"First. All of you must have received the curriculum for all your classes. Raise your hand if you didn't. For each lesson you teach I want a detailed lesson plan. You don't need to submit them to me, just have it ready, in case I decide to check.

"Second. Starting the day after tomorrow I want all of you to line up by the main entrance at seven thirty sharp. You will pick out random students as they enter. You will check their home assignment booklets and check that their assignments are done. I do not take kindly to students who leave their work undone, hoping to catch up during recess. Any delinquents must be reported to me. You will also hand the name of the offending students to their home room teachers. Home room teachers will keep permanent record of all infractions. One offense and no movie passes will be granted during the school year.

"Third. Teachers who have lived in this village more than one year need not volunteer to do community service. That leaves the four teachers from Baja. You four better make me proud. As proud as you made me during August. You have the time, use it wisely." The four of us gave each other knowing looks and once again I regretted my decision to board at Bacsbokod. "Six days a week I will be the volunteer with one other from Baja." I scolded myself for my stupidity, but I recalled the vast amount of study that awaited me for the State exams and I knew that I couldn't change a thing.

"Fourth. You might as well be told now that you will not be warned about the arrival of the inspection committee. They will come a few times a year and their supervision, their evaluation of your work, front of the whole staff, will be thorough. Stick to the curriculum...They expect to see you teach the lessons assigned for the days they are in your class rooms.

"Fifth. In the next room there are many large envelopes. All of them are labeled as to grade and subject. When I finish this meeting you will pick up your envelopes. Inside you will find the list of text book changes. You are to paste those over the designated paragraphs. This must be done today, before you are permitted to pass out the text books tomorrow to the students. One single mistake in this task and you are finished.

"Sixth. By tomorrow you must have purchased a sufficient supply of chalk. I don't appreciate teachers running to the store when they need chalk to write on the black-boards.

"Seven. You will find a roster of movie supervisors for every day. Two teachers will enter the only movie house in the village, five minutes after the show started. The policeman assigned to be with you will assist you to check all movie passes. Students of this school who do not have a pass will be taken out, their names will be recorded. Next day you will visit their homes and inform their parents. The offending students will be black-listed for the rest of the year.

"Eight. You are forbidden to use the only telephone that is in my office, and the typewriter and the duplicator, without my permission. The last two will be locked in the safe at the end of every school day.

"Nine. You are never to try to leave early. All the students must be out of the building before you can desert your post.

"Ten. All recesses must be spent outside by all students, regardless how cold it is. Half the staff will be with them one day and the other half the next day. You shall alternate. I leave it to you how you arrange it.

"Eleven. Each and every Sunday four of you will supervise student activities. These will be scheduled by me. The time we offer such activities will change. I will watch the priest and when he changes the times of Masses we will change the time of activities. Students must be attracted to our institution that offers meaningful learning experience, instead of religious lies, stupid opiates to fool the people."

"Twelve. When cold weather comes you are to see the janitor for your wood and one bucket of coal. It is your job to keep the class-room warm. I want no complaints from any of the parents.

"Thirteen. Physical punishment is a necessary component of your teaching. Do what you want, but do it with discrimination. There are a few students whose parents are powerful people; those kids must never be touched. I let you decide who these kids are and if you ever make a mistake it will be your head, not mine. Don't ever say I didn't warn you.

"Fourteen. The last day of each month you will come to my office, but only after school ended and there I will hand over your magnificent pay. And that reminds me of fifteen, which is most important.

"Fifteen. In October the bond sale committee will be at our school. They will take over my office for a whole day, as is their habit. They will call you in to sign up for a peace bond. You are expected to cooperate with them. Buy a lot of those bonds...Our staff's loyalty is proportional to the amount of bonds they can sell. My staff has always been at the top of the list of contributors. This year you must outdo yourselves.

I took copious notes on all of Pallosy's demands and as he announced the number of each order, as he shifted each time his position and punctuated his pronouncements with another issue of loud gas, I became more and more disgusted with the crudeness of the man.

"Since there are only fifteen commandments, I spelled them all out very clearly, you may leave now and attend to the tasks you were given." He rose, belched, cleared his gas filled bowel once more and left us to our own devices.

I saw staff members exchange glances; some wiped their brows; others spoke a few words to selected members and I decided that it was time to introduce myself, being the only new teacher.

"I am Laszlo Lichter..." My first attempt brought only a suspicious look. The second and the third had no success either, but my fourth target shook my hand warmly.

"And I am Pista Janics. Pleased to meet you Laszlo. It is time we get some fresh blood in here." I rejoiced hearing his words. "We will be friends, I seem to think. You could use a real friend Laszlo. These others are not very kind, except for my wife, Lenke."

"I don't really understand. I expected all staff members to welcome a new comer." I expressed my disappointment.

"They hate new comers," Pista announced.

"But why is that?"

"They know all about you being a university graduate. Rumor had it that you were a scholarship student."

"But so were all the others. The teacher shortage, you know Pista, made the Government offer scholarships to all who wanted to become teachers."

"They know that, but they think you too may be an informer."

"I cannot believe my ears! I, an informer? That is stupid."

"I know that Laszlo and I trust you. Be patient...When time permits we will talk again." Pista shook my hand once more and led me to the room where our envelopes waited.

I picked up the packets marked grade seven mathematics, grade eight chemistry and mathematics of the same grade. The three envelopes were very slim compared to others on the table. I turned to Pista.

"Why are my envelopes so thin?"

"Because you are a lucky devil. Be happy Laszlo you are a teacher of such subjects. Look at mine. I teach history." He waved his hand at a packet that was five times thicker than any of mine and with no more comment he picked them up and he was gone in an instant.

I approached my class-room and saw my name, just below the small square window of the door, and my heart jumped with the new found pride of being a teacher.

"Home room teacher: Laszlo Lichter." The small sign read and I was prepared to face anything. I opened the first envelope, removed the five bunches of replacement slips and began to read the instructions. Then I turned my attention to the others and found their contents almost identical. In each and every instance I was to turn to certain pages, to certain mathematical problems. I was to find Tito, the independent Yugoslav Communist leader, whose recent remarks about Stalin were not totally respectful. I was to paste over those sections that described that man. I read the problems that contained his name. In each and every one he was described as a kind, benevolent, faithful friend of his people, beloved ally of the Soviet Union. The newly issued paper, that I was to paste on top, read quite differently: 'an unscrupulous, cruel enemy of his own people, hated foe of the Soviet Union, chain rattling dog of the imperialists.' I was amazed by the skillful way my students' opinion of Tito was being manipulated. I chuckled about the possibility of a student repeating a grade and noticing how that Communist leader had changed in a single year.

Since it wasn't my place to question the wisdom of my leaders, I began the task of pasting. When all the books were finished, when not one kind word remained in them about that former, highly esteemed leader, I left my classroom and looked for Pista.

I found him in his classroom, almost pulling out his hair.

"You seem angry," I stated the obvious.

"Yeah. This is a time when I hate to be a history teacher. Hundreds of books and changes to make on many, many pages. Damn it. Even if I work all day and night I will never be finished."

"I finished mine. Maybe I could give you a hand?"

"That I would truly appreciate," Pista replied and he pointed to the stack of books that cried out for modification. We worked side by side, silently, slowly. We pushed aside the altered books and continued with the others. Then, around ten in the evening, we were finally finished and Pista thanked me.

"Will you have a drink with me? I am buying."

We entered the restaurant where everyone seemed to know Pista and an hour later, after many drinks, they also knew me.

"I hear you will teach my son," said one and bought me a drink.

"I was told that you will be my daughter's chemistry teacher. Is that so?" asked another and he too insisted that I drink with him.

"Down the hatch." Someone handed me a drink. "I have no kids yet in school, but it can never hurt to be on the good side of a teacher." The stranger winked at me and I searched for Pista. He was in the far corner of the large room, lifting his glass in a salute to me. I waved back and indicated in sign language that I wished to leave. Within minutes he was by my side and when the patrons began to object to my leaving, Pista raised his voice to make the crowd hear him.

"This new teacher - his name is Laszlo, if you don't know that already - needs his rest. He is not used to the way you and I live. He will learn, but for now he must leave and I will go with him to make sure that he finds his proper resting place. Good night my friends!"

"Good night Pista. Hope to see you again Laszlo," the drinkers shouted and resumed their favorite activities.

Pista and I stumbled over the poorly paved streets. When I stepped into a pot hole and almost fell, he grabbed my arm and steadied me.

"I must go home. I must have a good night's sleep," I told him and before he released me he whispered in my ear.

"And I my friend will neither go home, nor seek some sleep, instead I will find a willing wench and the two of us will engage in a delicious activity."

I found myself alone in the darkness. Not totally familiar with the village, I meandered from one street to another. My alcohol fogged mind found nothing that looked familiar in the darkness. Next morning I didn't remember how I got home and the sour taste of my mouth assailed me. I felt my throbbing head and an unfamiliar weakness.

"It was really stupid of me...For my first day of teaching I should be in my best form, not in this total mess. I am glad my dear Rozsa doesn't know how I spent my evening." I berated myself and punished my face and my stupid head with splashes of cold water.

***

My grade eight home-room class of thirty six students sat front of me and I tried desperately to say the right things.

"My name is Laszlo Lichter..." I wrote on the board and suddenly I was alarmed by what I have forgotten.

"In my eagerness to help Pista, to drink with him, to make him my friend, I forgot to buy chalk." I cursed myself. The small piece I had I found in one of the drawers will last me only a few minutes. To solve my dilemma I asked for a volunteer.

"Would someone go to the store for me to get some chalk?"

Several students raised their hands and when I made my selection, a boy, whose shabby appearance cried out for attention, I pointed at him and announced my decision.

"You will go...Here is the money, get me a box of chalk."

"Teacher, you cannot send him. Such jobs are always assigned to the leader of the Young Pioneers. That is me," one of the girls informed me.

"Well, this time we will make an exception. You go..." I pointed at the happy boy.

"Our principal will hear about this," the leader of the Young Pioneers threatened me.

"You do that young lady, but you will have to do it after my class is over," I stated indignantly and the rest of the students applauded.

"Now you will introduce yourselves and while you do that, I will have you put your name on the seating plan. As long as you are on your best behavior you will remain in the seat you chose, otherwise I will have to change that," I announced and they gave their names in the order they were seated.

The fifty minutes passed faster than I expected and I heard the ringing of a bell. That sound seemed to come from far away and as I wondered it seemed to come closer.

"What is that?" I asked my students.

"The janitor is ringing his hand-bell. This is the signal that the class ended." Announced one of my students and they filed out of my class in an orderly manner.

I drew first day duty, so I went to the yard and immediately I was surrounded by many students. Their questions centered around my age, my marital status, my education, my experiences at university and when the yard bell rang out loudly, the students ran to line up like an army of soldiers. Without shouted orders the first graders began to move, then the second graders and within minutes the eighth graders too disappeared.

I went to my class thinking about the students' obedience; their friendliness and I rejoiced. When I entered my class-room all the students jumped to their feet. They stood at attention until I told them to be seated. Whenever I addressed one of them, the student stood up and when he answered my question he waited for my command to take his seat. My lingering head-ache seemed to disappear. I began to lecture on the subject I most loved: chemistry. After twenty minutes or so of speaking about the Periodic Table, about the Russian who created it, I wrapped up with a review to check their understanding.

I looked at their seating plan and called on student after student. They stood obediently, each and every time I have received the right answer-that truly pleased me-and I nodded my head each time to have my student seated.

Then I called on Janos Karaj and his defiance surprised me. He remained seated and totally silent.

"Janos Karaj." I called out, hoping that he didn't hear me the first time, that this time he will stand and be ready to give his answer. Janos remained seated.

"You stand up when I call out your name!" I raised my voice. All the students looked at him and his seat-mate poked him not too gently. That brought on his reaction. He jumped to his feet, but did not face me. He looked at his class-mates instead and made his announcement.

"This teacher lied to me." He spit out the words and took his seat.

I decided not to confront him in front of the class, so I asked him to step outside the class-room.

"What are you going to do? Strap me?"

"I just want to have a word with you, young man." I stepped outside the class-room.

"So what do you want?" He stepped out, this time facing me.

"I don't want to send you to the principal. I made a mistake in the recreation room, but that was over a month ago. Please accept my apology."

"I never will. I cannot stand liars. Send me to the principal. Let him know that you are too weak to handle me."

"I don't want to do that..." I searched my mind for a solution, and then it hit me.

"Let's make a deal. In the class-room you will act like a proper student, but everywhere else we will act like friends, like you hoped us to be."

"I make no deals with liars," he announced flatly.

I recognized my own stubbornness in Janos and decided to give him time to forget his month old resentment.

"I am sorry you cannot forgive me. I will waste no more time with you, Janos. Return to your seat."

From that moment on Janos has ignored me; never reacted to any of my requests; he appeared to have become my sworn enemy.

***

I taught my students; carried out all of Pallosy's orders and as the school days passed, I realized that while many of my students became my friends most of the teachers still stayed away from me. My conspirators took the daily train journey and I, the foolish one, spent many of my non-teaching hours taking surveys and live-stock inventories for the local Government.

Now and then I was to enter the cinema to check our students' passes and to my great surprise I have never found a single student daring to defy the school authorities. My life beat its regular rhythm: Monday to Saturday I belonged to my students, but when my free Sunday came I belonged only to my darling Rozsa.

Once I had two months of teaching behind me I broached the subject that never left my mind.

"Do you think my love it's time to ask your parents?" There was no need to ask Rozsa if she was willing to marry me. There was never a conversation between us when we did not declare the immensity of our love for each other. There was never a time when either of us expressed a wish not to get married.

"I don't know what will be their answer Laszlo, but I sense that my Father's attitude changed greatly."

"I hope that change is not for the worse, but for the better."

"I know it is. He speaks about the fishing trips the two of you had together. He repeats some of your conversations fondly."

"If that is the case, my love, why should we wait?"

"I don't want to wait either. When do you plan to ask them?"

"If you have no objection I will do it today." Although I feared their possible reluctance, I feared even more the waiting.

The two of us returned to Rozsa's home, after our Sunday walk in the city, and found Rozsa's parents in the kitchen.

"Sit down Rozsa and you too Laszlo. Supper is just about ready," Mrs. Buja announced and the aroma of her dishes permeated her kitchen invitingly. Her hospitality never faltered; what she could afford to prepare for her family was shared with me and with the wine, Mr. Buja provided, I built up my courage and cautiously approached the subject.

"I have been teaching for two months now and I am sure my teaching wasn't found wanting. Although I haven't been supervised yet, in all modesty I can state that my students respect me and most of the parents like me. At the end of the year I will take my State examinations and I will be a fully qualified teacher. What I am trying to say is that I am happy, except for being unable to spend much time with Rozsa. During the week-days I rarely have the pleasure of her company and during the weekends..." I was unable to say what I intended, for Mr. Buja stopped me.

"I think I know where you are heading Laszlo. Would a few years of waiting be all that bad?"

"More terrible than I can tell you. We love each other...Life is so short...So many things could happen. Why not allow us to be truly happy?"

"And what about financial security? What about waiting until both of you are more established?"

"Mr. Buja I don't want to offend you, nor you Mrs. Buja, but how can you talk about financial security? I am a teacher, assigned to teach in Bacsbokod. Rozsa is a secretary. We both know that my earning potential will grow very slowly. Thirty-five years from now my salary will not even double. If on my salary and that of Rozsa we are doomed to starve, to be able to afford almost nothing, then why wait for something better, something that will never happen in this country?" As I spoke the truth, as I described my bleak future, Mr. Buja glanced at his wife, then at Rozsa and finally his gaze settled on me.

"I will ask you a question, Laszlo. Your answer must be nothing other than the truth. If you had a choice between marriage and financial security, which one would you choose?"

"There is nothing I desire more than to be Rozsa's husband. That is the only thing that would ever make me happy."

"And what about you my dear daughter?"

"My prospects are no better than Laszlo's. Waiting will not solve anything. If we could have your blessings, my dear parents, you would be giving me the greatest gift," Rozsa stated and her words evoked more emotions than any one of us could have anticipated.

Mr. Buja glanced once more at his wife and when she nodded, his words became the most beautiful gifts I have ever received.

"In this country one cannot even hope, that is true, I admit sadly. I don't blame either of you for reaching out for happiness. Rozsa is far too young in body, but not in spirit, not in character, not in maturity, that we can clearly see. Let's set a date for your engagement and when Rozsa becomes sixteen and one half years old the two of you will be allowed to get married."

The tears of happiness invaded my eyes, but I was not alone. Rozsa kissed both her parents; I gave a kiss to Mrs. Buja and pumped Rozsa's Father's hand with such power that he shouted in mock agony.

"Wait a second Son, don't break the hand that gave you the greatest gift. Now go get that calendar and let's find a suitable date for a party. We shall invite all the relatives and maybe a few friends and we will celebrate my daughter's betrothal to this teacher of many children. May God grant them happiness! May God save us from a calamity."

"Mr. and Mrs. Buja you never need to fear that. I will be a good husband to your daughter; I will work day and night to provide her with everything. I will love her until the end of my life and I will even love her from my grave. We shall grow old together and we will be always happy. We will be faithful to each other. We will never forget the wedding vows. We will..." I was once again interrupted.

"In your happiness Laszlo, you would promise anything. That we can understand. Not long ago we were almost as young as the two of you and I would have said the same things, but life has surprises in store for all of us. Once I was robbed of my rank, just after the war and later on I was removed from a position of authority. I would have liked to give my wife and children the whole world, but it didn't work out that way. Twice we had lived on the charity of our relatives. It is easy to make promises, but promises we cannot always keep."

"I don't earn much, I do admit, but to supplement the teachers' meager salary, the Government gave each of us an acre of land to cultivate. My acre I will plant with corn. I will cultivate it diligently. When harvest time comes I will gather in the crops and I will sell what we do not really need. That will help me to keep my promises."

"Have you ever farmed Laszlo? I think not! You will plant; you will cultivate, but to harvest is another thing. What will happen if your crops are destroyed by draught? If it will be wiped out by hail and sleet? Never count your chickens my Son until they hatch, that is what wise man had said for centuries."

"I will look for a second job...I will take a job during the summer...I will..."

"You will get the calendar Laszlo. That is what you will do now." Mr. Buja put an end to what appeared to be a long list of empty promises.

I jumped to my feet to obey him. Placed the calendar on table and the four of us turned its pages.

"I was sixteen on the sixth of June..." Rozsa began. "July, August, September, October, November and December will age me another half year. Maybe in January we could have the wedding?" Her deep blue eyes looked pleadingly at her Father, then at her Mother and both of them began to speak.

"January..." Mrs. Buja tasted the word.

"January?" Mr. Buja asked anxiously.

"January, Rozsa and I will become the happiest married couple in the whole universe," I announced and waited.

"No use for me to even try to delay the month of your wedding." Mr. Buja stated and made his proposal. "Maybe January thirtieth would be a nice date for a wedding?"

"January first would be much nicer. Don't you think my dear Rozsa?" My transparent attempt to shorten our waiting brought forth laughter from both of Rozsa's parents.

"I see Laszlo that you don't want to wait a single day. Maybe you would rather have the wedding tomorrow?"

"Dad please don't ruin our happiness by joking, by teasing Laszlo. We are grateful for your blessing, but what Laszlo said makes a lot of sense. On the first day of a new year people make thousands of resolutions, why couldn't we make ours on that day? A resolution that we would keep the rest of our lives."

"Maybe we should negotiate?" Mr. Buja smiled at me. "And besides the first of January falls on a Thursday. I think both of you would like to be free on your wedding day."

"I don't think that Pallosy, my principal would give me a day off," I admitted.

"Well, then it would make sense to plan for a Saturday evening wedding and a Sunday honeymoon." Rozsa and I both blushed hearing Mr. Buja's words and my heart beat with excitement.

I proposed January third; Mr. Buja tried to hold out for January thirty-first; Mrs. Buja displayed her generosity by suggesting January twenty-fourth; Rozsa asked for January tenth and when we became exhausted by haggling over the date, like so many bargain hunters at a market, Mr. Buja settled the issue.

"My pet asked for January tenth and that will be the date of your new beginning. You will have to tell your parents, Laszlo. We have a lot to plan: the place, the time, the kind of wedding, the food, the drinks, the guest list and a hundred other items. Well, the

Bujas and Lichters will take care of all that. Before the wedding everything is our responsibility; after the wedding it is up to the two of you. Just one thing I want you to promise us. For at least two years you should not think of having any children. Rozsa should be at least eighteen or nineteen, before she gets that added responsibility." Mr. Buja stated and none of us argued.

"Now what about the date of your engagement party? Rozsa you should decide that, we don't want to go through another set of negotiations." Mrs. Buja offered and Rozsa looked at the calendar and swiftly made her announcement.

"To give you time, my dear parents, I think it should be in December. When I was young I always loved Saint Nicholas day, on the sixth. Do you think we could have it then?"

"Consider it done Rozsa. A good choice indeed. Another Saturday to celebrate and a Sunday to get back to your senses."

"Are you happy my daughter? And you Laszlo?"

"Thanks to the two of you I am truly happy," Rozsa announced and I repeated exactly what she said.

"With this settled I think we will retire. The two of you shouldn't stay up too long and before we leave you I think you should be allowed to kiss each other."

I gave Rozsa a passionate kiss; she returned mine twice as passionately.

"Now let that kiss be the most ardent the two of you exchange, until the tenth of January." With those words spoken, the two Bujas were ready to retire but were delayed slightly by their Son's arrival.

"What are all those smiles about?" Joe inquired.

"About two dates we have agreed to," Mr. Buja replied cleverly.

"Will anybody tell me what the dates are and what will happen then?" Joe did not hide his irritation.

"I be glad to..." Rozsa spoke up. "On the first one we will have an engagement party. On the second I will become the wife of Laszlo." Her radiant face betrayed her joy clearly.

"Well, I be damned. Laszlo you have finally succeeded. Years ago you told me that the first minute you saw Rozsa you knew that she would be your wife. You brought water from the well; you cut wood and chopped wood at our house; you even shared my adventure with the out-house; you rejoiced when Rozsa spoke to you; you came to Szob and left disappointed. You persisted all these years; you never gave up...Well my friend my heartiest congratulations. The same to you my dear sister. May the two of you be always happy." He shook my hand and kissed Rozsa, then he planted himself by the table and with great gusto he began to devour his supper.

If Joe did not arrive when he did, I would have showered my wife to be with thousands of kisses, but his presence made that impossible. The two of us sat on Joe's cot, as was our habit. Rozsa's parents left their bedroom door open, as they did whenever I was present. We still dared not to sit in her room, the room that would have provided us with a measure of privacy.

I held her hand; stroked her arm gently; settled my eyes on her lovely face; I drank in her beauty and counted the months, the weeks, the days that remained before that happy day in January.

***

I ran home; woke up my family.

"I am getting married!" I shouted with joy, expecting censure, possible arguments, especially from my Mother.

"I have been waiting for this to happen. Congratulations Son!" My Father was the first to react. I was in his arms, when George and Mother joined him.

"Congratulations indeed...," said the woman who brought me into the world, who fed me, raised me, scolded me and was about to lose me to another woman.

"Congratulations brother," George shouted. "I will enjoy dancing with your bride. She is a lovely girl, that Rozsa."

"So when is the big date? Don't keep us in suspense any longer," my Father asked.

"On December sixth we will have our engagement; on January tenth we will be married," I announced proudly.

"We will have two big parties. We will have two real celebrations." My Father's joy infected my Mother.

"The wedding will be here Laszlo, I hope the Bujas will agree!"

"Whether here, or anywhere else it really doesn't matter." I stated boldly.

"It doesn't matter Laszlo says!" My Mother began to complain. "We have more room than the Bujas; we can accommodate more guests. Tell him Ferenc that I am right."

"I can understand Laszlo. It is not the place that matters to him, but becoming Rozsa's husband. We will get together with his future in-laws and we will plan the events together. Rest easy Laszlo."

"I would like that, but please no fighting." I appealed to my family and then added. "Please tell all our relatives and my friends that I am happy and will be even happier."

That night sleep didn't come to me and I rose early in the morning to catch the train. I reached the school beaming with pleasure. I stood in the door-way at seven thirty; I looked at assignment books and assignments, but my eyes saw only one thing: my beloved Rozsa's happy face.

I taught my lessons and during the recesses I sought out my few teacher friends.

I told Pista that I am getting married. I informed Tery, then Margit and finally Jancsi about the coming wonderful events and the dates. I received their congratulations, their hand-shakes, their kind comments and my heart danced many happy jigs.

During the afternoon I ran from house to house taking surveys or live-stock counts and in each and every place someone asked me.

"You seem really happy Comrade Teacher; will you share your happiness with me?"

"I am getting married. The hand of an angel was given to me." I spread my happiness around the village and when I have fulfilled my quota, dropped the papers on the desk of a Government official and ran to my boarding place.

"Just in time for supper Laszlo," Pista, my land-lord announced and Maris, his wife, beamed with pleasure as she set the food on the table.

We began to eat and Maris had noticed my changed demeanor.

"You seem different Laszlo...Did you have a nice Sunday?"

"The best ever...Rozsa's parents gave their blessing. We are allowed to get married in January," I announced the joyous news.

"Congratulations Laszlo...Please give the same to your beloved. Where will you two live?" Pista asked.

"I never thought of that." I admitted and immediately I got an idea. "Do you think you could put up with the two us?"

"Will you need any extra space?" Maris questioned.

"One room is all we need. Rozsa would be here for breakfast. She will keep her job at Baja. She will travel by train and would be back for supper."

"Well, we could put in a bigger bed..." Maris' eyes twinkled with unhidden mirth and I felt a blush invade me.

"You really don't need to do that..." I stuttered with embarrassment.

"I guess there is no need for a bigger bed...When we were younger I too wanted to feel Maris' closeness..."

"Stop that you old rascal. Laszlo need not hear such talk. All right Laszlo, your wife and you will live here. You will have the room you have now. I will provide breakfast and supper for both of you. I will even pack a lunch for Rozsa, as I have done for you my boy and I will do all these things gladly."

"May I ask how much more will you charge?"

"Well if we didn't know you we would haggle, but ever since you came we had nothing, but the pleasure of your company. We will enjoy having your wife too and if you invite us to meet your intended we will charge not a Forint extra." Maris settled the issue and Pista nodded his approval.

With supper finished; our future domicile established firmly, I went to my room to prepare for my next day's teaching. I placed Rozsa's picture beside my books. I glanced at the text books; I looked at my notes, but my eyes wanted to see only one thing: the picture of my dear Rozsa. I saw her sweet smile; her smooth face; her well shaped ears; her gorgeous eyes; her beautiful hair; her round shoulders under her dress and I began to dream.

"Just five weeks from now the whole world will know that we belong together. Another four weeks and she will be my darling wife, forever to hold and to cherish for an eternity." I thought about her and the promise of the coming joy, and my lessons, for the first time ever, remained unfinished.

***

I went to school the next morning, expecting nothing, but another simple day of teaching. When I entered my class-room my students jumped to their feet, but three strangers, sitting in the back, remained seated.

"Proceed comrade..," spoke up one of them and then it hit me.

"This must be the dreaded inspection committee, Pallosy spoke about. Should I go to them? Should I demand some kind of identification? Or should I simply obey that order?" I decided to forget the first two ideas, opened my lesson plan book and stared at the almost empty pages. I searched my mind for what I ought to teach. I wondered what lesson they expected to witness. Then I have made my decision.

"Today we shall review everything you have learned during the last two weeks of chemistry classes. From each lesson I will ask questions and you are expected to give your answers promptly." I told my students and began the charade.

I gave the name of a student who was to give the answer and when that student stood I asked the question. Their replies were almost always correct. By the time I asked thirty-five questions there was only one student whom I neglected.

"Janos Karaj will you please stand." I hoped with all my heart that two months of silence, that length of disobedience was finally over, but all my hopes soon vanished. Janos remained where he was, not even the presence of the three strangers was sufficient to break his stubborn spirit.

"I am sorry you are hurting...This time I will make an exception, you need not stand." I tried to mislead my supervisors, tried appease Janos with my statement.

"Who was the creator of the Periodic Table?" I asked my opponent and the tension mounted. Silence, a belligerent look and finally the bell that almost saved me.

"Class is dismissed!" I announced gladly.

"Just hold it for one more minute comrade. Be fair to all your students. I want to hear the young man's answer," one of the strangers, in the back, commanded.

Janos stood up, to my great surprise, and he turned to the back of the class room.

"It was a Russian scientist, if I am not mistaken. Dmitry Ivanovich Mendeleyev was his name. He was born in 1834 and died in 1907. That Russian chemist..." Janos would have displayed his vast knowledge; things that I have never taught them, had the supervisor not stopped him in his tracks.

"Well that is splendid...You are a credit to your school. Comrade Lichter dismiss your class. They must not miss their recess."

***

That unprepared period of chemistry was followed by a class of grade eight math. When my second group of students left and my third group, this time the grade sevens, arrived, the three strangers remained in the back.

Halfway through my third lesson of the day there was a knock on my door and without waiting a student entered. He handed to me the big, black book and without looking, I knew what was printed on the front cover: 'Announcements for the school year of 1952/53.'

I opened the book that contained today's commands from my principal and ordered the class to stand. This book came at least daily and sometimes twice a day. It was taken from class to class and after the commandments were read out loud, each teacher was to sign to attest to the fact that it was read, understood and will be heeded.

"Today's announcements are as follows:" I began to read.

"1. The Young Pioneers will meet this Sunday with their home-room teachers at ten o'clock in the morning. Every student is expected to be present. Teachers will take attendance and those absent will forfeit their movie privileges. All students, starting with grade three, are to write and bring a short essay on the assigned topic: 'I am grateful to our Soviet Brothers and Sisters.' Your home-room teachers will serve as observers and the class leader of Young Pioneers will conduct the meeting. You may be asked to read your essay front of your class. The best essay in each class will be rewarded.

"2. A staff meeting is called today for two o'clock. No teacher is exempted.

"Signed: Comrade Joska Pallosy, Principal of the Public school of Bacsbokod."

"That cagey bastard! He made sure by the first announcement that his loyalty to the Communists will be noted by the committee. That scum holds staff meetings very rarely, but with the committee being in our school our beloved leader wants to show off..." I thought while I affixed my name.

When I finished my lesson, that went rather well, or so I thought, I dismissed my students. The members of the committee stood up and without a single glance in my direction, without a word of praise or condemnation, they left my classroom. I had two more classes to teach before I could approach my friend, Pista.

***

He and I had many conversations during September, but the topics we have discussed then never touched politics. We spoke about his family and mine; I spoke about my beloved Rozsa and my hopes, my aspirations and all the other things that could be discussed safely.

Early in October he came to me: "Laszlo I truly enjoy your company. I came to trust you. Would you like to spend an evening in my home, with my family?"

I was pleasantly surprised and rushed to accept his invitation, before he could change his mind.

"What time would you like me there?"

"Come for supper. Lenke will prepare a feast. I think her fried chicken will be to your liking. We eat at six."

I knocked on the gate and Pista came to admit me.

"I always keep the gate locked. I trust very few people. Please come in, supper is almost ready. Lenke, bring a bottle of good wine. Laszlo is here." He issued the orders, leaving no doubt who was in charge in his household.

We sat by the table and he filled two glasses with red wine.

"Taste this wine. It is my own. Let's see what you think," Pista urged me.

I smacked my lips to show my satisfaction.

"That was good wasn't it?" Pista asked.

"One of the best I have ever tasted." I didn't need to lie.

"I have a vineyard, a few acres only. Lenke and I look after the grapes and when October comes we harvest. In the back I have a press. We make our own wine, both red and white. It is not adulterated like the stuff the Government sells to the masses. Where is the supper Lenke? We are hungry." His wife came out with the steaming dishes, placed them in the middle of the table and to my surprise she didn't join us. I looked at Pista curiously.

"I see you are surprised Laszlo. Lenke and I don't have the best of marriage. She is a good cook and a superb teacher, but her talents end there. I think you know what I mean?"

"I am not sure I know what you mean?" I said, while I was relishing the superb food we both began to eat.

"The bedroom...You surely know something about that?"

"I am afraid you have me at a disadvantage," I admitted shyly.

"I can't believe it. How old are you? Twenty-one and still..."

I didn't allow him to continue with the touchy subject.

"I hate to talk about your wife behind her back." I tried to change the topic.

"She is my wife, but it was only a marriage of convenience. I came to teach here years ago and she was single; she was handy and her parents weren't exactly poor. So we married. Did you ever take a good look at her?" Pista asked and I shook my head.

"I am sure nobody else did. She is tall and not shapely. I prefer women who are tiny, yet lack not a thing in the feminine department. I find them; pursue them and before long I enjoy them. I am like a butterfly. I love nectar, but always seek it from another flower." Pista finished both his boasting and his supper.

"Another glass of wine wouldn't hurt either of us," he announced and filled the glasses.

"Now I want to propose a toast: Here is to you Laszlo. May you always know who your friends are and may you never fall in the trap of your enemies."

We drank the wine and followed it with a glass of peach brandy. Then Pista stood up and excused himself. A few minutes later he returned with a picture and once again he began to speak.

"For weeks now I have debated what to do about you Laszlo, but today I have reached my decision. We are friends who can trust each other, I convinced myself and in spite of the possible danger, I decided to enlighten you. Do you know what an informer is?"

"I have lived in Hungary all my life. Your question is an insult to my intelligence Pista."

"That is the last thing I wished to do. Look at this picture Laszlo. This is our teaching staff. This here is Pallosy, as you can see. Do you know what that man did?"

"I heard some stuff, but I don't believe everything I hear."

"You are cautious Laszlo, I really like that, but what you hear from me is true in every detail. Pallosy was a teacher in another village. His parents were devoted Roman Catholics. Two of their daughters became nuns. One joined an order and the other became a teacher. She worked in our school when the church still had it. She lived in one of those cells, maybe in the one you use for your chemicals. Pallosy joined the Communist party and he wanted to advance. So one day he got a bright idea and convinced the authorities. The church schools were on the way out. The Communist Government wanted to control the minds of all the young people, so they weren't reluctant to confiscate this school, as they did all the others. All the teaching nuns were deported. Then Pallosy was given his reward. He was made principal of this school and he was given the apartment that once belonged to the Mother Superior. What do you think of that?"

"I was told a few things by the janitor, but I thought his words were generated by envy. To have a man instigate deportation of his own sister, that really beats me."

"Yet that is exactly what Pallosy did. About the janitor you are wrong Laszlo. That man is a decent fellow, not like some of our staff members."

"What do you mean?"

"When I have arrived to Bacsbokod I set about the task of identifying those that should not be trusted. It took a long time and a few jokes. One day I would tell a mild political joke to one member of the staff and then I would wait. A month would pass or even more, but sooner or later I would be interrogated and reprimanded for telling a joke against the Government. Thus I had one informer identified. Then I would tell someone else some mild thing I did. It took me more than two years and I have identified the informers. I would love to save you time, if you wish Laszlo. Do you want to have me continue or should I drop the subject?"

"It wouldn't hurt to know. I do appreciate what you are doing."

"Here is Bela Kovacs..." Pista pointed at the group picture. "He is working for the Secret Police. And this one is Otto Dome. He married the doctor's daughter. An ambitious son of a bitch. He too serves the same masters." Pista went on naming seven members of the staff and when he finished, he put away the picture.

"Now Laszlo I want you to remember this. Those seven cannot be trusted. Don't ever tell them anything. The others may be safe, but who knows? If you ever need my help, I will always be there for you. But even to me you should never say anything when we may be overheard. Not far from the school there is a brook. There are no houses around it. That and my home are the only safe places where we can talk freely. If you ever need to unload, just walk by me, raise two fingers of your right hand and I will leave the building. You follow me, but not too closely. I don't want anyone to know where we go. I want to keep that our secret."

"Thank you Pista. You took a great load off my shoulders. I really appreciate that. Now I think I must leave. Please thank your wife for the fine supper. And I thank you for the drinks and your trust and your sincerity."

"I am glad you came, Laszlo. Good night my friend. Remember everything I told you, but never repeat to anyone a single thing spoken this evening."

"I will never do that Pista. Your friendship is precious to me."

***

After classes ended for the day, I had recalled that early October evening and decided to speak with Pista. I searched for him and when I found him, I raised my right hand slightly, with two fingers extended. I left the building, went to the adjacent soccer field and I sat down waiting.

Pista walked by, never even looking in my direction, and cautiously, at a good distance, I followed him. I saw the brook, no wider than thirty feet. On both sides a small dike protected the village from its waters, but Pista I didn't see. I was about to turn back, thinking that I lost him, when I heard his low whistling. I moved to the top of the dike and below it I had found him.

"Come and join me. Here nobody will see us. This is where we will always meet. Now tell me what troubles you Laszlo."

"For three periods the committee supervised me," I announced.

"And I thought it was something important," Pista gave out a low chuckle.

"It is important as you will see. Last night I couldn't get my head around lesson planning. I never expected the supervising committee. I had no lesson plans...I wasn't able to follow the curriculum...During the first lesson I was double crossed by Janos Karaj, that obstinate student."

"Tell me all the details," Pista urged me and I told him everything.

"I wouldn't give Karaj another thought. Did they ask for your lesson plans?" Pista asked me.

"They never did, but they might, sometimes today. Maybe during the staff meeting..?"

"They may do that, but you should be able to think of something."

"I tried, but I have no idea what to tell them."

"It is rather simple. Between the end of classes and the staff meeting you went to your boarding place and took home all your note books, all your papers." Pista suggested.

"Why didn't I think of that? But...what will happen if they send me home to get it?"

"They will never do that. They are lazy sons of bitches, just like Pallosy. They will just tell us how you did...They may bark a lot about your teaching, but they will want to get out of there to join their cronies."

"Are you sure Pista?"

"I know the bastards. Whenever they come to a village their mind is really on entertainment. The top commies of the local Government always put on a spread for those commies who come from the capital. They give them food and booze and many times willing women. The powerful, almighty visitors from the capital take advantage of the hospitality of the ars lickers, so they will be anxious to begin the festivities as early as they can. What I suggest Laszlo is very simple. Whenever they give you an opportunity to say something, you should use your God given talent to articulate things slowly, deliberately and at great length. They will become impatient and will try to hurry up the process. Trust me Laszlo, that is what you should do and I promise you nothing terrible will happen."

"I trust you Pista, but I cannot make my fear disappear. I have a State examination yet to take and their evaluation of my teaching is very, very important."

"Laszlo you are truly naive. Do you think your professors would ever take their evaluation seriously? They know how well educated these men are. If you add up the years they went to school, remember not the years of their learning, the sum you get will be less than fifteen. They are Communist stooges, named to these so called supervision committees, not for their knowledge or their abilities, but for their loyalty to the Communist party. Don't give it another thought, they have been fooled before. Come to think of it I should tell you what I did two years ago.

"I had a terribly dumb class. I had fifteen knowledgeable, hard working students and twenty stupid loafers, I discovered early in the year. I didn't know how I will survive a visit from this committee. Then the idea hit me...They want to see an enthusiastic bunch of students and they want to hear answers coming fast. They have no idea whether the answers are correct or not, so they watch the teachers and know that if they try to pull a fast one, they will be given away by the more intelligent students. I worked on my idea and practiced it day after day. Then the committee arrived and everything went far better than I expected.

"I asked questions and every student had their hands up. They almost fell out of their seats, they were so eager to shine, to give an answer. I pointed at one student, then at another and almost every time their answers were correct. They have displayed great enthusiasm, eagerness and vast knowledge. My supervisors praised me during the evaluation session, front of all my colleagues. After they left the meeting Pallosy pumped me and so did other staff members. They wanted to know my secret of how I succeeded to turn stupid oafs into scholars. I smiled at them and spoke at length about my unparalleled teaching ability. They never found out how I did it, but you my friend will now hear it.

"I spoke to all the stupid students one by one. I bribed them to raise their hands whenever I asked a question. I asked them to display great enthusiasm whenever that was needed. I promised all of them a passing grade in my subject." Pista stopped with a smirk on his face.

"I still do not understand."

"Well it is an ingenious method I admit. All of my students are right handed, so those who didn't know the answer were to raise their left hand. Can you picture that Laszlo? After every question I asked, a class-full of students with their hands raised, clamoring to give an answer, made even the greatest skeptics believe seeing a bunch of scholars. Then picture this. I pointed at a student, who raised his right hand, and there came the correct answer. I became known as a teacher who could teach the blind to see; who could make the deaf to hear, who could do just about anything."

"I be damned...I would have never thought of something like that. I would never dare to attempt something like this. I would fear being discovered."

"No fear of that Laszlo. My students are loyal to me, with very few exceptions. The Young Pioneer leader comes from a Communist home; she is to be watched, to fear, she is the only danger. Fortunately most other students hate her, rarely speak to her, do not trust her. This is true just about all the classes. So the risk I took was minimal. Come to think of it I have faced risks much greater. One night, about two years ago, I watched a house where a shapely wench lived. I spoke with her several times and I knew she was willing and even eager. I waited until her husband left, then I went into her house and within minutes we were at it. Suddenly she stopped, I heard the sound too. Her husband arrived unexpectedly. I had barely time to get into my underwear, to grab my clothing and jump out of the open window of their bedroom. I walked home in the dark night. Didn't even bother to dress and I felt the thrill. Risking something for momentary pleasure; feeling superior to others; escaping the consequences, gave me more thrill than the act itself, I came to realize. That thrill I had time after time, but even that cannot compare to the thrill of fooling my supervisors."

"I understand, I think, but didn't any of your students ever make a mistake raising the wrong hand?" I drifted back to the subject that interested me more than Pista's sexual escapades.

"Sure they did, but not very often."

"So what happened then?"

"Laszlo I know that you are still quite naive. Nobody, not even the biggest fool, believes in perfection. Perfection would have made them smell a rat. A fool is keenly aware of the many mistakes he had made, so whenever I picked a student, who raised the wrong hand, and gave the wrong answer, my supervisors suspected not a thing. It added a measure of credibility to my classes' performance."

I listened to Pista's revelations, glanced at my watch and became alarmed.

"It is almost two o'clock, Pista. We must not be late for the meeting."

***

"I want to welcome the three comrades from the Ministry of Education. They are members of the Supervisory Committee." Pallosy addressed us from one end of the table and pointed at the other end, where the three officials were seated. "They believe, as I do, the wise words of our beloved Father, Stalin. 'The chain is no stronger than its weakest link.' My staff is the chain and I am the eye hook. I do all the planning; assure the smooth operation of this school; carry the burden of heavy responsibilities. They know my achievements, so I will not dwell on them, they are many. They have known your teaching abilities, after all they supervised all of you old hands. But this year we have a new teacher, he is that weakest link. Laszlo Lichter you stand up and face the eminent members of the committee. I will say no more. Comrades please proceed."

The first one to speak made me tremble.

"Laszlo Lichter, you are the weakest link indeed. In fact I doubt you will ever qualify to be a full fledged teacher. I am truly disappointed. I observed you for almost three hours and during that time you did nothing. You haven't mentioned even once Comrade Stalin and his great wisdom. You did not refer to our Soviet brothers and sisters during your classes. You did not praise the enormous efforts of our workers. Rakosi's name never crossed your lips. Love for our great ally, the Soviet Union, you did not instill in your students. Hate for the Imperialist war-mongers was totally absent from you lessons. I came to observe the political content of your teaching and I found it nil. Your political correctness is totally unacceptable. You are hereby commanded to remedy all these things. Can you do that?"

I should have been devastated by his comments-not even my class-mates criticized me this severely during any of my practice teachings-but instead I was overjoyed, I was given the opportunity to speak.

"Comrade with all due respect, I beg you to listen to me. Didn't Comrade Stalin urge his followers at a Congress of the Communist party to be beware of those who praise constantly. Didn't he urge them to speak about love for the leaders only at the right time, so that they would be believed. Praise that is given constantly, our beloved Stalin thinks, brings about negative results..." I would have continued to follow Pista's advice and drag things out endlessly, but the official became impatient.

"All you said Lichter is so, I too recall our beloved leader's words clearly. In my opinion there was at least one opportunity you could have heaped praise on Russian ingenuity. One of your students gave an answer about the Periodic Table, he even named its Russian creator, Mendeleyev. There was your opportunity."

"I beg to differ comrade...The student gave the name and the year the scientist died. It was 1907. Way before the glorious revolution. Had I praised Mendeleyev my student would have called attention to the fact that the chemist was a faithful servant of the Czar. I wanted to prevent that and I thought you did too, that is why you cut him short and ordered the dismissal."

"You are absolutely correct, but we are in a hurry. So I will turn this over to other members of the committee." I heard his words that gave testimony to what Pista told me.

"You Comrade Lichter didn't do too bad a job." The second member addressed me more cautiously. "That however doesn't mean that you need not grow. More experience no doubt will improve your teaching techniques and under the wise guidance of your principal you will become a better teacher." Pallosy beamed and I spoke up again.

"Comrade I would love to have the benefit of your experience. I am certain that your training, your education and all your observations enable you to give me a few specifics."

I saw his face flush, his limbs begin to tremble, but he decided to rise to the challenge.

"I will be glad to enlighten you Comrade Lichter. It would, however take many hours to share a small fraction of my vast knowledge." He began and I wasn't the only one who had to stifle a laughter that insisted on making an appearance. "Let me give you just one bit of advice. You made a student stand and then you asked your question. That approach stimulated little thinking on part of your other students. So what I suggest is to ask your question first, then select your target." I gave him a smile and thought of Pista's fabricated way of questioning his students.

The last evaluator took over.

"My job is to enforce the curriculum. In that aspect you are a miserable failure. Today, in all grade eight chemistry classes, everywhere in our beloved country, teachers teach their students about hydrogen sulfide. You dared to teach, no, that is incorrect. You reviewed all kinds of other things. You failed in the other two classes as well. There is no excuse for such action; it demonstrates far too much independence."

"Comrade may I react?" I asked.

"Do it briefly," he said and glanced at the other members of the committee who displayed signs of impatience.

"It is true that I did not follow the curriculum to the letter, but I wish to call your attention to one of the statements in the preamble. That statement warns all teachers that lessons must be mastered by all students. So how am I to ascertain mastery without a thorough review? That is what I planned to do comrade. And by the way you should have checked my lesson plans. That would have made it clear what motivated my independence." As I spoke I became bolder and took a calculated risk "You neglected to ask me for it, but now I think you should see it. I took it home after my classes. I think I should run there and fetch it for your inspection. It would take less than an hour and I would be back." I felt a thrill waiting for his answer, a thrill not unlike what Pista spoke about and when I heard him I knew that I was right to trust my instincts.

"Never mind that...We are in a hurry. Next time we supervise you we will remember to give your lesson plans a thorough examination." The three of them stood up; Pallosy declared adjournment. Pista gave me a knowing look; a slight touch on my arm, as he went by me, seemingly acknowledging my achievement.

***

It all began rather innocently. I sat in the back of my class-room at ten o'clock that strange Sunday. The blond, pig tailed, rather plump girl, stood front of my students, all of whom wore a red scarf around their necks.

"I stand before you as the appointed leader of our class organization. We shall begin the meeting with a song to our dear Father, Comrade Stalin." Her sweet voice surprised me, as she led her members in a rousing song of praise for the despised Soviet communist.

"You did very well comrades. I only wish the great man could have heard you. He is not here, except in our hearts. He is far away in that beautiful land of freedom and plenty." The platitudes poured out of her mouth and grew into a torrent. When she ran out of steam, she turned to face the picture of the bandit with the mustache and saluted Stalin's picture. Behind her all the students imitated her sincere action, but most of them with far less enthusiasm. She turned back to her flock of pretenders and asked for a volunteer.

"Who would like to be the first one to read the essay?"

The first volunteer began to read.

"I am grateful to our Soviet Brothers and Sisters, written by me.

"My Father was a poor peasant, he never got an education, but I am more fortunate than he was, thanks to our wise leaders. Comrade Stalin declared that only knowledge makes men free. I can attend school, learn about our great leaders and their glorious achievements. When I become an adult, I will become a member of the party..." He read on and on and I began to think of the hypocrisy.

"These poor students of tender age are already brain-washed. Privately they nurse their hate, but publicly they display only political correctness." I thought about that and many other things, while five or six readers stood and paid lip service. Then I sat up straight, I was riveted on the words of the next speaker, whose first few words I almost missed. She held no paper front of her, she didn't read. Her words contained nothing but bitterness and ironic sadness.

"You may think that I am not grateful, but that I truly am. I am really free. My Father died serving our beloved friends in far away Siberia. Now I do as I please, my Mother is unable to control me." Her simple words were spoken with courage; she showed no fear, didn't seem to fear retribution.

The flood-gates opened and many students raised their hands.

"I am grateful to our liberators for my well being. I love to stand in line, at the store, for more than two hours for half a loaf of bread...," cried out one.

"I am grateful too, for being able to walk five miles on my way to school and back, even in the dead of winter; my feet have no shoes, just a bunch of rags. My family is poor, although both of my parents are workers," another student lamented.

"Me too...I am grateful to the Russian soldiers, who raped my Mother. Who conceived my sibling, who made him a bastard? I am the only one here who can boast about having a beloved half Russian brother." I was amazed by what I heard. But it amazed me even more that the leader of the young Pioneers made no attempt to stop them. I knew that with the passing of each minute, with each word spoken, more and more of my students will put themselves in great danger. I heard their words that touched my heart; I heard a few students sobbing; and I heard some of my students' applause. It was time to act.

"May I say something?" I rose to my feet, not waiting for permission and I went to the front of the classroom.

"There were a few speakers who did very well..." The leader of Pioneers tried to stop me, but I would have none of that.

"You take your seat Comrade Leader. You are unfit to conduct this meeting." I didn't know then what was to take place just a day later and the leader obeyed me, with a smirk playing around her lips.

"Some of the speakers have made a mistake. They fell for stupid propaganda. Their words didn't come from their hearts. They didn't mean what they said. Some adults put bad ideas in their heads. As they mature they will come to know the truth. I think our time is gone. This meeting is over," I announced without clarifying which group of speakers were the target of my reprimand.

***

Once again Pista picked up my signal and that Sunday afternoon we sat by our brook, hidden by its high bank.

"I think some of my students are in trouble. I need your help Pista," I muttered and composed myself. I gave him all the details of what has happened.

"You are mistaken Laszlo. Our students are young...The Communist party Secretary will hear about these events and he will find a scapegoat, someone other than a student, for the mini revolution you have experienced."

"What should I do? Report what has happened or wait out the storm's coming?" I asked my friend, my advisor.

"Before I can give you an answer, tell me which student started it."

I gave him the information.

"Well that is rather interesting. The student you named is not an orphan. Her Father was never in Siberia, he is the Deputy Chairman of the local council."

"But why would she lie? Why would she say those things?"

"It is an old trick, my dear friend. It was you who was being tested. The leader of your Young Pioneers is the daughter of the Party Secretary. She and that other got the students going and the two of them waited to see how you will handle it."

"You still haven't told me what I should do."

"Wait and trust your instincts, as you did with the supervising committee. You did really well Laszlo...I couldn't believe how you took them on, how you made them squirm, how well you have succeeded. Do nothing my friend...There may be no repercussions. On the other hand, if I am wrong, then you must use your God given talents. Talk your head off, convince your interrogators about your best intentions. I think I better go...I shouldn't keep a lady waiting. That lady, I think you can guess, is not Lenke, but someone far more cute and eager for action."

I would have loved to go to Baja; to meet with my beloved, but only a small sliver was left from that wasted Sunday and the short time would have been insufficient. Instead, I went to my boarding place and busied myself with preparing all my lessons for a week of teaching.

***

"You don't need to stand here, wait for me in the staff room," Pallosy ordered me, as soon as I stepped inside the school, that Monday morning.

"But I must check the assignments...," I protested.

"You need to do no such thing. When I am finished here, I will have something to say to you and after that we will go and pay a visit." He pointed to the stairway that led to his office and to the staff room and I, with trepidation, climbed the stairs and began my waiting.

"You disgraced my school, you disgraced me!" Pallosy shouted for all to hear, after the bell sounded.

"What did I do?" I moaned in misery.

"We shall find out. You come with me."

"But what about my classes?" I asked.

"You have been relieved from your teaching position, until further notice." His words rang out and I was devastated, but this time it wasn't my tongue, it wasn't my action that brought me to this terrible ending.

"Just when I should be enormously happy. Just before our engagement and our wedding, this had to happen to me." I almost screamed out in disappointment, but my scream I was able to stifle. I finally came to my senses, still standing in the staff-room, as if I was rooted to the floor like an ancient tree.

"Where are you taking me?" I finally asked and Pallosy's answer didn't surprise me.

"The Party Secretary wishes to see you and I will make sure that I am there when you face him."

***

We entered the huge, ornate, brick house, that some time ago must have belonged to a rich farmer, but wherever I looked I saw something missing. Every farm house was built not for comfort, but for utility. The large stable, that must have stood in the back, was turned into a pile of bricks, lumber, roof shingles and other building materials. So were the *goras*, the wooden, slatted corn drying buildings. Only the main building remained erect.

We entered the huge room that echoed our footsteps and I thought of the family that must have occupied it, before the inner walls were demolished to create a large meeting hall. Pallosy led me to the glass door, that opened into a room where the mighty man sat, behind his heavy, oak desk, with his feet planted on the expensive table.

I judged him to be shorter than I, which was a rarity. His skin hung on his face like a badly rumpled suit; his eyes looked at me maliciously and they squinted. His pointy nose sniffed the air, which reminded me of a cunning weasel.

"Good morning Comrade Pallosy. You may take a seat." He ignored me and I remained standing.

"Good morning Comrade Party Secretary," Pallosy returned his greeting.

"It is a good morning indeed. We have flushed out a traitor and on top of that the party will get a pile of money." The weasel spoke through his nose.

"The traitor I know about, but not about the money that will enrich our coffers." The two of them spoke as if I wasn't even present.

"Oh, that my friend is the money we will get for all those building materials."

"I see you had the stable demolished and all the *goras*," Pallosy observed.

"I did indeed. We have moved into the house of this criminal about three weeks ago. The owner and his family were relocated. He was nothing but a German *swab*, you know the kind...Those Germans who came to our country to exploit our Hungarians. They stole our land; they took our riches; they tried to destroy our dignity. Well my friend the *swabs* are *kaput*, as our Soviet brothers would put it. There are camps for the likes of them, set up in the east of our country. There they are being re-educated and that task is not easy...It takes a long time and in the meanwhile we have their free labor. Well that is how those materials will enrich our party. What could I have done with all those buildings? We are not in the business of farming, but in the sacred task of leading, educating, protecting the masses." The two of them spoke on, like I no longer existed. My patience was running out fast; my fear seemed to have disappeared.

"Comrade Pallosy told me that I was relieved from my teaching position, however I wish to point out that it was the Minister of Education who appointed me, not you comrades, so let's get to the point, my students are waiting."

"You are far too bold for a young one." The Secretary punctuated his statement with a finger extended in my direction. "You of all people who betrayed this Nation by bringing about your students' revolution should stand there and shake with fear. Do you know what the Secret Police does with traitors? Do you realize that I have the power of life and death? Tell him Comrade Pallosy what I am capable of...Tell him what happened last year to that teacher." The small man of huge power was fully enraged, his narrow lips trembled.

"Do you really want me to do that?" Pallosy questioned.

"Yes! I do! I want to hear you tell it."

Slowly, carefully, he told me about the event. It seems that the Secretary's daughter took a dislike to her Russian language teacher and neglected one of her assignments. The old man, learned that language in a Russian prison camp, was eventually released and was allowed to resume his pre-war profession. He began to teach children that sacred language. From time to time he was prone to shout at his students and when shouting didn't do the trick, he resorted to pulling on the offending student's ear. This is what he did to the Secretary's daughter, upon finding out her negligence. The girl ran out of the classroom, but it didn't end there. She went to see her Father and together they went to see the only doctor. A brief examination revealed that the girl suffered from a bleeding gash behind her ear. It was more than an inch long and several millimeters deep. The doctor was anxious to please the party secretary and provided him with a written statement, as to the nature of the injury, which he attributed to the teacher.

Armed with that paper the party secretary marched into Pallosy's office and had the old teacher brought to him. The old man denied causing the injury and an argument ensued. The old man received a terrible beating. A few days later he disappeared. All of this Pallosy told me with great relish.

"Now that you know about my power, let me tell you about my trickery and the courage of my daughter." The party secretary smirked at me. "The teacher did not cause the injury. Her ears were intact when she came to me, but she was very bitter about that teacher. So my darling daughter and I talked at length about how to finish her hated enemy. She was game, accepted my suggestion and front of me she courageously used her finger nail to create the gash. She never shed a tear, not my daughter. She is smart as a whip, bright as a button, conniving like her old man, unlike her stupid Mother. She is really a chip off the old block. That is the girl that caused your problem young man. She is the one who planned, orchestrated and pulled off yesterday's event. You see Lichter I didn't mind to make a clean breast of it."

"This is beyond belief...Using your own daughter? Using the other students? Creating dissatisfaction amongst young people? What a way to live?" I gave voice to what bothered me.

"Well, as you can see Lichter, I am willing to do anything. I am even willing to hand you over to the State Security apparatus, let them deal with you as they see fit. Or I may be willing to forget the incident and let you go back to teach those children. Which one would you prefer young man?"

"I have no doubt you have already made your decision, but just remember one thing. Nobody is indispensable. Today you are a man of power, but tomorrow you may become a victim."

"How dare you threaten me?"

"I am not threatening anyone. I am simply stating a fact. You were reckless to say things front of me. You destroyed an innocent teacher...You urged your own daughter to encourage dissatisfaction and a mini revolution...And you will have to account for every Forint you make from the sale of those demolished buildings. If you have never done this before, you need not have any fear. On the other hand, if this is not your first time, you will be in great trouble. Profiteering is a grave crime in this country, even if it is done by a Communist. I have seen other men of great might being deposed, offered as a sacrifice to the masses. So hand me over to State Security and take your chances." My boldness must have surprised him.

"I never intended to do that. As you said I have reached my decision before you came. You will return to your school; you will keep on teaching. Yesterday's incident shall be forgotten and now and then I might ask you for a favor. It was nice meeting a bright young man like you, Comrade Lichter. I am pleased to know that my daughter is in such good hands, that she has your guidance. If you ever need my services I hope you will come to see me."

I couldn't believe my good luck...I couldn't believe all that happened...Once again my precarious action turned into a small victory.

***

The week passed without any further incident. Pallosy never brought up the subject of the Sunday revolution, but every opportunity he had he let me see his wordless resentment.

I would have loved to talk to Pista; to tell him everything I heard; maybe even boast about how I handled that ignorant man, who believed to be the master of people's destinies. My several efforts to have him come to our brook failed every time for the rest of the week.

"Why is he unwilling to talk to me?" I knew that my signals were received. "Maybe he began to suspect me...Maybe he thinks I too became an informer...," I thought bitterly, then it hit me. "Didn't the secretary say that now and then he might ask for a favor. When he said that, I thought he might ask for preferential treatment for his daughter. I knew I could pretend to do that. Was he hinting at something else? Wasn't Mr. Buja approached the same way? They took their time with that good man. Maybe the party secretary is taking his time with me? God curse this rotten country where men are forced to betray all vestiges of decency. I will never ever become an informer; I will die before I do that." I thought bitterly and put that possibility out of my mind, instead I concentrated on my teaching and the coming free weekend.

***

On Saturday evening I was finally at the Bujas and after two weeks of absence Rozsa looked more beautiful than I have remembered. It seemed that averted dangers sharpened my senses, intensified my love for Rozsa and made our togetherness sweeter than anything.

I thought of telling her all that has happened, but I didn't want to scare her. I wanted to talk to her Father about the possible similarity of demands made to both of us, but I have remained silent.

The day and a half that I was near my Rozsa belonged to us and her dear parents.

"How is the planning coming? I am sorry I wasn't able to come home for two long weeks, for not being able to take part in the planning," I told Rozsa and her parents on Saturday evening.

"Don't worry about a thing. We got together with your parents Laszlo and this is what we have decided. The guest list for the engagement will be rather short. Close relatives and very few friends will be invited. Our space is rather limited, but the wedding will be at your home. There will be lots of guests. Food and drinks will be plenty. Your parents will kill a pig a few weeks before and so will we. A Gypsy band is lined up to provide the music. So many of the details are lined up, while others will have to be decided," Mrs. Buja informed me.

"Thank you for all your hard work. I will thank my parents as well. I see that I wasn't really needed."

"In that you are wrong Laszlo. We haven't had a chance to find out where the two of you plan to live." Mr. Buja brought me back to reality.

"I am truly sorry. I should have consulted with Rozsa, but the topic came up unexpectedly. My landlord and my landlady made a very generous offer." I explained to them what those two old people did.

"We kind of hoped that you will live here. Rozsa's room will really be empty." Mrs. Buja expressed her disappointment.

"If that is what my beloved wants, I can change things. Wherever she is, that is where I will be happy. What she wants is exactly what I desire. So it is up to you my beloved."

"Joe had to sleep on this cot in the kitchen for a long time. So it might be fair to give him my room and do as Laszlo arranged," she announced simply.

"And what about your honeymoon Laszlo? Have you given any thought to that?"

Just the mention of that word set my heart on fire and in my confusion I didn't know what to say.

"We cannot afford a honeymoon, I think Laszlo." Rozsa came to my rescue. "After the wedding we should go to Bacsbokod, if you agree."

"I like the idea Rozsa. Our wedding will be on Saturday. We will have a Sunday together and if we are lucky maybe we will get Monday off as well."

"We will, I assure you. I already checked and found that when someone gets married the law dictates one paid day off. So will have two precious days together."

"And after that? Will Rozsa be traveling to Baja on the train?" Mr. Buja popped the question.

"I checked the train schedule and she can get on the train at seven o'clock. She will be at work soon after. She doesn't even have to walk far, just across the park at the train station and she will be in her office. That will be a great advantage. If I were to travel to Bacsbokod, I would have to leave her very early in the morning. Every precious moment we can spend together is important to me." I explained honestly what went through my mind and everyone nodded with understanding.

"Oh, there is one more thing Laszlo. That one thing is most important. The law dictates a civilian wedding at City Hall. We would love to have a church wedding as well, but we don't dare to risk that." Mrs. Buja informed me and my sigh of relief didn't escape them.

"You don't seem to mind it Laszlo. Why is that?" Mr. Buja asked.

"My job would be in danger and so would that of Rozsa. My principal and Szantai, Rozsa's boss, are one of a kind. They would need no more excuse than a church wedding and we would be finished."

"Very well then...There will be no church wedding the day the two of you get married, but you both must promise us that within two months you will find a way to be married by a priest," Mrs. Buja announced and the two of us made our solemn promises.

Laszlo S. Lichter

Laszlo Lichter

Rozsa Buja

The Lichter Family

My parents: Ilonka Lichter (1912-2008) and Ferenc Lichter (1907-1995). They had to remain behind when their son, daughter-in-law and grand-daughter escaped. We never saw them for seven years.

My mother, father, George and I.

My uncle, Jozsef Santa (1910-1955) and his wife Gizella Santa (1910-1989) tried to escape with us in 1955. Uncle Jozsef was killed by a landmine and Gizella was imprisoned for two years, but escaped in 1956.

Laszlo S. Lichter

The Buja Family

Maria Buja (1911-1988) and Jozsef Buja (1911-1983). Their heroic escape from Communist Hungary in 1954 was written by Jozsef and was translated by me and included in this book.

Joe and Rozsa

Rozsa and I at Dery Park, July 1, 1950

January 10, 1953

A picture of Rozsa's family in the early years: Jozsef, Maria, Rozsa and Joe.

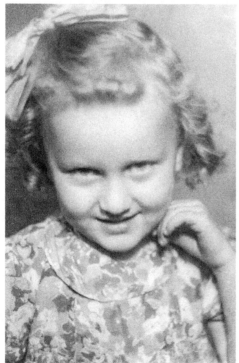

Rozsa as a young child.

George Lichter (1935-2000)

My brother, George, attempted to escape with us from Hungary in 1955 and failed; however, his second attempt in 1957 to Yugoslavia was successful.

Joe, my brother-in-law, escaped with us in 1956.

We were all accepted by Canada as refugees

Laszlo S. Lichter

Our escape started on two motorcycles, followed by a bus, two train trips, an eleven hour walk in snow, getting lost a few times, being captured by two guards and by sheer luck and stubborn determination we arrived in Austria. Here we are safe in Austria: Laszlo, Rozsa, Maria (Rozsa's happy mother) and Ildiko.

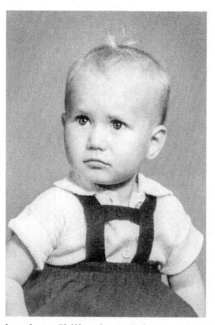 

Our daughter, Ildiko, born February 10, 1954 was only three at the time of our escape.

Chapter 11

The precious weekend with my darling and her parents was followed by a routine week. I began to feel a change in members of the staff. Slowly, one by one, they began to speak to me.

Bela Kovacs was the first one who approached me and I was weary, remembering Pista's words of caution, the picture he showed to me.

Bela checked the four stalls, assured that we were alone and then he began to speak.

"I am sorry Laszlo for having treated you with indifference, but after what you did in that staff meeting and after what I have heard about your students' mini revolution, my attitude toward you shifted. From you I have nothing to fear, I trust." He spoke those words in the only washroom allocated for the use of all teachers; the students were to use the two outhouses.

"Nobody needs to fear me. I am what you see - A young man trying to make a living. A happy man soon to be married. I wear my thoughts on my shirtsleeves. What is imy mind and in my heart, I say freely."

"I know that now...May I call you Laszlo? Or do you prefer to wait until we become better acquainted?"

"No, that won't be necessary."

"And you should call me Bela, if you don't mind. That would be to my liking."

"Thank you Bela." I saw no harm in using our first names, but as soon as he began to speak again, I became cautious, once again.

"Some of the other teachers asked me to approach you. I want to be honest with you Laszlo. I wanted to do that without them asking."

"Why did they not approach me?"

"You must understand us Laszlo. We live in fear, but if you would honor me with your presence, at my home, we could talk more freely. Would you like to come for supper? Say around five? It would be nice to have a visit from a young man."

I was about to give him a polite refusal, when Pista entered.

"I am in a rush...I must use the toilet," Pista announced and entered a stall.

I changed my mind and without another word I nodded my head in agreement.

***

The nicely furnished, three room flat, opened to the kitchen, where the table was set, in the middle a bunch of flowers. Bela showed me the living room, its walls covered with oil paintings. He pointed at the room that he called their bedroom. Then the two of us were seated.

A slim woman of about fifty came to great me.

"I am Anna. I heard a great deal about you Laszlo." She shook my hand.

I looked at Bela inquiringly.

"She heard nothing bad, I assure you." He pointed at the prematurely graying woman. "Anna is a librarian in your home city. She travels by train."

"That is what my intended plans to do...Maybe the two of you could travel together?" I was glad to make her acquaintance, to be able to find a traveling partner for Rozsa.

"It will be my pleasure, I assure you. How long have you known the girl you will marry?" She asked me kindly and I saw no harm telling her how we met, how we fell in love and how we have received her parents' blessing.

"You are a lucky man Laszlo. True love is the most glorious thing the dear Lord gave us. Cherish that young girl; love her with all your heart; protect her for the rest of your life and provide for her the best you can. Well I better get supper ready." She rose with a sweet smile and went to finish her preparations.

"What do you think of Anna?" Bela asked me.

"She is a lovely lady. Just like my Rozsa." I offered the highest praise I could think of.

"She is that...It has been thirty years, since we married. Not a single day of all those years do I regret. I hope your Rozsa and you will be this happy." I weighed the possibility of Bela being an informer and it entered my mind that Pista may have been mistaken.

"We will be happy...We have waited years for that special day when we will be wed."

"I know how it is Laszlo, but there is not much I can add to what Anna said. 'Cherish that young girl; love her with all your heart; protect her for the rest of your life and provide for her the best you can.' Those were the words my dear Anna spoke. In this country we are free to cherish, to love, but to protect and to provide, well those things we are not in position to guarantee." Bela spoke and my suspicions rose to the surface.

"Do you care to elaborate on that?" I asked him, tested him and hoped with all my heart that he will say nothing to intensify my suspicion.

"There are men in every village, in every city, who have the power of life and death. You met Pallosy, so you know what I am talking about and you met our esteemed party secretary. Both of them are dangerous men. You saw what Pallosy did to the Kochs...To abuse two old, dedicated teachers for attending masses is base, is crude, is unjust. In other countries it would not be tolerated. When that happened the first time in my presence I felt like standing up and demanding Pallosy's apology to those fine people, but I never stood, I never said a word, I remained silent. I knew far too much about Pallosy's ability and his power. He had his sister, who was a teaching nun, in this school, deported. How can we protect people we love in this country? That is one of the things I meant."

"And what was the other Bela?" Pista's efforts to educate me in the way people get trapped wasn't wasted, I became cautious.

"My Anna urged you to provide for your bride the best you can...How much do you earn Laszlo?"

"Eight hundred Forints a month, but that is no secret to anyone."

"And I, after thirty years of educating students, receive eleven hundred. My Anna brings home not much less. Two thousand Forints is not a princely sum, we can see that month after month. Less than two weeks after we are paid, we have almost nothing...Just waiting and scrimping until the next pay day..." His words died off.

I glanced around the room, took in the lovely oil paintings. Bela must have read my mind.

"If it wasn't for those paintings, some of which we had to sell during the last few years, we would have been even worse off. Before the war I was a teacher, but back then I was paid well. My Anna didn't need to work...That is when we were able to buy nice things. Now we are forced to sell them and to do something else." Bela appeared to be reluctant to come to the point, so I became impatient.

"If you want to say something Bela, please tell me. If you are afraid to bring up a subject, that is fine with me."

"If I fear to speak about something it is not because I doubt you Laszlo. I don't want to put you in any danger." Bela couldn't hide his misery.

"I am glad you no longer doubt me...I am sorry you feel fear about anything...Don't be concerned about me facing danger."

"Very well then...A told you we bring home two thousand Forints, well that is not entirely true, we bring home even less, thanks to that cursed peace bond."

"The peace bond Pallosy spoke about?" I asked.

"Yes that is the reason Laszlo. When that committee comes to the school, as they go to offices, factories and all work places, they make terrible demands."

"I heard about the peace bond and the committees that go around, but I never had to face them."

"You will Laszlo and you will be the first one."

"They probably call people in alphabetical order. You will see them Bela, before I do."

"That is not the way they operate. They call in the least experienced worker, one who has the lowest earning. Once they put their hooks into that person for a princely sum, the rest becomes putty in their hands"

"I am not sure I follow your line of thinking."

"Just think Laszlo. The lowest paid member of our teaching staff signs up, that is you Laszlo, let's say a month's pay. Then they call in the next victim. They show him the list and the sum. They will use you for leverage and the rest of us will not have a leg to stand on. All of us will have to surpass your donation. So those staff members, who asked me to talk to you, made a request. Hold out if you can for the lowest sum, give the rest of us a chance. Do you think you are willing to do that?"

"I will think about it...," I stated cautiously and we were called to supper, which we ate in silence.

***

A week later the principal's black book was brought to my classroom, where Pallosy's edict had to be read.

"To all teachers and students,

"Tomorrow the peace bond committee will arrive to Bacsbokod. As one of the outstanding members of this community I urge all students to talk to their parents. Convince them to sign up for a lot of bonds, our Nation depends on their help. We are surrounded by our enemies, who wish to destroy us, among them the yelping dog, Tito, on our southern border. Each and every Forint your parents give to the Government will help to assure the sanctity of our borders. The money is needed to build Communism; to defend your right to an education; to make our country strong and mighty. We know you, our dear students, are dedicated to our cause and so should be all you parents.

"My teaching staff is urged to set an example. I will watch them and students are to watch their parents.

Signed: Comrade Joska Pallosy, Principal of the Public school of Bacsbokod."

That night my sleep was troubled. My thoughts meandered around Bela's request, made on behalf of some of the teachers. I recalled the first two months of school, during which most of the teachers avoided me and my desire to make them become my friends was too strong, too compelling to ignore what they have requested.

***

Next morning, before the bell rang, Pallosy came to see me.

"Laszlo, you are wanted in my office," he used my first name. "The committee is anxious to meet you. Do as they ask. Don't let me down. I care about you my friend." His false words grated on my nerves.

"Today he calls me by my first name; I am his friend...Not long ago I was the weakest link; I was a bitching, complaining, puny, stupid creature, asking for extra privileges. I was a disturber of his line of thought, when I tried to speak to him. My university education didn't entitle me to argue with him. He had never called me a friend. He made me miss my early train to get me volunteer my services to the chairman of the village council. This is the man I am not supposed to let down." I told myself all these things and if I had any reluctance to do as Bela asked, that reluctance has now evaporated.

"Come in Comrade Lichter..." The trio stood and they all shook my hand. "Please be seated. We think this process will take little time...all you have to do is sign here." The man, who appeared to be the leader, placed the sheet front of me.

I saw the date, my name, the amount of eight hundred Forints beside it-written in pencil-a blank space and the amount of the monthly deductions, sixty-six Forints and sixty-six Fillers. The pen was handed to me and three fingers pointed at the blank place that was to receive my signature.

"All you have to do is sign here and we thank you for your generosity, your dedication." One of them urged me, with a smile around his lips, while the others nodded eagerly.

"So you want me to sign here?"

"That is correct."

"Maybe I should think about that," I announced, my voice shaking.

Three heads suddenly lifted; tension filled the room and the speaker's voice became harsher.

"Maybe you should think about the vast amounts our Government spent on your education...Maybe you should thank your lucky stars that we have allowed the Son of a capitalist to become a teacher. Maybe you should think about your future..."

"I will be thinking about all those things...," I became somewhat bolder.

"Are you telling us that you will not buy any peace bonds?"

"Did I say that comrades? I think not. You misunderstood. All I said is that I need to think about it. I am about to get married...I need every Forint to get established...A month of salary is nothing to sneeze at."

"Young man, you are not thinking clearly." The speaker no longer called me comrade. "Marriage means nothing, when the husband is absent."

"Am I going somewhere?" I became reckless.

"If you sign here you will go far...If you don't, you may be sent farther." The committee leader spoke and the others remained silent.

"I will go far...Thirty-five years to teach in this school, that is how far I will go, if I sign. And if I don't I will go farther. That sure sounds like a threat to me."

"Your stupidity I cannot understand Lichter. You are obstinate; you are careless; you are stubborn; you are an enemy of this Nation. We know how to deal with such man." The shouts came from all three of them and I was contaminated with their disgusting saliva. At this point I stood up, showed them my back and left them.

As I entered the adjacent staff room, I saw their next victim. His face was set in a stony white mask. Clearly what was to come was not to his liking. I should have gone back to my class room, but something held me and I waited.

The teacher spent with the committee no more than three minutes and when he came out he looked relieved. Never before did he speak to me, but this time he reached for my hand and whispered a few words of thanks.

The committee was scheduled to process their victims before two in the afternoon. Soon after one, I sat down in the staff room and watched the door that led to my principal's office. When one more teacher came out, when I was sure that they have processed everyone, I knocked on the door and opened it slightly.

"May I come in?"

"What do you want?" their leader inquired.

"It is not what I want that is important. It is what this Nation needs. I told you before that I must think and that is what I did. So let me just have that paper and I will be glad to donate a month's earning."

"But that is preposterous. You have refused to buy any peace bond! Didn't he do that?" The leader turned to the others and received their agreement.

"Why would I refuse to help the government that helped me to get an education? Why would I be different from my colleagues? I am no less dedicated than any of you comrades."

"You are scum...You threw a monkey wrench into our plans. Had you cooperated we would have done a lot better." The youngest committee member let the cat out of the bag and I felt gratitude to my friend, Bela.

Early that afternoon the committee left the building and the teachers milled around the staff room. As soon as I have entered, a silence descended. One by one they came to shake my hand, but gave no voice to their thoughts. It was a silent ceremony that was the beginning of many new friendships.

When Pallosy entered the staff room he was in a foul mood. He allowed us to smell his displeasure and he called me into his office.

"Lichter you are a disgrace to me. Your action will not be forgotten. Get the hell out of here."

***

After the third month of my teaching career my life in the village began to change.

Maya Floch and her husband, Istvan, competed for my presence for supper and card playing. Bela and Anna tried to outdo them by many invitations. Pista and Lenke sought my company, as did others.

Whenever I have entered the local pub, I was approached by strangers, who have let me know, one way or another, that they have heard things about my 'trickery with the evaluation committee'; my 'handling of the mini revolution'; my 'courageous way of taking on the mighty party secretary'; my 'skill of handling the peace bond issue'. Those were the phrases they used when they spoke to me and each and every time I was made to drink to my accomplishments. When I walked home, loaded to the gills, I vowed to stay away form the drinking establishment.

It soon became unsafe to walk around the village, especially in the evenings, before darkness came. Parents of my students stood in their gate-ways, as I tried to walk by, and they stopped me.

"Will you honor my home, teacher?" They asked in various ways and when I gave in, when I entered, food and drinks were immediately provided and the praises came.

When I was at last allowed to leave, I walked no farther than a few houses, when I was once again intercepted and an another invitation was extended.

I began to refuse politely.

"Are we less worthy of your presence than my neighbor whose house you left?" a man would ask and I would be made to eat and drink again, until I could consume no more.

This went on for a few weeks, then to my great relief my new found popularity began to vane.

***

December sixth came very slowly, but when I finished my teaching that day, I rushed to the railway station and my luck held, the train was running late. By three in the afternoon I was at my home in Baja and in no time I was fully prepared.

Early that evening the celebrants began to gather. First the Buja's bedroom became crowded, then the kitchen overflowed with guests. They came with their gifts and congratulations. The eight of us received them.

Mr. Buja opened the gate, each time someone knocked on it. He received the guest's congratulations, then Mrs. Buja, Joe, my parents, George were the recipients of good wishes and then it was Rozsa who accepted their many kisses. They shook my hand, pounded my shoulders and in various ways they expressed their doubts or their best wishes.

"Isn't Rozsa too young?" someone asked me.

"Congratulations Laszlo. You are a lucky man to become engaged to the most beautiful girl in this city! Maybe even in this country! Oh, the heck with it, I might as well say it. The most gorgeous creature in the whole world is more than a mere mortal, like you, deserves. That is what I think," someone else said and I was delighted and at the same time infuriated.

When everyone had arrived, Mr. Buja asked for silence. Through the open door of their bedroom, even the kitchen guests obeyed.

"I raise my glass to Rozsa and Laszlo. Maria and I have promised Rozsa to this young man. We have asked you to come and witness their engagement. To their happiness, to their good health, to their prosperity I ask you to drink with me."

Their glasses raised, their smiles abundant, they drank deeply and the celebration was under way.

I stood close to my darling, whenever I was able. I held her hand to feel the pleasure her touch always gave me. I looked at her sweet, beaming face and my heart palpitated, as guest after guest proposed a new toast to the loving couple.

The food, Mrs. Buja and my Mother, prepared with loving care, was consumed. The drinks, provided by Mr. Buja and my Father, began its magic and the singing started.

I sang with them, no longer afraid to give away the lack of my singing ability. I gave no thought to the troubles we will, no doubt, have to face in our doomed country. I forgot the school; the teachers; the volunteer work; the many dangers I had to face; the small room where I was to take my lovely bride, after the wedding; my coming State examinations; the possible danger I faced from the military; my former friends; the problems my family members had; for I was on a deserted island. Only Rozsa and I existed and I could think about nothing else, but the day of our coming wedding.

When the guests began to leave; when my own family said good-bye to us, when only the five of us remained, I couldn't leave.

"Rozsa became my fiancé, I will not leave her. She is mine; she is my beloved. She is my everything," I told myself and heard Mr. Buja's question.

"Are you happy my dear children?"

"I am truly so," Rozsa assured him.

"And I am the happiest man in the whole universe thanks to the two of you, Mr. and Mrs. Buja."

"And what about me?" Joe asked mischievously.

I looked at him, not comprehending.

"My parents gave the two of you their blessing, but if it wasn't for me this would have never happened," Joe announced.

"And why is that?" I asked befuddled.

"Well Laszlo, let's look at the facts. You may have decided to make my sister your wife, on the day you first saw her, but even with your determination you wouldn't have succeeded if it wasn't for me. Had I not allowed you to help me, when you offered; had I not accepted your friendship; had I not given you the opportunity to see Rozsa, the two of you now would be strangers."

I looked at Joe and in my rapture, I grabbed his hand and thanked him for all his kindness.

***

From that night on I began my countdown.

"Thirty-five days...That many nights...Almost eight hundred forty hours...Over fifty thousand minutes left. I don't even dare to count the seconds that tick away ever so slowly." I calculated on my way home from the engagement party and my immense happiness was tinged with the misery of waiting.

A day later I counted the time left, once again and I repeated the act each and every evening, as I lay in my lonely bed, before I began my evening prayer.

"Dear Lord you have always helped me. Please make the days pass a lot faster, please protect my dear Rozsa...Please keep safe everyone dear to her and all my loved ones. Please make this year come to a close, please bring me soon the tenth of January."

***

The Almighty must have heard me; time began to slip by in a flurry of activities. My parents killed a pig and so did Rozsa's, on two different Sundays, with the help of family members. Christmas of '52 came and went. Rozsa and I ushered in the year of our marriage and each time we were together, one more detail of our wedding plans were debated.

"My heart bleeds for my little girl. We won't be able to buy her a wedding gown," Rozsa's Mother stated one night, weeks before of our great event.

"Don't fret Mother. I found someone who is willing to rent out her wedding gown. That is what I will wear," Rozsa announced.

"Well, at least that is settled. So what will you wear Laszlo?" Mr. Buja inquired.

"I planned to wear the only suit I have, but my Father didn't think that would do, so he bought me a new one.

"Well, those two things are taken care of," Mrs. Buja brightened somewhat.

"Now what about a photographer? We must have a few pictures of Rozsa in her wedding gown and of course the groom should not be neglected."

"We will visit the photographer, just before our wedding. I have already made an appointment." Rozsa took care of that item.

"And how will you get there my dear daughter and you Laszlo?" Mrs. Buja popped the question.

"I will walk from my home to here. I will arrange for a taxi. Rozsa and I will get our first ride, then we will have another one waiting to take us to City Hall before five o'clock that evening. From the City Hall we will take another one to meet the wedding party."

"I only wish we had a car...I don't even know anyone who is able to afford such luxury. Bicycles are our usual mode of transportation," Mr. Buja sighed with regret.

"But this way you will see the bride before the wedding. That shouldn't be the way Laszlo. They say it brings bad luck my darling," Mrs. Buja complained this time.

"There is nothing we can do about that," Rozsa stated.

"Getting married to your lovely daughter can bring nothing, but happiness. I am not superstitious. I don't believe in fairy-tales," I announced, beaming.

"I suppose there is not a thing we can change. These things are then settled my children," Mr. Buja spoke again.

We kept on planning all the other details. At midnight Rozsa was to change from her wedding gown into a sweet dress; she was to cover her head with a headkerchief, following the ancient custom, that would declare to everyone her changed status from a free girl to a married woman. Then she was to dance with all the men who could afford to pay for that privilege. We were to say good-by to everyone, before one o'clock in the morning, and walk to the train station to begin our train journey together.

We laid our plans and hoped for no divine interference.

***

In my new suit, that fitted me well, I walked the long distance that I have walked many times before. This time my trek was different. My steps were light; I felt only joy; my heart sang all the way. "This is my last lonely walk, after which my beloved and I will never be separated." This axiom I kept repeating.

I entered the house where my darling waited and when I was admitted I saw an angel.

Her slim body was covered in white silk; it hid even her tiny feet. Her lovely head was crowned with a garland of small flowers. The fine, white veil cascaded down the length of her body, trailed behind that gorgeous being. Her lips were cherry red, inviting. Her blue eyes sparkled with animation. Her exquisite face lit up when she saw me. Her tiny hands, I held so often, were covered with crocheted, white gloves and held a bouquet of flowers. Her attractive ears were made even more beautiful by her long earrings. Beside her, on the top of a chair, a white fur piece waited.

I stood there, rooted to the floor. Maybe for the first time in my life, I was speechless. The strength of my emotions shook me...The sight of my beloved Rozsa made me feel weak. I have always known that she was beautiful, but the woman I saw before me surpassed all my expectations.

"So what do you think Laszlo?" Mrs. Buja broke the spell.

"I think, I do not know this heavenly creature...She is more gorgeous than anybody I have seen...Am I dreaming? Is she really the girl who loves me? Is she the angel who will be my wife? Are any of these things real, or am I dreaming?" I muttered my doubts, my questions with disbelief.

"You better snap out of this Laszlo or you will never make your own wedding." Mr. Buja brought me back to my senses.

"So many, many years ago, I saw a young girl, who carried a basket, while I was covered with the dust of our street. One look at her and I was in love. One glimpse of her and I vowed that her I will marry. So much has happened since that day...I courted her relentlessly. We were together and we were apart, but my feelings toward her have never changed. My love for your daughter Mr. and Mrs. Buja had grown day by day. I hoped, I wished with all my heart, for the coming of this day and now that it came, I have a hard time to face this reality. Later on I may not be able to say this, so please allow me to say this now. I am thankful for your gift of Rozsa...I am grateful for your understanding...I am happier than anyone could ever be...I promise you now that I will be good to your daughter...That I will care for her; provide for her; honor her for all my years. If I ever make her unhappy, even for a single moment, I will beg her for forgiveness...Mr. and Mrs. Buja, I promise you now that your exquisite daughter will be cherished, protected, loved and honored until my eyes hold her dear sight for the last time. I will keep these promises for an eternity." I didn't know what else to say to assure the concerned parents; to convince them about my best intentions, so I fell silent.

"We thank you Laszlo for all you promised. If you ever forget what you have said, you will have to face me. I will handle you like you saw me handle many fish. Now get going. The taxi must be waiting," Mr. Buja spoke with solemnity.

Rozsa took one look at her old room, probably saying farewell to the place of her childhood. Then she embraced both of her parents. She offered one of her arms to me and gathered up her long, white veil with the other and we went to enter the waiting taxi.

***

"You, young lady better stand here." The photographer pointed at the chair with its high back. I watched my darling Rozsa being assisted by the middle aged man, as she stepped carefully on the platform. I filled my eyes with the sight of my beloved, as she stood there.

Her smile was sweet; her posture erect; her two hands held the lovely bouquet of flowers; her veil flowed around her back, came to the front, by her left side, and the silky, gleaming material covered the two steps that elevated my queen far above me. Her white stole, placed beside her chair, made her look like a real princess. The tall, candle holder's electric light danced around my beloved. The gathered, silky drapery, behind her, emphasized the outline of her sensuous body and I turned, averted my eyes from my darling. My burning cheeks, my intense desire she was not yet to see.

"No this won't do..." The photographer announced, fussed around her and then he found a spread of ten white lilies, which he placed at the feet of my angel.

I blinked my eyes as the bulb popped and her loveliness, her innocence, her love, her desire, her anticipation was captured by the film for an eternity.

"Now I want the two of you together," the photographer announced and I was finally allowed to join my angel.

I stood beside her in my new, black suit, with my right arm behind her, our shoulders touching. My left hand clenched around my white gloves that soon became wet with perspiration. I was keenly aware of her presence, the fragrance of her flowers that were far less intoxicating than the aroma of her perfume which gave me a delightful shiver. I was happy beyond all measures and then the photographer's words stained my happiness.

"I think I must do something about your shortness," I heard him and I was devastated. I was always the shortest amongst all the boys I knew and the remarks made by many children and adults never failed to embarrass me.

"If Laszlo was any shorter, he could join the best circus and be the smallest amongst the midgets," I recalled what some of the boys used to say.

"Laszlo you are getting as tall as a flag pole," one of the shop keepers always taunted me, until I refused to enter his store.

These remarks and many others never failed to hurt me deeply and now the photographer joined them.

"Just take our picture...That is what we pay you for," I fired back in anger.

"Now hold on just for one minute. I am an artist...I will tell you how to pose. Both of you step down for one moment," he ordered us and we obeyed.

I helped Rozsa with her long veil, I held her arm very closely and my happiness was whole again.

While I stood there, I looked deep into my Rozsa's blue eyes and saw the promise those blue eyes held.

"Today she will be wed to me." My mind repeated the sweet promise and I have never noticed the photographer's treachery.

"Now you stand on the left, facing me," he told Rozsa and once again he arranged her and her long veil, her flowers, to his liking.

"You stand on her right. Well now that is much better. You young man appear to be taller. I think we are almost ready."

He moved behind his camera, gave us a few more suggestions and the flash bulb popped again.

"I think I have captured these special moments. The two of you look well together." I heard him say and I was grateful to him for making no further reference to my shortness.

"In a week I will have all the pictures ready. If you don't mind I will display them in the center of the city."

I thought about it only for a moment. Another display popped into my head. My beloved Rozsa smiling at that young officer, in that glass display case. The old women mistaking them for lovers. Their comments; my stupid quarrel with my darling, that almost ruined everything. I was ready to give him my answer.

"Please do that...It will please us...Don't you agree, my darling?" Rozsa stated sweetly and it was time to leave.

***

Arm in arm, we entered the cavernous gate of City Hall. We climbed the steps to the second floor, taking great care with Rozsa's veil. As we entered the office of the registrar, who was to officiate, we were led toward the front, walking in the clear space between the metal chairs.

I saw many of Rozsa's relatives and mine, present to witness our happy day. When we reached the front, where the official waited, I couldn't help but see the hated faces. Stalin glared at us from the center. On his left Lenin's picture was ready to witness the ceremony. On the right, Rakosi's pudgy face intruded.

"I wish those pictures were not here...," I told myself and tore my eyes away from the hated faces.

The official began to speak and it took me no time to realize that this was far from a proper wedding, but more like a meeting of the Communist party.

"These two young comrades have come before me and front of Stalin, Lenin and Rakosi they will pledge loyalty, not only to each other, but to their beloved leaders.

"They came here to declare their love...To declare their loyalty.

"Laszlo Lichter will you...." I listened to his words and when the time came, I gave my reply.

"I do with all my heart," my words sounded too loud.

"And you, Rozsa Buja, will you..."

Her answer came in a whisper, "I do!"

"Now put the ring on her finger...." I slipped the cheap wedding band on Rozsa's finger with as much reverence as I could muster.

"Now put the ring on his finger..." I felt Rozsa's finger touch mine and saw the wedding band find its place.

"Now in the power invested in me by the Republic of Hungary, I declare you to be man and wife. You may kiss the bride now."

In the presence of the despised pictures; after the simple State ceremony that made not a single reference to God; and in front of all those who raised us, supported us, guided us for many years, I turned to Rozsa and we kissed each other passionately.

***

I stepped out of the taxi, rushed to the other door and opened it for my darling. I reached for her arm-no longer fearing who might see us-and before I led her into the home of my childhood, I pointed at the dusty street, then at the gate of the house, where she once lived.

"There my love...I can see it ever so clearly. I saw you carry a basket and from that moment on nobody else existed. Do you remember my wife, my dear Rozsa?" I tried to resurrect the sweetness of that long ago moment; I tasted the words 'my wife' for the first time and her words surprised me.

"I see it too, very clearly. I saw a street urchin, among others, covered with dust, stood there transfixed and stared at me. As time passed the miracle of love touched me and now, my dear husband, you and I should think about the future, the past is behind us. The guests must be waiting."

We entered the house and suddenly I remembered that I was no longer the boy who-on his way from school-used to recite with each step: 'Does she love me?' or 'Did she write to me?' Now I was a happy man, whose arm held his beloved wife's and together we approached the kitchen.

"They are here...!" the shouting began and we were torn away from each other. People hugged and kissed my darling, others reached out for my hand.

The hubbub continued for several minutes. The women wept from joy, dabbed at their eyes with ever present handkerchiefs; the men were outspoken. Many of them whispered in my ears, causing me to blush, and I tried to hide my embarrassment, my annoyance upon hearing the things they suggested.

Rozsa was led out of the kitchen, where a dozen or more women were preparing the feast. Into my room they went, the room that was now almost empty. Gone was the bed, I once shared with George and from there they went to my parents' bedroom, where three long tables waited for the banquet. I followed them as fast as I could. I wanted to be close to my wife, to the angel, to my beloved Rozsa.

"Sit here..." Someone led her to the head table and there she waited. Within minutes I sat beside her and instead of admiring the cheerful guests, I stared at her sweet face and my body shook with my emotions.

"Give her a kiss! She is you wife!" someone shouted and the guests waited.

I needed little urging...I reached for her, drank in the fragrance of her body and my lips sought hers with thirst and fire.

The guests began to take their seats and when not one remained standing-except for the women, ready to serve the food-Rozsa's Father stood and commanded attention.

"I hope your glasses are filled to the brim and your hearts are filled with joy. Many years ago, we have moved into that house, across the street. A few days later a small, young boy began to make his appearance. First Rozsa's Mother and I thought that he was after our Son's friendship. He began to haul water from the distant well, then he moved up a rank and began to cut our winter wood. We still suspected nothing. If my recollection is not faulty, Rozsa, our beloved daughter, was barely past her twelfth birthday. The days and weeks and months had passed and our eyes began to open. That young boy sought no other than our sweet daughter, we began to see. When alone or with Joe or even with us, he never cracked a smile, but when our daughter made an appearance his face underwent great changes. He began to smile; a flush spread all over his face; his lips trembled and we began to fear.

"I am sure all of you heard the story of the outhouse, so I will try to make this rather brief. Our Son, Joe and Laszlo tried to jump out of the new hole, when the sewage broke through, but only Laszlo escaped. Joe stood up to his neck in that terrible stuff. According to an old saying stepping into that stuff will bring great luck, so I think Laszlo should have been the victim, for he is a lucky man indeed. He withstood all our attempts to break up this lovely couple. Not our moving to Szob; not his studies at Szeged; not my terse letter-demanding that he stay away from our young daughter-ever kept him from our dear Rozsa. He is as stubborn as his Father, so in the end we just gave up. He succeeded and we gained a Son, a successful teacher. Today you witnessed the ceremony that made them man and wife. They are young, deeply in love, as you can see. They have nothing, just each other and their love binds them together. May that love last forever. My wife and I wish them everlasting happiness; we wish them prosperity and we wish them something else, but that something I better not mention. Congratulations Rozsa. The same to you Laszlo. Now raise your glasses-after my speech you must be thirsty-drain them in one gulp and let's begin the celebration.

Speech after speech followed and each time we were congratulated with words of love and hearty drinks.

The guests at the head table were served, then the others and over the hubbub of clattering plates, forks and knives came the shouts, demanding that Rozsa and I show them the depth of our affection.

I needed little urging...One spoonful of soup and a kiss. One bite, that I never tasted, then a kiss. One sip of wine or some other strong liquor and another taste of her sweet lips.

When our guests could eat no more, supper was halted.

"The other room has been emptied, by now the gypsies are ready to play. Let's all move to that room and there Rozsa and Laszlo will start the dance," my Father extended the invitation.

The three member gypsy band began to play a slow number and I reached for my sweetheart's hands. My clumsy feet forgot their ineptness; my empty arms were filled Rozsa's sumptuous body. The distance between us began to diminish with each note the gypsies played and when the number came to an end, I was forced to relinquish my darling.

The dancing continued at a frenzied pace, but I never danced with anyone. I stood in one of the corners, unable to tear away my eyes from wife, the skillful dancer. Her body swayed; her face became flushed with exertion; her eyes danced with joy and happiness; her arms held, with skill, all the males at a respectable distance and I, like a hawk, followed her every movement.

The hours passed slowly, the minutes fell behind me with even less speed and I glanced at my watch, from time to time, suspended in the delirium of waiting.

Then finally midnight approached and Mrs. Buja made her announcement.

"The bride will now leave and when she returns, all of you will have a chance to dance with Mrs. Lichter. Before midnight her dance was free. When she returns, we will start the bidding." She reached for Rozsa's hand and the two of them, followed by two other women, disappeared.

Twenty minutes may have passed, during which many of the guests urged me to take a drink. I took a few sips, but my mind wasn't on other things.

"They took her to my Aunt Manci's apartment, in the back of the house. They must be taking off her wedding dress...," I told myself and my imagination allowed me to see.

"She was in her white slip that clung to her perfect body. Her gorgeous wedding dress was being placed on the bed. Her head was uncovered, her veil was gone, replaced by a scarf to mark her new status, she is now a married woman. She pulled a dress over her head; inspected herself in the mirror. The women made a last examination, nodded their heads with approval and began the short walk to return my beloved wife to me." Someone interrupted my reverie.

"What do you think they are doing?"

"They will come back in a minute," I assured the guest and positioned myself so that I would be the first to see. The door opened and the heavenly creature entered to the sound of our guests' clapping.

I stood there with my mouth open. The dazzling woman wore a blue dress that hugged her body. She was no longer the bride in the wedding dress, whose sight took away my breath, but a grown, mature woman, whose sight made my heart race with the force of a hurricane. Her head was covered with a beautiful red and white polka-dot scarf. Her face was aglow with unconcealed pleasure, as she rushed to me.

While the guests clapped, while they hollered, while the gypsies broke into a lively *csardas*, a Hungarian number that never failed so set hearts and feet on fire, we embraced, we kissed and she was torn away from me.

"The bidding will start now. Anybody who wishes to dance with this heavenly creature better get his Forints ready," Mr. Buja shouted over the gypsies' playing.

"We will start with ten Forints. Who wants to dance with Laszlo's wife, with my lovely daughter? You are disqualified Laszlo...You will have your whole life to do that. So who will give me ten?"

"I bid twenty," shouted someone and someone else shouted even louder.

"I bid thirty, I insist to have the first dance with Mrs. Lichter!"

"I will pay forty," came from the first bidder.

"And I pay fifty!" the successful bidder retorted and Rozsa began to dance with him.

The bidding continued and I would have given everything, I had in my wallet, to be able to dance with my angel, in spite of my lack of skill and my dislike for that activity.

The wicker basket on Mrs. Buja's arm began to fill with Forint bills and the frenzied bidding still continued. Rozsa swayed and stepped to the music; she was held by one male, then by another. Their fast movements became a blur and I envied every male; begrudged everybody who made a contribution.

"This is not right...This is my wedding night...I should be the only one allowed to touch her..." My mind was bombarded with silly thoughts; my soul suffered in silent anguish.

Slowly the gypsies began to tire, but not as much as did my Rozsa. Whenever she passed by me, she glanced at me, smiled at me, when she could, she touched my arm, but those precious seconds didn't last long. She was carried away by a man. The time passed very slowly and when half past one came, the gypsies stopped.

"Now the young couple will say their farewells. Uncle Pista and Aunt Maris, their chaperons and landlords, will take them to Bacsbokod. That is where the young couple will spend their wedding night. That is where they will live. The rest of you remain here. In a few minutes another meal will be served and after that there will be a lot more dancing. Not one of you should seek your home; not one of you should be in bed before sunrise. We are having a real Hungarian wedding," Mr. Buja announced to the revelers, using the old couples' names in a manner that became his custom after the first time they broke bread together in his household.

I became more enthusiastic than during the previous sixty minutes. Minutes that I counted secretly, while Rozsa entertained the guests and was building our modest nest egg. My hand found my darling Rozsa's and the two of us approached each guest.

To our parents we said a heartfelt thank you; to the guests we said our farewells; and when we were certain that nobody was neglected, we went to get our two suitcases and were ready to begin our one mile trek.

***

The four of us began our walk. Rozsa and I, side by side, as close as my two suitcases permitted and Uncle Pista and Aunt Maris a few steps behind us.

Four weeks before I checked the train schedule. A week later I inquired from the station master.

"The first train leaves very early in the morning...Two o'clock," he replied to my question.

On our way to the station I calculated.

"Two o'clock, if it's on time and we will be on our way. By two thirty we will be at Bacsbokod...a ten minute walk to our boarding place. Five more minutes to say thank you and good night to our escorts. At two forty-five we will enter our room and I will be at last alone with my beloved Rozsa!" The civilian ceremony was forgotten, but not the wedding promise we had made. The hated pictures of our leaders I blotted out of my mind, they were no longer important. The long waiting, while Rozsa danced, no longer meant a thing.

The four of us entered the deserted station, where we have said many tearful farewells during the years of my courting. We stood on the deserted platform and waited.

"This time we are not being separated...We will take this trip together, my dearest, my darling," I whispered in Rozsa's ear.

"I am so very happy Laszlo." She brushed my ear with her lips, as she returned my whisper. "On those occasions, when we were separated, lonely days and tearful nights followed, until we saw each other again. Not this time my love...We will always be together."

I looked at my watch and confirmed the time by looking at the station's clock.

"Where is that train? It is way past two o'clock. Something is wrong...There are no other people waiting," I observed with mounting dread.

"Maybe you should inquire at the ticket window," Uncle Pista suggested.

I went back inside, but not without my lovely wife. I held on to her hand and knocked on the window. The attendant rose slowly from his slumber, rubbed his sleep-filled eyes and his words were belligerent.

"What do you bother me for this late in the night? Can't a man have some peace around here?"

"I just want to find out how late the two o'clock train will be?"

"Two o'clock train? There is no such thing. Where are you planning to go?"

"To Bacsbokod..."

"Well you missed that one by one hour. It left at one."

"But that cannot be...," I stated in utter misery.

"Well it went and this being Sunday, there will be no other train until late afternoon," he stated, shut his window and resumed his place in his chair, ready to return to his disturbed slumber.

I looked at my darling Rozsa. My apology poured out, for what may have been my mistake.

"I am so sorry my darling. I am sure I was told two o'clock. In my excitement I may have made a mistake."

"I am sorry too Laszlo, but we do have a saying: 'Men make plans and the

Almighty makes the alterations."

"What should we do now? We cannot wait here until evening." I could have kicked myself, shot myself, I was so disappointed.

"We have little choice Laszlo. We must return to the wedding."

"Not that...That I couldn't bear."

"Do you have a better suggestion?"

"I cannot think...I am confused...I am angry."

"The first two I can understand, but for you to be angry on our wedding night is not what I have expected."

"I am sorry. Of course you are right. We must go back to my parents' place. Maybe they will find a solution."

We began our backward trek, after I confessed my crime, my mistake to our escorts.

Five houses before we reached my parents' home, we began to hear singing. With each step that brought us closer, the music and singing became louder. Then I summoned up enough courage to face the wedding party and I began to bang on the gate.

I heard their voices after many minutes. They came into the yard and shouted.

"If you can't sleep, join us...We will not stop, not until noon, at least."

The gate opened and George, seeing the four of us, burst into a ribald laughter.

"Already back. Did Laszlo chicken out? Did you Rozsa come back for another dance? I am game!"

"We want to see our parents," I cut him short.

"You missed your train...Is that what happened Laszlo?" he shouted while he helped me with the two suitcases. "Did you guys hear that? Laszlo couldn't even manage to take his bride..."

"Enough of this! I don't want to hear one more word from you. Get our parents. We will not go inside into that madness," I told him bitterly.

"Fine...Have it your way. Come on guys, Laszlo is sore as hell." George and his companions left us in the yard.

"What has happened?" Mrs. Buja asked.

"What is going on?" Mr. Buja joined her.

"I cannot believe my eyes. You are back," my Father lamented.

"Now I have seen just about everything," my Mother became sarcastic.

"We missed our train. It is my fault. I ruined our wedding night...I destroyed everything."

"I thought you were a lot smarter Laszlo, than your comments seem to indicate. Nothing is ruined...We will find a solution. Could the kids spend this night in Manci's flat, where Rozsa changed?" Mr. Buja raised the idea.

"I wish they could, but Istvan, Manci's husband, was three sheets to the wind, long before the kids left, and he is the one who occupies the bed now. And besides, in your excitement you forgot Gitta, your little niece. She sleeps in their room too," my Mother announced calmly.

"Well that idea went out the window. Rozsa and Laszlo need no company. I think I will ask the Gomoris. They have a big house and until late morning it will be empty."

"Please don't..." I began to plead. "I feel bad as it is. I don't want everybody to know what I did. Could we not go to your house? Rozsa's room is still there...You wouldn't mind the long walk. Would you my darling?"

"I go where my husband takes me," came her reply and I began to heal.

Mr. and Mrs. Buja exchanged a quick glance. A fleeting smile crossed Mrs. Buja's face, she was about to speak, but Mr. Buja's raised finger made her change her mind and she remained silent.

"It is settled then. Go there...Leave the suitcases here...You can pick it up tomorrow before the train leaves. By the way, what time is it going?"

"I never thought of asking," I admitted sheepishly.

"I can understand that. Now go my children. Maybe what happened is for the best. Rozsa lived in that room for years...That is where she spent her last night as a girl; let her begin her new life in familiar surroundings." Mr. Buja settled the issue and as I thanked him, I saw a mischievous smile, but I was thinking of other things.

***

We walked, arm in arm, across the dark, deserted city. We walked the length of Szamuelly Street and I recalled a thousand other times when we followed the same route.

"Do you remember my beloved how we used to talk about our future together? Whenever we did that I used to steal a kiss," I told Rozsa.

"Back then you had to steal one, now my kisses are yours my darling," came her reply and we stopped. I took her in my arms, gave her a fervent kiss in the wee hours of the dark morning.

"We better get going or daylight will find us here." She broke away from my embrace and as we walked, she continued. "Do you remember Laszlo how you used to speak about us some day having a boy? You wanted him to become a chemist. You were denied that opportunity, so you wanted our Son to take your place. But during the last year you always spoke about having a girl, instead."

"I know Rozsa...I had good reasons to change my wish. A boy would grow up and be drafted by the military. I don't want our child to be drafted. I hate and despise the Hungarian army. Maybe someday we will have a boy, but that should happen in another country."

"In the meantime we must remember what my parents asked us," she announced, perhaps wanting to remind me and I blushed in the darkness.

We reached the end of the long street and turned left where Lokert Row started.

"Not much longer to go my darling," I told Rozsa and then I began to laugh.

"Is there something you want to tell me?" Rozsa asked.

"I was just thinking. After your Father's letter, that ordered me not see you, we walked this street. Your parents sat under a tree, in the darkness and discovered our treachery. This time there will be no watchers; there will be no reprimand. Husband and wife will enter your house, your room and we will be free. That is what popped into my mind and I couldn't help my happy laughing."

"Husband and wife...That was our dream...Our dream came true. Thank God Laszlo."

We reached the house. I unlocked the gate with shaking fingers. Then came the task of unlocking the door of the kitchen, but by then I was trembling so much that I had to ask Rozsa to fit the key.

We entered her unheated room and my nose twitched, as it picked up the not unpleasant smell, but I didn't wish to divert Rozsa's attention from the joy of having reached our sanctuary. The first rays of the coming dawn made it unnecessary to turn on the light and in the semi darkness I saw her narrow chesterfield that could comfortably accommodate only one.

"So much the better...," I thought happily. "We will be very close to each other."

Within minutes we lay close together, under the down filled comforter, and for the rest of the night we were like one being.

***

The January Sun streamed through our window and its brightness woke me. My arm under Rozsa's head; my front fitting her back gently; I listened to her slow breathing; felt the slight tremors that shook her body. My eyes inches away from her silky neck; my lips almost touching her lovely shoulder; my thighs against her slightly bent legs, I lay there, as long as I could, not wanting to disturb her rest.

I became aware of the smell and slowly, very slowly, I turned my head. My eyes saw the ceiling and they glimpsed something totally unexpected. To the ceiling several hooks were fastened. The hooks held the ropes that held several broomsticks and from those wooden supports hung many items. I saw four large, smoked hams, several slabs of bacon and numerous pairs of sausages. The pleasant, faint smell of smoke came from those many items.

I made no further move, I just marveled.

"When Mrs. Buja was ready to say something, her husband stopped her. Was she going to tell us that Rozsa's room was converted into a storage room? Was she going to tell us not to come here? Probably today we will find out," I told myself and the marvel of where I was, who I was with and the manner of our being together, made me smile with the pleasure of my fulfilled dream.

I must have lain there for over two hours, before my beloved began to stir. She suddenly sat up. Although she wore a nightgown, she shyly covered herself up to the neck. When she looked at me, her face began to beam and she lay back down, turned toward me and she began to speak.

"I had a most pleasant dream Laszlo..." Her warm breath scorched my face. "We were in a lovely church. The priest began the ceremony...We made our vows, we exchanged rings, we kissed deeply and then came the wedding reception. I danced most of the night...We have received a great deal of money and even gifts...Then there was a train, yet there wasn't one...We were forced to come to my room by circumstances...Here we lay down together, as man and wife...And I was very happy. Tell me Laszlo that I wasn't dreaming. I couldn't have...You are here..." Before I could assure her we kissed deeply.

"Your dream is mostly accurate my beloved, but there was no church, no priest, but that will come, we promised your parents. You are my wife and I am your husband. The train we missed and we came here...We became one and I am truly happy."

She cuddled with me and closed her eyes. Then she asked a question.

"You don't mind what is stored above us?"

"I mind not that...I mind nothing. For over four long years I have waited for this special day, for this precious night. It finally arrived, that is all that matters."

"My parents had no choice. Many places were robbed in the last few weeks. The burglars always hit places where a pig was butchered...Our people are hungry...This is all my parents have for the long winter, so they wanted to keep the food-stuff safe," she kept explaining.

"I am hungry too, but I will not touch any of the stuff above us," I told her and found her lips.

***

A few hours later we heard voices in the kitchen.

"Maybe it's time to wake them up?" Mr. Buja spoke.

"Let them be...They must be exhausted. So many people. So much dancing. Such long walks." Mrs. Buja's voice filtered through the thin door.

"We should get up Laszlo. It must be late," Rozsa suggested and within minutes we were fully dressed and joined Rozsa's parents.

"I hope we didn't wake you? We tried to be very quiet," Mrs. Buja spoke, but her eyes didn't seek mine, nor that of Rozsa.

"We were awake...We heard you coming. Thank you for the lovely wedding." Rozsa spoke and I spoke likewise.

"I hope you didn't mind us supplying you with all that food?"

"I have actually never noticed." I tried to put Mr. Buja at ease.

"A likely story...That is a good one. Rozsa's room is just like a butcher shop and you never noticed?"

"Well, to tell you the truth, I smelled something when we entered, but I was too tired to bother with anything," I began to fib.

"Have it your way Laszlo. I will not pry. We have raised that pig for many months and after we butchered it the hams, the bacons, the sausages had to be kept in a safe place. We have never expected you to spend your wedding night under so many delicacies. Well, I am sure, you are the only couple in the whole world who spent a wedding night under such circumstances." Mr. Buja joked with us and then he turned his attention to more serious matters.

"Now that the wedding is over, now that the two of you fulfilled your dream, your real life is about to begin. We wish that all your days would be as happy as yesterday was, but that is not the way. If some day one of you is sad, the other one must chase away the shadows. When you face seemingly insurmountable problems, the two of you must work it out. When one of you begins to doubt the other, you will have to talk, to trust and the doubts will fade away. If ever you have a fight, kiss and make up, that is the only way. Your Mother and I, my dear children, love each other more deeply every day. Yet, as you know, we don't always agree. Sometimes we scold each other; we argue bitterly. We are like nature: one day the Sun shines with all its intensity and suddenly dark clouds begin to gather and the coming of a storm is near. The clouds dump their wet load and the world begins to look very bleak. When that happens we must remember that it will change.

"I am glad you missed the train. This gave me the opportunity to say all these things. I could have done this, before your wedding, but then the two of you would have thought that I was trying to change your mind. I had no desire to ruin your special day. Remember these things Laszlo and you too my darling daughter. If you do so, your unhappiness will last only for short moments and your joy will be everlasting. Now I said what has been on my mind, ever since we gave in to your wishes." Mr. Buja fell silent and I was grateful to the wise man for sharing his thoughts, for accepting me.

"Now let's talk about the gifts," Mrs. Buja changed the subject. "I have the money Rozsa earned with her dancing. I counted it. There is almost a thousand Forints. Here is the money..." She placed a paper bag on the table.

"I can't believe it...It is more than I earn in a whole month of teaching," I spoke up.

"It is really a magnificent sum," Rozsa added.

"That is not all. The women brought a few small gifts. An electric iron, a hot plate, a few towels. We put them in one of your suitcases. When you get to your boarding place, you look at them and treasure them for many, many years," Mrs. Buja told us.

"Now that reminds me about your leaving," Mr. Buja picked up the thread of the conversation. "You should take my bike Laszlo and find out when your train is to leave.

Maybe this time you should put the time on paper, just in case you are still too excited."

"I will go and this time there will be no mistake," I replied and was glad to do as told, but not before I gave my wife a fervent kiss.

***

The train began to move. This time my beloved didn't stand on the platform waving her hand, drying her tears; she sat beside me, with her hand in mine and Pista and Maris smiled at us from across our seats.

Whenever someone walked by, a person Maris seemed to know, she made an announcement.

"They are newly married. Aren't they a lovely couple?"

The strangers stopped just for a minute, expressed their best wishes and they moved on. Those few, whom I knew from the village, looked at my wife adoringly and made their observations, offered their congratulations and advice rather freely.

"What a lovely girl...Congratulations to the both of you...Teacher you take good care of her...Cherish her all your days."

***

"Now please go to your room. You two are in my way. Supper will be ready in an hour. I will call you then," Maris' eyes twinkled, as she spoke and we needed little urging.

In our room we glanced at the gifts, but a lot more at each other. The hour passed fast and we heard the knock, on our curtain covered door.

When the delicious supper was finished, I began to speak.

"Rozsa and I have tomorrow free. One whole day before we have to return to our working places."

"Tomorrow the two of you must have long rests," Maris announced.

"On Tuesday, Rozsa will catch the seven o'clock train. I will escort her to the station, each and every day. She will come back around five, in the evening and I will be there waiting for her every day." I informed the three of them.

"And that is the way it should be. You Laszlo will make a fine husband, if you will keep all your promises. And you Rozsa will make an even finer wife. Just look at you Rozsa...You were created by the dear Lord in the image of His most beautiful angels." Maris praised her, adored her, as if she were her beloved daughter.

"I will keep all my promises, I assure you. That reminds me, we need your help."

"You name it Laszlo and if it is within our power, our help will be given gladly," Pista replied.

"We feel bad that we were unable to get married in the house of the Lord. You know Pallosy and his power. Rozsa's boss, his name is Szantai, is no better. A church wedding would have gotten us fired and even Mr. Buja would have lost his job. Yet a church wedding we must have. We want it and we promised Rozsa's parents. Is there any way you could talk to the village priest, maybe he could figure out something?"

"Consider it done Laszlo. Our priest is a kind, understanding man. I will discuss the issue with him," Maris promised.

That night we retired early and before we fell asleep we talked in hushed tones, lest we disturb our host and hostess.

We spoke about our long courtship, our short engagement, the kindness of our parents, the kind Maris and Pista, the generosity of relatives and friends, our jobs, our cruel bosses, and when we have exhausted all the subjects, we moved closer and our words became endearing.

Sunshine greeted us when we woke on Monday and the hours grew wings, the passage of time sped up immensely.

"Isn't it strange my beauty how things can change in a short time?"

"What do you mean Laszlo?"

"When I was away from you, I used to look at my watch and observed how slowly time had passed. The passage of one single moment seemed to last an eternity. Then, while I was with you, the same minute sprouted wings and it disappeared, like it never existed. After your parents gave their permission to have us become man and wife, the passage of time slowed down immensely. I counted the days to our wedding; I counted the hours and even the minutes. Each day when I did that, the time remaining seemed to be no shorter. Now that we are finally together, now that we could enjoy each moment, even if it lasted for an eternity, our time seems to disappear. If time keeps galloping at this rate, we will soon reach a ripe old age."

"It was and is no different for me...An hour lasts for sixty minutes, that never changes, but that much time with you is a short-lived second and without you it's never ending," Rozsa told me and my heart filled with joy, with the pleasure of knowing.

"So the more time we spend together the sooner we will seem to reach old age. At least that is the way it will appear, I think."

"If that is the case Laszlo, then we will be old soon my beloved. Will you love me even then? I might grow fat and wrinkled; you may come to dislike me. You might lose your desire."

"That, my darling, will never happen. Time will pass; we will both change, but whenever I hold you in my arms you will be like you are now. My eyes will see this beautiful, young woman; my arms will feel your young body; my lips will feel not the lines in your face, but the lips that will remain sweet and young forever. May God grant that we will reach old age; that we will always remain together." When I finished talking, I sought her lips and its sweetness I found more satisfying.

***

Monday passed in speedy haste and when Tuesday came, Rozsa and I walked to the station. There we stood, once again forced to part.

"The hours will pass my love. You and I will have a lot to do. Before night falls we will be together. We will shut out the whole world; the night will belong to you and me." I told her, before a kiss and then she alighted. I stood there, waving to my darling and she waved to me cheerfully.

I went to school, accepted my fellow teachers' congratulations and that of my students. The ribbings came during recess.

"Come and see us, as soon as you can tear yourself away from the bedroom. Bring your young wife. We are dying to meet her," Pista teased me.

"Now that you are married, will we see less of you Laszlo?" Mr. Floch asked me.

"We would love to have the two of you for supper. Do you think you could take the time and honor us with your presence?" Bela inquired.

Each time I assured them that Rozsa and I will be pleased to do as they asked and I was relieved when the bell rang, when I was summoned to return to my class, to resume my teaching.

I never forgot the close brush I had with the evaluation committee. My lesson plans were well prepared with proper political content. I wanted nothing to endanger our happy life, our ecstasy.

Before my marriage, the problems I gave my students were never embellished, but I began to plan more carefully. If the students dealt with percentages, they also dealt with the advantages of living in this country.

"A Hungarian worker earns eight hundred Forints a month...," I would begin truthfully. "He pays fifty Forints for rent. Calculate the percentage that is left from his salary."

"Ninety-three point seven five," came the prompt reply, but only after I asked for a show of hands and picked someone.

"In the United States the same worker would earn only five hundred Dollars a month." I began the second part of the problem, but avoided to divulge the difference between the value of the two currencies. "That worker pays one hundred and fifty Dollars for rent. Now you are to calculate the percentage he has left."

"Seventy percent," came the reply accurately.

"Prepare a bar graph of the moneys the Hungarian and the American worker have at their disposal after the rents are paid."

Soon after they raised their hands and when I asked someone to copy his creation on the blackboard, the moral of the problem became quite apparent.

"The Hungarian has almost ninety-four percent disposable income, after rent, while the American has only seventy. Where would you rather live?" I hated myself for my duplicity, yet my life has thought me a few survival skills and I applied them diligently in all my subjects.

**

Six days a week I taught my students; gave an hour or so volunteer work to the local government; attended the staff meetings Pallosy held; spoke with my friends; planned my lessons; studied for the coming State examinations and as the hours passed, ever so slowly, by mid-afternoon my excitement began to mount and in the last minutes before five, I ran to the railway station.

The train slowed down and there she stood, on the top step, her hand waving. The train barely stopped, when she jumped off, straight into my arms and my world became a million times brighter.

We ate supper with Pista and Maris. Chatted with them, ever so briefly, and it was always Maris who made the announcement.

"The youngsters are tired. We will continue tomorrow. Now go to your room and retire."

Our private evenings always began with an exchange of the day's happenings, but before long we ran out of words, sought our bed and the world no longer existed.

***

The first week of our married life was behind us. While Rozsa was at work the time has passed slowly, but when she came home it slipped by with great rapidity. On Saturday, Rozsa finished work around one and when she came home a few hours early, I begrudged every minute we had to spend with anyone.

We were not ready to visit any of my co-workers; we were reluctant to enter into lengthy conversations, even with Maris and Pista, but on that first Saturday evening, we stayed up late discussing what Maris found out.

"I spoke to the priest. As I told you he is a kind and understanding man. I described your situation and explained your wish. The priest just shook his head. He explained patiently that it is the church's policy not to join those in holy matrimony, who are already joined by the State. He listened to all my arguments, and believe me there were many...Slowly he started to change his position and when he gave his agreement, he demanded total secrecy. I think he fears his masters as much as you do...You could lose your jobs for being wed in a church and he would have to face the bishop's fury. He decided to risk that, since you are also taking a big risk. He understands how things work in this country. So you will have a church wedding, my dear children."

"When? Who shall we invite? What shall I wear?" Rozsa popped the questions.

"On April twenty second...That is a Wednesday. That night, at half past eleven, the priest will open the back door, the two of you will slip in and he will perform the ceremony. There will be absolutely no guests. The priest made that very clear, but he must have two adults to witness your union. He asked me who those two will be. He trusts very few people. Some may pose a danger to the two of you and some good, fervent Roman Catholics will make it dangerous for him. Before I left he asked if I and my husband would be willing to stand in. What do you think Laszlo? And what about you Rozsa? I know we are simple farmers, maybe not the kind..."

"Please stop right there," I cut her short. "We couldn't ask for two nicer people to be our witnesses. Am I not right my dearest?"

"Laszlo is right. You have been good to us; you trust us; you put up with us...You are our best friends," Rozsa stated.

"If you really think...," Pista added. "We will be honored and your secret we will guard for ever."

"Thank you...It means a great deal to us." Maris took over. "Now to your last questions, my angel Rozsa. You should wear what you wore after midnight, last Sunday. When I saw you in that blue dress, I couldn't believe my eyes. You looked magnificent. All eyes looked at you with admiration. The men held their breath, not only Laszlo. You looked sweet, but then again, you don't need a dress to do that. There was something else I noticed. You looked mature, far beyond your young age. Your blue eyes were absolutely stunning. Even your headkerchief made you look more special, but I guess you cannot wear that. Oh, I know what I meant to say...In that blue dress you looked just like your Mother. She is such a lovely lady...Laszlo did you ever think about this: When Rozsa becomes as old as her Mother, her beauty will be just like hers. Men sometimes do look at the Mother, I know my Pista did. He told me that, the day of our wedding and he told me many times, at times when he was cross with me, that I look like my Father," Maris began to tease her old, blushing mate.

"Now you stop that, you are not bad, come to think of it." He looked at her with unconcealed adoration and for the first time I came to understand how even old people love, how they never change.

"Well, enough talk, you must be exhausted." This time it was not Maris, but Pista, who sent us to our room and within minutes, I knew that the old couple, much like us, were fulfilling a dream.

***

Before April twenty second, Rozsa's parents and mine knew about the coming event.

"My heart bleeds thinking about not being present," Mrs. Buja lamented, using almost the same words my parents spoke, when we told them.

"That cannot be helped my dear. In this damn country free will doesn't exist. God gave us free will, but the Communists overruled even Him. We will be with them in our hearts and thoughts. Let's be happy they are keeping one of their two promises."

"What was the other? I seem to forget," I asked without thinking and Rozsa grabbed my hand, but it was too late.

"You are just like a man...," Mrs. Buja stated.

"Yes, Laszlo...Promises we make, but we don't always keep them. You promised us to have a church wedding and we are pleased you found a safe way to do that, but if you break your other promise, before the two years are up, Rozsa will be unable to conceal that." I heard his words, begun to blush and his words of long ago echoed in my ears: 'For at least two years you should not think of having any children. Rozsa should be at least eighteen or nineteen, before she gets that added responsibility.'

***

By the time April twenty second came, slowly, grudgingly I forfeited some of the private time I had with Rozsa and the precious hours we spent in our small room became even sweeter.

We had a pleasant supper with Bela and his wife, Anna. We paid a visit to Pista and Lenke. We even took the time to have a card game with our new friends, Istvan Floch and his wife, Maya. As often as we could we visited our parents and even some of the relatives at Baja.

During our second visit to Baja we went to pick up our wedding pictures. Rozsa and I looked at those splendid pictures and as soon as we have paid the man, we began to walk to her former home.

"Those pictures I will always treasure," I told Rozsa. "Every moment of my life I will remember the lucky day you became my wife, but if ever my memory would fade, I will look at these pictures and I will see my bride's unsurpassed beauty."

"You always exaggerate Laszlo...," she told me shyly.

"There is no exaggeration my darling. I married a girl whose beauty has been immortalized forever." I whispered in her ear and we found ourselves front of the photographer's display case. Two beautiful, enlarged pictures, filled the case and one of the enlargements made me startle.

"How could he do that? What a rotten thing to do?"

"What do you mean Laszlo?"

"Can't you see? Look here...He placed a two inch board under me, to make me look taller, but he left one corner uncovered, for everyone to see. I want this picture out of here...I demand its removal."

"I see Laszlo...You go into a rage over nothing."

"Nothing? Is this nothing to you? For the rest of my life, whenever I look at our picture, I will be reminded of my shortness. I want it out of here. I want the whole thing redone...I want his apology."

"And I want you to talk to my Father. He is the only one who can bring you back to your senses." Rozsa began to walk and I followed her in raging silence.

***

"May I talk with you Mr. Buja?" I approached my Father-in-law, as soon as we entered Rozsa's former home.

"Are you having a problem, Laszlo?"

"I sure do, look at this. Tell me what you see." I handed him the picture.

"I see my lovely daughter, just before her wedding and I see you Laszlo."

"Look under my feet."

"Under your feet? What am I supposed to see there?"

"Do you have a magnifying glass?"

"I have. I go and get it," Mr. Buja announced and Rozsa shook her head.

"Now I am looking with the glass, yet I see nothing extraordinary."

"Do you see that board under my feet?"

"I do Laszlo. So what about it?"

"That incompetent baboon wanted to make me look taller, so he placed that board there. Then he displayed our picture in the city square. I thought he covered it up with the rug, but as you can see..."

"Dear God in heaven, now I can see it. You are being foolish Laszlo...That is what I see. How many people walk around with a magnifying glass? How many do you think?"

"Nobody...But that is not the issue. The picture displayed is enlarged greatly."

"And so is your vanity."

"Is that what you think Mr. Buja? Is it my vanity that makes me so angry?"

"Nothing else my Son, I assure you."

"So what do you suggest I do?"

"Do nothing. Come to think of it, you could have done something, before that picture was taken."

"What could I have done?"

"You could have selected a Soviet photographer. That is what I meant." I was too angry, too serious to note that he was joking.

"A Soviet photographer, Mr. Buja? Now you really lost me."

"Well, I better tell you a story. That ought to shed some light on the situation. The ruler of a small African country wanted to have a superb painting. That painting was to be duplicated and displayed in public places. He had a lame, disfigured leg; he was a hunchback and one of his eyes was badly deformed. He had far more short-comings than you have Laszlo. So the dictator asked for proposals and many offered their services.

"The first painter painted a handsome man and according to the bargain he was executed. The ruler had no desire to be ridiculed by his subjects.

"The second artist painted him as ugly as he was and he met the same fate.

"Then a third one came forward and made his offer. 'I will give you a painting that you can be proud of, but what will you give me in exchange?' The ruler explained the deal he made with the others. 'If you succeed you will get a bar of gold, if you fail, you will join the other two, no longer living artists.'

"The artist accepted the deal, but not before he set one condition. 'If you obey me and do what I tell you, I will give you a painting you will be proud of.'

"The deal was made and the artist gave his orders. 'Kneel down and put your disfigured leg behind you.' Once the ruler obeyed him, came his second order. 'Pick up this rifle and raise it as if you were to fire.' Then came the third request. 'Pick your target and close your deformed eye. Everybody aims a gun with only one eye open.'

"The ruler obeyed each and every one of the artist's orders and when the painting was finished he was elated. The badly formed leg couldn't be seen; the hump on his back was hidden by his position and the one opened eye looked completely normal.

"'So what do you think?' The artist asked and the ruler praised him, paid him, then he asked him a single question. 'Where have you learned your art comrade?'

"'I took several courses in socialistic realism, in the Soviet Union. Your faults are all there, but none can see them.' He told the dictator and both of them burst out laughing.

The people were fooled, yet the ruler walked, for the rest of his short life, with all his deformities.

"Now that you heard my story Laszlo, you should understand. Our artists are not completely trained in socialistic realism. Give them time and that skill they will acquire. You are an honest young man. Do you really want to be like that African dictator? You have Rozsa's love; she is your wife. What else do you need?" In this manner Mr. Buja put my problem in the proper perspective and I, whenever I look at that picture, which is often, smile at my stupidity, my immaturity and I recall his wise words and his funny story.

***

Then the big day came and I began to fret.

"What if Rozsa misses the train? But there is another, an hour later. What if someone finds out about our church wedding? What if the priest changes his mind?" I couldn't chase away the gloomy thoughts and later I stood at the railway station.

The train came, but there was no Rozsa. Passenger after passenger left the train and when it was ready to pull out of the station, I rushed to the conductor.

"Where is my wife? Where is my sweetheart?" I shouted at him the stupidity.

"You must be drunk" He shouted at me and signaled to the engineer to continue the train's journey. I jumped aboard, ran through the few compartments and I searched in futility.

I jumped off the train; stood at the station and my cursed mind gave me no peace.

"I knew this will happen. She missed the train. How could she do that? For over three months this never happened. Did Szantai keep my darling beyond the office hours? Why would he do that? That bastard! He likes her; he likes all pretty women. Maybe...No, that is impossible...My darling Rozsa would refuse all his attempts. Did she have an accident then? Did something happen to my beloved? Should I look for transportation to Baja? Should I go there and search for her? No, that is not a wise course of action. I will wait for one hour, until the next train comes, and if she is not on it, I will borrow a bicycle and pedal like hell, until I get there." My agony made me pace front of the station and when I heard the whistle of the next train, I stopped and began my short prayer.

"Please dear God let her be safe. Let her be on this train," I prayed fervently and my prayer was answered.

She stood on the train's platform, her hand waving and relief, joy replaced all my apprehensions.

"You are here my dearest darling. You came to me. I was so worried, so confused, so angry," I told her, after a kiss, as we began to walk.

"I was worried too when I have discovered that, for the first time ever, in my excitement about our church wedding, I got on the wrong train," she began to tell me.

"You got on the wrong train? What a likely story?"

"I did and I resent your doubting Laszlo. Don't ever do that again. I got on the wrong train, you better believe me. I discovered it when the train began to head south, instead of east. I asked someone where the train was going and when I heard Vaskut, without thinking, I ran to the door, yanked it open and jumped off. I scraped my knee."

"Dear God! Why did you ever do that?"

"I know you Laszlo, that is why. You worry too much, you are the jealous kind, I am sure you know that. So what choice did I have, but to jump, to limp back to the station and to wait for the next train?"

"I wish Rozsa...," I began to say, but did not finish my sentence.

"You wish what?"

"Nothing my darling...I am so very happy you are here." She didn't allow me to hide my ugly thought.

"What were you going to say Laszlo?"

"I wish you didn't work with Szantai...He is a skirt chaser," I spit it out.

"And what am I? Do tell me."

"You are a desirable woman. You are beautiful. You are what every men dreams of possessing," I tried to give her compliments.

"And I am your wife. I am a faithful, married woman...You better remember that."

"I do my love...I made a mistake...Please forgive me."

We reached our home, greeted Maris and went to our room until supper.

"I am so glad you are home my beloved." I reached for her hand, touched her face, just as she turned toward me. Her sudden movement made my touch a bit harsher than I intended.

"You slapped me," came her pain filled accusation.

"I did no such thing. I am not a fool...I love you."

"Yes, you love me, but you told me you were angry. In your anger you dared to hit me." She began to sob.

"I didn't mean to...It was an accident. Please forgive me."

She sat down on the wooden chair, her tears rolling down her sweet face and I knelt front of her, cuddled her slim body.

"My dear darling, please try to understand. I was so worried all day...I thought about the possibility of you missing your train...I worried about someone finding out about our church wedding...I feared that the priest might change his mind. I worried about many things." I kept on telling her and slowly her tears disappeared.

"You will never change Laszlo. You are an eternal pessimist. That you may not be able to change, but your jealousy you better get under control, otherwise our life will be nothing but days and days of misery."

"I only wish you didn't have to work. I can't stand thinking of you working with all those men."

"So here we go again...Can you support us with what you earn? Tell me that Laszlo. Look at us. We live in a small room. Everything you see here belongs to someone else. How could I stop working? And even if I did, would that cure you? You are jealous of the sun that shines above me; you begrudge every moment I spend away from you; you hate when someone looks at me, smiles at me, speaks to me. If you had your way you would shut me away; hide me from all eyes. Maybe I was too young to see your faults, to understand your nature, to comprehend your inability to trust, maybe I made a mistake." Her tears began to appear, once again.

Suddenly I heard her Father's words: 'If ever you have a fight, kiss and make up, that is the only way.' I stood up, leaned closer to her, showered her face with many kisses and as I reached for the top button of her blouse, her deep, blue eyes stared at me.

"Not on your life...Get away from me." Her words hit me hard. I must have paled. When I heard what she said next, I was once more experiencing ecstasy.

"Not until we are married and this time properly."

***

At eleven, that evening, we began to walk the dark streets. I chose our route that allowed us to avoid my school, that took us away from Pallosy's window, form his prying eyes and when I knocked on the church's small, rear entrance, we were promptly admitted.

"I am pleased to meet the two of you. Once your witnesses come we shall proceed. In the meantime I need some information." The kind man of God sat down by his desk and offered us a seat.

"I have two registers; in them I record all weddings and baptisms. One is for the authorities, be they church or secular. The other one is for people like you...So many of my flock is in danger...The farmers and the very few self employed Roman Catholics dare to get married openly or to baptize their children, but so many more, those who are employed by the State, do these things, like you do, in total secrecy. My bishop and the higher ups, forbade us to perform such secret ceremonies. 'A civilian wedding must be followed by an open church wedding, within a few hours and before the marriage is consummated...No baptism for any child who was born out of wedlock.' Those are the edicts we were given, but the edict givers are not very pragmatic. This is a country where these secret ceremonies must be performed...Now that I told you these things, I think you understand what made me reluctant first and why I must insist on total secrecy.
Now please let me have your names and that of your parents, including your Mothers' maiden names."

We gave everything he required and when he had all the information needed, he began to fill out a paper.

"While we wait for the arrival of your witnesses, I will fill out your wedding certificate. I will not sign it until the wedding is over. When you made your vows, I will affix my signature, hand it over to you and I suggest that you keep it in a safe place. Ah, I hear them knocking." He went to the door, his black vestment rustled with his rapid movement.

He led the four of us toward the altar, illuminated only by the red light given out by the everlasting oil lamp. He made Rozsa and I stand beside each other. Maris beside Rozsa and Pista beside me.

"I think we are ready...," he smiled at the two of us in the flickering red glow.

"Dearly beloved. We have come together for the marriage of Rozsa and Laszlo. May they continue to deepen their life with each other. We are gathered here..." His words, dictated by long tradition, he spoke clearly and with great emotion and I forced myself to forget, at least for the moment, the hated pictures, the empty lies that Rozsa and I experienced on the tenth of January.

"Marriage begins in the giving of words. We cannot join ourselves to one another without giving our word. And this must be an unconditional giving, for in joining ourselves to one another we join ourselves to our Lord, to Jesus Christ and to the Holy Church. Rozsa and Laszlo, we live at a time when very little in life is considered sacred. One thing must remain so, however, that is an agreement between two people. This day we celebrate a sacred agreement between the two of you. We live in times that are beset with problems. This marriage is not to be an escape from the world, but it is to be a commitment to greater service to the world. You shall not exclude the world but include it in your love. Together, in this marriage, you shall contribute more fully, for you shall be more full.

"Rozsa, Laszlo is God's gift to you, but he is not a gift for you alone. It is God's will that in your love, this man might find within himself a greater sense of who he is meant to be. You are asked by God to see the good in this man, to accept him for who he is and who he shall be, that thus he might be healed and made strong. In this way, God's purpose shall be accomplished in this relationship. May this man find, literally, the reign of heaven through the love you share.

"And so it is with you also, Laszlo, that although Rozsa is God's gift to you, she is not a gift intended for you alone. You are asked by God to so love this woman, that in your love she might find herself as God has created her, so beautiful and strong and brave and true, that the entire world might be blessed by the presence of a woman who shines so. May she relax in your arms as she has never relaxed before. May she know, from now on, that there is one whose love she can depend on forever.

"Courtesy and consideration even in anger and adversity are the seeds of compassion. Love is the fruit of compassion. Trust, love and respect are the sustaining virtues of marriage. Trust, love and respect each other.

"To both of you, I enjoin you to release at this time all impediments to your joy. In this moment may you forgive each other any past transgressions, that you might enter this marriage reborn. Allow the waters of forgiveness to wash you clean. You are given the chance to begin your lives again this day, as God grants you renewal through the power of this commitment.

"Now please repeat after me:

"I, Laszlo, take you, Rozsa, to be my wife...," I repeated the words of the priest with solemnity. Then it was her turn.

"I, Rozsa, take you, Laszlo, to be my husband, to be my partner on my path, to honor and to cherish, in sorrow and in joy, till death do us part."

"Now Rozsa and Laszlo celebrate their love and proclaim their union with rings of precious metal. The precious nature of their rings represents the subtle and wonderful essence they find by losing themselves in each other, and the subtle and wonderful essence they find individually, through their mutual love, respect, and support. The metal itself represents the long life they may cultivate together, not only in years, but in all the infinite dimensions of each moment they share." The priest blessed the rings and I read the text he gave to me.

"With this ring, I give to you my promise that from this day forward you shall not walk alone. May my heart be your shelter. And my arms be your home. May God bless you always. May we walk together through all things. May you feel deeply loved, for indeed you are. May you always see your innocence in my eyes. With this ring, I give you my heart I have no greater gift to give. I promise to be the best partner that I can be. I feel so honored to call you my wife. I feel so blessed to call you mine. May we feel this joy forever. I thank God. I thank you. Amen." After I finished, I handed the text to Rozsa and she began to read.

"With this ring, I give to you my promise that from this day forward you shall not walk alone..." I listened to her sweet voice and my heart filled with joy.

"Now that Rozsa and Laszlo have given themselves to each other by solemn vows, with the joining of hands and the giving and receiving of rings, I pronounce that they are husband and wife, in the Name of God the Creator, and of God the Creative Offspring, and of God the Creative Presence. Let us pray.

"Eternal God, creator and preserver of all life, author of salvation, and giver of all grace. Look with favor upon the world you have made, and for which your Son gave his life, and especially upon this man and this woman whom you make one flesh in Holy Matrimony.

"Give them wisdom and devotion in the ordering of their common life, that each may be to the other a strength in need, a counselor in perplexity, a comfort in sorrow, and a companion in joy.

"Grant that their wills may be so knit together in your will, and their spirits in your Spirit, that they may grow in love and peace with you and one another all the days of their life.

"Give them grace, when they hurt each other, to recognize and acknowledge their faults, and to seek each other's forgiveness and yours.

"Make their life together a sign of Christ's love to this sinful and broken world, that unity may overcome estrangement, forgiveness heal guilt, and joy conquer despair.

"Give them such fulfillment of their mutual affection that they may reach out in love and concern for others.

"Grant that the bonds of our common humanity, by which all your children are united one to another, may be so transformed by your grace, that your will may be done on earth as it is in heaven.

"Please kneel down front of me. Now you will feel no rain, for each of you will be a shelter to the other. Now you will feel no cold, for each of you will be warmth to the other. Now there is no loneliness for you; for loneliness no longer exists. Now you are two bodies, but there is only one life before you. Go now to your dwelling place, to enter into your days together. And may your days be good and long on earth.

"God the Father, God the Son, God the Holy Spirit, bless, preserve, and keep you; the Lord mercifully with favor look upon you, and fill you with all spiritual benediction and grace; that you may faithfully live together in this life, and in the age to come have life everlasting. Amen."

The devoted, skilled, understanding priest, finished and he extended his congratulations and his hand to Rozsa and me.

We sneaked out of the church, clutching the paper that attested to what we did and having murmured our thanks to the man of God and to our witnesses. Arm in arm, we walked in the darkness, but our hearts were at last illuminated.

When I struggled, more than forty-four years later, trying to recall all the kind words of that daring, great man, I was forced to cheat. His words and ours were long forgotten, but never their meaning. Time consumed those words like rust consumes iron, so I committed to paper all the words, in my old age, in my fullness of maturity I would have loved to hear.

Chapter 12

When May arrived, the flowers began to bloom and our love blossomed. Rozsa's daily trips to her work place and back to me gave me pain and joy. The manner of our morning parting never varied. Words of good-by and parting kisses were on the morning menu, and when evening came, we found our joy, as we found each other. During the early evening hours we ate our meal with Maris and Pista; went to visit some of our friends, and when we returned we closed our door, pulled in the curtain, exchanged our day's stories, as well as impassioned kisses.

Time passed with great rapidity and we had little to worry about, we were happy, we were together and my only fear, concerning the party secretary and his request, greatly diminished.

As was our usual practice, Pista Janics gave me the signal and within minutes we were at our brook.

"I have good news for you. I think you will be delighted," Pista told me.

"Good news is always appreciated."

"The party secretary of our village was demoted," Pista announced.

"Demoted? That is superb. What happened to him?"

"He lost his position. I heard that people complained bitterly about his cruelty; about his making too many enemies for the State, but that alone would not have done him in. His greed, his selling building materials and pocketing the money that belonged to the party, was his real undoing. He was sent back to the mine, where he worked for years as a miner. So what do you think of that Laszlo?"

"I am grateful to you for telling me and I am happy that he is gone. I was afraid that he might force me to do something that wouldn't be to my liking."

"Would you have become an informer, if he pushed you?"

"I really do not know. We never know what we are willing to do to protect the people we love. I am so happy with my wife, Rozsa, that I probably would have done almost anything to protect my love."

"You are truly lucky Laszlo. You married for love; you have a lovely wife; not like I."

"What you said Pista is all true, but Lenke is a nice woman too."

"She was never that, you know Laszlo. Well, maybe when we had our wedding. When she was my bride, when she stood front of the priest, with me beside her, I thought, but only briefly, that I am a lucky man. But that all changed within days and I have begun my philandering."

"I didn't know that you two had a church wedding."

"We sure had, but that was years ago. Many things have changed since then. Pallosy wasn't around and practicing our religion required no daring. In this new world very few people dare to stand up. Hardly anyone is brave enough to defy the authorities."

"We did...," my words slipped out.

"You did? I truly doubt that. You wouldn't want to put your future in danger?"

"Well, we didn't do it openly, not like that."

"I really do not understand."

I was about to change the topic, but I have recalled many of our conversations, none of which I had reason to regret and was overwhelmed by need to tell someone. I began with the promise we made to Rozsa's parents and then slowly, carefully, I told Pista about the time, the place, the priest and the ceremony.

"Thanks for trusting me, once again...There are so few who can be trusted. I am happy you kept your promise to your in-laws."

"That promise I kept, but we have made another one and neither of us are experienced," I admitted shyly.

"And what was the other promise?"

"For at least two years we will have no children." Once again I confided.

Pista began to take me under his wing and before our conversation ended, he expressed his hope that the advice he gave me was still timely.

***

We were about to finish the first school year and I was ready for the State examinations, when Rozsa stepped off the train. Her steps were no longer sprightly; her face looked drawn and pale.

"Is something wrong my darling?" I asked her before we took a single step.

"I really do not know. I feel weak and exhausted."

"Maybe it is that time of the month?" I asked her, hoping that nothing else was wrong.

"Take me home...There we should talk."

We entered our room and she burst out crying.

"For four days now I got sick to my stomach, during my morning train trips."

"Maybe you caught a bug? Maybe it is the influenza? Many of my students get sick every day." I tried to console her.

"And maybe it is something else."

"What do you mean?"

"You asked me earlier Laszlo if it was that time of the month. It is not that. Last month it didn't happen and this month it didn't come either."

"But how could that be?"

"I don't really know. We were always so careful."

"My darling we must go and see a doctor. Tomorrow please. I will go to Baja, in the afternoon and I will be with you. We must do this."

"Yes, I think we better do that," she told me and she lay down, not even wanting to eat her supper.

***

"Please come in," The doctor told Rozsa and I paced the corridor, then I went outside to wait for my darling.

She came out of the building, rushed to me, her arms around my neck and she whispered in my ear.

"We are going to have a baby."

I was first flabbergasted, then as I looked at her beaming face; as I saw her happiness, I began to cheer.

"I am truly happy my dearest. I hope it will be a sweet little girl. I don't want a boy."

"We will have what the Lord gives us. Maybe after the church wedding He decided to bless us. It must have happened within two weeks...The doctor seems to think that I am seven weeks pregnant. He was amazed...After the examination he told me that it is a miracle that I could conceive at all, considering what he observed."

"I hope he didn't find anything wrong?"

"No, nothing is wrong. I am just going to have a baby."

From that moment on we began to talk about the sweet little girl, who will enter our life and make it even dearer. We never doubted that our child will be a girl and Rozsa began her preparations accordingly. Everything she knitted was in pink; every word she spoke was full of love. Our joy would have been complete, but for her morning sickness, that completely wore her out and my concern about how am I to tell her parents. After one more week of watching her suffer, I asked her the question.

"Would you be willing to move back to Baja?"

"But that would mean giving up living here," came her answer.

"It would mean that, but there is no other solution my darling. I will not let you suffer like this. I can't stand the thought of you traveling any longer."

"But where could we go? You know that it is almost impossible to find an apartment."

"We should go visit your parents and mine too. We should announce the splendid news and ask for their help. We will do that after I return from Szeged. Once I pass my State examinations, your parents will be proud and understanding."

***

The grueling exams I had passed with flying colors. It pained me that I never met up with any of my former friends, but they were scheduled to appear a few days later and I wanted to rush back to my precious wife, to the Mother of our child, whose arrival we guessed to be sometimes in February. At the station, while waiting for my train to take me to Baja, I bumped into a former classmate of mine. We sat down together and began to talk.

"How was your second stint in the army?" I asked him first.

"That was dreadful. I was, like all other of our classmates, in a machine gun unit...But it must have been the same for you."

"I was never called up," I told him with a twinge of guilt.

"You were really lucky Laszlo. After two months of constant exhaustion, abuse and other things, we became sub-lieutenants. I wished they kept the rank and allowed our summers to be free."

"I remained only a corporal," I told him.

"But you were free. Have they called you up for this summer?"

"No, I never heard from them."

"You are a lucky bugger Laszlo. I was called up again. That is where I am going now. I don't cherish the thought in spite of my coming lieutenancy." I heard him, but not with envy and I decided to change the topic.

"Have you seen professor Kobor?" I asked him and felt great regret that I didn't take the time to look up that kind man.

"I haven't seen him, but I heard a great deal about him."

"What have you heard? Is he well?"

"He is really well and guess what...He got married."

"Married? I cannot believe that. He was devoted to his teaching; to his research. He had no interest in any woman."

"That is so, but he is also stubborn. Did you know that?"

"What does his stubbornness have to do with him getting married?"

"Do you remember that girl in our class, who had a bad heart condition?"

"Yes, her name was Eva. What about her? Tell me fast, my train will be soon leaving."

"Eva was ordered to teach at a small settlement school, where there wasn't even a doctor. Professor Kobor tried to change that. The Minister of Education refused his request for a better assignment for Eva. That was after we had left. Kobor tried again and again, I heard, and when he was unable to change the mind of the government, he married Eva and sent in his resignation. Within days the Minister called him to appear before him. He demanded that Kobor remain at Szeged. By then, according to the story I heard, Kobor did a great deal of research of our laws. What he discovered, he shared with the Minister. 'Husband and wife, if both teachers, must be given positions within a radius of twenty miles.' The law stated and Kobor took advantage of that. The Minister was outmaneuvered and Eva was transferred to Szeged."

"Well I be damned. I always knew that Kobor cared for all of us, but to marry someone not for love, but out of obstinacy is hard to accept," I stated.

"Kobor is a dedicated, caring, wonderful man. To teach young people is his devotion. To change the Minister's mind; to assist Eva with her medical problem; to beat the system took such a great man."

My class mate barely finished his story, when my train rolled in and I hopped on it with thoughts of that kind professor, that dedicated, unselfish, wonderful man.

"I hope some day I can be a teacher like him: beloved by all; respected by many; touching each life as we come in contact," I told myself as I sped toward home, missing my dear Rozsa.

***

The four of us sat in the kitchen and before we had a chance to inform Rozsa's parents, Mrs. Buja spoke up, giving voice to her dread.

"My dear daughter what happened to you? We didn't see you for a whole month and now you look quite different."

"Rozsa suffers from motion sickness...The train ride every morning..." I came to her rescue.

"If that is the case, you should move back here. I will not have my daughter suffer such inconveniences." Mr. Buja looked at me sternly.

"That is what we came to talk about. I want us to move...I can't stand Rozsa traveling in her condition...I should be doing that."

"In her condition? Whatever do you mean?" Mrs. Buja probed.

"We kept our promise to have a church wedding, but that other promise..." My voice died off.

"Are you telling us that Rozsa suffers from more than motion sickness?" To Mrs. Buja's question I nodded my head in agreement.

"Is it true Rozsa? Are you expecting?" Mr. Buja looked into Rozsa's eyes and he needed no confirmation.

"I think we should be angry with you Laszlo...I think I should rake you over the coals and yet I will not do that. A child, at any time, is God's greatest gift. Your love created this child and we congratulate you. Let's hope the baby will be healthy. May God grant that Rozsa have an easy pregnancy. We love you both and soon there will be one more person to love, to adore, to cuddle, to take to our heart. Maria and I look forward to the blessed event."

My relief was greater than I dared to hope. Rozsa's face regained its radiant sweetness and began to shine with a new intensity.

"I want...No, we want you to move back here immediately," Rozsa's parents announced concurrently.

"We will be happy to do that...I am so grateful for your understanding. Thank you both for not being cross with me," I spoke in relief.

"Having a new addition to any family is a joyous event. Instead of being cross we will have a celebration. Didn't I tell you Laszlo a long time ago that 'In your happiness you would promise anything. It is easy to make promises, but promises we cannot always keep.' Do you recall that?"

"I do recall...You said that when you gave us your blessing." I tried to prove that I have not forgotten.

"That is so my son and daughter...Promises we cannot always keep," Mr. Buja told us very calmly, yet with a great deal of sadness.

"I think we should go and inform my parents."

"Do that and afterwards we will expect you for a nice supper."

***

My parents received the news calmly.

"Congratulations Rozsa and Laszlo" my Father kissed her and shook my hand.

"Congratulations indeed," my Mother came next. "It will be so nice to have a baby. I will love her, like I love Gitta. I am glad you have decided to move, but why go back to that one room?"

"There is no alternative," I informed her.

"That is what you think. Manci and her husband, Istvan, were sent to another city to work. Their apartment of a kitchen and bedroom are fully furnished. There the two of you would be more comfortable and this place would be much closer to your work place Rozsa. You would be close to us and we could help. It is not easy to look after a child and to go to work. Think about that."

I couldn't believe our good luck. We were concerned about finding a place and suddenly we had two offers. I saw the wisdom of my Mother's suggestion, but I had no desire to hurt Rozsa's parents.

"May we think about it Mother? We should discuss it with Mr. and Mrs. Buja. I come to think of it, should we not ask Manci and Istvan?"

"Leave that to me, you don't need to do that."

***

The supper celebration was a splendid affair. Good food, a bottle of wine, friendly talk and no disagreements. Rozsa's parents saw the wisdom of my Mother's suggestion and within an hour we settled everything.

The following weekend we said good-by to our friends, Maris and Pista. We promised to see them often, to maintain our friendship. With our inconsiderable belongings we moved into the two room flat. I took a summer job for four weeks, at a distant collective farm; borrowed my Father's bicycle to make my daily journey. The extra income we badly needed. I would have liked to work during the entire summer, but Pallosy had other ideas. For the entire month of August he made me appear at the school, where I had nothing to do, but to mind an occasional student.

In order to do that useless, unnecessary task, I was to get up five in the morning to catch the unreliable train and I was able to return home, mostly in the late evening. Once more my services were volunteered to the local government, but not by me. Pallosy took great pains to pay me back for my 'peace bond betrayal'.

Then the news came that my Aunt and Uncle were returning to Baja, thus needing their apartment. We were on the move again and we were back where we started.

"Do you remember our first night together, in this room, my darling?"

"I will never forget Laszlo. This time however we are without hams, slabs of bacon and sausages." She smiled at me, as she reminded me of the spicy night and she and I and our little daughter to be, occupied a newly acquired, bigger bed.

A few days before I was to begin the new school year, Mr. Buja invited me to join him for a Sunday fishing.

We baited our hooks and cast our lines into the fast flowing current. We were silent for a few minutes and then he turned to me.

"I didn't want to tell you this, front of the women. I am in terrible trouble. I don't know how much longer I will be able to hold out. I told you, some time ago, that over a year ago I was to make reports on the progress of our building activities. I did that, in a half hearted manner, but what the secret police agent wants now I am not willing to deliver." He fell silent.

"What does he want you to do? Do you want to tell me Mr. Buja?"

"I will, but why don't you ever call me Father?"

"Father..." I tasted the word and it wasn't to my liking. "Could I call you Dad, instead?"

"I would like that. Now back to what I was going to tell you. Joe, as you remember, joined our construction firm, not long after I became established. I should have been wiser...I should have never gotten him the job...But that was my mistake, for that I cannot blame him. He is young, has an eye for girls and that got him in a great deal of trouble. Many months ago, before he was drafted in March of this year, he was delivering a small payroll to a distant job site and he met a fetching, willing, young girl. She convinced him to go with her to Budapest and there the two of them spent most of the money. When little of the payroll remained, some five days later, the girl dropped out of sight and Joe came home, asked for my help. I didn't have the money to replace what he misappropriated, but he is my Son, I couldn't let him go to prison. I went to see my boss and he promised to help me. The secret police agent came the next day.

"Up until then that unscrupulous scoundrel didn't have the upper hand, but after what Joe did, he didn't mince words, he spoke plainly. He told me how his female agent approached Joe; how she tempted him; how she seduced him; how she dropped him when her services were no longer required. Then he showed me the way I can save Joe. I am to visit a friend of mine, Balazs, we were in the army together. I am to slowly, carefully make him talk about his hatred for the Communist regime. I am to entrap him and when I succeed, I am to make my written report and Balazs will be finished. He will be tried for treason. I will have to testify against him. Those were the demands that were made and I was to deliver or Joe would spend a long time in prison." Mr. Buja's eyes bulged with the agony of his dilemma and he no longer watched the fishing rods; he cared nothing about the bites that came and went.

"What are you going to do?" I held my breath.

"I cannot let Joe go to prison and I cannot betray my friend."

"What will you do?" I asked.

"I have begun to plan."

"Plan what?"

"To escape from this country." His voice was hoarse. "We hoped to take you and Rozsa with us, but it will be a long and dangerous journey. We cannot do that, not now that Rozsa is pregnant."

"I am so sorry..."

"And so are we."

"And what about Joe? Will he join you?"

"I don't know. He is in the army. It is far more dangerous for a soldier to attempt an escape. Desertion is a crime, punishable by death."

"When do you plan to make the attempt?"

"We are at the planning stages...Lajos Miklos and I think that we may get a guide, but it won't be soon...Maybe not even this year. It all takes time; takes a lot of planning. In the meantime I will stall for time; I will visit my friend and drag out our conversations. I hope the secret police agent will suspect nothing."

"Thank you. I hope everything will turn out for the best...Dad."

That night we carried our empty fish bags home and our spouses were not happy.

***

I said nothing to my beloved about her Father's predicament.

"Let Dad tell her when he sees fit," I told myself and after much thinking I fell asleep.

The alarm clock jarred me awake, after what seemed a very short slumber. I looked at the luminous hand in the darkness and saw that it was only four o'clock in the morning. I was ready to fall back to sleep, when Rozsa spoke up.

"You better get up Laszlo..."

"But it is only four in the morning," I complained, my mind clouded with sleep, not understanding.

"You must get up. The train station is a long way from here." Her words cleared my head. I washed quickly, dressed, grabbed a piece of bread and munched on it on the way to the station.

"My circumstances became worse with the move. From my parents place the train station was only a mile away..." I told myself. "But from our new place it is almost three." Just for a single moment, I felt bitter, regretted what we did, but my bitterness was replaced with love and my mood brightened.

"My dear darling is with her parents. They will look after her; care for her. She will not need to travel on the train. Maybe she will not be sick. Maybe she will be, but less frequently. Time will pass...I hope her pregnancy will not be too hard...When the baby comes we will cherish her; we will play with her; we will provide for her; she will be a lovely little baby. How far away is February? Not even six months...The way time passes that time will come soon and Rozsa will be a Mother. She was always such a loving girl and even more loving after we became married. She will love the baby our love has created. It will be nice...We will think of nothing other than our happiness. The hell with the regime; the hell with the Communist party. We will lock our gate; we will close out the whole world; we will exist only for each other." My thoughts meandered during my long walk and when I reached the station, I got on the train and waited.

A few minutes later I saw Jancsi. Then Tery came with Magda and the three of them took seats in my compartment.

"What happened to you Laszlo? We thought you are still boarding with that old couple." Jancsi asked and I explained my changed situation.

Their congratulations were profuse. They spoke briefly about their summer and at greater length about other things.

"So you now live, like us, in enemy territory?" Magda asked me.

"What do you mean?"

"Didn't Pallosy tell you that he hates Baja and all of us who travel from that city?"

"He did tell me that he hates that city, but I never understood. Why does he feel like that?"

"Well that is a long story...His parents live there and so did Pallosy, until the deportations. When he denounced the nuns; when he rejected his religion, his parents cast him out. As far as they are concerned Pallosy, their Son, is dead. That is why he hates everyone who reminds him of Baja," Magda revealed.

"But that is preposterous," I told the three of them.

"You are wrong Laszlo...You have served, one year, under our esteemed principal. You put up with all his nonsense; you obeyed him in almost everything; you smelled his stink, quite often, and you consider what we told you preposterous? How much more proof do you need?" Jancsi asked me.

"I am sorry...I think you are right. That man is capable of anything." I no longer doubted what they said.

"That first August we enjoyed outwitting Pallosy. Then we lost you, but the three of us kept doing nothing less. Do you wish to join us again Laszlo?" Jancsi asked me.

"I think I better do that. I want to be home early, whenever I can, to look after my wife and a few months from now to take care of our baby." The train stopped at Bacsbokod, shortly after I made my commitment.

***

For two whole months the four of us practiced our deceit and Pallosy has never found out, or if he did, he never mentioned anything.

One day in four I was able to catch the early train and I was home long before Rozsa finished working. I used the time to visit Aunt Gizella and Uncle Jozsef, or when I didn't find them home, I went to see my Mother. Before four I walked to the Health Office building and there I waited.

It was the last Friday in October. The oak trees were shedding their leaves, covered every inch of the side walk and I kicked at them angrily, as I paced impatiently, up and down, front of the building. A few of Rozsa's co-workers came out the door and I approached them.

"Isn't Rozsa finished yet?" I asked one of the women and I imagined seeing a smile, a look pass between them.

"She will be quite late, I think," one of them spoke up.

"Why do you think that?" I had a miserable feeling.

"The chief of accounting borrowed her from Szantai. She has been with him since noon or so. They are closeted in his office." One of the women smiled at me and continued. "Maybe you should wait for her at home Laszlo."

"I will do no such thing," I announced with stubborn determination.

"Suit yourself. I think you will have a very long wait."

I paced up and down; I kicked at the leaves angrily and in spite of my better judgment, after two hours, I entered the building. I looked at the signs; walked the long corridors, until I found it.

"Chief accountant," I read and hesitated. I didn't want to bother Rozsa; I didn't want to appear jealous again, but my cursed nature wasn't going to be denied, I began my banging.

"Who is it? We are busy...," came the male voice and I didn't stop, until the door opened.

"Who are you? What do you want?" the tall, redhead demanded.

"I want my wife...I am Laszlo Lichter."

"Oh, you came to get Rozsa?"

"That is what I came for...She is not your slave; you have no right to keep her beyond working hours." My stupid complaints poured out.

"But she volunteered!" came his brief explanation. "And we are just about finished." He turned around and spoke to my wife. "Rozsa you may go...Your husband is here to get you. I seem to think that we can finish what we started, tomorrow if it is all right with you."

Rozsa came out. She looked sweet, in spite of her protruding tummy, but her eyes blazed with indignation.

"I am coming. I will get my things from my office. You can wait for me outside." Her words made me move. The manner of her speaking caused my regret.

"I am so sorry my darling. Perhaps I shouldn't have come for you?" I told her when she exited the building.

"Not the way you did. You humiliated me greatly. What did you think you were doing?"

"I have waited for you for over two hours. I heard from one of your co-workers what you were doing..."

"And what was I doing? Please tell me."

"You were in that guy's office...You were staying with him after the others left. I don't really know what you were doing."

"Here we go again. Your stupid jealousy took the upper hand. Look at me...You are my husband...It is you I married...It is your child I carry...Will you ever learn to trust me?" She spoke the words with tears in her eyes and I hated myself for her suffering.

"Please forgive me. I will never do this again." I reached for her hand and we walked the rest of the distance in sullen silence.

We entered the house, where our supper waited, and when we sat down by the table, beside my plate, I saw the letter.

"What is this?" I asked Mrs. Buja and saw her tears, as they rolled down her cheeks and noticed the paleness of Mr. Buja.

"We didn't want to open it. It is addressed to you. As you can see it was sent by the Military Draft Board." Mr. Buja could hardly utter the words and I tore the envelope open.

I felt the blood drain from my face and my shaking hand dropped the paper.

"What is it my darling?" Rozsa asked. Her anger, her humiliation, probably forgotten, she reached for my hand.

"I am being drafted...November twelve is the date of my call up, according to this paper." I announced the terrible news and Rozsa became sick to her stomach. I jumped to my feet, rushed out with her to the outhouse; I held her while she retched and when we rejoined her parents, to comfort all three of them I made my announcement.

"It is a mistake Rozsa, my darling. I will have it straightened out in a few days. I will not leave you...I promise you my dearest."

"I am sorry Laszlo, but you shouldn't make promises that cannot be kept."

"I will keep this one! I will go to the draft office and they will put things in order. I am not leaving my pregnant wife. I will not allow them to destroy our lives."

"I know you will try Laszlo, but you may be disappointed. Please do not raise false hopes. Rozsa has already enough problems. Joe's situation bothers all of us...Mine puts on us tremendous strain and now you, Laszlo, being drafted, well it is just too much to take," Dad announced.

"I didn't know, Dad, that you told Rozsa."

"One night I was terribly depressed. You came home around eleven. Before your arrival the topic came up...Rozsa heard something from her Aunt Gomori, that aroused her suspicion and when she asked me, I could no longer remain silent," her Dad explained.

"So Rozsa knows about what Joe did? She knows about your plan to escape? Have you told her when you will do that? Will all of us desert her at once? The thought of that makes me sick."

"We will try to take Joe with us, if we can...That has been decided. If he stays here, they will punish him, not only for what he did, but even for my duplicity. I told you before Laszlo that it will take a while to organize everything. Now with this new development I have no choice, but to promise our darling daughter that before her child's birth we will not make the attempt."

"You speak Dad as if I have joined the army already. I am telling you that I will beat the draft. I will move heaven and earth to stay with Rozsa. You will all see that I will not fail."

That night, when we sought our bed, we were closer than ever before. Our words of love were tinged with the pain of possible parting; every touch of Rozsa's hands sent shivers through my spine and I held her so close that I feared she may be smothered.

Saturday I approached Pallosy.

"I must take Monday off. I have official business to attend to."

"You will be here Monday and come to think of it, you better be here tomorrow for cultural activities."

"I can spend so few days with my wife and now you even try take my Sunday?" I challenged him.

"Am I trying? Is it what you said? I don't need to try, I am in charge and you will do as told, you stupid bastard."

"Why do you do this to me?"

"Think back lad...Remember the times you crossed me. You are my slave; I do as I please and besides, I hate the city of your birth and all its inhabitants. Listen to this...This is what I think of you." I heard the sound, smelled the expelled gasses and I left his office disgustedly.

***

The next day I rose, once again, very early. Caught my train; supervised a stupid political activity, that only five or so students attended and I rushed to the station to catch the one o'clock train, that pulled out, its whistle mocking me, when I was only a hundred yards away. My breath came in gasps; my legs shook with the effort of my running; my body trembled with the rage of anger.

I decided not to wait for the evening train, that would get me home close to eleven. I calculated carefully the extra hours I might be able to gain by walking home.

"I can walk three miles an hour...Four hours of walking will get me there. Even if I must take a half an hour rest, before six I will be with my angel. We will have five extra hours together." I figured it all out and began my trek.

I had hours on my hand to think. I thought about the draft letter. I thought about the possibility of it being a mistake. I recalled the time I shamed my military lecturer and began to fear that my drafting was the Hungarian Army's revenge. In order to chase away my gloomy thoughts, I thought about our courtship; our wonderful engagement; our wedding; the night that followed; our covenant, in the middle of the night, in the deserted church; Rozsa's pregnancy; the coming of our baby; my Father's hard life; how he lost his factory; how and why he was sent to prison on two occasions. Then my mind began to dwell on my new Dad's life: his military career; his switching to the River Police; his dismissal; his stints of being unemployed; the time he delivered newspapers and how even that job was taken from him. I recalled his happiness when he got the job as an engineer and his devastation when he realized that his two choices were reduced to becoming an informer or to plan to leave his homeland.

"All our joys were given by God and all our miseries by the new gods, the Communist plotters; the rotten spoilers. Pallosy is one of them...May God send His curse upon him! I will get even with that rotten man!" I promised myself, as I neared our home and forced myself to become composed before I faced my dear Rozsa.

"You look exhausted...When you didn't come home in the afternoon, I didn't expect to see you until late evening," she told me and gave me a sweet kiss.

I returned her kiss and told her: "I didn't want to be away from you, all Sunday. I walked home, my dearest."

***

Monday, Jancsi took my place and I got to Baja before two o'clock. I rushed through the streets, with my draft letter in my pocket and demanded to see the draft office's commander.

"What can I do for you comrade?" he asked me after we were seated.

I reached into my pocket, took out the letter and handed it to him, with words that I could hardly speak.

"It is a mistake, I am certain. Please take a look and tell me it is so."

"I see that we called you up. I also see that you are over twenty-one years of age and that you have not served your country in the military."

"That is not so...In 1951 I spent the whole summer in the military. I was promoted to the rank of Corporal. Surely you know that."

"Our records indicate no such thing," he announced patiently.

"But that is not possible. University students are exempt from the draft. Is that not so?"

"That is the usual way. They serve their time during the summers. Have you done that Comrade Lichter?"

"I told you...In '51 I did."

"And what about '52 and this last summer?"

"I wasn't called up. Is that my fault?"

"No, it is not, but someone, somewhere made a mistake."

"That is what I am trying to tell you."

"I understand. But you cannot blame us. We are not given the authority to deal with any of the university students."

"Then why do you deal with me?"

"You are no longer that," came his reply.

"So what can I do? I am married; my wife is expecting a child; she cannot survive without me. Please have compassion."

"Please understand that compassion I am not lacking. My hands are tied, unless you can straighten out the mistake, if that is what it is."

"How do you suggest I do that?"

"The mistake must have been made at Szeged. Isn't that where you attended university?"

"Yes."

"Well, the best advice I can give you is this. Go to Szeged. Speak to the commanding officer there and bring me a letter of exemption. I will be glad to act on it."

***

I walked home, full of hope and when Rozsa arrived I told her everything.

"When do you plan to go to Szeged?"

"I hope to do that tomorrow or the day after. I need Pallosy's permission. I think I know how to get it."

Tuesday morning I went to his office and when he allowed me to enter, I launched into my false story.

"I had a phone call from the Dean of the university. They are selecting candidates for this school year's top administrators. He wants to talk to me in person."

"But you Lichter are only a teacher. You are not even a vice-principal. Why would they want to talk to you?"

"The Dean didn't tell me, but I suspect that they are checking on a few principals, you may be one of them. I think that may be the reason." I lied, I mislead him and my carefully laid plan began to reap the benefits.

"My dear Laszlo, I cannot deny you this splendid opportunity. Let me call the train station, maybe there is a train you could catch before long? How long do you think you need?" His tone changed with great rapidity and I became not his enemy, not his betrayer, but his dear Laszlo.

"If I can leave today, by Thursday I could be back."

"Let me make the phone call." He reached for the only telephone, that we had in the whole school, and his face beamed when he made his announcement.

"There is a train Laszlo within an hour. You can be at Szeged early this afternoon. Remember any honor that may come this way is an honor for the whole staff, you included."

***

Four hours later I sat in the reception area, clutching my draft letter. The receptionist made me wait.

I sat there, my heart full of hope, with intense desire to clear up the terrible misunderstanding.

"You may go in...The Commander is now free," the female receptionist announced and I entered the office, my hopes almost shattered. The officer who received me was none other than the one who investigated my year and a half old treachery.

"Your name please and tell me what you want," came his command and I thought he didn't recognize me.

"Laszlo Lichter reporting, Comrade. Someone made a mistake in this office and I wish to bring it to your attention."

"What mistake?"

"I was a student here, between '50 and '53. I served in the military and I have received this letter by mistake." I handed the draft letter to him.

He read it slowly, shook his head and then he asked me to go out of his office and wait.

About thirty minutes later I was called in.

"I have examined your situation. I have discussed it with one of my officers. You are right..." My head was spinning with dizzying joy. I almost shouted with relief. "We will call the commander of your draft office, as soon as you have left. Rest assured young man you will be treated with due consideration. You may go now and thank you for allowing us to correct the mistake."

***

I was grateful to the great man. I ran all the way to the station; hopped on the first train and could hardly wait to share my joyous news with Rozsa.

"It is all straightened out. Just as I promised you my darling," I announced to her in the presence of her parents.

"What a relief. We are so happy Laszlo," Mrs. Buja shouted with joy. Mr. Buja shook my hand in silent congratulation and my dear Rozsa gave me her best kiss ever.

That night we talked long about the coming of our beautiful little daughter. I promised her to be with her every minute I can. I gave her my word that I will be a good father. Our joy was without bounds. Our relief made our togetherness sweet. We had no need to face another parting.

Next morning I went to the draft office, as soon as it was opened and I have entered with my spirits soaring.

"Good morning, Comrade." I was trying to be pleasant.

"You must have gone to Szeged, since I saw you last." The officer's words were not unkind, but his face showed something else. His face was white, his lips were drawn in a thin line, his eyes semaphored sadness.

"Did you get a call from my former commanding officer?" I asked him, knowing that he must have.

"Yes, I did. Yesterday afternoon," he told me, but said nothing else.

"I am glad the mistake is all cleared up," I announced and rose, ready to leave.

"I wish it was that simple." He took no pleasure in making his announcement.

"What do you mean?" Suddenly I was frightened.

"Your former commander called me, as I told you, but it pains me to tell you what he said."

"What could he say, other than what he told me? 'I have examined your situation. I have discussed it with one of my officers. You are right...We will call the commander of your draft office, as soon as you have left. Rest assured young man you will be treated with due consideration. You may go now and thank you for allowing us to correct the mistake.' Those were his exact words. Surely nothing more needs to be said." I tried not to lose my temper.

"He spoke the truth, yet he misled you. I am angry, otherwise I wouldn't tell you all this. Yes, he called. Yes, he told me that they have made a mistake, but the mistake was not in the draft call. He told me to make sure that you are not only drafted, but will serve out your full two years. He also told me that it is their wish not to allow you to get a soft job. 'Boot camp for that rotten scoundrel. Make him sweat blood...Make him suffer...' Those were his exact words. What did you ever do to deserve that?"

I sat there, listening to my two year prison term. My face drained of all blood and I was broken hearted.

"Do you want some water, comrade?"

"No...I want nothing anymore." I announced, forced my shaking legs to obey me and sought my escape. I went to the garden of Dery, across the street. Sat down front of our tree, where the enlarged, carved heart stood and I looked at the letters I carved there.

"Curse my nature...My mouth, my stupid daring, my blind desire to gain my fellow students' respect got me into this trouble. I have to leave my beloved for two long years...All the things I will miss...I will not be here to help her, to support her during her pregnancy. I will not be around when our daughter is born...I wish I was dead. My dear Rozsa would be free...How could I be so stupid? How could I have done this to my darling?" I blamed no one, just myself for my imbecility.

I sat front of our tree for a long time and when I could no longer stand my self-torture I went to visit my Mother and eventually Aunt Gizella. To both of them I announced the devastating news and their first reaction was that of anger. Later on their anger turned to offers of help.

"We will look after your dear wife. We will look after your dear little child, have no worry about that my Son," were my Mother's words.

"You can depend on us Laszlo. Jozsef has a good income, we will not let your wife starve, or your child either. Those two years will pass and you will be back. Your teaching position is secure. The day they discharge you will give all of you great joy." My Aunt Gizella assured me and I felt just an iota better when I went to wait for my Rozsa.

At four o'clock she came out of the building and she ran to me, to give me a chance to confirm the good news.

"Is the mistake really straightened out?" she asked me immediately and I didn't know how to tell her.

"Let's walk home my darling. There is no need to rush into this conversation."

"Are you holding back something Laszlo? You seem so pale, so drawn, maybe even angry. What is it my dearest? Surely you can tell me."

As we walked, I told her all that happened and with each bit of information I gave her, her hold on my arm increased, as if she never wanted to release me.

Later on it was Mr. and Mrs. Buja who shook their heads in disappointment.

"There is no end to the Communists' conniving. The commander at Szeged could have told you the truth, but that would not have served his purpose," Mr. Buja complained bitterly.

"Why do you think he did that?" I asked naively.

"He could have told you the news and gloated, but then he would have lost the advantage of letting you build up your hopes and ours. Those who have little hope cannot be robbed any longer. So the Communists constantly dangle hope front of us; they make our hope grow daily and that way they assure their enemies' bitter disappointment. That is what they did to all of us Laszlo."

"What hope do we have then?" I asked Mr. Buja.

"Hope is almost three hundred kilometers from here. Far in the west, between Hungary and Austria, stands the border some day we will cross. When we approach that 'fence of despair', we will face our lives' greatest challenge; once the Almighty helps us to cross it, that name will change, the 'border of hope' will be behind us."

***

Until November eleven I taught my students; said farewell to all of them, as I did to my friends, to my colleagues. My principal was another matter.

Within minutes after my return from Szeged, he called me into his office, where he treated me like a lost son.

"I am dying to hear what happened, Laszlo. Did you put in a good word for me? Am I going to be on the list of top administrators? Will this school be honored in any manner?"

"I lied to you," I confessed. I had no energy left to string him on. I had no desire to play games any more. My spirit was broken.

"You didn't do that Laszlo. You surely couldn't have?" He held on to the hope of undeserved recognition.

"I did lie, but now I must tell you the truth. I will be leaving your school. I have been drafted by the army." My telling him what happened to me made him first absorb the news, then came his gloating.

"I never swallowed your lie, you rotten bastard. I knew all about your real purpose for going to Szeged. The military asked for my advice and I urged them to draft you, to get you out of my sight. You will no longer be a teacher. You will rot in the military for two long years. You didn't want to part with your money to buy peace bonds, now you pay with two years of your life to defend our peace. Two of us can play this game and at playing games I am much better," he screamed at me, but I retaliated.

"Yes I know all about you...You sold me out, like you sold out the church, like you sold out your sisters." I turned on my heels and from that day on we never spoke until I approached the front door, at twelve thirty on the eleventh of November.

"Where do you think you are going? Your last class isn't over yet."

I brushed aside the big man with my puny body and without a word I opened the front door and with as much dignity, as I could muster, I left the flabbergasted man.

***

That night Rozsa and I shed many tears. We hugged each other like two lost souls in a life boat, shipwrecked with no hope of survival.

"When will I be able to see you Laszlo?" She smothered her tears against my chest.

"Rumor has it that new recruits are not allowed visitors in boot camp."

"And how long do you think that will last?"

"Some say three months and others say it is longer."

"Three months...That will be an eternity without you my darling."

"It will seem like an eternity, but once that time passes, you will be able to come and see me." I tried to cheer her up without any success.

"Three months from now will be February. The month of our little daughter's expected arrival. I doubt I will be able to travel. Where will you be?"

"I do not know, until I get there." I was angry, but not with my beloved.

"Can't you find out tomorrow, before they take you away from me my dearest?"

"I will try, but I dare not make any more promises."

"But I want you to make promises. I want you to tell me that you will always love me. I want you to promise me that you will be home when our daughter is born. I want you to give me hope that we will have a long and happy life together."

"My love for you Rozsa is as limitless as the heavens; as deep as the deepest ocean; as wide as the plains of Hungary; as intense as a raging fire storm. My love for you will never diminish, that I can promise you my darling, but my presence at the time of our little daughter's birth is not something I dare to promise. I will never again make promises to anyone, promises that I might not be able to keep. All I can tell you is that I will do my best."

***

The first rays of the November sun woke us, but we had no desire to rise. We clung together, trying to drag out the sweet moments before our bitter parting. The minutes ticked away and when there was no more time to spare, we rose, we washed, we ate, we packed and during all our activities I held her hand and looked at her deeply, trying to commit to memory her sweet face, her tiny nose, her blue eyes, every feature of my darling.

"It is almost ten o'clock. Aren't you supposed to report before eleven?" Mrs. Buja forced herself to remind me.

"We will be going in a minute...," I told her and the reality of our situation grabbed me. I checked my tears; I emptied my mind; I busied myself with a last minute check of what I was to take. "I have my identification booklet...Clothing I don't need...My tooth brush and other such items, I also have. What else do you think I should take Rozsa?"

"Take my picture...Take my everlasting love," she sobbed, but this time without tears.

"Those two things are always with me."

"Do you want us to go with you Laszlo? Maria and I?" Mr. Buja asked me.

"Thanks, but no thanks...I told my parents; my relatives not to come. Even if it seems selfish, I want to spend my last minutes with only Rozsa."

"Have it your way Son. We respect your wishes. When you get wherever they take you, write home immediately," Mr. Buja urged me.

"Will you be here to read my letter?" I asked him. He knew exactly what I meant and he gave his assurance.

"We will not leave Rozsa...Not in her condition. She is our daughter. We love her. We will care for her. Rest assured, Laszlo."

***

At the door of the large assembly hall that swarmed with new recruits the guards stopped us.

"You better say good-by here. Only those drafted are allowed to enter." I heard the disappointing news and the two of us stood there, unwilling to part and unable to stay together.

"Can you tell me at least where I will be taken?" I asked the guard and he shook his head.

"Farewell my darling," I whispered in Rozsa's ear and touched it with my lips.

"God go with you, Laszlo. Come back to me, soon."

"Keep well my beloved. Eat regularly. Take good care of our baby."

"I will not be alone Laszlo. When I touch myself there and feel her kicking, you will be with me, at least in my memory."

"And I will be with you every moment of my life. Remember that my beloved."

"Keep well, Laszlo. Make sure nothing bad happens to you…I couldn't stand the thought of losing you."

"I will be well, just very lonely."

"And so will I…," Her words were cut short by one of the guards. He reached for me, complained about us blocking the door, berated me for my tardiness and pulled me away from my crying Rozsa.

Our hands slipped apart with great reluctance; our fingers touched just for one more fleeting second and I turned my head to see her just once more, before the door closed behind me and I entered a new world, where I needed new skills to assure my survival.

***

Chapter 13

The confusion in the assembly hall and my wretchedness made my head reel with the unreality of it all.

Boys, not much younger than I, stood in small groups. Some of them cried, others whistled sad tunes, still others chatted and I, knowing not a single soul, stood there waiting. I listened to what conversations I could overhear, but learned nothing of importance.

"We will be taken to a faraway place," someone said and the boy he spoke to replied.

"You are crazy. Why do you listen to rumors? It serves no purpose other than to scare us."

"I heard they will take us to the Soviet Union," someone else said and the listeners raised their voice in unison.

"What stupid lie."

I feared before, to be far away from Rozsa, but now my fear turned into rage.

"The God damn Communists spread false rumors, just to make us suffer. I will not succumb to their lies; I will wait; I will take them on," I told myself and my waiting was over.

"Line up in a single file," came the order and I rushed to the head of the line, hoping to be the first to learn what will happen.

"Hand over your identification booklet," came the first order. I passed my red book to the officer and for the last time I glanced at its hard, front cover, that displayed the ugly emblem of the Hungarian Republic. The crossed hammer and sickle, with the five spiked star, stared at me and my old hatred ignited. The officer filled out a card, that gave my name and the number 'X 36874' and handed it to me.

"Now listen up... The card I hand out you must keep." The officer shouted. "In a few days you will be issued your military identification. When you receive it, you must keep it always in your possession. It will identify you as a soldier in the Hungarian Army. In order to travel you must also have a travel document. If you are ever found outside your unit, without this book and your travel pass, you will be treated as a deserter. The punishment for desertion is severe. The first twenty must line up there..." He pointed at a door and then he repeated his announcement.

I stood in front of the closed door and waited.

"They took away my identification booklet to prevent my desertion. Where could I go in this country? May be to Yugoslavia? The border is not that far...," I told myself and then my loss came clear to me. "On page eight of my booklet existed a special stamped notation. It gave the county where I lived. It identified the city where I was born; the village where I worked; the date it was issued; the official's signature and the red star with a number two beside it. That number entitled me to enter the twenty kilometer belt, still inside Hungary, that spread all along our border with Yugoslavia. In this manner the Government made sure that anyone who didn't live or work in that belt would not be able to get nearer to the border than the number designated. I heard from some people that beside Austria a number tree stamp was required and that meant thirty kilometers, instead of twenty.

"They sure take pains to prevent desertions," I thought and I cheered slightly. "If they take this great a pain to restrict us, there must have been a few attempts." The truth of what I thought I found sometime later.

"Five of you come in and strip. One front of each table," a soldier ordered us into the next room.

I moved to a table and there I waited.

"What are you waiting for? Strip completely. Everything you have you put on this table." The next soldier issued the order. I took off my clothing, placed them and my small, battered briefcase, on the table and when I stood in my underwear I spoke up.

"Is this really necessary? Why do I have to be completely naked?"

"Don't give me any lip. You are in the People's Army. You will do as you are told. Now get on with it."

I stood there naked, covering my private parts with hands and card, as I watched my few belongings being searched, then dropped into a cardboard container.

"You are a shy one...You will be cured, I assure you. Who is this?" He pointed at Rozsa's picture.

"My wife." I hated the officer for looking at my darling.

"Well that one is some fetching girl. I would fancy to show her my equipment..."

"Shut up! It is my wife you are talking about," I screamed at him.

"You better control your temper, soldier. I do what I want...You will not see her for a long time...She will forget you, just like other women did their husbands." His fat, gloating face, I would have liked to strike, but I used my brain, controlled my fist and curbed my tongue.

"Now move...Get into the next room," came his order.

"May I have her picture?" I asked.

"Everything you had now belongs to the army," he announced, still gloating.

"Very well then..."I thought angrily. "You broke us apart; you even took her picture, but you cannot take my brain; you cannot destroy my dignity."

I moved into the next room, where a doctor waited.

"Your card soldier!" His face, his words displayed boredom.

I handed the card to him, ever so carefully, not to expose myself completely.

"Take your hands away..." I did as he told me. "You are all right there. Now turn around, bend over and spread your cheeks." I obeyed him sullenly.

"You are completely fit, you are healthy. Stamp his card with 'Ka'" he ordered the clerk.

"Now move to the next room." He gave me my order and the card.

One glance at the card made quite clear what happened to me. Beside the 'Ka' stood the words: 'Fit for military service.'

I would have laughed out loud had I been dressed, had I not felt misery.

"One look at my private part and one look into my disposal system made me fit for this God damn army. This is what they call a medical examination. So be it. With one of my healthy parts I fill f...them over, whenever I am given the opportunity, with the other one I will drop on them whatever my bowels carry. After all, they determined them to be healthy." I felt slightly better having given thought to all my future actions and I cheered even more when in the next room I was given back everything.

Finally I was dressed; I was no different than when I said good-by to my darling. I sat down on a bench, in the long corridor, where we were made to wait for several hours, before the order came to have all of us form up, this time in a double column.

Two officers inspected us and located armed guards, on both sides of the column.

"You will be led to the railway station. You will be told when to board the train, then you will be taken to your destination," one of the officers explained.

"Are we going to get rations for our trip?" I asked, hoping to trick the stupid bastard.

"You get no food, until you get there. Less than two hours will not kill any of you. Now move out!" He gave his reply and the order.

I was elated. The stupid man gave me the answer.

"If they take us west, less than two hours will not take us beyond *Kaposvar* or *Sztalinvaros*. If we go east we will not reach beyond *Szeged*. The name of the city really doesn't matter. I will be only a short distance from my beloved." My first victory over stupidity made me happy; the small distance to our destination elated me, but it took no time for my cursed nature to turn my happiness, my elation into a painful discovery.

"They might as well take us to the end of the world. If we are not allowed to leave our unit; if we are not permitted to have visitors, does anything really matter?" My mind dwelt on this discovery and then I noticed our arrival to the railway station, that was always the place of our painful parting.

"I thought I was smart, but I was really stupid. Why didn't I think more clearly? Rozsa could have waited outside...She could have followed us to the station...Maybe we could have said good-by there? Maybe a final kiss we would have been able to give each other? Maybe we could have had a last hug to sustain me?" I cursed myself for my lack of proper planning, then I berated myself for my selfish thoughts. "Poor Rozsa would have had to wait for hours. No...I did the right thing...In her condition I am glad I didn't make her wait. She must be home by now...She must be crying...How could I let her know that I will not be far? I will write to her the minute we arrive. I will tell her where I am and I will inform her that we are not treated badly. Yes, I must not make her fret; I must give her hope and good news only." I closed my debate, as we began to board the train, that faced to the west and when it began to move, I stood by a window.

I looked at my beloved Danube, as we rolled across the bridge that spanned that majestic river. Far to the north I imagined being with my Rozsa, where we used to swim, where we have spent many happy hours. The train didn't stop at *Porboly*, it didn't slow down *at Bataszek* and later at *Szekszard*. My fear began to mount.

"What if that officer didn't take my bait? What if I didn't fool him into telling the truth? What if we will be taken far away?" My self-torture was born again and if I had the time I would have become miserable enough to do something stupid. Thank God that didn't happen...The train began to slow down and when I saw the sign '*Tolna*', my hopes were resurrected.

"Everybody out! Out!" the guards shouted the order and within minutes we began to march and entered the compound. From the moment the gate closed behind us, the pace picked up and many things happened.

We were assigned our bunk beds; over one hundred to each room. I put Rozsa's picture under my pillow and my briefcase on top of my lower bunk bed. Rushed to the spot where we were to line up. Entered the barrack where five barbers waited.

The hair of my fellow soldiers began to pile up, behind each chair. Red hair; black hair; blond hair and others littered the floor and as I waited for my turn, I was devastated.

Those who were given the three minute treatment stared in the only mirror that existed.

"Oh my God! You left nothing on my head," complained one of the soldiers.

"I did a good job. Didn't I? And I will do this to you every two weeks." The barber laughed in an uproarious manner.

"You are next." He pointed at me and I began my protest.

"You must cut the hair of every private. Isn't that so?"

"You got it right soldier. Take a seat."

"I am not a private...I am a Corporal. I think I will just skip this treatment."

"Show me your card," he demanded and I handed it to the butcher.

"It says nothing about you being a Corporal. When you can prove that to me I will leave something on. Now get in this chair...Others are waiting."

I sat down, rather reluctantly and as my black strands fell on the floor I have made my decision.

Next came the ugly, ill fitting uniforms. Then they issued our machine pistols, ordered us to line up under the stars.

"Now listen up. We need a few clerks, so if you meet our requirements you take two steps out. Everybody who graduated from high school, step out now."

I took two steps to the front, with several others.

"Let me see your card. You will do. Here is your assignment." The officer gave a paper to a lucky soldier. "You are to report to the processing office, over there."

The next three received the same treatment and I glanced at my card, but saw no special notation, so I felt quite confident that I will get the same treatment.

"Let me see yours," the officer stepped in front of me. "You take two steps back," came his order.

"But comrade I have attended university. I am better qualified than..." I wasn't allowed to finish my explanation.

"Your card has a corner missing. You are boot camp material. Step back and let me get on with my job." I stared at my card and saw that he was right, one of the corners was cut off and I had no choice, but to accept his verdict and to study the faces of all the lucky boys, who succeeded.

When late night came, I wrote a letter to Rozsa and gave her the good news of being at *Tolna*, no more than sixty kilometers from her, I estimated. Then I wrote another letter and gave my parents' address for the return mail. Finally I wrote one to my parents and informed them where I was and what I expected. Having completed the task I promised Rozsa and having taken the first step of the plan I formulated while the barber scalped me, I kissed Rozsa's picture and fell into an exhausted sleep.

***

Next day our cruel, demanding training began and I found myself at a disadvantage. The many farm boys and factory workers took the obstacles with ease, but I acted differently. I fell off the high bar; I dropped into the water ditches, we were to jump over; I couldn't scale the vertical wooden fences, no matter how others pushed me; I couldn't climb the ropes, in spite of our Sergeant's exhortations. There was not a thing I could do right, except what I accomplished during the free times, we had in the evenings.

I began to cultivate friendship with one clerk, then another, until I found the right one.

He was a simple boy, who attended a high school, but flunked his last year. He was impressed by my education and my constant efforts to help him. I went to his office many nights, helped him with the reports he was to prepare and in one week, I found out something that was to my advantage.

"My Captain is an uneducated man; he can barely write or read. So I have to do everything in this office. He has one passion though, he loves to play chess. He and I have spent a lot of time playing each other, but he grew bored with me for almost always losing. He loves a challenge, but he also loves to win."

"Too bad he is not here at night. I used to play chess and I think I could give him a beating."

"I could tell him...He is single...He is bored...Maybe he would stay?" my new friend made the offer.

"I would be grateful if you would do that," I told him and within two days he approached me.

"My Captain is looking forward to a game tonight. Do you think you can make it?"

"I wouldn't miss it for the whole world. Tell him I will be there this evening."

For several weeks, I spent almost every evening playing the Captain more cunningly than he knew. The first game, the two of us ever played, I won; the second one I lost to him. He was far from being a chess master. I made sure that the results of all games alternated. He kept meticulous notes on the scores and it took me little time to realize what he was doing.

"If he ever leads by one game, he will never play me again." I speculated and after I won a game, I made sure that I lost the next one, but never allowed him to take the lead.

***

Early in December the letter came that I have waited for over three weeks. My Father wrote very briefly, but what elated me most was what he enclosed from the office of the Minister of Home Defense.

That letter was very brief. It simply stated that my request to confirm my rank was received and the confirmation paper was enclosed.

I rushed to the personal office and gave the proof of my status. To my great surprise, without any argument, the stripes were given to me, but I didn't sew them on until later.

A few days later I have returned to the personal office; sought out another clerk, who didn't see the letter from the Minister of Home Defense and handed him my Military Identification book, that I have received a week after my arrival to *Tolna*.

"Please bring my book up to date...I recently was promoted." I made my simple request, depended on the carelessness with which most draftees worked.

"I will check your file. Please wait for a moment."

He came back shortly and made his announcement.

"Your file indicates that you became a Corporal on December 5, 1953." What he said was exactly what I hoped for, although the date was wrong, I have received my promotion in August of 1951.

"Can you make a notation in my military identification book? When I was promoted, that wasn't done."

"May I have your book comrade?" he asked, thumbed the pages. "Here it goes, on page seven." he announced and entered the note: 'Promoted to the rank of Corporal on December 5, 1953.'

I thanked him briefly. I didn't want him to know how greatly I have appreciated his service. That day I sewed on the stripes on my shoulder badges and all the Privates began to salute me. The barber no longer gave me the short version of what he considered a proper hair-cut and I began to cut my boot camp training.

***

Christmas Eve came and I was terribly lonely. I thought about my dear wife and my future little daughter all the time, but that evening, while playing chess, I pictured my darling and her parents around the Christmas tree. Even her dear letters, that came often, did not ease my pain.

"Check mate..," the Captain announced proudly.

"Indeed it is. You beat me rather badly." I praised him and hoped with all my heart that he will take me up on my coming offer.

"It would be so nice to be able to play with you, Captain, more often."

"We could do that if you became my clerk," he replied without any hesitation.

"Unfortunately, that is impossible." I took advantage of his love of a challenge.

"Nothing is impossible Lichter. If I decide to do something who will ever stop me?"

"I will. I cannot stand the thought of my dear friend, your present clerk, going back to boot camp. It would be unfair..."

"You just leave that to me," came his reply and I hoped for my Christmas present's delivery.

***

When the cold wind of January arrived it brought a heavy snowfall. The surrounding mountain tops glistened in blinding whiteness and my fortune changed.

"Come in Comrade Lichter..," the Captain called out and when I entered, he gave me the present I had waited for daily.

"Starting today you will no longer be cold; you will be my clerk. Now what do you think of that?"

"I cannot accept, unless..." He raised his hand and explained.

"My former clerk is gone. I have many friends and we stick together. The battalion's supply officer needed a clerk and he took mine, so this position is now open. Shall I look for someone else?"

"No. That won't be necessary. I will be delighted to work here and I will be looking forward to a few extra chess games."

He shook my hand, ushered me to my desk and began to explain the tasks my new position demanded.

"I hope you are good with percentages? All our reports require such calculations. My education is rather limited, I don't mind to admit. That is not my fault, but that of the former regime. Can you handle percentages?"

"I think I can and if I cannot I will learn fast, I assure you."

"What about typing? Preparing lectures? Maybe even teaching?" he asked and as I gave my answers, all in the affirmative, he expressed his delight.

"I think you will do a fantastic job. A far better job than my former clerk did."

"I promise you to do my best."

"It was a stroke of good luck that brought you here. I had a lot of difficulties with your predecessor. He was careless, made many mistakes and his chess playing gave me no challenge. Speaking of challenge, reminds me, that you will be challenged by many people. Officers will come to this office. They will demand things...When I am here I handle them, but when I am away, you are in charge Laszlo. Do you understand what I am saying?"

"I do and I don't. For example, if an officer gives me an order, when you are not here, can I disobey him?"

"It seems you are not very familiar with our chain of command. I will explain it briefly. A Private is at the bottom of the totem pole. A Corporal is just above him. Then come the other ranks, but I am sure you know that. What you don't know Laszlo is this: The chain of command goes from highest rank down, until it reaches a Private, but that is true only within each unit. When someone, from another unit, out-ranks you, let's say he is a Sergeant, who do you think has more power?"

"The Sergeant of course."

"Not true." He wagged a finger at me. "He is higher, as far as rank goes, but not in authority."

"Are you saying Captain that any officer, who is not in our unit, cannot give me an order?"

"That is exactly what I am saying."

"And why is that?"

"Well that is the way of our army. In each unit the highest ranking officer gives the order and that filters down to all soldiers under his command. Officers of another unit this way are unable to give contradictory orders, thus we avoid confusion. Do you understand now?"

"I do, but what does it mean? I am only a Corporal and if I refuse to obey a higher ranking officer's order, is that not subordination?"

"Outside this office it may be that, but in here and in my absence, you are the supreme commander." I listened to his words and I became what he told me.

***

Within days I was familiar with all forms, practices and knew about my Captain's wishes, even before he announced them.

When he gave me a topic to prepare a lecture on, be it the Bolshevik Revolution or a Party Congress, I sat down with the books I took out from the library, I reached for the ancient typewriter, and within hours his lecture material was ready.

For a while he made me attend the political lectures. I sat with the other soldiers, while my boss, my fellow chess player, read the words, written by me. I chuckled with amusement when he stumbled on a strange word that was not in his vocabulary.

"My clerk's handwriting is awful. Half the stuff he put on paper from my rough copy cannot be deciphered," he announced and gave me a look of apology.

Later he came to the office and put his look into words.

"Sorry Laszlo for blasting you...I had no other choice. I came to a conclusion: Would you like to lecture in my place? It would give me more time and your contribution would be greatly appreciated."

"I give it a try, if you wish. It would be just like teaching. I really miss doing that."

"Do you really? I think I can do something about that. We have upgrading classes in many subjects. What did you teach when you were a teacher?"

"Mathematics, chemistry, and I could even teach physics."

"Well I might not be able to do much about the last two, but it would be nice if you would be willing to teach math."

Within a few days I was not only a Corporal, in charge of an office, but a lecturer of political science and instructor in mathematics. Had I not missed my Rozsa; had I not worried about her high blood pressure, she wrote about, I would have been a truly happy man. I lectured, I taught, I did the office work; I slept on the cot beside my table, but never gave up my bunk in my barrack.

One day my Captain scratched his head, while he worked on a report.

"Can I help you?" I asked him.

"I wish you could, but this report is highly confidential. Every second day, I struggle with this combat readiness document, but for the life of me I can never get it right." He admitted.

"Are you sure I cannot help?"

"I cannot risk it. Someone might pop in any time and if they discover that will be the end, not only for me, but even for you Laszlo."

"I could do it during the night. I sleep here. I could lock the door and nobody would be wiser." I saw him ponder the offer and when he accepted, he locked the report in the safe and gave me the combination.

"Are you sure Laszlo? You know it must be ready by eight in the morning."

"I am sure and you have nothing to fear. It will be completed and will be back in the safe when you arrive." I promised him and the two of us became partners.

***

When night descended, I locked the door, opened the safe and removed the folder.

"Strictly confidential!" The stamped words glared at me and just for a few moments I thought about the irony of it all.

"I hated at university our political lecturers and I became one. No conviction needed to fool the masses, just words and lies and distorting of facts. Well they have made me what I am. No longer a Private, being punished for mocking my military instructor at the university, instead a Corporal and an instructor. They hoped to make me sweat blood and instead I am more comfortable than most soldiers in the army. They wanted to punish me, but they didn't succeed completely. The distance from my darling is my only punishment. Not being able to see her is punishment enough. I will continue to manipulate my superiors. I will find a way to return to my beloved." I cut my reverie short and turned my attention to the document.

"The questions are simple...The calculations no more difficult then I gave my students..." I observed and set to the task of answering each question, doing all the necessary calculations. An hour later, I double checked all my answers and when I was satisfied that there were no mistakes, I returned the file into the small safe.

"Tomorrow morning my Captain will be anxious to find out if I succeeded. What should I tell him?" I asked myself and weighed my options. Then I sought my cot, lay down, gazed at Rozsa's picture and I imagined being with my lonely darling.

"She must be asleep. I hope her blood pressure is under control. Oh, how I would love to hold her; to kiss her; to embrace her. How I would love to feel our dear little girl's kicking. Could I somehow talk my Captain into a transfer to Baja? I would be able to be with her during her labor. I could comfort her; care for her; cheer her up when she is sad. But that is impossible. I have worked for this man only for a few weeks. Surely he would not let me go." I kept thinking about ways that would allow me to be with my darling and when I woke early the next morning, I knew that somehow I will succeed.

"How did you do Laszlo?" the Captain couldn't hide his anxiety. "Is it done? Did you complete it?"

I was ready to tell him that it was a breeze, but to avoid making him feel mediocre, which he was, and to put him in my debt, I lied smoothly.

"I started around ten...It was a hard, difficult, complicated document to grapple with. By three in the morning I was ready to give up, but I couldn't let you down, so I worked until five. I finished it and double checked everything. I think you will be pleased."

"We will see," was all he said and removed the document from the safe, glanced at it and went to pass it to the battalion commander.

Two hours later he returned and his face sported a wide grin.

"You did a fine job, Laszlo," he announced, still beaming. "The battalion commander, his chief clerk and the Secret Police Officer spent an hour scrutinizing my report and when they finished they shook their heads. They told me that there wasn't a single mistake, that the quality of my reporting had improved greatly. Thank you Laszlo...I am so happy we have found each other. I dread the coming day when you complete your service, but that is far away. We will stay together until then." His words sent me into despair. My hope of ever getting a transfer lay in shambles and a few days later the Almighty's mercy touched me, granted me an opportunity.

***

My Captain and I finished our chess game. He beat me and his record showed that we were even.

"It is almost ten o'clock. I am getting tired. I think I go home," he announced, not wishing to be beaten in the next game and when he left, I locked the door, ready to retire.

The knock came first gently, then it became harsher. I opened the door and a stranger, a lieutenant entered.

"What can I do for you?" I asked.

"Tonight I will sleep here. All the officers' barracks are full. It was suggested that I come here. Now go...I shall retire."

"You may do that, but not here. This is my office. That is my cot and that is where I will sleep."

"Let's have no argument Corporal, I out-rank you. Your refusal will bring punishment for subordination."

"I am in command here...You are from another unit," I announced stubbornly.

"You are on dangerous ground soldier. Get out of here," he commanded.

"You may have to use your pistol to drive me out and even then you may not succeed."

"You are a difficult bastard. Why are you so stubborn? Why don't you go peacefully?"

"Had you come in here to ask my permission, I probably would have let you sleep here, but you came in here giving me an order and that I will not tolerate," I announced not without fear.

"Have it your way Corporal. Please will you let me sleep here?"

"Oh, that is much better. This is the way you should have asked in the first place. Now I will let you sleep here and I will sleep in my barrack."

"If I ever tell my friends at Baja how you defied me, they will never believe it." He stated calmly.

"You came from Baja?" I couldn't believe what he said.

"Yes, that is where I serve. I brought my ski team to your hills for two days of practice. It is good to be away from that cursed city." By the time he spoke those words, both of us were seated and we became more friendly.

"Is that city not to your liking?"

"You got it right. By the way, what is your name?"

"Corporal Laszlo Lichter. And yours?"

"I am Benedek Patkoi. My rank you know, I am sure, even if you do not respect it."

"I meant no disrespect comrade. I was told by my Captain that when he is not here, in this office I am the supreme commander."

"He is right of course. I should have remembered the chain of command. Had I done that we wouldn't have had this little conflict."

"You are absolutely right comrade. I always play according to the book."

"Good for you, Laszlo. Oh, I almost forgot that you asked me a question. What was it?"

"Is that city not to your liking? That is what I asked."

"Well, I don't think you would like it either. It is fine when we, officers, stay at our garrison, but when we go out for an evening's fun, trouble begins."

"What kind of trouble do you experience?"

"If I go to a watering hole and order a drink, I get the worst wine with spit in it. I saw a waiter do that, once and ever since then I have to go to private places. Bootleggers are the only people who do not hate us, officers, our money there is appreciated."

"What else?" I prodded him.

"If I go to a movie, I have to make sure that I am not alone. Even then I am attacked by the hoodlums of Baja. I hate to fight...Although, I give as good as I get, I must admit that I took a few beatings."

"Anything else?" I pushed him on.

"Now and then I went to a dance and asked a girl to dance with me. They like us; they are impressed by our uniforms, but when I try to see the same girl a second time, I am always getting the same answer. Someone in the city warned the girl not to see me. This is why I am so lonely. That city is no fun. It is full of danger. So the wise thing to do is to remain at my station. Play cards; have a few drinks; listen to some music, but I need more, those simple things don't make me happy."

"Would you like to be free to roam Baja? Would you like to be able to trust the waiters? Would you like to go to the movies without fear of getting a beating? Would you like to meet nice girls, who would not be harassed for seeing you?" I dangled my baits in front of him, like Mr. Buja taught me and when his reply came, I was ready to set the hook.

"Would I ever like to do all those things. But wishing is just that...Those things will never happen to me."

"Why not be optimistic? Let's assume that you meet someone who has influence in that city. Let assume that the man knows one of the most prominent waiters and could convince him to change a few things. Let's further assume that the man has many friends, he could influence them to give you the freedom of the city. Would that be to your liking?" I gave him my most enigmatic smile and waited.

"If such a man existed, I would make him my friend gladly. Give me his name and I will be in your debt for ever."

"His name is Laszlo and he is sitting right here," I revealed.

"I be damned. Are you telling me that you are from Baja? Are you trying to convince me that you could do all those things?"

"I was born and raised in Baja. My Uncle is a head waiter at the biggest restaurant there and among his peers he is well respected. I went to school with many of the boys in that city." I went on and on, telling him half-truths and complete lies, and when I finished, I hoped I didn't do all these despicable things in vain.

"How fortunate it is for me that I came to Tolna. I know it is too great a coincidence to find you here, but maybe, just maybe, we will become friends and if you are willing to help me, I would show my gratitude in some way. Are you willing to help me, Laszlo?"

"It will be my pleasure, but there is not much I could do from here." Out went the bait and I waited for the bite.

"You could write a letter to your Uncle...You could write a few to your friends at Baja...Maybe they would heed your advice? Maybe they would treat me differently?"

"I will be pleased to do that, but I cannot guarantee the outcome," I pulled the bait away slightly.

"Is there a way you could help me that would be more effective?"

"If I was able to talk to my Uncle; if I was able to talk to the boys; I could persuade them, that would be far more satisfactory."

"I might be able to arrange a few days leave. Would you like that Laszlo?"

I struggled greatly with this possibility.

"A few days with my dear Rozsa would be heaven sent, but to leave her again would give us nothing but pain. I better hold out...I will not sell my services for a mere morsel." I thought about it and announced my decision.

"A few days may do the trick. What might happen after I leave, I wouldn't be able to guarantee."

My new ally, the officer from Baja, looked at me and shook his head.

"I think I must agree with what you said. You have a commanding presence and guts. Just look at how you stood up to me. If there was a way I could get you transferred to Baja and keep you there, now that would be a better solution. Let me think..."I held my breath and prayed and waited.

"Why did I not think of that?"

"What?" I almost gagged on my single word.

"My drinking buddy, my regimental commander, Colonel Pasko is losing his chief clerk, shortly. I don't think he found a replacement yet. Would you like to become his clerk and my friend?" I swallowed hard. I became agitated by the opportunity presented.

"I never thought of that. My Captain will never allow me..."

"Forget that ,Laszlo. Pasko has great influence, where it counts. Your Captain will have no choice, but to accept when your transfer papers arrive. Are you willing? Should I act?"

I needed no more words. The hope he gave me, my dumb good luck was far too good to believe.

"Just a few weeks before the calculated arrival of my dear daughter and here I am being offered the chance of a life time. What am I waiting for? I have manipulated the former clerk of this unit; made him my friend; then I took his position. I have manipulated the personal office to record my rank...I have made almost everybody believe that I was an old hand in the army, not just a draftee of a few months. I handled this man from Baja to my own advantage and now when he has given me such an opportunity, I feel fear, I am hesitating. Why is that? I won't be able to deliver what I promised. When this officer realizes that I lied, he and others will be angry. Their retribution will be swift and without mercy." My realization and the consequences hit me hard, then I brightened.

"My Uncle will do what I ask, but the boys are another matter. I have so few friend in Baja...Who could I approach? Who could I ask for such a great favor? George, my brother...That is where my hope lies...He has many friends; he is a popular street fighter...He will help me and all will be well."

"Is there something wrong my friend? You haven't answered any of my questions. You are deep in thought. Maybe you have lied to me?"

His words woke me up. I rushed to repair the possible damage.

"Sorry... I was already making plans to protect you and in my enthusiasm I forgot to give you my answer. I am more than willing! I want you to act! How long do you think it will take?"

"Great...Then it is settled. Let me see. Two days from now I will speak to Pasko. He trusts my judgment. A week he will require to pull some strings. Ten days from now, I guess, you should have your transfer papers."

I thanked him; I made his bed and went to my barrack, but that night there was no sleep, just hope, fervent hope, anxiety and ten long days of waiting.

***

I worked each day, just to make the time pass and I played my Captain many chess games. When I began to lose, game after game, he looked at me strangely.

"Laszlo, is something wrong?"

"Yes, there is, but nobody can help me." I calculated what I was to say, to smooth my way; to gain his sympathy.

"Try me...You told me so little about yourself, about your family circumstances."

"I am married, but that you know. My dear wife lives and works at Baja. She is the nicest person that ever existed and she is pregnant. In a few weeks, she will have our baby...I won't be there...That is what bothers me."

"Maybe I could get you a furlough? A couple of days I think I could manage. Do you want me to do that Laszlo?"

"I thank you for your kind offer, but I couldn't accept."

"You are a strange one, my clerk. You explain your misery to me, but when I offer my help you rebuff me. What is your game Laszlo?"

"I play no games, I assure you. It is just that my love, my wife was heart-broken when I left and I cannot put her through that again. Not in her condition. Can you imagine two days of happiness followed by months of misery? It is better if I don't see her at all, until I can return to her for good."

"Are you sure Laszlo that is what you want?"

"I am sure...If only you could do more..." I let my statement hang, unfinished.

"What more could I do? I am only a Captain and my power is not unlimited." He stated kindly and I smiled inside, thinking of the coming week and of my transfer paper.

***

Two days later a brief letter came from Mr. Buja. He informed me that Rozsa's blood pressure went haywire. She was taken to the hospital and the doctor informed them that she should have been there days before. The doctors were doing all they could to help Rozsa. When I grasped my darling's situation I thought of deserting; rushing to her; helping her; but my better judgment overruled what my heart desired.

Six days have passed and a wire came.

"Dear Laszlo stop. Rozsa had a lovely baby girl, stop. She had a very hard labor, stop. Baby is well, stop. Rozsa is recovering, stop. She will remain in hospital for several days, stop. Congratulations, Laszlo, stop. Your Dad, stop." I read the telegraph and tears of joy came to my eyes, but bitterness and disappointment soon replaced them.

"I got my wish dear God, for that I thank you. I am the father of a little girl and her betrayer. Why did I hold out hope for a transfer? Why did I not accept the furlough offered me? Why did you allow me to be such a fool? Why did you not guide me to make the right decision?" I spoke to Him; I held Him responsible, but all the while I knew that it was I who made the wrong decision and for that I began to hate none other than myself.

I worked hard and slept little, waiting, hoping for the passing of the remaining two days. When the eleventh day came and nothing happened, my despair began to grow. Another day passed, then one more and my work became sloppy; my chess playing became more erratic, and I no longer harbored hope.

"I should have known better...," I told myself. "Mr. Buja told me, I must remember what he said. He spoke about hope, but what did he say?" I searched and searched, until the words came back to me. 'Those who have little hope cannot be robbed any longer. So the Communists constantly dangle hope front of us; they make our hope grow daily and that way they assure their enemies' bitter disappointment. That is what they did to all of us Laszlo.' "Yes, those were his words and that is what that officer has done to me." I came to my conclusion and my shattered hope I shoved in the background.

Two days have passed since my hope disappeared, when my Captain came into the office with my transfer paper and his disappointment.

"I must think that you have betrayed me. Here are your transfer papers...Tomorrow you shall leave me. I should have known better..."

I was too elated to feel sorry for my mentor, but I felt that I owed him an explanation and that I gave him. I told him about the officer who came from Baja. I said nothing about how I manipulated him. I explained to him that the officer brought up the possibility of having him get me a transfer, but I mislead him, by telling him that I considered that possibility nonexistent. I saw his expression soften and waited for his coming words.

"I have the power to appeal the ruling," he told me and my fear came like a tidal wave, ready to swamp me.

"Will you do that?" I didn't have to pretend that I was in agony.

"Maybe a few weeks ago I would have done nothing less. At least that would have delayed you, if not prevent you from leaving, but after our conversation about your dear wife, about you becoming a father, I will not allow myself to become a vindictive bastard. I will let you leave tomorrow. See your wife; be there for the birth of your child. I hope this will make you happy."

"Thank you...I am really grateful, but my child was born a few days ago. I got a wire from home, from her Father."

"Yet you said nothing to me." His simple statement sounded like an accusation.

"No, I didn't. I was first elated, then I was bitter and disappointed, not having accepted your generous offer. So I didn't say anything."

"I think I have been manipulated by a master," came his reply and then his question. "Was I Lichter?"

"Do I have your word as a gentleman that you will not interfere with my transfer?" I asked him.

"You have my word, but there are things I want to know. Will you tell me the truth?"

"I will!"

"You had ulterior motives to make my former clerk your friend. Is that true?"

"Yes."

"You manipulated him until you were able to play chess with me. Is that so?"

"Yes."

"Did you throw a few games to make certain that either you led or we were even, whenever we played?"

"I did that, but you are not a bad player." I offered him something for his kindness.

"Don't patronize me young man. That I do not need. You became my clerk and my friend, yet you were constantly looking for an opportunity to leave me. Am I correct?"

"Yes, but it was my way of survival. My way of realizing my dream. I never did a thing maliciously."

"I know that Laszlo. Now let me see if I am on the right track. When that officer came from Baja, have you sucked him in? Have you manipulated him too, with some kind of promises?"

"I did that, but what choice did I have? My wife, my baby, my family will always be the first with me. All others can come only after."

"If I was a married man, I would do the same, under the circumstances. Very well Laszlo. You have answered all my questions honestly. I will get another clerk and I will miss you. I will even miss your conniving. Let's part friends. What do you say?"

I gave him my hand. I gave him words of thanks for all his kindness and for his understanding. After he left the office, I never saw him again and when dawn came the next day, I rushed to the railway station.

Chapter 14

I couldn't sit down. My impatience outweighed my joy, if that was possible, for I considered myself to be the luckiest man in the world. Being in the army no longer bothered me. In my ill fitting uniform, I stood by the window and counted the markers, as they fell behind me. The passing of each power pole took me closer to my beloved and to my little daughter, Ildiko. The name we have picked with great care, long before I left for the army. We never doubted, even for one moment, that we will be blessed with a little girl, who will use that name proudly.

"I hope Rozsa is well...I hope she didn't suffer too much. I hope my darling, little daughter is striving. I will see both of them soon and I will see them daily!" I told myself repeatedly.

From time to time, I reached into my tunic's pocket, took out my transfer paper, just to assure that I wasn't dreaming.

"Corporal Laszlo Lichter, is to report to Colonel Pasko, commander of regiment nine-one-zero-five on February 15, 1954 before five o'clock in the evening.

"Regiment nine-one-zero-five is located at the corner of Honved and Hajnald streets." I read the words, that swam front of my eyes; eyes full of tears, not only from the rushing air that came through the open window, but far more with the intensity of the love that swamped me.

"Not only did I get transferred to Baja, but I will be located only two blocks from my parents' place." I told myself and began to calculate. "This train will be at Baja by one o'clock in the afternoon. That will give me time to go to the hospital...Move train...Go faster...Get me to the city of my birth. Do not delay me." I urged the train on and it picked up speed, taking me closer to my heart's desires.

Whenever it stopped at a station, I urged it to begin to move. Whenever it slowed down, I cursed it for its sluggish movement. When it finally reached the Danube, I looked at the beloved river and I, a grown man, shed a few tears that joined the regal waterway.

The train barely stopped and I jumped off, rushed through the park and down the streets. I finally reached the hospital's gate. I found it locked and began to push the buzzer.

"What do you want?" came the gruff voice.

"I want to see my wife and baby," I shouted at the bearded man.

"They must be in the maternity building. Is that what you are saying?"

"Yes...My little girl was born five days ago. I want to see them immediately."

"You cannot do that. Visiting hours are in the morning and in the evening."

"You must let me in," I begged, I shouted.

"That I cannot do soldier. Surely you can wait a few hours?"

"I cannot wait. Can't you understand that? I haven't seen my wife since November. I have never seen my dear little daughter. I cannot wait, by evening time I have to report to my unit. Please let me in." I spoke the words with such desperation that the guard took pity.

"All right soldier. I will make an exception. But only a short visit. Do you understand?"

"Thank you...I will stay only for á few minutes. I promise," I told him and he swung the gate open.

I ran over the walkway and within a minute I was front of the building. My eyes took in its great bulk. It was built a few years ago and the carved inscription, just above the entrance, still amazed me.

"For a single girl, to give birth to a child is a glorious achievement; for a married woman it is simply a duty." I couldn't believe my eyes. My mind seemed to deceive me.

"How can this be? Have we lost all sense of morality? The Communists must be desperate. Men and women of this country have no desire to beget children. The population must be falling. This is their attempt to convince us to bring new slaves into this world. Will my dear little daughter become a slave, like her Mother and Father? No, I will not allow that to be...My Father-in-law is right. Where the border of hope stands, there lies our salvation." My gloomy thoughts left me, when I entered the building.

I asked a nurse for the room number and when I received it, I rushed to find it. The door was closed, but I hesitated not, I opened it and saw several beds and finally my dear darling.

She was asleep; ravaged by her illness and the pain of delivery. I studied her face. I filled my eyes with her features and the change pained me. Her cherry lips were like thin lines; her paleness scared me. She trembled in her sleep. One wasted hand came out from under the cover and touched her temple. I felt sad, guilty, devastated.

"What have I done to my beloved? Her parents warned us that she was too young to have a child. I should have listened to them. I should have waited." I berated myself bitterly, but her waking put an end to my misery.

She looked in my direction, trying to focus on what she saw.

"Please tell me I am not dreaming." Her voice was drowsy.

"You are not dreaming my darling, my sweetheart, my beloved," I told her and touched her hand. "I am here..."

"I dreamt about you coming, many times. Am I still dreaming?" she asked and I touched her lips with mine tenderly.

"I am here Rozsa." She finally realized that I was real.

"Yes, you are really here Laszlo. Please don't leave me again. Please tell me that you are staying."

"I was allowed to have a short visit only," I told her and she misunderstood.

"No, I can't stand the thought of another parting. How long can you stay Laszlo?"

"A half an hour or so and they will throw me out."

"I meant how long can you stay before you have to go back to Tolna?" Her voice was weak.

"I am not going back."

"I don't understand."

"I have been transferred to Baja. I will be staying here...We will see each other daily." My words created a total transformation. Her face became radiant; her eyes regained their former fire; her lips brightened. She suddenly sat up, reached for me and this time we kissed less tenderly.

"How are you my darling? How do you feel?"

"I had a bad time of it. For two weeks, before our little girl arrived, I was in great danger. They tried to control my high blood pressure by starving me for five days, but her arrival and yours, Laszlo set things right. I will mend...I will be well...I am truly happy."

"Can I see Ildiko, our little darling?" I asked her.

"I will call a nurse. Ildiko must be hungry."

When our little daughter was brought in, I didn't dare to hold her. She looked so small, yet sweet and bright and smiling.

Rozsa offered her one of her breasts and I fastened my eyes on the feeding baby.

"She is gorgeous my darling."

"She is that and really hungry." Rozsa smiled sweetly, at both of us, and my gratitude, for her being the mother of my child, swamped me.

"Thank you darling for this dear little girl...Thank you for everything." I whispered in her ear.

"And I thank you for returning to us. I will no longer be lonely." Her words made me feel joy and I no longer felt guilt over what I did. After a much longer visit than I was allowed, I told Rozsa everything that happened. She reciprocated and before I had to leave the two people dearest to me, I made them a promise.

"I will see both of you each and every day, come hell or high water. I promise you my darlings, nothing will ever take me from you, nothing will ever again spoil our happiness." I believed firmly what I promised and with that in mind, I went to report to my new commander.

***

"Corporal Laszlo Lichter reporting, Comrade Colonel." I stepped inside the office, when the chief clerk allowed me.

"Come in. I have been expecting you Corporal Lichter," came the statement from the short, thick-set officer. He was not an inch taller than I was and that alone would have pleased me, but what came next gave me even more reason to be elated. "You come highly recommended. I don't know why, but Lieutenant Patkoi sang your praises, after he returned from Tolna. He tells me you are from this city. That you are married and your wife is expecting. When is the blessed event?"

I gave the answers to all his questions and he gave his sincere congratulation.

"Well that is splendid. I am glad your wife is out of danger and that the two of you are parents of a healthy baby. I have two children and my dear wife suffered like yours, but she had another illness. When is your wife due to leave the hospital?"

"In a few days, I think, she will be well enough to leave."

"I am glad to hear that, but now we should talk about your new assignment." He described all the things I was expected to do. None of it sounded too burdensome and my self-confidence told me that I will have little trouble to meet his expectations. When he finished, he stood up and was about to lead me into the outer office.

"May I ask you Colonel Comrade a question, please?"

"You most certainly may," he consented.

"Where should I report to get my billeting? Where should I sleep?"

"Well the first one is quite easy. I will ask my chief clerk to take you there; it is just across the street. But as to your second question, that quite frankly puzzles me. Are you not from this city? Are you not a married man? Are you not the father of a tiny baby?"

"Yes, I am," I stated proudly.

"Do you have no desire to sleep where they live? Isn't it the place where a husband and a father would like to sleep most?"

"Do you really mean it Colonel?"

"In your place I would not have even asked, but since you did, here is my answer. Get billeted in the barracks. Have a bed there, just in case some night you will need it. Give your address to my driver and he will pick you up in the dead of night, but only when you are desperately needed."

***

"I despise being a soldier...I hate the army." The chief clerk announced, after we have arranged my billeting and sat in his office, that next day was to become mine.

"So do I." I told him and described my circumstances.

"So what are you doing about that?"

"What can I do? What can any of us do?" I asked him.

"Yes, indeed. That is what I thought when I was drafted, but it took me only seven months to find a way out."

"You did? Are you saying that you are being discharged this early?"

"Exactly that is what I am saying."

"But how?" I didn't hide my admiration for the young man.

"How indeed? I cannot tell you the whole story briefly, but if you are not too tired...?"

"I am not tired. I am willing to sit here all night, if it takes that long," I urged him to tell me his story.

"I was drafted seven months ago, but I was lucky. I got this position, clerking for Pasko. He is a decent man, not like many others...I soon learned about his drinking problem and that of most of the other officers. I slowly, carefully began to listen; to learn all I could and this is what I found out.

"The officers of this unit are like members of a country club. They cover for each other; they assist each other in their various deficiencies. Do you know why they do that?"

"I don't have the faintest idea," I told him and was grateful to him for sharing with me his accumulated wisdom.

"It took them years to build up their friendship, their trust. They loath the thought of starting over, somewhere else. They fear a transfer...But what they fear most is the breaking up of this unit. That danger they face daily. Do you know what an extraordinary event is?"

"I don't...," I admitted.

"Suicide is one of them. Five months ago we have found one of the young Privates hanging by his neck, he was dead. That was one of the extraordinary events. The second came when they gave the new recruits live ammunition. A young Private turned his gun on a hated officer and he pulled the trigger. A long meeting of the officers followed and I heard them talk about their fear of one more extraordinary event, that must be prevented at any cost. They reviewed the rules under which a regiment must be disbanded. Three extraordinary events in any one year and that is what will happen.

"I began to search and I found the list of extraordinary events. Suicide, attack on an officer, desertion and a homosexual attack on anyone, are on the list and there are many others. That is when I got the germ of an idea and I formulated my plan.

"One night... No, I don't think I know you well enough to say anything more." He stopped.

"It is true that you don't know me well enough, but I didn't know my wife at all; I saw her only for one minute, when I fell in love with her. Love and trust are like brothers. They can come fast or not at all." I tried to convince him and his need to confide in someone must have been great and thank God, I was his confession's recipient.

"I guess you are right. The girl I love. The angel I will marry some day, lives in Budapest and she is lonely. It is hunger for her; it is my love for her; it is her face that made me do what I did. I will tell you what I did, but you are never to repeat it. If you do there will be one more extraordinary event, but it will not be an officer who will be killed.

"One night I sneaked into the bed of a soldier and I tried to kiss him. I hated myself for that disgusting act, but I had to carry out what I planned. When the soldier objected, when he slapped my face, I retreated, crying. Within a day I was called in by Pasko and in the presence of the Secret Police Officer, they grilled me. I confessed to being a homosexual and when they heard my confession they ordered a medical examination.

"I went to the doctor's office and there the learned man examined me. By that time I have read all about homosexuality and I knew that proof of being what I claimed did not exist. When I asked him what he found, he admitted that it is impossible to say with any degree of certainty.

"I grabbed the opportunity and was ready to convince the man. I offered to do things to him that were not to his liking. I offered the same things to Pasko and to any officer who doubted what I claimed to be.

"After a month of their probing and questioning, they found no way to determine my status, so Pasko approached me with an offer. He announced his intention of recommending me to be discharged from the army. My plan did work. I will be free, not only from the army, but also from the constant strain of pretending to be what I am not. I can return to being a healthy human being." He ended his story and it was my turn not only to thank him for his trust, but to enlighten him about many things that happened to me.

I told him about my first, summer stint, in the army; about what happened there. I spoke briefly about how the officers tricked us into believing that we had live ammunition; about the attack by one of the Privates and about my discovery.

"When I was drafted and discovered how they made it almost impossible for any of us to desert, I didn't understand. Thanks to you, I know now why all those extreme precautions," I told him, before we parted.

The following day my predecessor was gone, but not a single thing he told me.

"I must remember what I have learned. Maybe one day I will be able to take advantage of my new knowledge. Maybe one day I will be able to find a way to be dismissed from the army." These thoughts were chased by many others and to divert my meandering mind, I applied myself to the day's work, which began with a trip to the post office.

"I am your driver. My name is Laci Bozsik." The driver of the jeep was very friendly. "I will drive you, every morning to pick up the mail, whenever Pasko doesn't need me."

I introduced myself and we shook hands. I found out during that short trip that he was from far away and lonely.

Before we returned to the regimental office, I asked him if he had breakfast. When he gave me his answer, I asked him to drive me to my parents' place.

Having made the introductions, I asked my Mother to make us breakfast and the two of us had a hearty meal.

When evening came I rushed to the hospital, this time during visiting hours and the greatest of joys filled me. Rozsa was sitting up in bed. She was no longer sad, no longer sickly. Her face broke into a merry smile when she saw me and within minutes, the two of us watched our feeding little baby.

"When do you think you will be allowed to take our baby home, my dearest?"

"No more than three, four days. The doctor told me."

"I have splendid news my darling," I told her and her face was beaming.

"After all these months of lonely existence, good news upon good news is very much to my liking," she whispered lovingly.

"Once you go home, that is where I will spend my nights. Not one more night will we be lonely."

"Are you sure Laszlo? How can this be?"

I gave her a true and accurate account of my first meeting with Pasko and when I finished Rozsa spoke up.

"I didn't think I will ever bless a Communist, but this commander of yours deserves that and my thanks. You tell him Laszlo that I am grateful. Tell him that he made me immensely happy."

***

The next three days became very busy. The first hour of the morning I cultivated Laci's friendship and we had three hearty breakfasts in my Mother's kitchen. The rest of the daylight hours I spent in my office, doing my work and that of others. The evening hours I spent at home, with my loving wife and our beautiful baby. I even found time to talk to Uncle Pista, the head waiter and to my brother, George. The first one promised to talk to all the waiters of our city and he assured me that my benefactor will be treated more fairly. George was a bit more difficult, but in the end, he promised to talk to his friends and assured me that my officer friend will get beat up less frequently.

My hard work in the office paid off. Pasko was full of praise. So was his deputy, who held the same rank.

"Could you join me in my office?" Matyas Pete asked me on the fourth morning.

"It will be my pleasure Comrade Colonel."

He walked ahead of me, just a short distance, and stopped at his door. He unlocked the wrought iron gate that covered the heavy steel door, then he unlocked that too and we had entered.

"Sit down Laszlo. I can't stand formalities, so I will call you by your first name. If that is okay with you?"

"My pleasure, Colonel Pete."

"The day will come Laszlo when you will want to call me Matyas. I will wait. In the meantime I want to tell you about this office. I am the only person permitted to work here...I despise what I am doing. Maps, nothing but maps, keep me company all day. I am like an old maid locked in here and I get thirsty and horny. Booze and women are my only passions and not always in that order. But to guzzle booze takes less time than to seduce a woman. The two of them together need a lot of time and leave me very little time to revise these old maps. On top of that, I have to prepare mock battle plans. I have to figure out the number of soldiers needed, the equipment, the supplies and sundry other items. Frankly the work is not exciting and if I had a choice I would rather be away doing other things. Do you think Laszlo you could help me?"

"How could I do that? Didn't you say that you are the only person permitted to work here?"

"I did say that, but there is a way where there is a will. Do you think you could give me two hours a day?"

I pondered his question and knew that my own work I could do faster; I could spend less time at my Mother's place and by visiting Rozsa and Ildiko a little later, I could gain two hours without any difficulty.

"Yes...Two hours I could spare, but what would I tell Colonel Pasko?"

"That you can leave to me. We have an arrangement. When he leaves the building I must be here. Before I go he must be back. Too bad we cannot drink together, but that is the way things are. He drinks when he can and I drink and whore whenever I am free."

I was delighted to learn something more about my officers' weakness.

"Everything I learn may come handy," I told myself and to him I said something else. "If I give you two hours daily, except on Sundays, how will you get me here?"

"That is simple Laszlo. The two of us will enter my office together. There is no rule against that. Later on, I will sneak out and you will remain. I will lock the doors behind me and nobody will know that you are here, as long as you have the shades pulled down; as long as you work quietly and never answer the door, doesn't matter what may happen. Do we have a deal?"

"I will be glad to do it, but...," I was ready to bargain, but Colonel Pete interrupted.

"Don't ask Laszlo. Don't ruin our friendship by raising the issue. I will be grateful and having me for a friend will be to your liking."

From that day on, I gave him two hours of service daily, behind locked doors, while he took his pleasures and I became privy to a great deal of confidential information, amongst them the date and time of night exercises, that permitted me to prepare in advance the usual combat readiness reports, that Pasko would find in my safe, to which he knew the combination.

***

When my beloved was released from the hospital, she and I carried our baby daughter into our sweet room that was heated with a brick oven. Rozsa and I joked a few times about the strange contraption. It stood in a corner of her room. It's rounded, whitewashed surface, stuck out grotesquely. Much like Rozsa's belly, during the last few months of her pregnancy, she told me. The oven was just like a wood furnace, but it had to be fed fuel from a storage chamber that was attached to her room. I stoked up the furnace to provide heat and when it became hot it held it for many hours, making our room and our baby, in her swaddle, quite comfy.

We ate supper with her parents. We talked for a long time about my new found freedom and our love for each other.

When all of us tired, we went to our warm room and Rozsa offered sustenance to our little daughter. She made small sounds of delight, as she sucked the sweet milk from her swollen breasts that produced that precious gift abundantly. Ildiko was unable to consume all she was offered, thus Rozsa was forced to pump out the remnants. We weighed Ildiko before and after each feeding and her weight changes we have recorded. When there was nothing more to do we have retired.

Our nightly routine repeated itself for three days and then Mr. and Mrs. Buja turned the conversation to something that we have neglected.

"Ildiko should have a proper christening. Don't you think?" Mr. Buja spoke up.

"We would love to do that, but how and when? We don't want to put anyone in danger," Rozsa raised the specter of what she feared.

"I understand, but is there really any danger, my dear daughter? You are away from your job for three months of maternity leave. If your boss ever finds out about Ildiko's christening, which is not likely, he will forget it long before you return to your job. And Laszlo? If they find out, they might throw him out of the army. I am sure that would be to your liking."

"But what about your job, Dad?" I asked him.

"My job doesn't matter any more." I heard him declare and I began to fear, but decided not to probe, to let him confide in us when he wished.

"Who can we find to do the christening in secret?"

"I took care of that." Mr. Buja told us. "Father Balind Antal is a friend of mine. He serves at the Parish of Paduai St. Antal. He is willing to christen Ildiko without too many people knowing it. All he needs is your cooperation Laszlo and two people to stand as God-parents."

"I could ask Aunt Manci and her husband. They would never tell a soul." I made my selection.

"Go to them now. Speak to them and if they agree we should proceed with the christening."

"When?" I asked.

"There is no time to drag our feet. Tomorrow is as good a day as any." I noticed Rozsa's Father's haste and my fear sent its roots deeper.

That night I went to see Manci and her husband at their work place and they gladly gave their agreement.

***

Early evening, on the next day, I rushed home. I carried my daughter to the church, in the darkness. There, our little daughter cried out when she felt the cold, sanctified water and she became Ildiko Maria, on February twenty fourth in the year of the Lord of one thousand-nine-hundred and fifty-four.

That night the Bujas and the three of us celebrated and our joy was great, but it lasted only a few days, then our lives collapsed, sadness and bitterness replaced our joy.

***

Five days later, upon my return home, I felt the tension and saw many signs of Rozsa's parents' crying. Their faces were drawn; they were like two people whose hearts were broken; they looked totally devastated.

In our room, I asked Rozsa. "Are your parents ill?"

"I really don't know."

"Has something happened to your Father?"

"I do not know that either."

"Did they have a fight?"

"No, they couldn't be more loving and in peace with each other."

"What happened then?"

"I really don't know. I slept a little around noon and when I woke up my Mother was in tears, my Father was at work. I tried to talk to her, but each time I began, she just burst out crying. She held Ildiko, as if she did that for the last time. She hugged me more warmly and more frequently than ever before."

"Let's join them Rozsa and after supper I will find out."

Our supper was eaten in total silence and when we were finished Mr. Buja spoke up.

"Laszlo and Rozsa I have something to tell you. I ask you not to interrupt me, just hear me out." Rozsa and I nodded our agreement and Mr. Buja asked for our baby. He held on to her, from time to time his eyes sought that of the baby and his words came slowly, reluctantly, with an occasional sob that he tried to stifle.

"I told you a long time ago, that Joe was tricked by a secret police agent and that I was forced to become an informer to save his skin. I hated myself for writing an occasional report, but I never wrote anything that would harm someone.

"My friend, Peter Balazs, was their main target. I had to visit him many times to gather evidence against him. My reports I made sound neutral and meaningless, but my controller became impatient and ordered me to see him on a certain date, at a specified time. He told me to get him drunk and when he reached that blessed state to pump him for information on how he felt about Communism. I found it strange that my meeting with Peter was arranged that carefully, but I went and suspected nothing, until I got there. A secret police agent, I recognized, was already there and they were already drinking. I delayed my assigned duty, in the hope of being able to warn my friend. When the opportunity came, I did just that. I told him not to answer me honestly when I ask him a question.

"We continued to drink and with broken heart and fear, I asked him about Communism and when his replies came, I was delighted. He told us that he cared not a fig for politics; that he keeps his nose clean and all he cares about is making lots of money.

"I made my favorable report, but my controller was in a rage. He called Peter a rotten plotter, someone who is trying to overthrow the state. He has allies, I was told. He is planning a revolution and that I must do my utmost to find the evidence and his co-conspirators.

"Another meeting was set up. This time it was on the Danube and we were to fish together for a whole day. In the evening we were to make camp and begin to drink. Later two strangers drifted into our camp and they began to tear down the Communist party. Peter was loaded to the gills and he let down his guard, but before he could say anything too damaging, I decided to make my excuse. I blamed your Mother Rozsa for my sudden departure. I told them that I must go home, or all hell will break loose and that I cannot risk.

"Next day, my controller summoned me and raked me over the coals. He told me I was stalling; that I was responsible for what will happen. He informed me that no further delays will be tolerated. He really put the pressure on. I was given the choice to cooperate with him or suffer the consequences. During the last three months, your Mother and I have been scared out of our minds, on four different occasions.

"The first time a vehicle stopped front of our house. I heard its motor running. I found it unusual. Our street hardly gets any motoring traffic. I went to the window, pulled aside the curtain slightly and in the moonlight, I saw the uniformed policemen. I waited, with my heart in my mouth, for their entry, but nothing happened. They chatted under our window; they smoke a few cigarettes-I saw the flare of their matches-and after an hour or so, they left. The sound of their jeep receded.

"I went back to bed and hugged your Mother. We talked; we fearfully contemplated what could be coming.

"Each and every time, when I turned in my written report, a report that contained no damaging information, my controller raged at me; warned me and predicted my downfall. After each such meeting the jeep arrived, always around two in the morning, and they stayed for an hour, but never came in, never approached me. This is the tactic they use Laszlo to frighten innocent men, to break their will down, to turn them into traitors.

"I had decided a long time ago that I will not give up my honor; I will not be anyone's Judas. I will die before I harm anyone, but not without a fight...not without trying everything." Rozsa and I listened to Mr. Buja's revelations and Mrs. Buja nodded her head to confirm that she agreed with everything her husband said. I could no longer hold my tongue.

"What are you trying to tell us?" I asked and squeezed Rozsa's hand.

"Please don't interrupt me. I asked that before. I am not trying to be impolite; rather, I am trying to give both of you the background." I held my breath and promised myself to be more patient.

"So we have been terrorized; we have been harassed; we have been made to taste the bitterness of an uncertain future and while the Communists did that, I did something else." I almost asked him what he did, but his admonishment was fresh on my mind and I remained silent.

"I did something dreadful, that will cause you pain my darling daughter and you too Laszlo. I began to plan our escape from this cursed country. Yes, I told both of you that...but back then it was only a dream, yesterday it became a reality." It was Rozsa who could no longer control her tears, her words spilled out.

"You are not deserting me? Please tell me that is not so."

"I wish you didn't regard it desertion. I can no longer live in constant terror, nor can your Mother, Rozsa. Even after we leave all of you; even if we succeed escaping, we will be always with you...Our hearts and souls are wrenched by what we must do, yet they left us no choice, no alternative."

"When?" Rozsa whispered the word and I could hardly believe his answer.

"Tomorrow morning we will be on a bus, at five o'clock." Mr. Buja's announcement was like a death sentence.

Rozsa burst out crying, screaming in anguish and neither I, nor her parents, could calm her. My tears were not far below the surface, but I choked them back, not wanting to add to Rozsa's suffering.

"Why? Why, do you have to do that?" she cried out.

"I tried to explain it, my dear daughter. Have I done a poor job to make you understand?"

"How did you manage to find a way out?" I tried to steer our conversation away from the parting.

"As you know Laszlo, Lajos Miklos and I have talked about this endlessly. You also know that each and every Sunday we have listened to the Free Europe radio and it gave accounts of many ingenious escapes. The more success stories I heard the more certain I became that I will find someone. The failed attempts I tried to put out of my mind.

"One day I approached a trusted friend, who plies the waters of the Danube with his ship. He even goes to Yugoslavia. He was willing to hide us on his ship. To take us across the border, but from that point on he could no more. He revealed to me the many dangers. The Yugoslavian Government changes with the wind, as you all know. One day they are hated enemies of the Soviet Union and they welcome all refugees, but the next day they turn and those who cross their border are escorted back to Hungary. So that plan I had to abandon. Then I had a bit of luck.

"I knew that there are many false guides. People who take the money from would be refugees; lead them close to the border and turn the fugitives over to the border guards. That knowledge made me very cautious. I feared that I may never find anyone I could trust, then my luck changed. I got a new employee, Vilmos and we became friends. Month after month I learned a great deal about him.

"At the end of the war he left our country and took his family to Austria. There he tried to work in the Russian sector and when he found that his income was a pittance, he became an opportunist. He joined the Communist party and he began to strive. He acquired several trucks and cars and after three years he had his own transportation company. He attributed his good fortune to the Communists and being home-sick, he decided to return to Hungary. He came back, but not his many relatives. Slowly the State took away all he had and he came to work with me.

"His disillusionment was great, but his desire to return to Austria was even greater. We talked many times and one day out of the blue, he told me, that he could have a guide come for them, but he dared not risk the trip with his family. A few months ago, one of his two, grown sons was struck by a tram car and broke his thigh bone. A metal pin was placed to hold his bones together. He would need a great deal of help while walking and so would his five year old daughter. He asked me if we would be willing to help his helpless two children.

"I grabbed the marvelous opportunity and told him that my wife and I are strong and willing to help. We began to formulate a plan, but we ran into a snag. The guide will want one thousand American Dollars from each person. Vilmos had enough money salted away to pay five peoples' cost, but I had none. We talked about that problem and I convinced Vilmos to allow me to find three other, strong, capable adults to join the seven of us. I was thinking of Lajos Miklos and his wife, who offered to pay our cost, if I ever found a guide and I wanted to save my friend, Peter.

"I went to see Lajos and we settled the issue. The two of them were more than anxious to join us.

"Then I went to see my friend, Peter. I urged him, tried to convince him that he had no other choice, but to come with us. I confessed to him what I was forced to do and he forgave me. I told him that he was days away from being arrested. He will be tried for conspiracy and no doubt found guilty. He held out stubbornly. He didn't mind to leave his wife, but his daughter was another matter. With him I didn't succeed, until today, but finally he gave his agreement.

"Yesterday the guide arrived to Vilmos' home and there I met him. He is an experienced guide; he knows every inch of the western border. He is familiar with all aspects of how to cross it. He knows where the false borders are. There are places where the Communists set up barbed wire fences and other false fortifications. When the refugees cross these things, they find signs in German to designate which way to go, where to report to be received by the Austrian authorities. They follow the German signs; they are warmly greeted by Austrian guards, who turn out to be Hungarian agents. The rest you know. They are tried, sentenced and if lucky, only imprisoned for a long time. But our guide knows all the tricks the Hungarian border guards play and he made many trips, but never two at the same spot and that is to my liking." Rozsa and I have listened to Mr. Buja and as he spoke each word, as he revealed more and more details of their well laid plans, I began to cheer up and Rozsa's attention was somewhat diverted from her misery.

"Will you take Joe with you, Dad?" Rozsa asked.

"I wish we could. He is not where he used to be...I tried to find him, but I was informed that they are on secret winter maneuvers. We have to leave him behind too..." Mr. Buja answered.

"How far will you get before they miss you at your working place?" I asked.

"For two days they will not miss me. The guide did a good job. He thought of everything. He asked me if I had any relatives, outside this city and I told him about my sister, Lujza, who lives in Budapest. He promised that he will make the necessary arrangements and he did."

"What did he do?" It was Rozsa who probed now.

"Someone sent a telegraph. It came while you were asleep Rozsa." Mrs. Buja spoke up. "The telegraph said that Lujza was ill. That we must go soon, if we wish to see her alive. I knew all about the details of our escape plan, but it never seemed real, it was just like a dream, until the wire came. Than it all sank in and I began to cry; I felt the greatest pain of my life, but I promised your Dad Rozsa not to say anything."

"And I came home at lunch time. By then we had the bad news. I took the wire to my boss and got two days off to go see my sister. So they will not miss me at least that long and maybe even longer. By the time they twig to what we are doing, I think we will be across the border."

"What if something goes wrong? What if there are unforeseen delays?" I asked and began to think of my own situation.

"I work with a lot of confidential documents. I wish I didn't. Once they find out that my in-laws crossed the border, I will be in a great deal of trouble. I will be investigated and so will be my dear Rozsa. I must plan things very carefully. I must play my cards right. I must fool the authorities. How will I be able to do that? Now is not the time to think about these things. I will have all night, later." I turned my attention back to Mr. Buja.

"I am not telling you these things to cause you worry, but to have you understand the situation. We think we will be across in three days, but you may be right Laszlo. Something unexpected may happen. Double that time...Even under the worst case scenario we should be very close to the fence of despair, in six days, or perhaps on the other side of the border of hope. If something goes really wrong and we have to turn around, in six days we should be back or in prison, God perish the thought."

"What is your most realistic estimation of success?" I asked him and feared his answer.

"Even with our good guide I estimate it to be fifty-fifty."

"Why is it such a difficult task?" My inquisitive nature took over.

"Do you really want to hear this?" Mr. Buja shook his head, disbelieving.

"I do! Each and every day I will pray for your safety, but to do that I must know what you are facing."

"And what about you Rozsa? Do you want to hear?"

"I do Dad. I can't bear the thought of not knowing."

"It pains me to tell you about the dangers we will be facing, but you leave me no choice. So I will be totally honest. We will get on the bus tomorrow morning. Miklos and his wife have left already...They will get on the bus at Kalocsa. Vilmos and his family take a train and they will meet us at the southern railway station in Budapest, exactly at ten thirty. The guide will be there, as well. We will pretend that we do not know each other. Peter, if he doesn't change his mind, he is always vacillating, will hop on the bus somewhere along our route.

"At the railway station we are to get in the same coach as our guide. From there on we are to follow every move he makes. Any one of us may be followed. If one suspects that, he must break away from the group, he must turn back.

"First we have to avoid the border belt check, some thirty kilometers from the border. Once we leave the train we will have to walk, but only at nights. During the days we will hide in the woods or in big hay-stacks. Just before the fence of despair there is a raked strip of four meters of land. If it is frozen we have little worry about, but if the weather turns mild we must walk backwards and cover our tracks. The sentries patrol that piece of ground every five minutes. If they see human tracks, they alert the Russians, who occupy that part of Austria. I don't need to spell out what will happen then. Once we reach the fence of despair, we will have to avoid the guards and their blood-thirsty dogs. We are taking a great deal of ground pepper that we will spread to get them off our scent. We must attempt to cross between two guard towers. We must avoid the search lights and the deadly machine guns. We will have to cut the first barb-wire fence, but carefully, for on cold days the tightly stretched wires make a sound that the guards could hear even at a long distance. We have to make sure that no signal rockets go off...They have many of them placed on the fence. Once we cut the wire fence, we have to proceed carefully to avoid the mines that are placed all over the belt that separates the first fence from the next one. Our guide will go ahead. He will use a knitting needle and we are to step nowhere else than in his tracks. The second wire fence we have to cut just as carefully, but once that is done we will have reached Austria, we will have crossed the border of hope. The rest will be not too difficult; our guide knows how to avoid the Russians and the Austrians don't exactly cooperate with their despised occupiers." A weak smile crossed his face, he seemed to struggle with his emotions, and then he turned to something brighter. "We will send you messages, letters and many parcels."

"I wish I have never asked," my statement slipped out.

"I don't care about the parcels," Rozsa cried out.

"And I wish I didn't have to tell you," Mr. Buja spoke softly. "I wish I didn't have to put you through this, but you had to understand not only why we must go, but why we cannot take you with us. In your condition Rozsa, you would never survive the trip. This dear little girl, in my arms, is far to young to be exposed to the dangers. A year from now or maybe sometime later, I will make arrangements. A happy day will come when you will be able to join us in that land where we will find our freedom."

After those words there was a deadly silence.

"I know I don't have to tell you that letters are always censored, especially those coming from the west. How do you plan to communicate with us?" I asked.

For several minutes we discussed our future method of communicating with each other; worked out a code we both were to use when writing and after that came my painful parting.

"I have slept home for a few nights, but tonight perhaps I shouldn't sleep here?" I raised what I considered to be a precaution.

"Are you planning to leave me too?" Rozsa sobbed out.

"I must leave you my darling, just for this night. I am convinced that I will be interrogated. What could I know if I wasn't here?"

"Laszlo is right. He knew nothing. You too, my dear will be interrogated. You were told nothing either, just that we went to Budapest to say good-by to my beloved sister, who was dying. I know both of you are strong and wise. I know you will be able to fool the authorities." Mr. Buja gave his counsel.

"Dad and Mom..." I began and stood up. "You have a long journey ahead of you. You need your rest and so does my darling. I will leave you now. I will let all of you retire. As the days pass, I will follow your journey; my thoughts and prayers will be with you. I wish you success and I wish you a safe crossing. When the border of hope is behind you, may you find peace, may you enjoy your freedom, may you strive in your new country."

We hugged each other, we shook hands and as I was leaving, I heard Dad's dog's pain-filled barking.

***

The streets were dark and empty, but far less than my heart was. I got no further than a few hundred feet, when I stopped and felt a pull to return to my Rozsa.

"This night of all nights, I should have stayed with my beloved. I was stupid, selfish and brutal. Should I go back? I should be with her. I should hold her, succor her, dry her tears, and assure her that we will never be parted." I thought and took a few steps back, but my struggle went on and on and in the end I turned again and put a great deal of distance behind me.

That night I glanced at my watch very often and my thoughts came like gusts of swirling winds.

"Rozsa's parents will face great danger, but there is nothing we can do to change that. My responsibility now is to assure our survival. What should I do? My first duty is to help my darling. That is what I will do as soon as Pasko arrives. Can I do what Mr. Buja suggested?" I asked myself and recalled the words he spoke before our parting.

"Before they ever question you Laszlo, you should speak about your concern for my sister's serious illness. Mention it to your best friend, and then drop a hint in front of your commander."

"Yes, that is what I will do, first thing in the morning." I had decided in the night's darkness.

"When we don't return after two days, you should express your concerns about us. Let your commander know that you think that we may have been delayed by an accident. Go to the police, preferably with a reliable witness. Ask them to check all the hospitals in Budapest. By doing that you will not only establish your credibility, but you will also throw them off our tracks. You will give us some extra time to reach our destination. Please remember what I am asking. If you do these things well, in a believable manner, you will increase our chance of success." I recalled these instructions and made mental note of what must be done and in what sequence.

"When the fifth day passes, go to the police again, but this time be greatly agitated. Tell them that you began to suspect a plot. Inform them that the wire may not have come from my sister, but from the AVO, the Hungarian Secret Police. Use well your God given brain power. Convince them to make inquiries. If they do that, it will give us at least one more day. After this, one of two things may happen. They will deny our arrest, if we haven't been captured or they will take great delight in telling you that we were caught, somewhere this side of the border." Mr. Buja's further instructions seemed to be well planned and I hoped to posses the needed acting ability.

His last words gave me more trouble.

"After six days, provide the police with our picture and demand that they start a man hunt. If we have crossed the border this action will not harm us and will help you greatly. Had we failed and not returned home, your action will not matter."

"How could I do such a heartless thing? Will I have the strength to do that? I just have to wait and see," I told myself and I must have fallen into a restless sleep.

I woke with a start and when I saw the time, my heart wrenched with pain. It was already four in the morning. I imagined my dear wife holding our darling baby. I could see her beautiful eyes filled with tears, as she said good-by to her parents. I sensed the hesitations of those last few moments and their pain of parting. My every instinct urged me to get up, to run to her, to comfort her, but I forced myself to survive the next few hours, without doing anything that could put in jeopardy our well being.

***

By eight o'clock I sat in the jeep, beside my driver. I thought about those dear people on the bus, completing the first and least dangerous part of their journey. I didn't have to act to look haggard. The lack of sleep; the agonizing thoughts; my concern for Rozsa's parents and my worry about my sweetheart made me look as Laci saw me.

"You look like death warmed over Laszlo. Is something wrong my friend?"

"If I look as bad as I feel, I shouldn't show my face in public."

"What is going on?"

"My wife is still sick and she must look after our baby. Until yesterday her parents were able to help her, but now she is alone and greatly concerned about her Aunt's illness."

"Hold on. You lost me way back. Tell me step by step the whole story."

I forced myself not to ramble, but to tell him how sick my wife was. How her parents received the bad news and rushed to Budapest. I informed him that for two days they will be away and during those two days nobody is taking care of my sick wife; nobody is looking after our baby.

"God, I thought you had much greater problems," Laci laughed out loud.

***

After our return to my office, the two of us sorted the mail and when I was ready to deliver the letters that were addressed to Colonel Pasko, Laci stopped me.

"Would you mind if I took them in?" I heard my friend and my plan's first part crumbled.

"If I don't see my commander now, I may not see him for many hours. I should refuse Laci's request." I thought and my driver's words stopped my thinking.

"Let me do it. I know him better than you do Laszlo. I will assure that your problem will be solved." He spoke with such force of conviction that I had no choice, but to give my consent.

Ten minutes later, Laci came out and winked at me.

"Pasko wants to see you in his inner sanctum."

"Corporal Lichter reporting, Comrade Colonel Pasko," I addressed him, as I entered.

"You didn't bring in the mail, as you usually do. Is something eating you Laszlo?"

"What did Private Bozsik tell you?"

"What he told me is none of your business. I am interested in hearing your story."

"I am depressed. I have many problems," I spoke up, knowing not what my friend told my commander.

"How many days would you need to chase away your depression?"

"Two days from now I would be a new man."

"Then take two days off. Private Bozsik will drive you where you want to go. Two days from now I want you back and I want your depression to be past you."

I asked Laci to drive me first to where the Gomoris lived and there I spent five minutes. As fast as I could, I informed Mrs. Buja's sister about Rozsa being alone with Ildiko, her parents having left for Budapest and when Rozsa's Grandmother offered to be with Rozsa, I accepted her offer gladly.

Laci drove us to where my love and baby waited and two of us entered.

"I am back my dear, my beloved. I will be with you for two whole days and your Grandmother came too; she will be with you, as long as necessary."

"My dear Rozsa, you look pale. You are rather sickly. Give me the baby and off you go to bed." The kind, old lady announced and she accepted no argument.

Rozsa and I went to our bedroom and I made her lie down, sat beside her and cradled her in my arms, while she wept.

"What time did they leave Rozsa?"

"They left at four-thirty...The last half hour, before they left, we cried and cried and our tears mingled. When we had no more tears left, they kissed Ildiko for the last time, they hugged me and showered me with their kisses. Then they patted the dog and while it whined, like a crazed beast, they opened the gate and closed it behind them. I thought I will die; I felt my heart breaking and then the desolate silence came, and it made me cry even harder." Her words poured out and she pulled me closer.

"I am here my dearest, my sweetest, my beloved little Rozsa. We will be well. From this pain we will recover. Your parents will be across the border and they will no longer be in danger."

"When will they get there? When will we know?" in her agony she cried out.

"Today is Tuesday. Well, let me see. This coming Sunday we may have a message, we will be glued to the radio."

"I fear today, but I fear even more each passing day that takes them closer to the border. What if Sunday no message comes? What if they are captured? What if they step on a mine? What if they are shot to death? What if they never make it? How will I survive losing my parents?"

"They are in God's hands. We will pray, Rozsa."

"I did that all night. I never slept a single moment."

"Your prayers will be answered, my darling."

"How can you be so sure Laszlo?"

"I have faith not only in God, but a lot of faith in your Father. Had he not survived the war? Had he not found all of you when the hostilities ended? Had he not survived unemployment and later the conniving of the Secret Police? The good Lord granted His mercy to him whenever he was in need. He will not desert them now. In my heart I know that Rozsa. You must be strong and you must be fearless. Give it time and some days from now, we will look back on these trying days and we will have many reasons to be delighted."

"Do you really believe this Laszlo?"

"I believe it. I know it and so will you, my dear darling."

"Where do you think they might be now?"

"It is almost eleven o'clock." I told her, after I checked my watch. "They must be on the train, heading west. With the passing of each moment they are getting closer and closer. They will be across the border in no time and after that they will be really free."

For two days Rozsa and I were never farther from each other than a few inches. We talked about her parents endlessly and tried to imagine where they might be, what they might be doing. As the hours passed, we began to see their escape through rose colored glasses. Had we known the truth we probably would have contemplated something desperate, but the Almighty spared us from knowing it all, until much later.

A few years later, we heard about their ordeal from Mr. Buja and some twenty years later, he put it all on paper. This autobiography would be incomplete without including what he wrote. Forty-three years had passed, since they began their attempt to cross the border. I sit with the faded, typewritten sheets, long after those dear people have departed, and I am filled with deep emotions. I have read his long, pain-filled story and I am compelled to translate it.

***

Chapter 15

It is Tuesday, March second in nineteen fifty four. The time is just past quarter after five, in the early morning and after one last, painful, long hug, that we gave our daughter, we closed the gate behind us. For a half hour we stumbled with my wife, like two drunken people, all the way to the bus station. During the fifteen minute wait, that was left before our departure, I imagined seeing my dear daughter's swollen eyes, full of tears and anxiety. Then I thought of my friend, Peter and knew that he experienced the same kind of parting. I feared that he may not have been strong enough; that he may have changed his mind, in the very last moment. I tried to hide my tears, my fears and in a whisper I urged my wife to do likewise. I told her that our emotions we must hide, lest those betray us at the very beginning.

Amongst the travelers, I saw many familiar faces and to my greatest surprise I saw Peter a few paces behind me. In less than an hour, we had reached the city of Kalocsa and there Lajos Miklos and his wife joined us. They took a seat as far from us as they could; we have exchanged not a word. Now and then I searched all faces surreptitiously and my blood froze. Among the passengers sat a member of the dreaded Secret Police. I knew him, fortunately he didn't know me. I first considered his presence a coincidence, but my mind kept thinking of other possibilities. *He may be watching someone!* Suddenly I saw, once again, my dear daughter's face and her words reverberated in my mind. Her last glance at us now seemed like a final parting. I had to brace myself against the tears that lurked behind my eyelids. I glanced at my wife, who set beside me and sensed her hidden struggle none of which she showed and that heartened me.

We have reached *Budapest* and for two hours we rested at the home of a relative of Lajos. At the appointed time we approached the southern railway station. Our guide stood alone...Vilmos stood with his family...Peter stood about ten meters away from Vilmos.

I purchased two return tickets to *Celldomolk*. Our eyes scanned the crowd, but watched nobody more than our guide, trying to make sure that when he boarded the train we could follow him.

I watched him take a seat. Then came the family of Vilmos, but Peter never appeared. I became restless...I walked from compartment to compartment, but to no avail. Peter wasn't on the train. I had learned a year later that he was being followed by the AVO agent, who was on our bus and in order to help us, he took a return train to *Baja*.

The train chugged on and I forced my mind to dwell on nothing, but our desire to succeed. At *Szekesfehervar* we transferred to another train and we have reached *Celldomolk*, nine o'clock in the evening. The Almighty was on our side. The station was shrouded in heavy fog and hid our stepping off the train, on the opposite side from the station. We were able to avoid the guards, whose job was to check everybody's identification papers for the stamp that allowed entry into the thirty kilometer belt, on the east side of the border between Hungary and Austria.

Our guide took off and we followed him blindly, seeing not him, but hearing only his footsteps. Our walk took us around the village and on to the highway, heading west, but only for twenty minutes, after which we began to head north, but no longer on the paved road. We caught up with our guide, who stood waiting in the plowed field. The road we traveled on earlier was free of snow, but that was no longer the case. During the day much of the snow melted, but what remained was crusted over. Each step we took sounded too loud, but we marched on for no more than five minutes. A vehicle's lights came almost too fast and all of us fell on the ground to avoid being detected. When the car passed and disappeared around a curve, we stood up, fully drenched with water. We walked on, followed our guide, in a single file, but the ground became uneven and the mud holes became our first enemies. The mud began to pull on our feet, each step required a greater effort. Rivulets of sweat began to drench us. Our footwear was covered with heavy mud. Our small parcel, with two days of food, seemed to be too heavy. The five year old, little girl, walked quietly, but with great struggle and I have decided to ease her burden and to make good of my promise to Vilmos, her Father. I lifted her up, settled her on my shoulders and she was fast asleep. After an hour, Lajos gave me a break and from there on we shared that sweet burden.

My lack of sleep, during the previous night, began to take its toll. I was bone tired, but I knew that I wasn't the only one hoping for a break. Soon, our guide stopped, in a spot, where he and I could risk smoking a cigarette and while we did, all members of the group struggled to catch their breaths, to fortify themselves for the rest of the ordeal.

I looked at our small group that consisted of three women, five men, the young, injured boy, whose muscles didn't want to obey him, whose bones were held together with the steel pin and the five year old girl. I knew then that it will be far more difficult than I have ever imagined. After the first half hour of our walk, Vilmos' son needed a great deal of assistance. When I wasn't carrying the little girl, it was him whose arm was over my shoulder and I have felt his weight.

We put the cigarettes out and were on the march again. We skirted a settlement, where dogs barked, but saw no signs of any human activity. As the barking began to fade, I felt firmer ground under my feet. We were walking among vineyards, where the sand was hard packed, but our clothing was wet and steaming.

Our guide stopped suddenly. His announcement that we may be lost, surprised all of us, but when he decided to go ahead, to do some scouting, we welcomed the opportunity to take another needed rest. We sat down on a log, too tired to talk and there we waited.

My dear daughter's pain-filled face came front of my eyes, as she did many times before, and I wondered if we undertook a foolish thing. I knew our chance of succeeding being no more than fifty percent, but by now even those odds began to shrink. I thought and thought about those we loved and left behind and with each painful thought I got closer to the brink. *What bloody crime have we committed? Why have the Communists drove us to this desperate act?* I weighed our chances. *On the one hand, Communist headhunters, blood thirsty dogs, mines, guard towers are waiting for us. They will show no mercy, not even for a child. They will spare not the women; let alone the men. If they find us they will not spare anyone. On the other hand, if we succeed in crossing the fence of despair, we will be free. I will have my honor...* I reached for my wife's hand and I knew that she was thinking much like I; that her suffering over whom and what we left behind was just as intense as mine was.

I remembered many men and women who catered to the Communists, yet soon found themselves disillusioned and when that happened they were finished. Were not even able to choose the method of their deaths. It was the gallows, never a bullet. That recollection sobered me. *At least we are trying to find a solution and what we are doing is against the Communists' ten commandments.*

I was shaken from my reverie by a shouting voice that commanded someone to stop. I heard two shots. I thought the Heavens caved in, then came four more shots. I heard the groans of someone, probably a wounded man's and the screams of pain in the far distance. Audible footfalls came closer and two more shots rang out. I was ready to go to investigate, when our guide rushed to us. He was out of breath. He ordered us to move fast and took off like he was on fire. We needed no more. We didn't want to lose him, so with adrenaline pumping, we ran after him and the race was on.

After ten minutes the running came to a halt. Not one of us had anything more to give. The guide stood, bent over, his breathing labored and between the gulps of air he took, he told us what happened. He was stopped by two uniformed men, probably guards. They took two shots at him and he fired his pistol four times. He dropped one of the two, while the second began to run away. He ran after the fleeing guard and fired two more shots, with one finding him. He informed us that in case of one of the guard's survival or in the likely case of other guards finding their bodies, we will be mercilessly hunted. As soon as he told us about the frightening events, he took off at a steady speed. Had this happened just before the barb wire fence, perhaps my fear of being caught would not have been so terrifying, but we were still thirty kilometers from the border, having traveled not in a straight line, but at a angle.

My exhausted mind began to play tricks on me. I heard the guard dogs barking, imagined myself being hanged, then my mind cleared and I had realized that the barking came from a few dogs of the settlement we were passing. Soon we left the settlement behind, crossed a muddy, swampy patch of ground and to my relief, our feet began to sink in snow, but underneath I felt solid footing. Our breaths made rasping sounds; the fog began to lift and signs of the coming dawn appeared.

Our guide tried to calm us with promises of a whole day's rest in a haystack, after one more mad rush to find it. We followed him the best we could. The little girl on my shoulder, but not as heavy as my gloomy thoughts.

Laszlo S. Lichter

What will happen now? The chase, the capture, the terrible sentence and our life is over. There is no way back, our dear children, we were forced to leave you behind. I wonder if you feel our suffering? I still feel Rozsa's clinging, her kisses on my face as we parted. Now there is a whole world, an unscalable gulf between us. Your Mother Rozsa is beside me. Her face transformed by her rugged determination, ready to face all dangers. This is the kind of Mother you have my children, yet she was forced to desert you. I hope you understand that we had no peace, no security. How could we have stayed? How could we have faced our inevitable arrest, our forced parting? I see Rozsa that your Mother is suffering greatly, her soul is tortured, her feet must hurt greatly. She winces with each step, but that she tries to hide from me.

I force myself to stop thinking, I want to keep my sanity. Ahead of us only mud and snow, behind us the searchers with their dogs. Time and time again our eyes cheat us. We see in the distance haystacks, but as we drag ourselves closer and closer, they turn out to be just piled up manure and we are greatly disappointed. We search more desperately; daylight is coming, we must hide. They must not find us in the open. The next haystack is no less cunning and when we get close to it, its stench tells us that our eyes have cheated us, once more. We are like lost souls, in a desert, seeing nothing but mirages. We no longer care. We seek warmth where we can find it. Our hands reach into the manure pile, create holes to warm our half frozen bodies and we are grateful for the slight warmth it provides us. Our hands are covered with mud and so are our bodies, but mud is nothing compared to this awful staff. Yet we reach for our small parcels, open them with frozen fingers and reach for our food. *We must eat...We need strength...*Our bodies feel the minus three temperature and the wicked wind makes it feel like minus twenty. We talk, while our teeth chatter and decide to move on, in spite of the rising sun. We must find a suitable hiding place...We must move, although it is eight in the morning. After two more kilometers we reached a river. Our guide called it *Raba*. Close to the river we have a bit of luck. Cornstalks are piled in small bunches, they provide us with a new home and we feel grateful, we feel lucky. We seek its shelter, like we used to seek our own bed and within minutes my wife and I hide in one, while the others hide in others. Some of the others changed their wet socks for dry ones. I planned things ever so carefully, at least I thought, but now I knew the mistakes I made. We brought no spare clothing and even if we had, I would not have dared to remove my wife's shoes, to take her socks off. I knew that by then some of her toes must be frozen. The time drags on, each minute passes slowly...*Will the searchers find us? Maybe not.* In places, where the howling wind swept the ground bare, we sprinkled large amounts of ground pepper...That may confuse the dogs...Afternoon came and the heavens opened up. The rain came between the gaps in the cornstalks and when we were drenched to our skin, the rain let up and we began to feel the cold steel of hail lashing us. The elements conspired against us. We could stand no longer to stay where we were. We were all wet, frozen, stiff and devastated.

We resumed our desperate march on the dike of the river *Raba* to reach the bridge where we could cross. We heard a sound behind us. The man was on a bicycle. He looked after the small dams, that dotted the river, he told us. When he inquired about our destination, in such awful weather, our guide came to his senses and told him that we were assigned to work at a distant collective farm. That is where we were heading, but we must be lost. He explained patiently and that decent human being bought our story or decided not to betray us. He gave us clear directions and we thanked him warmly. We watched as he mounted his bicycle and began to paddle on the icy surface. I wondered then if the man pretended to be a friend. I considered the possibility of that man rushing to the nearest police unit. In either case, we could do nothing, but to trust in God.

We reached the bridge and began to cross. In the pouring rain we saw the guard house, but it was too late to stop. *Inside there must be guards. They will ask for our papers*. I was certain that we reached the end of our journey. Three heads appeared at a window and my heart took a jump. Then two men came to the door and I saw that they looked like us. No uniforms, no guns, just simple workers, who must have sought shelter from the rain and the pelting sleet.

Suddenly two lights appeared on the road and rushed toward us. A few seconds may have passed before we realized that the vehicle sported the police emblem on its front. It was too late to run, impossible to hide. The end was near. The car slowed down and two distorted faces stared at us, but the icy glass gave them little to look at. I broke out in a sweat, in spite of my shivering and a divine inspiration made me raise my hand to give them a friendly greeting. The Almighty must have moved my hand and the car began to speed up. Soon after that we climbed across the water filled ditch, walked a few hundred meters and there it stood. The huge haystack became our home, provided us with homely warmness and we consumed another part of our meager provisions. We planned to rest for two to three hours in the hay covered holes. Our rest was sleepless; our wet clothing dried slowly and began to tighten. It felt like being in a straight jacket and that made us restless.

At eleven, that evening, we were ready to continue, but with each of the Lord's blessing another trial popped up. My wife suddenly fainted, probably from exhaustion, but her recovery was fast. Another female suffered a pulled muscle, sometime during our walk on the uneven ground. Miklos ran up a fever, probably from the vast quantities of snow he consumed, but he had medicine with him, so after a while he recovered. Three sick people, one child and one cripple made it impossible to continue across the fields, so our guide decided to walk on the highway, where we would face much greater danger, but gain time and speed.

We have crossed one settlement that was brightly lit. We tried to walk as silently as we could. Soon we reached a second one and as we were about to cross that, a truck rushed toward us and we almost froze. The truck was loaded with armed soldiers and they could see us clearly, from two meters away, where it rumbled by without any sign of slowing. We were frightened out of our skulls. Even our guide was badly shaken. He took off...He was almost running...Then he must have taken control of his panic and slowed, to let us catch up with him. Our luck held...We found a large haystack, not far from the road and for half an hour we rested.

While my body cried out for rest, my mind examined many possibilities. *My two days of absence from my work is over. Today when I don't appear, my boss will notify the*

Secret Police agent. My poor daughter will be questioned...With her heart broken, with her spirit at its lowest, will she be able to follow my instructions? My controller possesses little intellect, but will it take not much to guess what I was doing. Probably he knows nothing about the others. He will call for a search, but the searchers will be looking for only two escapees. That will be to our advantage, but that will not last long. Lajos' parents will begin to miss them and when that happens, they will report their disappearance. Will they be able to put two and two together and search for a larger group? How long do we have before that will happen? I am fooling none, thinking of these possibilities. The two soldiers, possibly both dead, our guide shot at, must have been found...The searcher must be after us. Please God help us!

I had no more time to torture myself, at least not with my thoughts. We climbed out of the haystack and with chapped lips, with killing thirst, and gnawing hunger, we resumed our hike. I worried a great deal about the child, who was now sitting on my shoulder, but that child was a really wise one. Her parents prepared her well. She never complained, she never cried out. If she felt fear, which she must have felt, the only indication she gave me was by making her hand on my neck tighten.

We were approaching the third settlement and held a brief conference to decide if we should skirt around it, or if we should dare to march through it. The condition of most members of the group had badly deteriorated. We decided to march through the settlement's only street, in total silence. It was at that point that the armed civilian appeared form behind a house. Our guide, once again, described us as workers, going to a collective farm and in his excitement he forgot to inquire. After a few steps, he turned around and went back to ask for information. After his return, he told us that we will get on the road to Sopron, which was not far ahead of us. We approached another settlement, all lit up, but we were on its west side. To our left stood a vast body of water, its surface was slightly frozen. To our right, some three hundred meters away, we saw a larger building and a truck that drove out of the compound.

Panic gripped us, but only for a split second. Then all of us dove for the cover of the ditch that was full of water. The ice cover broke...Our bodies almost completely submerged; our heads behind withered reeds, as the truck sped by, then we were out. Sodden and cold and shivering and weak with exhaustion, we continued the only way we could...On the road by the illuminated compound. It took no time to recognize what the building was- a small military establishment that housed the border's guard units. The sounds that came from behind the walls were that of soldiers clanking metal on metal. We were terrified, expected the coming of the end and from behind the closed windows a few soldiers stared at us. To this day I don't understand why they have not rushed out, why they have not arrested us. There was only one explanation: Once again, the good Lord smiled upon us.

We marched by the building and beyond it. When we took a curve that hid us, we fell on the snow and tried to quench our thirst of excitement with that white stuff. The sun began to rise and once again finding a hiding place was most important. A mile away, we saw the outline of a forest and not our exhaustion, not the deep mud was able to impede our progress. Luck was with us...At the edge of the wood stood a huge haystack. We tore at the hay to create the cavities needed, but we made certain that the holes we dug faced away from the settlement and faced the woods, that stood close by. We settled in, covered our entry and after the deep mud, the ice and the water, we treasured our hiding place, like we would have treasured finding a palace. Had I known then that some of the others decided to take advantage of the warm sun to dry their wet clothing, I would have prevented the near tragedy, but I knew nothing about their stupid action and from our hiding place I saw three men come toward us.

    I watched them, as they came within fifteen feet, and my blood froze with fright and anxiety. One of the three stopped suddenly and surveyed what he saw. His harsh shouts came and four of us obeyed his order, we climbed out and stood there helplessly. They must have considered us gypsies and little wonder. Muddy clothing drying in the sun. Three men with unshaven faces. My wife with a drab, gray headkerchief on her head.

    They shook their heads and began to walk away, but after fifty meters they stopped and one, that carried a rifle, pointed at some of the trees. Then it dawned on me. *The man with the gun must be a forest ranger and the others are wood workers.* I hoped with all my heart that they will pay no more attention to our presence, when all three of them turned and came back to us. The forest ranger asked for identifications and after he checked two, he turned to me. I told him I had no papers. Our guide began to explain what happened to us. He informed them that we had tried to leave the country, but changed our minds and wished for nothing more than to be able to return home, without the authorities ever finding out.

    They looked quite skeptical, but the ranger took pity on us. With the help of the two workers he made a fire and told us to dry our clothing. The other members of the group, still hiding in the haystack, heard his words and the inviting, crackling fire and they appeared one by one.

    The additional number of strangers startled the ranger and he appeared to be hesitating. At that point I approached him with the intention of speaking with him, but the other male members of my group misunderstood what I was about to do and began to move, giving the impression that we were trying to surround him. He raised his rifle, pointed it at my chest. I called out to my companions, urged them to move back and when they obeyed me, I indicated that I just want to talk. We moved a few steps away from his companions and there I offered him my lapsed military identification. He looked at it, he was puzzled and when he heard me, he turned white. The news that I was a former, discarded military officer, without hope of any future in this country, took him by surprise. When I told him that we were not heading east, but were heading toward Austria, where my relatives lived and waited for our arrival, he was badly shaken. I asked him, I begged him, I appealed to his decency, to let us go in peace; to allow us to continue our journey. He just shook his head, chewed on his lips and contemplated. His decency must have fought a huge battle with his fear of what will happen if he doesn't inform the authorities. Then the battle came to an end. He told me I would have been better off have I not told him the truth, but soon after he added something that was really reassuring. He informed me that he hasn't heard a thing I said. Immediately after, he began to walk back to the village and this time it was I who had to fight a battle. On the one hand I felt like preventing him from reaching the village, on the other hand I felt an unexplainable trust toward that man and in the end the latter succeeded. I rejoined the group and we chatted with the two strangers as if were attending a party.

We have learned that one of them was forty years old and that he was the skeptical kind, especially when he was given a story like our guide gave him. The other one was much younger. He was twenty-four years old, we learned. A tractor driver and a young Communist, not by choice, but by necessity.

It didn't take us long to size them up and when we began to believe that they can be trusted, we informed them about our need for food. They looked at all of us, but in particular at the child girl and after our guide offered them two thousand *Forints*, they expressed their willingness to get us food. After prolonged negotiations, more money changed hands and our guide went with those two and we rested. Exhaustion caught up with all of us and we must have slept for all of five hours, when our guide arrived back with the two workers and woke us not only with the good news, but with the delicious food, they brought us.

We fell on the bread like hungry wolves; we consumed the ham, the sausages, the cheese and the boiled eggs. We gave no thought to the coming days, to further starvation, our good luck colored or wiped out our reasoning ability and so did the two bottles of rum. The two workers watched us with amusement, as we satiated our hunger, as we quenched our thirst.

When we finished eating and drinking, when not a morsel of food was left, they offered their services to help the weaker members of the group to get to the nearest railway station, to begin our homeward journey. I didn't think they believed our guide's story. I was certain they were putting us on. When we refused their help, they began to give us useful information. They described the deployment of the border guards; they told us where we can expect to meet with police units; gave us distances from one place to another. After two hours of friendly chat, they left us to our own devices. Our country depended on terror. Our leaders survived only as long as they remained constantly vigilant. Our people were forced to become informers and yet we have found that decency still existed. The forest ranger and his two helpers were the finest kind of Hungarians, as it turned out and although I have never learned their names, I have included them in all my prayers.

We rested for several more hours and the food, the drink, the warmer day, made me happy enough to cuddle up to my wife and to talk. That was the first time that she confessed how much her feet hurt, how they itched. I had no heart to tell her that she suffered from frost bite, the signs were far too familiar to me, for I have suffered from the same malady during the war. My concern for my dear wife mounted. *If she doesn't get medical help soon, she may have to have her toes or even her feet amputated.* That thought scared me so much that I began to urge our guide to get going. We decided to leave our palace of warmth at eleven o'clock in the evening. One of the women lost consciousness, just before we were to start out and that delayed us fifteen minutes, before the drug her husband gave her brought her around.

During the first thirty minutes, we walked in deep slush that the warm sun created. But the chill of night came fast and my wife's feet cooled sufficiently to hide her pain. Regardless of what the temperature was we suffered greatly. When it got warm the mud sucked at our footwear and to remove it from that dirty clutch required inhuman effort; when the temperature dropped greatly, several pounds of frozen mud clung to our footwear, as if they wished to stay with us, to leave this cursed country. Our small band of desperate men and women trudged on; those few who were still healthy aided the sick, the disabled, the child and the weaker women. We crossed a railway track and reached another road, that brought another truck and another dunking in a water filled ditch. We skirted around another settlement; avoided another border garrison, shied away from all populated places.

Five o'clock came on the morning of March fifth. We had completed the first three days of our escape plan. We were getting a lot closer to the border. The sounds of moving vehicles became more frequent...The appearance of guards could be expected at any moment, thus we have begun to exercise even greater caution. Our need to find another hiding place was made clear by the fast disappearing darkness. The forest of acacia trees stood front of us and when we went in we found out how small it was. We barely entered it and we could see out into a field and at the other end stood an inviting, huge haystack. I estimated the distance to be no more than one kilometer to our would be palace, but the daylight came far too fast to risk reaching it, so we stayed in that small clump of forest. We found a small, make shift hut, built close to the edge of the trees, that must have served no more than two border guards with an observation post and a bit of shelter. We tore it apart, built a windbreak a few feet from the edge of the small forest. We sat shoulder to shoulder, beside each other, facing away from the sneaky wind, that came in gusts and tore at our wet clothing. We were freezing, our teeth chattered, our limbs became stiff with the cold and with the seemingly endless waiting.

We had no food, nothing to drink, just plenty of cigarettes which we, men used to calm our nerves. Our little group lived on the hope of being able to endure everything the next seven kilometers had to offer. Our guide estimated that we were no farther than that from the border. In hushed voices he instructed us what we must do as we approach the border. Eleven o'clock came and we heard the fall of footsteps. An old peasant appeared from nowhere. He saw us and I couldn't tell who was more surprised, our small band of refugees or the old man. He looked at us, squinted at us and went on. We were in a trauma, we were benumbed by fear. Thank God it lasted only for a few moments and then I realized the danger of letting the man go. I ran after him and called him back, without trying to frighten him. To my friendly words he reacted and without hesitation he followed me back and made no secret of the fact that he was aware of our intentions. We gave him cigarettes, followed by a few hundred *Forints* and our small gifts loosened his tongue. He told us how six young men, just a few days ago, tried to get across the border. He described their fate, which sent us into a great gloomy depression. Three of them were killed when the guards opened fire, the three others were captured, carried through the nearest village, to set an example. We looked at each other and I am certain each and every one of us wondered what was waiting for us not far from here. He told us that this small patch of wood belonged to him and he came here, to make sure that the wood poachers weren't stealing him blind. There was a small hidden well, he told us, then he took us just a few feet from where we huddled and finally, thanks to the old, good-hearted Hungarian, we had plenty of good water to drink. He wished us good luck before he left us and I included another nameless Hungarian in all my prayers.

We suffered the cold and the hunger, but at least we were no longer thirsty. Around four, in the afternoon, we spotted someone in the distance. His stealthy movements and what looked like a rifle, on his shoulder, alarmed us. Our guide drew his revolver and rushed to intercept the stranger. Before the guide got within range, the man saw him and he broke into a run. Our guide told us that he was a young man, with a spade hanging on his shoulder and his direction was straight toward the border guards' garrison that we left behind us.

The guide informed us that soon we can expect horse mounted guards to appear. His statement caused panic. The child began to cry for the first time and half the group was ready to give up. Arguments broke out and my wife tried to calm them. Half an hour passed and the fear became a living, breathing monster. One woman began to tear at her hair in anguish and some others moaned softly, in their panic. Slowly the panic died off. It was replaced with quiet acceptance. We held hands, we hugged those we loved and for two more hours we have waited. Slowly evening began to fall and at six forty-five we rose from where we sat and with a new found determination began to walk the last seven kilometers. Our hope of being able to cross the border that very night, gave us strength and courage and in the darkness we began to see something. What looked like fireflies seemed to follow a pattern. Two flies moved, always in the same direction, until we could no longer see them, then sometime later another two appeared. I turned to our guide and inquired. What we heard gave us hope, yet it was terribly frightening. The fireflies were actually the light of two torches, carried by the patrolling border guards, in the far distance.

We walked, maybe only two kilometers, but we tired as if we had circumnavigated the earth. The plowed fields made us stumble and fall. The mud sucked us deeper and deeper and each addition step required more effort, more energy, more sacrifice, more of everything. Our guide pulled a muscle and he began to limp badly. The mud became deeper and deeper and there was no alternative but to form a chain and assist each other. Then the mud suddenly ended. We reached the side of a water filled ditch, that stood beside a roadway. Our guide stopped us and gave us the bad news. We must cross tonight...There is no alternative...If daylight finds us where we are, we will be finished. He decided, in spite of his pain, to go ahead and to do some scouting. We were to wait where we were, while he went toward a village, he called Zsira. We lay down on the hard ground, as he left us and we were all bone tired, hungry and in pain, but particularly my wife, whose frozen feet began to give her a great deal of trouble. We probably would have dwelt on our predicament, but were spared that, when the reflectors began to illuminate us. Five trucks of soldiers were being transported back to their compound, I judged from the direction of their travel. We pressed our bodies into the smallest of depressions to avoid being detected and when the trucks passed, my concern shifted from fear for ourselves to that of our guide. *Was he caught in those cursed lights? What will we do if he was captured?*

My self-torture didn't last long. My thoughts were interrupted. We heard the shout, commanding someone to stop, then everything became silent. We held our breath and waited. The sounds came from not too far. First the squeaking of something we couldn't see, then feet, many feet, from the direction of the highway. Then sucking sounds made by the mud and finally a welcomed announcement. . He informed whoever was in charge, that no human being is able to walk across this mud without being sucked down, immobilized and defeated. *Thank God the soldier did not know the strength of our determination.* The footsteps again and finally those sounds receding. I took charge. Made my companions move about fifty meters, along the ditch, in the direction of the border and suddenly footsteps came from behind us. Thank God, it was our guide and he got free after he met up with two soldiers, who ordered him to stop. He dove into a nearby ditch. Zigzagged to avoid being shot and the two soldiers jumped on bicycles and tried to head him off. Obviously they didn't succeed. What we heard earlier was the badly oiled bicycles and the sounds came again, but this time from the opposite direction. We speculated that the soldiers drove on, hoping to find our guide and were just now returning.

Our guide explained that we must resume our walking, but due to our close proximity to the border, we should be prepared for anything. His sobering, but realistic words, made all of us react. While the others spoke to their loved ones, I spoke to my wife. I told her that her behavior was truly heroic; I thanked her for the many years of bliss she gave me; I explained to her that these moments may be the last ones we can share. My broken heart didn't allow me to tell her what I expected. *If we are captured, we will be separated and we will never see each other again. We* said good-by to each other and our fervent kisses had many, many meanings.

I let go of my dearest, when a white rocket reached for the sky, illuminating the area around the settlement and just behind us. The bright light began to dim and when darkness fell, our shaking limbs received their orders and carried us over the deep, water-filled ditch, then across the road and into another field. Using every ounce of our energy, we walked beside a clear-cut forest in total silence. After five hundred meters of solid ground, we hit a plowed field that was more treacherous than any of the others. We were dragging ourselves out of the deep mud, no farther than one kilometer from the first fence. Our muscles began to give up, our feet would take no more steps; our guide must have realized and became agitated. Not far from us we seemed to see a haystack. *We must reach that hiding place, regardless of how much effort it will take,* I urged myself, then urged the others. *Four days, less one hour, had passed, since we began our journey and the time was four o'clock, the date was March sixth. This date I will always remember.* I thought sadly, but knowing not why exactly. *Will it be the day of our capture? Will it be the day of our deliverance?* I tried to see into the future, but all I saw was the need to hide, to assist those who could never make it to that haystack.

Fifty meters is not a long distance, but for ten totally exhausted people, fifty meters on muddy soil, where the water stood up to our thighs, was far, too far away and to reach it took an eternity. The haystack stood on high ground; all four sides of it were cut with care and on the one side, that faced the border, a large hole existed. It was clearly an observation post for the border guards, but now it was deserted. We tried to figure out what to do. To stay here promised great danger. To move on was total madness. Our guide informed us that he will go closer to the border to spy on the guards' activities. He left us within a moment and when Lajos noticed that he didn't take his small satchel that contained his map, his gun and his torch, it took Lajos only a few words to panic everyone.

"He has left us behind! He gave up on us! He is crossing the border without us!" The statements came from various people, but in whispers, not in shouts.

I saw Vilmos' wife whisper something in his ear, then I saw the five of them going into a huddle. When they broke apart, Vilmos' statement shocked me. He told us that they made all their relatives believe that they were going to Budapest for six days of shopping. He announced that they will be in no danger if they turn around and return to Baja. He announced that they will not take more risks. He, for the first time, told us that his wife had a heart condition that is why she was so weak and sickly. Vilmos' announcement was like the striking of a match setting others on fire. It was Lajos who followed their example. He informed us that they had misled everyone, by making them believe that they were visiting relatives. Not a soul knows about their escape plans, thus they will return too and urged us too to join them. There were now only three people, who had no other hope than crossing the border. Our far away guide, whom we may never see again and my wife and I who had nothing to lose and everything to gain.

The situation reached its most critical point, my wife must have realized and she exhorted them.

"You are badly mistaken," she told them patiently. "If you return after what happened on the first day, you will be charged with the murder of two soldiers. You will be found out. Think about the days, the nights, the dangers we have faced together. Think about the future of your three children in this country of slaves. But most of all, look in that direction." She pointed toward the border. "There is your future; there is your salvation, there is where freedom resides; there is where all of us should be heading. Are you all crazed with fear? Are you gripped by useless panic? Can't you see that there is no other choice? You have sacrificed so much and now you want to gain nothing?" Her words gave them no time to think. Her pleading; her arguments; her chiding made the two women burst out crying and Vilmos' two sons took a step to stand beside my wife, indicating clearly what they desired. We never noticed, until a bit later, that our guide stood flat against the haystack and listened to my wife's emotional appeal.

"I think you know that she is right. You have no energy left to go back...You will be captured and you will be punished. So what choice do you have? We will spend the day here, hiding. Now dig in and rest and sleep. Dream about success, dream about freedom, dream about the other side and after the day passes, we will cross the fence of despair; we will be across the border of hope and finally you will taste sweet freedom."

I measured our chance of success carefully. *The settlement is about a half kilometer away, behind us. We are separated from it by water covered fields. Front of us I can see the border. I judge it to be no more than one kilometer from where we were hiding. To our right, the deep, water filled ditch. To our left, the plowed field with its deep mud. Maybe the guards who use this hiding place will be loath to approach it. No doubt that danger lurks all around us, but what choice do we have left? Trust in luck and in the good Lord's mercy.*

At the very beginning of our long struggle, our guide taught us how to hide in a haystack, but this stack we had to handle far more carefully. All sides of it were very smooth; whoever built it was very crafty. The slightest disturbance could be detected. So we worked with the greatest of care. We lay down, on our backs, front of the stack, with our feet touching it. One kick at it, with both feet and our shoes were inside. Kick again and push and move deeper, until even our heads disappear. Now turn slowly, ever so slowly, until our torso was sufficiently twisted and we lay on our bellies. Now to free our hands and use them to cover properly the opening. That was the process and the energy it took left us even more exhausted. The weight of the hay helped too and within an hour, it settled to hide all openings.

A long day of fearful, nerve wracking waiting followed. Hunger and thirst and cold and misery and the feeling of weight above us, almost brought us insanity. Being prone and unable to move for twelve hours was hard, very hard.

We lay there, not even able to speak. When daylight came, soon after we hid ourselves, in the rising sun we saw the armed border guard, about two hundred meters away. His destination was clearly our hiding place. He was walking on hard-packed ground and his dog was pulling him. His steady progress brought him closer. I watched and prayed and cursed with each step he took and about fifty meters from us I saw him reaching the water covered field. *Please stop...Good Lord make him stop...Don't let him come any closer...*I prayed and knew that the guard will be hesitating, but not the dog, that trained animal. With determined effort it kept pulling its master toward the water and at the edge of it something made it turn and to drag his master away from us. *The dog must have picked up the scent of our guide, that he left behind, when he left us, a few hours ago.* Hammers were striking at my heart, sweat poured off my shivering body and I watched and watched with increasing hope as the dog, followed by his master, began to disappear.

It was a close call, a very close one and I suffered, like all the others, thinking about being discovered, being captured, this close to the border. *Will he come back? Will others approach us?* The thoughts rattled in my brain and minute after miserable minute I was unable to do anything, but hope and pray and wait and squeeze my wife's hand, which was cold and shaky.

I had made many friends during my forty-three years of living in this country and

Laszlo S. Lichter

I have made enemies too. But this day and what went with it, I didn't wish even on my greatest enemy. I have always believed in Heaven and in Hell, but I know now that the latter really exists.

An hour or so later, my confused mind heard groans of pain and my foggy mind was unable to determine where it came from. Then my mind cleared and I have recognized that the groans belonged to my suffering wife. Her frozen feet must have warmed up sufficiently to have her brain register the cruel pain. It broke my heart to be unable to hug her, to comfort her, to help her, but the heavy load of hay and the lack of energy no longer allowed even the slightest movement. My feverish mind called out for the Almighty and He granted my wish, for her groans died off. She had fallen into a feverish slumber and after a while I joined her in blessed dreamland, where pain no longer existed, where suffering was unknown, where no guards hunted for us, where only freedom existed. When I came awake, I was unable to look at my watch, but from the angle of the sun's rays I judged that my sleep was a very short one. Wakefulness, brief slumbers, unconscious existence alternated, in no particular order and what I felt must have been close to the experience of one who is taking his last breath of life, before he is called to his Maker.

Darkness fell and the hay began to rustle. Then I heard our guide's whisper. He urged us to emerge from the haystack and one by one, he pulled us out and made us lean against it. He rubbed my arms, then my legs and when my blood had finally circulated, the two of us began to work on two others. When we finished our task, two others were restored to living and some twenty minutes later, all of us were able to take a few staggering steps.

Our group was ready to move, but not before we whispered encouragements to each other and in hushed voices husbands said good-by to their wives; the young ones were given a final kiss, just in case we will never again be able to do that. We wade across the water filled ditch and on firmer ground we walk toward the border. We are some five hundred meters from it. We see the faces of the guards, who walk in pairs, with their torches swinging right and left, but we really see not their faces. It is only our imagination. We take a few more steps and hear the hiss and see the bursting red rocket. One of us must have touched a hidden wire and that set off the rocket to illuminate everything around us. We dropped to the ground and waited to have the rocket fall back to earth, right beside us. The little girl is in my arm, she fell from my shoulders when I dropped to the ground. She makes no sounds, just clutches my hand, letting me know that she knows her duty: stay flat against the ground and remain totally silent. That is how our guide prepared us for this terrible moment.

Our guide gave his order in whispers and the male members of the group all sprang into action, doing their duty in four different directions. Ground pepper all around us is being sprinkled in a liberal manner.

We knew that the bursting of a red rocket will activate the guards and their ever present tracking dogs...The pepper will render the dogs useless, but the guards are another matter. We began a mad rush to cover the remaining distance and after another hiss, another red rocket, our last hidden reserve of energy, that we didn't know existed, sends us, drives us closer and closer to the fence. We come to a paved highway and on the other side, some three hundred meters away, we can see the fence. We cross the road in total silence, our movements are now more stealthy, but the crunch of gravel, under our feet, sound like thunder in our ears that are used to silence. The slight breeze brings voices of the hunters and we step off the highway. The terrain front of us looks smooth, but after a few steps, we find nothing but mud, sucking mud that drags us down. After the first few steps all of us begin to sink deeper and deeper. The mud reaches up to our knees. We pull ourselves out and with the next few steps it reaches higher. It must be close to seven in the evening, night fell early on this cloudy day, and not one of us is able to take a step without assistance. Our guide was at the head of the column and he reached back, pulling me and helping me to gain one step. Then one by one he assists the others, until he becomes the last one. Now it is up to me and after many moments I am the one at the end. This continues for a few hours, until we gain a hundred meters. The searchers are not close to us...They must consider this section of the field to be impossible to cross, but we have no other choice, so with inhuman effort we continue. The guards, no longer fireflies, walk front of the fence and are a lot closer. I turned to the good Lord, like all the others must, and beseeched him to help us just a bit more, to save us from drowning in this swamp, to help us cross the border.

We begin to see the outline of a guard tower, some two hundred meters to our side, but the search lights never come on. We hear voices carried by the breeze. *Thank God for their ineptness...Thank God for the way they operate...Mechanical failures, in this country, are very common and the expediency of repair is almost nonexistent.* My thoughts are disrupted, alerted to another danger. *We are halfway from the edge of the swamp to the fence. The mud is pulling us down, but never deeper than our thighs. What if we take a step and there is no bottom, just a muddy, watery grave awaits us? Dear God, please don't allow nature to do the job of the man hunters. Please don't allow us to disappear without a trace. Please let us survive, please let us be free.*

A few members of the group, until now, kept their few parcels, that may have contained a few pieces of extra clothing, but now silently they give them to the swamp, no energy left to carry them any farther.

The sounds become louder and we begin to make out the words. "Nobody can walk through this swamp. Follow me...We will search the other sector." The speakers must have been on the earthen walkway, just beyond the four meter wide, raked strip that serves as an identification belt. They took great pains to keep it in good condition, so that every track would show clearly. *Front of the walkway stands a forty to fifty meter wide mine field. The mines are of two types. One kind is activated by the weight of an average human being. This kind poses less danger in very cold weather, once their soil cover freezes hard, these mines are rarely activated. The other kind poses much greater danger. They are wired together with trip wires and the unfortunate soul who touches the wire sets many mines off.* The words of the guide, spoken at Baja, come back to me like the words of a harmless lecture. *Thank God my wife wasn't there...Thank God she doesn't know what awaits us...*

Laszlo S. Lichter

I am thinking about our desperate situation. *Our progress is slow. The manhunt continues, in spite of the two hours that passed since the second red rocket. They don't give up...They are determined to find their prey...They love the hunt...They love the rewards...Three weeks of vacation and a watch for each guard, who captures a refugee alive, or two weeks of vacation for a dead one. They want those vacations...The watch doesn't matter much...So we are in great danger of being shot.*

We move carefully, silently, like the hunted deer does. When we see the light of approaching guards, we lay down and rest until they pass, then for two to three minutes we walk, just to get a few meters closer. Seeing into the land of freedom gives us new lease on life, gives us hope and more energy. For three more hours we walk and we find ourselves just fifty meters from the barbed wire. We are on the ground, our bellies touching the soil of the land where we were born, the land that now is our enemy. We breathe, but even that we must do slowly, carefully, to avoid making the slightest sound. Mud surrounds us, trying to reach our mouths, our nose, trying to suffocate us. We are almost unconscious. My fog-filled mind conjures up the kids we left behind us. It shoves front of me the faces of my relatives and the home I loved so much. *But there are no kids now, there are no relatives and we have traded our home for manure piles, for haystacks, for muddy marshes. There is only one goal, one desire, one wish, we must succeed, we must reach freedom.*

We moved on, in three minute burst and I began to lose all hope, when we got to the edge of the withered, grass covered field. Our guide ordered us to hide at the edge of the field and as soon as the guards passed, he began his painstaking probing. With knitting needle in one hand, he is on his knees. In goes the needle, but ever so lightly and when it encounters resistance, our guide puts another probe down, just a few inches away. In this manner he marks out a spot, where he can plant his foot and knee. His progress is slow, but before the next guards' arrival, he uses his own footsteps and hides beside us. Then it starts over and over again. In one hour he has the route and in a single file we begin the crossing. I watch where he steps, and when he moves one foot, I replace his and so it goes. My wife watches me, she is watched by the next one and although our progress seems to be slow, we complete the crossing of the minefield and the walkway, before the appearance of the next guards. We hide again, check our breathing and wait until they pass us.

Now we cross the raked belt, but this time our guide is behind us and he sweeps all signs of our crossing. When the next group of guards shine their torches on that strip of ground they will see nothing, but undisturbed earth and they will move on while we press our bodies against the ground, hoping against hope that we will not be detected. God was with us...They passed us by and now we must cut through the two meter high, thickly wowed wire fence, that is laced with booby traps and trigger wires to set off more red rockets. Three wire cutters are being operated by three males. The guide cuts, then he points at where I am to cut, then he does the same for Lajos. The child girl is in her Father's arms and she is still quiet, but the night's silence is shattered by the sound of snapping wires.

When the breech is wide enough to pass across the fence, our guide stands there with a mine between his feet, trying to assure that we will not step on it. Our steps become lively, our hearts beat with renewed hope and when the last of us left the fence behind, our guide came after us, no doubt greatly relieved. The second fence stands only two meters away, much like the first one and in between a deep ditch. The water in it provides us with another soaking. A few more cuts, hacking the second fence to pieces and when we cross it we kiss the ground...We are on Austrian soil, we cannot believe it. We hug each other; we shower each other with many kisses. We are finally free. We stand there, just meters from the fence of despair. Our hopes are resurrected...Our eyes fill with tears, with tears of joy and with the tears of suffering and with the tears of sad parting. We gained freedom, but the price was great. Our children, our grandchild, our relatives and all our possessions we have traded in.

Then the sounds come, the terrible sounds of shouting. Suddenly we realize the grave danger we are in. The guards can no longer reach us, but their guns are still within range. We begin to run. Only God knows where the energy comes from, but we run up the hill for dozens of meters and when we reach the hill's summit and run a few feet downwards, we fall down totally exhausted. We are behind shelter from the guns of our enemies, who are our countrymen, but who were subverted by the cursed Communists to become hunters, to become the executioners of all freedom loving beings.

I don't know why, but I thought of the last mass I had attended many months ago and heard the last words of the priest: " And God be with you." Those words never meant much, until this day, until this place and from that moment on His presence, His being with us, we never doubted again.

**

Through our inhuman struggle, we became a closely knit family. We surveyed each other. A woman lost one of her boots; another one sprained her ankle, but nothing mattered any more.

After a happy rest, much kissing the ground and each other, we rose and limped close to the nearest Austrian village. At its edge we found a haystack and having no more energy to walk on, we sought its shelter and for two and a half hours we had rested. There was no sleep, just endless talking. We spoke about various phases of our escape; we reminisced about the dangers we had faced together, but most of all we spoke about the Divine guidance and enormous luck that brought us here. We knew that we were still in the Russian occupied sector. We knew that we were not totally out of danger, but our state was so euphoric that for now we paid no heed to anything.

When it was time to move again, to catch the four o'clock bus, to continue our journey, lady luck had deserted us. It was Sunday and no bus service ran on the Lord's day.

Laszlo S. Lichter

We looked for a glebe house, but found none, at least not at that end of the village. When the lights came on at a nearby house, our guide asked us to remain quiet and he went to investigate. In no time he was waving from the house's gate and one by one we sneaked into it.

The Austrian woman and her son could not have been more friendly. They urged us to get rid of our muddy overcoats and as we took them off, as we dropped them on the floor, we dropped beside them. In no time at all, the woman gave us deep plates, filled with hot chicken soup. The steam rose to meet our tears and we all cried unashamedly. The host pulled down the curtains to hide us from prying eyes. For six long days we have experienced nothing like this. For two whole days we had nothing to eat. And now when food and drink became plenty, we spent a great deal of time crying. I will never forget our first Austrian hosts; I will never forget their kindness.

After we have had our fill of food and drink, our hostess' son led us to the stable. There we settled down, beside our new neighbors: two cows, a couple of horses and three pigs and basked in the heat they generated. None of our limbs functioned properly; we were exhausted, but in spite of that, we began to clean ourselves, in the hope of being again, looking again like human beings. Paramount on my mind was to remove the shoes and socks from my wife's aching feet. The removal of socks and laced shoes, that were on her feet for six solid days, required a sharp knife and a pair of large scissors. When I have finally succeeded, I was sick. Her feet were purple and black. The mud worked its way under her skin, where the shoelaces cut into her flesh. From four toes on her right foot and from three on the left, some terrible, grayish, whitish, fluid exuded. I looked at her suffering face, then at her feet again and I marveled at the strength of her character, at her determination. *Here is a woman who has known great pain, yet rarely complained. This is my wife who walked many miles with these frozen toes and found the inner reserve to help others. She is something else. My soldiers, during the war, demanded hospitalization for far less of a frost bite and my wife instead of complaining urged others to move on, to seek freedom. That is just far too amazing. When we wed we gave our oath to stand by each other in good or bad, but to do, what she did, was far beyond that pledge. It exceeded all my expectations.* We brought lots of hot water from the house and began administer our treatment. Hot soaking, followed with cold, seemed to ease her pain, but her feet began to swell grotesquely.

The rest of us were better off. We were encased in caked mud. The men sported several days of unchecked growth of facial whiskers. We began to wash, to scrub, to shave, until we began to look like human beings. We slept and woke to the comings and goings. The neighbors came, brought a portion of their Sunday dinner and we sampled the delicious food they brought. They eased our hunger, they satiated our thirst and our bodies began the long process of healing.

Then March eighth arrived and three in the morning we began our preparations for the long bus trip. We dressed my wife's feet the best we could and an old pair of large boots she was able to tolerate, but just barely. She limped to the bus station and in the alcove of a gate we waited. An Austrian policeman sauntered by, in a leisurely manner, and he either didn't notice us or didn't care.

The bus arrived and our guide went to talk to the driver. When he returned, he led us one by one and made us take a seat in the very back. The bus was transporting workers to a factory in the Communist zone of Vienna and the outside of it was plastered with tasteless, Communists slogans, with the red star, with the hammer and sickle. Seeing these symbols of Communism did not allow us to forget that we were still in danger and not exactly free. The bus filled up slowly, as it picked up more and more workers at its stops. We were warned by our guide not to converse. Hungarian words would bring us doom. In this silent manner we entered Vienernaisstadt, on the outskirts of Vienna.

Our fear began to mount as we saw six buses ahead of us. Their passengers stood outside, as two Russian soldiers were in the process checking their papers. *We have spent six dreadful days to get this far. All our efforts, all our sufferings, all our sacrifices were for naught. The arm of the Communists was far reaching and now we are within their grasp, we are in mortal danger.* I saw the outcome very clearly. *First the arrest, then the separation. After that will come the beatings. The Communists would make sure that our sufferings will be hard and long, before they allow us to face the hangman.*

Two Russian officers stepped on the bus, although we understood not much in Russian, their command was understood by all. They ordered us to get off the bus. I squeezed my wife's hand and she returned my touch. Without words we said good-by and it seemed that our life together was over. To our surprise the driver stood up and in fluent Russian he began to argue. After what seemed like a heated debate, one of the officers spoke one single word, "Karaso" and the two of them left the bus. Our bus pulled out from behind the others and passed by the six buses and as we put distance between us and the Russians, we glimpsed once more the miracle of a loving God.

It was sometime later that we found out what was said and what had happened. The driver told the officers that all on this bus had security clearance. That we were working in a secret establishment, that was run by Russians and only those were allowed to step on the bus who had their passes. The bus was behind schedule and even one more minute of delay would bring swift retribution. When the officers still insisted on checking everyone, the bus driver demanded a written note to explain the reasons for his lateness. He told them that the responsibility will fall on their shoulders. It appeared that the officers were quite low on the totem pole, thus the ruse worked and they gave in. Thanks to that fast thinking, kind driver our lives were safe, our efforts paid off.

In a few minutes we entered Vienna and our bus stopped just fifty feet from the factory entrance. The workers began to leave the bus and as they did, we took up our new seats, as were instructed, before the bus trip, by our guide and now we were scattered around the bus and each of us ducked below the windows. From the outside the bus appeared to be empty. When the bus pulled out and sped away, our guide waved to us to sit up and he was laughing. Finally we were out of danger. Ten minutes later the bus stopped front of a bakery and our guide announced that he will make a phone call.

He left the bus, but within a few minutes he returned with buns and other baked goods and the ten of us fell on the food like hungry wolves, but the fresh baked goods didn't taste as good, as the taste of our new found freedom.

Ten minutes later the bus stopped at the mouth of a narrow alley and there we alighted. The military truck, with its engine purring, stood ten feet away and the hands of American soldiers lifted us, piled us in the canvas covered back of the truck. Two black soldiers joined us and gave us chocolates, candies, chewing gum and far more than that. They gave us their caring and our final freedom.

The bus entered a large building, which was obviously an American compound and there our new life began. We were treated like heroes. We were greeted, congratulated, wined and dined. All of us received immediate medical attention and when the doctor examined my wife, in perfect Hungarian he made his pronouncement. She needed immediate medical attention...She was to be flown to Linz, to an American hospital, where she will receive the best of care. I hated the idea of parting and begged them to take me too, but that was impossible. The plane available could carry only the pilot and my wife, so we had a tearful parting.

After my beloved, courageous wife, the mainstay of our group, our inspirer was taken from me, I turned my mind to other matters. I sent a message through the Free Europe Radio to our daughter. They must know as soon as possible that we were safe, that we were finally free. Then came the debriefing and I took my thoughts back to the second of March when we began our perilous journey. Step by careful step, I told my entire story. When I came to the end, my listeners shook their heads and one of them made a suggestion.

"You should write this all down, so that others could read it. Millions upon millions of people take freedom for granted. You should let them know what treasure freedom really is."

I spent my two weeks, while away from my beloved wife, to write an outline of our escape and twenty years later, when I finally had the time, I typed our story.

Chapter 16

"Welcome back, Laszlo. I hope your depression has passed," Pasko approached me, after my two days of absence.

"Thanks to you, I was able to help my loved ones. As to my depression, it seems to get deeper every day." I stopped, not wanting to push my luck.

"Maybe you should tell me all about it. Maybe I could help?"

"I know you mean well, Colonel Pasko, but nobody can really help us."

"You will never know until you try me."

At that point I was ready to do as my Father-in-law suggested. I told my commander about the wire; about our relative being on her deathbed. "My wife's parents expected to be away for two days only, but they have not returned yet. My wife and my baby are without care." My last statement wasn't exactly true, but the truth wouldn't have served me.

"I think you should return to your wife and baby for one more day. I am sure that by the end of the day your in-laws will return safely."

I needed little urging. Thanked my commander and gained one more day for the escapees.

***

The third day has passed-since Rozsa's parents left-and when I returned to my office, on the morning of the fourth day, Pasko was nowhere to be seen. I turned my mind to the accumulated tasks and whenever the door opened, I, without great effort, acted devastated.

Pasko came in, he sat down beside me.

"So how is my chief clerk?" he asked me kindly.

"I wish I was a lot better, but I am not in the habit of lying. There is no word from my wife's parents, they seem to have vanished. My wife cries day and night. She is unable to eat, to sleep and that upsets our baby."

"I do sympathize with them Laszlo. Could you not contact that sick lady?"

"I don't know which hospital she is in. I never thought of asking Rozsa's parents, before they left. Maybe they had an accident? Maybe they are dead or dying?"

"If that is what you think I should send out an inquiry."

"Where do you think you would inquire?"

"I will check first if there was a bus accident. Didn't you say they traveled by bus?"

"That is the way they went to Budapest."

"Then I would check with the Police department of Budapest to see if there was an accident in their city. They would check all the hospitals, I am sure and they would be glad to accommodate me."

"How long do you think all this checking would take?"

"No more than a day, I guess, and while they are doing the checking, you better look after your family."

I thanked him for his kindness and rushed home to my wife and baby.

***

"I am sorry, yet I am glad Laszlo," my commander told me on Saturday, the fifth morning.

"I do not understand."

"I am sorry I found out nothing and I am glad that your in-laws were not in any accident. Where do you think they may have gone?"

"I wish I knew. This is not like them...They are kind, caring, responsible people. If they had a choice they would have come back. They would be looking after Rozsa and my little daughter." I made my voice quiver, without much trying.

"Are you hiding something from me, Laszlo?"

"Just one thing; one possibility."

"Then tell me what is that?"

"I don't know if I can. It is not that I don't trust you, but I don't even dare to seriously consider the dreadful possibility." I put on the act and hoped that he will push me.

"You have no choice. This matter seems to be getting out of hand. If I were you, I would spill it all out. I wouldn't try to hide anything."

"My father-in-law was a former officer in the army. The AVO didn't exactly treat him kindly. Night after night, AVO agents came to their house, always around two o'clock in the morning and they parked under their windows, they talked, they smoked a few cigarettes and then they left. Those experiences frightened them and may have been...Oh, I don't know any more what to think." I pretended to hesitate, but he pushed me to continue my story.

"When they didn't come back, after two days, I began to think of this possibility and with the passing of each day I began to fear that my thinking may not be far off. I didn't even tell my dear wife what I was thinking."

"Will you spit it out? Quite frankly I don't have the whole day." Pasko became somewhat impatient and I judged the time to be right to improvise on what Rozsa's Father suggested.

"The AVO works in mysterious ways. What if the wire was sent by them? What if they tricked them to go to Budapest? What if they made them disappear?" I made my questions indicate anguish.

"Do you have that relative's address?"

I was prepared for that question and I wrote down the address for Pasko.

"I will make a quick phone call. If your relative is not dying, then you maybe on the right track. I will call the Budapest Police Department. Give me five minutes, and then you come in." Pasko stood up, went inside his office and I waited.

I entered his office, when he just put the phone down. He had one of the two phones; the other phone was in his Deputy's office. Not even I, the chief clerk, was allowed to have one.

"Sit down Laszlo...I spoke to someone in Budapest and gave him the address. A policeman will be sent there soon and when he reports back, we will have the answer."

I thanked him, went back to my office and there I sat and worked for most of the day. I knew what the news will be and tried to prepare myself for my life's greatest role, tried to summon up my limited acting ability.

"Please come in..." Late afternoon, Pasko called me in and I saw his pasty face, his sagging jaw. He was a kind man; he suffered more than I did, while he told me the story.

"Laszlo, you must be brave...The news is not good...I wish I didn't have to tell you."

"Please...Please, don't tell me that I was on the right track," I moaned and groaned and forced out a few tears.

"I asked you to be brave...Stop your crying."

I wiped away my tears and looked straight into his eyes.

"Now that is much better. This is what I found out: Your relative, her name is Lujza, is as healthy as can be. When the policeman went to her apartment, she opened the door and she looked frightened...She is not sick; she is not dying. The official spoke with her at length and he is convinced that she did not send the wire."

"How could that be? It cannot be true! If it is, my worst fears are coming true. They were arrested, like so many others...My poor Dad and his wife, tricked, arrested, made to disappear? Why would anybody do that? We will never see those dear people...How will I be able to give the bad news to my darling?" I lamented, letting Pasko observe my misery.

"You are letting your imagination run away with you Laszlo. All I found out that the wire came from someone else. You are jumping too fast to the wrong conclusions."

"What else could I do?" I cried out.

"You could let me do what I can, before you say a single thing to your wife."

"What can you do?"

"First I must admit that I don't have the power to push the AVO. But I have a friend and he will find out. It will take time...Let me see. Today is Saturday. If you go home now and spend what is left of the weekend with your wife and daughter, I think by Monday morning we should have the answer."

Once more I spoke words of thanks and my driver drove me home to enjoy the rest of Saturday and all of Sunday.

***

Sunday morning, I began to fiddle with the radio's tuner. I sat it carefully on the short-wave band and selected the proper bandwidth. Silence greeted us, but it was too early yet. An hour of waiting was nerve wracking, but when ten o'clock arrived the radio came to life and we were glued to the old set.

First came the somber music that lasted only for a half of a minute, then: "The mills of God grind slowly..." The announcer's voice intoned the usual words with which the Free Europe Radio signed on. Our ears were only inches from the radio's speaker. Rozsa and I strained to hear it. Then came the buzz, the cursed Communists were at it and the voice was drowned out. I played with the dial, hoping to escape the jamming.

A male voice began to give the news items, but what we heard came in spurts and it was far from clear.

"A group..." We heard, then came the loud buzzing. I moved the dial just a fraction and a few words came through the speaker. "Several people..." Buzz again. I moved the dial. "Their valiant struggle..." More and louder buzzing. Another moving of the dial. "The details are..." Buzz...Frantic twisting and turning of the dial.

"Try harder Laszlo. Please do it fast...We must find out," Rozsa's cried out. Her Grandmother returned to her home, at Rozsa's request, to get something, earlier in the morning. We didn't want her to witness our frantic efforts; we didn't want her to become suspicious.

My struggle continued for one half hour, while the broadcast lasted, but what we were able to hear amounted to almost nothing.

"What do you think Laszlo? Did my dear parents get out?"

"They probably did." I tried to assure Rozsa.

"What makes you think that?"

I tried to recall all we heard and began to put them on paper.

"A group...Several people...Their valiant struggle...The details are..." The announcer's words accumulated, but those few words, we were able to hear, meant so little, meant almost nothing.

"We heard so little, but what we heard is encouraging," I told Rozsa.

"No...You are trying to mislead me...They must have failed. They must have been captured." Rozsa was in agony.

"No! Look at these words. Let's try to fill in the gaps." I told her and took another piece of paper. I wrote down what we heard and added my own words in italics.

"A group *of people escaped from Hungary. The escape was* a valiant struggle, but it *paid off. They are free.* The details are *not yet complete. Further details will be provided as they become available.*"

"You are just trying to make me feel better...What we heard really says not a thing." Rozsa spoke up and I decided to burn both pieces of paper, to make certain that the Communists would never find them.

"We will listen again this evening. I know, I feel it in my heart, that your parents made it my beloved." I assured her, kissed her and we found what little comfort we could by admiring our little darling.

Evening came slowly on that terrible Sunday. From time to time, again and again, we brought up the subject of that jammed broadcast and when we became no wiser than before, I began to talk about getting a better set.

"But we don't have the money," Rozsa announced and suddenly I thought of what never entered my mind, not even in passing.

"Rozsa is right. I no longer earn anything more than the sixty *Forints* a month, the army pays me. Her maternity pay equals her salary, but with her parents gone, her Father's income will no longer supplement Rozsa's earning. How will we pay the rent? How will we survive? I must turn to Aunt Gizella and to Uncle Jozsef for financial help. I must find a way to milk the army." My thoughts were interrupted by the arrival of Rozsa's Grandmother and for the rest of the day we tried to hide our pain; we tried to avoid speaking about the broadcast. Rozsa's Grandmother was in the habit of retiring early and when she did, we have waited with anxiety for the Free Europe Radio to sign on.

I turned the radio on, but this time set the volume lower and to my great surprise the jamming fell into the background and the announcer's words came more clearly.

"Six...men...to escape. The sad...follows: Three...dead...Three...captured. They...price...freedom." We heard and shed a few tears for those who lost their lives trying to gain their freedom. It was quite clear that the announcer didn't speak about Rozsa's parents and their companions, but about another group that perished at the border.

That night I said a silent prayer and begged the dear Lord to grant His mercy to Rozsa's parents.

***

Monday morning I took a photograph of Rozsa's parents from an album and put it in my tunic's pocket. As soon as I arrived to my office, Pasko called me in and introduced me to an officer, who was the AVO agent assigned to our regiment.

"This is a friend of mine...He made the inquiry you requested Laszlo. I will let him tell you what he found out."

"During the weekend I have contacted our headquarters in Budapest. Every AVO unit received an inquiry and their replies came back, shedding no light on your in-laws' disappearance. We drew a complete blank. Your suspicions were unfounded." The officer's words didn't hide his resentment.

"Now that I know I must do something," I announced.

"What do you want to do?" Pasko asked.

"I want the authorities to start a manhunt. A crime may have been committed. I want to know if my in-laws were victims or perpetrators. They may have been robbed. They may have been killed. Or they may have staged their own disappearance. This last possibility I hate to admit, but I have no other choice than to provide you with their picture. Have this picture circulated...Let them be hunted without mercy. If they have done this terrible thing to my sweet, innocent wife, then I want them to be found, I want them to be punished."

"Only the police could do what you suggested," the AVO officer spoke up.

"In that case I want your permission Comrade Colonel Pasko to go to the police now."

"My permission you have and the three of us will go together."

***

Half an hour later, we sat with the Police Chief of Baja and he asked me many questions.

"Why have you not come to us after the first two days?" the Chief asked me, after I told him my story and what I wanted them to do.

"Corporal Lichter came to me," Pasko spoke up. "At that time I saw no need to involve the police."

"You were wrong Comrade Colonel Pasko. This is not a military matter...It is a matter that clearly falls within our jurisdiction." The Chief took Pasko on.

"That is why we are here..."

"Okay, let me have the picture. We will begin the manhunt," the Chief announced. "Corporal Lichter, you wait outside, just in case we have any further questions."

I paced the corridor with great impatience and thought and thought about what I did.

"They left last Tuesday...They had six full days to get across the border...I hope they made it...But what if they didn't? What if they ran into a snag? If they needed more time to cross the border? Did I do the right thing or did I betray them? I did nothing more than what my Father-in-law asked me. I had to do this. I have to think of my wife, my child and of my precarious situation." My guilt-filled, doubtful thoughts chased each other and in my misery I didn't notice that Pasko was beside me.

"Laszlo come with me." His order sounded harsh, but it may have been only my imagination.

Front of the Police Station our driver waited, but Pasko dismissed him and announced that we will take a walk.

Side by side, we walked in silence, then Pasko turned to me.

"We put our heads together, I mean the Police Chief, the officer of the AVO and I. We have figured out what had happened. The other two must never find out that I told you about our conclusion and the action that now will follow." I listened to him and gave my word never to divulge anything he tells me.

"Our conclusion is not a pleasant one, but that is the only one we could agree on Laszlo. Your Father-in-law is a former, high ranking officer of the army and besides he was the Captain of the River Police, he had two postings. In the jobs he held he came across a lot of confidential information. Our enemies are many. Amongst them the Americans are number one. They are always looking for information about our military strength and about our country. Your Father-in-law must have been their target. They sent him that false telegraph...They lured them to the capital and from there they whisked them across the border. I am afraid your in-laws were kidnapped by a conniving bunch of bastards."

"I cannot believe that. That is dreadful. I never thought of that possibility." I made the announcement and almost laughed out at Pasko's stupidity and that of the others.

"Believe it Laszlo. And I might as well tell you what the AVO officer decided. He will inform his superiors and when he does, the State apparatus will spring into action. Their arms are long, those arms reach into many countries. Austria is not far away and there they have many, capable agents. Give it a few weeks, may be a few months and your in-laws will be brought back, they will be kidnapped once again, if it need be."

I was swamped with my emotions and not to betray what I felt, what I thought, I stared ahead and remained absolutely silent.

"They got out! They succeeded! Dear Lord I thank You! I must let Rozsa know, as soon as I can. She will be truly happy. We will celebrate...We will rejoice...We will have to pretend to be in pain...And we will have to warn her parents. Dear Lord don't let them succeed in bringing them back. You allowed them to be free. Please protect them from the AVO monsters. Please allow us to join them soon. Please make us free."

"You are very silent Laszlo. What bothers you now?"

"How can I tell my wife the terrible truth? How can I inform her that her parents are the victims of the Imperialist enemy?"

"Don't tell her what happened to her parents. She will know the truth soon enough. I think letters will come. The enemy will find out the position you are in and no doubt they will force them to try to enlist you. Will you ever pass on information, Laszlo?"

"I will die first...I would never betray my country." My words were believed or so I thought and that evening I rushed home to tell the great news to my darling.

***

"Are you sure Laszlo? Are you absolutely certain?" she asked me, over and over. We were in our bedroom, talking in hushed voices.

"I couldn't be more certain of anything."

"How can you be so sure? The AVO is an evil organization. What if they are lying?"

"We must look at what I was told in a logical manner," I began to explain. "They had six days to get across the border. Had they been captured, the AVO would have told us, they would have gloated. So we must assume that they got across the border. The AVO hates to be out-foxed by anyone. They would never admit a successful escape from this country. So they cooked up a plausible story. Your parents were kidnapped by Imperialist agents. Just think about this Rozsa. Your parents were harassed by the AVO and they have slipped out of their clutches. They don't want to look inept; they fear to admit failure; they don't want the responsibility and the inevitable punishment that would follow. That is why they have concocted this story. There is another thing, I just thought of my darling. After what I was told neither of us will be interrogated. They must have told Pasko to inform me, but to make it sound like he was sharing with me confidential information. I think my darling that we will be safe and that we will have news from your parents, by next Sunday."

I was right. Neither Rozsa, nor I, were interrogated about her parents' disappearance and our luck has changed greatly.

Two days later we received a letter and a cheque for one thousand *Forints*. It took us a few moments to absorb the good news. The Peace Bonds I have bought, during my first year of teaching, were entered into a draw, as all bonds were and this time an anti-Communist won something.

"Someone made a terrible mistake my dear. Only the Communists win anything in these draws. This time they must have slipped up and it would serve them well if we spent this amount wisely."

"What are you suggesting Laszlo?"

"I know it is an ironic suggestion, but I think you will like it. Let's buy the most powerful short-wave radio with this windfall. The stupid Communists deserve that my darling."

"I am all for it...Let's do it, Laszlo," she told me, cheered up and began laughing. "By next Sunday we should be able to hear a lot better." Rozsa settled the issue and after two days of careful shopping, our old radio was replaced with a new one.

***

Before Sunday came I have worked each and every day in the office. I feared what I thought might be coming. To lose my position of trust and comfort would have changed everything, but I was truly lucky. The two hours of work, I was asked to do every day in Colonel Pete's office came to an abrupt halt, but that I didn't mind. It provided me with more time to do my own job and to spend more time with my darlings.

After we had acquired our new radio, we have tried it out and it sounded fine, but the real test came on next Sunday.

The Free Europe Radio's theme song came in very clearly. Then came the announcer's voice, crisp and clear and in the background the inevitable, but much lighter buzzing.

"The mills of God grind slowly, but surely...." The announcer intoned and then read many news items. Before five minutes passed we sat up straight, my hand holding on to Rozsa's and the words set our hearts on fire.

"Last Sunday a group of ten people have crossed the Iron Curtain." I squeezed Rozsa's hand, real hard, but she didn't seem to mind it. The tears that came to her eyes and to mine, sprang not from pain, but from our joy, from our relief, from us being delighted. "Six males, three females and a five year old girl have escaped from bondage and are now free. One of the women suffered bad frostbite; she is being treated in a hospital. Her condition is not considered life threatening. We salute these brave people. We condemn the Communists who drove them from their homeland."

The rest of the news items held no interest for us, so we kissed, we hugged, we told our little baby daughter that her Grandparents had succeeded. The news came to an end and the last fifteen minutes of the broadcast consisted of messages from self exiled Hungarians to their loved ones.

"Do you think they will send us a message Laszlo?" Rozsa whispered and I concentrated on the voices of strangers.

"It will come my dearest. Your Father always kept his promises," I whispered back and adjusted the tuner to avoid the increasing interference.

Message, after message, was read by the announcer and we almost gave up, when suddenly our hands tightened.

"To our beloved children, who spent their wedding night under hams and sausages..." The announcer read the unmistakable code and Rozsa cried out.

"They are safe Laszlo...You were right...They are free."

I placed a finger across her lips to force her to control her joy, to listen and we had missed only a few words.

"After six days of constant struggle we are safe, we are free and we miss you. Your dear Mother is doing well. Her feet froze, but she is getting excellent care and treatment. We love you all and may the good Lord keep you safe. We will do this every Sunday. Good-by our children." The message ended and was replaced by another.

The joy we felt I cannot describe. The relief that washed over us was without bounds. The tears we shad, during the last two weeks, were replaced with the tears of joy and gladness.

"They are out!" Rozsa kissed me.

"They are free my dear darling." I expressed my delight and the rest of the day, each time we had a free moment, we smiled, we kissed, we hugged and whispered sweet things to each other.

When evening came, we sat by the new set. We had to hear the news again and we had to let Dad's words warm us. The news items were repeated and so was the message to the young couple, who spend their wedding night under hams and sausages. When that message ended, we went to the room where we have spent our first night, but this time there were no hams nor sausages, just the three of us, filled with joy, relief, hope and love.

***

Monday morning, before I left, Rozsa raised the question.

"Shouldn't we tell our relatives?"

"I agree my love, we should. You tell your Grandmother, who still doesn't seem to suspect anything and as soon as I can, I will inform the others. I will just tell them that your parents are in Austria, but I will not tell them how we found out."

"They will not be so easy to put off. They will want to know more."

"They will, I know that, but to speak about the message, we had yesterday, would serve no purpose. Soon it would get out. That we must not risk, Rozsa."

"You are right Laszlo. I will not say anything, if you think that is wiser."

"I do my love."

That morning I went straight to my parents' home and I informed my Mother that Mr. and Mrs. Buja fled to Austria.

She looked at me with eyes wide and then instead of probing, she berated my absent Father.

"If your Dad had any common sense, we too would be out of here. He was dragged through the war; he was robbed and lost everything. He was imprisoned twice, falsely and yet he thinks this is his homeland. He is a stubborn man, your Father, not like Mr. Buja. I am glad for what they did...I always knew he was wise and decisive, not like your dear Father, who always hesitates, always contemplates, but remains indecisive."

"Some day Mother, some day he will change his mind." I tried to stop the flood of her complaints, but she would have none of that.

"He couldn't leave his beloved Danube. That is where he is now. He is on that ship, as he calls it, but truth be told, it is nothing but a barge, yet he feels like a captain in charge of an ocean liner."

"He suffered enough Mom...Don't make him suffer more by destroying his illusion."

"Just you wait until I tell him where his friend went. This is not the first one Laszlo. Do you remember Berkovitch, his former partner? After the factory was robbed, after they couldn't resurrect it, his friend left the country, but no, not your Father. We will rot here in this cursed land, until we become old and worn and useless."

"I must go Mother. My commander must be looking for me."

"Go...I will tell the other relatives."

"You do that Mother, but please let me be the one who informs Aunt Gizella and Uncle Jozsef."

"Very well. I will not even ask why. I let you keep your secrets."

***

So I went to serve my masters and I did that for several hours, then I got permission from Pasko to leave a little bit early.

I went to see Aunt Gizella and to my great delight, I found both of them home.

"I have great news. You will be pleased," I told the two of them. They knew nothing about my in-laws' absence.

"Thank God you came. We were really puzzled," Aunt Gizella announced.

"Puzzled about what?"

"About what your Mother told me," came Aunt Gizella's reply.

"Was she here?"

"She sure was, but she behaved rather strangely. She came around nine in the morning and she seemed to possess a great secret. She told me that you will come, that you will have something to tell us and that we will be delighted. I pushed and probed and prodded my sister, but she wouldn't spill the beans. So tell us the great news Laszlo."

"Mr. and Mrs. Buja got out!" I announced triumphantly.

"I didn't know they were in. Do you mean prison Laszlo?" Uncle Jozsef spoke up for the first time. He was the quiet one in the family.

"No, you misunderstood. They were not in prison, except the big prison, that we call our country. They got out...They escaped to Austria," I clarified my great news and my Aunt grabbed me.

"You are not lying, Laszlo? Is this really true? Is it really possible to get out of this rotten country?"

"They did! It took them six days." I said more than I intended, but my Aunt's enthusiasm was infectious and I wasn't able to hold back, thus I told much more than I told my Mother. I told them everything.

"There is a God! There is freedom, even for us imprisoned human beings. You brought good news Laszlo, but you brought more, a lot more than that."

"I am not sure I understand what you are saying Aunt Gizella."

"We have money; we have possessions we could sell. The only thing we do not have is freedom Laszlo. Now that your in-laws are out of this country, they will not rest until they find a way to have you join them. When you decide to go, I want us to be with you. I want to leave this loathsome country. Promise us Laszlo that you will include us. Promise us that you will not desert us. Help us and we will help your dear wife and your little darling."

I thought about what she offered and about my earlier resolve to ask them to help my family.

"I am loath to beg, but she has given me a great opportunity to be of service to them and to gain their help without even asking." I thought and in my youthful exuberance, in my naivete, I decided to make a pledge, to enter into a most dangerous activity.

"They send us coded messages on the Free Europe Radio, every Sunday. Before they started their journey, we have worked out a code that we will use when we write to each other. As soon as they settle in their new country, I will ask them to send a guide for us and when that guide comes I will alert you. I would love to have you come with us and I thank you for your offer, which by the way is very timely." Then I spoke briefly about our financial plight and my Aunt handed to me five hundred Forints, which she called the first payment of many.

"This is just great! Don't you think Jozsef?"

"I didn't think much about it, but..."

"There are no buts! You will come with me!"

"Where my wife goes that is where I will be heading," came Uncle Jozsef's reluctant reply and the stone was cast; the ripples began to travel and the future, thanks to the Almighty, I couldn't see.

Before I left, I asked them to remain absolutely quiet about our plan.

"You must not breathe a word to anyone. Not even to my Mother," I told them and received their solemn promises.

My next trip, although brief, took me to Gomories. I told Rozsa's maternal Aunt, Margit the splendid news and in her joy, in her elation, she asked me no questions. She was too busy crying.

***

Two weeks have passed before the first letter arrived and before I had great reason to feel fear and greater reason to become more manipulative.

The first letter I read to Rozsa and she wiped her tears. The news was good. Her Mother was fully recovered and her parents were reunited in a place my Father-in-law called Linz. They had freedom and they had food and many new clothing. The first they earned. The last two they received from the Red Cross, he informed us. He wrote not one word about the details of their six day journey. He held back on the details, probably to avoid frightening us with all the dangers, with the tremendous difficulties.

After I have read the letter to Rozsa, she took it from me and slowly, carefully, she read her Father's neat handwriting. When she finished, I took the letter back. Went to get the small book, her Father left with me, and after checking the pin holes on page one, I broke the code and the hidden message became clear.

"We will look for a guide and when Ildiko becomes a year old, when Rozsa is fully recovered, we will send to you someone. Try to get out of the army before that time comes." Mr. Buja used the code and gave us hope and reason to be delighted.

When Rozsa wrote them an innocent reply, I applied the third page of the code book and this is what I added.

"I will try to do as you told me. We will be patient; we will be ready and two of my relatives want to leave too. They must be accommodated."

***

The fear gripped me the following morning.

"Are you ready to pick up the mail Laszlo?" Laci approached me, but he was no longer the cheerful driver. He looked pale, drawn, something disturbed him. We got in the jeep, but my mind was so full of hopeful thoughts, that I never thought of asking what bothered him.

Once we picked up the mail, Laci began to drive the jeep, but not in the right direction.

"Where are you heading Laci? Are we not going to my Mother's place for a good breakfast?"

"Today I want to go somewhere else, we must have a talk. We need privacy." Laci's words came and he stopped the jeep on a side street, off the city's main square.

"Where are you taking me?" I asked him.

"I found a small delicatessen, where we could take a booth in the far corner. It is just a block away." He told me and I walked beside him, wondering what may have happened to cause him to be so agitated.

The restaurant was almost deserted. Only one of its fifteen cubicles was occupied and that one was right by the door and we sat down in the far corner. We ordered a glass of *palinka*, the favorite alcoholic drink of Hungarians and after Laci swallowed his, in a single gulp, he took out a few sheets of paper.

"What I am about to tell you will put us both in great danger," Laci began and I sensed what was coming, but I remained absolutely silent.

"We have become friends...I ate at your Mother's table...All was well, until a week ago...Then my world collapsed and I didn't know what to do. I slept little...I agonized over my decision, but once I have made it, I was relieved." He stopped. I didn't know the cause of his hesitation, but sensed that it was for real.

"If I tell you what they are trying to make me do and what I have decided, will you promise never to tell anyone?"

"I promise you...We are friends."

"Promise me on the life of your beloved Rozsa."

"I promise you even that."

"When you were no longer asked to work in Colonel Pete's office..." I stopped him immediately.

"How did you know about that?"

"I am the jeep driver. I drive many officers to the bootleggers and to their mistresses. When sober, they are tight-lipped, but when they are drunk, they spill everything. A little over a week ago, I was to pick up Colonel Pete, after one of his visits to an illegal establishment and while I drove him back, he mumbled something that tipped me off."

"What did he mumble?"

"He was drunk...He spoke about how good it was that you helped him and how bad it was that you are no longer trusted."

"I see..," was all I said. The news didn't surprise me.

"I don't think you see it Laszlo. I wrote off what he said while he was inebriated, but two days later I found out that the AVO officer was about to do serious business. He called me to his office and there he gave me these papers. He first tried to sweet talk me into becoming an informer. He offered me several days of furlough; he offered me a few privileges and when I refused, he told me about the alternative. My dear Father was a landless wage worker, before the Communists divided up the large landholdings. My Father got ten acres of land. For the first time he was able to cultivate land that was his. When the collective farms started to pop up, the men who earlier were given land were told to give it up, to join the collective farms. Many have resisted, amongst them was my Father. That is when the Hungarian Communists began to use the term '*kulak*', any man who still cultivated land that belonged to him. Thank God my Father owned only ten acres. Those who owned more and were too stubborn to do as they were told were arrested and disappeared. My Father is still free, but not for long, if I refuse to cooperate with our AVO officer. That is the alternative I was given: I become an informer or my Father will be arrested, he will disappear."

"Who are you to report on?" I asked him.

"Sometimes you are really dense Laszlo. Who do you think?"

"It must be I. Is that what you are saying?"

"It is you my friend. It is your in-laws who deserted this country; who betrayed all Hungarians. By association you became a traitor, the AVO officer informed me."

"If they no longer trust me, why don't they just get rid of me?"

"Because they want to watch you...They want to use you to get back your in-laws."

"But they were kidnapped by Imperialist agents," I exclaimed.

"I cannot believe it Laszlo. You of all people bought their concocted story? If you did, my controller is right. He told me that you are stupid, that you believe everything you were told, that you were instrumental in starting a manhunt for your in-laws, that you will be easy to report on. He even told me that during their escape your father-in-law killed one guard and wounded another one." This last revelation shook me and I began to think hard for a way out of the dilemma.

"So you are to write a report on me or if you don't your Father will be finished?"

"Those are my choices Laszlo, but I have made my decision."

"So what have you decided?" I asked him and held my breath.

"First I tear up this cursed paper." He was about to do that, but I stopped him.

"Don't, not yet at least. I want to hear the rest."

"I will not become an informer! I will desert the army and try to escape from this God forsaken country." His forceful words left no doubt that he would do what he said.

"And your Father will still be here. Do you think they will let him live Laci?"

"But what else could I do?"

"Give me a minute...Let me think." I assessed the situation and then I brightened.

"Of course I should have thought of this before," I told Laci.

"Thought of what?"

"Of the perfect solution. My possible ticket out of the army."

"You speak in riddles Laszlo. You must be insane."

"It will be all clear, once I explain it. I am telling you I have never been saner. This calls for a great deal of manipulation, but together we will learn how to do that."

"For God's sake Laszlo, why can't you make things clear?"

I looked around to assure that our total privacy still held and then in whisper I told Laci what I hoped to accomplish.

"Would you be an informer if you passed in a report to the AVO that was written by you, but dictated by me?" I asked Laci and gave him a wink.

"What? Did I get this clear? You want to dictate to me a report on yourself? You want me to pass it in, as if I wrote it?"

"Why not? Just think of it. I would dictate each report to you. I would include in it what may benefit me. You would pass it in and nobody would be the wiser. You would be safe; your conscience would be clear and your Father would remain untouched. And besides, the bond of our friendship would become much stronger. This arrangement would be our own small, private conspiracy and we could have an occasional laugh about it. The AVO has the power, but you and I have the brains to outwit them. What do you say Laci? Is this not a better solution than your desertion, your attempt to escape, which would do nothing to save your Father?"

"Dear God in Heaven...I thought my life was over. It must have been Divine guidance that made me tell you the whole story. It is brilliant; it is to my liking. Let's get to it. Dictate on Laszlo. The first report is due tomorrow morning."

"Not here my friend. We don't want to be found out. Put away those papers. We will go to my Mother's place and there we will trick the f...ing morons."

***

"Would you like to have me prepare breakfast?" were my Mother's words, as soon as we arrived.

"Please make it Mother and give us some privacy."

"That too? What else would you like Laszlo? You want to deny me the pleasure of seeing two young men eat what I cooked?"

"It is not that Mother. You sat with us every morning, but from now on we must work while we eat."

"Now I have heard everything. Make our breakfast...Leave us alone...You are just like your Father," she complained and after that she remained silent.

"Take out your papers and pen Laci." Without delay, I began to dictate the first of many more reports, and as I warmed to the task my words came more smoothly.

"I, the undersigned, had the opportunity to talk with Corporal Lichter on several occasions and to observe him carefully, during the last week.

"Here are my findings. Lichter is a bit guarded, but I don't think he is hiding anything. He is quite bitter. From time to time, he curses the Imperialist dogs, who kidnapped his in-laws. He must have bought the story Colonel Pasko told him, but Lichter never made any reference to that fact.

"He received one letter from his father-in-law and he even let me read it. He found it strange that there was no mention of the kidnapping, but he explained that his Dad is a proud man and had he fallen victim to the enemy, he would be too proud to admit it. The letter I read said nothing, but the normal stuff a parent would write to his children.

"One thing though bothers Lichter greatly. His wife is still convalescing and he cannot afford to get hired help. They are very short on money and since his in-laws were kidnapped, it is his responsibility to pay the rent. He is afraid that he may be unable to pay, that soon they may be evicted.

"Lichter seems to be slightly depressed, but I think there is no reason to think that he would do anything rash, by that I mean he is not suicidal, he doesn't hate his superiors; he hates only the kidnappers.

"There is nothing more I can report this time. If I am to find out more, I must gain his full trust, I must spend more time with him and I must be able to help him in some tangible manner."

"Now I think you should sing it, seal the envelope and give it to that moron." I told Laci and I was pleased with my new status of being a self-informer.

"Do you think the AVO officer will be satisfied with such a short report? He gave me two pages and I don't even have the first one filled."

"Before I answer your question, let me make a suggestion. Between us to speak about the AVO officer is awkward, let's call him the moron, whenever we refer to him. The moron will be satisfied and will find your report truthful. Just think about it Laci...First you tried to refuse him, then you thought about it for a whole week. Is it not logical that you should still feel some reluctance? That explains the shortness of your report. The moron will find it quite natural and he will buy all you said. I even think you will be given some money."

"You must be crazy Laszlo. He would never pay me and even if he did, I would never accept his payment."

"Am I crazy? I assure you that I am more sane than I ever was. The moron will read your report and he will be dissatisfied, I do admit, but not with you, but with my lack of trust. Now what would I do in the moron's place? I would first put my victim at ease, so I would arrange a few days to have my victim look after his wife and baby. Then I would give some money to my informer, but not a payment, just money that he could use to help his victim, by doing so he would gain Lichter's trust. So that is what I think. If I am wrong, no harm is done. If I am right, I will get a few days off and a bit of money for my pain of being a strange kind of informer."

"You amaze me Laszlo. If you were not my friend, I would even fear you. If you were doing this to anyone, other than the moron, I would have to consider you a conniving bastard."

"So the way things are, what do you consider me to be?" I asked him smiling.

"I consider you a real friend of mine and a skillful foe of all your enemies."

I loved the way he defined my being and from that time on, that is what I always tried to be: A real friend to all my friends and skillful foe to all my enemies.

***

For three whole days nothing has happened, then things began to move and my calculations proved to be correct.

The moron happened to drop into my office and without being told, he sat down and watched me work. I was in the process of filling out forms for those going on furloughs and calculating the allowance they were to receive. The army had some strange policies. Each private received no more than forty *Forints* each month, regardless of the family responsibilities they had, the children they had to support. The amount was barely enough to buy a package of cigarettes every three days, thus those who smoked resorted to begging from the more fortunate smokers and that kind of begging was not tolerated by the army. It was considered to be an act that no self-respecting defender of our peace should resort to. Thus many soldiers were forced to resort to stealing and many fights broke out. The wiser soldiers, especially in their second year of service, found another way to supplement their income. They applied several times a month for a furlough. The army allocated twenty *Forints* of allowance for each day a soldier was allowed to leave his unit and those who were lucky to get the approval and had no families, chose to accept their allowance, but took no advantage of leaving.

The forms: approval of furloughs; travel passes and approval of allowances; I was to prepare and it was my job to make all the payments in cash to the lucky privates. To cover their tracks, I began to falsify the list of combat soldiers. The officers were lax in checking my reports, against those who were present during training and exercises, thus many second year service men supplemented their income and cheated the army.

It was a dozen or so forms that I was preparing while the moron watched me. I began to scratch my head and reached for my ink eraser that became very busy.

"Damn it. I made another mistake...," I mumbled under my breath, at least five times, before the moron spoke up.

"Comrade Corporal Lichter, I have never seen you this sloppy. I have never seen you make this many mistakes before."

"You would make them too Comrade Colonel, if you were in my place," I retorted.

"Would I?" he asked me and pulled on a corner of his black mustache. "Why would I do that?"

"Because your mind would be on something else. That is what is happening to me."

"If something bothers you, probably you should tell me." I heard his words and knew without a doubt that he was trying to verify the report he received from Laci.

"My blasted in-laws are not home to help my wife," I cursed almost inaudibly.

"I know Lichter, but what else?"

"I am behind the rent...I earn almost nothing...And besides my wife is sick."

"I understand," the moron stood up and went to see Pasko.

That night my commander gave me one week of vacation and I rushed to prepare the papers and paid myself the princely sum of one hundred and forty Forints. I was about to leave, to go home to my dearest and then an idea hit me.

"I will scan the list of second year soldiers and find those who didn't have a furlough for a long time. I will process furlough applications for them; get my commander's approvals. I will falsify the number of soldiers who are not in the sick bay, who are not on furlough, who are battle ready. The amount of money they should be paid, I will pay to myself and by doing so I will be able to help my loved ones. A dangerous undertaking...But what else can I do? Am I not facing more danger by fooling the moron?" I thought about these things for a while, and then I began to refine my plan. When I was satisfied that the likelihood of being found out was close to nil, I turned out the lights, locked the door and promised myself to put my plan in action, as soon as my courage would permit me.

I had to walk home that night and spent my time thinking about how I changed.

"There was a time when I was unable to make friends and now I have made many. I was timid, but the Communists changed that. I became bold, daring and conniving. A few years ago my own shadow frightened me, but now I am willing to face all kinds of danger. Tricking the moron, added to my formalizing an escape plan, are bad enough, but now I am ready to become a thief." I kept telling myself that I became foolish and reckless, but the circumstances have changed, forced me to survive in this hostile country, like so many other Hungarians.

I recalled the slogans the Communists loved to spout and smiled at that recollection.

"In our country everything belongs to the people!" they declared endlessly and I knew that their slogan was partly true.

"The huge prisons, they built, do belong to the people, so they make many of us use those people owned facilities. Amongst them was my Father," I thought and chuckled bitterly. Then I recalled a joke, that wasn't a joke at all, but a generic description of most Hungarians.

"A poor factory worker was in great need of money. He worked in a factory that manufactured wheelbarrows." The story began. "He figured out a way to make some money and he began to starve less. The years have passed and starvation was far behind him, he even became a bit wealthy. Each evening, after he finished his shift, he pushed his wheelbarrow, covered with his jacket and at the checkpoint-where all workers were searched for tools, for nails, for anything that they might steal from the State-he was stopped and searched and night after night, the vigilant guards found nothing. A good, trusted friend of his noticed the change in his financial situation and asked him to reveal his secret. He obliged, in the following manner.

"I push a wheelbarrow to the checkpoint. They lift up my jacket and search under it, then they search me, but they never find a thing. Yet day after day I became more wealthy. How am I doing that? Well it is very simple. I steal only one thing each and every day: a wheelbarrow, my dear friend, but they never caught on and never will. The good Lord, probably as a joke, put us under their power, and in His mercy he blessed them with a good dose of stupidity. Blessed be the Lord for all His kindness."

The recollection of this story made me laugh and I hoped with all my heart, that I will be as lucky as the wheelbarrow collecting Hungarian.

The following day, in my Mother's kitchen, Laci handed me two hundred Forints.

"Take this my friend, you really deserve it."

"Where did you get all this money?" I asked, but I already suspected.

"The moron gave it to me. He told me to lend it to you, but never to tell you where it came from. He wants me to gain your complete trust. Your report paid off, just as you predicted. You gave him the right name Laszlo. He is a moron, there is no doubt about that."

***

The days passed and they flowed into each other. Work during the day, precious moments in the evenings with my little angel and joyous nights with my Rozsa came and went.

Ildiko seemed to change each day. Her smiles became more frequent and with a healthy appetite she consumed a part of her Mom's milk. Rozsa reported to the doctor, who gave her an almost clean bill of health. Since her maternity leave expired, he put her on sick leave, with reduced pay. He informed her that the Government regulations required that she sell any of her milk, not required by our sweet baby. In this manner she began to supply milk to two other infants, whose mothers were unable to produce the badly needed sustenance. By selling milk she almost recovered what she lost by being on sick pay, thanks to the Government's pricing policy. My Aunt Gizella made regular, willing contributions and so did the army, but they knew nothing about that.

Each week, I had two or three soldiers, processed for a furlough, at least on paper, and the allowance they didn't deserve went into my deepening pocket.

Each week the moron received a further written report from Laci and his concern began to mount, especially after the fifth one.

***

"Are you sure you want me to write this?" Laci asked, when we were half way in the fifth report to the moron.

"If I wasn't sure do you think I would dictate it?"

"I know what happened each time Laszlo, but how far do you want to push this?"

"Come on...Don't you trust me?"

"I trust you Laszlo, but there must be an end to your daring."

"There is a lot more where the other reports came from."

"I don't doubt that...The first one was short; the others much longer. But none of what you have dictated during those first two occasions put you in real danger. Then you started to get bolder...Let me see...The third one described your deepening depression and your grave financial problems. In the fourth one you hinted that you may have found a solution. But to say that you are on the brink of committing suicide is far too bold, it is not something they will take lightly. Please reconsider Laszlo; don't force me to even mention such a terrible possibility."

"But you must do as I say Laci. That is part of my greater plan."

"Maybe it's time you leveled with me...What are you trying to accomplish Laszlo?"

I thought about what he asked. I appreciated his decency, his kindness and decided to tell him everything. I told him about the conversation I had with my predecessor, who was willing to pretend to be a homosexual, in order to escape from the army and how he succeeded.

"I think you understand now Laci what I am trying to do. I must get out of the army. When I made you write about my depression they gave me time to spend with my family. When your report spoke about my lack of trust, didn't the moron give you money, to gain my trust? If I raise the specter of one more extraordinary event this year, in this unit, namely that of my suicide, they will want to prevent that. Maybe they will throw me out? That is my final objective. Do you understand me Laci?"

"I do, but it is too bold, too daring. Could they not put you in the stockade to prevent you from ever trying?"

"They would never want to do that. Didn't you tell me that they want to use me to get back my in-laws? I am the bait, I am their only hope, I am their only means of succeeding. So let's not argue more...Continue your writing. The last thing you wrote down you should read back."

"His depression is getting really deep. He, at times, becomes incoherent, and..." Laci read and waited.

"Yes that is where I was when you refused to continue. My dear friend please write down what I am dictating." When I saw his pen poised over the paper, I gave him the words that I hoped will bring my deliverance from the army.

"...today I saw him do something that made me fear for someone's life. He was loading his revolver. I thought he might attempt to shoot someone, but when I tried to find out what he was up to, he started to jabber. I couldn't make out all he said...Something about the rotten kidnappers...Something about life being worthless...Then he raised the revolver to his forehead and I had to grab the gun, before he had time to cock it. I fear that he is getting desperate enough to kill himself...So I rushed to prepare this report, that is why I am passing it in early.

"Someone must do something and soon, otherwise I fear what might happen."

"Did you get it all Laci?"

"I did, but I am still fearful."

"Don't be my friend. I know how to manipulate the bastards. Now sign it, seal it and early this afternoon, pass it to the moron. Tell him that you are two days early, but you wanted to have him know everything that happened. Put on a good act Laci and I will do the same when the moron calls me into his office. It will not take him long to become alarmed, to decide on some sort of action."

"Against my better judgment, I will do as you suggested. Consider it done, Laszlo."

***

The afternoon came and I imagined what must have happened.

"Laci must have passed in his report. The moron must have read it. When he went in to see Pasko, they must have discussed it and decided what to do about me. But that was two hours ago and the moron left, without saying a word to me. Maybe I did a foolish thing? Maybe I have false illusions of invincibility? Maybe I put my dear wife in danger and even my baby? Why was I so stupid to take all these risks? Have I not gone far enough? I broke the law by listening to the Free Europe Radio; I began to steal from the army; I received and wrote letters, containing coded information; I am planning an escape from the country. How much more risks can I take?" My reverie was interrupted.

"Corporal Lichter report to me," Pasko's voice thundered and it lacked the usual kindness.

"Now we must have a talk," Pasko told me, after I took a seat. "First I want to ask you something. Do you love your wife? Do you love your little daughter?"

"I do love them both. I love them very deeply."

"That is what I thought. Do you remember when I saw her and your daughter the first time?"

"I do remember Colonel Pasko. I made a bad mistake in my judgment."

"You did Laszlo." He became kinder. "You knew that to take off your uniform and to prance around the city in civilian clothing is against regulations, yet that is what you did one Sunday."

"I know and you have found out."

"How could I have avoided it? My wife and I went for a walk and who do we happen to see? My chief clerk, with his beautiful wife, pushing the baby carriage. You were a bit taken aback, but so was I. Then you introduced us to your wife; you showed us your lovely baby. Do you know Laszlo why we have walked with you for almost half an hour?"

"That I never found out."

"If the M.P.s found you out of uniform, you would have faced a court martial. To avoid that possibility I walked with you, figuring that no M.P. would dare to stop you while I was present. I care about you Laszlo...I would hate to have anything happen to you. Do you understand me?"

"I do and I am truly grateful."

"If you are grateful I want you to end all this nonsense."

"Am I doing something wrong?" I asked him and for the first time I began to fear that I was found out.

"What you are doing is above reproach. The way you look is another matter."

"What I am doing is above reproach," I repeated the words in my mind and I almost smiled with relief. "I wasn't found out." He noticed a flicker of my smile, his next statement indicated.

"That is what I am talking about Laszlo. For many weeks you looked like a condemned man, but now you gave a small smile. Why can't you do that more often? Have I not been good to you? Furlough after furlough, I gave you. You can sleep home, with your wife, every night. When night exercises are sprung on other soldiers, are you made to march with them? Have I ever sent my driver to wake you in the middle of the night, when I was woken? I know, you would love to be out of the army...You were drafted when you shouldn't have been, but I can do nothing about that. Time will pass Laszlo and you will be free again; you will return to your school; you will be teaching and all this will be behind you. In some ways you are more fortunate than I. Why do you think I drink so much? I hate the army no less than you do Laszlo. Well I have said enough. Maybe too much already. I want you to look at the good things; the privileges you have. I want you to get rid of morbid thoughts and I ask you to promise me one thing. Promise me Laszlo that you will look after your dear wife and your lovely child. Think of what their lives would be without you."

I didn't allow myself to smile. "My reports have made their impact, but from this day on I must make them milder. Besides, I must stop stealing from the army," I thought and put Pasko at ease.

"Thank you Colonel Pasko for being so kind. I was ungrateful; I was carried away by false thoughts; I have contemplated a cowardly act, but I assure you, I promise you that it is all over."

"I am glad we had this talk. Now you can leave me, I am no longer worried. When a friend makes a promise I know he will keep it." With that said, Pasko dismissed me and from that day on the furlough requests slowed down and the tone of my reports became milder, yet they contained nothing ever that the moron could use against me.

***

Rozsa was happy with the knowledge of her parents being safe and I was relieved by having ceased at least one of my dangerous activities. On Sundays we visited various relatives and every one of them admired our little, bright girl of three months. They gave her small presents, they showered her with kisses and whenever we visited Aunt Gizella and Uncle Jozsef, we came away with a small amount of money.

Each and every time we spoke about the progress of our escape plan, I assured them that I was really trying. During one of those visits, Aunt Gizella made another request.

"We have two friends and their little daughter...Do you think they could join us?"

"Have you said anything to your friends? I asked you to keep everything totally confidential."

"Do you think I am that foolish? I said nothing to them. We were just chit-chatting about conditions in our country and about the people who succeeded to escape across the border. They just happened to mention that they had money and they would pay anything to get out of here."

"The time is still far away. Ildiko is far too young. Let me think about it. In a few months I will give you my answer."

In the meantime, our code used by our Dad, every Sunday, was discovered by Aunt Margit. On a Monday night, as I walked home, Aunt Margit saw me and rushed across the street. She was unable to contain her excitement and began to shout before she reached me.

"I heard it yesterday...Those hams and sausages sure came handy..."

I was more rude than I intended.

"Keep your mouth shut! You are putting all of us in danger."

"I am sorry Laszlo...I got too excited."

That night I took out the code book, turned to the right page and wrote to my in-laws a letter that to the censors would mean nothing, but our Dad would understand the hidden message clearly.

When Sunday came, he signed on the same way, but a week later he did that differently.

"To the young man, who came home early one morning with three little piglets and a bottle of *palinka*..." Rozsa and I looked at each other-by that time her Grandmother was no longer with us-and kept listening to what my Father-in-law had recorded. When his message was over, I turned the radio off and spoke to Rozsa.

"Thank God. Your Father got my meaning. He changed the code...I think we better do this more often, before the authorities catch on."

"Thank God indeed. You know Laszlo I forgot all about that episode. It happened several months before we got married, I think, or was it after?"

"You are right my love...It happened in September of '53. Had your Father not used that as a code, I probably would not have remembered. At *Bacsbokod* I got permission from the local Council to purchase three little pigs. I bought a bottle of *palinka* and the former owner of the piglets harnessed up his horses and was kind enough to drive me here. I remember your parents' surprise when I gave them two of the piglets. One was for them, one was for us and the third one was for my parents. But the bottle of *palinka* was for us and your Dad and I became quite tipsy."

"I never ever thought that this episode will become so significant," Rozsa told me.

"There will be many others your Father will use. Bless his good memory and bless him for his caution and kindness."

***

We went on many Sunday walks, but by then I wasn't daring enough to take off my uniform. I, the shabby looking soldier, my beautiful wife, Rozsa, and in the nice baby carriage, our cute little girl, Ildiko, strolled around the city. Our favorite places were the *Korzo*, where many people took their Sunday stroll and the flower filled park of *Dery*.

By the end of May the acacia trees flowered and the air was sweet with their aroma. The flowers bloomed, the trees swayed in the light breeze and we stopped by our tree, sat down on our bench and when Rozsa smiled at me, my pain was resurrected, that came with Pasko's announcement.

He came to my office, five days before and told me what was coming.

"Check your roster of those on furlough. Notify everyone that by next Monday all soldiers must be on base. There will be no furloughs, beginning that day, for many months.

We will begin our summer exercises."

"I will do it immediately."

"And one more thing Laszlo...I am sorry I have to tell you this, but we have been ordered to spend several months at our summer camp. The accommodations will not be fancy. We will not have the pleasure of being close to our families. There will be pain in parting."

"I am sorry to hear this. My wife really needs me."

"And so does mine, but this is the army."

For days I was about to tell Rozsa, but each time I was about to begin, I became a coward and besides, I promised her that I will never leave her, and now I would have to tell her that I was unable to keep that promise.

Every night, when I cuddled with her, before I turned away, I thought of telling her, but I have waited.

"There are several days left before I have to leave her...," I told myself and turned away, after our last kiss that night.

"There is still one more day, but then I have to give the bad news to my darling." I told myself the night before Sunday.

Sitting on the bench, beside my beloved and rocking gently Ildiko's baby carriage, I could no longer hide the news from my darling.

"Do you remember when I carved this heart and our initials in the bark of this tree?" I pointed at the heart, just behind us.

"It was so long ago...We were just kids; we were dreamers; we talked about some day getting married," Rozsa spoke and I took over.

"How many times did we have to part my darling, after our initials were carved there?"

"Too many times. So many painful times, that I don't care to count them."

"Each time Rozsa, when we had to part I came back to you. Going away gave us pain, but my returning gave us more joy," I told her, gathering up my courage.

"Are you trying to prepare me for some bad news Laszlo?" She knew me well; she knew how I operated. "For the last several days, before you fell asleep, I sensed your disquiet. Were you hiding something from me?"

"Yes, my dear...Yes, my darling...I promised not to leave you ever again and now I have to break that promise."

"Where do you have to go this time?"

"Tomorrow my unit will go to summer camp," I gave her a part of the bad news.

"Where are you going?"

"To *Fadtolna*...It is not far away."

"It is not far, if you will be home each night...It is at the end of the world, if I cannot see you daily."

"It is not for good my darling, just for a few months, Pasko told me."

"It is not for good, I know that, but you are still holding back something Laszlo."

"I wanted to tell you; I still want to tell you, but I hate to see you suffer, my beloved."

"I have suffered before. Suffering is not new to me. When you had to leave me I was able to console myself with the thoughts of your return. When my parents left, I had to learn to suffer in silence and without the hope of ever seeing them Laszlo. I gave birth to our little daughter. I was in labor for twenty-six hours. That was another kind of suffering. Each time I had suffered, I became stronger, so you can tell me what you have been hiding."

"Pasko told me there will be no furloughs, while we are at summer camp, my darling."

She looked deep into my eyes and pointed at the carved heart.

"That heart will be there, as it has been for many years. I will be home for you when you return Laszlo. I am sure we both are strong; we will survive anything."

***

Early Monday morning, I kissed our baby, I embraced my wife and before I left, I gave my last minute instructions.

"Listen to the radio every Sunday...Write me letters, whenever you can, and I will write to you my darling. Write me nothing about the messages, I don't want the censors to find out...Tell Aunt Gizella that our plan has been suspended temporarily, but as soon as I get back, I will do all I can to make our dream come true...In the meantime I will find a way, somehow, to get out of the army...Kiss our baby for me each day...Tell her many times that her Father loves her, as he loves you my dearest, my beloved, my sweet darling."

After a long, lingering kiss, our lips parted and behind me the key turned in the gate's lock and with broken heart I took my seat in the jeep, beside the driver and I was whisked away to *Fadtolna*.

***

Chapter 17

For several, long, almost unbearable months, I was separated from my wife and daughter. Rozsa's letters came and her loving words, her accounts of Ildiko and the magnitude of her love, eased my pain somewhat. By that time Rozsa became the stronger one. She never complained. In her letters she described the sweet little things Ildiko was doing. She was making sounds that nobody could understand, yet those sweet, baby sounds chased away Rozsa's aloneness. She made faces that made Rozsa laugh. She was a delight and her presence, her existence made Rozsa feel much better, but not me, who was forced to miss what Rozsa saw; who experienced nothing but a desolate loneliness.

During the days, I tried to find escape in work and in the middle of the night, Laci and I huddled in my miserable office, and worked on another of the never ending reports to the moron.

Regardless of what I have dictated I have not received a single furlough and there were no more payments. The moron came to see me, but no more frequently than did the other officers of our regiment.

Since they spent an enormous amount of time on endless marches, during their short stay in camp they came to me. Inside information was what they sought and there was no better place to get that than in my office. 'Chief clerk', my title, was a misnomer. I never had another clerk work for me, thus I have become the only clerk the officers could turn to for a favor. They were always short of money and I found ways of padding their expense accounts, thus helping them and short-changing the army. They also sought information about the mood of Pasko.

I handled the two personal rosters. The first one listed the 'core group' and the second 'the enlisted men.' The first list began with Pasko's name, followed by all the officers, according to rank, in descending order. I was the second last person listed and last one on the list was Laci, my friend, my accomplice, our jeep driver.

Each time I did someone a favor, I made a brief note beside the name, on a second copy that I kept hidden. The hot summer days came and went; my notations grew greater in number.

When I had three favors noted beside a few names, I grabbed the first opportunity to speak to the owners.

"Comrade.......I have a wife and a child. They need me very badly. Do you think you could support my application to be released from the Army?" I raised that question, time and time again, but only in casual conversations, and each and every time I received negative answers.

I couldn't understand what made them so unfeeling, until I heard an innocent comment.

"My reports seem to do very little good," I told Laci, just as we were starting to prepare another one.

"The moron must have grown tired," came Laci's reply.

"Maybe I should start dictating something drastic?"

"I begged you before not to do that Laszlo."

"If I don't, how am I ever going to get out of the army?"

"By serving your time...Two years will pass...," Laci began.

"No! A thousand times no! I must get out soon."

"My dear friend you must never speak like this. You must accept that very few soldiers get out before their time is up."

"Did I hear you right? Did you say 'very few soldiers get out before their time is up'?"

"That is exactly what I said," Laci stated.

"Then you must know at least one who got out early."

"So do you Laszlo...You told me about your predecessor. He was the pretended homosexual, if I am not mistaken."

"Yes...He was wise and very daring, but for me that is no solution. Do you know anyone else Laci?"

"Yes...Well not exactly...I heard of one."

"What did you hear?"

"A private in another regiment was released after ten months."

"How did he ever do that? Did he do favors for the officers? Did he put them in his debt? Did he get them support his release request?"

"According to what I heard he became quite contrary."

"I really do not understand."

"What is there to understand Laszlo? If you do favors to people, they want you around, but if you make them hate you, as that soldier did, then their natural reaction is to find a way to get rid of the trouble maker. I heard that is why that soldier was released from the army."

That night we began another report to the moron and I gave it a new slant.

"Corporal Lichter is under a great deal of pressure from many of the officers, he told me, but refused to name names. Some of the officers force him to short-change the army...They always need money and use Lichter to steal for them...They take advantage of Commander Pasko too...They go to Lichter, dig for information on Pasko and when they find what they want, they take advantage of the commander.

"Lichter gets letters from his wife, quite regularly, but those letters never speak about his in-laws. Unfortunately there is nothing else I can report." I finished my dictation.

"You are playing with fire Laszlo...You should think about the consequences," Laci urged me.

"Could the consequences of this report be worse than being here, away from my beloved wife, from my little daughter?"

"You know it could...They could put you in the stockade...They could have you court-martialed."

"If they put me in the stockade, I would be at least in Baja. Rozsa could visit me..."

"A ten minute visit would do no good at all. While she is there you would be happy, but think of how you would feel after."

"I know you are right, but I must do something."

"Tear this report up...Dictate another one that would be more to my liking."

I thought about what my wise friend suggested. "They probably would not have me tried for stealing from the army. There are too many officers who would be implicated. But they could keep me under arrest...They could keep me for a long time from my darlings." I reached for the sheet of paper and while tearing it up, I searched frantically for another way to get out of the army.

***

The days have passed, the letters came and went, but my deliverance remained a dream, an unlikely possibility.

Our last report to the moron was so mild that he became angry. He told Laci to find something, anything on me or his services will be terminated, not in a favorable manner and someone else will be found to report on me. When Laci told me what happened, we put our heads together and I began to dictate the report that I hoped to be to the moron's liking.

"Finally I found something that Lichter has done, that may allow you to take action against him. He told me that some time ago he subscribed a month's salary for Peace Bonds, but then he was teaching. He explained to me that this year he will refuse to subscribe a single Forint to that cause. He doesn't care what will happen to him. For the first time ever, he admitted that he knows how you feel about him. You consider him an enemy of Hungary and if that is the way he is thought of, he might as well act like one.

"I was really surprised how bitter Lichter was and I think that when the Peace Bond Committee begins its subscription drive, this coming fall, he will do as he stated."

"Pass that report in Laci and the moron will be pleased."

"He may be pleased, but what about you, Laszlo? You are sticking your neck in a noose. The moron will act swiftly, he will be truly delighted."

"Let him do whatever he wants. He is nothing, but a stupid man. I thought about this for some time now and the time is here to trap the misbegotten bastard."

"Will you tell me please what you propose to do?"

"The outline of my plan is almost complete, but not even you must know its details. Believe me Laci, it is safer this way and the less you know the better it will be. If the moron swallows the hook I throw him, I am sure I will be released from the army."

"I wish you trusted me completely Laszlo. I wish you would not play with fire, but I know you well and I dare not argue."

***

Before the Peace Bond Committee arrived to our regiment, life dealt me a blow that I never expected.

Rozsa's letter came, but this time she was terribly bitter, she was no longer the strong one. She returned to her workplace in the middle of September and immediately her boss, Szantai, called her in.

"You are fired," she was told by the Communist bastard. She wrote down details of their conversation.

"You cannot fire me. I know the law. No woman of a child, without the financial support of her husband, can be fired," she told her boss.

"The law doesn't apply to the daughter of a traitor. That is what you are. You better pack your things. Get out of here." I read and reread her bitter letter and decided to speak to Pasko.

"I am terribly sorry, I have to bother you with my problem. I know you cannot give me a furlough, but once you read what my wife wrote, maybe you can do something," I told my commander and handed to him Rozsa's letter.

He read it and reread it and shook his head.

"That guy thinks he is above the law. Your wife is right. No wife of a soldier can be fired and besides, the mother of a child under one enjoys the State's protection. I cannot interfere in civilian matters Laszlo, but I want to help you. Are you willing to go to see that man? Are you willing to confront him? To threaten him with court action?"

"I am willing to do anything to that bastard."

"Very well then...I will order the jeep driver to drive to Baja. You will be ordered to bring back some documents from my office. While you are at Baja, give the bastard hell."

"I do thank you for your kindness. How long do you think I could stay at Baja?"

"To find the documents I require you will have to search many files. It is not a furlough, I hope you understand. If you take your time; if you do not apply your usual efficiency, it may take more than three days to search for the non-existent document. Do your search and if after a week you do not come up with anything, notify me. I will send my driver to fetch you immediately."

***

Two hours later we were on our way and I explained to Laci what has happened.

"Pasko is a kind man," Laci commented.

"He is kind and understanding," I gave my reply and the rest of the trip we made in silence.

I found Rozsa home with my little daughter. Her eyes looked red and swollen, but in place of her tears, came her sweet smiles, her ardent hugs, her feverish kisses, then her words of love.

"I cannot believe my eyes. You are home my dearest Laszlo"

"Just for a short while...A few days perhaps, until I can straighten out that bastard."

"You must mean Szantai," Rozsa spoke that name with anger.

"That is whom I meant my darling. Today I will go and see him and by tomorrow I hope you will have your job back."

"I wish I could hope the same Laszlo, but I know Szantai better than that."

"He is not above the law, Pasko assured me."

"He may not be above the law, but just the same, he has the power. He is high up in the Communist party. I should know, he bragged about that many times before and especially when I was fired."

For a few hours Rozsa and I talked about the details of what happened and when Rozsa had nothing more to say, I went to see that man, the misbegotten scoundrel, the dirty bastard.

***

"I want to see Szantai," I announced to Rozsa's replacement.

"Do you have an appointment?"

"I don't need one. I am a soldier. I was sent to see him by my commander."

"You take a seat. I will see if Comrade Szantai is free."

The tall, well built, sandy haired, mustached man came out and with unbelievable friendliness he shook my hand, which I accepted reluctantly. He invited me into his office, made me sit down and my anger simmered under the surface, when I heard his first words, witnessed his conniving.

"What a great pleasure to greet a soldier; to face one who dedicated two years of his life to defend our peace. I sleep well at nights knowing that men like you stand on guard. Well, I said enough...I am sure you didn't come here to listen to my sincere compliments. You must be Mrs. Lichter's husband."

"I am he. That is why I came to see you. There is a misunderstanding that must be straightened out."

"I am sure there is, as you said. May I call you by your first name? It is Laszlo, isn't it comrade?"

"Yes. I am Laszlo."

"Well Laszlo, I am glad you came to clear up the misunderstanding."

"Do you really mean that?"

"I mean it with all my heart. You are a soldier, a member of our army. Am I correct?"

"You see my uniform; you know that is what I am."

"There is no need to get huffy, comrade. Tell me what is the duty of a soldier."

"To defend our country."

"I see that you are well versed in what is required. Have you started divorce proceedings?"

"What the hell are you talking about?"

"I thought you came to make that announcement, but I may be mistaken."

"You most certainly are mistaken." Our conversation took a turn. No more friendliness, just animosity.

"I surely am. A member of the armed forces is always on guard and searches for the enemy. Your wife's parents escaped from this country. Your Father-in-law killed a border guard and almost murdered another. The seed of that traitor created your wife. By birth, by upbringing, by association she has become a traitor. I, a simple civilian, have recognized that fact and acted accordingly. A member of the armed forces cannot do less. You must divorce the traitor; you must desert her; you must cast her out of your life, as I did from this office. Are you not willing to do your duty?"

"You, Szantai, are a rotten bastard."

"And you, Lichter, are a foul mouthed little prick, a traitor, a bad example of a soldier. I am sorry...We shouldn't insult each other. Let's start over...Your ill mannered comments are already forgotten. I cast that woman out, that was my sacred duty. Will you do the same?"

"You broke the law, Szantai. I will never break my vows. Rozsa is my beloved wife. She committed no crime...You had no right to fire her."

"And what law did I break?"

"You cannot fire any woman whose husband is in the army. You cannot dismiss the mother of a young child. That is what my commander told me."

"Who do you think makes the laws?"

"The Government does."

"And who do you think the Government is?" He didn't wait for my answer. "We are the Government...The Communist Party...We make the laws and we break the laws, whenever it suits us. I have a great deal of power and I use that power wisely."

"You take her back! Do you hear me?" I screamed out loud.

"Vow! You are insolent; you are rude; you are stepping out of line. Is this any way to conduct a civilized meeting?"

"You are speaking about a civilized meeting? You fired my wife; you condemned my child to starvation; you insulted me and my in-laws. How civilized are your actions Comrade Szantai?"

"I see we are getting nowhere. You come here questioning my actions, my authority. You shout at me, you insult me, you demand that I undo the firing. You have a lot to learn young man...Get up...Go back to the army...Keep on defending our precious peace...Forget your wife, that little traitor...Do you understand me?"

"I understand you too well. You are nothing, but...Oh the hell with it."

"If you have nothing more to say Lichter, go back to the army, defend our peace. Forget your wife...Just get out of here."

I reeled with his words, from his uncaring and if I was armed, I would have killed that slimy bastard, but instead I stood up, walked out of his office and slammed the door behind me.

***

I have hated before, but my hatred this time reached a higher level.

"This country is run by devils, not unlike Szantai. This may be where I was born; where my parents raised me, but it is no longer my homeland. This place is a prison; a home to scoundrels, to snakes, to unfeeling liars; it became a den of inequity. I must find a way out of here. I must allow my child to grow up in a free country. I must get them out. I must get out of the army." My thoughts were clear. My resolve to escape from this cursed land could no longer be debated.

From Szantai's office I rushed to Aunt Gizella's home, where I made a bold announcement.

"Aunt Gizella, I need a great deal of money. I am going to get out of the army and within a year we will get out of this country. Your friends, you spoke about, will be able to join us." I made the request and the promises blindly.

"I am really pleased Laszlo. I have waited for these words for a long time, but finally you came, you made this announcement. My friends will pay and so shall we. We have lots of nice things. We will sell them all and the money will be yours. We will be grateful, we will prepare for our escape, we will find freedom in some other country."

***

For several days, after my meeting with Szantai, I could find no peace of mind. I contemplated to start a law suit; I considered asking someone to intervene on my wife's behalf, but the more I thought about these actions, the more I understood the futility of trying.

On the one hand my wife was unemployed, without any hope of ever finding a job and I had no legitimate income, just what I could start stealing again from the army. On the other hand, Aunt Gizella made her word good. She gave us all she could and added to that was the amount paid by her friends, whose only desire was to leave the country. Rozsa had received two parcels from her parents and when she showed me their letters and their beautiful gifts, I was really delighted.

I was no longer worried about my family's survival. I was obsessed with my desire to leave the army and with getting out of our doomed country. I took out the code book and wrote the letter. I begged my in-laws to find a guide; to send him into Hungary.

When five days have passed, when I have spent many hours searching for a solution, as I have pretended to search my office for the non-existent file, I have decided to make the call and return to *Fadtolna*.

Our parting was painful, but I tried to convince Rozsa that next time I come home I will be free from the army.

***

I told Pasko everything that happened in Szantai's office and that good, decent man, promised to do all he can to assure my family's survival.

A day after my return, the political officer came to see me, but he did not come alone, the moron came with him.

"While you were at Baja, Comrade Corporal Lichter, the Peace Bond Committee arrived and we put you down for fifteen *Forints*. We hope you have no objection." The political officer announced and the moron watched me.

"Is it not customary to ask someone before he is signed up to buy Peace Bonds?" I asked and saw the moron brighten.

"He read the last report, Laci passed in and he has waited for this opportunity. He had me signed up, hoping that I will object and that he will finally get his chance to finish me." I thought and saw my plan unfolding.

"We would have asked you Comrade Corporal Lichter, but you were away and we figured that you will be more than happy to support the national effort with what you can afford, with this small sum." The moron spoke up and his beady eyes brightened with the possibilities.

"Well you were both wrong comrades. I know the law. Without my signature on that subscription sheet, the purchase is null and void."

"We know that Lichter. That is why we came. You only need to sign it," the political officer stated and gave me the sheet that listed everyone on the core roster; showing the amounts of Peace Bonds each individual purchased and their signatures in the last column.

"So where would you like me to sign, if I am willing?"

"Over here," the political officer pointed at the spot and the moron held his breath.

"How long can I think about this?" I asked and the moron seemed to exhale slowly.

"There is not much time…Let me see…Within two days this list must be sent to the Peace Bond Committee and a copy must be submitted to the Minister of Defense. I give you one hour to make up your mind. We will be back" the political officer announced, but the moron objected.

"I am not prepared to give you any time...You sign right now or suffer the consequences."

"Did I say I am not willing?" I tantalized the moron.

"If you are willing than you must sign it right now. Although your willingness I doubt," the moron spoke again.

"I thought I had an hour to think about it." I tortured the moron a bit more.

"So be it." The political officer, whose job it was to suck everybody into subscribing, gave in and the two of them left me to my own devices.

***

I placed the list on my desk and from a filing cabinet I took out the core list that contained all the names and the salaries received by everyone. I began to compare the two sheets and made a few calculations. What I found was very much to my liking.

"Pasko signed up only for the equivalent of one week's salary. All the officers did likewise. I was put down for no more either. Well that is splendid. When I was teaching, I was coerced to give no less than what I earned during a month. So were all other civilians, but these Communist officers are getting away with far less, in spite of their huge earnings." I observed and examined the possibilities.

"Here is the moron. He earns two thousand *Forints* a month and he is donating only a week's earning. Now that is really generous of him. His loyalty is beyond reproach. And here is the political officer. How much is he donating? Five hundred *Forints* only. Wow! That is truly a magnificent sum. It seems that if one is a Communist, one doesn't need to give up his earning to the State, after all that nonsense was created for the masses. And all the officers were proved to be just as stingy. One week's earning from every single one. That is why they have signed me up for no more than that paltry sum." I thought about what they did and what I must do to modify things. I examined carefully the plan, I formulated before I dictated my last report to Laci, and found that all the officers unwittingly played into my hand.

***

Before I noticed the hour's passing, the two officers were back.

"Have you made your decision Lichter?" The moron tried to irritate me, no doubt hoping to get me refuse. I was no longer Comrade Lichter. I didn't even have a rank this time.

"I thought and thought about this, but I regret to say that it is not to my liking."

"You heard him comrade. Lichter refuses to buy Peace Bonds. Let me deal with him," the moron couldn't hide his enthusiasm.

"Are you sure Lichter? Are you really sure?" the political officer tried once more.

"I have never been surer of anything," I announced defiantly.

"I am sorry to hear it. It seems this issue is out of my hands," the political officer announced and the two of them were ready to leave.

"Just one moment, Comrade Officers. You may have misunderstood." The moron went pale.

"What do you mean?" the political officer asked.

"I said earlier that it is not to my liking. I also stated that I have never been surer of anything. But I have never said with a single word that I am not willing to buy any Peace Bonds. Have you heard me say that, comrade?" I spoke to the political officer.

"No I did not. But what is not to your liking?" he asked more kindly and the moron became infuriated.

"Let's get the f... out of here. We are not going to negotiate with this traitor."

"Am I a traitor? What makes you think that? A traitor wouldn't buy any Peace Bonds, so just to prove how wrong you are, I ask you to change the figure and I will sign the document gladly."

"Sure...Fifteen Forints is too much for you. Is that what you are saying Lichter?" The moron spit out the words.

"Not at all comrade. That is far from what I am saying. May I explain?"

"Do that, but do it fast...Time is being wasted." The political officer gave his permission and I began to explain, all the while watching the moron blanching.

"Hungary is my country. It is my homeland. I treasure our freedom and I want to protect it." I lied like a trooper and the moron became paler. "To donate fifteen Forints only would cheapen the concept of peace; would be an insult. Just think comrade about the value of that sum. It is worth no more than two packs of cigarettes. It doesn't even buy two bottles of beer. Is our freedom; is our peace; is our wonderful life worth no more than that? I hardly think." I stopped and almost laughed out seeing the moron's contorted face. "He is beginning to see my plan. That is good. I fooled the bastard. His plan of finishing me off is getting beyond his reach," my thoughts almost made me chuckle.

"I see Comrade Corporal Lichter that I misjudged you…Well, let's make it thirty *Forints* and be done with it." The political officer was ready to settle the issue, but what came he couldn't have expected.

"Even that amount would be an insult. The Imperialist enemies kidnapped my in-laws." I turned to the moron. "Isn't that true comrade."

"Yes, it is."

"Our State apparatus promised to bring them back. Is that not so comrade?"

"We are working on that hard, I assure you."

"To aid their effort I will buy a hundred twenty *Forints* worth of Peace Bonds. That is what I get for two months of service in this army. Change the figure and I will sign gladly." My announcement shocked them both.

"Comrade Corporal Lichter, that is really unnecessary. You earn only sixty *Forints* a month. We are not monsters. We cannot ask for such a great sacrifice. Two months of salary is unheard of," the political officer argued. "Think of your wife; think of your child. You will cause them to starve, if you give up this much of your money. Maybe we could settle on a smaller sum?"

"My wife and child have never been a concern to the army. Let me be the judge of their best interest. I will settle for no less than the sum I stated. Change the figure and I will sign right now."

"The hell with you, Lichter. You are a conniving man, an unmitigated bastard. You just don't want to buy any Peace Bonds…That I understand. That is all I expected from the enemy. So let's just forget it. We will let the authorities deal with you, you scoundrel." The moron tried to extricate himself from the conundrum I created.

"Let them deal with me…I will be glad to tell them that my generosity was not appreciated," I issued the threat and both of them looked quite worried.

"I cannot let you make this great a sacrifice. I will not change the sum and I believe you will not sign Lichter. Am I correct?" the political officer seemed to accept the impasse.

"You got it comrade," I stated and they left my office.

***

There were three regiments stationed at *Fadtolna* and the overall command was given to three high ranking officers: the military commander, his political equal and the highest ranking AVO commander. It was those three I had to face within an hour.

"I want to ask you why your signature is not on this paper?" the military commander asked me.

"I refused to sign!" I announced stubbornly, but my voice shook with fear, but my resolve never wavered.

"I take it that you are not willing to buy any amount of Peace Bonds," the political commander spoke next.

"That is not true. I was not allowed to buy the amount I want."

"We were told nothing about that," the AVO officer spoke up.

"I have explained my situation to those who put me down for fifteen *Forints*. I told them that my gratitude to the State will not be properly expressed by that sum."

"Well, it seems that we have no problem. Let me change the figure to twenty *Forints* and let's get this paper signed," the political commander offered.

"I have already refused that amount. One hundred twenty *Forints* is what I want to buy and I will settle for nothing less." I stood my ground.

"But that is an enormous amount of money for a Corporal," the three of them stated together.

"And so is my gratitude to the State. Is that a crime? Am I not allowed to exercise my free will; to show my generosity?"

"Every citizen in this country is given that opportunity, you are no exception Corporal," the commander stated.

"Change the figure to what I want to buy and I will sign gladly."

"Please leave us for a few moments. We must discuss your offer, your foolhardy insistence," the political commander requested.

I sat in the outer office for more than twenty minutes, before I was called back.

"It seems that we have little choice," the commander took the lead. "We have decided to permit you to sign for that princely sum."

"I am pleased. I am truly delighted." I made my announcement and signed the paper and hid my pleasure; I didn't dare to gloat over how well my plan had succeeded.

***

The following night, Laci came to see me.

"You sure kept me in the dark Laszlo. The last report you have dictated, I didn't understand, but now, with all I heard, I am beginning to see your plan."

"So what have you heard my friend?"

"I heard about the huge sum you have donated Laszlo."

"If that is all you heard then I just wasted my money."

"I heard a lot more, I assure you. The whole camp is buzzing with the news and the officers are full of anger."

"Why is that?"

"Officer after officer were called in by the top political commander and they were made to increase their subscriptions. They are in a rage, with the exception of Pasko. He is the only one who just smiled when he was forced to give up two months of salary," Laci told me.

"Were the others treated in a like manner?"

"I heard they were and they swore to get rid of the conniving bastard who stirred up this fuss."

"Their wish is not unlike mine...You gave me good advice Laci."

"You baffle me, my dear friend. I gave you no such advice, if I recall correctly."

"But you did Laci. Just think back...Didn't you speak the following words: 'If you do favors to people, they want you around, but if you make them hate you...then their natural reaction is to find a way to get rid of the trouble maker.'?"

"You were blessed with a fantastic memory Laszlo. Yes, I spoke those words, but your action I never expected."

"I know my friend, but what is done is done. The officers have good reason to hate me and that gets me one step closer to achieving my dream. Do you think you could help me once more?"

"Tell me what you want me to do and if I can, I will do it gladly."

"The officers speak freely front of you, especially when they are inebriated. That is how you found out what was done to all of them. Am I correct?"

"Yes...That is how and when I hear things."

"Next time you hear an officer speak about me will you be willing to give the speaker an idea?"

"What idea?"

"I think you will hear them speak again about getting rid of me...No doubt they will contemplate bold actions. Some will think of laying charges against me. Others will even speak some more drastic actions. When you hear them talk like that, please drop a hint about how conniving I can be. Tell them that you think that I have documented each and every time, how they padded their expense accounts, how they stole from the army. Those documents were placed in safe hands and will be revealed if anything happens to me. Tell them that and they will not dare to bring charges against me or to try to harm me."

"You may be right, but how will that get you out of the army?"

"That alone will not do the trick. You must say something else Laci."

"So what should I add?"

"Drop the word that you think that the Minister of Home Defense was asked by someone to discharge me. Add to it that one request is not enough, but if many officers ask for the same action, the Minister might think about it."

"I will be glad to drop the hints, but once again you are playing with fire."

"Give it time Laci and do what I have asked, then we will see."

***

Two weeks later we had returned to Baja and thanks to Pasko, I was allowed to resume my former practice.

Each day I worked, as I have done for many months, and when evening came, I rushed to my dear Rozsa. Our nights of togetherness began with admiring and playing with our little daughter. When a letter came from Rozsa's parents we read their kind words and broke the code to find that they were working hard to find a guide who will lead us out of this damn country. We wrote our reply. We admired the many gifts that came in the more frequent parcels and when late night came we sought our bed and held on to each other.

"Do you think you will be discharged Laszlo?" were Rozsa's last words, before we turned from each other and each and every night I gave her the same answer.

"Maybe tomorrow my love...Or maybe the day after."

***

The days have passed and turned into weeks, but no news came about my discharge and I almost gave up, when on November twenty fourth, Pasko called me into his office and opened a bottle of *palinka*.

"Are you in the mood to celebrate Laszlo?"

"I have nothing to celebrate."

"That is what you think my friend. You have been like a son to me Laszlo."

"I don't think I deserve this, after what I have done to you Comrade Pasko."

"Isn't it time to drop this nonsense Laszlo? Don't call me comrade...Don't address me as your commander. Just call me by my first name, you lucky bastard."

"Am I lucky?"

"I think you are, but before I say anything more, let's have a drink, let's tip back our full glasses."

I swallowed the searing drink, in a single gulp, and waited.

"Now here is the good news: You are discharged from the army."

"What did you say, Antal?"

"You heard me right and if I did too, I am glad you called me by my first name. And why shouldn't you? You are a lucky civilian, Laszlo."

"I cannot believe it. Say it again, please...I must hear the good news ten times before I can believe it."

"Well, I am not going to waste my time to say it ten times, just once more. You are discharged from the army."

"When did this happen? When am I going to be free?"

"The order came today and it is effective immediately."

"Can this be true? Am I really free? Can I be this lucky?"

"The Minister's order is clear. You are free, but it is not luck that brought you this far. When you came to me, highly recommended, I considered myself lucky and it took me no time to begin to like you. When you began to steal from the army to support your family, I couldn't bring myself to tell you that I had found out. I closed my eyes to all your conniving and pretended to be dumb. I let you do all your manipulating. I watched with fascination how you led all of us on a merry chase for your in-laws, when you knew all along that they were trying to escape from the country. I watched you like I watch a good play and I was amazed by the play's plot, that you created Laszlo. Your last bold action cost me a bit of money, but I don't really care, I will just have to steal a bit more from the army. When you pulled that last stunt, I decided to recommend to the Minister of Home Defense that you be discharged from the army. I knew that my recommendation will not be heeded, but a miracle happened. Do you know what that was?"

"I don't have a clue...," I stated sincerely.

"A few days after your stunt with the Peace Bonds, one of my officers came to me. He asked me if I knew anything about a request to have you dismissed from the army. I don't know how he ever found out, but when I told him what I was contemplating to do just that, he asked my permission to allow him to sign too. He must have blabbed around the news and within days all my officers queued up to sign my request. They didn't even ask what reasons I gave, they just wanted you out of their hair. This is how you became free. I was blessed with two good chief clerks. Your predecessor pulled a different stunt; he was disgusting, but your action Laszlo was nothing short of brilliant. You should some day write down all that happened. Let people know how they can be manipulated. Now let's have one more drink...Then you must turn in your gun, your uniform and must sign out of this hell hole. May God bless you son...May all your wishes come true...Think of me now and then...When you do, please think of me kindly."

That was the last time I saw Pasko, but that kind man was never forgotten.

***

I knocked on our gate, that was always locked and Rozsa rushed to open it. Within a second we were in each other's arms and her kisses tasted sweeter than honey. When we separated after two, three long moments, her eyes appraised me and my small suitcase that I took with me when I was drafted.

"What is the meaning of this? You dared to take off your uniform? That is foolhardy. You brought home your suitcase too? What is going on my love?"

"Come in...Sit down...," I told her. I picked up my ten month old baby and with Ildiko in my arms, I told the good news to Rozsa.

"I was discharged today. I am free. I will be with the two of you until my day of dying."

"Did I hear right? Can this be true?" Her questions would have continued, but I sealed her lips with mine and she knew that this time I really meant what I said and when our lips parted, she cried out.

"You kept your word...I am so happy my dear, my darling."

***

After two joyful days I returned to *Bacsbokod*. As I entered the school, that I left a year ago, I was warmly greeted by my former students and by most of my colleagues, but not by Pallosy.

"What do I see out of uniform?"

"You are seeing me. I am back to resume my teaching duties."

"You may be here, but just wait until I notify the army. Deserters are not treated kindly. This time you have shot yourself in the foot Lichter. One phone call is all I have to make and you will be finished, you rotten bastard."

"Make your phone call, if you wish, Principal Pallosy, but before you do, you might want to read my discharge paper." I handed him the Minister's order and he blanched during the reading.

"Welcome back...," he changed his tune. "I am really glad to see you. A year early, you have been released. Well that is quite an accomplishment, I ought to congratulate you. Now as to your classes..." He began to explain what I was to teach and listed all my duties, amongst them the most important: "Of course you will keep living in Baja and as a non-resident of this community you will be required to volunteer your time to the Government."

"That is nothing compared to the army," I announced gladly and at the end of the day I approached the Chairman of the local Council.

"I have just been released from the army comrade and my family and I need accommodations. It is my wish to reside here. How soon can you provide the three of us with a flat?"

"I wish it was that simple Comrade Lichter. The waiting list is long, in fact there are people, who have waited for more than two years."

"Some have waited that long comrade, but others, I know, were given a house, even before their arrival."

"I do admit that there have been a few such cases, but the orders came from above and we had to provide the accommodations."

"Am I less deserving than some others?"

"I wish I could say that you are not, but who am I to make those judgments? I am a servant who must carry out orders. When a new Communist Party Secretary is sent to my village, they wield an awful lot of power. The calls come from the Ministry of Interior and I am made to do things that are not to my liking. I have always tried to be fair, to be impartial, but I am sad to say that I have rarely succeeded. I don't know why am I so frank with you comrade. Maybe the fact that you served time in the army? Maybe I am hoping that my soldier Son, will be treated the same way by someone? Perhaps a time will come when you will give me reasons to regret my frankness?"

"I doubt that comrade...That is not likely." The Chairman's simple sincerity impressed me, he reminded me of Pasko. "Not all Communists are evil, thank the Lord for His kindness," I told myself.

"I take you at your word Comrade Lichter. Now let me see if I can find a solution. The waiting list is long, but there may be a way to solve your problem."

"I hope there is...I need a place badly."

"Let me see...We have a house that belongs to us, but it is a registered child care center. Do you know the place I am speaking about? Have you seen the sign, just six houses from here, toward the station?"

"I think I know that house, but that house is never used."

"No, it is not. Our people are not willing to send their young children there. They prefer to look after their early education, even if that means taking them to the fields, where they toil daily."

"I know what you mean. They don't want their children brain-washed." My words were out before I could think clearly.

"I haven't heard what you have said, so please never repeat it," the Chairman said kindly.

"So what about that house?"

"It could be taken off the list and if it was, I promise you that your waiting will be over. You will be allowed to move into that house, but only after."

"Have you tried to achieve that?"

"Such a request couldn't come from me, but if it ever came from someone else, it could be done. I do believe it."

"Has anybody ever tried?"

"I have never dared to mention this approach to anyone, until now."

"Would you like me to try it?"

"It would require a formal application and many signatures from parents."

"I will do that. I will do almost anything to avoid the early train rides and to have my family close to me."

"I am glad I confided in you...You seem to have a great deal of initiative."

"Thank you comrade...I will start right away and if I succeed, when I succeed, will you notify me?"

"You have my word that I will do that, but please remember that the idea came not from me. In fact I know nothing more than your need for a place to live."

***

Within two days I had put the school's only typewriter to good use and after two weeks of volunteer work to the Council, I had over one hundred signatures on the petition required.

I kept Rozsa fully informed about my actions and when she asked why am I doing that when we are trying to leave the country, I gave her my explanation.

"I am not trusted by many people. I will be watched for quite a while. What better way is there to mislead the watchers, then to indicate my desire to move to Bacsbokod?"

"I always knew that you were thinking ahead, but this action of yours surprised me."

The two of us have waited for the outcome of my petition, but not as much as we have waited for the Sunday messages and for the coded letters.

In December of nineteen fifty four we had celebrated Ildiko's first Christmas and looked forward to the New Year that we hoped would bring us freedom.

Our plans have progressed nicely. My father-in-law found a guide, he could trust and in one of his messages, followed by a letter, that is what he indicated.

"Within two months a guide will cross the border. He will contact you to start your preparations," his coded message and letter indicated, but before the two months had passed, two members of our family made things more complicated.

***

My brother, George, paid us a visit and he announced that he wanted to join us.

"Join us in what?" I was flabbergasted.

"I too want to get out of here," he stated clearly.

"What made you think that we are planning of going?"

"A couple of things: I know your in-laws and I know that they will want you to rejoin them. And besides, I am not blind. Aunt Gizella is slowly selling off everything. I visit them often and notice that each time a piece of their furniture is missing. When I tried to find out what is happening, they became very tight-lipped. I think they will be part of your group and that is what I desire."

"Do my parents know anything about this?" I asked and feared that they too may have noticed what my Aunt and Uncle were doing.

"No...They never suspect a thing. Mother thinks that her Sister grew tired of the old things and wants everything cleared out, so she could pressure her husband to modernize everything."

"And what does Father think?"

"He is rarely home, always on his ship, so never visits the Santas. Mother tells him nothing when he comes home, which he does quite rarely."

"They must never find out. You know Father and his constant fears. If he ever finds out what we are contemplating, he would do his utmost to change our minds. He probably would do anything not to lose us and his only Grandchild. Please tell him nothing George."

"I will say not a thing, if I am included."

"I will raise the issue with Rozsa's Father, but I don't expect any difficulties."

"I am really grateful, if there is anything I can do, you just have to name it."

"Just stay mum on the whole issue, otherwise you will stay behind when we start our journey."

***

The other surprise came from Joe, Rozsa's brother. He served his two years in the army and upon his discharge, he came home.

For a few days we spoke about nothing, but his parents' successful escape and their regret that they were unable to take him. Then slowly we began to tell him that soon a guide will come and that we, as well as his parents, will want him to be ready to leave his homeland.

He expressed no reluctance, in fact, he was extremely enthusiastic. The possibility of an escape appealed to his adventurous nature.

My next letter to my in-laws openly stated that their Son was home, that his service in the army was over, but his desire and that of George, to join our group I wrote in code and soon the message came, indicating that both of them are included.

In this manner, by early spring of nineteen fifty five, our escape group was fully formed and our excitement mounted.

"There will be two children..." I was telling Rozsa. "Ildiko will have to be carried all the way; she is only a year old. The other little girl, almost five, will need a great deal of help as well. But that is no problem. Uncle Jozsef, Joe, George, Joska Bago and I, will be able to carry the two children. The three of you: Aunt Gizella, Mrs. Bago and you, my beloved will not require too much assistance. So there will be ten of us. May God grant that we get out safely."

A month had passed before Joe made his announcement.

"I changed my mind. I am not leaving this country."

"Are you insane? Our parents will be heart-broken," Rozsa told him.

"I do not care. I met a girl and we love each other."

"When did this happen?" Rozsa inquired.

"A few days ago," Joe announced it as if he and his new paramour have known each other for an eternity.

"Joe, you must come to your senses. Your parents want you in Austria; they wish for nothing more than to have their family together. You have been in love before. How many times? I do not know, but I do know that you do not even remember all the girls you thought you loved. Am I correct?"

"It is none of your business Laszlo." Joe was infuriated.

"Your love affairs are none of my business, I know that Joe. Normally I wouldn't say a thing, but this time is different. We will risk our lives to gain our freedom. Freedom is a precious commodity. I am sure you too want to be free."

"I want to be free of your constant nagging."

"When have I bothered you with anything?"

"Haven't you been after me to take a job? Haven't you asked me, berated me for my lack of willingness to become a slave? You started that the day after I came back from the army."

"I did that almost every day, ever since your return, but I did that to assure our survival."

"Your survival is all you care about. You go away very early in the morning and you come home very late. When you arrive you always scold me. I know you don't mind getting up early, so you want me to do the same. Get up early; go to a boring job; sweat for eight hours; come home to get a plate of bean soup. That is the way you would have me live. Well, my dear brother-in-law, it may come to you as a surprise, but that kind of life is not to my liking."

"Joe, you are my brother, but sometimes I don't understand you. Laszlo is the only one who brings home any money. What we eat; the roof over our heads, the little we have is what Laszlo provides. I wish I was allowed to work to help out. You are young, healthy and strong. Don't you think that your contribution would be badly needed?" Rozsa's words poured out with more bitterness than I expected.

"Well I am not like Laszlo. I like to sleep in; I would like to have fine food and nice clothing. If I could find a job that would pay me a lot, I would take it. To work for the kind of wage Laszlo gets would destroy my dignity. Do you want me to be like Laszlo?" Joe appealed to his sister.

"No, I just want you to help out. I want you to escape with us. Once we are in Austria you can do whatever you want, you will not be our responsibility."

"Oh, I see. My own sister begrudges me the little happiness I have. You are not like my beloved. She is kind. When I go to her parent's place, at the small train station of Borsod, they feed me like a king. My girlfriend, soon to be my fiancé and her parents, don't mind me not working. They appreciate what I am, they truly like me."

"You are a hopeless case Joe. I will let your parents know what you have decided. I am too tired to argue every evening."

"Then stop your quibbling. I be glad to see all of you go. I will be truly free."

I was amazed hearing Joe's words, to see how he lacked a shred of understanding.

"He can hardly wait to see us go, but thinks not even for a moment that he will have to pay the rent; that he will have to fend for himself, that he will be without our support." I thought and decided to give up on him and to concentrate on what was coming.

***

The middle of March came and the cold, struggle filled winter seemed to be over. A few flowers poked their heads out of the thawing ground and the new shoots of greenery gave notice that Spring was coming.

"The spring of hope, the spring of our delivery cannot be far away," I thought and within a few days a parcel arrived from my in-laws.

We have always put some money aside to be able to pay the stiff duty and ever since my deliverance from the army, Rozsa waited for my arrival, so we could enjoy together looking at those precious parcels.

"Was the duty steep, my love?"

"I had to pay four hundred Forints, Laszlo."

"I know that it is never cheap, but everything they sent will be worth it," I told my beloved and cut the strings, opened the cardboard box and as we removed each item, we sighed with delight.

"Look at these red, little boots they sent for Ildiko." I lifted out the shiny, red boots and when Rozsa ran her fingers over the fine leather, she began to cry.

"My poor parents...They send so many nice things...They select all the items with love. I can just see them when they are getting the things ready. Their fingers touched each and every item. It is not goods they send, but a part of their hearts and all their love." Her words came out, between sobs and I wanted to end her sadness.

"Let's try the boots on Ildiko."

"They are too large...," Rozsa announced, after trying.

"She will grow into it my darling."

"We will put it away for her and in a year or two she will be able to wear it, by then she will be walking."

We touched, admired, each item. Bags of candies, chocolate bars, chewing gums, nylons, silk scarves, blouses, skirts, jackets, pants, and many other fine things piled up on the kitchen table. Then came a bag of something that neither of us has ever seen. The long, brown, fruit like items, filled the bag, but inside the bag looked slimy.

"What could this be?" I asked Rozsa.

"I don't know. I have never seen anything like this."

"Do you mind it if I open the bag and take out one of these things?" I didn't wait for Rozsa's answer, instead I opened the bag and tried to pull out the seven inch, brownish-black shriveled, yet oozing item.

"Now what should I do Rozsa?"

"I give you a plate. Put it on that. I think you should open the skin with a knife."

I did as Rozsa suggested and the insides spilled out.

"Now what my love?" I was puzzled.

"Should we taste it?"

"We might as well." I told my beloved and I found that it wasn't to my liking. "It tastes strange, yet a bit sweet. I wish I knew what this strange thing is, before letting you try it," I told Rozsa.

"Maybe we could check the list." Her parents always listed every item, hoping that the custom people will be deterred from stealing any of the items.

We scanned the list and found only one thing that we have never heard of and the two of us decided that the gooey stuff must be that. It was listed as bananas. Then we noticed the date of the parcels mailing, it was sent in mid January.

For half an hour more, we unpacked and enjoyed our windfall, after which we had checked the contents against the list that was in Rozsa's Dad's handwriting. A few of the items were underlined, but one of the underlining seemed wavy.

That item, underlined with what appeared to be a shaking hand, was a red, knitted scarf, with a peculiar pattern.

We tried to read some hidden meaning into that underlining, but in the end we gave up, having decided that it carried no special meaning. We were wrong, we found out on Sunday morning.

"To the young lady who now has a red scarf. When I listed it, my hand shook with excitement. Soon you will have two identical scarves and when the second one arrives you will have what you most desire...," the announcer read.

We were certain that the message was for us; that Dad changed the code, once more and that it was getting us closer to our greatest desire. Sunday night we listened again, but we understood no more than we did that morning.

When two days later, a letter arrived and I broke the code, I read the clear message to my sweetheart.

"You have one red scarf, knitted by your Mother. Trust the one who will take to you an identical scarf."

We talked about what Rozsa's Father wrote, in code, and our hearts began to beat much faster.

"What do you think Laszlo his message means?"

"Your parents must be getting close to sending a guide for us," I told Rozsa.

"Do you really think that Laszlo?"

"Your Father was always a meticulous planner. They sent the package. They knew that it will take two months to have it reach us. He underlined a few items, but the scarf was underlined differently. He hoped that we will notice and when he thought the time was right, he sent us that letter to further clarify things. The last thing he sent was that message. Your Father planned well...A hint in the parcel; a coded message added to it, then the Free Europe Radio's announcement, all add up. I don't think there can be any doubt: we will soon receive a visitor. When someone comes my beloved, while I am away, have that person wait for my arrival, or have him return, later in the evening."

***

A few, rare visitors came the following week, but they were relatives or friends. Each time I heard a knock, with my heart in my mouth; I went to unlock the gate and hoped to see a stranger. Then on March twenty first, it finally happened.

I opened the gate and saw a slim, young woman.

"May I help you?" was all I was able to say to the stranger.

"If you are Laszlo Lichter, if your wife is Rozsa, if you have a daughter that goes by the name of Ildiko, then you better let me in," she spoke with urgency.

"This is my wife Rozsa and Ildiko, our baby." I introduced to her to my family, as soon as the two of us entered.

"If you don't mind I will not give my name," she spoke up. "How many people in your group?"

"I don't think I understand. What group are you talking about, lady?"

"I see you are being cautious. That is appreciated. Maybe this will make you open up." She unbuttoned her coat, removed a red scarf from around her neck and gave it to Rozsa. "Does this look familiar?"

"I have one, just like this," Rozsa announced and brought out her scarf from the bedroom. She compared the patterns of the two scarves and their stitches.

"The patterns are identical and so are the stitches."

"They should be. Both of them were knitted by your Mother, my dear. One was sent to you in a parcel, that also contained a bag of rotten bananas and the other one was given to me."

"Who gave it to you?" I asked.

"His name I will not reveal. I was not authorized to do that. I can tell you this: He is now in Hungary. He gave me the scarf and this picture." She handed over a photograph I took of our baby, at the time of her first birthday, a copy of which I sent to my in-laws. I saw my handwriting on the back and a brief, cryptic note from Dad.

"Our first Granddaughter, February 10, 1954. May she succeed to grow up in the land of freedom." His handwriting couldn't be mistaken.

"Thank you for the scarf and for the picture. We have been waiting for you for some time. Do you have our instructions?"

"That is why I came…You must not write down a single word. I was told you will able to remember."

"You were told right. Please tell us what we are to do."

"I understand you are no longer in the army, so that will not pose any problems. You are teaching and your Spring break will begin on March twenty-eight, that is next Monday."

"That is so. My Father-in-law thought of everything."

"He did, I assure you. You have one week off, so you will not be missed, so it will be safe to begin your journey. Now here is what you must do." She laid out the instructions and when she had finished, she asked me kindly.

"Will you remember all this? Will you be able to follow all the steps of these instructions?"

"I swear I will," I told her with mounting excitement.

"Very well then. I must return home. I was never here. Do you understand me?"

"We do!" Rozsa and I assured her and before she left she wished us luck with words that were truly appreciated.

"May the good Lord watch all your steps. May you have His blessing for your dangerous journey."

***

The following day, in the dead of night, I visited my brother, then my Aunt and Uncle and finally their friends, the three Bagos.

I gave my brother detailed instruction. I did the same with the two families and before I said good-by, I told them one thing.

"Next time I will see you, we will have to pretend that we don't know each other. May God bless all of us. May He help us to succeed. May we be strong enough to reach that free country."

***

On what we hoped to be our last Sunday in Hungary, we went to visit my parents and later on Rozsa's Aunt, Uncle and their only Son, Sana. We spent at least two hours at each place and tried to be strong, not to betray our intentions, with tears or words or with any sign that this was the time of our parting.

It was a very difficult time. To hide the truth from people we loved, was not in our nature, but somehow we managed to say good-by and after we have reached our home we began our crying. Ildiko must have sensed that something was wrong and her baby cries mingled with ours. What little time was left of that sad, yet hopeful day, we spent packing. One suitcase was filled with sundry items: extra shoes, socks, cloth diapers, bottles of food for Ildiko, who was no longer breast feeding, some food for us and medicines for headaches, for fever and a mild sedative for those who may need it. When we have closed the small suitcase, I lifted it up and found that it was light enough to carry for many kilometers, should it become necessary.

"Have we forgotten anything?" Rozsa asked, her voice quite unsteady.

"I don't think so. Do you have your identification book my dear?"

"I do. I keep it in my coat pocket. Do you have yours?"

"In the inside pocket of my jacket."

"How many days will it take Laszlo?" she asked me again, although she knew what the messenger told us.

"No more than three. Tomorrow, around noon we will be in Budapest. We will spend the night at your Aunt Lujza. The next morning we will catch the trains to reach *Gyor*. By early afternoon, we will be there. Then one night's of traveling on the hay wagon, under straw. A day of hiding at a farm and when night falls the hay wagon will take us closer to the border. That night we will cross into Austria. I think we will be able to cross the border on March thirtieth, my dear." I repeated what the lady told us. It really sounded simple and straight and reassuring, so I left it that way not wanting to frighten Rozsa.

"I wish Joe would get home soon. Maybe we could change his mind?" Rozsa expressed her wish.

"Don't get your hopes up my darling. Joe is in love," I told her simply and dropped the subject.

By eight o'clock Ildiko fell asleep and Rozsa and I sought our bed, hoping to get lots of rest before our journey.

"What if something goes wrong Laszlo?" Rozsa cuddled with me and her whispered question I had to ponder, before giving her an answer.

"We have survived so much my darling. I am sure we will survive this last trial."

"Is there something you don't want to tell me?" she asked, her breath warm against my face.

"We cannot see into the future. I suppose it is just as well. We must be courageous my beloved. We must accept what the good Lord planned for us. Our love is strong, together we will be able to face anything."

"What if we get killed by the border guards?" Her whole body shook.

"If we all die my love, at least we had each other to love, to hold, to cherish. That is more than I ever thought I will live to see," I whispered in her ear.

"What if we get captured? What if we end up in prison?" her breath seared my face.

"Even there we will remember each other. We will recall our time of courtship; our engagement; our wedding; the birth of our baby and we will remain strong. Some day they will have to let us out and we will be together again; we will still love each other and our little girl." I tried to reassure Rozsa, but there was only one way left to really console each other.

When we were totally exhausted and ready to go to sleep, ready to refresh our spent bodies, Rozsa whispered in my ear.

"I love you Laszlo. Have some rest and when you pray, as I will, beseech the Lord for His mercy."

***

After an almost sleepless night we got up, got Ildiko ready and woke Joe, who came home around one o'clock in the morning.

"This is the last chance Joe," I told him, while he rubbed his sleep filled eyes.

"The last chance for what?" He either did not comprehend or pretended not to do so.

"To change your mind. To come with us. To see your parents."

"If that is all you want then you should have let me sleep."

"I couldn't do that. This may be the last time you will ever see your Sister and Ildiko too."

"Where are they?"

"In the kitchen." Joe slept in Rozsa's old room.

"Well, they should come in. I am not going to get up," he announced and within minutes we said good bye to Joe, in the room where we spent the first night after our marriage. He was cold, unmoved, uncaring and in some strange way that made parting from him easy.

I locked the gate behind us, dropped the key into the mail slot and my heart beat very strangely. It caused me great pain to leave the house where I spent so many pleasant hours, courting Rozsa. The kisses we stole while preparing corn in the attic for the pigs, suddenly came to my mind and the sweet memories made my leaving a lot harder. The yard where we have spent many hours, pouring over an old Sears catalogue fell behind us, but not the memory of that time. The recessed gate, where we spent many moments with my beloved, especially during dark evenings, where we had exchanged many kisses, I will never see again, and that made me gasp with sadness. The tree that stood front of the house, under which sat the two Bujas, when they had discovered that Rozsa and I disobeyed them, could no longer be seen, but that tree stood out in my memory, for by that tree my life have changed forever.

As we walked from our former home to the station, I said a silent good-by not only those I loved, but to the many places that held special memories for the two of us.

"We will never again sit in our back row of the cinema of *Urania*. We will never stroll on the *korzo*. We will never hold hands under our tree with the carved heart, displaying our initials. We will never..." I tortured myself, but thank God we arrived to the railway station.

***

We sat in a compartment with many people, that prevented us from talking about important things, so we stared out the window and pointed out to our uncomprehending little daughter the villages, the towns, that we were about to leave forever.

Aunt Lujza greeted us with kisses, hugs and admired our little baby.

"We would like to stay here, until tomorrow morning," I announced and was glad to hear her warm words of agreement.

"Over a year ago a policeman came to see me. At that time I didn't know that your parents used me to escape from the country. I had a few letters from them since they got out, but they gave me no explanations. Can you tell me what was that all about?"

I told her as much as she needed to know and when I finished relating the story, she took a guess.

"And now it is your turn. You are trying to leave this country."

I looked at Rozsa, not quite sure as to what to say and she nodded her head.

"We are trying to join Rozsa's parents," I told her simply.

"For that I cannot blame you. If I were younger I would leave this place gladly, but my age, my Sons, keep me here. The three of you are young. Your whole life is ahead of you. So stay here, until tomorrow morning and when you leave remember me."

***

The following morning we left Lujza and after the tears that the women shed, we traveled by trolley to the railway station.

Rozsa and I stood close to a sign, as we were instructed and I held our blanket wrapped baby. In the fold of the blanket, close to Ildiko's chin, a small corner of her picture showed, exactly as we were advised. A few minutes later I saw the three Bagos, some twenty meters from us; then George, almost that far, but in the opposite direction and finally I saw Uncle Jozsef and Aunt Gizella, by the main entry.

We have waited, not knowing exactly what was supposed to happen and when a stranger walked toward us, my heart gave a jump and my mind screamed: "That must be our guide!" When his footsteps carried him past us, I was troubled. "Did something happen to our guide? Is this the end of our escape plan? Did he desert us?" I couldn't stop my awful thoughts, but I didn't want to scare Rozsa, so I smiled at her, patted our baby's face and hoped for the next stranger to approach us.

The footsteps came and went by us, but then the man turned and stopped in front of me.

"What a lovely child. May I take out that picture?" I heard the right words and nodded my head.

"I see the baby and the writing. Buy tickets to *Szekesfehervar*, make it a return trip," he whispered and went into the station.

"Two return tickets to *Szelkesfehervar* please. And one for the baby, if she needs it."

"How old is she?"

"She was one year old, last month."

"There is no charge for her. For your tickets you pay two hundred eighty."

I counted out the money and knowing that one family was behind me and my brother and the other family at the next wicket, I thanked the man quite loudly for the return tickets to that city.

We have waited in the waiting room and I watched the others walk by me. I noted when each male bent down, as was instructed, to tie his shoe-laces.

"Thank God, they heard me and bought their tickets too," I thought having picked up the prearranged signals.

By the door to the platform, our guide waited and when he boarded the train we did the same, entered the same coach and took our seats a few rows away from him. The others followed our example and I gave a sigh of relief, as the train pulled out.

Before we have reached *Szekesfehervar*, our tickets, our identification booklets were checked, by the conductor and another male.

"When do you plan to return to Budapest?" the second male asked.

"In two days, maybe three."

"The purpose of your trip?"

"A visit to relatives. To show them our baby."

"May I have your relative's name and address."

I gave him what he required. I had no difficulty to recall the name and address of real people who lived in that city. I hoped with all my heart that all the others will be able to supply the information I gave them during my visit, last Tuesday. There were four sets of names the lady gave us during her visit, those we were to use during this leg of our trip and four more when we will be checked on the second train that will take us to *Gyor*.

The AVO officer seemed to be satisfied, for he moved on to check on all others. I was certain that he belonged to that dreaded secret police organization; that it was his job to check everyone who dared to travel toward a western destination.

After a few hours of travel and a few diaper changes, we have arrived to *Szekesfehervar* and there we all purchased another set of return tickets. We were scrutinized even more carefully before we reached Gyor, but the names and addresses seemed to serve us well. All of us have reached that city safely.

Our guide took off, after our arrival and he was nowhere to be seen. We milled around the station park and when after an hour we became quite tired, Rozsa and I took a seat on a park bench and fed Ildiko, exchanged a few words of concern about the unexpected waiting.

The guide reappeared, but this time, he didn't seem to be composed; he looked worried. He sat down on the bench, next to ours. Unfolded a newspaper and from behind it he spoke, loud enough for us to hear.

"Our plans have changed. Go to the first church, three blocks on the road to your right. It is open, wait there." He folded up his newspaper and stood up. Within minutes he was out of our sight and my earlier thoughts of desertion were resurrected.

"What could have gone wrong? What are we going to do now? What is happening?" I didn't share my thoughts with Rozsa, instead I got up and we walked to the Roman Catholic Church. We found it open, as was the usual practice in Hungary, in spite of the Communist Government's attempts to curtail religious freedom.

We took a seat in the back pew and watched as the rest of the group walked in and took seats far from us and each other. In spite of my disturbed state, I couldn't help, but be awed by the quiet place of worship. It was large; the Sun sent its rays through the colored, stained-glass windows. The statues, the pictures, the fresco that covered the dome, the altar-full of fresh flowers-created an aura of peace and deep devotion. I could smell incense. I stared at the crucified Christ that hung behind the altar. Everything around us promised salvation, but wherever I looked suffering was depicted.

"Good God in heaven," I thought. "Are we going to be crucified for what we are doing? Others come here to offer You their prayers; to worship You, but how many people have You ever seen who bring their suitcases? Lucky for us this place the Communists loath to enter. Dear God please keep them out of here, please give us sanctuary and help us to get across the border." Rozsa disrupted my thoughts and prayer.

"I must change Ildiko, please give me a diaper." I did as Rozsa asked and then I heard her next request.

"This poor little baby has a rash. I must wash her backside. Please take out a dry cloth and dip it in water."

I went outside the church, looking for a well, but found none and when I entered the foyer I saw no other source of water, than the stone basin, that stood by the entrance, containing Holy water.

"It would be a sacrilege to wash her bottom with this sanctified water." I told myself, but I had little choice. I asked the Almighty for His forgiveness, as I dipped the cloth into the stone basin and once again, when I handed the wet cloth to Rozsa.

"I am glad you found water, Laszlo. By the way where did you find it?"

"Never mind, just look after our daughter," I told her and I sensed that she perceived clearly why I had hid the truth.

"You couldn't have. Did you get the water where I think?"

"I did my love. There was no other place to get any."

"May God forgive us. May God grant us his mercy."

***

We spent over two hours in that holy place and with the passing of each moment, my dread grew; my fear increased; my certainty of being discovered got itself more firmly established.

The guide came into the church; knelt down front of us and began to speak.

"The driver of the hay wagon was arrested, two days ago, while he tried to take a group of refugees to the border. The AVO agents and the border guards are on full alert. Drivers we have used in the past, are terrified and unwilling to undertake the journey. We will have to walk all the way to the border. We are almost fifty kilometers from our crossing point. It will take two nights of walking. During the days we will have to hide. There is a restaurant, 'The Five Stars', six blocks away, on your right from the church. Five minutes after I leave, go there. Have something to eat. All of you will need energy. I must tell you the truth...It will not be easy...We will face many more dangers than I have anticipated. After dark I will come for you and we will start out."

"Couldn't we take a train to get a little closer? There are two children and the women to think about," I mumbled to the guide.

"I wish we could, but we couldn't get off the train before the western border belt. Our identification books would give us away. We most certainly would be arrested, if we tried to enter the thirty kilometer border belt," he said no more, stood up, genuflected, left the church and I was broken hearted.

"What are you thinking Laszlo?" Rozsa whispered in the silence and from time to time I saw the others turn their heads toward us, no doubt wanting to know what was amiss.

"We will have a very hard go...Are you up to it my beloved?"

"I will walk for days on end to join my parents, to find freedom."

"It is settled then my darling. Let's go to the place our guide mentioned. There is nothing else we can do, unless we are willing to give up our dream," I told Rozsa and this time it was our turn to genuflect, but first we asked the good Lord to help us; to deliver us from this country.

***

We sat at four different tables and ate hearty meals, trying to command our bodies to process what we have offered, to fortify our bodies for the coming ordeal.

The darkness began to fall around five o'clock and our guide made no appearance. We ordered a few light drinks, we sipped them slowly and when Ildiko began to cry, we gave her a sedative.

The guide entered. At the bar he sipped his beer for a few moments, then he left the place and slowly we followed him through the dark streets.

It took us more than twenty minutes to get outside the city and ten more minutes to cut across a cultivated, mud covered field. We reached a dike and in the quiet of the night, in the moonlight, beside a tree, our guide waited. In clipped sentences he explained to the assembled group everything he told me and Mrs. Bago began to sob.

"We will never make it," she cried out in the quiet night.

"We will make it, but it will not be easy. I will walk ahead and all of you are to follow, but do not bunch up. We must not be seen together. The moon will soon be covered by clouds. I will walk only when and where we will not be seen. We can't waste any more time. Thirty kilometers tonight and twenty the next evening we must cover. God be with us..." His words died off and soon he was so far away that we could hardly see him.

The Bago family were the first to start out and after they got a hundred meters ahead of us, Rozsa and I, with Ildiko in my arms, began to walk. George kept close behind me and as I tired, he took my sweet burden. My Uncle and Aunt followed us, after we had walked a fair distance.

"Are you all right my darling?" I asked Rozsa and in the night's silence, she reached for my hand and squeezed it.

We must have walked for over three hours. Rozsa staggered quite often, but she walked on without complaint, without a word. Her perspiring face, her clenched teeth, her body bent with the effort of the long walk showed her resolve. We have walked on for a few more minutes when Ildiko began to whimper and in spite of my petting her face, making for her comforting, cooing sounds, her whimpers turned into loud crying. I touched her forehead and I was alarmed.

"Touch her forehead. Do you find it hot Rozsa?"

"She is running a fever. Should we give her some medicine?"

"We must my dear. She must be made to quiet down."

The four of us stopped and Rozsa gave Ildiko an aspirin and then, after some debate, we made her swallow a sedative as well. In the meantime, my Aunt and Uncle caught up with us.

"Why is Ildiko crying?" Aunt Gizella asked us.

"She is sick. She is running a high fever," Rozsa replied.

"What rotten luck. I think I should catch up with the guide. We must get his opinion." Gizella announced and she ran ahead.

"What should we do now?" Rozsa asked me.

"We might as well rest, while we are waiting."

"Waiting for what?"

"Aunt Gizella will bring back the guide. He will look Ildiko over. He may be able to help somehow." I told Rozsa and the rest of our small group agreed with what I was saying.

"It does make sense," George announced and sat down on the grass. The rest of us joined him and Ildiko's crying pierced the quiet night, making me realize that the sound must be heard even at a good distance.

Within fifteen minutes my Aunt and the guide came into sight and when they reached us they sat down too.

"Her forehead is hot; she is running a high fever," the guide sounded angry. "Have you given her any medicine?"

"Hours ago we gave her a sedative and a while ago another. An aspirin too, but it doesn't seem to work. She has been crying."

"She sure has. I could hear her two hundred meters away. That is why I have turned back. We are doomed. This child will give all of us away." He sounded more angry.

"No she won't!" I told all of them. "We will not let all of you be captured, because our little angel got sick." Without asking Rozsa, I made my decision and made my announcement. "Rozsa and I will turn back. We will not endanger anyone."

"A wise decision. I was about to suggest the same," the guide stated and although I knew that there was no other way out, his words hurt me, destroyed my dream.

"If they go back, I am going with them," George's announcement surprised me, and my emotions ran so deep, that I was unable to utter a single word; instead I reached for my brother's hand and squeezed it.

"Well I will not stand here any longer. Time is being wasted. God see you home safely. Those who want to find freedom follow me." The guide took off; he was clearly troubled and agitated. Without any hesitation, only with a brief good-by, my Aunt took off and ran after our guide, but my Uncle just stood beside us, clearly hesitating.

"What am I to do now?" my Uncle finally spoke up. "I have a terrible premonition. I would love to turn back with you, but I cannot lose my wife. Her dream of being free is too strong and my wishes have never been important." I thought he was going to say something else, but he added nothing. He embraced Rozsa, then shook hands with George, kissed our baby and he turned to me.

"Good-by Laszlo. You were like a Son to me." The two of us embraced, held each other for what seemed an eternity and with tears in his eyes, he let go. I had a terrible feeling.

"Maybe I should stop him from going? I do not want to lose this dear man. But how could I tell him to let his wife continue alone? I would never leave my dear Rozsa, so how could I ask Joseph to give up his wife? How could I stop what I put into motion? How could I have known what fate will bring?" These confusing thoughts ran through my mind and by the time I have recovered, I could see only my Uncle's back, fast receding.

***

We covered the distance back to the station in total silence. My limbs ached; Ildiko was constantly crying and I imagined how my beloved felt, how her heart ached, how she regretted our failing.

"She has lost her chance to live in a free land. She will never see her parents again. She seems composed, but inside she must be crying," I thought and reached for her arm, while George carried our baby.

We spent the wee hours of the morning at the railway station and after one train trip, followed by two more, we were back where we started. In the dead of night, we pounded on the gate, until Joe came to unlock it.

"I see you didn't make it. You and your big talk about freedom; about seeing our parents. I was the wise one who wasted no time and energy," he said no more. We have entered our home, the place where we dreamt about freedom. We comforted Ildiko, we gave her medicine and finally she was no longer crying. She fell into a deep sleep and we followed her example. We were utterly exhausted.

"We must pray Laszlo for all the others. May God help them to get across. With the Lord's help, some day my love, we will give it another try. By then Ildiko will be older and with God's help we will succeed," Rozsa told me, I turned out the light and we fell asleep.

Chapter 18

"We have failed. We will never be free," came my bitter thoughts, during the first day after our return and tried to avoid Rozsa's eyes. I dared not give words to what ran through my mind, to what I feared and anticipated.

"The group of six must be getting close to the border. Maybe tonight they will try to cross? Will they succeed or will they fail? Will they fall prey to the manhunters?" I thought during the day, then when darkness descended and to hide my fearful thought, I sat down front of our radio, twisted and turned its dials.

"What are you doing Laszlo?" Rozsa asked me while she fed Ildiko.

"I am trying to see if there is any news about them."

"It is far too early and besides the Free Europe Radio broadcast is not until Sunday."

"I know my love, but I cannot think of anything else, but those poor people. Maybe they got across already?"

"I wish it was so, but they must be still walking."

"You must be right my love, but I see the face of my Uncle, as he stood by us and hesitated. I must try to find out what is going on."

"Maybe tomorrow you will. Maybe then there will be an announcement."

***

I rose early Friday morning and turned on the radio. I scanned station after station, but heard little that interested me. By noon all that has changed and when I picked up the broadcast from the BBC, I heard the announcement.

"A brave group of six Hungarians tried to escape to Austria..." The announcer began to read the news item and I called out for Rozsa. We held hands, as we listened, and my happiness soon turned into sadness. The news hit me like daggers, stabbed at my heart, I was devastated.

"Two males, one female and one little girl got across the border. They were badly injured by an exploding mine. The Austrian doctors were in the process of treating their injuries from the mine fragments, when Russian soldiers rushed in and at gun point, in spite of the medical team's objections, took them off the operating tables and dragged them out of there. We can speculate only on what happened to those courageous Hungarians. They were probably interrogated and handed over to the Hungarian border guards. One of our reporters was present when they were treated and heard their story. There were two others who didn't make it, our reporter was told. They refused to give the names of the failed escapees. A male, in his mid forties, was killed by a mine and his wife stayed where he fell. A few minutes later, she began to scream and they saw her running in the minefield, probably trying to join her husband.

"We will keep our listeners informed as we learn more details of this tragic event."

"Oh my God, what have I done?" I screamed.

"Laszlo, please, don't jump to conclusions. It may have been another group." Rozsa tried to ease my agony.

"It all adds up. Can't you understand? I killed my Uncle and God only knows what I have done to my Aunt."

"Please, my darling, don't torture yourself. We don't know that it was Uncle Jozsef."

"I know it in my heart. I can still see his face, his hesitation, before we turned back. He wanted to come back with us. Didn't you hear what he said? 'I have a terrible premonition. I would love to turn back with you, but I cannot lose my wife. Her dream of being free is too strong and my wishes have never been important.' Those words of his echoed in my ears all the way home and ever since. He must have felt that the end was coming. Why did I ever include them in the group? I knew it was my Aunt whose wish it was to leave this country, but my Uncle was quite contented. I am guilty. I don't deserve to live."

"Maybe tomorrow we will hear something else. Maybe they are alive. Maybe they are out of this country. Will you please chase away your morbid thoughts?"

"I wish I could, but that is not possible. You must understand my dear that I will never be able to forgive myself."

"But there is nothing to forgive. All members of the group made their own decisions. You didn't force anyone to undertake the journey."

"I didn't force them, that is true, but if I didn't tell them that we were trying to escape, my poor Uncle would be alive and they would be home."

"Can you stop and think just for one moment. We don't really know that it was our group. We know not a thing. Not a single name was mentioned."

"I know that my love, but look at it the way it is. The guide had to be one of the two men who got across. The other one was probably Mr. Bago. His wife must have been with him and with their little girl. Who else is left? Uncle Jozsef, the poor, unfortunate man stepped on a mine and my Aunt was the one who tried to join him."

"Let's wait a day before we allow ourselves to go to pieces. Maybe by then we will hear a different story."

"I wish we would Rozsa, but I doubt it. We must be strong. We must let Lujza know that we are home. I told her what we were trying to do. What if she hears the news and she thinks the worst my darling?"

"Then send her a wire. Do it now Laszlo."

***

Within an hour, I did as Rozsa suggested. The telegraph was short, but at least Lujza could rest easy. After I have done that task, I began to walk home and met George.

"Have you heard the terrible news, Laszlo?"

"What news?"

"It is on every western station. I heard it just an hour ago. I was on my way to see you."

"I heard something, but I don't believe it." I lied only to myself.

"But what if it is all true?"

"If it is then I am guilty. Please tell me, George, that it is not so."

"I know how you must feel, but you must think of Rozsa and Ildiko. If the rest of the group was captured, do you think they will be able to keep mum about us?"

"I don't believe what I am hearing. Nobody will talk, you will see."

"You forget about the child. They will trick her and she will spill the beans." I heard what George was saying and I wasn't in the mood to argue.

"If that happens we are all finished." I accepted what I couldn't change. We talked for a few more minutes and carefully laid our plans. I rushed home to spend as much time as I could with my two angels, both of whom I loved dearly, yet I put in mortal, danger.

***

"I sent the wire, as you suggested," I told Rozsa and sat down, my mind in turmoil.

"If George is right, how much time do we have before they come for us?" I asked myself and the dreadful answer came instantly.

"Tonight or tomorrow we will all be arrested." I kept that terrible thought to myself and when we put Ildiko to bed, I said a silent good-by to my dear little daughter.

That night I held on to Rozsa tighter than ever before and in the dark night I have waited.

"Can't you sleep love?" she asked me after an hour.

"No, I don't deserve a peaceful night, after what I have done," I whispered in the darkness.

"You are too hard on yourself Laszlo," Rozsa whispered back.

"Am I really?" I asked her and my tears began to flow, as did my words, although I had no intention to frighten my beloved.

"I met George and his understanding of the broadcast is no different than mine. This may be our last night together Rozsa. The child will give all of us away and they will come for us. They will tear us apart. I may never ever see you again. I may never hold Ildiko in my arms. How can I survive that?"

"If that is what God has decreed then who are we to fight it? Love me Laszlo, that is all I ask of you. Love me like you have never done before and if we get torn apart, some day we will be reunited."

I held on to Rozsa and for the rest of that night we were like one being. We fell into an exhausted sleep that was shattered by the noise, the crash, the shouting voices.

"They are here...Good-by my darling." I was able to say no more, when the bright light blinded me and the gun was pressed against my head.

"Get up you bastard. You are under arrest." One of the armed men shouted and I heard another, similar shout, from Joe's room. "Get dressed...Make no sudden moves or you will regret it."

"There must be a mistake, comrades." I began my feeble protest, but they dragged both of us out of our bed and pulled us into the kitchen where the light shone brightly.

Joe stood in his underwear, but by then I began to dress.

"Hurry up!" came the order. "Put on warm clothing. You will need it where you will be taken."

"Dear God! They will take me to Siberia," I thought and began to beg.

"Take me if you must, but spare my wife, my child and Joe."

"You are all traitors, but we are compassionate men. Your wife and child will remain here, under house arrest."

"Thank God," I thought and looked at Rozsa's face, at her tear-filled eyes and at Ildiko in her arms.

"Good by my dears. Don't be afraid...I will be back."

"How touching," one of the six announced and his brutal face shone with the satisfaction of their accomplishment.

"Please don't arrest my brother-in-law. He is totally innocent," I tried to plead with my new masters.

"Laszlo is right. I did nothing," Joe protested.

"Shut your mouths you vile creatures," one of the six spit out the order and Ildiko began her earsplitting crying.

Two of them held on to my arms, and led me away, not even allowing me to kiss my wife, my daughter. They took me to the waiting car and once inside, they drove me to the police station.

I recall that in spite of being terribly frightened the irony of that car trip wasn't lost on me.

"I have never sat in a car, other than the taxi, at the time of our wedding, and now that I became the enemy of the State, I am being driven like I was somebody important." I thought and under different circumstances I would have laughed out loud, but instead I was crushed, I was without hope.

"This is the end of my sweet dream of a happy life with Rozsa and Ildiko, in a free country." I thought in misery and if my pride permitted I would have let them see the tears that gathered behind my eyelids.

***

Once in the yard of the police station, they hauled me out of the car and I took a quick look around, but saw neither Joe, nor George.

"Maybe they lied. Maybe they left Joe alone. Maybe they know nothing about George." I tried to convince myself and braced myself for the punishment that was to come for the crimes I have committed.

They led me into a small room, where two civilians waited.

"Give us your name," the taller one ordered.

"My name is Laszlo Lichter."

"Do you have a middle name?"

"Yes, it is Sandor."

"Whose name were you given when you were baptized?" The reason for that question didn't become clear, until later.

"My uncle Jozsef's middle name was Sandor," I told them and I felt the pain again that the mention of my poor Uncle created.

"Where is he now?"

"I do not know."

"Have it your way. When we finish you will not be in the mood to lie," the shorter one announced and I steeled myself for what I expected.

"They will begin the physical torture soon. How many times have I heard about the cruel ways they use to force their victims to talk? Many, many times and very few people were ever able to hold out. I know I will sing like a bird. I will not be able to withstand it," I told myself and tried to check my fear.

"Are you married?" The tall one and the shorter one, alternated in asking the questions and each time I turned my head to give them my answers.

"You know I am."

"How long have you known her before you got married?" I heard the question and wondered why have they become kinder.

"A number of years."

"It must have been a very nice courtship. Tell us how you met. How you fell in love. We want to know all about it."

I was puzzled, confused, but I obeyed them and slowly I warmed to my story. Now and then, when I stopped, one or the other urged me to go on.

"We love to hear more...Your wife is such a gorgeous creature."

"She is that." I was pleased and re-lived all the beautiful days I spent with my beloved Rozsa.

"When was your little daughter born?"

"February ten in nineteen fifty four."

"So that little girl is barely past her first birthday?"

"She is almost fourteen months old," I told them proudly.

"So you have a beautiful wife and a lovely little daughter. Why aren't you with them? Why are you here?" My interrogators made me think.

"I really do not know. I was arrested. I was brought here. I committed no crime, comrades."

"Well, we have heard many others affirm their innocence, but you deserve a prize for your acting ability. Have you not tried to cross into Austria? Have you not gotten together a bunch of traitors, escapees? Have you not killed your Uncle Jozsef, the man whose middle name was given to you? Have you not caused the imprisonment of several people? You keep telling us that you are innocent and you think we are stupid enough to believe you. No more lies. Tell us the truth. Tell us what has happened."

"I made a mistake, comrades."

"Stop right there. Traitors are no comrades of ours."

"Then what should I call you?" I asked.

"Call us your enemy."

"But that is not what you are. We are all Hungarians."

"Hungarians indeed? You tried to escape from this great country and you dare to call yourself a Hungarian?"

"I tried and I forced my wife and my helpless baby, but I came to my senses long before we got inside the border belt. I turned around and regretted what I did. I tried to convince the others, but they wouldn't listen, they wouldn't join us. They wouldn't come back."

"So you became a patriot, all of a sudden?"

"I had a lot of time to think, while we walked. I wanted to return home and we did. If doing that is wrong then I am guilty."

"Guilty as hell." One of them changed his tune. "Do you know what we do to people who are found guilty? You will rot in prison until you are an old man. Your wife will be released soon, so she can divorce you. The girl you courted and love so deeply will find someone else to please, to kiss, to love, to make happy and she will forget you. Your little daughter will be brought up by the State. We will teach her to hate men like you. Many years from now, you will see her on a street and she will know who you are. She will spit on the sidewalk when she sees you. That is what will happen to Laszlo Sandor Lichter, the rotten traitor."

Had they spoken these words, shortly after my arrival, I would not have minded, but after making me re-live-for almost two hours-all the wonderful times I had with Rozsa and later on with my little daughter, I felt my love for those two people far more keenly and I became a lost soul. My suffering was far greater than any manner of torture would have created.

"We will accomplish these things, we assure you," the shorter one hissed at me. "Unless you are willing to do what we tell you."

"What do I have to do?" I asked them.

"A simple confession is what we want. You are to write down all your anti-State activities."

"Give me the paper. I want to start right now."

"Well that is a lot better, but if we don't like what you write, you will have to do it again." The taller one handed over a pen, several sheets of paper and I began to write.

***

"My dear wife and I were unjustly treated. I was drafted by the army, when I shouldn't have. My dear wife and my soon to be born baby no longer enjoyed my support. Then my in-laws were kidnapped by imperialist agents and the AVO promised to bring them back, but they never did. I found out that they mislead me, that my in-laws left this country on their own. I began to hate those traitors. The two people I thought I loved, deserted their daughter and their only grandchild. I would have never dreamt of joining them, but my dear wife was fired by her boss, Szantai. Her firing left my family without any income and I had no choice but to appeal to my in-laws for a guide to take us out of this country.

"Somehow my poor Uncle and Aunt found out what I was contemplating and they begged me to allow them to join us. They have been good to us. I couldn't refuse them. Nor could I refuse their friends, the three Bagos. When I got word that the guide has crossed the border and he was ready to take us out, my dear wife bagged me not to do it, but I was stubborn and bull-headed, at least until we got within thirty-five kilometers of the border.

"I began to see that my wife was right. I became concerned about my little daughter growing up amongst foreigners. We are Hungarians, I thought proudly and told my wife that I wish to turn back. She was delighted; she jumped from joy, but it was too late to convince the others. God only knows how hard we tried. We begged my Aunt and Uncle to come back with us, but they were under the influence of that evil guide, as were all the others. We turned around; traveled to Baja and we knew that we will be found out, but that didn't concern us, we wanted to make things right."

I re-read my confession and hoped that my wife will say the same, should she have to give an account of what happened. I knew that George will remember our agreement and back my story, if he is arrested. When an hour later, my interrogators returned, they read my confession and shook their heads.

"You are a rotten scoundrel. You lie through your teeth. You didn't turn back, because of your non-existent conscience. There was another reason. Wasn't there?"

"There was no other reason. What I wrote is the truth," I insisted.

"You didn't mention your dear brother. He is spilling his guts in the other room and you are trying to mislead us. Let me show you what I think of your confession." The taller one grabbed the papers and tore them up.

"Now start again. We must have the truth, not only about your reason for turning back, but also about your spying. If you try to lie once more, you will put your wife and child in more danger. Your wife spied too. She sent to her parents confidential, medical journals. If you want to save her neck you must write down the truth. Start over." I had my instructions and I was willing to do anything to save my beloved.

***

My new confession gave them more than the first one. I admitted that I organized the group; that I hated the army and that I desired nothing less than to leave Hungary. I described how I forced George to join us and tried to clear my wife of all wrong doing.

One of my interrogators seemed to be in a better mood when he read the second report.

"Now that is closer to the truth prisoner," the tall one announced and passed my confession to his partner, who barely looked at it.

"The f...it is. You are still hiding the truth, but so be it. We are your first line of interrogators only. In a few hours you will sing a different tune. You will be eager to spill your guts. The whole truth will be known."

I wondered what his threats meant, but failing to find an answer, I began to think about what more could I confess.

"I must protect my wife. It doesn't matter what it takes. If they want me to confess to spying, I will do that. If they want me to implicate the dead, I cannot harm my dear Uncle, he is safe in God's hands. If they want me to condemn all other members of the group, I will do that too. They are in Communist hands now. Nothing I could say or write will harm them." I made my hard decisions and as soon as I made them, I got other ideas. I weighed them carefully. I tried to find the best alternative, but I was confused.

"How long will I survive in prison?" I asked myself and the answers came, but those answers gave me no peace, no comfort, just misery and lack of will so badly needed for survival.

My interrogators returned and put on me the handcuffs. I tried to twist my wrists, ever so slightly, and found that with each movement the cuffs tightened. I gave up any further attempt to move my hands. The cuffs cut into my skin and I was frightened. They led me out of the police station, one on each side, my arms in their grips. They shoved me beside the driver of the car and the tall one sat down beside me. I was jammed in the front seat, very close to the driver and my handcuffed hands on my lap; my eyes staring straight ahead. Then I heard the back door slam shut and I glanced in the rearview mirror and I saw three faces.

"Poor George. He didn't escape my fate. He was made to sit behind me. The shorter of my two interrogators between him and Joe, who was also arrested, in spite of his total innocence, in spite of his refusal to join my group of escapees." I thought bitterly about their fate and promised to do what I must to save them.

The car began to roll and I could see the familiar places. We stopped at the railway tracks, where a train was gathering speed.

"This must be the train that took me away, so many times, from my dear Rozsa, but each and every time our separation was short, our reunion was sweet. Will I ever see her sweet face? Will I ever see my little daughter? My interrogators think not. They should know what awaits me. She will grow tired of waiting. She will find someone else to love. She will kiss another man. She will divorce me." I couldn't avoid those false thoughts, yet I had to admit that the outcome will be likely. "How long will she be able to survive without a job, even if they allow her to remain free? Not long I guess...She is young and sweet and good looking. Guys will pursue her relentlessly and after a long while she may forget me." This last bitter thought lingered in my mind and I saw the ancient, thick trees that stood beside the road, invitingly.

"If I could grab the steering wheel, just for one moment, I could cause a crash, we could be killed. Maybe that is what I should do? Maybe it would be better to end it all now?" I almost reached for the wheel, but something held me back, nibbled at the edge of my mind. "Maybe George and Joe would be killed too? Have I not killed my Uncle? Do I have the right to kill them too? Dear God, please give me a sign. Please tell me what am I to do. Please do not desert us." I prayed silently for Divine guidance and suddenly the trees disappeared. Vast fields of new corn, barley, wheat and oats, rushed by us, the terrain was flat, not a tree close by.

"Maybe this is a sign from the Almighty?" I asked myself and the tension that built up in my body, slowly dissolved and in total silence, we have completed our terrible trip, that ended at *Kecskemet*.

I was taken out of the car first and I was given the order sharply.

"Keep your head down prisoner. Don't look up. We will lead you."

I heard the metal gate open noisily. I saw front of my feet the tiles and step after step my dread grew, until I was led into a small room, where I was handed over to my new minders.

"Strip prisoner." I heard the order and as I took off my heavy winter coat, as I removed my cap and the rest of things that covered my skinny body, I saw the finger rack and other strange things, that I took to be instruments of torture. At the police station of Baja, I would have gladly suffered physical torture in place of what they did to me, but my courage deserted me seeing those items.

"Please God don't let them torture me," I prayed to the Almighty.

I stood completely naked, in the cold room and I shivered with fear, with cold, with shame, but dared not utter a single word. I was no longer the old Laszlo.

"Turn around...Bend over...Spread your backside..." I obeyed and felt rough fingers violate my body.

"Now get dressed, but remove your shoe-laces and your belt. Those items you are not to have. Your watch, your wallet, your identification booklet will be returned to you when you become an old man."

I did as I was told and regret flooded my mind not only for what I did, but also for not grabbing the steering wheel, while I had a chance.

"I should have grabbed the wheel. I should have tried to kill us all, but now it is too late. I will not be able to kill myself. They took away that opportunity."

"Now move...," the order came, once I was fully dressed. One hand closed on my arm and the guard began to guide me. I heard his snapping fingers...Click after click came and the sound continued, until my cell door opened and I discovered that I was isolated.

"This is your new home prisoner. The rules are simple. We will tell you when you are allowed to sit, until then you must stand. We will tell you when you are allowed to lie down. When we let you do that, you must cover your body with the blanket, but your hands must always be kept on the top, so we can see it. You are always to sleep on your back. If you turn to your side we will wake you. When you are not in bed, you must not take off a single item of clothing. We don't care if you are too warm or if you are freezing. Through the peep hole we can see everything you do. You better not break prison rules or you will be severely punished." The guard finished my indoctrination and slammed the door, but only after he gave me a wide, cruel smile. I just stood there and saw a single eye looking at me through the peep hole. I tore my eyes away from my watcher and looked around my cell.

It wasn't more than two meters wide and maybe four meters long. At one side I saw the iron bed, the thin mattress and the single blanket, not even a pillow. I noticed the foul smelling bucket and almost lost my last meal when I thought of using it with that eye watching me. There was no chair, there wasn't a table. I was bone tired from the almost sleepless night, from the arrest, the interrogation, the car trip, but most of all I was tired of life in our beloved country. I had no permission to sit, but I decided to test my guard. I put my backside on the edge of my bed and the door opened immediately.

"Did I give you permission to sit down?" the shout reverberated in the small cell.

"No," I said and promptly stood up. I kept standing for a few hours and then the bottom of the door opened. A small metal tray was slid inside.

"This must be my supper." I thought and saw a piece of stale bread. A tin cup of water or soup, I couldn't distinguish between the two. A small *csajka*, not unlike the one I was given by the army, but what was inside it turned my stomach. I decided not to even try the foul meal, yet my parched lips cried out for some water. I raised the tin cup and the taste of that fluid made me spit it out.

The door swung open.

"You are to eat and drink what we gave you," the guard ordered and he raised his revolver.

I gagged on the bread. The fluid, that was neither water nor soup, I sipped and it went the wrong way. The *csajka*'s contents offended my nose. I found that it was a tasteless, moldy millet. In spite of my stomach's revulsion, I obeyed the guard and before he left, he voiced his approval.

"You will get used to it prisoner. After five years or so this food will be very much to your liking."

His announcement made me shiver with that possibility.

"Have I committed such a great crime that I could be imprisoned for five years?" I asked myself and one part of my mind denied that possibility, but another part, the realistic one, took command.

"Some people got five years for telling a simple joke. What you have done is no joke at all. You have become a thorn in the side of the Communists. Twenty years is more likely." My mind told me and I let the two parts argue. Back and forth they went.

"Not even five years. Laszlo will be released soon." One part expressed a faint hope, but the other part wouldn't let go.

"Lucky if he will not be shot for his treason."

I listened to my thoughts that seemed to originate somewhere else and the more exhausted I became with the constant standing, the more I began to hope for simple things.

"You can go to bed now," I seemed to hear, but the voice came from my own head and I remained standing.

"Didn't you hear me prisoner? Are you trying to disobey me?" This time I heard the voice more clearly.

"I didn't hear what you said."

"You are to go to bed. Take off everything, except your underwear. Remember the rules. Blanket over your body. You lie on your back. Your hands always over the blanket."

I obeyed my keeper like a dog and once I was in the bed my tired body began to relax, but my active mind kept on its nagging.

"In the army you found ways of being disobedient. You always outsmarted your superiors. Have you become chicken-shit Laszlo?" One part of my mind urged me to disobey, but its adversary didn't give up either.

"Do what they tell you. Don't dare disobey them. They will punish you without mercy."

"Am I going insane?" I asked myself and found that possibility not unlikely. I began to shiver, with my naked arms over the blanket and slowly turned on my side and hid my arms under the cover.

The door opened. My watcher made me stand up.

"Repeat the rules," he demanded. I must have repeated his instructions accurately, his next words indicated.

"Now I am convinced that you are trying to defy me. You know the rules, yet you do things that are not permitted."

"I am sorry...I didn't mean to disobey..."

"You better not. Go back to bed and demonstrate to me what you just stated."

I lay on my back...Arms over the cover...I tried not to feel the cold. I struggled to put out of my mind all the discomforts. Merciful sleep saved me. The dreams came and I was a happy man. I was in my Rozsa's arms, our little girl beside us.

"Do you know where we are?" Rozsa asked me.

"Beside each other."

"I meant in what country."

"Hungary of course, where else my beloved?"

"In Austria, Laszlo. Can you believe that?"

"How did we ever get here?" I was flabbergasted.

"We escaped...We crossed the border."

"I thought we turned back."

"Don't be so foolish. Do you think I would do such a thing?"

"I am confused. I thought we did and I was arrested."

"That was only a nightmare. You are with us...We are free."

I must have shouted Rozsa's last words loud enough for the guard to hear me. He was beside me, shook me awake and when I snapped out of the dream, I heard his words and in my disappointment, I almost cried out.

"You are not allowed to talk prisoner."

"But I was asleep. I was with my wife," I said lamely.

"Fat chance...You will never see her again. Now get back into bed and no more talking."

I was afraid to fall asleep. I was fearful of having another dream, another disappointment. I didn't dare to risk speaking in my dream, to break prison regulations. I tried to stay awake, but my eyelids became heavy and after a while I shut my eyes, I was back in dreamland.

***

Rough hands shook me awake. I may have slept only ten minutes, but it could have been five hours for all I knew. In my confusion I looked at the watch that I no longer had.

"Is it night still or is the next day?" I wondered.

"Get dressed fast. Put on everything you have," the guard waited.

Within two minutes I was fully dressed, expecting to be taken out, to be shot or transferred or interrogated.

He grabbed my arm with far more force than required and I winced in pain. He said nothing more, as we walked on the corridor, but his fingers kept making the clicking sounds, exactly as he did after my arrival.

"What is he doing with his fingers? Why is he doing that?" I asked myself. A few minutes later I found out.

I heard another series of clicks, but those came from a distance. My guard's beefy arms shoved me against the wall. His hands held me there and no more clicks came from him, but the other clicking continued. That eerie sound came closer. I heard shuffling feet and then silence. My guard pulled me away from the wall and we continued our walking, while his fingers resumed their activity.

"Click, click, click." The snapping fingers went on, until we faced a door. He opened it, shoved me through it and I saw two uniformed officer, sitting by a table, across from each other.

"Stand over there prisoner." Chubby ordered-that was the name I gave to him- pointed at the huge, ornate heating unit, built from ceramic tiles. Its surface radiated intense heat and I tried to take one step back.

"Get close to the stove," Chubby spoke again and Skinny remained silent. I stood just inches from the hellishly hot heater. Within minutes sweat covered every inch of my body. I tried to divert my attention from the intense heat and thought about my guard, the sounds he made and the sounds made by that other.

"I was put in an isolation cell. I am not allowed to see the other prisoners. That must be what they were doing. The guards, who led prisoners on the endless corridors, made those sounds to warn each other. One of the guards would stop his clicking, thus signaling to the other. One prisoner would be shoved into the wall to make sure that he doesn't see the other. That is what my guard was doing...Was it my brother who was led by me, or was it Joe?" I wondered and my attempt to occupy my mind, to forget the heat, was futile. I was terribly hot. I was awfully tired.

"May I take off my coat comrades?" I heard my question and then the answer.

"What else would you like to do? Maybe you want us to release you? Maybe you would like to see your wife and daughter? We do no favors for traitors. You raise both of your hands above your head, that I will allow you," Chubby again.

I obeyed my tormentors and tried to withstand the heat. Tried to strengthen my tiring body.

The officers chatted with each other.

"I don't exist any longer. I am just a piece of furniture to these two men. To them I am less than nothing." I thought bitterly and found no comfort in the fact that I wasn't being interrogated.

Skinny finally spoke and I was surprised by his kindness.

"Would you like a cup of coffee?"

"No thanks comrade, but I would love to sit down." I gave my reply and he just chuckled.

"That is a laugh. You refuse the coffee. You are not willing to accept that from your enemies, but you would love to sit in comfort. The hell with you. Stay as you are. You will change your mind soon. Your pride will melt from that hot fire."

I stood where I was and bitter thoughts increased my suffering.

"These are rotten bastards. They are truly my enemy. But why don't they question me? Why don't they ask me for my confession? What the hell are they trying to do?" The answer didn't come for almost an hour.

Chubby summoned the guard, who must have been stationed front of the door.

"Take him back to his cell," he gave the order.

We made the walk back to my cell, exactly as we walked before, but this time there was no other guard clicking.

"Strip to your underwear and go to bed. Remember the rules," my guard spoke up.

I hurried to rest my worn body and in no time I fell asleep, but the shout cut my rest short.

"Up. Get dressed. Put on everything."

Another walk followed to the same office. The officers were still drinking coffee.

"Would you like to sit down?" one of them asked.

"I would comrade."

"Would you like to have some pastries and a cup of coffee too?"

"Yes, I would like that." I accepted the offer without hesitation.

"You betrayed your country. You spied for the enemy. You did many terrible things and yet you expect us to be kind, generous and understanding?"

"What did I do comrades?" I asked them, my voice shaking.

"I am sure we will know soon, but now I will allow you to sit down and enjoy our offering."

"I sat, I sipped the hot coffee and I even consumed one piece of pastry."

The two officers ignored me and began to tell each other jokes.

I heard the funny stories, but I wasn't in the mood to laugh. I just sat there, hanging my head and waited for the interrogation.

"Have you heard all the jokes we told each other?" I nodded my head.

"Did you like them?" I nodded again.

"Well how about this one? A gypsy decided to escape from Hungary. He got as far as the Austrian border, but before he was able to cross, he was captured and interrogated. 'Where were you heading, gypsy?' 'To the Soviet Union, comrade.' 'To the Soviet Union? Who are you trying to fool?' 'Nobody comrade, I assure you. If anybody was fooled it was me. I was told by many that the earth is round. I was told if I go west and keep on walking I will reach that paradise eventually." I listened to the joke I heard before. A joke punishable by imprisonment.

"Dear God. This is the joke I told only once, to my dear friend Pista." I thought and decided that my captor's telling of this particular joke could have been nothing, but a coincidence.

"So what do you think of this joke, prisoner?"

"I found it funny."

"You did. What a surprise. Maybe you were trying to reach the Soviet Union too?"

"I was on my way to Austria and the closer I got, the more my country pulled me back. I was born here comrades. This is my homeland. I made a mistake, but I corrected that mistake by bringing back my wife, my daughter and my brother."

"You mentioned your wife, let's talk about her and you. When did you get married and where?" Skinny asked.

"On January tenth, in nineteen fifty-three," I told them the truth.

"Where? I asked!" Skinny shouted.

"At City Hall in *Baja*."

"And where else?"

"I don't know what you mean."

"You are a lying bastard. Think again. Think hard. I will not tolerate anything but the truth," Chubby remained silent.

"They must know about our church wedding. But how could they know that?" I tried to think back to recall who knew about it. "Our witnesses would never breathe a word. My in-laws are out of the country. Who did I tell? Pista Janics knew. I told him beside our brook. If anyone betrayed us, it must be him. He has been a friend of mine ever since '52. Maybe I am mistaken? I must know. I must find out."

"I still don't know what you want me to say. You told me that joke, then you switched to our wedding. You totally confuse me."

"Well let's go back to the joke about the gypsy. Was this the first time you heard that joke?"

"I think so."

"You are lying again. You told that joke to many people. We know about that."

"But I never heard that joke before." I was lying. I knew then that I was betrayed. Pista Janics was their informer. Our failed attempt to escape from the country; the death of my Uncle at the border; the capture of all the others; our arrest; the prospect of never ever seeing Rozsa and Ildiko and other members of my family, were blows I somehow survived, but this last one, added to all the others, plunged me into hell. "I can never ever again trust anyone. I was betrayed by one whom I considered a trusted friend. Janics showed me the staff picture. He pointed out to me the known informers. From the first day on, after we met, he was nothing but a rotten informer," I thought bitterly and decided to level with my interrogators.

"I am sorry comrades, before I didn't remember. Yes, there was another time when my wife and I had a wedding, but I forgot all about it."

"Now we are getting somewhere. Tell us all about that."

"On April twenty second, at eleven o'clock, we went to the Roman Catholic Church in *Bacsbokod* and in total secrecy we had our church wedding."

"Who else was present? Who were your witnesses?"

"Just my wife and I and the priest. Nobody else," I lied after I recalled that I didn't tell Janics about our witnesses.

"That alone was a crime, deserving of punishment. Why did you ever do that? A teacher must set the right example for his students, but you chose to do otherwise."

"Had I done it openly, I would agree. No student was aware of what I did, thus I didn't set them a bad example. I had no desire to wed in a church, but my in-laws insisted. I just obeyed them."

"Very well. We will just include this in your confession. We will not make a great deal about it. Now about some of your other anti-State activities. Have you told to anyone anti-government jokes?" Skinny continued and Chubby remained an observer.

"Only to one person and even that I did rarely." My answer must have surprised the observer.

"Just let that go. We are not interested in his jokes, but his real crime is another matter," Chubby spoke up.

"I can see what just happened," I told myself and felt good about having outwitted my interrogators. "Skinny slipped up; allowed me to know that Janics was an informer. Had I told jokes to anyone else, he would have gotten away with his statement, but as soon as the other one heard what I said, he knew that the cat was out of the bag. My interrogator is no more skilled than the moron was," I told myself and my spirits rose.

"Now tell us about the escape attempt," Chubby took over.

"What do you want to know?"

"I want to know everything."

"Where should I begin? Maybe you could ask questions?"

"I will do that. Whatever you say will become part of your confession."

"That is fine with me."

"Did you know about your in-laws' escape attempt, before their leaving?"

"I knew about it, but they told nobody else. Not even their daughter."

"You did nothing to prevent their leaving. Am I correct?"

"I did nothing for a few days, but after, I began to feel bad so I went to the police and gave their picture to the Chief. I wanted them apprehended."

"Yes we know all about that charade. How long after their crossing the border did you start to organize your escape group?"

"They escaped in March. My wife was unjustly fired by her boss, Szantai. That must have been early in October. Shortly after that, I asked my in-laws to send a guide for us."

"How did you communicate with them?"

"They sent us messages through the Free Europe Radio and I wrote letters to them. I used a code."

"Tell us about the code you used."

Slowly, carefully, I described the book I used to craft the messages.

"Is this the book you spoke about?" Chubby removed the book from a drawer.

"That is the one...," I admitted.

"We found it during the search of your home. We almost missed it, but the holes were noticed and the book took on new significance. Show us exactly how it works."

I became the patient teacher and instructed them like they were my students.

"Are you willing to keep on using this code, if we tell you what message to send?"

"It depends on where I am."

"So you are trying to negotiate now?"

"From prison, I couldn't really help."

"Let's just go back one step Lichter." The use of my name surprised me. I was no longer called 'prisoner'. "Would you like to be free? Would you like to be allowed to return to your wife and child?"

"I would like nothing better."

"You committed many crimes, Lichter. How could we ever trust you?"

"A man always learns. I have learned many things, since my arrest."

"So tell us what have you learned."

"I learned that Communists, even members of the AVO, can be compassionate."

"Are you saying that you would be willing to cooperate with us?"

"That is what I said."

"What would your wife think?"

"I wouldn't tell her."

"That is a wise decision, Lichter."

***

Within minutes I was back in my cell. The rules remained the same. I was to get in bed and before I fell asleep, I thought about what sounded like an offer.

"Should I allow myself to hope that they will set me free? What is it they want? My in-laws back," I concluded. "Would they come back, if I was to write what my masters might request? Never. They would not fall for any trick. These AVO officers are just like the moron. Would they really release me? Would they buy my false promise of cooperation? If they do, what will I do? I will write what they tell me, but I will find a way to let my in-laws know that I was being coerced," I had decided and with my hope of seeing Rozsa again and my little daughter, I fell asleep.

Once more the guard woke me. Once more I was with my interrogators, but this time neither of them spoke about any release.

"Give us the name of your guide," Chubby ordered.

"I have never been told his name."

"You are lying."

"I met the man, but he did not introduce himself and I didn't ask him for his name. I didn't think it was important."

"Did he go to your home? Is that where you have met him?"

"No. It was at the railway station in *Budapest.*"

"Describe to us your meeting with him."

I told the two of them exactly how he came to us; how he looked at Ildiko's picture and how he spoke the right words.

"You slipped up Lichter. You are not as smart as you thought. Someone gave you the instructions and the right words, before you went to meet him."

"Stupid me...I was brought here, then back to my cell...I cannot even remember how many times. Back and forth...Sleep, followed by sudden waking...Total disorientation...Confusing questioning...They are not as stupid as I thought...They made me fall into their trap." I realized with great disappointment, but the hope of being allowed to return home I felt so keenly, that I cooperated.

"A woman came to our house. She gave us the instructions. She told us what the guide will do and what he will say."

"You must prove to us that we can trust you, otherwise you will never see your sweet wife," Chubby threatened me.

"How can I prove that?"

"By giving us her name."

"I am glad that our visitor refused to tell us who she was. Had she not done that I don't think I would have the courage to withhold her name. Thank God I have nothing to give away," I told myself and something else to the investigators.

"She refused to divulge her name."

"Don't give us that. We must have that information," Skinny shouted.

"They have the guide in custody, but he must have refused to talk. Otherwise they would not be pressing me," I thought and took courage from the guide's assumed silence.

"I would gladly give you her name, but I have never learned that."

"Where did she come from? Where does she live?"

"I don't know that either."

"Get him out of here," Skinny shouted and my guard returned me to the cell, where he made me stand for what seemed to be many hours.

"They must have changed their minds. They will never release me." I was convinced, once more, that I will never see those dear people whom I loved and my pain intensified. My suffering was endless.

***

"Do you know what day this is?" Chubby asked, when I was taken back to the room of my interrogators.

"I lost track of time..."

"Do you know the date of your arrest?"

"Yes...I was arrested Saturday morning, around two o'clock."

"How long do you think you have been here?"

"I do not know. I was taken back and forth between my cell and this office. I alternated between sleep and the guard waking me. I have no watch...No way to tell the time. Maybe two days? Maybe three?"

"It is April fourth...A day of great significance. When you are taken back to the cell think about it. Your confusion we understand, but your lack of cooperation is not appreciated. Well maybe a few weeks from now, or maybe a few months from now you will come to your senses."

"I told you everything I know." My agony showed, but no pity was extended.

"You told us what we already knew, but you refused to give the name of that woman," Chubby complained.

"How could I tell you what I don't know?"

"Give us her description," Chubby demanded.

"I am not very good in describing anyone. My memory for faces is almost non-existent."

"Give it a try."

I began to give a vague description of the female visitor. My description could have fit several thousand females, thus I put her in no danger. Yet my description was close enough to what Rozsa reluctantly might give them.

"Well if you lied, we will know," Chubby told me.

"I didn't lie, but my lack of memory for faces may have misled me," I told the investigators.

"Back to your cell..." The order came from Skinny and this time another finger snapping guard led me to my cell.

***

"April fourth...So it is Monday. I had been here only for three days, yet it seems like an eternity. This is a Communist holiday, ever since they took power. The day of Hungary's Liberation. After the holiday became established, enemies like me, used to refer to it as the day when the last of our cattle was driven across the border into the Soviet

Union; the day of our last factory being demolished and shipped to the east; the last day of our hope of being free." I thought about that special day, just as my investigators told me.

"Have they called my attention to this special day to raise my hopes, or did they do that to fool me?" I asked myself and hoped with all my heart that on this day I will be liberated.

"Get ready. Bring all your possessions," the guard ordered.

"What possessions? They took everything."

"So they did. Well never mind, just get dressed and say good-by to your cell."

"Am I being released?"

"You must be stupid. Your release is out of the question. You will be further interrogated," the guard announced and I found it unusual to have one in his position know anything.

"Did they tell him to frighten me; to mislead me?" I asked myself and followed the guard. He kept snapping his fingers and then I heard another guard snapping. The distant snapping stopped and we continued. As I walked by the prisoner facing the wall, I recognized Joe and I almost made the mistake of saying something.

"Poor Joe," I thought. "He refused to join us. He wanted to stay in this rotten country. He wanted to enjoy life with his fiancé, yet here he is. I will do everything to gain his release. I must not forget my brother either."

"Sit down Laszlo. Your confession is ready. All you have to do is sign and then we will talk about your future." Skinny called me by my first name and gave me the document to read.

It detailed accurately many of my activities. I confessed first of all to organizing an escape attempt. I confessed also to getting married in a church; telling anti-government jokes; spreading anti State propaganda; spying for the Americans and having misled the authorities about my in-laws disappearance.

I finished reading the document that could condemn me to a life in prison and shook my head sadly.

"Is something wrong Laszlo?" Skinny asked and offered me coffee and pastries. In spite of being hungry and thirsty, I refused both, their offer and the signing of the document.

"That is too bad. We have been authorized to release you," Chubby told me.

"Release me after what this paper says I did?" I couldn't believe my ears; I was certain that they tried to raise my hope just to dash it, to devastate me.

"You doubt our word? How can we ever trust you?" It was Skinny's turn to dangle the bait.

"Some of the things in this confession are true, but other things I never did."

"Give us one example of what is false and we may change it," Skinny offered.

"I didn't spy." I picked on the most serious crime.

"You confessed using a code. We have your code book. You described how to use it. Only a spy needs such tools. Don't you agree with me?"

"I sent my in-laws no confidential information. I sent them only personal messages."

"Does it really matter Laszlo, if we set you free?"

"It may not matter today or tomorrow, but you could arrest me any day after and I could be sent to prison for an eternity."

"You are right my friend, yet you are wrong. We have you in prison now. We can keep you here as long as we like. We may even torture you. Force you to sign this confession. What would happen then? Are we not offering you your freedom?" Chubby dangled the bait and I nibbled at it.

"What more can I lose by signing it?" I asked myself and saw my dear wife's face and that of my daughter. "I could see them again...Maybe only for a short time, but is that not better than what I am facing now? Maybe they will let me be free, long enough, to escape across the border? Then we would be truly free."

"What are you contemplating Laszlo?" Skinny asked.

"I was only thinking about my brother and my innocent brother-in-law. What will you do with them?"

"They are small fish. Not even good for bait. They would be released too. We don't even need their confession," Chubby told me and that settled the issue.

"Let me sign my death warrant," I announced and affixed my signature.

"You like to dramatize things Laszlo. Your death warrant it is not. As long as you don't step out of line; as long as you don't try to commit another illegal act," Skinny announced.

"When can the three of us head home?"

"Your co-conspirators are ready. They are waiting in another room. Just a couple of more things and you will be on your way," Skinny pushed front of me a blank paper.

"So here comes the catch," I thought bitterly and felt great regret over having signed my confession.

"What else do you want me to do?"

"We just want you to sign this Laszlo," Chubby pointed at the paper.

"Sign what? There is nothing here."

"We didn't want to delay you any further, but if you are not willing to sing, so be it." Skinny stood up and called in the guard.

"Can I say something?"

"We are getting tired of all this nonsense," Skinny said, but waived the guard out. "Say what you want, let's be done with it. If I call the guard in once more, you are finished. You will never see your charming wife. You will never see your sweet little daughter."

"Would either of you be willing to sign a blank paper? That is what I wanted to ask."

"Sure we would sign a receipt for travel money," Chubby chuckled.

"But it doesn't say that."

"Very well. We will prepare it properly, but once we do that, you must sign it."

"I'd be glad to do that," I announced and watched as Skinny began to scribble on the paper. When he finished it, he handed it to me.

I read his short statement and realized that I almost lost our freedom over nothing. Yet the text bothered me.

"I the undersigned, have accepted three hundred Hungarian Forints on April 4, 1955 for services rendered."

"What services have I rendered?" I asked them.

"We are not allowed to give civilians travel money. So we had to word it that way Laszlo. If it is not to your liking, if you refuse to sign it, then just forget our offer." Skinny's threat was clear and I was too tired to object to anything.

"I will sign it," I told them and reached for the pen.

"Here is your travel money." Chubby counted out fifteen twenty *Forint* bills and shook my hand. "I hope there is no hard feeling. We did our job and you are free."

His words echoed in my mind and I couldn't believe my good luck; I still couldn't trust them.

"Oh, yes, there is one more thing."

"Oh God...Here comes the catch...," I told myself and was ready to give up all hope.

"You cannot say anything to your wife. You cannot say anything to anyone about your confession. You must not say anything to anyone about the interrogation. If you do, we will know and I am sure you know what will happen," Skinny spoke the last words and my relief was so great that I almost burst out crying.

The prison's door slammed shot behind me and I stood in the wonderful sun-light. I looked around for George and Joe, but I was alone.

"Did they lie to me? Did they mislead me? If they did I will make the bastards pay." I issued the threat, under my breath and I knew I was being foolish. I asked a passer-by how to get to the railway station and within ten minutes I stood in the waiting room.

Hands touched my shoulders and before I turned around, my fear took hold of me and I imagined being tricked, re-arrested, taken back to prison, condemned to a life sentence. I felt my face turn pasty white. I felt my limbs shake with fear and disappointment. I had to slow my heart beat, lest I have a heart attack. Then two voices penetrated my fog-filled mind.

"Laszlo!" Joe whispered.

"Laszlo you are free!" George stated, no more loudly.

We fell into each other's arms. We kissed each other's cheeks, on both sides. We soaked up each other's sight and then we came to our senses. I led them to the window to buy our tickets.

"Do you have any money Laszlo?" George asked and Joe looked at me eagerly.

"I had three hundred *Forints*, when I was arrested. They gave it all back," I lied to them.

We boarded the train and the two of them spoke excitedly, but I wasn't in the mood for conversation. I knew that somehow my life had changed and that the AVO will not leave me alone, they will demand payment. My anticipation to see my beloved wife and daughter made me extremely happy, yet I felt the gathering of storm clouds. The loss of my Uncle Jozsef made me feel a deep sadness and the loss of my friend, Pista Janics, caused me deep disappointment and made me terribly angry.

"Why do you think they have released us?" Joe asked me, but I was still thinking about other things.

"I asked you a question Laszlo," Joe persisted.

"How would Laszlo know? How would anybody know?" George saved me. "When they came for me, Dad was home and he put up a great fuss. He screamed at the AVO. He told them that he has influential friends. Maybe Dad was able to pull a few strings?"

"That may be..," Joe gave in and for the rest of the journey we traveled in silence.

***

I knocked on our gate and when it was finally unlocked, when I finally saw my beloved Rozsa, we kissed, we hugged, we ran into the flat and I lifted up my little daughter.

"Dad is home!" Rozsa told her and my little daughter tried to say something.

"Dada...," she seemed to say and all my pain, all my suffering, all my fears I was able to shove in the background. For the time being I was free and immensely happy.

"How long were you guarded my darling?" I asked Rozsa.

"They left me the day after you were arrested."

"How can that be?" I asked her.

"I don't understand it either, but does it really matter? You are home Laszlo! We are free."

***

On April fifth, I returned to *Bacsbokod*, to my school, to my students, but it was no longer the same. Pista Janics, my friend, my mentor, had betrayed me.

After classes ended, Janics crossed his fingers, as he left the school and I picked up his signal; followed him to the brook, where I used to confide in him.

"How are you Laszlo? I was worried about you," Janics announced and I marveled at his audacity.

"He must have been told about me. He must know something and I must play him like he had played me. I will tell him things, just to make him believe that I am the same Laszlo," I told myself and turned to him.

"Why would you ever worry about me?"

"I don't really know. I had a strange feeling."

"Maybe you ate the wrong food? Maybe you drank too much during the school break? Maybe you whored around too much?" My remarks oozed with sarcasm.

"Or maybe I missed my friend. I haven't seen you for nine days."

"I was with my beloved Rozsa and my dear daughter, Ildiko."

"I know, but I missed you just the same."

"I missed you too Pista, believe me, but who wouldn't miss a true friend? That is what you are. Aren't you Pista?"

"True friends always stick together and tell each other everything."

"Sure thing Janics," I told myself. "The AVO already briefed you. I don't know how much they told you, but I am sure that you were told to keep an eye on me. You are no friend of mine. I will play your game. I will pretend to be your friend, but I will never forgive you." To Janics I said something else.

"What would you like me to tell you?"

"Are you happy Laszlo?"

"I have never been happier. This last week made me see things very clearly," I told Janics and to myself, 'Tell them that, you rotten bastard."

***

A week later, I caught the afternoon train and as I walked across the park, front of *Baja*'s railway station, I saw a man sitting on a bench, with his newspaper unfolded.

"Sit down beside me Comrade Lichter," he spoke quietly, as I was about to walk by and I dared not ask for his identification. I sat down, checked my fear.

"Do you know who I am?" He looked like a weasel. His beady eyes squinted; his sharp nose sniffed the air; his pointed forehead perspired.

"I most certainly don't," I gave my reply.

"From this day on, I am your controller," he announced and his sly smile sickened me.

"My controller? What do you mean?"

"You volunteered to be an informer. Isn't that true Comrade Lichter?"

"I did no such thing."

"Well, I have a copy of a paper you signed. Do you want me to show you?"

"You better do..," my fear gripped me.

"Read it comrade." He handed over the short document and I paled as I read it.

"I the undersigned, have accepted three hundred Hungarian Forints on April 4, 1955 for services rendered." My signature under that one sentence took on a new meaning.

"But it was travel money they gave me," I told the weasel.

"Do you think anybody would believe that? We could accidentally leak this document, but first we would put on it the AVH's stamp. Who would believe anything other than the truth? You are working for us, Lichter."

"I am not that..," I told him.

"Well that remains to be seen. Here is what we want: In your next letter, use the code and this is what you are to write to your in-laws. 'I was arrested. So was Joe, but we have been released.' Can you remember that?"

"I no longer have the code book. I am not able to do that."

"You are wrong comrade. Do you think we are idiots? The code book was returned to your wife today, with a few other items."

"I see."

"Don't disobey us or you will lose your freedom. Am I making myself clear?"

"I will do as you ordered." I gave in; after all there was nothing in that message that would harm anyone.

"There is one more thing. Your Father-in-law had a friend. He was to inform on him, but he escaped this country. You will take over. You will visit him; gain his confidence and after a while you will be given further instructions. We are sure you know who that man is." He stood up and left me.

I was stunned by my new status.

"Can I live with being an informer?" I asked myself and began to think about others, who had faced the same predicament.

"My poor Father-in-law had little choice. The AVO used Joe's misdeed to force him to become an informer. He was to inform on Peter Balazs, but he never harmed that man. He dragged things out as long as he could, then he took the only way out, he escaped from Hungary. Maybe now that I was forced to take over, I will have to follow the course set by him, in spite of grave dangers.

"Then there was my dear friend in the army. Laci was forced to become an informer. He was decent, he came to me, he told me everything and we found a way to fool the bastards. Maybe I could do what he did?

"And my former friend, Pista Janics. Was I just condemning him? What hold did they have on Janics? They must have forced him, much like they forced me.

"How many other poor Hungarians did the AVO press into their service? A quarter of the population? Maybe half? Or maybe even more? If that is the case, informers are informing on each other. Well the hell with it...My family's survival is the only thing that really matters. I will do as they ask, but I will drag things out, like Rozsa's Father did. I will never hurt anyone. In the meantime I will find a way to get my family out of this disgusting country."

I walked home, my mind in disorder, but when I saw my little daughter's smile, when I tasted Rozsa's sweet lips, I was whole again and life went on, almost like before.

In the coming weeks and months I had to do a lot of pretending.

***

I wrote the first coded message, I was ordered to write and I looked up Peter Balazs.

"I am so glad to see you Laszlo," Peter greeted me with genuine pleasure. "I heard a great deal about you from Rozsa's Father."

"Hope you heard nothing bad?"

"No, he never spoke a bad word about you. He always praised you for your hard work. He spoke about your decency, your studious nature and how much it pained him that he had to leave you behind too, like he had to leave Rozsa, Joe and Ildiko, amongst other people. They did the right thing to escape this country," Peter spoke.

"I only wish you went with them," I stated.

"Your father-in-law talked me into doing just that. He told me how the AVO forced him to inform on me. I was on the way to escape, but I had to turn around."

"Why?"

"I was followed by an AVO agent, when I got on the bus. In *Budapest* I tried to lose him, but that didn't work. I didn't want to endanger the others, so I caught the next bus back to *Baja* and here I am, stuck in this country."

"And so are we," I told my Father-in-law's friend, for whom I felt great affinity.

"Maybe someday you will make an attempt to get out of here." He told me innocently and I couldn't help but tell him how we tried; how we turned around; how my dear Uncle died; the fate of the other escapees; how we were arrested; how I was tricked into becoming an informer.

"You too Laszlo? Half the people I know are in the same boat. You may not believe, but there are three people who came to me and told me that they are being forced to inform on me. Well one more, namely you Laszlo, really doesn't matter. In fact I am getting pleasure out of being this important."

"But how can I write reports to the AVO? How can I survive as an informer? How can I look my wife in the eyes? How can I bring up my child with this knowledge?" I allowed my self-pity to show.

"How can any Hungarian survive in this country? Have you ever asked yourself that question Laszlo?"

"I did many times."

"And have you ever found an answer?"

"I may have, but that answer is little consolation now."

"Tell me Laszlo. What answer have you discovered?"

"The answer lies in fooling them," I told Peter and I brightened.

"So have you ever been able to fool them?"

"Yes, I have." I told Peter and without waiting for his next question, I spoke about Laci and the reports I dictated to that army friend.

"So, in a peculiar way, you have been an informer before?"

"But I was only informing on myself."

"Well I have a piece of advice for you Laszlo. Do you want to hear it?"

"Please tell me. I need advice badly."

"Very well...The reports you dictated to your friend were always designed not to harm you, but to give you an advantage. Am I correct?"

"What you say Peter was true."

"Then here is my advice Laszlo. Whenever you are made to report on someone, put yourself in the place of that person and never write anything you would not be willing to write about yourself. That way your conscience will be clear and you will even experience the joy of fooling the authorities." Peter finished giving his advice and from that day on I did exactly as he suggested.

***

Chapter 19

Summer came early in '55, but my inner cold never thawed out. I remained cold from the botched escape attempt, from the hopelessness of our lives and from what I became. Yet somehow we have survived the next few months. My teaching I have never neglected; my volunteer work has never suffered and whenever I had the opportunity to inquire about the house that was promised to me, I have received the same answer.

"Your petition is under review," the Chairman told me. "Soon, I think, they will make a decision. Have patience, Laszlo."

I was never short on patience, but my controller lacked that quality. He found me, at least once every week, in the most unexpected places. A few times he sat down beside me on the train; a few other times he intercepted me, while I was walking and when he grew tired of hunting me down, he gave me his order.

"I am getting tired to chase you around and I am tired of waiting for information on Peter Balazs," he told me in June.

"Balazs is not an easy man to befriend. His best friend was my Father-in-law, yet even he could not gain his confidence. How do you expect me to succeed, where my Father-in-law failed?"

"Don't make me laugh Comrade Lichter. Your Father-in-law had no intention to betray his friend. He held out on us, but you will make up for that. Don't think for a single moment that we are fools. We will not tolerate delays. We will not accept failure. Balazs will rot in prison for all his crimes and if you do not do your duty, there are others we can tap."

"But I am really trying comrade..."

"Try harder. Starting next week you will come to me. There is a small pond, in the woods, not far from your home, by the main entrance to the School of Gardeners. Do you know the place I mean?"

"I do."

"Wednesday evenings, at eight o'clock, unless I tell you otherwise, you will wait for me by the pond. If I don't show after an hour, you will go home and return the next day. Your report better be good, for if you fail you will suffer the consequences."

"I don't really think I can make it."

"I will not accept any excuses."

"It is not an excuse comrade. In order to keep the times you gave me I have to get on the one o'clock train. My principal makes that difficult; I can rarely get away that early."

"That will change. Just leave it to me," my controller announced and I don't know how he did it, but Pallosy told me a few days later, that he is releasing me early, on Wednesday and Thursday of every week.

"Pallosy gave no sign of knowing what I became," I told myself. "He is a devoted Communist, who rarely asks questions, when he is ordered to do something. He may have been told by his superiors that he must allow my early leaving and he obeyed."

Next Wednesday, at the designated time, I went to the small pond and sat down on its grassy slope. I envied the frogs that sang freely. Around me the reeds swung in the gentle evening breeze and memories of my early childhood came to me.

"How nice it was when I was a young child. My friends and I used to go to ponds like this. Our fishing poles made out of reeds and a small container of worms were all we needed to catch dozens of perch and sundry other fish. How sweet and simple my life was then. Back in the prewar years, I was an innocent child, but time has a way of changing everything. My innocence had been destroyed and the same thing happened to my country. The good Lord created good and evil. He had given us free will. There was a time when I firmly believed that good always triumphs over evil, but that is not the way. I have known many good men. My Father is one of them, but he was made to suffer and slowly he lost his hope, his enthusiasm for a better future; he lost almost everything. Then there is Mr. Buja. His devotion to God and country was a shining example of the goodness of men, but he had to escape from his homeland to guard his honor, to retain his decency. The best of them was my Uncle Jozsef. He lived a simple life. He survived Siberia. He worked all his life and never hurt anyone, but where is he now? Somewhere in an unmarked grave? He was unable to cross the border of hope. He fell on a mine, made by Hungarian hands, and died on this side of the fence of despair.

"Then there are men like Pallosy. God gave him the power to be good or evil and in everything he did he chose the latter. His own sisters, he condemned to hard labor. He denied his God, his Maker. He hounded all who practiced their religion. He mistreated all his teachers. He was supposed to be a leader of knowledgeable men and instead he chose to be their tormentor. God curse Pallosy; Rozsa's boss, Szantai and all members of the AVO..." My deep, bitter thoughts were interrupted by approaching footsteps.

"I see you have found the place." My controller sat down beside me.

"I did."

"Have you also found something on Peter Balazs?"

"Nothing much, I am afraid to admit."

"But that cannot be. That man is a traitor; I have been informed by others."

"If that is so why do you need me?"

"We live in a just society. We do not condemn men on the say so of a couple of people. We need more collaborating evidence. It would have been nice to add your denunciation to all the others."

"What can I tell you that you don't already know?"

"You could report that he told you anti-Government jokes."

"He never did."

"You could tell us that he is planning to overthrow the Government."

"A hundred thousand men couldn't do that. Our Government is strong and popular and beloved." I contrived to say what was untrue.

"Yes...We are strong, popular and beloved."

"Those are the exact words Balazs used, in our last conversation. It is included in my report."

"I can imagine. Others told me otherwise. You are lying Lichter."

"Why would I ever lie to you? My child, my wife and I are in grave danger. Do you think I would risk losing our freedom?"

"You better not...I will give you another assignment. Do you think you would like that?"

"I do what you tell me to do. I am willing to do anything," I lied and almost choked on my statement.

"Fine...You will stay away from Balazs. Do you know Istvan Lorant?"

"He was our best man at our wedding."

"Have you seen him lately?"

"I am afraid not. For a little while after our wedding, my wife and I went to see him, but after I had to join the army and we lost contact."

"Well...that is not exactly true. Didn't he give you and your wife a present, after the birth of your little daughter?"

"He made my little girl a baby carriage, but it wasn't a gift, we paid for it."

"It wouldn't hurt to go and see him. Find out what is he up to. Are you prepared to do that?"

"I will do it, if that is your wish."

"Very well. For a month I don't need to see you, but five weeks from today you come back here. By that time you should be able to write down all you have found out about Lorant. I will leave you now. You stay here for ten minutes and after that you may leave."

I was greatly relieved that I didn't need to spy on Balazs, yet I was concerned about my new assignment.

"Starting out with Istvan will give me a new opportunity for further delays." I thought and consoled myself with the fact that I gave my controller no derogatory information on his first target.

***

Within two weeks, I looked up Istvan Lorant and we chatted for an hour like two old friends. I found out that his business was flourishing; that he married his former housekeeper and I told him about my stint in the army; my job as a teacher and we spoke at length about my beloved Rozsa and our little Ildiko.

Before we parted he invited the three of us to pay him and his wife a visit, which we never did. I didn't want to involve Rozsa in the things I was forced to do. I wanted to spare her from being asked about Istvan Lorant.

I alternated between the happiness of being with my family and the despair of what might happen, once they find out that I am not cooperating.

The month, following my last trip to the pond, was filled with work; with the constant struggle of obtaining enough food for the three of us and with the need to prepare for the coming winter.

By the summer of '55 the food shortage was rampant and abuse by the authorities reached new heights.

To get a loaf of bread, Rozsa was to stand in line for many hours. To get a half a kilogram of meat took many trips to the butcher and maybe once a month Rozsa succeeded to get that precious commodity. On Wednesdays and Saturdays, she went to the market, clutching her almost empty purse, and when she was able to buy some potatoes, flour and beans, she beamed with pleasure, as she told me about her achievements.

"I bargained with the farmers until I got the price of their goods down sufficiently. I am sure I have enough staples for a whole week and you will never guess what else I got Laszlo."

"With the small amount of money I give you each month, I am surprised that we are not starving. No I cannot guess what else you got."

"I went to the butcher and I stood in line for two solid hours. Pregnant women were allowed to enter the store without waiting and two women got quite a beating from the enraged crowd." Rozsa began to tell her story. "You see Laszlo those two poor women weren't really pregnant. They just pretended, but somebody found out and they were made to suffer for their small conniving. By the time I got close to the door, the butcher came out and announced that they had no more meat. So after that I went to the market. You know what I saw in one of the store windows?"

"I don't my love." I was beginning to get tired of waiting to hear what Rozsa got, but I sensed that her way of telling had its importance.

"I saw a terrible sign and bags of sugar, cans of lard and big chunks of butter."

"What did the sign say Rozsa?"

"It gave the name of the man who got six years in prison for hoarding all that food. The sign blamed the hoarders and black marketers for the food shortages. I couldn't believe my eyes, seeing all those rare goods. Then I saw two other store windows, with the same displays, with the same signs, just the names different. That was when I have decided to spend less money on beans, potatoes and flour and buy something with what I saved that would allow us to eat meat every Sunday. But we will have to wait for that quite a long time."

"I understand what you said my darling, but you still haven't told me what you bought."

"I purchased a dozen chicks...I put them in the storage room for the night. During the day I will let them out in the yard. Once they grow up, I will prepare your favorite dish Laszlo. Chicken soup and fried chicken will be on the menu my beloved."

"What a magnificent woman you are Rozsa." I praised her; kissed her; held her and we talked on.

"Do you think those people really hoard food? Do you think they cause the shortages?" Rozsa asked me.

"That is only propaganda Rozsa," I told her and shared with her some of the atrocities the authorities committed.

"I am made to volunteer my time to the local Government and while I go from house to house I hear many things. Farmers, who own a small piece of farmland are made to give half of their crop to the Government and the other half they must sell to them. The amount of their crop is pre-calculated. When their crops fail their obligation remains the same. To feed their own families they hide what little crop they have. But even that small amount of food is uncovered and confiscated. The farmers who dare to do this are arrested and sent to prison. Those posters give the names of innocent men. I also hear that many times they even lose the roof over their heads.

"A recent case I heard about was even worse. A high Communist party official took fancy to the home of a farmer. When the whole family went to cultivate their field, two civilians broke into the house, but they took nothing, instead they hid in the loft a few bags of potatoes, onions and other stuff. The family knew nothing about that. In the dark of night their house was searched and the goods were found. The man was sent to prison; the rest of the family were thrown out of the house and it became the home of the Communist official." Rozsa was about to say something, but I was wound up.

"In another case the Communists became even bolder. A family went to work and when they arrived home, they found their furniture on the street. When the head of the family tried to complain, he was told that he broke the law. He was shown food he never hid. Food that supposedly was found in his house and for that they lost everything. Their possessions were ruined by a rain storm; their home was confiscated; they became homeless," I told Rozsa.

"In spite of our problems, we have a lot to be thankful for. We are not farmers. We are not homeless. Although we have little to eat, we are not starving and when those chicks get big enough we will have many feasts my darling." Rozsa counted our blessings and I turned the conversation to the coming winter.

"When winter comes we will have wood too."

"What do you mean Laszlo? Where will you get wood?"

"I know that last winter we had nothing other than bundles of corn stalks and even that I had to beg for, but this winter we will be warm. I found a way to get wood my darling. When school closes, three teachers and I will go to *Rezert*. I got permission to cut wood all summer. Half of what we cut will belong to the Government, but the other half we will be allowed to buy my darling."

"Isn't *Rezert* a few kilometers north?"

"It is six kilometers from *Baja*. Your Father used to fish there, Rozsa."

"But how will you bring the wood home?"

"For four weeks we will cut and pile and after that we will build a raft to float the wood down the *Danube*. By the middle of August we will have lots of wood, my beloved."

"That is too good to believe. Grown chickens to eat and plenty of wood to warm our house, will make us feel like prince and princess."

***

At the end of June we closed our school and during the last staff meeting, we received our summer schedule from Pallosy.

"One quarter of the staff will provide our students with summer activities, during the first two weeks of July. Then another quarter will take over. By the last two weeks of August all of you have served for two weeks. You may work out the details. It doesn't matter to me what arrangements you make, as long as it is done fairly." Pallosy left us and we put our heads together, until the schedule was worked out to everybody's satisfaction. When the other staff members left, the four of us smiled at each other.

"We got our way. We will serve during the last two weeks of August," we told each other and made our plans.

***

Two days later, at six o'clock in the morning, we met where my Father's small boat was moored and when the four of us were seated in the *csikly*, we found that we were badly overloaded.

"Do you think it is safe with all of us in this boat Laszlo?" Jancsi asked me.

"Is there any other alternative? If we make no sudden moves; if two of you sit down on its floor and if only two of us paddle, I assure you that we will get there."

Within an hour we went far enough north to begin to cross the wide, majestic river. Within another twenty minutes we turned into the old branch of the *Danube*, that was called *Rezert* and shortly after we have reached our destination.

The forest ranger was already there and gave his orders.

"This is the section you are allowed to cut. All wood must be cut exactly two point four meters long. You are to pile the logs one point two meters wide and to the same height. When you have a cord of wood piled in that manner, you are to begin a new one. You have permission to cut all through July and you must get your half out of here after you paid me, but no later than the end of August. After that the woods will be out of bounds." Once he gave his orders, he went to see another group.

The four of us sharpened our axes and began to chop the trees like four hungry wolves. We fell the trees at a good rate, but by the afternoon we became tired.

"I cannot lift my ax anymore," I announced to my friends and I thought I will die from exhaustion.

"Nor can we..," said the others.

"Maybe we should cut up what we have and pile it," Jancsi suggested and all of us welcomed the change; picked up the two cross saws and began to cut them to the required length.

By five o'clock we could barely feel our muscles and when we sat in the *csikly*, to begin our journey home, we were grateful to our beloved river, whose swift current took us back to *Baja*.

"That was some workout," I told the others.

"Tomorrow it will be easier," Jancsi informed us. "We are not used to such physical work. That is why all of us are exhausted."

That week we had made six return trips and although we did not find the work any easier, our efforts began to pay off. By the end of the week we had fourteen piles of wood and I began to calculate aloud.

"If we keep this tempo up for four weeks, we will have cut fifty six cords of wood. Half of it we will be allowed to buy. Once we divide it four ways we will have seven cords each. Maybe we could slow down a bit? Five cords of wood would do me nicely."

"We will not slow down Laszlo. If we can cut seven cords, we will do that. Who knows if they will allow us to do this next year?" Three of us nodded our heads and worked like devils all through the following week.

It was usually around seven that I got home. That gave me no time to make my Wednesday meeting. I had to try to change the arrangement.

"Would it not be good to knock off early each Wednesday and Saturday?"

"I guess it wouldn't hurt. We have made a great deal of progress and all of us are bone tired," Jancsi stated. My co-workers, my friends didn't suspect that they were being manipulated, thus they readily gave their agreements.

***

"How are you getting along with Lorant?" My controller asked me and I wished he had given his name, so that I could call him something other than comrade.

"We are getting along fine. A few more months I think and he will be willing to open up. He talks about his wife quite openly. He told me about her...Well that is not important. It is all in my report, there is no need to repeat things, comrade."

"You are reluctant to call me comrade, even after a dozen meetings. Aren't you Lichter?"

"I will admit that I find it awkward. I would rather use your name."

"We don't give out our names. That information is confidential. But if you like you could call me 'friend'. What would you think of that?"

"I got myself trapped. Curse my stupidity. I have no desire to call him 'friend'. That he will never be," I thought and hesitated.

"I see that 'friend' is not to your liking. Would you rather call me 'foe'?" my controller played with me.

"I have no difficulty to call you my friend. You misunderstood my hesitation. I am just not thinking clearly."

"And why is that? I hope it is not something that Lorant told you?"

"No...Not at all. It is just that I am terribly tired."

"Tired of us or something else?"

I saw no harm in telling my 'friend' about the long days of wood cutting; about the boat trips on the treacherous river and my difficulty of meeting him, especially on Thursdays.

"I see. Well to show you that I am really a friend we will change the arrangement. If I don't make it on Wednesday night, you are to come here on Saturday. Would that be more suitable to you Laszlo?"

I thanked my *friend*, this time sincerely and fifteen minutes later, I entered our home.

***

I found Joe home, which was unusual. He rarely came home until we were asleep and I rarely saw him, except on Sundays.

"Where were you Laszlo?" he asked me, as I ate my late supper, a plate of bean soup with a piece of bread.

"I had work to do." He never suspected what I was made to do.

"Work...I think you are about to give me another lecture, but you need not bother. Tomorrow morning I am leaving the three of you. I am getting out of this cursed city."

I was greatly surprised. I put my spoon down and turned to my brother-in-law.

"You are leaving? But why?"

"I broke up with my fiancé. The bitch found someone else. I am heading to Budapest. I think I will live with Aunt Lujza."

"Have you asked her if she is willing to keep you?" I asked Joe.

"Why wouldn't she?"

I just shook my head and wondered.

"Joe has lived with us for a long time. He had an occasional job, but after a few days he grew too tired to work. His nature has never changed and now he wants to impose on someone else. Well that is fine. That will suit me. It will be easier to provide for the three of us," I thought and didn't argue.

"You will write to us sometime, I hope?" Rozsa asked her brother.

"You will get a letter, I assure you. Now I better go to bed." He rose and without another word he retired.

The following morning I was up and out of the house, too early to say good-by to Joe and by the time I got home we were alone.

For over a week life became sweeter. I didn't have Joe to scold for his unwillingness to help support the family. Not even his letter was able to ruin the new found tranquility of our household.

Rozsa handed the brief letter to me, with tears in her eyes and I was astonished.

"To Rozsa and Laszlo,

"I got to Budapest and I am living with Lujza. She is kind, considerate and she doesn't nag me, like you did Laszlo.

"I kept my promise to write to you Rozsa, as I always keep my promises.

"Accept my thanks for all the bean soups. If I am not mistaken, I consumed a hundred sixty plates of that stuff.

"Keep enjoying the life you live, I will enjoy my new found freedom.

"Tell Ildiko that her Uncle sends his love.

"Joe."

"I am glad Joe wrote to us my beloved. At least we know where he is and what he thinks of us. Wipe away your tears my darling. We got what we deserved. Now we must look after each other," I told Rozsa and after a while she gave me a big smile and we were happy with each other.

By the end of July, our happiness was shattered.

I came home on the last Thursday of our wood cutting adventure and Rozsa handed to me the unopened letter.

"It came in the mail today, Laszlo."

"It looks like it came from *Bacsbokod*," I told her and hesitated.

"Open it love," Rozsa urged me.

"I will in a minute. Just let me catch my breath. I am so tired, but we have almost all our wood cut. Next week we will build the raft and I guess in two weeks I will be able to show you the result of our effort."

"I get your supper Laszlo. In the meantime read your letter."

I opened it, like it was my death warrant and when I read it, I cursed loudly.

"Pallosy is a f...ing bastard."

Rozsa almost dropped my plate.

"What is wrong Laszlo?"

"Listen to this my beloved? Can you ever believe this?"

"What am I to believe? You told me not a thing."

"I am so sorry Rozsa. I am upset. I will read it."

Rozsa picked up Ildiko and with her on her lap she listened intently.

"Comrade Lichter,

"My plans have changed. You are to report to me on August first, next Monday. You will be supervising students during all of August.

"Your disobedience will not be tolerated.

"Principal Pallosy."

"Can you believe Rozsa what Pallosy is doing?" I cried out.

"I know that this may ruin your plan, but maybe there is a misunderstanding?" Rozsa tried to calm me.

"There was no misunderstanding when Szantai threw you out. That rotten Communist bastard is a twin brother of Pallosy, at least in spirit. He must have found out that we are cutting wood. He must know that we will lose it all. That is why he is doing this to us," I told Rozsa.

"Maybe your three friends will be able to bring the wood home? Maybe they will help us out?" Rozsa raised the possibility and my spirits rose.

"I know they will. They are decent guys. I will talk to them tomorrow."

***

I could hardly wait to get to the boat, to ask my friends the big favor. The three of them were already by my Father's boat and they seemed to be greatly agitated.

"Curse Pallosy!" shouted Jancsi, when I was a few meters away.

"F... that bastard," shouted the two others and my hopes were dashed. Each of them had a letter in their hands.

"What is going on?" I asked them.

"I am sure you know. Didn't Pallosy write you too?" Jancsi asked me.

"He did...But I thought I was the only one he hated."

"It seems you were wrong Laszlo. All of us have been ordered to report to him on Monday."

"What are we going to do?" I moaned in misery.

"We will go up to *Rezert* and speak to the forest ranger. Maybe he will give us permission to take the wood home on Sundays?" We followed Jancsi's suggestion and two hours later we had our answer.

"We have been ordered to go back to school for all of August. We will be unable to take all our wood out before September," Jancsi told the man of authority.

"You will be unable to take any of the wood, unless you pay me. You each have six cords of wood, if I am not mistaken?"

"That is what we have and soon we will be ready to pay you."

"I am glad to hear. Each cord will cost you a hundred twenty Forints."

We stood there with our mouths open.

"We were told the price is seventy Forints per cord," I shouted at the official.

"That was the price in June, but since then it was raised."

"But we had an agreement," I tried to argue.

"Do you have that in writing?"

"We were never given a written contract," I admitted and hung my head.

"You will have to pay the new price and you will have to do that before Sunday."

Not one of us saw a way out, so we have promised to do what he requested.

***

That night I visited my parents and borrowed the missing sum from my Father. The next day we paddled to *Rezert*.

"Here is the money for twenty four cords." I counted out the princely sum of two thousand eight hundred eighty *Forints* and asked the man for a receipt, which he made out promptly.

"We will be hauling our wood out on Sundays," I informed the ranger.

"Sunday the woods are closed. I be damned if I will work on Sundays," the ranger retorted.

"But we have no choice...," Jancsi took over. "If you don't allow us to work on Sunday, the wood will never be taken."

"You are totally wrong. The wood will be out of here by October, even if you do not take it."

"But we have paid for it. You are putting us in an impossible situation. We are free only on Sundays. Who else could take it?"

"Look around you. This is a flood plain. The Danube will begin to rise in late September. It does every year and by October it will be in a rage...It will take everything."

"Please let us do the work on Sundays."

"That I will not do. Our business has been concluded. You paid the price. The removal of your wood is your responsibility. Now get out of here. I am a busy man."

We drifted down the river in silence, but before we have gotten half way a terrible south wind came up and the frothing river conspired against us. The waves lashed our boat; threatened to sink us. Two of us picked up the paddles, while the other two did the bailing. The rain began to pour and our frantic paddling, bailing did little good, as did the arguments with the ranger.

"Pull harder!" I shouted at the paddlers and increased my frantic bailing. "Head toward shore!" I shouted next and our problem with the ranger; the action of our cruel principal, faded in the background. Nature conspired against us. It joined our other enemies.

We reached the eastern shore, about an hour later and having no more energy left, the four of us tied the boat up and sat on the bank of the treacherous river. We were soaked to our skins; we were worn out; we were crushed.

"What are we going to do now?" Jancsi asked.

"We will wait out the storm. Then we will rush home. My wife must be worried," I answered him.

"I didn't mean that. What are we going to do about the wood? We worked like horses for four solid weeks. We have paid for the wood, almost as much as we earn in a whole month. We can't just give up. We must think of something." Jancsi was at least as bitter as I was and the other two remained silent.

"We will report to Pallosy Monday morning. I will try to talk him into letting us supervise for two weeks, as he proposed originally."

"Fat chance of that Laszlo," Imre spoke up.

"You don't know the bastard, if you think he will give in," Miklos added.

When I got home I told Rozsa about the setback, but I said nothing about our dangerous trip home.

"Did the storm catch you Laszlo? Did it hit while you were on the river? I was terribly worried. I was really frightened."

"It was nothing my darling. A little rain; a bit of wind. I have faced the Danube when it was far worse. I think you probably remember my adventure with Joska."

"Thank God for that. Do you think you will be able to get Pallosy on side?"

"I will beg him, if that is what is needed. I will appeal to that scoundrel. I will not let you and Ildiko freeze, after all the money we paid for the wood; after all our back-breaking labor."

***

Early Monday morning the four of us boarded the train and before six we were at *Bacsbokod*.

"Let's have a glass of *palinka*," Jancsi suggested.

"I don't mind if I do," Miklos announced and the four of us entered the drinking establishment, across from the station.

"We will have to choose a spokesman," Jancsi announced.

"Not me," Miklos spoke up. "All through July, I hardly said a word."

"Not me either. I am the quiet type. I am not a good arguer," Imre announced.

"Well that leaves the two of us Laszlo. It was your idea to convince Pallosy. I think you should be the one to do that."

"If that is what the three of you want, I will give it a good try." We settled the issue and celebrated my election with another drink.

Before eight o'clock we entered the school and sat around until ten. Not a single student showed and Pallosy didn't appear either.

"Where do you think our great leader is?" Jancsi asked me.

"Probably in bed. It is his habit to rest until late, I found out the first time I came here. He will come soon to check on us. He will want to know if we were derelict in carrying out his order." As soon as I finished my sentence, the great man entered the staff-room and greeted us with unabashed farting.

"Well this felt really good. But not as good as seeing the four of you doing your duty. I see that all of you got my letters."

I glanced at my friends. Saw that they waited for me. I began my negotiating.

"Comrade Pallosy, we have been here since eight o'clock and no student showed up. Who are we to supervise?"

"Supervise each other, if that is to your liking," Pallosy announced and polluted the air once again.

"What was to our liking was your original plan to have a quarter of the staff supervise in two week shifts."

"It was a good plan then, but I changed that."

"What do you mean?"

"I took pity on the female teachers, they are no longer required to do duty. Some of the male teachers were on duty for the first two weeks of July, from eight in the morning until two. Then another group of males took over for the rest of July. They put in a lot of hours, but they had very few students to supervise. Only the four of you are left to look after things during August. To be fair to you, I shortened the hours. You will be here, from ten to one, excluding Sundays," Pallosy chuckled, like an intoxicated man, but he was intoxicated only by his power.

"You know that our train gets here before six o'clock. Having us start at ten means four wasted hours."

"That is your problem, not mine."

"And besides, if we are to stay until one, we will miss the afternoon train. We will not get home until late in the evening," I argued with Pallosy.

"Are you trying to blame me for the train schedule?"

"I am not blaming you for anything, but the four of us made plans, based on what you told us at the last staff meeting."

"That was long ago...Am I not permitted to change my mind?" Pallosy challenged me and his beady eyes shone with pleasure.

"It is one thing to change your mind; it is another to be unfair to the four of us." I was getting angry.

"I thought you were teaching mathematics Comrade Lichter. I pity the kids you are teaching. The other teachers served six hours a day. Twelve times six is equal to seventy two hours. I ordered the four of you to do three hours a day for four weeks. Can you figure out how many hours is that?" Pallosy began to mock me.

"Seventy two hours is what I get."

"Seventy two hours from all other male teachers and seventy two hours from you too. Where is the unfairness in that?"

I knew I was losing ground. I began my begging.

"You are being fair...I am sorry for not having told you at the very beginning the real problem we have."

"Tell me now and I might decide to help."

I told Pallosy about our wood cutting; the money we had to pay; the inflexibility of the forest ranger. Then I appealed to his nonexistent decency.

"If you would let us do duty for two weeks, we could give you eight hours a day."

"And during the last two weeks of August you would deprive my poor students from using the school's facilities?"

"Maybe we could propose something else?" I was becoming desperate, besides being angry.

"I am all ears. Let me hear your proposal."

"The first two weeks two of us would supervise for eight hours a day. Then the other two would take over." I surprised my three friends with the new offer. It was an offer we have never discussed, but I had to give it a try.

"Maybe two could build the raft? Maybe two would be able to float the wood down the Danube?" I thought and hoped that Pallosy will give his agreement, that my friends will raise no objections.

"I wouldn't think of doing that. The four of you are such good friends. I have no heart to deprive you of each other's company."

"Please think about what will happen to my child this coming winter."

"And what is that?"

"She is a little baby. She needs to be in a warm place. I cannot provide her with that, without your help."

"Did you and your wife need my help when she was conceived?" Pallosy was becoming nasty.

I ignored his rotten remark, as I tried to ignore his constant farting. I made one more stab at making him understand.

"If you had a child, would you not try to keep her warm? Would you not be more understanding?"

"I have no child, that you know well. So my child will never freeze. You should have thought of the consequences of your acts. A church wedding; jokes against the State; manipulating the Peace Bond Committee to foil my plans; the incident with the Communist Party's Secretary. How many more of your crimes do I have to list?"

"Not a single one comrade. Punish me, but please don't do this to the others," I begged the rotten bastard.

"They are your friends. They deserve what they get. Now go and supervise each other."

We walked out of the staff room like scalded cats and in the recreation room we began to plan.

"We could cut our supervision short; catch the one o'clock train and get our wood out by working late into the evenings," Jancsi raised the possibility and Miklos immediately objected.

"We would get home around two; we wouldn't get to *Rezert* until four. How much do you think we could accomplish before dark?"

"Not much...I grant you that, but what else could we do? We wasted our energy; we wasted our money. It was useless to try to talk to Pallosy, especially the way Laszlo did." Jancsi spoke, like I wasn't even present.

"There is one more thing we could try."

"And what is your brilliant idea this time, Laszlo?" Jancsi spit out the words and his eyes blazed with unconcealed hatred.

"We could go to the Inspector of Schools. He may overrule Pallosy, once we tell him our story. He may be a more compassionate man."

"Be our guest, Laszlo. You go and see him. I wish I have never listened to you. It was your idea to spend July cutting wood; to pay the ranger; to talk to Pallosy and where did it all get us? We wasted our summer; we lost a pile of money and we have nothing to show for it, except Pallosy's animosity, which we earned by being your friend." Jancsi didn't try to hide his anger and I realized that our friendship was over.

***

The following day I skipped out of school to catch the early train and once at Baja, I went to see the Inspector of Schools.

I introduced myself, provided him with my identification paper and after he gave me permission to describe my predicament, I told him about how the four of us spent our July; what we were about to lose and why.

"I wish I could help you Comrade Lichter. I really wish, but to overrule one of my principals is not that easy."

"You are my last hope Comrade Inspector. You seem to be a compassionate man. Please help us. I beg you comrade."

"There is only one way I can help you."

"Any help you could give me would be really appreciated."

"Does that include advice? That maybe the only thing I can give you."

"Even getting advice from you would be appreciated," I told the man.

"My advice is very simple. You need two weeks off to get your wood home. Am I correct?"

"That is all we need."

"In that case you go to your school, each and every day. Watch Pallosy very carefully. I know how moody that man gets, but even moodiness has it uses. Wait until he seems to be in a good mood, then just ask him for the time off. I hope my advice will really help." He stood up, extended his hand to shake mine and I knew that I lost, that our wood cutting adventure was over.

***

For all of August the four of us traveled to *Bacsbokod* to supervise no more than two to three students daily. We no longer spoke about the wood; about my failed attempt to solve the problem. We just drifted apart and that depressed me.

Friendship was always important to me, probably because as a child I had great difficulty in making friends. Pista Janics' betrayal hurt me very badly and having lost the friendship of my three wood-cutting partners added to my misery. I probably would have wallowed in self pity, all during the coming months, but by the middle of August life dealt me a new set of cards that made me forget my small problems and made me concentrate on what was really important.

I will never forget the sixteenth of August. I managed to get home early and found our gate locked. When Rozsa opened the gate, instead of letting me in, she stepped outside and whispered in my ear.

"Be very, very careful Laszlo. There is a man in our kitchen. He insisted to wait for you. He wouldn't even talk to me."

"I will take care of him. He must be an AVO man," I told Rozsa. I couldn't think of any other possibility.

Hand in hand, we entered our kitchen and I felt Rozsa's fear.

"Are you Laszlo?" the skinny, sickly looking, white haired, old man asked me and when I found my voice I told him that I was.

"Thank God you came home early. I would have hated not to be able to talk with you. Yet I must catch the evening train out of this city."

"I am not stopping you. You can go right now. If you are selling something, I am not interested."

"So you mistook me for a salesman? That I am not. I am something else."

"Even then I am not interested."

"Please hear me out first, then make your decision."

"You got five minutes, no more. Then you better get out of my house," I told the stranger.

"My name is Gyurka. My family name doesn't matter. Now let me ask you a question. What would you do if a man came to you, telling you that he is working for American Intelligence?"

"I would immediately rush to the police and report such a man's presence." I told Gyurka and the more I thought about it, the more convinced I became that he was an AVO man, who came to trick me.

"They resent my non-cooperation. They are trying to entrap me. I must be very careful," I told myself.

"So you would report such a man? Would you do that if I told you that I work for the CIA?"

"I would do exactly that!"

"Even if I was sent to see you by your wife's Father?"

"I wouldn't care if you were sent by God Himself."

"Well that is who I am. I am putting my life in your hands Laszlo. Go...Be an informer...They will hang me, I am telling you. My blood will be on your head. I believed your father-in-law that you would never betray me. Was he wrong? Did he misjudge you?"

"He must have. I will go to the police. I don't care what will happen to you, but right now I am exhausted. It is a long way to the police station. Before I go, I must have a rest and maybe something to eat, Rozsa."

"I will set the table. We will have an early supper," Rozsa announced and occupied herself.

"Do you mind if I take my jacket off?" Gyurka asked and without waiting he removed his jacket, which he hung on the door handle.

"You came this far and you came for nothing. We are loyal Hungarians. We have nothing to do with spies. We have no desire to associate with enemies of our homeland." I told Gyurka, just in case he was a plant. To myself, I said something else.

"What am I to do? Inform the police to save ourselves and cause his death, if he really came from the west? I must delay things...I must try to find proof...."

"I understand Laszlo that you have to be cautious. I don't blame you for that. I wish I could convince you to believe all I said. Had I thought of this possibility I would have brought a letter from your Dad. Isn't that what you used to call him, ever since a fishing trip the two of you had?"

"If he is a plant, would he know that?" I asked myself, but I dared not abandon caution.

"My calling Mr. Buja 'Dad' is well known fact. Yes, I began to call him that after a fishing trip we had. But that changes not a thing. After I had my supper, I will report your presence to the authorities, even if you left now."

"I will leave, if that is what you desire, but before I do you must listen to me. I promised Rozsa's Father that I will find out what happened to you all. He had a letter from the authorities, but he has to have confirmation of the letter's content. He was informed that your escape attempt failed and all of you were tried in court. You, your wife, your child, Joe and George were all sentenced to one year of imprisonment, but your sentences were suspended. The action of the Hungarian Government your Dad should consider an act of mercy and good faith. Should he and his wife decide to return to Hungary they would be treated with the same thoughtfulness. Should they decide to do otherwise, your sentences would be reactivated. Did you really have a trial? Were you really given those sentences? Should your in-laws return to save all of you? Or should they ignore the AVH's letter? If they do, will you survive? Will you remain free? These are the things Mr. Buja asked me to find out. Will you give me the answers Laszlo?"

"Dear God, what am I to say? If he is really who he says he is, then I must not breathe a word to the authorities. How will I know the truth? How will I find the right course of action?" I struggled with my thoughts and the deadly possibilities.

"I see you are not willing to talk to me Laszlo."

"I am hungry and I am tired. Maybe you would like to have supper with us? At least we could provide you with your last supper, before I inform the authorities."

"I accept gladly...But before I eat, I would like to use your bathroom."

"Rozsa, please show Gyurka where the outhouse is. Please watch the chickens too. I don't want any of them to get into the backyard." My dear wife must have understood what I desired, for she showed the stranger the outdoor facility and I saw her stand guard by the fence.

I rushed to check Gyurka's jacket pockets and found his revolver. I opened his unlocked briefcase, that stood beside the door, and stared at the map of the western border; the bundles of leaflets-calling on all Hungarians to start an uprising-and the compass.

"He must be CIA...," I told myself, but I still couldn't risk to accept his statements. "If he is a plant, he would make sure that he had things like these, just to fool me. Maybe he gave me the time to search his things? Maybe he hopes that I will be foolish enough to believe him, after what I found? What should I do? He put his life in my hands. Can I risk putting ours in his as well?"

Rozsa and Gyurka came back into the kitchen, just after I put his things back where he left them.

"Come have supper with us," I extended the invitation and sat down at the head of the table.

"It is hot in here...You don't mind if I roll up my shirt sleeves?"

"Do what you want." I told him and that is what he did. It took me only a second to notice something that required a closer examination. I stood up, walked over to the stove and took a furtive look at Gyurka's right wrist.

"Dear God. That watch is just like my Father-in-law's. He may have come from Austria." I told myself and made a mental note to probe why he had that watch, as soon as there was an opportunity.

"Do you enjoy the food comrade?"

"That I enjoy, but not your way of addressing me. I hate the Communist bastards. You don't know how much I hate them." I let him talk on, just in case he would say something that would give him away or prove to me who he is.

"During the war, I served my country as an officer of the Hungarian army. I was a land owner, had many servants and a dear wife and two little girls. May they rest in peace. Before the end of the war, I deserted and went to my estate. The Russians burned it to the ground...They raped my wife repeatedly...They violated my little girls, although neither of them reached their tenth birthday...One of my loyal servants tried to stop them and he paid for it with his life. Another servant of mine saw what was happening, from his hiding place. He told me that once my wife and daughters could provide the Russians with no more pleasure; once they lay helpless and bleeding, they shot them like dogs. When I found out what happened to my loved ones, I went into a rage. I swore in front of my servant that I will avenge them. Two days later I crossed into Austria and volunteered to work for the CIA. After a great deal of training they sent me into Hungary to spy. I have been back and forth for almost ten years and I can assure you that in spite of the harm I caused the Communists, my desire for revenge did not abate." His emotional account of what may have happened had great impact on me, but to trust him I still didn't dare.

"I am sorry for what happened to your family, if what you said is true, but even that changes not a thing. I will report you, that I know and I think it's time, it is getting late," I announced my decision.

"It is not even four thirty," Gyurka said, after he glanced at his watch.

"I couldn't help noticing what a nice watch you have," I told Gyurka, grabbing the first opportunity to find out what he will say.

"Oh, this watch is not mine. It belongs to your Dad." He said no more.

"I am almost convinced now that Gyurka is not lying, but I must have more proof before I am willing to trust him." I told myself.

"I have never seen that watch before," I lied and added. "My Father-in-law must have gotten it in Austria. Take a good look at it Rozsa."

Rozsa stood up to see better and stared at the watch for a few seconds, then she sat down and under the table she reached for my hand, giving it a squeeze.

"Maybe I am wrong. Maybe I don't remember the watch your Father had Rozsa," I urged my wife to give me an answer.

"My Father had a watch, just like that, but that one had an inscription," Rozsa surprised me.

"I have never seen the inscription Rozsa. What did it say and where was it?"

"My Father showed me many years ago. It is inside the back cover."

"Would you mind taking the back cover off, Gyurka?" I asked him and handed to him a sharp knife.

He pried the back off the watch off and handed it to Rozsa.

"Always an officer. Love, Maria." Rozsa read the inscription and shed a tear.

"Why would you have his watch on you?" I asked the obviously surprised Gyurka.

"Before I left Austria, I visited Rozsa's parents. Before I said good-by to them, your Dad saved me from a great blunder. He noticed my expensive, gold watch and pointed out that such a time piece is rare in Hungary. He felt that it would be noticed; it would create curiosity. He was the one who gave me his watch to wear while I am in this country and I gave mine to him for safe keeping."

"What more proof could a man give?" I asked myself and yet I hesitated. "He could have my father-in-law's watch, but only if he was apprehended. Had the AVO gotten back my poor Dad, they would no longer need us for bait. We would be in prison by now. They have my confession; they wouldn't need to entrap me."

I fought against my last morsel of suspicion and put an end to my doubts. I stood up; went to Gyurka and reached for his hand.

"Please forgive me for not trusting you before. We live in a country of evil. I was afraid you might be working for the AVO and that you were sent here to test me. I now know that I was wrong. I know that you are really what you said. I almost made a very bad mistake by reporting you to the police, please try to understand."

"There is nothing to forgive Laszlo. Had you bought my story at the very beginning, I would have been concerned about you being too naive. I fear nothing now. I will be happy to tell your Dad that you are a cautious man, that his daughter is in good hands." Gyurka gave me the undeserved kudos and the dam of my reticence broke, I told our story without restraint. I began with our escape attempt and half an hour later, I finished.

"I suspected before, but now I know that we were freed from prison for one reason only. They wanted to use us for bait."

"I thank you both for trusting me. Now I would like to repeat the questions, I asked about an hour ago. Did you really have a trial? Were you really given those sentences? Should your in-laws return to save all of you? Or should they ignore the AVH's letter? If they do, will you survive? Will you remain free?"

"I will answer them in the order you asked," I replied and continued. "We never had a trial. If they held one, we were not informed, we weren't present. This is the first time we ever heard about being on probation, so I doubt that it is so. My in-laws should never ever return to this country. Dad would be executed for the killing of one border guard and for wounding another, although we are sure that he is innocent of those charges. The AVH's letter to them is a barefaced lie. It is a fabrication of everything. They should ignore it! You can tell Dad that we will survive, but I cannot guarantee that we will be free. This is a country of ten million prisoners. Some of the prisoners are inside prison walls, the others are outside, yet behind the fence of despair. Does it really matter what kind of prisoner one happens to be? I will stall for time...I will gladly act as bait...I know the good Lord will watch over us and some day we will be free. Tell these things to my Father-in-law," I finished giving the answers.

"And tell them that we love them. Tell them that their only granddaughter is a lovely little girl. Tell them that we want to join them. That we will risk escaping again and again," Rozsa added.

"I will tell them everything, once I cross the border," Gyurka promised.

"When do you expect to do that?" I asked.

"Not for the next three months. I have work to do, not unlike many others. Whether I succeed or fail, I will have to be back in Austria before the end of November."

"Couldn't you return to Austria right away? If you stay in this country, you will face many dangers. You may be apprehended. You may be interrogated. You may even give us away," my thoughts tumbled out.

"My masters want me to prepare the soil for an uprising. My visit to you, they know nothing about. I must stay. The dangers do exist, as those dangers existed for almost ten years, but I was always able to elude the enemy. Look at me. Tell me what do you see?"

"What should I see? I don't understand." I was somewhat confused.

"You see a man whose hair is completely white. A man in his sixties. If I ever get picked up, my enemy will see that and something more."

"What?" Rozsa asked.

"A man whose speech is confused; who has no memory of anything that happened a few minutes before; a broken old man who poses no danger to anyone; they will see only a shattered, harmless, pitiful creature. I assure you that I have been trained well, that I will be safe."

"How will we know that you got back to Austria?" I asked Gyurka.

"I will send you a message on the Free Europe Radio, just like your Dad does."

"They use a code that they keep on changing. We should agree on something you will use so that we will know that you returned safely."

"Well, let me think. I think I got it. The message will come from 'the death head butterfly'. What do you think?"

"I think that will do nicely. If we don't hear those words in the first two weeks of December, we will know that you have been captured; maybe dead. On the other hand, if we hear those words, we will know that you are just like a butterfly, really free. Where will you go now?" I asked the agent.

"I will catch the first train to *Budapest*. That is where I will do what I must," came his reply, but he gave no details.

When Gyurka was about to leave us, we hugged and kissed and gave each other words of good wishes. Then we locked the gate behind him and fell into each other's arms, totally drained; our hearts full of hope and filled with fear.

***

"It will be a long three months Laszlo, before we get a message from Gyurka." Rozsa told me, while she fed our sweet, innocent daughter, who had the misfortune of being born at the wrong time, into a family that was plagued with trials and tribulations.

"It will be that...But he will get out...He will give all the information to your parents and the next time they send a guide, we will try again and that time we will succeed Rozsa."

"I know you are right Laszlo, but I can't help it. I am full of anxiety." Rozsa's words resurrected my earlier doubts and I have decided to do some checking.

"I will walk to the railway station to check on our new friend."

"If you think that is necessary, then do that, but I want you to be very careful."

"He will not know that I followed him. I will watch him from a distance. I have to satisfy myself that he is heading toward *Budapest*."

Almost an hour later I saw his white head in the station's waiting room, but he never saw me. I hid behind the corner of the station as the train pulled in to disgorge its passengers and was about to take on new ones.

I saw Gyurka mount the train and then I saw two men jump into the same compartment, both of them I believed to be AVO agents.

"Dear God don't let them capture him. His life is now in your hands and so is ours. Please help us. We never needed your help more than we need it during the next three months. Beloved Lord please grant us Your mercy," I prayed and the train pulled out, began to speed up and Gyurka was on his way the capital of Hungary.

I walked home and on my way I wondered.

"Was I right to trust the stranger? He had Dad's watch. It was Rozsa and I who discovered that. If he was an agent of the AVO he would have behaved differently. He would have offered the watch as proof. He would not have waited for us to discover its existence. But what if he was a very skilled agent? I have never met one with great skills. The moron who received my dictated reports was fooled for a long time...My interrogators were not smart either. They made the mistake of letting slip that Janics was their informer. My handler is just a country bumpkin. So what am I afraid of now? It must be my overactive imagination; my pessimistic nature. I always see danger where there is none. I always fear the worst happening." I tried to find peace of mind, but each time I was about to achieve that state, something new, something unexpected happened.

***

Saturday, late afternoon, I went to the post office to mail a letter to my in-laws. The letter contained a simple coded message, I was ordered to include, but I wasn't able to write anything about the strange visitor we had. The AVO knew the code and I dared not risk being discovered.

"Hello Laszlo. You stopped coming to see us. Just as well." I heard a woman's voice and I spun around. I was facing Mrs. Balazs.

"I am glad I ran into you. There are a couple of things I must tell you." She spoke loud enough to turn a few heads.

"Not here!" I hissed and walked away. I reached a house with its gate open and entered the dark, cavernous entrance. Mrs. Balazs joined me, after a few minutes.

"Are you concerned about the CIA agent Laszlo? Is this why you don't dare to talk to me?"

"Lower your voice woman. You are putting all of us in great danger. I have no idea what you are talking about."

"Sure you don't. Do you think I will believe you? Your father-in-law sent an agent to visit my Peter and he didn't ask him to see you? Who do you think you are fooling Laszlo?" The woman would have prattled on, but I didn't want to spend much time with her, so I ordered her to be brief.

"The agent came to see Peter last Wednesday morning. Didn't he tell you?"

"Nobody came to see me."

"Well he sure came to see us, but he was late by a week."

"Late in what way?"

"Peter was arrested by the AVO, a week before the agent's arrival."

"I am really sorry to hear that. Tell me about that man who went to see you."

"He had white hair. He must have been in his early sixties. He was sent by your in-laws, as I told you before...," I didn't let her finish her story.

"You have been fooled by the AVO. Can't you see that?"

"But he was real, I am telling you."

"Did he give you any proof? Did he convince you in some way?"

"I asked for no proof. I never thought of that."

"Then you are a foolish woman. You have been duped, I suspect. Peter was arrested; he was interrogated. Then the AVO sent to you someone to find out if Peter confessed everything."

"But that couldn't be...He asked me why Peter had turned back when your in-laws escaped. How would an AVO agent know that?"

"Peter must have confessed it."

"I never thought of that. If you are right Laszlo, what can I do now?"

"You should keep quiet. Never say a word to anyone else about that visit. If you are arrested, which I think will happen in a few days, you are to deny everything. That is the only hope you have now. How could you be so foolish? How could you fall for a trick like this?"

"I know now that it was the wrong thing to do, but I am just a simple, uneducated woman."

"So use your lack of education to your advantage."

"How should I do that?"

"You must play dumb. That wouldn't be difficult for you. Pretend that you remember nothing. You had no visitors since Peter's arrest. You talked to nobody. You cannot even remember what you had for breakfast. You do these things well and you might be safe." I hated to scare the poor woman, but I had little alternative.

"Her knowing about Gyurka put all of us in grave danger." I have realized and decided to do something bold, to prevent this calamity from reoccurring.

***

I returned home, scared out of my wits and after I told Rozsa about my chance meeting with Mrs. Balazs, the next blow came from a different quarter.

"A wire came from Lujza. You must go to see her, as soon as you can."

"What did the wire say?"

"Here, read it Laszlo."

"I need your help. Please come and see me."

"Tomorrow is Sunday. I will make the trip." I assured Rozsa and for the rest of the day we tried to guess why Lujza made that strange request. All our guesses centered around Joe and the possible difficulties Lujza may have experienced with him. So it was only natural that I fumed about the possible misbehavior of my brother-in-law and that Rozsa tried to cool me with her words, then with her kisses and later on she urged me not to think, but to try to get some sleep.

***

Before I went to catch the train to Budapest, I searched through a couple of drawers and found a post card that might do the trick. It was the picture of the monument of Jelky, the Hungarian hobo, who walked around the globe in search of fame.

I addressed it to my in-laws.

"Dear Dad and Mom,

"Just a brief note to let you know that we are well. Ildiko is growing nicely. I am sure you recognize Jelky, who was born in this very city. He is much like my brother, Gyurka, restless, always wandering. He came to visit us recently and since we don't get along, I would rather not have him come to see us. 'Evil men have their hair turn white..,'" according to an old Hungarian saying. I wonder if that is why he grayed so prematurely?

"Love to both of you, from the whole family.

"Laszlo, Rozsa and Ildiko."

When I finished, I gave the card to Rozsa.

"What do you think my love? Will your parents understand me?"

"I am sure they will, but aren't you playing with fire?"

"First tell me what they will make of this note, when they read it and when they see that it wasn't postmarked at *Baja*?"

"Where do you plan to mail it, Laszlo?"

"I will get off the train at a small station, somewhere between here and *Budapest*. I will drop this in a mailbox, hoping that it will get by the censors," I explained my plan to Rozsa.

"In that case this is what I think. My Father will judge from the postmark that you are being cautious Laszlo. He will understand that it is not your brother you wrote about, but the CIA agent. He will know that you don't want another visit. They will get the message, I believe, but what I fear most is simply this. If the censors pick this up, will they not suspect that you are writing not about George, your brother, but someone else? After all you are writing about Gyurka."

"But that is the beauty of my plan. My brother's proper name is George, but his nickname is really Gyurka. We have called him by that name, until he became a grown man. Besides, I think your parents must be warned not to endanger us again the way they did. Especially now that we know that Gyurka visited Mrs. Balazs. As long as we were the only people in Hungary to know about Gyurka's existence the danger was minimal, but with other people in the know, the danger is increased greatly."

"Maybe you are right. Maybe you should mail it," Rozsa gave in and I slipped the card into my pocket.

In a little while I hopped on a train and began my journey, all the while thinking about what mess Joe may have created. I interrupted my thinking only at the station of *Sarbogard*, where the train stopped for five minutes.

I slipped the card in the mailbox, with a fervent wish not having it intercepted.

***

I reached Lujza's apartment early afternoon, with the greatest of apprehension.

"I am glad you came, Laszlo. I got your wire, after your failed escape attempt. Thank God you turned back, thus saved the life of Rozsa and Ildiko. But Joe got himself in a heap of trouble."

"That is why I am here. That is what I suspected. Please tell me exactly what happened."

"What I tell you I heard from Joe, after he arrived here and when I was allowed to visit him once."

"Visit him where? He told you what?" My apprehension grew.

"In prison, where he is awaiting trial."

"Dear Lord, I thought it was something much simpler. What did he do to be arrested?"

"I think you know that his fiancé dumped him."

"Yes, we knew that, but nothing else."

"He went to see Sana, before he came to me. He got a handgun from his cousin. He was dispirited, lay around day after day, doing nothing. I had to force him to talk. He did mention killing himself, but I thought I talked him out of it. Then about two weeks ago, he went to see a movie. He bought some candy and passed it around to kids. The police noticed what he was doing and began to question him. During the questioning, he acted strange. They took him to the police station. He asked for permission to visit the outhouse, but before they allowed him to do that, they searched him and found his gun."

"That is terrible. Why didn't you let us know immediately?"

"I didn't want to bother you. You have had enough problems already. So I hired a lawyer, a friend of mine. He went to see Joe; he listened to his story and proposed a line of defense. Joe refused him. He was unwilling to state that as a last act of kindness, he bought candy for a few kids; then he was going to shoot himself over his lost love, his failed engagement. The lawyer tried to persuade him to have his former fiancé testify. She would have backed up his story. I would have told the police that Joe spoke about suicide a number of times, but Joe wanted to do something else."

"What is he up to now?" I asked her and knew, even before her answer, that Joe was up to something foolish.

"He wants to confess that he was on the way to the Austrian border and if anyone tried to stop him, he was ready to use the gun; he was ready to kill."

"But that is insane. Why is he doing that?"

"I don't understand it either. When he came here I embraced him; I fed him; I took care of him. After all he is the son of my dear brother, but he is different. He wouldn't look for a job. He would laze around endlessly. When I finally berated him for living off me, for not helping me, he went into a frenzy. He took off, but not before borrowing some money. That is when he got himself in trouble. I feel so bad. Did I drive him to doing what he did? Did I let him down? Tell me Laszlo."

"You did nothing wrong. We had the same experience with Joe." Then I told

Lujza about the only letter Joe wrote to us. How that letter upset my dear Rozsa.

"He never told me that he wrote to you. He rarely spoke about you and Rozsa."

"That is Joe. He lives in his own world. He lives only for himself."

"What should I do now, Laszlo?"

"There is nothing any of us can do. His mind cannot be changed. We were unable to do that when we asked him to escape with us. If he is unwilling to accept the help of the lawyer, we will just let him be. If there is nothing else you need to tell me, I must return to *Baja*."

"I wish there was nothing else, but there is. Joe was arrested on August sixth, I think that was a Sunday...Yes it was." She looked at the calendar, then pointed at August nineteenth.

"On this date Laszlo, someone pounded on my door. I was already in bed, fast asleep. My heart in my mouth, I crawled out of bed. I expected that some day the police will pay me a visit, but when I woke hearing that pounding on my door; when I saw that it was ten o'clock in the evening, I knew it must be the AVO coming to get me."

"Why would they bother you? You have done nothing wrong."

"Well, it wasn't them. It was a white haired stranger." Her announcement sent me into a bottomless pit.

"Stupid bastard...CIA trained imbecile...How much more risk could he create?" I asked myself and kept my thoughts to myself.

"Who was he?" I asked Lujza.

"He was a CIA agent. He was sent by my brother from Austria to take Joe out of Hungary in about three months time, but he timed his arrival badly."

"I hope you didn't talk to that man."

"Why shouldn't I have?"

"Because in all likelihood, he was a fake."

"No, he wasn't. He described my brother and his wife, down to the last detail."

"Sure he did. Didn't you think that Dad and Mom are well known to the authorities? Did it not occur to you that he was an AVO agent and he came to trick you? You put yourself into terrible danger."

"That couldn't be...," Gyurka described his train trip that brought him here. Shortly after he got on the train, he was approached by two AVO agents. At least that is what he told me. They asked him for his identification papers and he reached into his two pockets, pretending to search for the precious document. After some searching, he shook his head. He forgot his papers again, for the third time this month. He told them he was getting feeble. He offered to pay the fine willingly. One hand in one of his pockets clutched the bills, needed to pay the fine, but the other one clutched his revolver. He took a great gamble, he was either to pay the fine or three lives would have ended. The dead ones would have been the two agents and him. The agents took pity on the old, feeble minded wreck of a man; they didn't even fine him. Now that you heard what he told me, do you still believe that he was an AVO agent, Laszlo?"

"I have never been surer of anything."

"What should I do now? I told him a great deal about myself and I even told him everything about Joe. I just wanted him to tell everything to my brother..." Lujza began to cry.

My heart went out to her. She was the second woman whose life I upset, whom I made to feel real fear. I couldn't tell her the truth; that would create even more danger, so I gave her the same advice, I gave to Mrs. Balazs. When I sensed that her fear was sufficiently great to have her remain silent; that she will deny that late night visitor's existence, even under torture, I left her to her own devices.

***

On my way home, I thought about what I was and what I became.

"I was a shy, almost friendless, book-worm of no significance, until I met my Rozsa and I underwent a complete metamorphosis. My shyness was replaced with a relentless desire for the girl I loved. Having few friends no longer mattered and I was forced to study not only textbooks, but more so the skills of survival." I acknowledged the many changes I have underwent and had not an iota of regret, in spite of the problems I was facing.

"Being married to Rozsa; having Ildiko for a daughter were like treasured dreams. I have transformed into what?" I asked and I saw myself as juggler of many things.

"A juggler indeed?" I thought bitterly. "I have tried to juggle many balls: the AVO; Szantai, Pallosy; the CIA agent; Mrs. Balazs and Lujza too. Szantai and Pallosy I have juggled badly; I dropped the balls, that were those cursed bastards. Will the same thing happen to any of the others?" My rambling thoughts went on and finally the train pulled into my place birth, *Baja*.

Border of Hope, Fence of Despair

An hour later, I told all that happened to my beloved Rozsa and for quite a while she cried over her brother's imprisonment. She was disconsolate for three solid days, full of fears and when the knock came, in the middle of the night, she had even more reasons to be frightened.

***

There were only two of them when I opened the gate, around two o'clock in the morning. I knew neither of them, but that mattered not. The time of the night and their behavior left no doubt that they were AVO agents.

"Get dressed," ordered one of them, after he led me into the bedroom.

Rozsa was about to slip out of bed, but she was told to remain where she was. The agents wanted only me.

"Am I permitted to kiss good-by my wife?" I asked the officers.

"If I were you I would do that," came the reply.

"Am I under arrest?" I asked next.

"I am not at liberty to say."

I held Rozsa's pain-filled face with my two hands; looked deeply in her eyes and after a brief kiss, I asked her to say my good-byes to our dear little daughter.

The two agents led me out of the house and I feared that I may never be able to return. The car waited, just two houses away and I was made to sit beside the driver.

"Don't look back; you must not see our faces." The voice came from behind me and I sensed the presence of two men. I saw the rear-view mirror tilted at an angle that prevented me from seeing them, but their voices I could hear clearly.

"You are no longer needed." I heard the statement and froze suddenly.

"Is he talking to me?" I asked myself. "Is this the end? Have I dropped another ball? Am I really that poor a juggler?" Then relief washed over me, when I have realized that the statement was meant for the two agents, who got me this far, but were no longer needed.

The car began to move and for a few minutes we traveled in silence. I watched the streets that we left behind and when we crossed the railway tracks, I was certain that they were taking me back to *Kecskemet*.

"This time I must grab the wheel. George and Joe will not suffer. Will I succeed to kill myself and the three AVO agents?" I was about to act, when I realized that the car slowed down and traveled on a dirt road, beside a well known cemetery. Only when the car stopped did the silence end.

"How long have you been in our service?" the voice was deep, that asked me.

"Since early April."

"That is more than five months...What have you given us?" a high pitched voice came next and from that time on the two voices alternated.

"I don't understand, comrade."

"It is us who don't understand. Peter Balazs was your first assignment, but you gave us nothing. We had to use other assets to finally put that traitor away. Then you were given Istvan Lorant. You produced nothing useful on him either. What explanation do you have Lichter?"

"Before Balazs came to trust me, I was ordered to stay away from him. I haven't been able to gain the confidence of Lorant yet, but that will come soon, I believe."

"And we believe that you are playing with us."

"I swear comrades that I am doing my best."

"Are you indeed? We were sent from the capital to find out."

"To find out what?" I whispered in the darkness.

"To find out all about you and your family. Tell us about your Father, about your Mother."

"What do you want to know?"

"Every single detail."

I began to speak about my Father, then about my Mother. I described them as good people, who suffered a great deal and have accepted what fate dealt them. Then I fell silent.

"Do you have any sisters and brothers?" I was asked and I became more careful than before.

"They must know that I have only one brother. No AVO agent would question me without knowing my background. They must have intercepted my post card. They are trying to have me speak about my brother, George and Gyurka, the CIA agent. I must follow the advice I gave the two women and deny knowing anything about the spy or I will be dead and so will be many others." I tasted my own fear and bile filled my mouth, but my resolution to lie, to deny everything was my only salvation.

"I don't have any sisters and only one brother," I told them.

"What is his name?"

"Gyurka, I mean George." I was sure they have seen the post card. They were onto me, so I made sure that my mention of Gyurka on the post card, matched the name of my brother.

"Which one is it?"

"Well, for a long while, after he was born, we all called him Gyurka. Only during the last two or three years did we call him George. So it is both."

"I see...Do you ever write to your in-laws in Austria?"

"Sure I do...I wrote to them almost every week. Sometimes I even included coded messages my AVO controller gave me."

"That is superb. Your co-operation is appreciated. When did you write to them last?"

"I am not sure...Maybe a week ago?"

"It is a letter you always write. Isn't it true?"

"Well, now that you mention it, I want to tell you that it is not the case."

"Explain that!"

"The last time I wrote to them, I didn't write a letter."

"Not a letter? Then what was it?"

"A post card," I admitted, knowing full well that they had it intercepted.

"Where do you normally mail things?"

"At the post office of *Baja*. But that post card I mailed somewhere else. Let me think. Yes, I remember now...My wife's Aunt, Lujza, sent us a wire. She asked me to see her as soon as I can. She lives in Budapest. At the station of Baja I saw a post card of Jelky, so I bought it on an impulse. I was bored on the train and decided to write a brief greeting to my in-laws. Shortly after I finished it, we stopped at *Soroksar* and that is where I had mailed it." I sang like a bird, hoping that my willingness to reveal this much will fool them, if they didn't know the truth.

"If they had captured Gyurka, then I am dead anyway," I thought and hoped that it wasn't so.

"And what did you write on that post card?"

"Just a simple greeting..."

"Who did you happen to mention?"

"My wife...My little daughter...And my brother, Gyurka."

"Give us a bit more about that. You told us that during the last few years he was always called George. But on that post card you referred to Gyurka. We find that strange."

"There is nothing strange about that. I was on the train. I was thinking about my childhood and in that frame of mind, I thought of him that way."

"Describe your relationship with your brother, in fact you should describe what he looks like."

"Which one do you prefer first?"

"His looks might be appropriate."

"He is taller than I; stronger than I; better looking too. Black hair, a prominent nose; good, strong muscles and he is a snappy dresser."

"Now about your relationship."

"We don't really get along. I was always an introvert and Gyurka an extrovert. I had few friends and he always had many. We always ended up debating everything. If I said something about any topic, he seemed to know it better and he proved me wrong, time and time again. That always infuriated me."

"We can understand that. But something is amiss. Black hair you said?"

"Yes...Just like mine and my Father's."

"Well that is really surprising. You are a traitor; a disgrace to this country. You sit here lying your head off about your brother. You wrote the post card we have intercepted, and it wasn't your brother you wrote about. You think we don't know the truth? If you tell us everything; if you make a clean breast of it, we might let you live." The words, the tone of voice grated on my ears, but I sensed that he was only guessing; he was only trying to intimidate me and besides, I had no other choice than to protest my innocence, to keep on falsifying everything.

"I wrote about nobody else than my brother. If you want to send me to prison for using his nickname, so be it. I didn't know it was a crime...The AVO had my full confession of the crimes I have committed, yet I was allowed to go free."

"We know all about that, but associating with spies is a very serious matter." His use of plural, instead of singular, I picked up and I knew that they were just fishing.

"If one of you is a spy or both of you are spies, then I am guilty of such association." I was getting too cocky for my own good, but my approach seemed to be effective. Neither of them spoke again about Gyurka. Instead, they both jumped at a totally different topic.

"What do you hear about us?" the deeper voice asked.

"About members of the AVO. That is what my partner means," the high pitched voice piped up.

"Nothing...I hear nothing...Nobody speaks about members of the secret police."

"That is a crock of shit and you know it comrade. People talk about nothing, but us. We raided many homes, in the dead of night. We dragged men and women out of their beds, made them disappear. At least that is what our enemies say. Have you not heard about our achievements?"

"I never did."

"You must have heard that we take great pleasure in picking up innocent Hungarians and drive them close to a cemetery like this?"

"If anyone told me that, I would not have believed it."

"That is before we did this to you. Is that what you mean?"

"Yes...," I admitted and the possibility of them having sinister intentions began to terrify me.

"Have you also heard why we choose a spot like this?"

"As I told you before I never hear anything about the AVO, so how could I have heard what you accuse me of hearing?"

"It is time to enlighten you. We do this every time, before we dish out well deserved punishments. Close to the car, there is a ditch. It is big enough to accommodate a body. Two shovels in the trunk, some fresh earth on the other side of the ditch and five minutes of work, that is all we need. Do you get my drift?"

"I do understand what you are saying, but I will never believe that a Hungarian would do that to a country man of his."

"Very well put...We are human beings. As long as you keep your nose clean Laszlo; as long as you promise to report to us all misdeeds; as long as you turn in to us all traitors, spies and enemies, you are safe. We thank you for this night's pleasant conversation. Driver, you better get out. Open the door for our guest. He is free to leave."

The door opened. I stepped out of the car and began to walk away. I heard the driver cocking his revolver. I took another few steps and waited for the gun's report or for the bullet's impact, whichever would come first. The shot didn't come during the first sixty seconds and it didn't come the next minute either. I picked up my pace; I began to run and by the time I changed direction, at the corner, I was in full flight...I was heading home to my Rozsa, to my little Ildiko. God granted His Mercy. A reprieve I was given again!

Chapter 20

"I thought I was dead. I figured I was finished, but the good Lord saved me again," I told Rozsa, after I have described all that happened.

"The merciful Lord has been with us. How long do you think that will be Laszlo?" She asked the question and I hoped that our Protector would never abandon us.

Two days later Rozsa got sick and I felt helpless. I had witnessed many times my Father's collapsing and I ran to get a doctor to save his life. I was on the run again. I seemed to grow wings, I seemed to fly to seek help, but this time I did that for my beloved.

"My wife is very sick...She needs a doctor very badly." I could hardly speak the words when the door opened and it took me a few seconds to realize that I was speaking not to the doctor, but his elderly wife.

"Tell me, what is the nature of her illness? The doctor is not in the office."

"My dear Rozsa suffers from head-pains; she is totally blind. I fear that she may not survive the coming night."

"How old is she?"

"She was only nineteen last June. Please make sure the doctor will come to see her. I am frantic...Please promise me that you will send him to attend to my darling."

"Just give me your name and the address and I will see what I can do."

Having done what she requested, I flew back home, thinking about nothing else but my beloved.

"Is it getting any better?" I asked, out of breath, as soon as I arrived home and her answer gave me new lease on life; I was rejuvenated.

"The pain is gone...I can see...Don't be so worried Laszlo."

"How could I not be worried? You know how I am. Always thinking of the worst possibilities."

"I know my darling, but please try to think clearly. I have recovered. We have our beautiful baby. It doesn't do much good to worry constantly."

"I know my love that you are right, but I have lost my Uncle Jozsef. I haven't heard for months from Aunt Gizella. I am being questioned and pushed and tormented by the AVO."

"I know all that Laszlo, but this time it was not them you were worried about. It is only me."

"Yes, my love. I always fear losing you. I couldn't live without you...Don't you see?"

"You will never lose me, Laszlo! I am well, as you can see. Which reminds me...Shouldn't you go back to tell the doctor not to come to see me?"

"His office is two miles away...I am really tired...He is an old man; he must be worn out. He will not come, my beloved."

We ate our supper, played games with Ildiko. When she tired of our silly, little games, she pointed to her swing, that hung from two large screws on our bedroom's door-frame. She laughed and chuckled with the pleasure of her swinging and when she got sleepy, we put her to bed and removed the swing. By ten o'clock we were totally exhausted.

***

Around midnight, we were jarred awake by a loud banging.

"Not again!" Rozsa moaned and the noise continued.

I went to unlock the gate and when I saw the doctor, I gave thanks to God for having spared us from another visit by the secret police.

"I came to see your wife. I was making house-calls...When I got home, my wife gave me the message. It sounded bad, so I am here."

"I am really grateful doctor, but...," I almost blurted out that my dear wife was no longer in need of his services, but I felt so guilty, that I bit off my coming words and led him toward the bedroom to have him examine Rozsa.

I forgot to warn him about the three inch screws. Rozsa and I were both too short to be bothered by those sharp, dangerous items, but the doctor was much taller and as he stepped into our bedroom, he received a nasty cut.

The sight of blood always upset me. The feeling of guilt overwhelmed me and I shouted to Rozsa.

"Get out of bed...Give me some bandages..." She jumped out of bed, rushed to get what was required and within minutes, we tried to stem the bleeding from his forehead.

"I am so sorry, doctor," I gave a cry of distress.

"And so am I. I did join your wife in having a headache."

We nursed him the best we could and when he felt a lot better, he told us what he intended.

"I will examine your wife, young man. How do you feel Rozsa?"

"My headache almost killed me. I really thought I was dying. I couldn't see," Rozsa informed him, but spoke not about the improvement.

The doctor gave her a thorough examination and he raised three fingers.

"How many fingers do you see?"

"Three?" She announced with pretended uncertainty and I almost burst out laughing.

"Rozsa is not a good fibber...She is not like me," the thought ran through my mind.

"I suggest you see a dentist. I think it is your tooth that gave you all that trouble. Take consolation from the fact that you are well, you are the one who is really healthy."

The old, conscientious, kind doctor left our home around one and in the darkness of the night he got on his bicycle and I watched him disappear in the darkness.

"God bless him. He gave his time; he spent his energy; he hurt himself, yet he didn't blame us. Why aren't we all like this doctor? Why have we allowed ourselves to be corrupted, twisted, manipulated by the hated Communists?" I thought and condemned myself, along with many others.

***

In a few days, the doctor's diagnosis proved to be flawless. The dentist did his job and my beloved Rozsa's terrible pain didn't return, instead the pain came to me.

My Mother brought a letter, on the following Sunday.

"Read this letter Laszlo. The first letter from your Aunt Gizella."

> *"Dear All,*
>
> *"This is the first time I am allowed to write to anyone. I have received a five year sentence for my crime, but I suppose, I deserved it...I miss all of you, but most of all I miss my dear Jozsef.*
>
> *"I finally got permission to have a relative visit me for ten minutes. Would one of you come to see me? Visiting hours are from nine to five on Sundays. Each Sunday I will be waiting to see one of you. If I am allowed to make a suggestion, I would suggest that my late Jozsef's favorite come. As you well know it was Laszlo.*
>
> *"Love to all, from Gizella."*

After a few words with Rozsa, I promised my Mother that I will go and see my dear Aunt.

Ever since our failed escape attempt, I tried to avoid thinking about my Uncle, whose blood was spilled by the exploding mine.

"Those mines were made by Hungarian hands; planted by Hungarians to kill their own countrymen. My Aunt Gizella, was incarcerated by them too," I thought many times, but in the light of day, I was able to avoid thinking about the two of them. Then night fell, I lay awake, I saw their faces; I remembered their kindness and the pain of what I did plunged my spirit into total darkness.

***

During my trip to Budapest, where I was to see my Aunt, the pain became even more profound. I have re-lived the planning of the escape; the beginning of our trip; the moment of turning back and finally the news that came on the radio.

"Will my Aunt blame me for what happened?" I asked myself and listened to the train's clattering wheels.

"No blame...No blame...No blame...," my mind registered the imagined sounds, but my heart sensed something else.

"You did it Laszlo! You cannot escape the consequences. You planned it...You started it...You didn't make your Uncle turn back..." My heart didn't hesitate to shout its condemnation, but my mind tried to find an escape hatch.

"Why blame Laszlo?" my mind whispered.

"Who else could I blame?" my heart retorted and I, the doomed creature, kept listening to the contest.

"Blame the Russians and their Communist cohorts. They are the killers, the destroyers of all freedom."

"Don't be an ass. Many, many of the ten million Hungarians learned to submit. They learned to accept their fate; they became docile. Why didn't Laszlo do that?"

My heart and mind kept up the debate, as the train chugged in to *Budapest*. It pained me to listen to my heart's condemnation and not even my mind's attempts to exonerate me could ease that.

"Men are weak. So is Laszlo," my heart concluded.

"Men are stubborn and that includes Laszlo. He cannot help taking after his Father." My mind suggested and both of them fell silent.

***

I finished my early morning train journey and rushed to catch a tram to take me to the prison of *Kobanya*. When I got within three blocks, I saw the huge, imposing, red, brick building that dwarfed its surrounding brothers and sisters.

"Somewhere inside my Aunt is hoping, waiting and she will be happy to see me. She will be delighted for ten whole minutes," I thought and picked up the pace of my walking. It was already eight thirty.

The long line of waiters surprised me.

"Are all these people here to visit someone? Have all those they came to visit committed a political crime? This prison holds only the enemies of the State. There must be over three hundred people here...Far worse than the line-ups at the butcher shops. If I stand here all day long, will I be able to see my poor Aunt?" I asked myself and my heart sank when I joined the line, that grew fast behind me and diminished very slowly, as groups of five visitors were allowed to enter.

I looked ahead; I looked to the sides of the sinister building and saw the high brick fence, with its small gate, but I couldn't see behind it.

A woman, who stood beside me, spoke up.

"I saw you glance in that direction. Do you know what is there?"

"I couldn't imagine..."

"Nor could I, over two years ago, but I have made several visits to other prisons, all over the country. I have learned, during those visits, that every one of these prisons have one of those...It is the prison cemetery."

"Why would they need a cemetery?"

"You are young and quite naive...Prisoners die. Some pass away from sickness; others from the lack of will to live and many more are executed." The slim, well dressed, attractive woman-not much older than I, I guessed-spoke like we have lived in a free country. Her speaking out, seemingly without fear to a total stranger, surprised me.

"Maybe we shouldn't talk...," I couldn't think of anything else to say.

"Why shouldn't we?"

"Well, there may be informers in the line. They may hear us and report us if we say something wrong," I tried to explain what concerned me.

"Let them do that...Could they hurt us any more? Would it be worse to be condemned to a smaller prison than our country?"

"I spent a few days in prison and I can tell you that it is no fun." My reluctance to speak, to confide in a total stranger, seemed to evaporate and she smiled sadly.

"I see...Do you want to hear my story? Do you want to know why I am here?" she asked and I saw no harm in listening; in spending the long wait by learning something about her, so I nodded my head in agreement.

She began and for a whole hour I was engrossed in listening to her story.

***

"I was a young, carefree university student, when I fell in love with a dear man, who, soon after, became my husband. Our parents were members of the Communist party and they have enjoyed many privileges. We were in love; we were totally carefree. We decided to get married, just three years ago and we were even given an apartment. We hoped to live a long, happy life, but that was not to be.

"My husband was invited to a bachelor party. We were married for two months only and he promised that by midnight he will return to me. He never did. After two, long days of waiting, I went to see those who attended the same party.

"His friends...or should I say his former friends, were not very keen to talk to me.

One by one I asked them what may have happened to my husband, but only one was willing to tell me and even that one made me swear that I will never repeat what he told me. He informed me that everyone at the party had a lot to drink, including my husband, and they all began to tell jokes; they tried to surpass each other. One of the guys proposed that they hold a contest. The one who tells the funniest joke will be rewarded, that chap suggested and when the contest was over, my husband was declared the winner. The initiator of the contest left to fetch the prize and within an hour my husband was arrested. The guy who left early must have worked for the AVO, I was informed and I was broken hearted.

"I went to the police, but got no help from them. They suggested that I should contact the Minister of Justice. After three weeks of constant badgering, I got an appointment with that great man. He informed me that he will be glad to review my husband's case, but first I must find him. If my husband committed a political crime then he must be in one of the prisons run by the secret police and he had no jurisdiction over those facilities. He seemed sincerely interested in my husband's case. He even gave me a list of all prisons run by the AVO.

"I left his office and began an intense campaign of writing letters to all the prisons. I asked them to let me know if my husband was incarcerated in that facility. In some cases the reply came fast. My husband was never in that prison, they informed me. The others waited for several months, before they sent a reply and even those replies came sporadically.

"When I had received the first letter that admitted my husband's presence, I rushed to that prison, hoping to see my dear husband. When I got to the first one, when I was allowed to speak to one of the officials, he informed me that my husband was transferred to another facility. The location of his new home they did not reveal however, that was a State secret, they informed me.

"I have visited five such prisons and that many times I was told the same thing. I almost gave up hope and then an unsigned letter came. A prisoner was given amnesty. My husband and the writer spent several months in the same facility. That kind man, who risked everything by writing to me, was in this prison just five days ago. Finally I know where he is...Today I may even be allowed to see him." She finished her sad, haltingly told story when one of the guards shouted at her.

"You woman...Who do you want to see?"

"My dear husband..."

I didn't catch the name she gave, but I saw her enter the iron gate and watched her disappear. Ten minutes later, I was still outside, when she reappeared. She was pale; her eyes full of tears; her former beauty seemed to have vanished and as she walked by me, she was about to collapse. I grabbed her, supported her and listened to what she had to say.

"He is here...This time they were quite willing to tell me...They even gloated..." Her misery I couldn't understand.

"If you finally found him, then why the tears?"

"I searched for my beloved for almost three long years, but they always lied to me; mislead me... But this time they couldn't hide their joy, as they showed me where my husband is."

"So where is he?"

"He is over there." She pointed behind the high, brick fence and the realization came to me.

"The poor man is dead. He was buried in the prison cemetery," I thought and offered my sympathy.

"Thank you, young man. I know you mean well, but nothing will ever heal my wound. This country is an evil place. If you treasure your life and the life of those you love, get out of here." After those few, dreadful words she staggered toward the burial ground.

***

A few minutes later, I sat by the dirty table and across from me sat my Aunt Gizella. She was never fat, but it seemed to me that her whole body melted. She was pale; she was unwell, but her eyes shone with the old fire.

"Some day I will avenge Jozsef's death," she said it without fear and I saw that the nearest guard was out of hearing distance.

"I was so sorry...I will never forgive myself for what I did." I wanted her to know.

"Don't you dare blame yourself...We will do it again. I will not remain in this country."

"Are they treating you well?" I hoped to change the subject.

"After seeing my Jozsef fall, with his guts hanging out, but still alive. After watching the high ranking AVO officer kick him until he felt no more pain. After six months of solitary confinement, to think about what I saw and experienced, being in a cell with three other women, I suppose I cannot complain about the treatment."

"You will be free soon...," I offered her the only thing I could.

"I have more than four years yet to serve. After that they will release me, but I will be no freer than the rest of the Hungarians. Enough of this Laszlo. Ten minutes is not a long time, so tell me about Rozsa and Ildiko and all the others. How are they?"

I told her what I could and before I finished, the guard cut me off.

"Your time is up. Get out of here." His rough voice didn't bother me, but seeing my Aunt grabbed by that ruffian and being dragged away rekindled all my old hatreds.

"Rot in hell all of you stupid bastards...I curse all the Communists who entrap decent men and women in this hopeless country. Some day my Aunt will be released...Some day all those I love will find new hope, a new life, a bright future, but it will have to be in another country." I muttered under my breath, as I walked out of the prison and without thinking I went to the adjoining cemetery.

There were no headstones; no crosses, just many, many simple markers. On the markers I saw no names. They contained only a date and a number.

"While we live, we are treated like dirt; we are considered less than nothing in this country..." I thought bitterly. "Even these unfortunate men and women, who died of unnatural causes, are robbed of their names. Even after their deaths they are condemned to remain just numbers."

***

I returned to my sanctuary and found relief in the arms of Rozsa.

Life had to go on. In spite of our miseries, we have experienced great joys. In spite of our joy, misfortune lurked all around us.

Even in the smallest of things we have experienced failure. The chicks Rozsa bought, months ago, some day to provide us with a few good meals, brought us a few surprises.

During Ildiko's first six months we have weighed her before and after each feeding, to know exactly how much milk she had sucked from her mommy's breasts. But for a long time it wasn't Ildiko we were weighing, it was our slowly growing chicks that got that treatment.

"When one of them gets close to weighing a kilogram, I will have you kill it Laszlo and we will have a feast my darling," Rozsa told me while we were in the process of weighing each one before we closed them away for the night.

"Do you think any one of them ever reach that weight?" I kidded Rozsa. "The heaviest is only half of that."

"The corn I use to feed them will get them there," Rozsa replied and she was right. At the end of September, one of the chickens got close to the magic weight and we were ready to celebrate that coming weekend.

Each morning Rozsa counted them, as she let them out and each evening she repeated the process and did the weighing. When I was home, I was her assistant.

Saturday night she told me that the next morning I will have to become the butcher.

Sunday morning we rose early, after all that was the day of our first chicken harvest.

"One, two, three...," she kept counting and she stopped after eleven.

"I thought we had twelve?" I told Rozsa.

"Maybe I miscounted. Get them back Laszlo."

I called them and like the good pets they were, they came willingly, but there were only eleven.

"Let's weigh the biggest one," I suggested and we soon found out that the one missing was the bird that weighed the most.

"Rozsa what do you think is happening?" I asked and the two of us were puzzled. Always the one, destined for our table, fell victim to some strange destiny.

"This is stupid," I announced, a few weeks later. "Out of twelve, only one puny chicken is left. It weighs not even half a kilogram. A neighbor must be weighing them too. They must be less fussy then us. You bought them; we feed them, but not a single bird graced our table. I wonder which neighbor is doing this. Let's not wait any longer...Tomorrow let's have the only one left."

"You are absolutely right Laszlo," Rozsa announced and on Sunday we ate well and had more reason to be delighted.

We have never missed a single broadcast of the Free Europe Radio and were always happy to hear the messages that came from Rozsa's parents. This Sunday's morning broadcast was meaningless to us, but the evening one gave us joy.

"This message is from the Death Head Butterfly," the announcer read slowly and I reached for Rozsa's hand. "The metamorphosis is complete. The butterfly is back safely."

"God was with us again...The CIA agent is out...At least that worry is off our shoulders, Rozsa. God helped someone else to our chickens, but in this matter He gave us His mercy."

***

The joy never failed to come when, after work, I was reunited with my little girl and my loving wife. We talked; wrote letters; admired the contents of parcels that came from Austria, once every two months; played with Ildiko, tried to teach her many games; listened to her growing vocabulary and sought our bed and reassured each other.

"Maybe tonight we will sleep well. Maybe they will not come for you Laszlo?" was Rozsa's usual last words, before we fell asleep. If we had a week of undisturbed sleep, we felt lucky. If we were lucky enough to have four weeks of that luxury, we tried to pretend that the AVO no longer existed.

Our pretending never lasted too long. My weekly meetings with my handler never ceased, but he received no information from me that was of any use, thus more and more frequently he became angry.

Slowly the pattern emerged. When his anger grew, after four to five weeks, our sleep was disturbed by another late night knock and once again I was taken from Rozsa and Ildiko.

They questioned me; they threatened me; they tried to sweet talk me, but in the end they always let me go and when that happened, at least four times, I knew without doubt that they still hoped to get back my Father-in-law, that they still needed me.

***

"Two weeks only and it will be Christmas again and there is nothing I can afford to give you," Rozsa told me.

"I have your love. I need nothing more...And besides, I have nothing to give you either. For Ildiko we will set up a small tree...Get her a toy and maybe a piece of clothing."

"I saved up some money, Laszlo, to get those things. We will have a wonderful Christmas...You will see."

Rozsa was right, but the most wonderful Christmas present came not from her, not from the relatives, but from the Chairman of the local Council.

"I asked you to come to see me, because I have good news for you Laszlo," he announced in his office, once I was seated.

"Good news I could use," I told the man.

"Your petition has been approved. The nursery will be closed down soon and you will have a home, here in *Bacsbokod*," the Chairman informed me.

"That is splendid. To have my family with me is like a dream. To be able to spend more time with them is beyond my comprehension. To stay with them late in the morning; to get back to them early afternoon, I will really enjoy. I don't know how to thank you."

"Well there may be a way. I could use your cooperation." He sounded reluctant to bring up the subject.

"I will be more than glad to do what I can."

"Very well then...Let me tell you what my problem is. When I promised you that house, I should have known better. Now hold on, just for a minute...I am not trying to break my promise. I am just trying to placate the Communist party. That house is the nicest building in our entire village. As soon as the party secretary got wind of the nursery being allowed to close, he came to me. He announced that the party wants it. I was left with no choice, but to appeal to you Laszlo. I hope you understand my situation and will accept my slightly modified offer."

"It depends on what you are offering." I wasn't pleased at all, but I had no desire to frustrate the Communist party.

"What I am offering is a roof over your family's head. Not as sumptuous as the nursery building, I do admit, but what else can I do under the circumstances?"

"I really do not blame you Comrade Chairman." I still didn't dare to call him by his first name; he never invited me to do that. "The nursery building is prime property, that I understand. Once it must have belonged to the richest man of the village."

"It did...Those poor people have been deported. They were *swabs*, or should I say that they were of German ancestry? The house was taken over by the State and that is when it became a nursery. Now it seems it will belong to the Communist party."

"The roof over my family's head...You haven't told me yet where will we live." I wanted to get him back on track.

"Yes, you are absolutely right...The place I am allowed to offer you is the former headquarters of the Communist party. Do you know the house?"

I recalled my visit to that place with Pallosy. The former owners of that large building were also *swabs*, who were deported. The stable, the barns, the *gore*-where the corn was kept-were all demolished and the building materials were sold by the party secretary. Only the large meeting hall and the smaller office were still in existence when Pallosy took me to see that cruel man.

"Yes, I do. I was there once."

"Do you think you could live there?"

"The where is not important...I will live anywhere where my wife and little daughter can be close to me. When could we move in?" I have made my decision and I wasn't eager to rock the boat any more than I already have.

"I am really pleased. To show you how pleased I am, I will get a flat-bed carriage, two horses and a driver to assist you with the move. Would you like that Laszlo?"

"When?"

"You may want to spend Christmas in your old home? In January, I am sure the building will be empty." The chairman made his promise and on January fourteen '56 he did deliver.

***

Saturday, January 14, I was freed from my teaching duties. No doubt Pallosy made this great concession to me at the request of the Chairman.

Once we have loaded all our scant possessions on the flat-bed, with the kind help of the driver, I said good-by to Ildiko and Rozsa.

"Catch the first train to our new home my darling. I will meet you there," I told Rozsa and my heart was full of joy, in spite of the apprehensions I felt about Rozsa's opinion of our new home.

A few hours later, I found out what she thought.

"Don't misunderstand me darling...I am not a fussy person...I am happy, as long as we are together," she began with a great deal of reluctance, while our belongings stood in the middle of the meeting hall. "Look around you Laszlo...We had trouble heating our small rooms, but this? How are we ever going to get it warmed up? This room is like an enormous cavern."

"Come look at our bedroom, I think you will be pleased." I lead her by her hand

and I carried Ildiko into the former office of the party secretary.

"We will put our bed here, right close to the stove. And Ildiko's crib, right over there. We will be warm enough here my darling. That other room we will use rarely. Maybe we will hold in it a party. A house warming party is what I mean."

It took Rozsa no more than a minute to make up her mind and she gave me a sweet kiss.

"Give me a few days darling and I will make a home out of this monster, then you can invite all the guests you wish."

"I knew you will like our new home. Thank you for your understanding. How many guests should I invite?"

"If I consider our wealth, I think we can have eight or ten. If I reflect on the size of our living room, you could invite at least a hundred fifty."

We spent the rest of the day placing our furniture, where Rozsa fancied.

"Well we have done it my precious Laszlo. It is not exactly what I have imagined, but it will do...Ildiko will have no choice, but to grow up in an almost empty warehouse." Rozsa laughed out and the three of us danced around the living room that would have been coveted by the manager of the largest dance hall.

That night we have retired early and when I fell into an exhausted, but happy sleep, I dreamt about the party secretary.

In my dream, the rotten bastard cursed me for having taken over the place that once was the seat of his power. He told me how much he envied me for the beautiful woman who lay beside me. He complained about the ugly, stupid wife he had to contend with and before he vanished from my dream, he warned me that bad things were about to transpire. I woke with a start and tried to banish the fear the dream created.

"Thank God he is no longer in power...He is gone...He won't be able to cause us trouble...It was only a stupid dream."

***

Two weeks later our guests arrived. They came in pairs, greeted us warmly, but the chill of our home touched all of us, at least until I served the drinks. After a while the wine and *palinka* began to loosen our guests' tongues.

"Are you going to form a new political party Laszlo? You have the meeting place already," Bela Kovacs began to kid me.

"You should do that. You have the room and also has the gift of gab." Pista Floch added, while Rozsa and the women surveyed the apartment.

"How are you ever going to heat this?" Mrs. Floch asked Rozsa, when she sat down beside my wife on the old chesterfield. "Maybe you should build two walls across. You could make it into three smaller rooms."

"Not a bad idea," Rozsa replied and turned to me, "Don't you think Laszlo?"

"I would have to apply for bricks. Monday I think I will do just that."

"While you are at it, you might as well find out how to dry out the walls. They are dripping with water," someone else suggested and I have made mental notes of everything required.

We sat down by the small table, placed on the bare floor, in the middle of the cavern. Our meal, although not sumptuous, was well prepared-by then Rozsa became a fine cook and a gracious hostess-and the ten of us ate everything, Rozsa and I were able to offer. Our glasses filled with red wine, my heart brimmed with happiness and joy, as I listened to Bela's toast.

"I have known Laszlo for a few years and admire his determination. Without that he would have never been able to get a place from the authorities. His lovely wife, our friend, Rozsa and their little daughter, Ildiko now have a home. May they be always blessed with plenty; may they enjoy each other's company; may they have a fabulous new year. I know my dear friends that my wishes for you seem like impossible dreams, but the winds are changing...'56 will bring us good things, I feel that in my bones. To Rozsa, Laszlo and Ildiko, I command all of you to drink."

"Now that Bela spoke, I cannot remain silent. All he wished this happy couple, I wish them too, but the change Bela feels, in his bones, is only the chill of this huge cavern." Pista Floch finished his short speech and while the others chatted, I contemplated my next step.

"Monday I will talk to the Chairman. I cannot allow my family to suffer any more...I brought them here. I must bring about a few improvements."

***

"So how do you like your new place Laszlo? Is your wife pleased? Is she happy?"

"I don't want to sound ungrateful, Comrade Chairman, but the place needs a lot of work. I am not afraid to do that. But I need bricks, materials to make mortar and two doors at least. Do you think you could help us?"

"In a little while we shall see."

***

The weather began to turn much colder and when I arrived home from school, the chill of the cavern hit me. We could find comfort, warmth and joy only in the small room- which served as kitchen, living room and bedroom. Under the thick, feather bedding we were warm and snuggled gladly.

"Is there any news from the Chairman?" Rozsa asked me day after day and each and every time I gave the same answer.

"Have patience my love. The Chairman is a decent man. I know he will soon do something."

Two weeks have passed with great rapidity. From eight to one I taught my students and I enjoyed every minute of my teaching. I attended the rare staff meetings, but rarely learned anything of great importance. I have suffered through the supervising committee's visits, but by then I was crafty enough, thus I was rarely criticized and never reprimanded. Now and then I offered my volunteer services to the government, but I did that more rarely.

My time with Ildiko and Rozsa were far too precious to share frequently with anyone, thus most of the time-from one to seven thirty, the next morning-I was with the two people I most loved and not even the cold, the shortages, the occasional harassment by the AVO, my weekly meetings with my controller-at a new location-could ruin our bliss.

One night, about three weeks after my last meeting with the Chairman, Rozsa went to visit a friend and I stayed home to mind Ildiko. I heard the car door slam, under our bedroom window and turned out the light, peaked out from behind the curtain and saw three figures approach our gate, in the darkness.

"What am I going to do? They came for me, I am sure. I cannot leave Ildiko alone. Dear God don't let them take me again." Suddenly I realized that they couldn't be the AVO. The time was wrong. It was only eight. I opened the gate, saw their extended hands and shook them gladly.

"These two comrades are from the Ministry of the Interior," the Chairman announced, but made no attempt to introduce them. "They wish to talk with you…They would like to look at your house. I have urgent work to do, so I will leave all of you for now. Please give your cooperation to the comrades, Mr. Lichter," the Chairman announced and I sensed a measure of his annoyance.

"We have been charged with the task of examining your place. May we call you Laszlo?" The taller one seemed to be in charge and the other one remained silent.

"Call me Laszlo, if that is what you wish, but what will I call you comrades?"

"Call us your guardian angels. You complained about the condition of your living quarters and we came." For a minute I was truly flabbergasted.

"They came from the Ministry of Interior. They seem to be powerful men...Their nice, big car; the suits they wear seem to indicate that. They want to improve this place; they are here to help us," I thought and yet I had an uneasy feeling.

"So what improvements would you require Lichter? We desire nothing less than to make this place warm; to make it dry; to turn this place into a proper home. Don't think of the cost Laszlo, just tell us what is needed."

I led the two of them around the large room; pointed out the dripping, brick walls.

"These need to be dried out," I suggested meekly.

"What else?" the second official spoke up.

"This meeting hall must be walled off, to make three rooms out of it." I recalled Mrs. Floch's suggestion and proposed it with boldness.

"Is there anything more we could do to make this place suitable Laszlo?" The first official took charge again.

"A new stove in each room, so that those rooms could be heated."

"Anything else. You better tell us now, you may not have another chance. Tonight we are going back to Budapest. You probably know that *Rakosi* is gone and so is the terror our former leader had created."

I couldn't believe what I heard. I knew that Rakosi fell from favor in '55. I was aware that we had a new Communist leader, Gero, but I saw no lessening of the terror, until now. I began to feel comfortable with my two guardian angels.

"Would it be too much to ask to have a few rugs in each room? I cannot afford such luxuries...But that would make the place more fit for human beings."

"Thank you for your suggestions Laszlo. We have made notes of everything you requested. I assure you, in the name of our Government, that the improvements will be carried out soon. Now we must go...Our job is done...You have been really helpful." The leader extended his hand to shake mine and the other official followed his example.

I could hardly wait for Rozsa's arrival and when I heard her footsteps approach the door, I rushed to her, kissed her, held her in my arms and made my announcement.

"Bela was right."

"What do you mean, Laszlo?"

"Do you remember his nice toast? Do you remember what he said Rozsa?"

"I think I do, but for the life of me I do not understand what makes you so cheerful."

"'The winds are changing...'56 will bring us good things, I feel that in my bones.' That is what Bela said and he was right," I informed Rozsa.

"It may be true my beloved, but I see no improvement in this place. It is bitter cold and wet. The Chairman did nothing for us."

"But he did, my beloved...While you were away, he brought two officials to see to the improvements. They even called themselves my guardian angels."

"Are you kidding me, Laszlo?"

It was then that I told Rozsa everything that happened and our joy was limitless, until the next morning, when I found out that there was no end to the Communists' conniving.

***

I was called out of my class by one of the teachers.

"You better see your wife. She is waiting for you downstairs." I was told and I almost broke my neck, running down the stairs. I found her crying.

"What is the matter my dearest?"

She was too upset to tell me what happened.

"You must come home, at once Laszlo."

The two of us ran to our place and not even my hand holding Rozsa's could stem her crying.

In the yard stood a large wagon, loaded with bricks and other building materials. In our cavern, stood two policemen and three busy workers.

"You stop right now!" I screamed at two of them, who were in the process of taking out our chesterfield.

They obeyed instantly, hearing my shouted order and not knowing who I was.

"You better not interfere with our orders," screamed at me one of the policemen.

"What orders are you talking about?" I turned to him.

"You are to vacate this place. That is what we were told."

"Who told you that?"

"The Deputy Chairman issued the order."

"The Chairman gave us this place. I will not let you move a thing. We are going nowhere."

"You are...Your furniture is being taken to the street," the policeman retorted.

"The hell it is!" I shouted even louder.

"You take it up with the officials, but in the meantime you better let the men do their job." The policeman made a threatening move and I knew that I must take my fight elsewhere.

***

"I must see the Chairman at once," I shouted at the secretary as soon as I entered.

"He is expecting you Comrade Lichter," she told me and led me into the inner office.

"What the hell is going on?" I wasn't in the mood to use his official title.

"I don't know how to tell you how sorry I really am." The Chairman sat behind his desk, he was truly shaken.

"You better tell me...I have little time. We are being thrown out of our place. Two policemen and three workers are harassing my wife; are taking our furniture to the street; upsetting my little daughter. They are taking bricks into our flat."

"I know Laszlo. I wish it wasn't so."

"Are you not in charge? Are you not the Chairman?"

He extended his arms above his table, put his two wrists side by side and asked me to look at them.

I was puzzled, but soon my impatience returned.

"What am I supposed to see?"

"The handcuffs."

"You should be handcuffed for what you are doing to us, but you are not."

"In that you are mistaken. There are no real handcuffs on my wrists, I do admit, but that makes me no less a prisoner. Let me explain Laszlo.

"Before I took those two officials to your house, they didn't tell me their real reason for the visit. When they came back they revealed everything. First they told me that any property that once belonged to the Communist party remains their property forever. Then they informed me that one of the collective farms is getting a new Communist party secretary and it was their job to find a place for him. The improvements you suggested will be made, just as they promised you, but it will not be for your benefit. It is being done to make comfortable that Communist bastard.

"I objected to what they were doing, but all my arguments, all my pleading, produced only smiles and threats.

"They told me not to interfere with the Communist party's plans. I asked them how they picked that place. They told me that my Deputy made the suggestion. That God-damn bastard is mean, rotten to the core, but he has the real power. I am only a figure-head. I hope you can see now that even without real cuffs I am handcuffed and unable to reverse what is happening."

Although I was greatly disturbed by his revelations, I began to understand.

"The poor man is risking his life by telling me the truth...He is decent...I must always remember the risks he took."

The door banged open and a skinny, red faced man, with an arrogant, narrow mustache, came in and grabbed one of my shoulders.

"You should be home...You should help getting your belongings out of the party's house. You are wasting your time here, Lichter."

"I am staying in that place, unless you kill me!" my words tumbled out, without thinking.

"I can oblige, I assure you. What are you? A traitor and so is your wife. Do you think anyone would object? You are nothing...Get the fuck out of here, before I kick your balls, so hard, that you will be unable to make another kid."

I shook with rage...I was ready to take him on...I lost all control...I was like a maniac. I began to scream at the Deputy.

"I got your party a brand new house to plunder...That wasn't enough you thief?" I would have gone on, but the Chairman stood up, towered over the two of us and began to shout.

"Shut your mouth Lichter. Not another word or you will regret everything you say. Please leave us Comrade Deputy. I know how to handle this obstinate bastard. I assure you the apartment will be empty before night falls."

The Deputy was about to leave, but his parting shot made me feel real fear.

"You better be out of there Lichter. Soon! And you better keep watching your back, for I swear that I will get you some day," he screamed as he left the office.

"I am sorry for what I said," the Chairman began. "If I allowed you to say one more word, he would have finished you off. You would not have been his first victim."

"I know what you were trying to do and I appreciate it. But what will I do now? Where will my family live? We gave up our place in *Baja* and tonight my family will have to spend the night under the stars. In this bitter cold they will freeze." Before the Chairman was able to say anything, I got an idea and rushed out of his office.

***

Twenty minutes later, I led Rozsa into our bedroom, while the workers were doing their job. I explained to her what I planned to do and asked her to do certain things. I grabbed the portable typewriter-with lies and conniving I was able to convince Pallosy to trust me with it-walked into the huge room, brought inside a small table and chair. Placed them in the middle of the cavern and began to type. Two men carried bricks in. One began to build the walls I suggested to my 'guardian angels'.

Within two minutes Rozsa stood beside me and as instructed she asked me loudly.

"Who are you writing to Laszlo?" From the corner of my eyes, I saw that one of the policemen was within hearing distance.

"Have you ever heard of the National Board of Control Committee?"

"I don't think so."

"After Rakosi was removed, a committee was set up to investigate any and all anti-Communist activities. Well maybe that is not the correct way to describe it. The people of Hungary were becoming very restless, thanks to the constant terror. The new Communist Government figured that there are people in power, who by committing atrocious deeds, are intentionally creating anti-Communist sentiments. The Committee, I heard, is trying to find out who these criminals are. I am writing to them, Rozsa."

"What will you tell them?" she asked what I wanted to hear.

"Atrocities committed in this village. That is what I will bring to their attention," I informed her, loudly enough for the policeman to hear; turned back to my typing and was delighted to see the policeman take off.

I had typed for over twenty minutes, detailing how families were thrown out of their houses; how they were robbed of all their possessions. I described the atrocities, but gave no names or dates. I implicated the Deputy; the Police Chief and a few others. Before I was able to finish the lengthy document, I heard the rough voice of the returning policeman.

"The Chairman and Deputy Chairman want to see you immediately."

I took my time to complete the document and wondered how it will all turn out.

"I am taking a terrible risk, but I will do anything to save my family. I will lie; I will connive; I will threaten those in power." I had decided before I stepped inside the Chairman's office.

***

"We had a long conversation, after you left," the Deputy announced and his statement, his tone of voice was no longer threatening.

"I am glad to hear. What have you decided?" I asked and thought about the advice my Father gave me, before his first imprisonment.

"There are small tyrants and there are tyrants above them. Our new society was built on fear. Imagine a long ladder with many rungs. On each rung sits a group of tyrants, but there are other tyrants above them. On the very top sits Rakosi, but the ladder doesn't end there. It continues in the Soviet Union and on top of that enormous ladder sits Stalin himself. The ladder shakes and swings endlessly, but it is not the one at the very top who fears the fall. That fear exists in reverse order.

"'Will I be able to climb any higher? Or will the one above me cause my fall?' they ask themselves constantly and keep wary eyes on all above them." The lesson my Father taught me, I used once before with success. "This time it is the deputy who fears the swinging of that ladder," I assured myself.

"Well we talked about your predicament Laszlo." The Deputy was almost kind, tried to show me that he was understanding. "Maybe you could give us what you typed? Consider this whole thing a misunderstanding."

"My furniture is in the yard...We have no idea where we will sleep tonight...We have been dispossessed. Do you call all that a misunderstanding?"

"If you got another place to live...If we helped you to move into another flat, would you be willing to forget this incident?"

"I doubt I will ever forget what you put us through, but in exchange for a place I will give you the document. Although it is expected."

"Expected by whom?" the Deputy raised his voice.

"The Chairman of the Board of Control Committee. I wrote to him last night. Alerted him to my coming detailed letter. I wasn't fooled by the two officials, who came to see me last night. I knew that something was fishy about them. The letter is already mailed by a trusted friend."

"You are lying, Lichter," the deputy screamed at me.

"If you really believe that I am that stupid, then call my bluff," I suggested boldly and held my breath.

"I wouldn't have you and your family live on the street. I cannot be as cruel as you Laszlo. The movers will move you this afternoon, into your new apartment. I know your wife will be pleased. The place is neither wet, nor cold. Now hand over the document," the deputy ordered.

"And what will I say if the Board's Chairman happens to inquire?"

"I have no doubt you will think of something." The Deputy reached out for the document.

"I will not be tricked again. You will have this after we are in the new place."

"I could have you thrown into prison...I could make you disappear."

"You could, I am sure, but the outcome may not be to your liking," I closed the conversation and by mid afternoon we were in our new apartment.

***

It was a very large farm house. When the movers opened the huge wooden gate, a large, covered, entry way greeted us. The horses and the carriage they pulled emerged from the entry way into an enormously large yard. The yard widened out and behind a low stone fence, two barns, several pig pens could be seen.

One of the workers unlocked a door, to the left of the entrance. Rozsa, carrying Ildiko, and I stepped inside the hallway, explored the two rooms with their high vaulted ceilings. Saw the beautiful, ceramic covered, floor to ceiling stove. We entered the small kitchen and descended the three steps to the pantry.

I saw Rozsa's eyes taking in everything and was delighted to see that her tears were replaced with smiles of pleasure as she surveyed our palace. We stepped outside and entered a large storage area, where steps ascended to a huge attic.

"So what do you think my love?" I asked her when we have completed our tour.

"I can't believe our luck. This place is a hundred times better than what we had. How did you ever manage to get this Laszlo?"

"If I knew I would tell you. Some day we may find out. Now let's go to make sure that the movers put everything where you want them Rozsa."

An hour later the men left us and we fell into each other's arms and celebrated our good fortune with fervent kisses.

"I wonder who lives in the other apartment," Rozsa said, after we ate our supper.

"Maybe we should go over to introduce ourselves," I suggested and we walked across the yard, knocked on a door and were greeted promptly.

Their name was Bencsik. They worked in one of the collective farms and behind the yard they grew vegetables. They had several pigs in the pig pens. Five milking cows in one of the barns. Behind the fence chickens, ducks and hissing geese lived, we were told by Mr. Bencsik, who prided himself in being a hard working farmer.

"You have a really nice place," I complimented our neighbor.

"A place is only that...What really counts is my hard working wife and my girls Mr. Lichter." He spoke slowly, with the drawl of a real Hungarian peasant and in spite of the hospitality he extended to my family, by insisting that we eat from his home made sausages and from his wife's home baked bread; that we taste the wine he made; and that Ildiko drink a glass of fresh milk provided by his milking cows, I felt that he harbored some resentment.

We talked for at least an hour and before we parted, I expressed my hope that we will become good friends.

"I try to make friends with all my neighbors, as I did with the old lady, who lived where you live now Laszlo," Lajos Bencsik stated and I sensed that behind his words there was something else.

"The old lady...Why did she move and when?"

"Maybe you know the reason far more than I? She never moved, as you put it Laszlo...She was moved by someone else."

"But how could I know? I never knew her, for that matter, I never knew about her anything. Nobody made mention of a former occupant."

"You mean a former owner."

"I am not sure I understand. If she owned this wonderful flat, then why did she give it up?"

"I don't know that and I don't think she knows that either."

"What do you mean Mr. Bencsik?" Rozsa listened to our conversation and she became paler by the minute.

"I don't think she knows that you are living in her place."

"How could she not know?" I asked and began to fear what may have happened.

"It is like this Laszlo. The old woman lived here for several years. Each year she went to visit her daughter, who lives quite far away. When she did that she just locked up everything and went, as she did a week ago. Then around noon today, to my greatest surprise, three men and a policeman arrived. They opened up her place and took out all her belongings. I tried to find out what was going on, but they were rather close mouthed and ordered me not to ask any more questions. Then you and your stuff arrived and that was that."

"But that is preposterous...They moved us here without her knowledge; without her permission?"

"That is what I suspect." He closed the conversation and when we put Ildiko into her crib, we fell into bed totally exhausted.

"Do you think Laszlo that we have caused someone to lose her home?" Rozsa asked.

"Tomorrow I will find out. Now sleep my darling. There is nothing I can do tonight...We are living in strange times...We should be happy we are here and not under the start, not in the cold. We must look after our little daughter." I turned away, but sleep didn't come to me. I was thinking about that poor, old lady.

"What will happen when she comes home? Will she blame us? Will she blame the regime? Will she understand that we are all pawns in a great chess game?"

***

Next afternoon I went to see the Chairman again and I was happy to find him alone.

"Will you tell me whose apartment was I moved into?"

"Just an old woman's."

"Did she give her permission to have us moved there?"

"My Deputy needs no permission to do what is expedient."

"How can I live there knowing that I dispossessed someone?"

"You must take from this life what you can, Laszlo. Principles no longer matter."

"But principles matter to me."

"Your family should matter to you more..." His voice died off, he seemed to tire of answering my questions.

"Just tell me one thing. Will she be compensated for her loss?"

"Compensated in what way?"

"Well she lost her apartment and all her belongings. Will she be given money and her stuff back?"

"Her apartment we considered abandoned. She spent a lot of time with her daughter each year. By her being there made her a resident of another place. So for the apartment she will not be paid, but her stuff she will get back. All of her things are kept in storage. Does this answer all of your concerns Laszlo?"

"I suppose it does, but I sure don't feel good about this whole thing."

"Nor do I, but remember what we are and where we live. I promised you roof over your family's head and that you have. Don't try to rock the boat...Try to understand political reality."

For many days I struggled with my conscience, but as time passed it fell more and more silent, until the old woman walked into our place.

"May I speak with Mr. and Mrs. Lichter?"

"I am he. Please come in, make yourself comfortable." I suspected who she was the minute she entered. She looked around the room. A tear drop appeared in the corner of her eye and she began to speak.

"I used to live here...Did you know that?"

"We knew someone lived here," Rozsa told her.

"May I ask you a question?" the woman replied.

"Please do," I suggested.

"Are you a powerful man?"

"I am only a teacher."

"Are you a Communist?"

"I am not and I will never be."

"Then how did you manage to get me dispossessed?"

It was time to unburden my soul, to tell her everything. She listened to my story of how I fought to have the nursery closed; how I was promised that house; how I was moved into another. Then I told her about our need to have the place improved and described the visit by the two officials. I continued to tell her as much as I could, hoping that she would understand.

When I finished, she wiped away her tears and made her pronouncement.

"I came here to show you my anger, but I cannot do that. You have suffered more than I; you have been manipulated. I can now clearly see what happened. I will live with my daughter and now I have an excuse to do that all the time. You have a lovely wife, treasure her. You have a beautiful child, look after her. You have scruples; make sure you will retain that. Now that I know that it is not a family of Communists who will live in my place, I will not be unhappy. The best of luck to all of you. Enjoy the place, as I have enjoyed it. I feel no anger; I do not blame you. May the good Lord deliver all of us from the Communists' yoke. May He correct all injustices."

From that night on we were able to truly enjoy our palace and lived there month after month in almost complete bliss, marred only by events that were not of our making.

***

In a few weeks Bencsiks and us warmed to each other. One of their little girls, Marika, only a couple of years older than Ildiko, began to play with our daughter. Rozsa and Mrs. Bencsik commenced their friendship. When we had the time, Lajos and I had long conversations.

During one of these bull sessions, shortly after the old lady's visit, Lajos enlightened me.

"I owe you an apology Laszlo. The first time I set eyes on you, I was bitter about how you moved next door. I was wrong to be like that."

"How did you come to know that Lajos?"

"The former owner, that old lady, came to visit us, after he saw you. She told us everything. After that I had no reason to blame you...I want to make friends with you. Will you accept my apology?"

"You owe me no apology, but if that makes you feel better, I accept it gladly."

"Now let me teach you a few survival skills Laszlo," Lajos offered.

"I am the teacher, but I will accept your suggestions gladly."

"First, you should buy a piglet. You should feed it and by December it would feed you."

"Do you know someone who would have one for sale?"

"I have several piglets. I will be glad to sell you one, if you could get the necessary papers."

"Consider it done. What else should I do?"

"You should think beyond this year. For the following year you should raise two pigs."

"But that would take a lot of corn."

"Yes, it would, but aren't teachers entitled to an acre of land. Have you claimed your acre yet?"

"I never did. I lived in Baja. It would have been impossible to cultivate that land. Besides, what do I know about farming?"

"It takes hard work; a bit of luck. The rest I could teach you," Lajos offered and within a week, I was granted permission to buy a piglet and to cultivate an acre of land, but not without strict conditions.

"The pig you cannot sell, it must be for your own use. The land you must use to grow corn only. Half of your crop you must donate to us. The other half you can use any way you wish," the official informed me.

When I showed the papers to Lajos, he sold the piglet to me for almost nothing.

"Did you get your land Laszlo?" Lajos asked me.

"I got one acre, but there are conditions attached to my using it."

"There are always conditions in this country, I know that well. Half of what you grow, you must donate, the other half is yours Laszlo. Am I correct?"

"That is exactly what I was told, but I was told other things as well. They even made me sign a paper."

"What are you allowed to grow?"

"Corn only."

"Corn is a precious commodity. The government needs it badly. How much do they expect you to harvest?"

"Eight tons is my quota." Lajos gave out a whistle after he heard about my paper harvest.

"Pray for enough rain; for enough sun-shine. Ask the Lord not to send us hailstorms. If He grants all of your wishes and you work very hard, you will fulfill your quota Laszlo," Lajos informed me.

"What happens if I harvest less?"

"If your crop will be only four tons, the Government will take their share and your attic will be empty."

"Do you mean Lajos that they will take it all? I believed that I have to give them only half of my harvest."

"Half is right, but it is half of what they expect you to grow, not half of what the Lord will give you."

"What happens if my crop fails completely? Can that happen Lajos?"

"Once, two years ago, that is what happened to me. If you are unlucky Laszlo and all of your crop gets wiped out, you will still owe the Government four tons of corn. You will have to buy that and give it to the bastards."

"I cannot believe that. I wish I have never agreed to farm that land. A crop failure could bankrupt me."

"I wouldn't worry about that Laszlo. Now that you became a teacher/farmer, you will have to live like I do. Early morning you go out to your field and work like hell. After you finish your teaching, you go back to your land to keep on working. Always watch the skies, always pray to the good Lord and always hope for the best."

"But my land is seven kilometers from here. How will I get there?"

"You cannot afford to walk that far, it would cut into your working time. Buy an old bicycle and paddle back and forth, but tend your land well."

I thanked Lajos for all his advice and within a week, I was the owner of an old, beat-up bicycle.

***

Once I informed my parents about our changed circumstances, my Mother and Father decided to pay us a visit. The train that brought them to *Bacsbokod* arrived around six o'clock in the morning and the three of us walked the long distance.

My Mother held Ildiko to her chest and showered her with her kisses, until Ildiko began to protest.

"Enough Grandma..."

"But I love you!" She followed her statement with a few more kisses.

"Let me show you the apartment, Mother." I wasn't sure if Rozsa wanted to show off our new place or just wanted to rescue Ildiko. The two of them walked around and when they returned, my Mother turned to my Father.

"Now this is a place to my liking, not like the dump we live in Ferenc. Laszlo is only half your age and they have a nice apartment. But you had to waste all our money on that stupid factory and what did that get us?" She would have continued to berate my Father, but his action and mine stopped that.

"I see you are still playing the old record. It will be completely worn out before long," my Father interjected with good humor.

"Let's go to the kitchen and have a good breakfast," I suggested to make my Mother become silent.

We sat around the table, set with many fine staples, most of them bought from Mr. Bencsik.

"Now this is really nice. Laszlo is a good provider..." My Mother would have gone on and on, but the banging on our gate stopped her.

"I will go and see who it is." I stood up and for a few seconds I felt relief. It always bothered me when my Mother berated my Father; when she was unfair to him. Thank God it only happened when she had an audience and since my Father spent most of his time on a ship, that happened quite rarely.

When I opened the door, I almost fainted. My controller stood there, his face sporting a grin.

"Aren't you going to invite me in?"

"We have company...And besides I don't appreciate you coming here."

"I know you have company, but only your parents. You don't appreciate an agent of the AVO visiting your home, that I appreciate, but I am not here in that capacity."

"Then what are you doing here?"

"Just a friendly visit. I hope you will introduce me to your parents as an old friend of yours. Well? Let's go in and invite me to have breakfast. I am famished."

I did as I was told and soon after the six of us, including Ildiko, sat around our kitchen table.

"Where did you ever get this butter?" the agent/friend asked.

"Where do you think?" my Mother's sharp tongue sprang into action. "He sure didn't get it in one of the stores. Empty shelves and useless stuff is all we can find there. He bought it from the farmer, right across the yard."

"Well it is the best butter I ever had. And the sausages are truly magnificent." The agent smacked his lips together. "Too bad your in-laws Laszlo cannot get such fine food in Austria."

My Mother needed no further provocation.

"You don't know what you are talking about, young man. Austria is a free country. A neutral country, I hear. They are no longer occupied like..."

"Mother, please eat and drink. Really there is no need for this discussion. Didn't you teach me not to eat and talk at the same time?"

"In that case I will stop eating, if my doing both bothers you Laszlo."

"Let her talk. I am fascinated," the provocateur suggested and I was unable to control my Mother's tongue. She had the audience; she had the right topic and she wasn't going to let my friend remain ignorant.

"Now as I was saying the Austrians are free. Have you ever seen a parcel Rozsa got from her parents? I guess not. Well some day you should go and see. The shoes and clothing that they send are better than anything our glorious workers produce in this country. The chocolates and candies melt in your mouth." I couldn't stand the thought of my Mother getting herself in trouble and seeing that my Father remained silent, I tried to stop her once again.

"Don't exaggerate Mother, please."

"So I am exaggerating? Didn't you yourself brag to us about all the fine things they sent? Didn't you tell us about the silk scarves they sew into the coat sleeves? The scarves you sell to your customers? Tell your friend how much do you get for one scarf Laszlo."

"Forget it Mother. My friend is not interested in these topics."

"But I am. Do as your Mother asked Laszlo." My controller was like a bulldog, he wouldn't let go, once he realized that my Mother was a gold mine of information.

"A hundred *Forints* for one scarf," I grunted out my confession.

"Do you hear that? They send at least a dozen scarves in each package. One thousand two hundred *Forints* Laszlo gets for them. How many months does it take for you Laszlo to earn that much money?"

"A month and a half..," I forced out the words.

"But that is not all...They even get two or three half kilograms containers of cocoa in each package. Do you know how many decagrams that is young man?"

"One container must contain fifty decagrams, I reckon."

"You reckoned right. Laszlo has a lot of buyers for that stuff too. Tell him Laszlo...Don't be so shy...What are friends for, but to confide in them. Am I not right? What was your name young man? I don't think I caught it when Laszlo introduced you."

"Just call me Arpad." The agent didn't remind my Mother of the fact that I used no name, introduced him only as a friend.

"Well, will you tell Arpad how much cocoa you sell to each of your customers and how much do you get?"

I could have screamed at my Mother; I could have shaken her for what she did. During all our meetings, my controller got less information than he did during this cursed breakfast.

"I really don't think...," I began lamely, but Mother would have none of it.

"Oh Laszlo is so foolish. He has a suspicious nature. If he didn't tell us that you were an old friend of his, I would have thought that he suspects you too. You can tell your friend Laszlo, how much money you make by selling the cocoa. And you might as well tell him, how you cheat your customers."

"That is enough Ilonka. If you don't shut your mouth, I will find a basin, full of cold water," my Father issued the threat.

"We are not home Ferenc! May I remind you? You will not degrade me front of Laszlo's friend." My Mother's eyes blazed and my Father just gave up.

"Now back to where we were. Tell your friend Laszlo all about the cocoa."

I glanced at Rozsa. She hung her head dejectedly. I looked at my Father, who spread his arms to indicate that he was helpless. I found no escape hatch, so I told 'my friend' what I did.

"Once I told a few people that we have received cocoa from Austria, they begged me to sell them a small quantity. The first time I did that, I made up packages of one decagram and satisfied all of them. They use it for baking a special Hungarian cake, as you well know. Soon others have found out, but by then I didn't have any to sell, so I took their orders and promised them some, when the next shipment arrives. When the cocoa arrived in the next package, my orders amounted to more than what we had, so I mixed the cocoa with icing sugar and I satisfied all my customers. They were delighted. This way I disappointed nobody and I even made more money." I made my confession.

"I never knew Laszlo how talented you were. Being a black marketer is punishable in this country, but I assure you nobody will find out from me. In fact I wouldn't mind to have some cocoa either. Do you think you can sell me some the next time you get a parcel?"

"You will have some..," I gave in.

"Is there anything else you want Arpad? Nylons, scarves, all kind of nice things, Laszlo could get for you. He could even do more. Couldn't you Laszlo?" My Mother was getting on even more dangerous grounds and I had to stop her.

"I see everybody finished breakfast. Rozsa I am sure you want to wash the dishes. Mother will help you," I suggested and was happy to see the two women leave us.

"She is a bit touched, I am sorry to admit Arpad. I hope you didn't take anything seriously my wife said during breakfast?" my Father whispered, probably hoping that he will not be heard by Mother.

"Give it no more thought...I enjoyed both the breakfast and the free flowing conversation. I think I better go now Laszlo. Guide me out." Arpad waved good-by to the women, caressed Ildiko's face, who by then sat on my lap.

I handed Ildiko over to her Grandpa and followed my guest out of the house.

"The AVO sure made a mistake Laszlo."

"I don't know what you are talking about." I was fuming inside. "My Mother should have known better than to talk the way she did. This conniving bastard, who gave himself the name Arpad, sure set me up good," I thought bitterly.

"We should have forced your Mother to be the informer. Nothing escapes her and we would know everything." Arpad laughed as he made that statement.

"Leave my Mother alone...She is a simple woman, as you can see. She just enjoys hearing the sound of her own voice. Please don't bother her...Let her be."

"It depends on you Laszlo. From this day on you better cooperate with us. If not, you will find that not only you, your wife, your child, but even your parents will face our wrath. Oh, by the way, you no longer need to meet me. When I need you, I will find you." Arpad/my friend/the AVO agent left me and from that day on I saw him rarely.

***

Bela was right. The early part of '56 brought many changes, but the greatest of change wasn't exactly to my liking. I was a teacher/farmer, who had many students, but not a horse, not a plow and to find someone to plow our land took quite some time. All those who could have done the job were too busy with their own plowing and planting. I would have been helpless, but Lajos and the dear Lord intervened.

"My field is plowed; my seeds are in. I will skip a day from work at the collective farm. I will do your plowing," Lajos announced and a few days later, Rozsa and I bent double with the task of planting.

I took Rozsa on my bicycle to our land and watched, not without envy, how the small, green shoots began to appear everywhere, except in our plot of land, where we did our late planting. A few days later came the frost and the tiny green plants were wiped out, but our little corn seeds rested under the rich earth, still protected. As time has passed the green shoots appeared and ours were healthy.

Two weeks later the Danube and its many tributaries were in full flood. Our classrooms were no longer used to teach children; instead in each classroom dozens of flood fighters were billeted. They slept on straw; they had inadequate washroom facilities; they had no time to look after themselves. Our school was soon infested with lice and fleas and bed-bugs. When the flood receded, so did they and Pallosy ordered to have the school opened immediately.

"This is horrible," I told my friends. "Pallosy is asking for big trouble. Many kids will get sick from the filth the workers created. We should demand a complete clean-up, before the students are allowed in."

Most of the teachers were afraid to fight for what was needed, although they agreed with me. But there was one exception and the help came from an unexpected quarter.

"I am with you Laszlo. Let's go and tell Pallosy what we think," Pista Janics announced and I welcomed his help. I knew that he was an informer, but so was I in a way. I lost my right to condemn him.

"Let's go and talk to Pallosy," I told Pista and the two of us waded through garbage to reach the principal's office.

He sat behind his desk and Pista addressed our great leader.

"We came to see you, although I came reluctantly. We have something to ask you Comrade Pallosy."

"Ask, if you must, but be quick about it."

"Maybe Laszlo should do the asking, he is much better with words than I." Pista tricked me, but I was so angry that I was unable to control myself, unable to see the trap, my former friend set me.

"I want you to delay the school's opening. The place is filthy...It should be cleaned up. Our students deserve to be protected." I said my piece.

"I am the principal and I am not going to be ordered around by someone like you Lichter," Pallosy shouted at me, but I stood my ground.

"I object...I will urge the parents not to allow their children to enter this place, until it is cleaned and disinfected."

"You do what you want and so will I. The school will open now and this conversation is over. Get out of here," Pallosy shouted and I heard and smelled the loud escape of his foul body gases.

"I am sorry Laszlo that I let you speak for me too. It seems we have accomplished nothing, but we are not finished yet." Pista turned to me in the corridor.

"There is nothing more we can do." I was ready to accept defeat.

"You are wrong Laszlo. Come with me." I followed him like unwary sheep follow the butcher. He walked to the main entrance, unlocked the door and faced the waiting students.

"The place is filthy..," he shouted at the top of his lungs.

The students milled around, seemingly unable to decide whether to enter or to head home. I didn't know what to do. I have decided to let Pista handle the situation.

"I know that not many of you trust me. I am sure you trust Mr. Lichter more." Pista shouted over their heads and his words propelled me into the limelight.

"Mr. Lichter should we go in or should we go home?" came many voices, all of them looking for my guidance.

"Go home...The place is not even fit for pigs," I urged them and within a few moments, Pista and I stood alone.

"You did well Laszlo. I am proud of you. The parents of our students will reward you," Pista praised me.

"I did it not for reward...I did it to protect them."

"You did protect them and you protected all of us teachers. I think we should disappear too. Let's go and celebrate your victory." Pista was all smiles.

"I think I will just go home." I experienced enough misery that morning.

"I will not let you do that Laszlo. Surely a little drink will not hurt you?"

"All restaurants are still closed, as was ordered by the Government, when the flooding began. They haven't lifted the order yet," I tried to avoid going with Pista.

"I am not without influence in this village. Let me demonstrate what I said." Pista began to walk away and I followed him.

Pastry shops, in our village, also sold alcoholic beverages and it was the closer of the two shops Pista approached. He exchanged a few words with the manager and within a few seconds we entered through the back door.

"Now let me tell you how we dealt with Pallosy." Pista began to tell the manager what had happened, but this time I wasn't the one who crossed swords with Pallosy. He heaped credit only on himself. For some stupid reason I felt cheated and disappointed. For ages upon ages, Hungarian men have been known to turn to drinking whenever life dealt them a blow and I behaved similarly.

We drank *palinka*; we tilted back peach brandy; we mixed it with wine and beer. The more I drank the less control I had. In no time I was drunker than I have ever been.

"I am going back to school. I am well fortified to face Pallosy. This time he will not get words, but a proper beating," Pista boasted and the two of us staggered outside.

"I go this way...You take another street Laszlo. I will meet you in Pallosy's office. We will beat the shit out of that bastard," Pista announced. I watched him stagger toward the school and I did likewise.

In my drunken stupor, I climbed the stairs to the second floor and tried to remember why I came; where the principal's office was and who I was supposed to wait for.

"I see you had come back Lichter," Pallosy approached me in the corridor. "Just as well, the Police will not have to search for you. Yes, I did report your sabotage. The Police Chief was outraged...He ordered your arrest. Then came a phone call from the

Laszlo S. Lichter

AVO. They too are after you Lichter. If the Police don't finish you, the AVO will. I will go visit your grave, not out of respect. I will go there to fart so loud that even in your grave you will hear me." Pallosy walked away, grinning like a moron.

I didn't know then that he lied about the police. I didn't know that his news about the AVO was a fabrication. All I knew that I was alone. Pista didn't arrive. I felt like I was in a spinning black hole, where life was worth nothing; it had to be ended.

I took drunken steps toward my small laboratory, where all my chemicals were stored, including the poisons. I reached the former cell that once belonged to a nun and fished out my key, tried to unlock the door, but in my condition I found even that small task impossible to achieve.

Stupid or not, I staggered to the staff room and begged one of the women teachers to assist me in opening the door.

"You are drunk Laszlo, you should sleep it off somewhere. Do you want me to fetch Rozsa?" I heard her voice, but I was too far gone to see her face clearly; to recall her name.

"You don't get her...Get me to the lab...Poison is there...I got to end it."

When I opened my eyes, for a few seconds, I didn't know that I was in my own bed. The setting sun's rays came through the windows. I saw the halo around her lovely head and I was sure I saw an angel.

"I escaped all of them. All my miseries are over. Pallosy; the police; the AVO cannot reach me where I am," I thought and must have smiled.

"You sure gave me a fright Laszlo. You wanted to commit suicide and you are grinning like an ape." Rozsa's sweet voice was scolding me. I came fully awake, by then I was sober.

"Did I do that?" I felt like a lost child.

"You almost did. First you had a fight with Pallosy. To make things worse you got drunk and went back to school. You spoke to Pallosy, if you can call your incoherent utterances that. He took advantage of your condition. He told you things that were untrue, just to frighten you. That stupid man almost succeeded. Thank God you couldn't unlock your lab door. I will always be grateful to your colleague, Terry. She refused to open that door for you. She tried to talk you out of that stupid act. Then you collapsed and she came to get me. The two of us brought you home and I might as well tell you that it wasn't easy. You have been asleep for six solid hours. I hope you got back to your senses. If you ever do something stupid like what you did, you can forget about us Laszlo."

I begged for Rozsa's forgiveness...I promised her to change...I pledged to her never again to forget all the precious things the good Lord granted me: her love; the existence of our little daughter; the hope of some day being able to leave this country.

Never again did I lose hope the way I did. Never again did I allow myself another moment of weakness. I became the husband and the father I should have been.

Laszlo S. Lichter

Chapter 21

Rozsa and I pined for nothing more than a bit of tranquility and the good Lord granted our wish, at least for the time being. I felt comfortable with my students; Janics for quite a while avoided me. My small family had a home and the three of us were together.

The shortage of food didn't bother us. We had lots and lots of practice. Once in two weeks we were able to buy two eggs; once in a month Rozsa placed some meat beside the potatoes, that became our main staple. Once, one of my students came to me with a message from her Father. I was to go to the grocery store he managed, where-in the dark of night-I was able to buy five decagrams of butter, he put away for us, saving us from the futility of standing in line for hours. All these things and the long absence of my controller helped our serenity.

We lived like slaves during the days, but when darkness fell and the stars shone in the heavens, we locked our doors; shut ourselves away from the world and the three of us were together.

When I didn't teach, Rozsa and I went to our field and tended to our corn. Our grateful little seeds, that we planted with loving care in the spring, became high cornstalks, that swayed in the wind like so many graceful, green dancers.

Rozsa and I walked between the rows that reached far above our heads and she shouted out her joy when she saw the first sign of reward for our many, many hours of toil.

"Come over here. Come quickly, Laszlo."

I rushed to her side and watched as her loving fingers caressed a tiny ear of corn.

In an awed voice she began to count the tiny, barely formed treasures on the cornstalk.

"One, two, three...," she stopped at ten.

"It is a miracle, my love," I told her in amazement. "I have never seen corn plants this tall, this full. I think we will have a bountiful harvest."

"Let's check a few others," Rozsa suggested and we held hands, as we walked by our plants and saw that all of them did at least as well as the first one.

I left Rozsa, ran around our marvelous acre and when I returned, I expressed my joy with a kiss of happiness.

"What were you doing Laszlo?"

"I counted the rows; I counted the plants in each row. Then I multiplied them together."

"Oh, you and your calculating mind, Laszlo." She teased me with her words, with her dancing eyes, with her smiling lips and I was full of desire.

"You better behave yourself, Laszlo...We came here to pull out the weeds. So get to it and no more of this nonsense." She escaped from my embrace and bent to pull out the growing weeds. I had reluctantly followed her example.

After a few hours of work, she sat front of me on my bicycle and I peddled home not without disappointment.

"What bothers you Laszlo." Finally Rozsa broke the silence.

"Nothing..," I lied and peddled on.

"Nothing, you say? I know you better," Rozsa replied and I thought about how I loved her; how great my desire was; how I would have loved to celebrate our good luck between those towering cornstalks. I didn't have the courage to tell her what bothered me, so I changed the subject.

"You never asked me Rozsa about my count."

"We had work to do then Laszlo, but we have the time now. So why don't you tell me what you found out."

"I counted the number of rows we have, then I counted the number of plants in a couple of rows. Can you guess Rozsa how many plants grow in our field?"

"Judging from my aching back, we must have a lot," Rozsa replied and I felt a stab of guilt.

"I promised her the moon and the stars and what I gave her is struggle, endless labor and not much happiness," I told myself and returned to my story.

"I figure we have over thirteen thousand plants, Rozsa."

"That sounds a lot. Do you think your figuring is right, Laszlo?"

"I took great care; I assure you that the figure is just about right. But what is more significant is what you found Rozsa."

"And what is that?"

"You counted ten, tiny corncobs on the first plant. The others are doing no worse either, but to be on the safe side I figured on an average of eight corncobs on each plant." I dragged out sharing my conclusion with my darling.

"You are keeping me in suspense, Laszlo. So how many corncobs do you guess we have altogether?"

"Would you believe around a hundred six thousand?" I asked her proudly, as if I fathered all of them.

"It is a big number Laszlo, but what does it mean?"

"Just think my love. If those little corncobs grow well, during the rest of the season, eight of them will make up a kilogram of corn."

"So how many kilos do you figure on, Laszlo?"

"Almost eleven thousand kilos is what I figured out. That makes eleven tons my darling. Quite a bit more than our calculated quota." I beamed with pleasure; planted a warm kiss on Rozsa's neck and paddled on.

"I know you mean well, Laszlo. So did I when I bought a dozen chickens."

"Those were chickens my beloved and I know that only one graced our table, but this will be different. Late September you will see. I think we will have a good harvest."

***

When we got home, I went to get Ildiko from Bencsiks.

"So how was it today Laszlo?" Lajos asked me.

I told him about what we did and what we found and just to assure myself, I asked Lajos what he thought of my reckoning about the harvest.

"Between the Danube and the Tisza, in the lowlands, eleven tones of corn from one acre is not unheard of...That amount of crop I had a couple of times, when I cultivated my own land. Only in my garden, behind what used to be a stone fence, do I have a real good crop. On the collective farm it is a different story. Everybody owns those lands and nobody cares about them. We plant and toil, but our hearts are not in what we are doing. We let the weeds choke the plants and most of them die off. An acre of land barely provides a ton of corn; most of the time even less. That is why the authorities need corn so badly and why the quota is set so high. I think Laszlo that you have nothing to worry about. Keep on working; love each and every cornstalk and by harvest time you will reap your reward. Which reminds me, we had a bit of bad luck today. Or should I say, you had?"

"What are you saying, Lajos? Bad news is the last thing I need."

"Look over there, Laszlo." He pointed where the brick fence stood, when Rozsa and I left the house.

"What happened to your fence Lajos?"

"I think you can see..."

"When did it collapse?"

"While we were away. I planned to reinforce it. I feared that this may happen," Lajos said with regret.

"Don't be so sad, Lajos. It is only a fence. I will help you rebuild it."

"Thanks for your offer, but you may change your mind when you find out what else has happened."

"Nothing can change my mind. I am stubborn like my Father."

"And as unlucky. Didn't you tell me that about your Father?"

"What does his luck have to do with your fence?"

"Come with me Laszlo and you will see."

We went to where the fence lay in a heap and beside the bricks, I saw the two dead chickens.

"I left them where I found them. Look at the right wings," Lajos suggested and I saw that the right wingtips were clipped.

"These were my only two chickens, Lajos. How many of yours were killed?"

"Not a single one, Laszlo. I think now you know what bad luck is."

"But how could that be, Lajos? You had over a hundred and not one of them killed?"

"Only yours, Laszlo. I wish they were both mine, but as you can see..."

I was angry; I was envious; I was confused, but I didn't want to hurt Lajos.

"So be it...Tomorrow we will have a feast. Do you think they are fit to eat?"

"They are hardly touched. The bricks must have hit them on the head. You ate worse Laszlo. Didn't your friend, Mr. Floch, come on his bicycle a couple of times to tell you that the butcher had received a shipment of pigs? Didn't you rush then and stood in line for several hours to get a piece of meat?"

"You lost me Lajos...What does that have anything to do with these chickens?"

"These chickens perished only a few hours ago. The pigs that were shipped to the butcher were long deceased, before he ever got them. Your friend told you that, yet you were happy to get that pork. Am I right Laszlo?"

"Of course you are right. I told you all about it, but when Rozsa prepared that meat, I tried to forget what my friend told me."

"Do the same with these two chickens and I will replace them from my own flock, if you permit me," Lajos' offer came from his heart, but my refusal came from my stubbornness.

"I thank you for your generous offer, but the Lord gave me no luck with chickens, so let's just leave it at that. Corn is where my luck resides. Once I harvest my crop we will have plenty of everything."

***

When the end of June approached, school was almost over and according to custom, the teachers were called together to hear about the closing ceremonies.

"I want this group of graduates honored in grand style...," Pallosy's voice droned on and on, while I thought about his many misdeeds; I thought about one particular student.

The young, slim boy was about to graduate. His name was Peter. He was in my homeroom when I began my teaching career in '52. One harsh winter morning, he arrived to school, his feet covered with rags. I wished I had money to buy him a pair of shoes. I wished I had an extra pair to give that little lad. I was poor, just like that boy, but Pallosy had the means to help a few of our children. I took Peter to Pallosy's office, where I described the plight of the helpless boy. His half-frozen feet; his wasted body; his family's abject poverty, described by the boy-with such feeling that I almost cried-were insufficient to move my principal.

Pallosy told the boy that he should be glad to walk through even three feet of snow, bare feet and that. He was given by the well fed, sufficiently clothed man nothing more than platitudes. Then Pallosy offered the boy a great concession.

"You have my permission to stay home when there is snow on the ground and the mercury dips below ten." The man had no pity for the boy. The money the State provided for just such occasions, Pallosy wouldn't dip into, to help anyone other than himself.

The little boy's reply came back to me.

"My Father has eight children...All of us are condemned to starve, because my Father was unable to get an education. I can walk six kilometers, each way, rain or shine, warm or cold. I will not miss a day of school. My kids will have a better life...I will become a learned man."

"For four, long years that little boy had perfect attendance and now he was to graduate. He should be praised; he should be decorated, for his heroic achievement..." My thoughts were suddenly interrupted.

"You were not paying attention, Lichter. Had you heard what I said, you would have applauded."

I looked around me, hoping for someone to help me out and I heard Bela's whisper.

"No more summer duties..."

"I heard what you said Comrade Pallosy," I lied and didn't fully comprehend what Bela told me.

"Well, I have good news for all of you. I will repeat it." Pallosy spoke again and this time I missed not a word of his.

"I thought about the coming summer and I have decided that the school will remain closed. No more summer supervision...All of you will have two months off. What do you think of this Lichter?"

Flashbacks-of cutting wood; paying the Government for several cords; leaving it for the Danube's flood-assaulted me.

"I would have been grateful to Pallosy, had he given us the time to bring our wood home." I thought and remembered the cold of that winter without wood and my bitterness made me hard, devoid of joy, in spite of the good news.

"You haven't answered me Lichter!" Pallosy raised his voice and I knew that I had to speak.

"I was told by someone, not long ago, that the winds are changing. That man was right. That is what I think."

"I hoped you will show some gratitude Lichter, but you have been always a hard man to please. You have always been a thorn in my flesh, but some day I will pluck you out...I will be free of you!" the great man announced.

"When plucking time comes it may be you who will get plucked," came my stupid retort. I cursed my mouth for being so outspoken.

"I am truly my parents' son...My stubbornness came from my Father and other things...Well those things I inherited from my Mother," I told myself and headed home at the end of the staff meeting.

***

"My whole summer will be free Rozsa." A little later I made my announcement. "I have a lead for a summer job. I think I will take it."

"What about our corn field Laszlo? It needs your time; it demands attention."

"If I get the job, I will need to work only six days. On Sundays I will look after our corn field." I settled the issue and within two days I got lucky.

Monday morning I said good-by to my two darlings and hopped on my bicycle to make the fifteen kilometer journey. Within five kilometers my bicycle tire gave out. Not even the string I used to bind the worn, outer tire was able to withstand the long trip. Had we been still getting silk scarves and cocoa, I would have had the money to buy two new tires, but after my controller's breakfast visit, those badly needed goods, although sent, no longer reached us. The coat sleeves were empty and the round cocoa boxes never reached their destination either. The customs officials must have gotten wind of those treasures' existence and the money those goods generated must have gone into their pockets.

I fixed my bicycle the best I could. The inner tire I patched; I used my hand pump to inflate it and applied new strings to the outer tire.

I was nearing the small settlement of *Gara*, when a car passed by me and disappeared around the first bend. I drove on, unconcerned, until I reached the turn. I saw the man standing by the roadside. There was no car; he was alone. As I neared him, I recognized my long absent master.

"Fancy meeting you here Laszlo," my controller spoke up when I reached him.

I jumped off my bicycle like an obedient little boy and stood beside the bastard. I was out of breath; I was already tired, but most of all I was broken hearted.

"Fancy meeting me indeed...The car brought him to intercept me. What does he want now?" I thought and remained silent.

"Cat got your tongue Laszlo? Not even willing to greet your long lost friend? By the way, how are your parents? How is you dear Mother?" My controller called my attention to the precarious situation my Mother's candor created.

"They are well. At least they were when I last saw them."

"I am glad to hear...Heading to your new job?"

"That is where I am going."

"And how is the silk scarf business? And where is the cocoa you promised me?"

"We got no more scarves. Nor did we get any cocoa." I told him the truth and saw a fleeting smile spread over his face that seemed to betray him.

"What a pity. You have to work all summer long, just to make a bit of money."

"I don't mind the work. I am glad to have the opportunity."

"And why is that? You know you could tell me."

"We need the money," I stated simply.

"Is that the only reason you took the job, so close to the Yugoslavian border?"

"Why else would I have taken it?"

"Across the border you would be free from me. That may be one reason. The other one I don't even want to think about."

"And what would that other reason be?" I was getting exasperated.

"Well, no more scarves, no more cocoa, no more extra income, may have made you think about deserting your family."

"You are out of your mind. I love my wife. I adore my daughter. I would never think of deserting them."

"I am glad to hear, but just a small reminder of what will happen-should you decide to skip across the border-wouldn't hurt. Would it Laszlo?"

"I need no reminders, not from you, not from anyone," I spit out the words, unable to camouflage my hatred.

"In spite of that, I will give you a hint. Your wife would go to prison...Your child would be raised by the State...And your dear Mother, well that woman would be made to take your place. And there are others who would suffer in some manner. Remember what I just told you Laszlo. Do your job well and when you get on your bicycle, head home; paddle north, never south or you will lose everyone you love. Did you hear me?"

"I heard you...Never fear. I will do my job well and never leave this country."

"Well thanks for this little chat, Laszlo. I am sure we will see each other again." The car appeared on the road, came toward us and stopped to pick him up and I was once again alone with my thoughts and fears.

"Never leave this country..." My words, my promise kept coming back, as I neared the collective farm and I had to constrain myself from shouting out loud what I thought.

"Just give us one chance Lord and my family will head toward the fence of despair and once across the border of hope, I will shout back: 'F...you all, you rotten Communists.'"

***

I spent ten hours a day recording the amounts the old, almost useless, trashing machine wrestled from the bundles of wheat, oat and barley the workers brought to it. The toiling men, women and children uttered loud curses from time to time, but they were driven on by the Communist foremen with slogans like these.

"Keep on working for the greater glory of our homeland!"

"In the name of Communism don't leave a single stem in the fields."

"Sing while you work. Your lips should praise our beloved friends in the Soviet Union."

I was amused by what I heard and thought about how these same slave masters must have praised Stalin, before that invincible, great leader fell.

"They no longer dare to mention the name of that Communist divinity. The twentieth Communist Party Congress-held in February of 1956 took care of that. Leader, after Communist leader denounced Stalin at that Congress. They tried to outdo each other in blaming the wise Father. Khrushchev, the first secretary of the Central Committee, accused Stalin of being responsible for mass murders and deportations, the German invasion during World War II, and the USSR's break with Yugoslavia. After Stalin's death, Khrushchev must have forgotten that he himself been involved in Stalin's purges and terrorism. He became a righteous, converted man. Stalin's henchman, Beria, head of the secret police (known as the KGB) was arrested and executed in 1953." I recalled the bits and pieces the newspapers and radio fed to us, long after Stalin's death and these thoughts brought back to me a memory of what happened in March of '53.

The announcement book was brought to my class, shortly after nine o'clock, and while my students stood, I read Pallosy's decree.

"Five minutes before ten o'clock all teachers are to gather in the staff room. At ten o'clock sharp an important radio announcement will be made and after the broadcast is over all students will be informed about what was happening. Students, while your teachers are absent, you must stand and remain absolutely silent!"

I wondered then what may have happened and my teaching became disjointed. I was greatly distracted.

"What could it be?" I asked myself. "This has never happened before. It must be terribly important."

It was indeed, I found out when the radio was turned on, just a minute before ten o'clock. The gloomy music came across the airways and then came the somber announcement.

"All of you who were asked to gather together to listen to this announcement, are asked to stand up and observe three minutes of absolute silence. Think about the years of prosperity you have been given since our country was liberated. Think about the great Soviet leader, who gave you your freedom. Think about our wise Father; our great Friend; our Deliverer from bondage! Think about the man we all love! Think about Stalin, whose name will never be forgotten; whose memory is etched in all our hearts. Remember Him, like you remember nobody else! Whenever you are inspired to sing, include Stalin's name in your song...We are filled with pain. Our beloved Father passed on! Grieve with us comrades! We have lost the greatest world leader we ever had. The Communist party will live on; it will march on for the greater glory of mankind. Our grief is great, but our determination is even greater. There are millions to be liberated, our Father, Stalin taught us that. We will always remember the Leader; we will never forget the Teacher; we will cherish the name of Stalin, who was born Iosif Vissarionovich Dzhugashvili, in the glorious year of 1879 and lived only for us until he was seventy-four years of age. Revere the man we have called Stalin; pay tribute to the 'man of steel'."

I heard the announcement, as did the others. My thoughts almost made me cry, but not from grief.

"There is justice. A despot was taken by God, may he punish all the other

Communists in a like manner. Please do that soon...Bring us our delivery."

We filed out of the staff room, trying to appear sad, but very few of us succeeded.

I felt a tap on my shoulder and watched, as my friend, Janics, headed to the washroom, instead of his class. I followed him. He checked the stalls, to make certain that he would not be overheard, then he turned to me and began to whisper.

"Do you believe, Laszlo, that Stalin is dead?"

"Why would I not believe that?"

"Because the Soviet leaders couldn't believe it a week ago, when the beast actually died."

"I don't understand," Janics's serious tone fooled me.

"Well, let me tell you what really happened. Stalin collapsed. The top Soviet medical specialists gathered together to determine if he was alive or dead. They couldn't believe that Stalin was a mere mortal, thus they stood around helplessly and shook their heads.

"They dared not announce that the great leader departed. 'We must call in at least three doctors from other countries to determine what we suspect.' One of the doctors suggested and after hours of debate they did just that.

"The top American doctor touched Stalin's pulse and he shook his head.

"'He is gone!' he announced his findings.

"The French doctor held a mirror front of Stalin's nostrils and made the same announcement.

"Then came the most famous Hungarian specialist, but instead of administering a standard test, he spoke in the following manner.

"'Comrades, we are not dealing with a mere mortal, but with the man of steel. He was far more than a mere man. I have a way to determine whether or not he is really dead. Will you permit me to carry out a foolproof test?'

"The Soviet leaders nodded their heads. The Hungarian doctor took off his expensive gold watch. Placed it a few feet from where the great man was laid out and ordered everyone out of the room. Five minutes later they all returned. The gold watch was where it was placed and the Hungarian made his announcement.

"'The watch is still there. Stalin must be dead!"

As I recalled Janics' joke, he must have coined, while listening to the radio announcement, I laughed out loud.

"You are a strange one...," the thrasher operator shouted at me, over the roar of the gas powered engine. "Are you telling yourself jokes, you never heard before? You should pay more attention to what is going on. The carriage drivers will steal the State blind, while you are amusing yourself Lichter."

I didn't doubt the veracity of what he said. During my first days on the job, time after time, one driver tried to distract me, so that another one could take off with an unrecorded load.

"I will pretend to pay attention," I told myself and looked the other way to allow the pilfering to continue.

"These men have families that need food as much as mine. The Communists declared that everything belongs to the people. I will let that become a reality," I resolved and whenever it was safe, I permitted a bit of robbery.

***

When the first Wednesday night arrived, I left the bunkhouse. My heart ached for my loved ones. I wanted to be with Rozsa and Ildiko, so my bicycle and I headed north, not south.

I paddled on and on in the dark of night and when I entered our home, I was exhausted.

"I didn't expect you home until Saturday night Laszlo," Rozsa told me, after her warm, kiss filled welcome.

"That is what I planned my love, but I could no longer stand being away. How is Ildiko? How is my little darling?"

"Ildiko is already asleep, but she is well. She misses her Daddy. I missed you too Laszlo and every night I prayed for your safe return."

I went to see my little daughter and stared at the sleeping little girl. After I filled my eyes with her beauty, I took Rozsa in my arms and experienced ecstasy.

"When do you have to get back to work?" Rozsa asked me, before we turned from each other.

"By six o'clock I have to be there."

"Set the alarm and go to sleep Laszlo. You need sleep, you need your energy."

The alarm clock woke us at three. Rozsa rose, made me breakfast and it was then that I remembered the small parcel.

"I brought this for you and Ildiko. In my excitement, last night, I forgot all about it."

Rozsa unwrapped the small paper bundle and stared at the cured, paprika covered pieces of ham and bacon.

"Where did you get this Laszlo?"

"We are fed well. These pieces I saved for the two of you," I told Rozsa and remembered the meals we had at the collective farm. The food wasn't exactly grand, but whatever I could, I put aside and thanks to my small appetite I didn't remain hungry.

"I will be back on Saturday night," I told Rozsa. I held her in my arms for a brief moment and then we parted.

***

After that first visit, my routine was established. During the day I worked. I looked the other way when the carriage drivers took their share from the State. I entertained myself with almost forgotten stories. I hid the scraps of goods, I would take to my darlings and made the trip home every Wednesday and Saturday night. On Sundays we went to our field and tended our striving corn plants.

Back and forth, I paddled for eight weeks and while standing or sitting beside the thrasher I thought about what was happening.

About half the grain, the thrashers produced, went to the central storage area that was guarded day and night by armed soldiers. The trucks were to come twice a week to haul away the harvest-at least that was the State's plan-but according to what I heard that plan was poorly conceived and badly executed.

The trucks broke down, almost regularly and the crop was rarely hauled away. The rain fell on the uncovered crop and it began to rot. We had heard words about the trucks being sabotaged; about drivers and dispatchers being arrested. We learned about the hasty, show trials of saboteurs and about the lengthy sentences they received.

The State apparatus was clearly in shambles. Every detail was planned by

Communist planners, who knew nothing about farming, about the treatment the crops required. Their plans were handed over to Communists organizers, who lacked the skills and by the end of my summer, I understood clearly why we have experienced great food shortages; why most of us experienced hunger.

"A bunch of bumbling idiots are in charge and they mismanage almost everything," I told myself often enough and knew that it was true. I experienced the lack of skills in the army. I had firsthand experience with the inaptitude of the secret police. I saw how ill equipped Pallosy was to run the school. My opinion of the dictators plummeted even more. Yet I was grateful.

"Thank God they are what they are; otherwise, I would have been found out a long time ago. I couldn't have locked horns with the authorities. I wouldn't have been able to manipulate them. If they had any skills, they would have finished me."

***

My experience at the collective farm faded into the background by the middle of September. Teaching and preparing for the corn harvest were my new priorities.

I sought Bencsik's advice about harvesting.

"It is a hard, back breaking job Laszlo. You should ask a few people to help you. You will have to break off every ear of corn. You will have to husk them where they are picked. Husks make good fertilizer for the land; your work will be repaid next year. Then you must haul the corn to a central spot, accessible to a carriage. I will bring home your corn, whenever you are ready. The least I can do for a good neighbor. And by the way, don't forget to cut all the cornstalks. Dried cornstalks make excellent fuel. That will come handy when winter comes."

I accepted Bencsik's offer gladly, but he shrugged off my thanks and continued.

"Once you get your corn home, then comes the worst of it. Basket after basket of corn you must carry to your attic. You are to spread it out, as well as you can, so that it can dry out. After two weeks of drying you will have to reverse the process. You will have to bring down four tons and take it to the Government depot. You will have a lot of work to do Laszlo."

"The work I do not mind, but why not get the four tons that belongs to the Government straight to them from the field?"

"Now that would be simple. Wouldn't it be Laszlo?"

"Simpler by a lot. Why couldn't we do that?"

"The Government wants dried corn. Besides it gives them a lot more, once it is dry, not like the fresh stuff you will be harvesting."

"But all my crop will weigh less, after it dries, if I am not mistaken."

"You got it right, Laszlo. If you harvest ten tons, by the time it dries, it will be not much more than seven."

"That is outrageous...They are robbing me."

"The Communists are robbing everyone, so don't feel they singled you out Laszlo."

"Suppose there is nothing I can do, but submit."

"Submitting to the authorities is what life is all about. You are learning fast Laszlo."

***

I got the badly needed help from my parents and the four of us began to harvest. We began our enthusiastic work, very early one Sunday, but our enthusiasm didn't last long. Separating the large ears of corn from their mothers wasn't easy; husking them made our fingers bleed after the first few hundred. Carrying the heavy loads to the edge of our field seemed an endless task. Loading carriage after carriage with the half dried ears of corn sapped our remaining energy. Cutting out all the stalks proved to be harder than I thought, but two weeks later we stared at the large pile of corn and all the cornstalks.

"How much do you think Lajos all this might weigh?" I asked Bencsik.

He walked around the large pile of corn that stood in our yard and after some reckoning, while I held my breath, he made his announcement.

"I judge all this corn to weigh at least nine tons."

I let out a cry of joy and all the pain of hard labor was momentarily forgotten.

Whenever I had some time, I climbed the attic stairs, with a loaded basket. I spread our treasure, with Rozsa's help, on the wooden floor of the attic and when the last basket reached that dry place, Rozsa and I stood in awe.

"We did it my love," I told Rozsa.

"We did it Laszlo," came Rozsa's reply and kisses and hugs.

***

Two weeks later, we filled basket after basket with dry corn and I descended with the heavy loads, until I judged that I had four tons. To my greatest disappointment, I found out at the Government depot that I made a misjudgment.

"You are a ton short comrade," the official announced. "Within a day you must turn in another one."

Rozsa and I stood in the attic and surveyed the corn that remained.

"Another ton out of all this will leave us less than three tons, I guess," I told Rozsa.

"Even that will be a lot more than we ever had Laszlo," she announced and when we finished trading corn for other commodities, we had good reason to be delighted.

We traded some corn for bags of flour; we exchanged some for wine, sugar, butter and to our delight we saw that we had at least a ton of corn left for our future livestock.

Our fortunes have changed and our luck continued. In the middle of October Joe arrived home from prison, unexpectedly. He came to live with us in *Bacsbokod*.

"It is so good to see you Joe," Rozsa announced and broke out crying.

"It is nice to have you home Joe," I added and inquired. "This is a great surprise. I thought you had a few more years to serve. Why have they released you early, Joe?"

"There was an amnesty announced. I understand that thousands of others were treated just like me. I reported back to *Baja* and the police gave me permission to enter the border belt so that I can live with you Laszlo."

A few months before I wouldn't have been delighted, but having raised a pig, gotten it fat enough to slaughter-sometimes in December-meant meat and besides, we had fuel, flour, sugar, butter and wine. We had, for the first time in our married life, a lot and I was glad to share our good luck with Rozsa's brother.

A few days later, we got a message from my Mother.

"Your Aunt came home. You should come and see her."

The following Sunday we got on the train and took a trip to *Baja*. The minute we stepped into my Mother's kitchen our tears began to flow.

"I thought I will not see any of you for a very long time. I cannot believe my eyes how Ildiko has grown. Come give your Auntie a kiss." Aunt Gizella was overcome by emotion.

"I knew you would come home. I knew you will be free," I told my Aunt.

"If only my dear Jozsef could be here..," she bit off her words for some hidden reason.

"Tell them everything that happened. Tell them about your time in prison. Tell them about why you were released. Tell Laszlo and Rozsa what you are planning," my Mother urged her and Aunt Gizella dabbed at her eyes with a handkerchief.

"When we were about to cross the border, one of us must have touched a trip wire. A red rocket soared towards the heaven and we fell to the ground, as instructed by our guide..." Her pain stopped her and we heard her deep sob.

"It happened all so fast. One minute my Jozsef and I walked, hand in hand. The next minute we were on the ground and the land mine exploded. I saw his blood spurt at me...I saw his pain and saw him hugging his open belly...The others ran toward the border and I must have lost my mind...I ran circles in the minefield, trying to find a live one; wanting to join my beloved Jozsef. I had no luck at all...I ran blindly into the arms of the waiting border guards.

"Even today, I feel confused when I recollect that awful scene. I wanted to die, but even in that I couldn't succeed. The guards dragged me to my beloved Jozsef. By that time they must have taken him off the mine field. He lay on the ground; his insides ripped out, yet breathing laboriously. He seemed to see me with unusually huge eyes. I thought I saw fear and regret and hate in his eyes, but it may have been only my imagination. But what I saw next, I will never forget. I will carry the memory of that to my grave...It was horrible...I have seen evil before, but this was more than that..." She began to moan. For several moments, she struggled for the words and strength to continue her story.

I took her in my arms and rocked her gently, unable to control my tears. Rozsa joined us and then my Mother and our crying infected even Ildiko.

"Rest Aunt Gizella...You don't need to tell what happened next. Try to forget it." My stupid urging suddenly transformed her and she cried out.

"I will never forget it! I will not rest until I had my revenge. You know what that evil man did?"

"No," I moaned in misery.

"He came to me. He was a high ranking officer. He grabbed my arm and told me to watch what happens to traitors.

"'Is this heap on the ground your husband?' he asked me and I gave a truthful answer.

"'He is still alive you know. Look at him. He would be begging for mercy, but he has no energy to speak. How long do you think he will live?'

"I refused to give the officer the satisfaction of an answer.

"'Well, we will find out soon enough. One kick or two may finish him,' he whispered in my ear and his booted foot shot out so forcefully that my dear Jozsef slid a meter or so.

"'Check him. Is he still alive?' the officer asked one of the border guards.

"'I am being told that your stubborn husband, you bitch, needs several more kicks to send him to hell. So be it.' He kicked once more.

"At that point I screamed at the officer. I begged him to let Jozsef die in peace. He didn't listen to me; he just kept on kicking him, long after Jozsef expired.

"'So how did you like the demonstration of my power, bitch? Are you getting the idea of what we do to traitors? Answer me!' In spite of his frenzied screaming, I remained absolutely silent. I held back my pain and tears. I wasn't going to give him the satisfaction of letting him enjoy my grief.

"'Take the bitch away!' I heard his order and I looked into his moonlit face, memorized every feature of that animal. I carried his face in my mind to the prison, where I was made to spend six months in solitary confinement. None of you will ever know how much I cried; how I regretted not turning back, when you did Laszlo. For the first two months I nursed my pain, then for another four months, I nursed my hatred for all Communists, but in particular for that officer, who administered the Communist style last rites to my Jozsef. I swore to God that I will take my revenge on that evil man and I prayed to Him constantly to have Him allow me to remember; to have Him give me the time and strength and opportunity to pay him pack.

"Once I was allowed to join the general prison population, neither my sorrow, nor my hatred eased, but I found solace in the company of others, who were no more fortunate than I. In prison I met hundreds of women, whose crimes were no more serious than mine. I learned a lot from each and every one of them. They were simple, innocent women, who were imprisoned on some drummed up charges, brought against them by a neighbor or a so called friend. It took them no time to whip up their hatred against the Communists. We spoke endlessly about the revenge we will take, once we are given the opportunity. A week ago the bastards surprised us. Most of us, so called political criminals, were given amnesty. They expected us to leave with our hearts filled with gratitude, but that is not what I felt; that is not what any of us spoke about, once we learned the news.

"Revenge. Payback. Retribution. Punishment. Vengeance. Avenging. These were the only words spoken by all of us. These words all have the same meaning, but different lips used different words to express the only feeling left in our hearts. I have a paper, allowing me and an escort to go to *Mosonmagyarovar* to visit Jozsef's grave. He was buried at the edge of the cemetery. Within a week I will go there with a friend and I will kneel down beside his grave. I will tell him that his death will be avenged. I will also tell him that you cannot be there Laszlo and Rozsa...I will let Joszef know that his favorite nephew is well and so is his family. Once Jozsef hears my words, I know he will be able to rest in peace. I will also tell him that once I avenged his death, I will leave this cursed country."

Her story ended there and I had no doubt that she meant every word she said.

***

For several days after our meeting with my Aunt, I had night-mares about what happened at the border. My self-defense mechanism developed to a point where I was able to wake myself, able to escape my dreams, but not life's reality. I lay in bed, staring at the ceiling, but seeing nothing other than the bleeding body of my Uncle Jozsef.

Only in school, while I taught my students, was I able to forget the horror story, but even there my peace of mind didn't last long.

Pallosy opened my door and shouted at me one early afternoon. It happened on October twenty third, on the day of my likely doom and our deliverance.

"The AVO wants you on the phone. Hop to it Lichter." Then to my students: "Say good-by to your teacher. I suspect you will never see him again. I always knew this day will come. He is your enemy and mine. Good riddance to this bastard."

I couldn't believe Pallosy's cruelty. To have him announce my predicament to all the boys and girls was far more than I expected from even him. I took one look at my students and gave them a feeble wave of my hand, and then I went to pick up the phone.

"Do you know who is speaking?" I recognized my controller's voice.

"I know...What do you want?"

"You are to come to the railway station at once." The line was disconnected.

I rushed out of the school and for one fleeting second I thought of going home instead.

"If they are going to take me away, I might as well wait for them at home. Just once more I would like to see Ildiko and Rozsa." I thought, but my heart and mind were no longer in command. My feet marched in the direction of the station.

I saw my controller and beside him stood a stranger. My fear intensified, as I neared them.

"Nobody has ever been arrested by one member of the AVO. They always found strength in numbers. I should have gone home...I will never see Rozsa and Ildiko...I am gone...Many were given amnesty...There are lots of prison cells empty...They lost many free laborers, so now they need new prisoners..." My fearful thoughts ran through my mind and by the time I reached the two of them, my legs were shaking, my mind was confused, my heart skipped a few beats, I tasted my fear's intensity.

"They no longer wait for the dark of night...Now they are willing to do this in broad daylight. Day or night, does it really matter?" I thought and almost laughed out at my stupid thoughts.

"I wish to introduce you comrade to Laszlo Lichter," my controller spoke up and something in his voice made my spirits sore.

"He sounds more fearful than I. He is shaking. What is going on?" I asked myself.

"I am happy to meet you Laszlo," the stranger reached out to shake my hand.

I was unable to give him a reply. I forgot my manners, but not for long.

"You bastard, you can take off. Go! Disappear! Our country needs no man like you. The likes of you are all traitors." I heard the words, the anger they conveyed and for a brief second I thought he spoke to me, but those words were directed at my controller.

He sauntered away; looked devastated and my hopes began to soar.

"Bela was right. 56 brought us many changes." I remembered my friend's prediction and thought about our improved situation; the amnesties I have learned about, and in spite of my fear, that didn't recede completely, I found my voice.

"I am happy to meet you too," I told the stranger. "I didn't catch your name, comrade."

"Call me Janos. And I will call you Laszlo. We can drop the 'comrade'. That is no longer required."

I couldn't believe what I heard. After eight years of constant use of that rotten word, to have it suddenly disappear was very much to my liking.

"What can I do for you Janos?" I inquired.

"The table has turned. It is far more important to find out what can we do for you Laszlo. My Minister and I are anxious to repay you."

"What Minister? Where are you from?"

"The Minister of State Security sent me. I work in his Department. I would love to talk with you more Laszlo, but not here on the street. Where could we go? Suggest a place where we could sit and have a drink."

For one moment I thought of inviting him to our home, but I didn't want to frighten Rozsa.

"There is an inn, just across the street. Maybe there we could talk."

"Let's go then." Janos replied and in the dim interior of the inn, Janos selected a corner table.

"What would you like to drink, Laszlo?"

"Nothing for me, but thanks anyway."

"I will not hear of it. You must have a drink of forgiveness."

"I really don't care to have a drink," I stated stubbornly.

"But you must have one or even more. Or do you want to insult me?"

"That is the last thing I want to do." I gave in.

"Then let's have something really expensive. What is the most expensive drink here waiter?"

"Chocolate liquor," the waiter replied.

"Bring us a whole bottle," Janos placed the order. "After we get our drinks, I want to tell you something Laszlo."

The bottle and two glasses were placed front of us and Janos began to pour. Then he clinked his full glass to mine and to my great surprise he spoke words that even in my wildest dreams I have never expected to hear.

"I came here to beg for your forgiveness. You have been abused; you have been arrested; you have been forced against your will to become an informer. Those deeds were committed by the enemies of the Communist party. Your former controller has been dismissed. From this day on he will have to earn his bread, by the sweat of his brow and so will many others. All of those bastards were stripped of all power. Men like you Laszlo are asked, all over the country, for their forgiveness. Will you drink with me to the new era?"

I raised my glass, looked deep into his eyes and I saw nothing there, but sadness.

"I will drink with you to the new era," I announced and swallowed the tasty drink.

"Very well then...We want to repay you for all your suffering. We want to make amends Laszlo."

"There is no need to repay me. Nobody owes me anything. All I want is to be left alone."

"I would feel better, if you accepted at least a small token of our regret. There must be things you and your family need?"

"We have everything we need, but thank you for your kind offer." I found it easy to talk to Janos. He seemed sincere; he appeared totally devoid of deception.

"For weeks and weeks I have examined your file, Laszlo. It was my job to study the injustices committed against you and that led me to seek information about people close to you. I know all about your Father. The false charges...The two imprisonments...The loss of his factory. When I read about these things, I was horrified. I was even more aghast when I read all about Mr. Buja. How that talented man was treated; how he was driven out of this country. Your family and you Laszlo, sure suffered a lot, but I assure you, all that is over.

"Under Stalin, terror existed and it took some time for the new Soviet leaders to rectify the injustices. Did you know Laszlo that in our homeland there are new voices of freedom? University students were allowed to form a new forum for free speech. They call it the 'Petofi Sandor Circle.' Each and every day they have more and more members. What is happening in *Budapest* is happening all over our country."

"I know little about what is happening elsewhere. Here in my small corner of the world things remained the same."

"I know that Laszlo. Your principal, Pallosy, is another conniving bastard. His days are numbered. I can tell this only to a friend. Reading about how you were treated; how you almost ended up on the street, made me feel that we are friends. We desire the same things. We want good will to permeate our country. We want past mistakes to be forgiven and forgotten. We declared an amnesty to thousands of people, who were imprisoned unjustly Laszlo. But amnesty is not enough! Those who suffered must be compensated!" He spoke with such passion that my fear dissolved completely.

"Compensated in what manner?"

"Those who were imprisoned unjustly had to be liberated. Those who suffered shortages must be provided with plenty. Families that were torn apart must be reunited. Every step we take in the right direction is designed to heal the deep wound men like your controller has created."

"For years this is the first conversation I had that warms my heart," I told Janos.

"We want to do more than that Laszlo." He let his statement make its impact.

"There is nothing more you can do. I came here expecting that I will be arrested and sent to a prison or Siberia. I feared I will never see my dear wife, my darling little daughter."

"I cannot blame you for how you felt. I am here now...I told you the truth...The only thing I haven't accomplished is finding out what we could do for you Laszlo."

"I told you before there is nothing more I desire."

"Well let's have a few more drinks, maybe after you will think of something Laszlo?"

We drank once, then we drank again and I began to feel the effect of the alcohol.

"I think I should go home and tell my dear wife all the good news." My words were slurred and I stood up a bit unsteadily.

"Stay just for a few more minutes. Good news can wait and besides, there is one more thing we must accomplish. Then you will have a lot more to tell your dear wife."

"What could you give that would make her happier?"

"I could let you pay a visit to her parents," Janos made his unexpected announcement.

"What? Did I hear you right?"

"You most certainly did. Let me see. You haven't seen your in-laws since '54. Am I correct?"

"I haven't seen them for over two years."

"Would you like to see them Laszlo?"

"I would, I do admit, but I never thought I could do that."

"You are not being totally honest with me, my friend. You have attempted to escape once. Didn't you hope to see them then?"

"That was long ago...That was a mistake...I would never try to do that," I lied, hoping to convince Janos.

"This time around you could travel in comfort. We would finance your trip to Austria, if you would like that Laszlo. A small gift of our good will. How about that?"

"What about my wife and child? Could they come with me?"

"I didn't want to tell you before, but we are not finished with our enemies. There is a great power struggle going on in our homeland. Your travel I could arrange easily, but that of your family would be looked upon, by some, as foolhardy. Maybe, in a year or two, we could manage that, but this time you would have to go alone Laszlo."

"I understand."

"Do you accept our generous offer?"

"I accept it gladly. When would I be able to go?"

"Now that is much better. To have your agreement means a lot to us. A month from now, one of the Hungarian soccer teams will play in Vienna. We will have you travel with them. You will have two free days to see your in-laws."

"Will my principal agree to my absence?"

"He will have no choice, but to accede to our request for four weeks off and with full pay at that."

"But I thought I will spend in Austria only a few days." Suddenly I began to sense a trap.

"That is all you will spend in Austria. The rest of the time you will receive your training." His manner of speaking was no longer kind. For the first time during our conversation I realized that I was being manipulated.

"What training are you talking about?"

"We want to be fair with you, Laszlo. We wouldn't think of sending you over to Austria without proper training."

"You want me to spy?"

"You may call it that, but there may be a better description of what we expect you to do."

"And what would that be?" I was shattered. "Year after year, I was the manipulator, but this time they sent a skillful operator to manipulate me," I thought bitterly.

"Serving your country. Helping us to make valuable contacts. I told you we are in a power struggle with our enemies."

"I refuse your offer comrade. I will not go!" I spit out the refusal.

"If that is your final decision comrade, so be it. You don't seem to care about your wife. You endanger the life of your little daughter. You are a foolish young man. You will do what we tell you, after all you have volunteered. If you refuse, you will suffer a lot more than before. You are no longer controlled by that stupid officer. You are mine and you will do whatever I command you to do."

I stood up and staggered out of the Inn. To my great surprise, he made no attempt to stop me.

While I walked home, I thought about my choices.

"If I become their spy, I will be in constant danger and I can forget about my principles. To serve the Communists, I hated so long, is not an acceptable alternative. If I don't go, I will be arrested. My family will be destroyed. We were so close to have a happy life and now this. Dear God, I ask you once more, to help all of us. I am no longer able to withstand the pressures. I don't want to lose my wife...I don't want to endanger my daughter. Please help us dear Lord." I thought, I prayed, I begged, all the way home and a few hours later I found out that the Eternal Father was really listening.

***

When I reached our home, Rozsa informed me that Joe left us again; he went to get a job at *Baja*. Normally that news would have cheered me, but in my devastated state, I didn't rejoice over what Rozsa said. I dismissed the subject and told Rozsa everything. We sat in our living room, hugging Ildiko, contemplating the tragedy that was about to destroy us.

"What will you do, Laszlo?" Rozsa asked me.

"What can I do? Either way we are finished."

"Think of something. Whenever we have faced great danger, somehow you found a way out."

"This time, my love, only a Divine intervention could save us," I told her somberly and we heard a knock on our front door.

"Turn on your radio. Do it fast Laszlo. Something momentous is happening in *Budapest*," Lajos Bencsik told me and ran back to his apartment.

I rushed into our room; switched on the radio and heard nothing other than music, for a couple of minutes.

"I cannot believe what you are doing Laszlo. Our life is in peril and you are listening to music. Have you taken leave of your senses?"

I raised a warning finger toward Rozsa, when the announcer, clearly shaken began to speak.

"...I repeat it. We have been under siege by armed bandits. Criminal elements mounted an attack on our radio station. Shots have been fired...Thanks to our AVO contingent the rebels are being repelled. Erno Gero, our Premier, asks you to return to your home. Nothing important is happening. A few shots were fired by reactionaries. They are being dealt with. Soon peace will return! There is nothing to fear." Rozsa and I listened to what was said with our mouths open. Then came silence, the radio went dead. We left it on, hoping to hear something more.

"What is happening, Laszlo?"

"I don't know my love, I can only speculate. For eight long years free speech was dead. The Communists built an enormous dam of fear. Only their dam held us back. Then suddenly the authorities gave the people a trickle of freedom. They opened the dam just a tiny crack. I think they misjudged us. The crack must be getting wider. If they can't plug it soon, it will break everything down. I think that is what is going on...I believe the Almighty had enough Godlessness." Just then the radio came alive.

"The mob broke into the station...They are coming...I hear shots coming closer and closer. We must leave our posts. Farewell to all our faithful listeners. Have faith! The Communist party will not allow this to happen." The radio went dead again.

"Thank God for all His mercy," I said to Rozsa. "We must hear what will happen next. Maybe the people of *Budapest* had enough...Maybe they will succeed and resurrect our freedom. If they succeed others will join them, all over the country. I will no longer have to face that awful prospect."

"They have the army. They have the AVO. They hold the weapons. How could our people ever defeat them?" Rozsa asked, still disbelieving in the coming miracle.

"They also have the Soviet Union on their side, but don't forget Rozsa that the Turks had dominated our country for over one hundred fifty years, yet we had regained our freedom."

"That was then. Maybe you are right Laszlo? Maybe we will get rid of the Communists. What will we do then?"

"What do you mean, Rozsa?"

"Shouldn't we join my parents?"

"If the Revolution succeeds my darling, there will be no reason to do that. We could live and prosper in a new Hungary. It will be the Communists and the AVO that will need to cross the border. I think your parents would return and your Father would be glad to offer his talents."

"I suppose there is nothing we can do, but wait and see and hope, my love." Rozsa gave in. We put Ildiko to bed, but the two of us couldn't tear ourselves away from the silent radio, that after almost two hours of silence came to life. The announcer sounded excited, out of breath.

"The freedom fighters of Hungary liberated the radio station. Just minutes ago the last of the Communist personnel were expelled. Some have died. A few of them escaped and so did many members of the AVO. We urge all decent Hungarians to hunt them down. Now we will give you a brief description of what happened during the last several hours.

"Hours ago we began a peaceful demonstration, front of the radio building. Our demands were simple and our insistence on having the Communists broadcast them was strong. Our committee of students and workers drew up a list of twelve demands. We first demanded to have the Communist party abolished. Our second demand was the immediate withdrawal of all Soviet forces from our homeland. The authorities refused to air our demands. We shouted them front of the station and our ranks began to swell.

"We could see behind the windows the armed men, but they watched us silently for the first few hours. We sang old patriotic songs. We milled around, unarmed, threatening nobody, but when the loud speakers boomed at us repeatedly, ordering us to disperse, we didn't budge. A young man climbed the steps of the radio station and began to recite a beloved poem of Petofi.

> "Stand up Hungarians,
> "Your Nation calls.
> "The time is here,
> "Now or never.
> "Should we be slaves,
> "Or free of bondage?

Laszlo S. Lichter

"That is the question!
"You make your choice!

"The words of this poem, that ignited the Revolution of 1848, washed over us; set us on fire.

"Freedom! Freedom! We made our choice!

"Our voices thundered and so did the guns. The shots came from behind the windows. Machine pistols began to chatter and our ranks were decimated. We began to run to seek shelter, but the guns kept on spitting out their lethal bullets. We pulled the dead and the wounded out of range. Then truckloads of guns arrived from somewhere. Young hands grabbed those loaded guns and returned fire. Confusion reigned all around the station. A few Soviet tanks, that guarded the station, remained silent for quite a while. When the AVO began to fire at us with heavy machine guns, the tanks' turrets began to turn and instead of shooting at us, they turned their fire on our executioners.

"Encouraged by the Russians switching sides, we stormed the building, and as more and more guns arrived, we overwhelmed the defenders.

"We found out later that the guns came from *Csepel*. The workers of that industrial island heard the news of the attack on peaceful demonstrators and threw their support behind us.

"What began as a simple outcry for freedom turned into a bloodbath. All over *Budapest* people acquired arms and began to take over key Government buildings. At Jozsef Bem square another crowd gathered. They shouted for hours for the removal of the Soviet troops from our homeland.

"Russians go home! Russians go home!" Their shouts thundered on. Petofi's famous poem was read there too. Some of the people found some cutting tools and began to cut out the hammer and sickle from the center of Hungarian flags. The symbol of our Revolution was born in that manner. Our new flag with the ancient red, white and green now has a gaping hole in the middle. Rally behind our new flag Hungarians! The Hungarian Army barracks overlooked Bem square. For a short while Hungarian soldiers hesitated, then one by one they joined our cause...They took the old flags and cut holes in them...They are with us! We are proud of them!

"Outside the Parliament building, another crowd gathered to hear Imre Nagy. He began with the word 'comrades' and the crowd booed him. He changed that hated phrase to 'friends' and the crowd roared its approval. Imre Nagy, who served time in prison during our dark years, who was appointed Premier in '53 and deposed for being too liberal in '55, led the crowd in singing our National Anthem.

"God bless the Hungarians..," sang over a thousand men, women and children.

Not an eye remained tearless. The long forbidden song fuelled our new Revolutionary fires.

"We have just received reports that the hated statue of Stalin is gone. As you all know, the almost fifty foot statue of Stalin, on its high pedestal, stood in the middle of Heroes Square, but it is no longer there. According to reports received, hundreds of Hungarians cut Stalin's feet at the knees and toppled the huge monument. From little kids to old women, people lined up to spit in Stalin's face.

"A new report just arrived! Ropes have been attached to the head of the statue and right now trucks are dragging it, back and forth on *Korut*, the main street of *Budapest*.

"Our committee, created by freedom loving Hungarians, is calling on all of you. Fight for freedom! Throw off the oppressors! Free our country! We will continue our broadcast as we have more news. Freedom to all Hungarians!" The radio went dead.

"It is happening Rozsa. Our freedom is just around the corner!" We were jubilant. Divine intervention came and my future as a chained spy seemed to be over.

"Thank God we lived to see this day!" Rozsa cried out and in no time our tears mingled as we hugged and kissed and loved each other.

***

Our next few days were full of excitement. In school the students spoke about nothing else, but what was happening in our country. They talked endlessly about how the Revolution seemed to be succeeding; how it was spreading all over the country. They took sides. Most of them pro-revolution and as success story after success story were announced on the radio, the opposing students fell silent.

The staff room's climate was no different either.

"We must do something," Janics announced on October twenty sixth. "We cannot remain idle."

"What do you suggest my friend?" I asked him and the rest of the teachers gathered around us to hear his answer.

"Teachers have always been the intellectual leaders of a small village. We must demonstrate that we are supporting, with all our hearts, what is happening in our homeland."

"So what do you suggest Pista?" Bela raised his voice to be heard by all of us.

"Someone should draft a list of demands. Demands that would improve the life of the villagers. We should then call a mass meeting."

"He is absolutely right. We should join the fight...We must help liberate our country." I didn't see Pallosy arrive and his words truly surprised me.

"What an unmitigated bastard. His nose is always sniffing. His finger always in the air to determine the political wind's direction. A few days ago he was a dirty Communist, now he wants to join the freedom fighters," I thought bitterly, but I had my fill of fighting that shyster. I decided to remain silent.

"Here is what I think, if any of you are interested. Laszlo, my dear friend, suffered most under the Communists." Pallosy spoke again and I was getting sick to my stomach. "Just a few days ago he was about to lose his freedom. The AVO bastards were after him. It pained me that I couldn't help Laszlo, but all of you know how it was. Why shouldn't Laszlo receive the honor due to him? He should be the one to prepare our demands. He should be the one to announce them to the people of this village, but before he does he should receive our support. We should hear what he composes and endorse the demands as ours. So what do you think of my suggestions my dear friends?"

"A splendid idea," Bela shouted and all the others joined him.

"Now that this is settled, I will give Laszlo time off and provide him with a typewriter. Use all the paper you need Laszlo. Use your God given talent. When you finish the work, let me know and I will call everybody together."

I was puzzled by Pallosy's move, but I relished my new found importance. Typewriter front of me, I began to compose the text. At the beginning the work was easy. For three days I have heard not only about the success of the freedom fighters, but also the lengthy list of demands made by various groups. From those news reports, I have borrowed freely and after each demand I typed on the paper, I read it, re-read it, revised it, until it reflected my greatest of desires.

It took me several hours to finish the job and when I did, I asked Pallosy to call a staff meeting.

***

Pallosy stood up at the head of the table and my colleagues looked at him expectantly.

"Laszlo informed us that he finished the job. He made enough copies for all of us. I wish to thank him for his labor of love. We will listen to him, then we will debate what needs to be debated and if the majority so wishes, we will endorse what he created." Pallosy spoke like he never did before. He was kind, considerate, suddenly a firm believer in democracy.

I stood at the other end of the long table and with a shaking voice that soon steadied, I began to read.

"The following list of demands has been prepared by the teaching staff of the Public School of *Bacsbokod*. Should these demands be endorsed by the population of this village, we will forward it to the new Revolutionary Government.

"We demand all of the following:

"1. The Communist Party be abolished.

"2. Free elections to be held within ninety days and all parties, except the Communists, be allowed to run candidates.

"3. To assure free elections, the Soviet forces must be withdrawn to the Soviet Union before the election date.

"4. Lands, factories, homes and other assets must be returned to their former owners, within one year after a new Government is elected." Until I have read this point there was no debate; no applause, just silence. After hearing my fourth demand, one of the teachers raised his hand.

"Let me get this straight, Laszlo. I owned ten acres of land, but a few years ago, when I was unable to join a collective farm, due to my teaching commitment, my land was taken away by the Government. Are you advocating that they give it back to me?"

"That is exactly what I had in mind," I replied and a few teachers began to cheer.

I waited for others to speak up, but they urged me to read on.

"5. All political prisoners are to be released immediately.

"6. Hungary must become a neutral country, like Austria became late last year.

"7. The AVO must be officially abolished.

"8. All former members of the AVO must be tried, in open court, for the crimes they have committed against the people of Hungary.

"9. The system of informers, that caused so much suffering, must be abolished immediately." When I read this point I saw relief on Janics' face.

"10. Free enterprise must be restored within a year, after the free elections.

"11. The Army, the Police and all institutions must be purged of Communist leaders." Another hand was raised and Bela began to speak.

"Explain all institutions. What do you mean by that Laszlo?"

"Factory bosses; heads of all offices; managers of banks; Deans of Universities; principals of schools; and all others, too numerous to list, have been appointed by the Communist party. If these leaders have the qualifications and the talent to remain where they are, that I don't mind, but if their only talent is that they were members of the Communist party, then I advocate that they be relieved.

"Your last demand doesn't say that," Bela insisted. "You used the word 'purged'. I think that is too strong."

"Maybe it is. Suggest something else, Bela."

"This is what I suggest: 'All leaders of all institutions be relieved of their duties, until their past actions can be investigated."

"If that is the wish of the majority here, I will be glad to change it," I announced and invited a show of hands for Bela's amendment. His version of demand number eleven was unanimously approved and I made the necessary changes.

"12. Religious freedom must be instituted immediately." I finished reading the last point and received a standing ovation.

Pallosy stood with all the others; he kept slapping his beefy hands together. His face took on the colors of a rainbow. He was on his feet and when the applause died off, he took over.

"Our sincere thanks to you, Laszlo. I assure you that your effort, your enthusiasm, your twelve demands will never be forgotten." I sat, somewhat embarrassed and missed Pallosy's real meaning, but many days later I had the opportunity to understand it well.

"I call for a formal vote. Those who are willing to endorse the twelve points, as amended, raise your hand." All hands were raised and Pallosy nodded his approval. "Now I suggest that we authorize Laszlo to go to the Chairman of the local Council and to have him arrange a mass meeting. That meeting should be held within two days. We wouldn't want anyone's enthusiasm to wither. I am really pleased with everything we have accomplished. Now go my friends, this staff meeting is over."

***

The mass meeting was arranged for October twenty eight. It was to begin at two in the afternoon and for the next two days, the village drummer moved to every street corner, to make the announcement.

Each time the drummer began to beat his drum, in the usual manner, the crowd gathered and listened intently.

"The teachers of Bacsbokod declared their support for the freedom fighters. They ask you to join them Sunday at two o'clock in the yard of the Government building. Their demands will be read and you will be asked to endorse them. Be there on Sunday!" He gave another beat of his drum, to indicate the end of the announcement and moved on, followed by a large group of youngsters.

I waited for the coming of Sunday, not without some apprehension.

"Why did Pallosy favor me? Why did he give me this great honor? I have never stood in front of a large group of people before. Will I be able to speak to them?" I asked Rozsa on Saturday.

"You will do well, I am sure Laszlo. I will be there with Ildiko. When you stand on the podium, just look at the crowd and look at us my beloved. You will find the words, you will be inspiring." Rozsa tried to put me at ease and after a while she suggested that we turn on the radio.

First we listened to the Hungarian station and were delighted with what we heard.

"Colonel Pal Maleter and his tank battalion, stationed at the Killian barracks, joined the Revolution. Most Russian tank units, that remained loyal to the Soviet leadership, have been destroyed by makeshift anti-tank guns, by Molotov cocktails and sometimes by puncturing their spare petrol tanks, mounted on the side, and the leaking petrol ignited by simple lighters. Children, less than ten years old, have been decimating the Russian ranks.

"We also like to report that donation boxes have been erected all over the city to aid those families who lost someone. Donations are pouring in. Bills are being placed in those boxes and not a single soul has been seen pilfering. This is a credit to all Hungarians.

"The fight is raging on at the cinema of Corvin against the remaining members of the AVO and the Russians that didn't switch sides. Our famous Hungarian sense of humor has been evident even during fighting. It has been reported that our freedom fighters, at Corvin, borrowed several signs from the movie house. These signs have been placed on the outdated anti-tank guns. The signs read as follows: 'Held over, by popular demand.' 'Only for those over sixteen.' 'Box office will be open.'

"And now a news item on the lighter side. A story is making its rounds around Budapest. A young, six year old boy, is standing a few meters from a Soviet tank. The Russian tank crew is freezing inside. The boy holds a thermos of hot coffee. An adult walks by him and he is asked by the little boy to give the thermos to the soldiers. The adult tells the boy to do it himself. The boy replies with a smirk: "I cannot do that...Can't you see that they are terribly afraid of me.

"This story illustrates clearly how the Communists failed to brainwash our children.

"Another report I have just received. At *Mosonmagyarovar*, not far from the Austrian border, a crowd gathered front of the State Security building. They demanded that all Soviet emblems be removed immediately. The AVO opened fire on them. The latest count indicates eighty five people dead. After this atrocity, members of the AVO tried to flee, but most of them didn't succeed. The crowd took their revenge."

The news items came in dribs and drabs and we got tired of repeat items. So we switched to the broadcast from the Free Europe Radio. The news was not unlike what we had heard before, but the promises were something else.

"The world is with you. Troops are being mobilized to help you throw off your shackles. Don't give up! Fight on Hungarians. We are with you! The West will not tolerate your oppression any longer." Rozsa and I heard the news and talked about it for a while.

"Do you think, Laszlo, they will help us?"

"It is in their best interest," I gave my reply.

"If they do, we can rest easy," Rozsa stated and we sought our bed.

***

Sunday came with great rapidity and the news was still good. Success of the freedom fighters, all over our country, was being reported and promises again of Western help.

By one thirty, that afternoon, the three of us stood in the yard of the Government house, surrounded by hundreds of others. As the moments ticked off, as two o'clock approached, the huge yard was filled to capacity. I estimated that half of the village's six thousand inhabitants were present.

At two o'clock sharp, the Chairman of Council went to the podium and with the microphone turned on, he cleared his throat and announced what will happen.

"My dear friends. You might find it strange to have me open this meeting. Strong, new winds are sweeping over our homeland. We are in the middle of great upheavals. I want you to listen to Laszlo Lichter. He is a teacher and the spokesperson for the staff of our school. I urge you to give him your attention and I hope you will do what he says." He left the podium and I approached it with fear, joy and great anticipation.

"I am grateful to all of you who came to listen to us today, my friends. As you know the fight for freedom is evident everywhere in our homeland. The freedom fighters are fighting for you and I. Many have fallen, many more will perish, but their sacrifices must not be in vain. The Turks held us in bondage for over one hundred fifty years, but our forefathers threw off those shackles. We have been subjugated for eight long years by the Soviets and their Communist puppets; it is now up to us to join the fight others have started. We have prepared our demands and we want to share them with you, we want you to endorse them. People of *Bacsbokod*, do you want me to proceed?"

"Let's hear them! Let's hear them!" their voices filled the yard.

I held the paper in my hands and my emotions took hold of me. I was about to read out those twelve demands, when I happened to spot Pallosy in the crowd and his grin froze me. I glimpsed something evil in his eyes and without thinking, acting on impulse, I continued to speak.

"I was given the honor to read to you these twelve points, but I really don't deserve this great honor. I am new here. It shouldn't be I who does that. A man whom you have known for many years; a man under whose care your children have been educated is far more deserving than I will ever be. So I ask your principal, Mr. Pallosy, to come to the podium. He should read the twelve demands to you; he should convince you to endorse them." I stepped aside and saw Pallosy's contorted face, his unbridled hatred.

He walked slowly to the podium. His great bulk towered over the microphone. I handed him the sheet of paper. I saw in his eyes surprise, confusion, anger and hatred.

"Mr. Lichter did me a great honor...It is not too late to change your mind, Laszlo. I am happy to do what you thrust upon me, but reluctantly I will relinquish this spot, if you so desire." Pallosy tried to escape and I knew that I did right by changing the plans, by springing this task upon him.

"I will not rob you of this great opportunity," I stated loud enough for everyone to hear. My eyes fell upon Rozsa, holding Ildiko and her smile I found reassuring.

"The following list of demands has been prepared by the teaching staff of the Public School of *Bacsbokod*. Should these demands be endorsed by the population of this village, we will forward it to the new Revolutionary Government.

"We demand all of the following:

"1. The Communist Party be abolished..."

The more Pallosy read, the louder his voice became. The crowd mistook his shouting for enthusiasm and were inflamed. I, instead, heard the anguished cry of a wild, trapped animal. When he finished reading the first demand, thousands of people roared their approval.

"Down with the Communists! Down with the bastards!" The shouts came from all around and when the voices died down, our beloved principal was forced to read on.

As he read point after point, the crowd shouted a portion of what they heard.

"Free elections! Out with the Russians! Give us back what you stole! Free the prisoners! Make our country neutral! Get rid of the AVO! Punish the AVO bastards and also their informers! Give us free enterprise! Get rid of the Communist leaders! We want religious freedom!" There was no need for a show of hands to know that our demands have been endorsed by almost everybody present, except for the next speaker.

A young man rushed to the podium, pushed aside Pallosy and began to incite the crowd.

"Nice sentiments...But those things are nothing, but empty words. What we need is real action. Have we not suffered enough by the hands of the Communists?"

"We did!" The multitude roared its agreement.

"They stole from us! They tortured us! They made our families starve! They imprisoned us! They closed our churches! They persecuted us! They carried on false trials! They killed whenever they felt like doing it! "The accusations poured out and each and every time the speaker received the crowd's agreement. "You know why? Because they had the power! We have the power now! We are a force to be reckoned with! Bring the rope; let's string up at least one Communist bastard." The speaker whipped the more radical elements into a frenzy.

One young man produced a rope. Another one climbed a big oak tree and fastened the rope to it.

"Pick one Communist bastard!" The three of them shouted and someone grabbed the Chairman. The helpless man was dragged under the tree and the rope was around his neck. Nobody objected.

I saw his white face, his trembling body and I also saw what happened to me in his office. He was kind to me; he was decent; he declared himself to be a handcuffed slave, just like the rest of us, many months ago when my family was about to become homeless.

I had to do something. I rushed to the podium and surprised even myself with what happened next. I had no time to think clearly. My words rushed out trying to bring them back to their senses.

"Before you hang the wrong man, you'd better listen to me."

"Enough talk, just hang the bastard!" someone shouted.

"Hear him out...," shouted many others, and slowly the tide turned, the crowd fell silent.

"When you take a life, you must remember that the act is final. No amount of remorse will bring him back. Killing a man is not to be taken lightly. Especially when you are about to kill the wrong one."

"Who deserves it more?" they began to shout.

I knew that the day after the Revolution broke out, the Deputy Chairman escaped to Czechoslovakia, so I saw no harm in suggesting him as a replacement.

"Before I tell you, please listen to my story. This man was no less a slave than you and I, during the last eight years. I was in his office a few months ago and this is what happened..." In five minutes I painted with words an accurate picture of the man's decency. As the crowd listened to my story, their yearning for blood seemed to decline and even the rope was taken from around the man's neck. When I was about to finish, I threw out the challenge.

"If you are still in the mood to kill, find his Deputy." I was relieved to see that the Chairman, still shaken, was released and the three young blood-hounds began to search for the suggested victim.

One of them rushed to the podium and made his announcement.

"The Deputy is no longer in Hungary. What shall we do now?"

Cooler heads seemed to prevail. An older man came to the podium.

"Enough talk about killing someone. I have lived all my life in this village. I know all of you. You are not killers! You are not Communist bastards, just the victims of a cruel Government. Let's not turn on each other, instead let's elect a new Chairman. Let him lead us toward the light, shed by our new found freedom."

This speaker's simple words were embraced by the crowd.

"Let's elect our leader," many people shouted.

"You heard the teacher's story! He spoke of this man's decency. We almost hanged him...Thank God we didn't do that. Let's repay him for those terrible moments. I have known him all my life. I have known his Father and his family. You couldn't find a better man in this village. I recommend him to you highly. Raise your hand, if you approve my choice!"

The would-be hangmen were the first to raise their hands and their example was followed by everyone. We had a freely elected leader. The crowd began to disperse. I pushed and shoved to get to Rozsa and Ildiko, but three times I was intercepted.

An old woman shook my hand.

"I am glad I came. I heard an angel speak with a golden tongue. It was you teacher. I will never forget that."

The second one was our new leader.

"I owe you my life! I will never forget what you did."

The third person I would have loved to avoid.

"You will die for what you did to me," Pallosy hissed in my ear and all the way home I heard only the last speaker.

***

Good news, after good news came over the airways, and before the end of October came, I decided to go to *Baja*, to pay my parents a hasty visit.

To my greatest delight, I found my Mother, my Father and even Aunt Gizella home. Only George, my brother was missing, who was serving his time in the military. My Father, who was always a worrier- a trait he passed on to me - immediately, began to speak about George.

"What is going on in this country couldn't have happened at a worse time."

"Why do you say that, Dad?"

"Your brother is in the army. God only knows what happened to him."

"George is quite capable to look after himself," I tried to assure my Father.

"Do you think he too joined the freedom fighters?"

"Why wouldn't he? He hates the Communists as much as I do."

"Do you think he is alive? Do you think he is well? Do you believe he will come home?" My Father would have continued, but my Mother intervened.

"You came back from the war. Didn't you Ferenc? Do you think your Son is less talented?"

"It is not that, but there has been so much killing." His statement seemed to touch my Aunt, who until then was absolutely quiet.

"There was much killing...But some of it was necessary." She began to speak like someone in great pain. "I was there, I saw everything."

"What do you mean Aunt Gizella?" I was happy to steer the conversation away from the worries about George.

"My friend and I got on the train...Was it the twenty third of October? Yes, I think that was the date. We traveled on, but our journey took a lot longer than I anticipated. Something was going on...It was terribly strange. The train made many unscheduled stops. It stopped not only at stations, but between them. We waited for hours, on several occasions...Rumors, always rumors, came with each new passenger, but there were always rumors about our coming freedom, when I was in prison. Eventually I learned to disregard them. I did the same thing on the train.

"I could think of nothing else, but how will I face my dear Jozsef's grave. I cried a lot all the way to *Mosonmagyarovar*, not even my friend's presence could console me. Two long days, after we began our trip, we left the train at that city. There was great excitement on the streets. It was all so strange...People running...People congregating...Singing patriotic songs...Voices shouting about freedom, but all of these things meant nothing to me. 'My Jozsef is dead; he is in a nearby cemetery. I must go and see his grave. I must fall on my knees to beg for his forgiveness.' I couldn't think about anything else.

"I was in a daze...My friend inquired for directions and I went wherever she led me. I seem to remember people shouting. 'Off with all Soviet emblems.' I think that is what they shouted repeatedly. Then people began to fall, like my Jozsef fell, so long ago and the sight of blood, screams, wounded all around us resurrected all my pain. Suddenly I was aware of everything that happened. The shots came from a building. Above the entrance I saw the huge red star and under it the letters 'AVH Station'. I knew what those letters stood for: Border Security Force. Those people inside were the people who captured me, who killed my Jozsef. I couldn't leave. People were still dropping, some to their knees, others fell all the way, as they got hit by the bullets of the killers. Then some in the crowd began to fire back.

"We just stood there. I was rooted to the spot. My friend tugged at my arm, wanting to lead me to safety, but I couldn't move. Some inner voice commanded me to remain, to witness what was happening. An hour may have passed and the shooting from inside seemed to die out, but from the outside the building was being pelted. More and more guns seemed to go off...I saw bullets shatter windows; pock mark the clay siding and I saw here and there someone hit. I heard the screams and people coming out, holding up white flags, strangely enough they were in civilian clothing.

"All of them cried out 'We were prisoners of the AVH. Thank God you have liberated us.' They didn't look like prisoners to me. They seemed to be robust, well fed men. I knew what prisoners looked like. I forced my way closer to the building, by then the shooting stopped.

"I will never forget that terrible moment...An officer, stood facing away from me, but his voice I couldn't mistake. He was, without a doubt, the high ranking AVH killer, who kicked my Jozsef repeatedly, until he died at the border.

"'I was held prisoner by the AVH. I am so happy to be free.' I heard him and was about to reveal his real identity, when someone else got ahead of me.

"I know the bastard. He was the commanding officer of this AVH unit!" A man began to shout and my husband's killer turned around, his face was white, he must have known that retribution was coming, that his end was near.

"Search the bastard!" someone else shouted.

They found no identification papers on him, only money... many large denomination *Forint* bills.

"The money gives him away...I told you who he is." The same man shouted again and I, who, for over a year and a half wanted nothing but revenge, couldn't force myself to speak, but someone else did.

"'Spare my life and I will tell you who he is,' the voice belonged to one who emerged also with a white flag.

"'We will not harm you. Tell us about him.' A man gave his word.

"'He was my commander. He ordered us to capture or kill all refugees. He abused us whenever we had failed. This man is an animal..." His voice died off.

"'Spare my life. I will give you all this money. There is at least a hundred thousand *Forints* here,' the commander pleaded, tried to bribe the crowd, but misjudged them badly.

"'You can keep your dirty money.' A guy, who appeared to be the leader, spat in the AVH officer's face and ordered someone to get a container of gasoline.

"I was horrified and at the same time fascinated. The officer was held by two strong men, while the leader soaked bill after bill with gasoline. The gasoline soaked bills were placed under the officer's cap, in his shirt, in his trousers, under his arms, between his shaking legs and the last batch was shoved into his screaming mouth.

"'What you suffer now hardly pays for all the suffering; for all the deaths you caused. In the name of our free country I condemn you to die. You and your money can go to hell.' The crowd roared its approval and I saw the officer released. He made one last desperate attempt to run away from his fate, scattering money around him, but he was too late, the burning torch caught him and his anguished screams filled the square.

"I should have been delighted. My thousands of prayers for revenge were answered, but I felt nothing but enormous sadness.

"An hour later I knelt in front of Jozsef's grave. Through my tears I could barely see the simple inscription. 'Jozsef Santa 1908-1955'. I prayed to God to forgive all my trespasses. I begged Jozsef too for his forgiveness and when there were no more tears to shed; when I ran out of prayers, I stood up, ready to leave, but then I remembered.

"'I must tell you this, my dear Jozsef: In prison I prayed for two things only.'

"'I wanted revenge on the man who last touched you. He is dead my darling. If you meet him in that other world tell him something from me: 'God's mills grind slowly, but surely. The powerful and the helpless all come to the same end.'

"'The other thing I prayed for was deliverance from this country. I will go back to *Baja*. I will tell those you loved that I paid my last respect to you. Goodbye my love...In a few days I will leave this cursed land, but not your cherished memory.'

"I came home with a heavy heart. Revenge is not as sweet as I imagined. It didn't bring back my Jozsef, yet it is good to know that crimes do not go unpunished. Now we better say good-by too Laszlo. If God wishes, we will see each other again, but not in Hungary."

***

Two days before the end of October, Bela came to me.

"Your twelve demands were well received by the people of *Bacsbokod*. There is a lot of talk about what you did. You saved a man's life, you saved many of us from becoming killers, but Pallosy is still in power. How can we allow a dirty Communist to keep on poisoning the minds of our young people?"

"Are you suggesting something Bela? If you are then you should just tell me."

"Demand number eleven, the one I amended read as follows, if my memory serves me correctly: 'All leaders of all institutions be relieved of their duties, until their past actions can be investigated.' Why should we wait for the Government to act? We should take action, concerning Pallosy."

"What do you have in mind Bela?"

"We should contact all our teachers and if we can gain their agreement, we should have the new Chairman attend a staff meeting. He owes you his life Laszlo...He wouldn't resist you to have Pallosy put aside. A new principal should be appointed by him. Just think of the possibilities."

I gave no thought whatsoever to have us get rid of Pallosy, but the idea became more and more appealing.

"Who would make all the visits to the other teachers?"

"I would be glad to do that, with your help of course, Laszlo."

"When?" I was getting quite excited.

"Tomorrow, after school we should begin."

"You have a date Bela."

***

The next day Bela was absent from school. Rumor had it that he was sick. I went to his house after school closed and I found him in bed, he did seem sickly.

"What rotten timing Laszlo. Just when I want to do something, I am given a head cold and as you can see I can hardly speak."

"We can wait a few days Bela," I suggested.

"Please don't...It may take too many days before I regain my health. You could do the leg work Laszlo." He urged me to get on with the job and I did.

The next two nights, I went to the homes of every teacher. They listened politely to my plan and gave their agreement to attend the proposed meeting.

I needed no more and went to seek the help of the Chairman. He was willing too, at least to come and chair the meeting. We set the date for November third.

***

I was afraid that Bela might not be well enough to attend, but when I entered the staff room, I was relieved to see him seated with all the others. The Chairman and Pallosy sat at one end of the table, I sat at the other end and between us I saw all our supporters.

"This meeting has been called to examine the leadership of Principal Pallosy. Should this staff find him unfit to carry on, I am prepared to appoint a temporary replacement. Now let me hear from those who wish to speak." The resurrected Chairman spoke. I watched Pallosy and he didn't seem surprised, in fact I imagined that he was gloating. Minutes of silence dragged on; the tension hung thick in the staff room.

"For God's sake Bela, start the ball rolling...It was your idea...Why are you so quiet?" I thought and didn't wish to be the first speaker.

"The idea came from Laszlo. I wish to hear what he got to say." Pallosy found his voice and I began to smell the stench of betrayal. I couldn't help myself. I jumped to my feet and my condemnations of Pallosy poured out.

"I am one of the youngest teachers here, yet it seems that it must be I who reveals Pallosy's past misdeeds. So be it! When I came here I expected to work with a principal who is compassionate, understanding, who has principles and treats his staff and students fairly. I was wrong. Pallosy was not the man I imagined.

"He proved to be a persecutor of anyone who dared to practice his religion. Did he not rake you two over the coals for attending mass?" I pointed at the old couple, but I got no help from that quarter. Even now they feared their master.

"He had the sisters, who ran this school, deported. He did that when his own sister was a nun." Total silence.

"During the Communist regime Pallosy proved to be the worst of Communists. I can forgive those who truly believe in an ideology, but Pallosy believed only in power. He was worse than the worst opportunist." I saw a few heads nodding, ever so slightly and I paused, hoping that someone will take over. Everybody remained silent.

"Did he not order us to give up our summers? Did he not play God Almighty and cause four of us to lose all the wood we cut?" I looked where my fellow woodcutters were seated, but they just hung their head in silence. "Did he not endanger the lives of our students by opening the school after the flood, when it was still infested with lice, fleas and God knows what else?" This time I looked Janics in the eyes and saw him flinch, but even he remained silent.

"Pallosy was and is an unmitigated Communist bastard. He pretends to support the freedom fighters, but in his heart he hopes for the return of our previous masters! You all know that. Show your courage...Speak up my friends...You all supported the twelve points we have drawn up...We are dealing with the eleventh demand. Isn't that true Bela?"

Bela stood up, clasped his hands, as if in prayer and I was stunned by what he said.

"Your version of the eleventh demand is what you are dealing with Laszlo. 'Purge' is the word you tried to use, but I have changed that. We are all followers of the Christian teachings of Jesus Christ. Didn't he teach us to forgive our enemies? I am prepared to do just that. Pallosy made mistakes in the past, as other human beings did, I will not deny that, but I forgive him. I do more than that. I offer him my hand of forgiveness and urge him to lead us into a glorious future." Bela's words devastated me; his actions betrayed me as he walked toward Pallosy, as he extended his hand to that bastard. He embraced him with both arms, he kissed him on both cheeks, and then he turned to me.

"Laszlo, follow my example."

I stood with shaking legs. My life seemed to drain out of me, but my stubbornness took the upper hand. I looked at Pallosy, then at all the others.

"This is what I think of this Communist bastard." I spat on the floor, offering the greatest insult a Hungarian could to another, then I staggered out of the room, out of the school.

"I made my stupid stand. He was my enemy before, but from this day on he will be more than that. I lost everyone. Bela set me up; he wanted to become the new principal, that is why he pretended to be sick, he sent me alone on the errands. I am finished....I let my family down...I am at Pallosy's mercy. Dear God help us...It is Your mercy I need, Pallosy has none of that."

Chapter 22

My assumption about Pallosy was right. He possessed no compassion; he didn't know the meaning of mercy; he was the worst kind of Communist. He was just like the new Soviet leaders.

Early in November, in spite of the chaos that existed, the news was still good. Pal Maleter was promoted to General, and appointed Minister of Defense, by Nagy. The Soviets promised to withdraw their forces and leave Hungary to decide her own fate.

We welcomed this news; we were jubilant, but not for long. News item, after news item, poured in. Documents from AVO headquarters were captured and what they revealed were beyond belief.

We began to hear about prisons, where prisoners were tortured until they confessed, to crimes they did not commit. Evidence was found of the physical and psychological tortures. Prisoners were put into rooms without windows and with only one light bulb. They were told to lie on their backs and if they failed to do so they were beaten. They got food irregularly and soon their concept of time was destroyed. The length of their perceived days varied. Sixteen hours was sometimes only six. They became totally disoriented. A few weeks of such treatment brought results. They were ready to confess to everything.

We heard about the deaths of many prisoners and how their bodies were disposed. The method of disposal, exposed by the documents found, were hideous. They were lowered into a bath of acid, which dissolved them. The remains were flushed down the drains, to pollute our beloved river.

"How many of those poor men and women may have been still alive when put into those baths?" I shuddered, when asked myself that question, after that radio broadcast.

The worst story, fully documented, according to the announcer, was about 'Major Meatball', a pock-marked, ugly female AVO guard. A prisoner was taken by Major Meatball into her room. She had him tied to a chair, and then she stripped herself naked. Her AVO guard husband, with several other guards, burst in and declared the prisoner-who was still tied to a chair-a rapist. They inserted a thin glass tube into his penis and beat him until the tube broke into many pieces.

I thought about the horrors my countrymen had suffered and my own suffering seemed quite insignificant.

For the first time ever, we heard about *Recsk*, where the AVO held hundreds of prisoners. They made them work for many hours each day. They paid them for their labor. Then they charged them for the slop, that was called food and besides they were charged rent for their accommodations. The documents found, clearly indicated what these prisoners were told.

"We are Communists, we don't make slaves out of our prisoners, like capitalist fascists do," the announcer read.

Hearing these news items, I thought about what happened to my Uncle.

"Uncle Jozsef lost his life for wanting to be free. At least he didn't suffer long. His life was extinguished by that Communist bastard. He escaped lengthy torture, but not this terrible country." I tried to find consolation whatever way I could and these news items, in some demented way began to help me.

Many news items were given about how the Hungarians had captured the AVO buildings. In some cases the AVO men ran into the basements and would not emerge from where they hid. The freedom fighters took hoses and flooded them out, like one would flush rats out from their hiding places. When they emerged, the crowd's fury was unleashed on them, killing many members of the organization that held them under their control for over eight years. According to the reports there were over thirty thousand members in the AVO, before the Revolution began. It warmed my heart to know that many of them no longer existed.

Another story that made its way around concerned an AVO building in *Budapest*, a crowd ransacked. Voices could be heard below the floor. The freedom fighters and the prisoners below, were able to hear each other, thus it was learned that two hundred and fifty prisoners were under the building. All attempts to find an entrance failed for several days. In the meantime all of the prisoners had perished.

In spite of the horror stories heard, between October twenty third and the first two days of November were days of glory for all of us, who hated the Russians, who despised the Communist regime. We could live without fear of the AVO coming for us; imprisoning us; torturing us; bringing about our end.

The most encouraging news was that the Soviet soldiers were being withdrawn toward our eastern border. It appeared that we were indeed free. Several newspapers were published. After eight years of total censorship, writers were able to write the truth.

The demands that were sent to the new Government, led by Imre Nagy, were met one by one. Political prisoners were released from prisons. Cardinal Jozsef Mindszenty, Prince Primate of the Hungarian Catholic Church, was also released. He spoke to us; he motivated and inspired us to work for a new beginning.

Hated symbols of Communist oppression slowly disappeared. Stalin's statue was only the first; soon statues of Russian soldiers that overlooked *Budapest* were pushed over by freedom-fighters.

Imre Nagy renounced the Warsaw Pact and declared Hungary a permanently neutral nation. He dissolved the one-party system and for the first time, since 1946, multiple parties emerged. He repeatedly demanded permanent removal of all Soviet units from Hungarian soil. He seemed to succeed and each and every time we heard about demand after demand being met, Rozsa and I found more and more reasons to rejoice.

Each news of success made us decide to stay in Hungary, but every setback, we heard about, re-ignited the debate of whether we should stay or leave.

Nagy asked for assistance from the west. Ten million Hungarians joined him in asking the Americans; the English; the French and especially the United Nations to safeguard our new found freedom, but the world was too busy with the Suez Canal crisis, we soon found out. The Soviets began to re-supply their army. They brought new, Asiatic troops to our border. They were poised to attack us, it appeared.

The Free Europe Radio kept on encouraging us. Their messages never varied.

"We will support any nation in a bid for its freedom from an outside force." The announcer kept reading those words, day after day, and we were naive enough to believe the false promises.

"Western forces will arrive to help us keep Hungary free," I told Rozsa in those precarious November days, just before the Soviet invasion began. I did that in spite of the news reports that tanks and men were streaming into our country.

We heard about thousand of Hungarians simply walking across the border into Austria. The mine fields were no longer there; the guards couldn't care less; the border was almost free.

"After what you did to Pallosy, maybe we should get out of here," Rozsa raised the issue again, but by then it was November third and the announcement came on the radio, that the Austrian border, the only border to a non-Communist nation, was sealed.

In the morning of November fourth the Soviets attacked *Budapest*. Our freedom fighters were in need of food and ammunition. But they held out against the modern, well equipped army of the Soviets. Caravans of trucks could be seen on every highway. Hungarians, who produced food, were on their way to the capital to feed our boys and girls and they supplied everything they could; they did it for free. Food, drinks, blankets, used clothing were their contributions to a cause that was not totally lost yet.

When these courageous men and women returned to their homes, they spoke about what they saw.

"I saw Soviet tanks firing into buildings," one man, who just returned from the capital, told me.

"I witnessed the Soviets and the AVOs shooting at freedom-fighters and unarmed civilians. They killed freedom-fighters, as easily as they killed a weak old person, or a young child," another man lamented.

We began to fear that the Revolution was about to fail. It was rumored that Imre Nagy sought protection at the Yugoslav embassy, which he was granted. Cardinal Mindszenty, a strong anti-Communist from the start, took refuge in the American Legation, another rumor indicated, but the radio made no such announcements.

The most devastating rumor was about General Maleter, who no longer led the freedom fighters. Days earlier he was kidnapped by the Russians, during peace talks.

In spite of these dreadful rumors the fighting went on. Barricades were set up in many cities; forcing the Soviet tanks to enter narrow streets, where with Molotov cocktails, machine guns, grenades and many times by the ingenious use of simple dinner plates, many Russians were killed by the freedom fighters.

One young boy would watch for the coming of the tanks, another one, in the recessed entrance of a building would pull a string, with an upside-down dinner plate attached. The dinner plate would be left in the middle of the narrow street, where the lead tank couldn't go around it. When a soldier was forced to climb out of the tank to investigate the nature of the obstacle, that could possibly be a mine, a sniper from a roof top would pick him off. The second soldier, sent out to investigate, would meet the same fate and it continued until the tank was empty. Young boys and men would swarm the tank, plant on it a Hungarian flag, with the hated Soviet hammer and sickle cut out and hide the bodies of the Russian soldiers. Then they would wait in their hiding places. Sooner or later another tank would enter the street and seeing the Hungarian flag fluttering in the breeze, they would destroy the first tank and later on they would be destroyed by yet another one, thus creating many new barricades.

News came, but by this time, not from the official radio station, instead from transmitters set up in hidden places, that many Russian troops changed sides and helped the remaining freedom fighters. The new troops that had arrived were told that the Danube was the Suez Canal. They were urged to fight to the death against the American capitalist fascists. Many were fooled, but not for long. When they had learned that they were mislead; that they were tricked, many of those troops changed sides and some simply deserted.

The next bit of news shook me, as it must have shaken everyone, who still believed in what we were doing.

"Imre Nagy left the Yugoslav embassy, believing the promise of the newly installed Premier, that he wouldn't be harmed. Nagy and fifteen other families of his cabinet boarded a bus that would take them home. The bus they traveled in was stopped by

Russian tanks and armored cars. The bus was driven to Romania where all of them are facing an uncertain future."

The news kept pouring in from the two or three illegal stations, operated by freedom fighters, who were unwilling to do as the resurrected, Communist radio urged constantly.

"Lay down your weapons. You will not be harmed. You are innocent Hungarians, who were duped by the imperialists. They don't care about you; they will not help you. Your future is assured by our new leaders." Day and night we have heard the false promises and the replies, broadcast by the clandestine stations.

"We will fight on to the last man. We appeal to all western Governments. Send us help immediately." The broadcasts were short; the speakers spoke desperately and in less than two weeks, the last voices crying out for freedom fell silent.

From that time on, Rozsa and I turned our full attention to the Free Europe Radio. We hung on every word of every announcer.

"News came about the great number of refugees who crossed the border into Austria. The border is being patrolled not only by Hungarians, but by Russians, who on November twenty first dynamited the bridge at Andua. We estimate that at least a hundred fifty thousand Hungarians left their country to find freedom, most of them escaped after the Soviets reentered Budapest. It has been reported, although unconfirmed, that tens of thousands of Hungarians were deported to Siberia to Soviet slave-labor camps."

By the middle of November all seemed lost. The confirmation came from the Free Europe Radio.

"The United Nations debated long and hard what to do about Hungary. Unfortunately, the debate is over. It grieves us to announce that the promised help will not be sent...Instead the UN passed a resolution to lower its flag to half mast, thus expressing its empathy with the Hungarian freedom fighters."

I was enraged. I turned to Rozsa.

"That useless organization...They debate and debate again, but the meaning of the word 'action' is alien to them my darling. I was a fool my beloved. I should have listened to you. I should have asked your parents to send a guide for us. We should have left this country."

"Is it too late my darling?" Rozsa asked and I had decided.

"I am writing to your parents at once. I will ask them to send a guide. We still have a better chance to get out of here, than we had in '55," I informed Rozsa and set to the task immediately.

***

The next afternoon I decided to pay a visit to my parents. Due to the general strike, called by tens of thousands of workers, the trains stopped running and I was forced to find another mode of transportation. I approached a few truckers, who, from time to time, took shipments to *Baja*, but none of them were planning a trip soon. I considered driving my bicycle to my parents' home, but the cold and snow made that difficult. A day later, I found a truck that was about to go to the city, to pick up supplies for our grocery store. The store manager was a kind man, the same man who supplied us, at least on one occasion, with a little packet of butter.

"My truck will leave around three. You can go with my men and you can return by early evening," he told me after I approached him.

I expressed my thanks and three o'clock I climbed on the back of the truck, hoping to find my parents unaffected by the backlash that followed our days of success.

"I am glad you came, Laszlo." My Father greeted me with a warm hug. "I was afraid that you may have followed your Aunt Gizella."

"What are you talking about Dad?"

"She is out of here...Thank God she got across the border. She sent us a message Laszlo, just two days ago. Ask your Father why we haven't joined your Aunt," my Mother took over.

"Thank God Aunt Gizella is out." I could say nothing more.

"I would thank God if all of us were out of this rotten place," my Mother resumed her complaining.

"You don't know what you are talking about. This is our home. This is our homeland. This is where we stay. Don't you agree Laszlo?"

"I wish I could. I wish we had left in October."

"You don't really mean that Laszlo. I couldn't bear losing all of you. I have only one grandchild, you wouldn't make a second mistake trying to take her away from us."

"Dad I must be honest. During the days of hope, I wasn't willing to try to leave, but now that all our hopes are dashed, I have an obligation to Rozsa and Ildiko. Besides Rozsa's parents have only one grandchild...If we take her from you we are being unfair. If we don't try, we are being unfair to the Bujas."

"Think clearly, Laszlo. If you try to escape and fail you are going to take Ildiko not only from us, but also from her other Grandparents."

"No...We will get out."

"Haven't you heard the news Laszlo? The Russians are patrolling the border now. They shoot people on sight. Then there is the AVH to think about. Those bastards didn't disappear for good...They are back on the job and they are taking revenge on everyone for the death of many of their comrades. I heard so many horror stories...People shot dead at the border; others captured and shipped off to Siberia. Is that the kind of danger you want to expose your daughter to? Do you want to lose your beloved Rozsa?" My Father would have gone on and on. My Mother shook her head, but remained silent. I had to escape from my Father, whose fear began to nest in my mind. So I said a hasty good-by. I let my Father believe that he succeeded in changing my mind, but within minutes I posted my letter to Rozsa's parents, hoping that in the chaos, that still gripped our country, it will not be intercepted by the authorities. Two hours later I entered our home and saw that Rozsa was terribly frightened.

***

"My parents are as well as can be expected. I wish I could say the same thing about you Rozsa. Did something frighten you my darling?"

"Two policemen came to talk to you." Rozsa could hardly speak the words, she was crying.

"Came to see me? What did they want?"

"They came to investigate a complaint. I told them you went to see your parents...That you went to *Baja*. They gave each other a knowing look. Then they told me that you are to report to the Police station, immediately upon your arrival. That is all I know Laszlo. Why haven't we escaped when we could have? Why have we waited for so long? What will I do, if they take you away my darling?"

"Don't fret my love. I will go, talk to the Police Chief. I will be back within the hour." I tried to reassure her, but I couldn't stop her crying.

I thought about putting my arms around her. I wanted to kiss her and my little Ildiko, just in case...But I knew that such actions would only add to their fright, so I left the house, like someone who felt no fear, who was about to perform a simple chore, but my heart was full of fear, it didn't allow to deceive me.

"Pallosy must have sprung into action. Or maybe retribution is about to reach me, much sooner than I thought. My actions, during the Revolution, were nothing compared to that of tens of thousands of others. It is far too early for the Communists to turn their attention to me. It must be only Pallosy."

***

I entered the Police Station and soon I sat front of the Chief, who greeted me like a long lost brother.

"I am so sorry Laszlo for my men frightening your wife. Scaring you too, but it couldn't have been avoided."

"Am I under arrest?" I popped my fearful question.

"No, you are not," I heard with relief.

"Why am I here then?"

"To clarify a few things. Where did you go this afternoon?"

"I went to see my parents in *Baja*."

"That is what I was told by others, but you went with an empty truck. Why did you do that?"

"Are the trains running again?"

"Not to my knowledge, Laszlo."

"That is why I had to find other transportation."

"I understand, but others are not inclined to do that."

"Who are you talking about?"

"Pallosy for one...And the parents whom he riled up."

"So what did Pallosy do this time?" I was relieved to know that my guess was right.

"He went to see a number of parents, all of them former Communists, I don't mind to tell you. Then five of them came to see me. They demanded your immediate arrest to prevent a bloodbath."

"A bloodbath? What am I a monster? How would I bring about that?"

"According to them you took an empty truck to Baja, where you were to pick up guns to arm your students. The truck returned fully loaded, they informed me much later. What did you bring to our village, Laszlo?"

"I brought nothing. I was only a passenger."

"They told me a different story. You tried to have Pallosy removed. That was back in October...Then you have decided to kill that man and many, many others. Is that true, Laszlo?"

"If you believe them then you weren't at the mass meeting, where I spoke and saved the Chairman's life."

"I was there and I know what you did then."

"Then you also know that I had no stomach for killing. What would have happened if I didn't speak up?"

"The Chairman would have been hanged."

"Do you think that would have satisfied our people? Don't you think that other hangings would have followed?"

"I know what you say is true, but I had to take their complaint seriously."

"If I let the Chairman die, you probably would have been next."

"I know that too, Laszlo. That is why I will let you off with a warning. You can go home...We will not harm you, but for God's sake be very careful. What I am doing will not be to Pallosy's liking. He and his cohorts may take the law into their own hands. Sleep lightly Laszlo and make sure that you are well armed. Your family needs your protection. That is all I can do for you now. My hands are tied. I am in handcuffs, just like all decent Hungarians."

***

Another quick trip to Baja had to be made and I obtained a pistol, with several round of ammunition from Rozsa's cousin, Sana.

"Why do you need the gun Laszlo?" he asked me as he handed the gun over.

"My family has been threatened. I will not sit idly and watch them being attacked. If they come for us, we will die, but so will a number of others. I pray to God to give us enough time to have a guide come for us; to have us get out of the country."

"Why haven't you left, when the border was unguarded?" Sana asked.

"When success was still in sight, I didn't want to leave. So we have waited."

"You were stupid Laszlo. I hope you don't mind me speaking the truth. You swallowed the promises of help. The US and the others gave Hungary to the Soviets, after World War II. They feared a nuclear war. Did you think anyone would risk that? They showed their enormous courage by demanding that the UN lower its flag to half mast. When I heard the news, do you know what I said?"

"I have no idea."

"I told my Father that I will rejoin the Communist party and will do all I can to have the free world experience the slavery they cast upon us. My Father agreed and I think that is what millions of Hungarians will do."

"But that is absurd. Our only hope is the free world."

"You are still an idealist, Laszlo. Well I suppose I cannot do anything about that. Try to get out of Hungary. Get Rozsa and Ildiko out of here."

"That is what I am planning to do, but I am being watched constantly. I will have to find a way to fool Pallosy and his Communist gang."

"If there is anything I can do, you just have to ask Laszlo."

"There is one thing you could do Sana."

"Tell me and it will be done."

"Inform Joe to return to *Bacsbokod*, as soon as he can. When the guide arrives, he should go with us. Convince him of that."

***

I hid the loaded gun in the stove, that stood beside our bed, no longer used to provide us with warmth. For many nights we have slept little. I listened to the slightest noise, ready to grab the gun and fire at the enemy. Our nerves were frayed more than ever before and when a night passed, without any sign of danger, we gave thanks to God and dreaded the coming of each night.

"This is no way to live my love...," I told after seven nights of vigil to my Rozsa.

"Of course that is true Laszlo, but what else can we do?"

"We could try to get across the border without the help of a guide. Others have done that successfully." I searched desperately for a solution.

"We could try, but my guess is that we wouldn't get too far. Don't you think Pallosy is having us watched?"

"I am sure that is what he is doing, but guide or no guide, he will keep on watching us."

"You got to play it smart Laszlo." Rozsa gave me a sweet smile and she continued to elaborate. "What has always been most important to a Hungarian?"

"Food and shelter, besides always pining for freedom."

"Freedom we had, but just for a brief period of time. I think that futile kind of pining is over, but food and shelter is still treasured my darling."

"I think you are right Rozsa, but I still don't get your drift."

"We have a fat pig that would give us all kinds of food, once slaughtered. Hams, bacon, lard, sausages and goodness knows what else. If we slaughter the pig, what will people think, Laszlo?"

"They would think that we have settled in for the winter."

"Let's do it then....Let Janics know. He will inform others that we are planning to kill the pig. Once Pallosy finds out, he will reduce his vigilance. What do you think?"

"You are a wise woman Rozsa. I will let the news slip and we will go through with what you suggested. Maybe we will invite the family for the great event. We will have a feast and when they least expect it we will bring about our disappearance."

"It is a good plan. Now we just have to live long enough to carry it out," Rozsa added and I promised her that we will do that.

***

Night after night we kept up with our fearful vigil and when daylight came I got ready for school. Most of my colleagues rarely spoke to me. They either feared to associate with Pallosy's enemy or were ashamed of how they let me down when their help was desperately needed.

Only Janics showed any friendliness. I was ready to use my 'friend'.

"What are you going to do Laszlo? You made Pallosy your sworn enemy. While the Revolution still had a chance of succeeding he left you alone, but I guess he will become very active."

"I know Pallosy would love to finish me off, but he has as much to fear as I. He read the twelve points to the people of this village. If need be, many will testify to his enthusiastic delivery."

"What you say is true Laszlo, but he is a skillful man. Once things settle down, he will be after you. You should perhaps try to get out...," Janics suggested and held his breath.

"I thought of that, but my parents objected to our leaving. My Father convinced me to stay and promised me his friends' protection."

"Protection you will need Laszlo."

"I need a lot more than that. Once our school closes for the winter break, we will slaughter our pig and we will be set for the winter," I informed Janics, hoping that he will spread around my intention.

A few hours later, Pallosy came to summon me.

"There is a phone call for you, Lichter."

I rushed to his office and the two of us have entered. I hoped that he will give me some privacy, but he remained, listening intently to my side of the conversation.

It was Rozsa's cousin, Sana, who called to invite us to the traditional pork supper on the following Sunday.

"I don't think the trains are running yet," I told Sana.

He informed me that in our region the strike was over and insisted that the three of us be there.

"Very well then. You can count on us. We will take the first train on Sunday. Thanks for everything." I signed off and noticed a smug, satisfied expression on the face of my enemy.

***

The big event was attended by all the relatives and while the pig was being processed into seasoned foodstuffs, we ate and drank and tried to forget what has happened to our country.

Rozsa and I took the time to listen to the Sunday broadcast of the Free Europe Radio and our heartbeat quickened when we heard the message that was sent to us by my in-laws.

"Santa Claus will arrive a few days early..." The coded message that was meant for only us made its impact.

"The guide is coming," I whispered to Rozsa.

"What a Christmas gift that will be," Rozsa replied and we rejoined the feasting crowd.

On the late evening train we have returned to *Bacsbokod* and looked forward not only to our coming pork feast, but far more to the arrival of our guide, to our day of possible freedom.

***

I returned to school Monday morning and I was surprised by the way my former friends greeted me.

"I can't believe it Laszlo...You are here." Bela was the first to express his surprise.

"Where else would I be?"

"Never mind. I said nothing." Bela walked away and Janics greeted me.

"What a surprise! I can't believe my eyes, Laszlo."

"You are the second one to greet me in this strange manner. What is going on Pista?"

"Not here my dear friend. If you wish I will meet you after school...You know where." He walked away, like Bela did and I was greatly perplexed.

The news must have reached Pallosy, within a few minutes after my arrival to school. My class room door opened, just a few centimeters and I saw Pallosy take a peak. His face went white. The door flew open and he took a second look. Rage began to shake his tall frame, as he backed away from my room and for the rest of the day he couldn't be seen.

Each and every teacher, I saw that day, expressed the same surprise and I could hardly wait to talk with Janics.

He was already beside our brook when I arrived and in spite of the cold, the snow on the ground, we set down just for a few minutes and we talked, like we used to, before he betrayed me.

"I couldn't tell you at school what happened."

"I know Pista. Now you can tell me why did you behave like you saw a ghost."

"According to Pallosy, you were dead."

"Do I look dead?"

Janics disregarded my question and began to speak with great gusto.

"Last Sunday, Pallosy came to my home. I was truly surprised, he never did that before. I found out from him that he had visited a few other teachers. He was jubilant; he was beside himself, he announced that you were dead meat."

"Well, only Pallosy would be stupid enough to do something like that."

"He told me that he heard a telephone conversation you had with someone last Friday."

"He sure did. He listened to every word I said."

"He told me how he found out that you and your family were getting on the first train on Sunday. He was certain that you were on your way to get out of Hungary. He bragged about how he passed that information on to the authorities. He gloated over the fact that two secret agents were traveling with you and your family. 'Lichter and his brood will be arrested, taken off the train, as soon as they leave *Budapest*, heading west.' That is what he said. He timed his informing us well...I could no longer reach you, to warn you about the danger you were in. It was only natural that your reappearance sent all of us into a tailspin."

"Now I understand Pallosy's behavior," I told Pista and described my principal's visit to my class room.

"I am glad it is him and not I," Janics told me. "Can you imagine how Pallosy must feel? He thought he had his revenge and suddenly you reappear. He informed us, bragged to us, that you were arrested and here you are free. How did you ever escape your escorts?"

"Have I committed a crime by going to *Baja*? Do you think they could arrest me for that? I am glad Pallosy jumped the gun. I am elated that my phone conversation was misunderstood. Had he known that I intend to kill our pig…Had he heard that I plan to spend the winter in a warm place with plenty of food, he could have saved himself a heap of embarrassment."

"That he could," Janics agreed and I terminated our brief conversation by complaining about the bitter cold.

***

That evening I told Rozsa what happened at school and we had a lot to talk about. Our conversation focused on the topic of how we will get out of *Bacsbokod*, once our guide arrives.

"It will be during school break, so it will be easier," I told Rozsa.

"Don't you think that Pallosy will have someone watch the train station?"

"He will do that, I am sure my beloved. He and the station master are good friends. It would be easy for him to enlist his help, but I am not stupid either. I will think of getting away from this village in some other manner."

Next we turned our attention to the big event of killing our pig and who should be invited for the pork supper. We have prepared a list of several relatives. We had no desire to be stingy with the food and drinks; after all, if everything worked out well we wouldn't need all that foodstuff.

"The more guests arrive on the train, the more attention our settling down will receive." The two of us agreed and on the first day of our winter break, our fat pig gave up her life, so that our guests and us would have plenty to eat and that event gave us the cover we needed to carry out our not yet formed escape plan.

My parents left our house happy, particularly my Father, who was completely convinced that we will stay put. The others left a bit puzzled, for during their stay neither Rozsa, nor I, have said a word about escaping.

Joe came to the feast and remained with us.

"You don't mind my staying?" he asked me after everyone else left.

"I prefer you do that Joe. Didn't Sana speak to you about us wanting you here?"

"He did...He tried so hard to convince me to join your upcoming journey to Austria. Poor Sana didn't know that he was wasting his breath."

"You mean you are not coming with us?" Rozsa cried out.

"I would be foolish not to go," Joe announced with a smirk and I couldn't help, but remind him of the time when he refused to join us.

"That was then. I think I did the right thing, judging from what happened to you. I have spent some time in prison...They made me work in the coal mine like a slave...I don't need any more of that. Sana didn't need to work on me, I was ready to go without his urging. I waited only for your say so Laszlo. I am glad you finally came to your senses."

"We expect the guide before Christmas, at least that was the message we have received from your Father, Joe."

"But that is only six days away," Joe replied and I began to think about our past and contemplated the short time we had left in this country.

"I met my beloved in '48...We got married in '53...Ildiko was born in '54, the same year my in-laws escaped from here...We failed in our attempt in '55...A flood; a terrible earthquake, close to Budapest and a failed Revolution, all in '56. Just six days from now it will be Christmas. Will we spend that sacred holiday here or in prison or in a free country? If only I had a crystal ball...If I could see into the future, that would really come handy. Am I making another mistake? I am about to expose my loved ones to a perilous journey, but maybe it is better not knowing what the future holds for us. If I knew I would probably chicken out, yet there are no alternatives."

***

The minutes passed on with unbearable slowness; the hours have dragged on; night fell and another morning came, but no visitor approached us, until December twenty-first. On that glorious, yet fateful day somebody was knocking on the gate.

It wasn't the first time that someone banged on the door, but each and every time I opened it, with my heart in my mouth, it was someone who came to see Mr. Bencsik. This time the short, youngish looking man asked for me.

"So you are Laszlo Lichter. I am glad to meet you...Your picture I was shown, before I left *Linz*. You are just as skinny as your picture portrayed you. May I come in? I want to meet your beautiful wife and your lovely little daughter." I still feared a trap, but nothing seemed to matter anymore. I had to trust this man. I invited him into our home.

"I am happy to make your acquaintance." He shook Rozsa's hand and glanced at Ildiko first, then at Joe.

"Your daughter is really a lovely child. And you are Joe. Your parents are waiting for you too. Tomorrow we will be on our way. Oh, I almost forgot the letter. Here, read it...It is from your parents." He handed it to Rozsa.

"Our dear children,

"This will introduce you to Mihaly. He is a good guide. Trust him; do everything he says. He will lead you out of slavery. In a few days you will be free. We are waiting.

"Your loving, hopeful Dad and Mom." Rozsa read aloud the brief note and verified that it was indeed her Father's handwriting.

"Did you come by train?" I asked Mihaly.

"I did."

"Did they check your papers anywhere?"

"There was no checking...Just as well. I have no papers at all."

"No papers? That is incredible! How did you dare to travel all this way without them?"

"It wasn't hard. The country is still in turmoil. There is chaos everywhere. Hardly anyone is doing his job, except of course at the border, but there they are not looking for papers, just for escapees."

"What is the plan?" I asked Mihaly.

"Tomorrow we catch the first train out of here."

"We cannot travel by train. They are watching for us at the station."

"Then we got a big problem. You better think fast Laszlo."

His urging made me remember Sana's offer of help.

"Joe would you do us a favor?"

"You name and I will do it. Your inability to leave this village by train is a problem that must be solved. What do you want me to do Laszlo?"

"Get on the train tonight...Go to *Baja*...Ask Sana and his Father to come for us on their motor bikes, early tomorrow morning, before five o'clock. Tell Sana that his offer to help was never needed more. If anyone asks them why they are travelling that early in the morning, they should say that our daughter got very sick. They should explain that they will take her and us to the nearest hospital, which is in *Baja*."

"I am on my way," Joe announced and our guide began to give us his orders.

"Pack very lightly all you need. Two days of food you should bring. Warm clothing will be required and don't forget to wear your winter boots. Ildiko, of course will have to be carried. So bring a blanket and plenty of sleeping pills. We will cut a pole, tie the blanket to it and two of us will carry her across the border."

Rozsa began to prepare all that was needed, but she couldn't find any boots for Ildiko.

"Your parents, in one of the first parcels, sent her a pair of lovely red boots. It was too large for her then, but since she doesn't need to walk it should do nicely. Do you remember where those boots are Rozsa?"

"I do now my love. I seemed to have forgotten about them." She left the room and within minutes the boots were tried on Ildiko's feet. They didn't seem too large anymore; our little daughter grew a great deal since '54 when the boots were sent by her Grandparents.

Our guide surveyed the package, Rozsa assembled.

"This is good...But you should add a change of clothing for all of you, just in case you get really wet."

"What about my revolver? Should I take that with us?"

"I cannot permit you to do that. We could be searched. If they find it...that will be that." I knew Mihaly was right, so I went into our storage shed; lifted up one of the paving stones, dug a hole under it. Wrapped the gun in an oil-cloth and hid it there.

"If we fail...If we have to return...I will need this gun to protect my family," I thought and went inside.

Our guide was in the process of checking our small, full suitcase. He didn't find it too heavy and gave his approval.

"Before we put Ildiko to bed, don't you think my love we should celebrate Christmas?"

"You read my mind Laszlo. We should at least give Ildiko her gift." With that said Rozsa disappeared and came back with a doll. We bought it a month before. It was the only present we could afford to buy our little daughter.

Rozsa handed the doll to Ildiko, who hugged it lovingly to her chest.

"This is our Christmas gift to you Ildiko," Rozsa began. "We will take a small trip tomorrow and just in case we don't get back before Christmas Eve, little Jesus brought you this doll early."

She kissed both of us; murmured her thanks and within minutes she was asleep, still clutching the precious item.

"Now go to bed. Have a good night's sleep. You will need your energy," Mihaly spoke up.

"I must go over to say good bye to the Bencsiks," I told our guide and Rozsa.

"You shouldn't do that. You must not trust anyone," Mihaly began to argue.

"The Bencsiks are decent people. They have been our friends for almost a year. I will not go without saying good-by to them and besides, I want to give them a spare key to our apartment."

"If you must," the guide gave in.

Rozsa and I went next door and told Mr. and Mrs. Bencsik what we were about to do.

"You are wise to get your family out of this country," Mr. Bencsik began, trying to control his tears and to some extent he succeeded, but neither his wife, nor Rozsa could follow his example. "You go with our blessing Laszlo and Rozsa. Take care of little Ildiko. We will pray for your success. We will not tell our little daughter, Marika, the truth. We will just tell her that you went to *Baja* for a week."

We embraced; we cried a little when our tears could no longer be checked and returned to our apartment. That night Rozsa and I slept fitfully.

"Will Sana make his promise good or will he chicken out? How will all of us be able to travel on two motorbikes? What shall we do, if Sana comes alone? Should I go to see my parents? Would my Father talk and talk until he succeeds to have me change our plan? We said good-by to the Bencsiks and that was hard, but how many others will we have to embrace for one last time before we leave the city of our birth? Will we ever see those dear people again?" These questions ran through my mind, in a random order, and with each new question another was born.

"Will the AVO watch the bus? Will someone stop us before we reach Budapest?

Laszlo S. Lichter

If we get to *Mosonmagyarovar*, will I have time to visit Uncle Jozsef's grave? I cannot leave this country without paying my final respect to that dear man. Will Rozsa be strong enough to leave our home, all our belongings? There is not much to leave. The foodstuffs will not cause a problem, but the precious heirlooms, Rozsa inherited from her Mother and Father are going to cause her pain. My poor darling endured a lot. I know she is strong, but there will be a lot of crying. Her parents worked all their lives for what little there is in our apartment and so did we. Help her, dear God."

I must have dozed off, for I woke hearing the sound of motorcycles.

"Thank God the two of them came." I thought, even before I opened the gate and the Gomoris pushed their bikes into our yard.

Once inside, the older Gomori gave us the dreadful news.

"There is a barricade, just two kilometers from here. We were lucky. The single policeman guarding it bought our story, but I think on the way to *Baja*, he will want all the identification papers. Do all of you have the needed documents?"

"Mihaly, our guide has no papers," I replied and began to search for a solution.

"We must not fail now. I must find a way," I thought and got an idea.

"Is it AVO that guards the road? Or is he a local policeman?" I asked the Gomoris.

"He knew of you Laszlo. He expressed his regret that your child was sick. He even spoke a few words about how you saved a man's life..."

"In that case I have a plan. I think it will work. I am going to walk ahead...Give me thirty minutes, then all of you start out. I will meet you on the road after the barricade."

"I want us to stay together Laszlo," Rozsa stated and for several minutes she hung on to me, but eventually her tears dried up. She must have realized that there was no other way to get out of *Bacsbokod*. With a passionate kiss she sent me on my way to carry out whatever I had planned.

I approached the barricade, some twenty minutes later, and greeted the policeman, whom I recognized to be the parent of one of my students.

"I was sorry to hear about your little girl. I hope she will get well." The guard sounded sincere and he waved me on.

I walked a hundred meters or so, before I turned around and shouted back.

"I forgot to show you the identification papers."

"I know you, Mr. Lichter. There was no need for that."

"But I have all the papers for all the others, except of course the drivers."

"Who else is coming with them?" he shouted back.

"My littler girl; my wife and my brother in-law. Do you want me to walk back?" I held my breath; my heart skipped many beats; sweat was pouring off my body.

"Will he do as I expected? Or will he call me back? If he does, all is lost and our dream of escaping will be shattered." The thoughts came to me with great rapidity and so did his answer.

"Go on man...You have a long distance to walk..." I turned away from him and picked up my pace to get out of his sight, just in case he would change his mind.

Ten minutes later, I heard the sounds of the approaching bikes and within a moment the two of them came to a halt beside me.

"You are a foxy one Laszlo," Sana announced. "The guard never even bothered to ask us for our papers. He just waved us on, as we approached him."

Rozsa set behind Sana, holding Ildiko front of her and the older Gomori invited me to sit behind him and front of Mihaly.

"It will be a little crowded...It is illegal of course, but after what you have done Laszlo, I am sure you are not reluctant to break the law. We will drive a little slower. Sana you go ahead. We will meet you at the house soon."

I held on for dear life and in the coming dawn I saw Sana disappear with my darlings.

***

I heard the commotion, as soon as we entered the yard.

"Oh my God...Look what happened to Ildiko," Rozsa's voice sounded shrill and full of pain.

I rushed into the kitchen, expecting a dreadful setback.

Rozsa's Aunt, her Grandmother and Sana were examining the right, red boot that Ildiko wore for the first time. Its bottom was worn away, exposing her sock underneath.

"God, look at this. We got here just in time. Her boot must have been rubbing against the rear wheel. Another kilometer and her foot would have been caught. What a tragedy that would have been," Sana exclaimed.

Rozsa's Grandmother took over: "A sign from the Lord...You must stay home."

"That is nonsense. It was just an accident waiting to happen. Rozsa and the rest of them must go on. If they stay in Hungary, they will lose a lot more than part of a boot...They will lose everything. So be quiet Mom," Mrs. Gomori urged her Mother not to make the parting even more difficult.

"How long before we have to go to the bus station?" I asked Mihaly and was relieved to know that Ildiko was unharmed. Her escaping a serious injury I considered a Heavenly sign from our Lord that He wanted us to go on.

"Not for almost two hours. It is not far from here," Sana gave the answer and I fell silent, contemplating what I was to do.

"Should I go and see my parents? How could I leave them without saying good-by? I couldn't even do that to the Bencsiks. I may never ever see them again," I thought and announced my decision.

"I will go home, to my parents' home, I mean. I must see them before we leave."

"I go with you," Rozsa offered, but I feared the emotional drain that would mean to my Mother and Rozsa, so I declined her offer and took off alone.

***

I thanked God for finding only my Mother home.

"What an unexpected visit Laszlo," were the first words that my Mother uttered, but within a split second she was onto me. "Oh my God, you are about to leave the country."

I didn't know how to confess that I was determined to leave not only the country of my birth, but more so the parents who brought me into this world. I just nodded my head in agreement.

"I am ready to cry, but I will not do that. You are doing the right thing Laszlo. Life is not worth living in this country. I only wish your Father listened to me long ago. You are lucky he is not home. He would plead with you; he would appeal to you; he would try to frighten you and I know that you would give in. Why isn't Ildiko and Rozsa with you? I must say good-by to them as well."

"They couldn't come," I told my Mother and she shook her head.

"I will not let them go without a kiss. I will not allow them to leave without my good wishes. We will never see any of you again Laszlo. How are you leaving Baja and when?"

"In less than an hour and a half, we will go by bus to Budapest."

"I will be at the bus station," my Mother announced and I pictured what would happen.

"She will hug Ildiko and Rozsa and she will burst out crying. Her actions will be a dead give-away. I must not permit that."

"Mother, please listen to me. We may be watched. Your presence may give us away. Do you want us to fail? Do you want us to go to prison? Please don't come...Please don't make our leaving harder than it is."

"Where are they now?" she asked with her tears appearing.

"At Gomoris"

"They can say good bye to Rozsa. They can kiss Ildiko for the last time. And you dare to deny your Mother, what you allow others to do?"

"I am not. All morning Rozsa has been crying. To leave our home, all our belongings was very hard for my darling. She may change her mind, if she is forced to face you too. Is that what you want to do Mother?"

"That is not what I want. I must see them once more, Laszlo."

"I cannot allow you to come to the station. Neither can I allow you to come to the Gomoris. If there is something else you can think of Mother, so be it."

I could see her brighten, but her plan I couldn't figure out.

"Go then Laszlo. Don't miss your bus. I will say your good-bye to your Father and George too, when I see them. It will be hard. Your Father may never forgive you. He will be devastated."

"Remind him what our life was like. Tell him that we love him, as we love you." My last words made me cry.

"No more tears Laszlo. That is enough. Be a man." She hugged me and in spite of the advice she gave me, her tears rolled down her cheeks while she held onto me. I broke the embrace, but never the ties that bound us.

***

I ran back to the Gomoris and I had to repeat the same performance. All of them wanted to be with us, until the last minute, but I couldn't permit that.

"You must not come...I denied my own Mother that form of parting. We will say our good-bye here and then we will walk alone to the station. Mr. Bencsik has a key, Sana, to our apartment. Give us a week and if we don't return, take everything out of there and split all our belongings with my parents."

"We will do that..." Sana promised.

"Thanks to both of you for all your help," I told them and reached out to shake the hands of the men who got us this far. Then I kissed both women. The tears could no longer hide themselves. Crying, sobbing, laments of the final parting came and we could still hear those heart-wrenching sounds, as the gate closed behind us.

***

Tickets in hand, we climbed on the bus, after twenty minutes of fearful waiting. There were people, I knew, all around us, but neither them, nor were we inclined to enter into conversations.

"If they are watching out for us, we will know before the bus pulls away." I thought and glanced at Rozsa, her eyes red and badly swollen. I looked at Ildiko, sitting on her Mother's lap, hugging her new doll.

"At least our little darling is too young to understand our fear, the pain and the sacrifices we were making," I thought, as the bus pulled out of the station.

"Thank you dear Lord...You helped us this far...Give us your protection for the rest of our journey."

Still in Baja, the bus came to a stop, at the corner of Szt. Laszlo and Budapest Streets. There stood my Mother, her eyes covered with a handkerchief. I lifted up Ildiko for my Mother to see her Grandchild for one last time and controlled my tears.

Ildiko may not have recognized her handkerchief covered face, thus she didn't cry out and I was enormously grateful to the woman who brought me into this world and during the most crucial moment hid her face.

I lifted my hand, ever so slightly and waved before the bus pulled out. We were on our way.

"Hey, you are Laszlo Lichter. Remember me?" The man surprised me and my fear, in check until then, suddenly assaulted me.

"I don't think so," I blurted out.

"You worked at *Gara*, last summer. I was the bookkeeper at the collective farm. Do you remember me now?"

"I am sorry. I do now."

"So where are you heading Laszlo? Is this your wife and your daughter?"

I had no choice, but to introduce them.

Ildiko answered his question.

"We are going on a holiday."

"How nice," the bookkeeper stated. "I am going to a conference. Well it was nice to see you again. Maybe next summer we will work together again."

"Sure, I would like to do that," I lied to him, but something told me that he was misstating the facts too. "He is doing just what we are doing," I thought and I began to wonder.

"How many others on this bus are heading to Austria? Many, many I guess, yet we pretend, we lie, we mislead each other. What a terrible life. Nobody dares to trust anyone. This is what we have become. This is what the Communists did to us. They turned us into a bunch of hypocrites; they thought us how to fear."

Three hours later, we left the bus and our guide described the next step.

"We will go to Rozsa's Aunt Lujza. We will spend the night there. It is all arranged."

"Oh, dear God. I thought the time of good-bys were over," I told myself, but we did as our guide commanded.

Lujza fawned over Ildiko, whom she saw only once, at the time of our previous attempt. She greeted Joe with great warmth and relief.

"I was so worried about you Joe. You did a foolish thing. Why have you refused the lawyer's help? Why have you not gone along with his story? You probably would have been set free."

"Let it go Auntie. That was in the past. It no longer matters," Joe spoke up and that night he rarely spoke again.

A night with Lujza, who fed us, gave us drinks and many messages to her brother wasn't unpleasant, but what came next truly surprised me.

"I have a favor to ask from all of you," Lujza announced around ten o'clock in the evening.

"Anything we can do for you we will do," I promised her not expecting to be trapped.

"I have a really good friend. She lives next door. She and her boyfriend and her grown son want to go with you. I hope I didn't make a mistake telling them that they probably can?"

"How could you?" I blurted out.

"I had to...They are in terrible danger. If they are not out of here soon, they will be arrested. They will die a horrible death. Please help them Laszlo...At least come with me and meet those dear people."

I looked at our guide, expecting his objection, but that never came.

"Let's go," I told Lujza.

We entered the nice apartment and Lujza made the introductions. I noticed, not without surprise, that they were already packed.

"Can you help us Laszlo?" the woman popped the question.

"I don't really know."

"Why are you escaping?" This time the son spoke up.

"It is a long story. Let's just say that we are in danger, if we stay."

"And so are we," the boyfriend announced.

I wasn't sure what to do.

"To carry Ildiko, all the way, would need more than the three of us: Joe, Mihaly and I," I thought and gave my consent.

They expressed their eternal gratitude. Their praises sounded gushy and insincere. I didn't care, thus our small group of four swelled by another three.

Another almost sleepless night, another tearful parting and we were on our way to the railway station.

"Thank God this part is over. Rozsa has cried, each and every time, she had to leave someone behind. I cried inside only; I didn't want to show my weakness. Joe and Ildiko were the only two, who took everything calmly. To Ildiko the trip was a great adventure. Joe, for some unknown reason, remained unruffled by the many partings.

At the station-after we bought our tickets to *Szekesfehervar*-we had a long wait and I saw a group of three boys, who attended school with me in *Baja*. For a while they didn't seem to see me, and then one of them walked by me and feigned surprise.

"I cannot believe my eyes. It is you Laszlo. What are you doing here?"

"It is good to see you Sanyi. My family and I are going to visit someone."

"Someone in Austria?" Sanyi asked, but did so in a whisper.

"Oh, no. Just someone at *Szekesfehervar*," I replied and Sanyi turned pale.

"Too bad...My two friends and I are trying to leave the country. You know them Laszlo. Laci and Ocsi were in the same class with us when we have attended the Public School of *Baja*. We don't know the way across the border. We are going blindly." I felt sorry for my former classmates and made a quick decision.

"I lied to you Sanyi. I hope you didn't mind my caution. We have a guide; he knows the way and if you wish you could join us."

"That would be splendid. What should we do? Where should we buy our tickets?"

"To *Szekesfehervar*. Get in the same compartment we do. Watch us and when we leave the train you do the same. I will give your further instructions, as I receive them."

"But that city is down to the south. I thought you were going west?" Sanyi asked me.

"Our guide is following the safest route possible. He knows what to do, just follow our example."

At *Szekesfehervar* we switched to a train that was heading to *Gyor* and from there to another one to reach *Mosonmagyarovar*. Once we reached the last city, we would dare to go to by train; I spoke to Sanyi once more.

"We will be heading to a safe house. Follow us and once we get there we will talk more. Let's hope we get there safely." I walked away, having given him the instructions needed.

***

Mihaly was walking ahead, never looking back to see if we followed. The four of us followed his example. I imagined the three adults from *Budapest*, behind us and behind them Sanyi, Laci and Ocsi following.

Our home and those we loved were only a distant memory. The loss of all our possessions no longer gave me pain; the only thing that mattered then was to reach the safe house.

Mihaly banged on a gate and waited. After what seemed like a long time to me, he was admitted and was swallowed by the large house.

As soon as we reached the gate, as I was about to bang on it, it opened.

"Hurry up...You must not be seen!" the jolly, rotund man told us.

"There are two more groups of threes to come," I informed our helper.

"I will let them in. By the way call me Vitez. When they arrive we will sort things out."

The gate opened two more times and finally our group of ten were inside. We were one short.

"I thought there were three of you Sanyi. Isn't that what you told me?"

"We lost that stupid Laci. I wish we didn't go to *Szekesfehervar*. That is where he bailed out."

"What happened?"

"I tell you. Laci's Mother and step-father live close to the station. He went to visit them and never came back."

I thought of my own visit to my Mother and could imagine what happened to that young man.

"His Mother or his step-father, or maybe both, scared the daylight out of him. Must have persuaded him to give up his dream. It is really too bad. Had I found my Father home, I would have suffered the same fate, if I showed any weakness."

Soon we were seated in the kitchen; enjoying the meal the lady of the house prepared for all of us. When we satisfied our hunger, Vitez spoke up.

"I expected only three escapees. Your guide and I were paid for nobody else." Vitez announced, no longer jovial. His announcement surprised me greatly. Mihaly never said anything about payment.

"How much were you paid for each of us? And tell me who paid you," I asked and wondered what will happen next.

"Some people charge an enormous amount, but I am a patriotic Hungarian. I have led many to freedom..." He probably would have gone on and on about how great he was, but I realized that I was dealing with a businessman, who exploited the opportunity the exodus from Hungary gave him. At the risk of being rude, I cut him off.

"How much, I asked!"

"Two thousand *Forints* for each person, that is what it costs. Five extra people would cost you ten thousand, under normal circumstances, but since I am a patriot, I will make it only nine. That is a bargain you people are getting."

I looked at our late comers. Sanyi and Ocsi forked out their share of the cost. Lujzi's three friends just shook their heads.

"We have nothing. We are poor people. We cannot pay. Please don't make us turn around," the boyfriend began to plead and the two others joined him.

"We have lost so much during the Revolution," the son added.

"We were never told that we have to pay. We should have been told. Telling us now is unfair. Don't you think Laszlo?"

I knew that I was being suckered, yet I felt responsible for what happened. I searched for my few remaining bills and handed them over.

"You are still short of five thousand," the businessman counted the bills. "Are you trying to take advantage of my kindness?"

Sanyi began to hand over a few bills, then Ocsi followed his example.

"Still too short...A thousand short," Vitez shook his head.

"I have nothing more to give...You can't get blood out of a stone. If you are still dissatisfied, maybe you should give it all back, including the money my in-laws advanced.

Maybe we will try to get across on our own," I bluffed and Vitez paled.

"I wouldn't hear of such nonsense. I am a patriot. You owe me nothing more. I am glad this is finally settled."

All the while the bargaining went on, Mihaly stayed out of it. I couldn't tell if he did that, because he didn't care about money or because he was not the one in command.

"I want to know when do we start?" I was annoyed by the greed I witnessed.

"At five o'clock it will be getting dark. That is when we will leave the house." Mihaly gave the information.

"How far are we from the border?" I asked next.

"Maybe twenty, maybe more kilometers," Vitez gave the vague answer.

"Don't you know? Are you just guessing? You told us, you took many people out of here."

"And so I did, but you don't seem to understand. As the crow flies it is no more than twenty, but can you fly my friend? We will have to walk through many snow covered fields. Here and there we will have to take detours and there may be unexpected obstacles."

"Very well." I decided to give in and hoped that my unease was unjustified. I changed the topic of our conversation.

"Could someone tell me where is the Roman Catholic cemetery? I would like to go there."

"At the edge of town. I will give you good directions." Vitez seemed to be pleased with getting me out of his hair.

I embraced Rozsa and hugged Ildiko. "You two, my love, should take a rest. I will be back long before we are to start out."

"Please be very careful Laszlo. Don't be late coming back and say a prayer from me too."

Vitez gave me directions and when I was satisfied that I will not get lost, I left the house and twenty minutes later, I was there.

I approached the caretaker and told him whose grave I wanted to find.

"I don't rightly remember," he shook his head.

I tried another way to find out.

"My poor Uncle died at the border, back in '55. The authorities gave him a burial."

"Well that is different. All of them are in that far corner. That is where all traitors are buried." He pointed toward the setting Sun.

Being that close to my Uncle's grave, made it improper to curse at the caretaker for using the term 'traitors'. I walked away, without thanking him and disregarded his extended hand with his palm up.

I found many snow covered graves. With my gloves, I wiped the snow off the markers, one after another and stared at my Uncle's resting place. The inscription was, as my Aunt told me: Jozsef Santa 1908-1955.

I uncovered my head and knelt in front of the grave.

"Uncle Jozsef, I beg for your forgiveness. I wish you were alive! I wish you were with Aunt Gizella. You must know that she is in Austria; that she is safe. She came to visit you, a while back; she must have told you that your killer died a horrible death.

"I couldn't leave this country without coming to you. You were more than an Uncle to me...You were my friend. May God give you rest. Rozsa, Ildiko and I are heading toward Austria. We don't know if we will get across or join you where you are now, but whatever will happen will be better than the lives we have.

"I promise you Uncle, friend, that this time we will not turn back. We will either find freedom or we will find eternal rest.

"Good-bye Uncle; farewell my best friend. I will never forget you! This grave and all your kindness I locked away in my heart. To my dying days you will be remembered. Now I must go..." My tears rolled down my face; I offered a brief prayer and with great sadness, a heavy heart, I walked away, amongst the graves of those poor souls, who had found only this kind of freedom in the land of sadness.

***

I was back at the safe house a few minutes after four and the singing that came from inside the room, clashed with my sad memories.

When I stepped inside, the singing stopped and I faced three drunken men.

Vitez got up, reached for my hand and swayed. Joe couldn't even stand up; he just stared drunkenly into his half filled glass. Mihaly seemed to be embarrassed to have me see him in his intoxicated state.

"What the f...is going on here?" I couldn't control my rage.

"We are just having a little celebration...," came from Joe.

"We had a few drinks, that is all. After the lives I saved, am I not entitled to a bit of imbibing?" Vitez's slurred words came to me.

Only Mihaly had enough sense to remain quiet.

"Get some cold water...Get lots of coffee...," I shouted at the frightened wife of Vitez and for a half an hour I poured coffee down their throats and kept pushing their heads into a basin of cold water.

"Where are the others?" I demanded to know.

"In that room...Your wife and daughter rest."

"What about the boys?"

"They are resting in there," Vitez pointed in the opposite direction.

I glanced at my watch. It was getting near five. I roused Rozsa and Ildiko. Then I went to wake the others.

"Look at your dear brother. I found him and our guides, drunk as skunks, when I returned." I know my words hurt my dear wife, but I was beside myself.

"How in hell do they expect to get us across the border?" I wish I didn't speak those words, but it was impossible to retract them.

"It was a stupid thing they did Laszlo, but had you not left..." Rozsa didn't finish what she was about to say.

"Let's get going. It is getting late," I announced and looked at our two guides, who huddled together, talking in hushed tones, but I couldn't make out what they said.

Mihaly picked up his small valise and without a word he staggered toward the gate we used earlier.

"Where is he going?" I shouted at Vitez.

"He is going...ahead. We will meet up. Now grab your things...We are on our way." He lead us to a gate, at the opposite end of the yard from where Mihaly left.

"Why are we going the other way?" I demanded to know, still inside the yard.

"Trust us! Now listen to me all of you. You, you and you will follow me in two minutes." He pointed at Rozsa, Joe and I, with Ildiko in my arms.

"You, you and you come after them, two minutes later." He pointed at our non-paying guests.

"Then the last two of you wait two minutes. We must not be seen leaving the house together."

***

Our guide left the house and within two minutes we followed him through the almost empty streets. The Sun was behind the western horizon; the gray skies threatened to dump their load of snow, but the streets were bright with the white snow that covered them.

The guide seemed to have sobered up. At least he was no longer staggering. I only wished the same thing was true about my brother in-law, whose uncertain steps betrayed his state. I took the suitcase from him, wishing to ease his burden and carried Ildiko, as well, until we reached the edge of the city and began to cross a vast, snow covered, cornfield. The corn stalks no longer existed, just the stalks, under the snow. The ground was uneven. Where the corn grew there were rows of humps and between, what used to be rows, depressions existed. The deep snow hid the strong stumps of stalks. It was no longer a road that we walked on and soon ankles were bruised, tortured, twisted and our clothing became soaked with sweat. Ten minutes later, at the edge of a patch of woods, we stopped and waited. Slowly the others arrived, but Mihaly was not amongst us.

"Where is our other guide, Mihaly, I mean?" I asked Vitez.

"He was...He is not here? What the hell... We will go without him. Where is the blanket? We will cut a pole here...You will tie two corners of the blanket close to one end and the other two corners close to the other end. Then two of you can carry the girl inside it...She will be warmer and it will be a lot easier on all of you."

"What are we going to cut the pole with?" I asked.

"Use the axe."

"What axe?"

"Did I forget to bring one?" Vitez's words were slurred again.

"You are a moron...," the insult slipped out. "We barely began our trek and we are already in trouble, thanks to this patriotic, greedy, drunken bastard." I thought and searched the patch of woods, until I found a suitable pole. We tied the blanket; tested the pole's strength and having found it strong enough, we placed my little daughter inside the sagging blanket.

Sanyi and I lifted the sweet burden and followed our guide on the uneven ground, heading away from the city. The suitcase and the pole on my shoulder made me tire fast, and it seemed that none of the others fared any better. We heard soldiers singing, in the far distance and just the thought of running into them made me taste real fear.

We must have walked, stumbled, struggled for about an hour. The lights and sounds faded from the city. We walked in the fields; trudged in the knee deep snow; slipped on the ice of brooks. Our breathing became labored and my concern began to mount.

"Are you okay my love? How are you holding up?" I whispered to Rozsa.

"I am managing Laszlo," she replied, but her voice sounded weak.

"It won't be long. We must be five kilometers closer to the border. Just hold out for a while yet. We will be there..." I reached out for her hand and gave it a reassuring squeeze.

"I will survive it Laszlo," she told me and I felt her hand tighten on my arm.

Our guide suddenly lost his footing, fell to the ground. I hoped it was the slippery surface and not the alcohol that made him fall. We lifted him to his feet. He groaned and demanded that we rest for a few minutes.

We sat on the snow, until we began to shiver. I held Ildiko in my arms and Rozsa sat close to me.

"I want home...I am cold..." Ildiko cried out and to muffle the sound we covered her mouth with a scarf that Rozsa wore and gave her the first of several sleeping pills.

"Soon my love..." I lied to my child and felt self loathing for misleading someone I loved.

"At this rate we will never get to Austria," I thought and urged our guide to rise. His movements were sluggish, his gaze uncertain and when he finally rose, he looked around and began to walk.

From time to time Joe needed assistance, but thank God he was less and less under the influence of the alcohol.

The skies opened up...Heavy, fat, wet snowflakes fell on us and those flakes that settled on our lips, helped ease the dryness that came with exhaustion. For another two hours we have marched on. The blanket covered Ildiko got new carriers, more and more frequently. Our stops, our rest periods were more often needed and when I glanced behind us, I saw that our footsteps no longer showed, the snow covered them, as it began to cover our exhausted bodies.

The guide lost his footing and fell, time and time again. Only with our assistance could he get to his feet and with great difficulty, he marched on.

The snowfall went as fast as it came. The stars began to shine above us, but none of us knew how to use them for navigating. Another dreadful hour passed. Rozsa began to drag her feet; the rest of the group were in no better shape. Being tired; being wet would have been enough, but we were most disturbed by what we have discovered.

"Stop," I commanded and my order was obeyed. "What do you make of this?" I pointed at the impressions in the snow.

All of us, except Ildiko, who was asleep, examined the prints and then Sanyi spoke up.

"They are ours. There is no doubt about that. Look at this one...Then look at the sole of my boot...They are identical. We have been going around in circles. We are lost."

I dropped the suitcase. Sanyi and Ocsi were carrying Ildiko. I grabbed the patriotic, still drunken fool, who fancied himself to be a guide and savior of many Hungarians.

"Which way is the border?" I hissed in his ear.

The 'guide' raised his hand and pointed in one direction, then in another.

"You don't really know! Do you?" I hissed once more.

"It must be...I think, but that stupid snowstorm made me confused. Let me see..." He stood there, turned around several times and then he pointed once again.

"It must be ahead of us."

"Ahead of us indeed. You are no more a guide than I am, you greedy fool. You can boast and celebrate and make empty promises, but you are incapable to lead us out of this country. Thanks to you we will never get across." I was out of control. I could have killed that bastard.

"Laszlo please, don't make things worse by being so angry. Think of something," Rozsa pleaded with me.

"If we stay here we will surely not get out of Hungary. Let's get going," Sanyi urged me.

"You don't seem to trust me. I might as well turn around." The guide seemed to be offended.

"You are a moron. You know your way home, as much as you know the way across the border. You were paid well. You will come with us and if God allows us to get across, at least you will have made one successful journey. That way your next group of paying victims will be better off. Now let's get going." I took command.

Another hour of stumbling, falling, slipping followed and when we seemed to have no more hope, no more energy left, we saw a faint light. Without discussion, we headed toward it. It came from a window of an isolated farm house.

Our desperate group came to a halt and we began a whispered conversation.

"We must ask someone to help us," Ocsi suggested.

"There is no other way," Sanyi agreed.

"What if they are Communists? What if they will turn us over to the border guards?" The woman from *Budapest* found her voice.

"We got to give it a try or we will freeze to death. We will surround the door. There are enough of us to overpower them, if need be," I told the group.

In two minutes flat, we were by the door. My two friends on one side; Joe and I on the other side. The rest of the group flattened themselves against the wall. I raised my hand to give the door a knock and sent a silent prayer to the Almighty.

"Please help us Lord to find decent people in there. We don't want to harm anyone...Just need some food, some drink, a little rest and good directions."

My knuckles hit the door and a man peered out.

"Who is it?"

"Please let us in. We are lost."

The door opened all the way and we filed in.

"Dear God. Another group of refugees. Come in, come in. You must rest. Wife get some food and drinks into these poor people."

Our exhausted little group needed little urging. We fell into the wooden chairs around the large, plank table. The heat of the room embraced me, I suddenly felt more fatigued than I was anytime during our journey.

"You too must be worn out my darling," I spoke to Rozsa.

Her eyes shone brightly, not only with love, with relief, but with feverish exhaustion.

"If I can rest for a little while, I will be as good as new Laszlo." She tried to look brave, but it was only a front, I knew. My darling's store of energy was almost depleted.

The woman of the house served us hot soup, home-baked bread, plenty of bacon and sausages. We ate ravenously and answered the hosts' questions.

"Where are you coming from?" The man wanted to know.

"Our so called guide is from a city near-by. My family and friends are all from the city of *Baja*. These three people lived in *Budapest*." I pointed to the individuals as I spoke about them, and although I despised our greedy, ignorant, opportunistic guide, I didn't tell our hosts where he was from.

"You were lost. Weren't you?" the hostess asked us.

"Lost and without hope, until we found this place and its wonderful inhabitants." I expressed our gratitude and the woman seemed to be embarrassed.

"We are just simple farmers, looking out for our fellow men." She shrugged her shoulders and turned her attention to replenishing our plates.

"You are all wet...If you have a change of clothing, you should change. If not I might find something you could wear for the rest of your trek."

All of us, except our guide, hurriedly changed into dry clothing and we left the table, crowded around the hot stove.

"Can you tell us which way is the border?" I sought our host's help.

"It is only five kilometers from here. I will explain how to get there." He fell silent. Something seemed to bother him and then he resumed talking. "I will do better than that...I will lead you quite close to the border."

"We would be ever so grateful. But there is a problem...None of us have any money. We couldn't pay anything...," I began to explain our predicament.

"Stop right there. Have I asked you for any money? What do you take me for? Am I not a countryman of yours? Why do you insult me in this manner?"

I glanced at our guide, who hung his head.

"I am not like those who exploit their fellow men." The host spoke again and it was clear that he knew that our guide did, but not out of love, out of greed for payment.

"The last two months I have seen many kinds of people. First the AVO and AVH men and women were pouring across the border. I helped none of those people, and then November four came and went.

"Group after group struggled toward the border. Some on their own and others led by conniving businessmen. More than not those so called guides, knew nothing about how to get people out of our country, but were quite skillful in making those desperate souls part with all they had. A few groups, much like you did, stumbled on our place and when my wife and I saw them, we knew our duty. Food and drink; shelter for a few hours we have provided. With rest and my guidance they had a better chance to make it across the border and so will you people, I promise you that. I did nothing during the Revolution, I admit it freely, but once it failed, we were determined to make up for that and the good Lord showed us a way to help.

"You got here around twelve. It is one o'clock now. Rest for another hour and then we will start out. Pray that we will not meet any border guards, especially Russians. They are brutal killers. The Hungarian border guards have no desire to decimate their countrymen. Like all soldiers, in our country, they were drafted. They were less lucky than thousands of others, having been ordered to guard our border. They are decent young fellows. They too are victims of the system, not unlike most of us. Yet we will have to try to avoid all of them. I know how we will accomplish that."

We have rested and warmed our chilled bones, until our host began to dress. Ildiko, who also had some food and fresh milk from our benefactor's cow, was still asleep and we had to wake her, at least until we placed her in her blanket.

All of us left the house, but not before expressing our profuse thanks to the woman who shared with us what little they had.

The new, knowledgeable guide, walked ahead of us and when he found it safe to proceed, he waved back, making us follow him. In this manner, with many stops and short waits, we have covered about three kilometers, when we came to a dike.

"Up to this point our route was tricky, but from here on it is really simple. If you stay on this dike; if you walk on it for two kilometers, you will come to a deep cut in it. This side of the cut is still Hungary, but the other side belongs to the Austrians. Go quietly all the way. In the still night voices carry far, so don't give yourselves away by talking. Did all of you understand what I said?"

"We do, I assure you. What about the mine-fields?" I asked him and began to probe for the dangers that we were yet to face.

"There isn't any, any more."

"What about the wire fences?"

"Thousands of Hungarians have cut them to ribbons. Those fences have been demolished."

"Any guard towers?"

"Those still exist, but if not manned by Russians, you are likely to find them deserted. Besides, the route I suggested to you, will take you out at a spot about half way between two guard towers."

"You have been very kind to us. You saved our lives." I didn't know what else to say.

"I have been nothing more than what the good Lord made me: a simple, God-fearing Hungarian. I hope you will find what you are hoping for."

"We will never forget your kindness." I assured him and one by one we shook his hand. We stared after the man who got us this far and accepted nothing for his kindness; who shared with us what little he had; who risked his life to help a group of total strangers. The longer we stood there the more impatient our paid guide became.

"What a foolish bunch you are. He got you three kilometers closer to the border and you look upon him like he was your savior. I promised to get you all out and I be damned if I fail. Let's go."

'Don't fool yourself. You did nothing for us, you drunken bum. From this moment on, you are only an observer."

"Then I might as well turn around." He tried again, but I would have none of his nonsense.

"You do no such thing. You will cross the border with us. This time you will learn the route that might help some of your future victims." I turned from him and we began to walk.

The dike, we walked on, protected the land from the narrow river that slept under the thin ice and some thirty meters away, on the other side, we could see the dike's sister.

Laszlo S. Lichter

Moonlight glistened on the ice cover and here and there we could see the open water.

We marched on, but the effect of the refreshing rest didn't last long. Less than a kilometer sapped our energies once more and the group began to straggle.

"Keep up...Don't fall behind. We are getting closer with each step. Don't dare give up now," I urged one after another.

All was silent in the wintry dawn. Not a living soul anywhere nearby, except our desperate little group, probably dreaming about the border of hope, beyond which existed freedom.

I thought about all that was behind us. The bad times we have experienced; the bleak future our homeland held and once more I swore to myself the promise, I made at my Uncle's grave.

"I promise you Uncle, friend, that this time we will not turn back. We will either find freedom or we will find eternal rest." I kept repeating this solemn promise and my eyes settled on the face of my sleeping little daughter.

"You will grow up in a free land!" I barely finished whispering to her what I thought, when the stillness of the night was torn to shreds by a dog's barking.

It stood on the opposite dike, shaking with excitement, took a few tentative steps to cross the ice, but changed its mind. It returned to the top of the dike, but never stopped its snarling barking.

"It is only a stray dog...," I tried to assure Rozsa, but I was wrong. Two gun toting border guards crested the dike and shouted their command.

"Stop or we will shoot!" I could see their machine pistols aimed at us.

All of us stopped.

"Only two kilometers to freedom and all is lost," I thought bitterly. I couldn't think clearly; I couldn't breathe; I felt my rage taking control of me; I lost my mind; I wanted to die, yet somewhere, in the back of my mind, the kind farmer's words reverberated.

"The Hungarian border guards have no desire to decimate their countrymen." My mind cleared for a brief moment and I began to sort out the possibilities.

"I have to believe that these guards will not pull the triggers. I will have to act accordingly." I thought and a voice floated across the river.

"Where are you heading?"

"Are they imbeciles or are they making fun of our desperate situation? Three o'clock in the morning we are heading to the nearby border. How can they ask such a stupid question?" I thought, but decided not to give them a reply. The others too remained silent.

"We will take you back to the station. You must keep walking, but must not run or we will open fire."

"We will not go back! You have to kill all of us! You should start with the child!" The words were out of my mouth and my stupid utterances I couldn't take back, yet something in me sensed that my statements confused the guards. I could hear them arguing with each other, but their words couldn't be comprehended.

"Keep walking in the same direction," came the next order.

Our group stumbled before, but now none of us dared to fall. We walked a short distance, unable to guess why they were leading us toward Austria.

"Maybe they will let us go?" I hoped against hope and then it hit me. "There are only two of them! They have the weapons to kill all of us, but they will never do that. If they are not willing to shoot us, they will be unable to take us back, as long as all of us are willing to resist."

I turned to Rozsa: "We must agree not to turn back. Pass the word to the others my darling."

The message went from Rozsa to Sanyi and all the way back to the others. Then a message was passed to me.

"With the exception of the 'guide' they all agree."

A few hundred meters closer to the border, the border guards' plan became clear. We saw the bridge that we were nearing and when we reached it, came a new order.

"Stop right there! One of us will go across the bridge. The other one will cover you, just in case you have any stupid ideas."

One of the guards stood beside us, after a little while and waited for his comrade to cross the bridge. The dog was given a shouted order to remain on the other side of the bridge.

"Who was the fool, who urged us to kill all of you?" one of the guards demanded to know. I took one step closer to him.

"It was I."

"Whose child did you speak about?"

"My beloved little daughter. She is in that blanket." I pointed between Sanyi and Ocsi.

"You must be insane."

"I am. That is what Communism did to me."

"Don't you think there has been enough killing?"

"Even one killing is too much, yet thousands of our countrymen were killed for their love of freedom," I announced boldly.

"We are not killers...," stated the other guard and the moment arrived to appeal to their greed.

"Do you want my watch? My cigarette lighter? My ring?" I took the items, one by one, and held them in my extended hand.

They hesitated. Looked at each other. Retreated a few steps from us and when they came back, I heard the question and exhaled with relief.

"What else can you offer?"

The clamoring began. Someone found some money in his pocket. Someone else offered up his last treasure. Their eyes fell on the few suitcases, still in our hands and the question came.

"What about those suitcases?"

"You can have those too. Our few remaining treasures are in them." Without even asking the owners, I lied. My offer tipped the scale.

"Hide those suitcases below the dike," one guard told the other and the task was carried out instantly.

"We will help you across the border," came the welcomed news and so did our tears. "We must go with great caution. The Russians are asking no questions, they just kill everyone they see."

As if the guard's statement needed proof, the chatter of a weapon came from far away.

"Do you hear that?"

I nodded my head and my earlier relief was replaced by fear.

"If we run into them, we will have to open fire," the guard stated. "It is either them or us. We too hate those bastards. Now let's go."

They led us across the bridge and I began to protest.

"Aren't we supposed to stay on this side?"

"The gun fire came from this side. We know what we are doing. We patrol the other side...The Russians look after the sector here. Waste no more time. Get going fast. We must get below the dike, so we wouldn't be seen."

Each step became more difficult and soon Rozsa collapsed. The two guards scooped her up. One guard on either side dragged her toward the border. The silhouettes of two guard towers could be seen in the moonlight.

"We are almost there," one of them encouraged our little group and we heard the gunfire much closer than before.

"Bastards...," one of the guards hissed. "They are not far from the other dike. We must hurry."

Five more minutes of desperate struggle and they stopped in the snow covered field.

"We got you this far...Do you see that light? Head toward it and you will be free."

Before I could say anything they let go of Rozsa and they began to run. We had no idea whether they got us to Austria or if they tricked us, but there was nothing we could do, except what they suggested.

Rozsa had to be helped by two of us and I was happy to hold her up on one side and Joe too rushed to her aid. Ildiko, our precious little daughter, was being carried by Sanyi and Ocsi. In this manner we reached a bridge and not far, on the other side, the light beckoned to us like a beacon of freedom.

I was the first to see the sign, although my language skills I couldn't brag about, it was clear to me that the language was German, denoting the bridge's carrying capacity.

"We are in Austria...," I shouted and all members of the group hugged each other; kissed each other; shook each others' hands, jubilated. The 'guide' stood silently beside us.

"You can go back now. We have reached freedom, no thanks to you," I told the man, still bitter about what he has done to us.

He just turned and without a word he headed back to Hungary.

Two more minutes and we were across the bridge. The light we saw from the distance, shone on the railway station's clock. It was four o'clock in the morning. A man walked toward us...His question, in Hungarian, shook me to the core. I was devastated.

"Are you lost?"

"We were tricked...Those damn bastards led us back into Hungary," I thought.

"We thought we have reached Austria," I moaned with disappointment.

"You have my friends! Just like me."

EPILOGUE

Thanks to the world leaders after the Second World War and the imaginary lines that created all countries, millions upon millions of human beings were condemned to live under tyranny.

On December twenty fourth, the day before the birth of Christ, we were no longer amongst them. The border of hope we have crossed and the fence of despair no longer held us back.

It was time to celebrate.

A few years ago I was asked to write a Christmas message for one of the newspapers and as I finished this book, that article came to mind. A part of it I decided to include here.

"I have lived fifty six years, thus celebrated that many Christmases, but none of them were as special as the Christmas of 1956.

"It wasn't the splendor of a Christmas tree, for there was none; it wasn't the many gifts received, for there were few; it wasn't the gathering of family members, for beside my wife, daughter and brother-in-law, all other members were far away; it wasn't the warmth of a fire in our home, for we had no home and little warmth in the cold, huge, strange gymnasium that was populated with strangers; it wasn't the comfort of our bed, for we willingly exchanged that for the floor that was covered only with straw and blankets; it wasn't any of the above that made the Christmas of 1956 so special, and yet, special it was.

"The two hundred or so Hungarian refugees, who were our new family surrounded us, sat on the straw-covered floor, that Christmas Eve, praised the Lord through songs and as their voices swirled toward the heavens, as their salty tear-drops escaped, they touched their neighbors' hands and wished each other a Merry Christmas. Through these simple acts we became brothers and sisters.

"I still remember those people of that Christmas Eve well, although not their names. Smiling faces, in spite of being homeless; generous to each other, although without possessions; fearless, in spite of facing an uncertain future, in an unknown, faraway country that may open her door to them. All these things I remember, and whenever I think back on that one night of my life, as I always do when I think of Christmas, I know what raised them above human frailties: they were finally free."

***

Laszlo S. Lichter

Yes, I remember them and recall what happened to the others we loved and even those I hated.

Our family was scattered around the globe. Elisabeth, her husband Sanyi, her parents, Tercsi and Pista and their two small children crossed into Yugoslavia in January of '57. My brother, George followed their example. The United States of America and Canada gave these people sanctuary and that is where they live now.

Many others were taken by God in the intervening years.

My Father, who never left Hungary, except for visits to Canada and the US, when tyranny eased somewhat.

My Uncle Istvan, the paratrooper, who always loved the skies and probably looking down, watching over his descendants.

Rozsa's parents, with whom we were re-united on Christmas Day in Austria, whom we were forced to leave behind when Canada opened her door to us. Who, after seven years of our fighting with the Canadian Government, were finally allowed to join us.

My Aunt Gizella, who lived in the United States for many years. Whose fate took another twist. Many years after her escape, she moved back to Austria to be closer her husband's grave and to her relatives in Hungary. During her first week in that country she was badly injured in a car accident and as a cripple she was taken home to Hungary by her sister Manci.

Aunt Tercsi and Uncle Pista, two unfortunate, but beloved parents of Elisabeth, who were given only a few years of freedom, before they were taken by God.

Uncle Sanyi, whose motorcycle carried us from *Bacsbokod* to *Baja* and his dear wife, Margit.

Rozsa's beloved Grandmother, who cried her eyes out when we were heading toward the border.

Aunt Lujza, who offered us night accommodations, both times we were on our way.

My friends, Joska's parents, are no longer alive. His Father died while on a fishing trip; his Mother took her own life, perhaps she couldn't face life without her husband or she was not willing to suffer any more.

Janics, my friend/informer, drank himself into an early grave.

May all of them rest in peace.

***

Then there are others I think about.

My former classmates, who helped us carry Ildiko, were gone within a day, never to be heard from, never to be seen again.

Our non-paying guests, who were so poor before crossing the border, turned out to be quite wealthy. They hid their money; they kept their jewelry, while the rest of us paupered ourselves for their benefit too. Once across the border, they bragged about how smart they were, but to my mind they were no better than our greedy guide, who by the way got shot in the leg on his way back to his home. His injury was not serious. He spent some time in prison for playing at being a patriot.

Our real guide, Mihaly, we never met again; his fate still bewilders us.

Oh yes! I must write a few words about my enemies.

Pallosy remained principal of the school, but only for the rest of the school year. His enthusiastic reading of the twelve points earned him a teaching post in a remote settlement that he could reach only on a bicycle. He worked and traveled for a few years; then he gave up the ghost.

My controller lost his position with the AVO and as luck would have it, he became one of the rock pushers, supervised by my Father. During one of his many visits to Canada my Father spoke about him.

"Do you recall that breakfast when you introduced to us a friend, who pumped your Mother for information?" I nodded my head. "Well he got his just deserts. My workers found out who he was before and what he did. From that time on, quite frequently he was tripped, while pushing his wheelbarrow full of rocks. He fell many times into our beloved Danube and not always when the water was warm. Too bad he never drowned."

Szantai, Rozsa's cruel, Communist boss, I dreamt about killing, by sending him a parcel of poisoned food. I mellowed with the years and I never did, but God's mill took care of him too, as He took care of many of the Communists of my story.